HOW TO BUILD ANDROID APPS WITH KOTLIN

A hands-on guide to developing, testing, and publishing your first apps with Android

Alex Forrester, Eran Boudjnah, Alexandru Dumbravan, and Jomar Tigcal

HOW TO BUILD ANDROID APPS WITH KOTLIN

Authors: Alex Forrester, Eran Boudjnah, Alexandru Dumbravan, and Jomar Tigcal

Reviewers: Niharika Arora, Gaurav Chandorkar, and Kaushal Dhruw

Managing Editor: Anushree Arun Tendulkar

Acquisitions Editors: Royluis Rodrigues and Anindya Sil

Production Editor: Salma Patel

Editorial Board: Megan Carlisle, Mahesh Dhyani, Heather Gopsill, Manasa Kumar, Alex Mazonowicz, Monesh Mirpuri, Bridget Neale, Abhishek Rane, Brendan Rodrigues, Ankita Thakur, Nitesh Thakur, and Jonathan Wray

First published: February 2021

Production reference: 2160321

ISBN: 978-1-83898-411-3

Published by Packt Publishing Ltd.

Livery Place, 35 Livery Street

Birmingham B3 2PB, UK

Table of Contents

Chapter 2: Building User Screen Flows 57

Chapter 3: Developing the UI with Fragments 123

Chapter 4: Building App Navigation   187

Chapter 9: Unit Tests and Integration Tests with JUnit, Mockito, and Espresso 393

Chapter 10: Android Architecture Components 457

Chapter 12: Dependency Injection with Dagger and Koin 575

Chapter 14: Architecture Patterns   659

Chapter 15: Animations and Transitions with CoordinatorLayout and MotionLayout   681

Chapter 16: Launching Your App on Google Play   727

PREFACE

ABOUT THE BOOK

Android has ruled the app market for the past decade, and developers are increasingly looking to start building their own Android apps. *How to Build Android Apps with Kotlin* starts with the building blocks of Android development, teaching you how to use Android Studio, the integrated development environment (IDE) for Android, with the programming language Kotlin for app development. Then, you'll learn how to create apps and run them on virtual devices through guided exercises. You'll cover the fundamentals of Android development, from structuring an app to building out the UI with Activities and Fragments and various navigation patterns. Progressing through the chapters, you'll delve into Android's RecyclerView to make the most of displaying lists of data and become comfortable with fetching data from a web service and handling images. You'll then learn about mapping, location services, and the permissions model before working with notifications and how to persist data. Moving on, you'll get to grips with testing, covering the full spectrum of the test pyramid. You'll also learn how AAC (Android Architecture Components) are used to cleanly structure your code and explore various architecture patterns and the benefits of dependency injection. The core libraries of RxJava and Coroutines are covered for asynchronous programming. The focus then returns to the UI, demonstrating how to add motion and transitions when users interact with your apps. Towards the end, you'll build an interesting app to retrieve and display popular movies from a movie database, and then see how to publish your apps on Google Play. By the end of this book, you'll have the skills and confidence needed to build fully-fledged Android apps using Kotlin.

ABOUT THE AUTHORS

Alex Forrester is an experienced software developer with more than 20 years of experience in mobile, web development, and content management systems. He has been working with Android for over 8 years, creating flagship apps for blue-chip companies across a broad range of industries at Sky, The Automobile Association, HSBC, The Discovery Channel, and O2. Alex lives in Hertfordshire with his wife and daughter. When he's not developing, he likes rugby and running in the Chiltern hills.

Eran Boudjnah is a developer with over 20 years of experience in developing desktop applications, websites, interactive attractions, and mobile applications. He has been working with Android for about 7 years, developing apps and leading mobile teams for a wide range of clients, from start-ups (JustEat) to large scale companies (Sky) and conglomerates. He is passionate about board games (with a modest collection of a few hundred games) and has a Transformers collection he's quite proud of. Eran lives in North London with Lea, his wife.

Alexandru Dumbravan started Android development in 2011 working for a digital agency. In 2016, he moved to London, working mainly in the FinTech sector. Over the course of his career, he has had the opportunity to analyze and integrate many different technologies on Android devices, from well-known applications like Facebook login, to lesser-known tech, like proprietary network protocols.

Jomar Tigcal is an Android developer with over 10 years of experience in mobile and software development. He has worked on various stages of app development for small startups and large companies. Jomar has also given talks and conducted training and workshops on Android. In his free time, he likes running and reading. He lives in Vancouver, Canada, with his wife Celine.

AUDIENCE

If you want to build your own Android apps using Kotlin but are unsure of how to begin, then this book is for you. A basic understanding of the Kotlin programming language will help you grasp the topics covered in this book more quickly.

ABOUT THE CHAPTERS

Chapter 1, Creating Your First App, shows how to use Android Studio to build your first Android app. Here you will create an Android Studio project and understand what it's made up of, and explore the tools necessary for building and deploying an app on a virtual device. You will also learn about the structure of an Android app.

Chapter 2, Building User Screen Flows, dives into the Android ecosystem and the building blocks of an Android application. Concepts such as activities and their lifecycle, intents, and tasks will be introduced, as well as restoring state and passing data between screens or activities.

Chapter 3, Developing the UI with Fragments, teaches you the fundamentals of using fragments for the user interface of an Android application. You will learn how to use fragments in multiple ways to build application layouts for phones and tablets, including using the Jetpack Navigation component.

Chapter 4, Building App Navigation, goes through the different types of navigation in an application. You will learn about navigation drawers with sliding layouts, bottom navigation, and tabbed navigation.

Chapter 5, Essential Libraries: Retrofit, Moshi, and Glide, gives you an insight into how to build apps that fetch data from a remote data source with the use of the Retrofit library and the Moshi library to convert data into Kotlin objects. You will also learn about the Glide library, which loads remote images into your app.

Chapter 6, RecyclerView, introduces the concept of building lists and displaying them with the help of the RecyclerView widget.

Chapter 7, Android Permissions and Google Maps, presents the concept of permissions and how to request them from the user in order for your app to execute specific tasks, as well as introducing you to the Maps API.

Chapter 8, Services, WorkManager, and Notifications, details the concept of background work in an Android app and how you can have your app execute certain tasks in a way that is invisible to the user, as well as covering how to show a notification of this work.

Chapter 9, Unit Tests and Integration Tests with JUnit, Mockito, and Espresso, teaches you about the different types of tests for an Android application, what frameworks are used for each type of test, and the concept of test-driven development.

Chapter 10, Android Architecture Components, gives an insight into components from the Android Jetpack libraries, such as LiveData and ViewModel, which help you structure your code, and Room, which allows you to persist data on a device in a database.

Chapter 11, Persisting Data, shows you the various ways to store data on a device, from SharedPreferences to files. The Repository concept will also be introduced, giving you an idea of how to structure your app in different layers.

Chapter 12, Dependency Injection with Dagger and Koin, explains the concept of dependency injection and the benefits it provides to an application. Frameworks such as Dagger and Koin are introduced to help you manage your dependencies.

Chapter 13, RxJava and Coroutines, introduces you to doing background operations and data manipulations with RxJava and Coroutines. You'll also learn about manipulating and displaying data using RxJava operators and LiveData transformation.

Chapter 14, Architecture Patterns, explains the architecture patterns you can use to structure your Android projects to separate them into different components with distinct functionality. These make it easier for you to develop, test, and maintain your code.

Chapter 15, Animations and Transitions with CoordinatorLayout and MotionLayout, discusses how to enhance your apps with animations and transitions with CoordinatorLayout and MotionLayout.

Chapter 16, Launching Your App on Google Play, concludes this book by showing you how to publish your apps on Google Play: from preparing a release, to creating a Google Play Developer account, to finally launching your app.

CONVENTIONS

Code words in text, database table names, folder names, filenames, file extensions, pathnames, dummy URLs, user input, and Twitter handles are shown as follows:

"You can find it in the main project window under **MyApplication** | **app** | **src** | **main**."

A block of code is set as follows:

```
<resources>
    <string name="app_name">My Application</string>
</resources>
```

In some cases, important lines of code are highlighted. These cases are presented as follows:

```
<?xml version="1.0" encoding="utf-8"?>
<resources>
    <string name="app_name">My Application</string>
    <string name="first_name_text">First name:</string>
    <string name="last_name_text">Last name:</string>
</resources>
```

Words that you see on the screen, for example, in menus or dialog boxes, also appear in the text like this: "Click **Finish** and your virtual device will be created."

New terms and important words are shown like this: "It is the official **Integrated Development Environment** (**IDE**) for Android development, built on JetBrains' **IntelliJ IDEA software** and developed by the Android Studio team at Google."

BEFORE YOU BEGIN

Each great journey begins with a humble step. Before we can do awesome things in Android, we need to be prepared with a productive environment. In this section, we will see how to do that.

MINIMUM HARDWARE REQUIREMENTS

For an optimal learning experience, we recommend the following hardware configuration:

- Processor: Intel Core i5 or equivalent or higher

- Memory: 4 GB RAM minimum; 8 GB RAM recommended

- Storage: 4 GB available space

SOFTWARE REQUIREMENTS

You'll also need the following software installed in advance:

- OS: Windows 7 SP1 64-bit, Windows 8.1 64-bit or Windows 10 64-bit, macOS, or Linux

- Android Studio 4.1 or higher

INSTALLATION AND SETUP

Before you start this book, you will need to install Android Studio 4.1 (or higher), which is the main tool that you will be using throughout the chapters. You can download Android Studio from https://developer.android.com/studio.

On macOS, launch the DMG file and drag and drop Android Studio into the **Applications** folder. Once this is done, open Android Studio. On Windows, launch the EXE file. If you're using Linux, unpack the ZIP file into your preferred location. Open your Terminal and navigate to the **android-studio/bin/** directory and execute **studio.sh**. If you see an **Import Settings** dialog pop-up, select **Do not import settings** and click the **OK** button (this usually occurs when there is a previous installation of Android Studio):

Figure 0.1: The import settings dialog

Next, the **Data Sharing** dialog will pop up; click the **Don't send** button to disable sending anonymous usage data to Google:

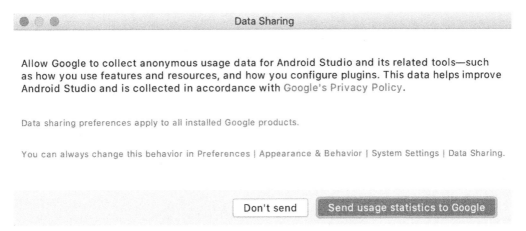

Figure 0.2: The Data Sharing dialog

In the **Welcome** dialog, click the **Next** button to start the setup:

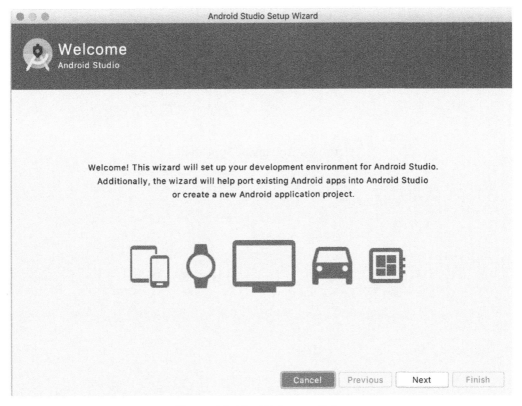

Figure 0.3: The Welcome dialog

In the **Install Type** dialog, select **Standard** to install the recommended settings. Then, click the **Next** button:

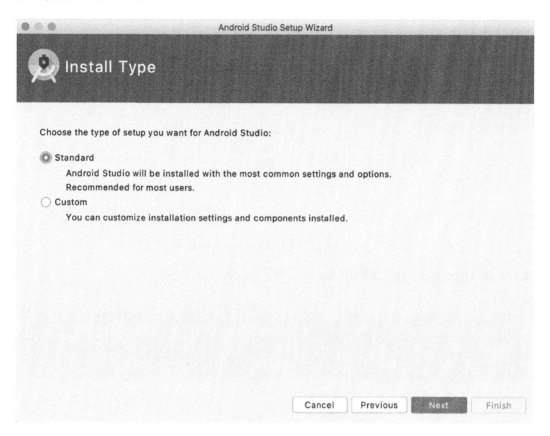

Figure 0.4: The Install Type dialog

In the **Select UI Theme** dialog, choose your preferred IDE theme—either **Light** or **Dracula** (dark theme) - then click the **Next** button:

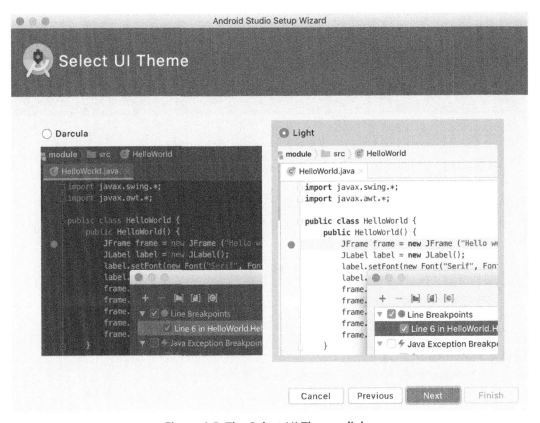

Figure 0.5: The Select UI Theme dialog

In the **Verify Settings** dialog, review your settings and then click the **Finish** button. The setup wizard downloads and installs additional components, including the Android SDK:

Figure 0.6: The Verify Settings dialog

Once the download finishes, you can click the **Finish** button. You are now ready to create your Android project.

INSTALLING THE CODE BUNDLE

You can download the code files and activity solutions from GitHub at https://github. com/PacktPublishing/How-to-Build-Android-Apps-with-Kotlin. Refer to these code files for the complete code bundle.

GET IN TOUCH

Feedback from our readers is always welcome.

General feedback: If you have any questions about this book, please mention the book title in the subject of your message and email us at `customercare@ packtpub.com`.

Errata: Although we have taken every care to ensure the accuracy of our content, mistakes do happen. If you have found a mistake in this book, we would be grateful if you could report this to us. Please visit www.packtpub.com/support/errata and complete the form.

Piracy: If you come across any illegal copies of our works in any form on the Internet, we would be grateful if you could provide us with the location address or website name. Please contact us at `copyright@packt.com` with a link to the material.

If you are interested in becoming an author: If there is a topic that you have expertise in and you are interested in either writing or contributing to a book, please visit authors.packtpub.com.

PLEASE LEAVE A REVIEW

Let us know what you think by leaving a detailed, impartial review on Amazon. We appreciate all feedback – it helps us continue to make great products and help aspiring developers build their skills. Please spare a few minutes to give your thoughts – it makes a big difference to us.

1

CREATING YOUR FIRST APP

OVERVIEW

This chapter is an introduction to Android, where you will set up your environment and focus on the fundamentals of Android development. By the end of this chapter, you will have gained the knowledge required to create an Android app from scratch and install it on a virtual or physical Android device. You will be able to analyze and understand the importance of the `AndroidManifest.xml` file, and use the Gradle build tool to configure your app and implement UI elements from Material Design.

INTRODUCTION

Android is the most widely used mobile phone operating system in the world, with over 70% of the global market share (see https://gs.statcounter.com/os-market-share/mobile/worldwide). This presents great opportunities to contribute and make an impact by learning Android and building apps that have a global reach. For a developer who is new to Android, there are many issues you must contend with in order to get started learning and becoming productive. This book will address these issues. After learning the tooling and development environment, you will explore fundamental practices to build Android apps. We will cover a wide range of real-world development challenges faced by developers and explore various techniques to overcome them.

In this chapter, you will learn how to create a basic Android project and add features to it. You will be introduced to the comprehensive development environment of Android Studio and learn about the core areas of the software to enable you to work productively. Android Studio provides all the tooling for application development, but not the knowledge. This first chapter will guide you through using the software effectively to build an app and configure the most common areas of an Android project.

Let's get started creating an Android project.

CREATING AN ANDROID PROJECT WITH ANDROID STUDIO

In order to be productive in terms of building Android apps, it is essential to become confident with how to use **Android Studio**. This is the official **Integrated Development Environment** (**IDE**) for Android development, built on JetBrains' **IntelliJ IDEA IDE** and developed by the Android Studio team at Google. You will be using it throughout this course to create apps and progressively add more advanced features.

The development of Android Studio has followed the development of the IntelliJ IDEA IDE. The fundamental features of an IDE are of course present, enabling you to optimize your code with suggestions, shortcuts, and standard refactoring. The programming language you will be using throughout this course to create Android apps is Kotlin. Since Google I/O 2017 (the annual Google developer conference), this has been Google's preferred language for Android app development. What really sets Android Studio apart from other Android development environments is that **Kotlin** was created by JetBrains, the company that created IntelliJ IDEA, the software Android Studio is built on. You can, therefore, benefit from established and evolving first-class support for Kotlin.

Kotlin was created to address some of the shortcomings of Java in terms of verbosity, handling null types, and adding more functional programming techniques, amongst many other issues. As Kotlin has been the preferred language for Android development since 2017, taking over from Java, you will be using it in this book.

Getting to grips and familiarizing yourself with Android Studio will enable you to feel confident working on and building Android apps. So, let's get started creating your first project.

> **NOTE**
>
> The installation and setup of Android Studio are covered in the *Preface*. Please ensure you have completed those steps before you continue.

EXERCISE 1.01: CREATING AN ANDROID STUDIO PROJECT FOR YOUR APP

This is the starting point for creating a project structure your app will be built upon. The template-driven approach will enable you to create a basic project in a short timeframe whilst setting up the building blocks you can use to develop your app. To complete this exercise, perform the following steps:

> **NOTE**
>
> The version of Android Studio you will be using is *v4.1.1* (or above).

1. Upon opening Android Studio, you will see a window asking whether you want to create a new project or open an existing one. Select **Create New Project**.

   The start up window will appear as follows:

Figure 1.1: Android Studio version 4.1.1

2. Now, you'll enter a simple wizard-driven flow, which greatly simplifies the creation of your first Android project. The next screen you will see has a large number of options for the initial setup you'd like your app to have:

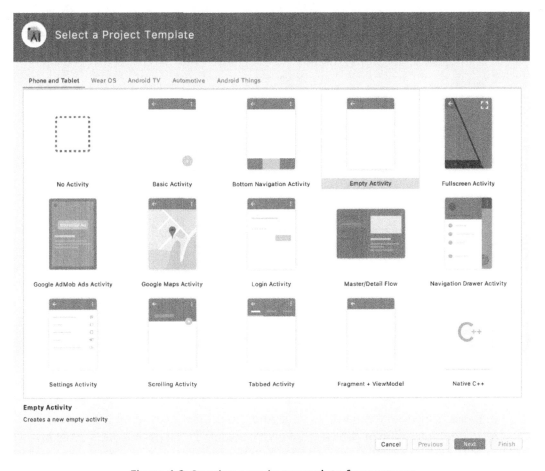

Figure 1.2: Starting a project template for your app

3. Welcome to your first introduction to the **Android development ecosystem**. The word displayed in most of the project types is `Activity`. In Android, an `Activity` is a page or screen. The options you can choose from on the preceding screen all create this initial screen differently. The descriptions describe how the first screen of the app will look. These are templates to build your app with. Select `Empty Activity` from the template and click on next.

The project configuration screen is as follows:

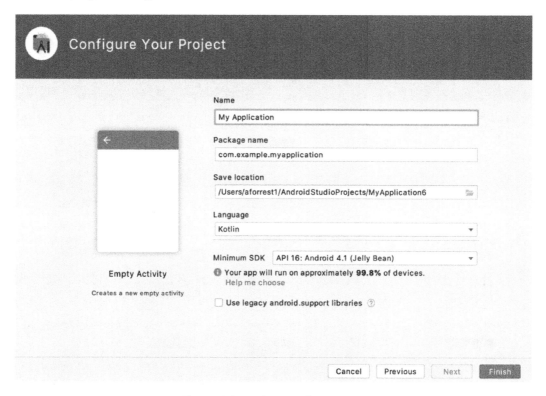

Figure 1.3: Project configuration

4. The preceding screen configures your app. Let's go through all the options:

   a. Name: Similar to the name of your Android project, this name will appear as the default name of your app when it's installed on a phone and visible on Google Play. You can replace the **Name** field with your own or set it now to the app you are going to create.

   b. Package name: This uses the standard reverse domain name pattern for creating a name. It will be used as an address identifier for source code and assets in your app. It is best to make this name as clear and descriptive and as closely aligned with the purpose of your app as possible. Therefore, it's probably best to change this to use one or more sub-domains (such as `com.sample.shop.myshop`). As shown in *Figure 1.3*, the **Name** of the app (in lowercase with spaces removed) is appended to the domain.

c. Save location: This is the local folder on your machine where the app will be initially stored. This can be changed in the future, so you can probably keep the default or edit it to something different (such as **Users/MyUser/android/projects**). The default location will vary with the operating system you are using.

d. Language – Kotlin: This is Google's preferred language for Android app development.

e. Minimum SDK: Depending on which version of Android Studio you download, the default might be the same as displayed in *Figure 1.3* or a different version. Keep this the same. Most of Android's new features are made backward compatible, so your app will run fine on the vast majority of older devices. However, if you do want to target newer devices, you should consider raising the minimum API level. There is a link, **Help Me Choose**, to a dialog that explains the feature set that you have access to with a view to development on different versions of Android and the current percentage of devices worldwide running each Android version.

f. (Checkbox) use legacy android.support libraries. Leave this unchecked. You will be using AndroidX libraries, which are the replacement for the support libraries that were designed to make features on newer versions of Android backward compatible with older versions, but it provides much more than this. It also contains newer Android components called Jetpack, which, as the name suggests, "boost" your Android development and provide a host of rich features you will want to use in your app, thereby simplifying common operations.

Once you have filled in all these details, select **Finish**. Your project will be built and you will then be presented with the following screen or similar: You can immediately see the activity that has been created (**MainActivity**) in one tab and the layout used for the screen in the other tab (**activity_main.xml**). The application structure folders are in the left panel.

Figure 1.4: Android Studio default project

In this exercise, you have gone through the steps to create your first Android app using Android Studio. This has been a template-driven approach that has shown you the core options you need to configure for your app.

In the next section, you will set up a virtual device and see your app run for the first time.

SETTING UP A VIRTUAL DEVICE AND RUNNING YOUR APP

As a part of installing Android Studio, you downloaded and installed the latest Android SDK components. These included a base emulator, which you will configure to create a virtual device to run Android apps on. The benefit is that you can make changes and quickly see them on your desktop whilst developing your app. Although virtual devices do not have all the features of a real device, the feedback cycle is often quicker than going through the steps of connecting a real device.

Also, although you should ensure your app runs as expected on different devices, you can standardize it by targeting a specific device by downloading an emulator skin even if you don't have the real device if this is a requirement of your project.

The screen you will have seen (or something similar) when installing Android Studio is as follows:

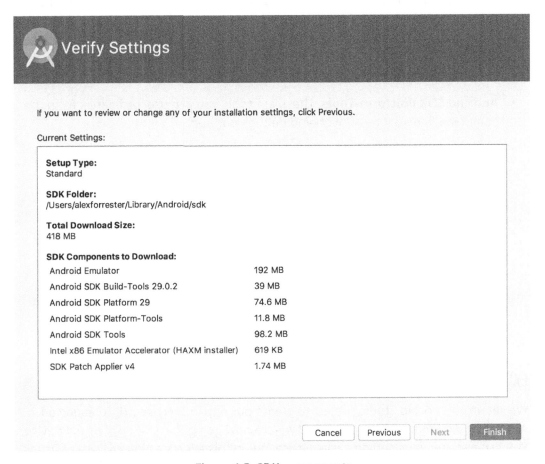

Figure 1.5: SDK components

Let's take a look at the SDK components that are installed and how the virtual device fits in:

- **Android Emulator**: This is the base emulator, which we will configure to create virtual devices of different Android makes and models.

- **Android SDK Build-Tools**: Android Studio uses the build tools to build your app. This process involves compiling, linking, and packaging your app to prepare it for installation on a device.

- **Android SDK Platform**: This is the version of the Android platform that you will use to develop your app. The platform refers to the API level. The Android version for API level 30 is 11 and the name is Android 11. Before the release of Android 10, the version of Android was also known by a code name, which was different from the version name. The code names used to follow a sweets/dessert theme; therefore, the name `Jelly Bean` was selected above in the Create Project wizard for configuring the minimum API level of your project. From Android 10, the versioning will no longer have a code name that is different from the version name. (The versions of the Build-Tools and Platform will change as new versions are released)

- **Android SDK Platform-Tools**: These are tools you can use, ordinarily, from the command line, to interact with and debug your app.

- **Android SDK Tools**: In contrast to the platform tools, these are tools that you use predominantly from within Android Studio in order to accomplish certain tasks, such as the virtual device for running apps and the SDK manager to download and install platforms and other components of the SDK.

- **Intel x86 Emulator Accelerator (HAXM installer)**: If your OS provides it, this is a feature at the hardware level of your computer you will be prompted to enable, which allows your emulator to run more quickly.

- **SDK Patch Applier v4**: As newer versions of Android Studio become available, this enables patches to be applied to update the version you are running.

With this knowledge, let's start with the next exercise of this chapter.

EXERCISE 1.02: SETTING UP A VIRTUAL DEVICE AND RUNNING YOUR APP ON IT

We set up an Android Studio project to create our app in *Exercise 1.01, Creating an Android Studio Project for Your App,* and we are now going to run it on a virtual device. You can also run your app on a real device, but in this exercise, you will use a virtual device. This process is a continuous cycle whilst working on your app. Once you have implemented a feature, you can verify its look and behavior as you require. For this exercise, you will create a single virtual device, but you should ensure you run your app on multiple devices to verify that its look and behavior are consistent. Perform the following steps:

1. In the top toolbar in Android Studio, you will see two drop-down boxes next to each other pre-selected with **app** and **No devices**:

Figure 1.6: Android Studio toolbar

The **app** is the configuration of our app that we are going to run. As we haven't set up a virtual device yet, it says **No devices**.

2. In order to create a virtual device, click on the **AVD Manager** (**AVD** stands for **Android Virtual Device**) to open the virtual devices window/screen. The option to do this can also be accessed from the **Tools** menu:

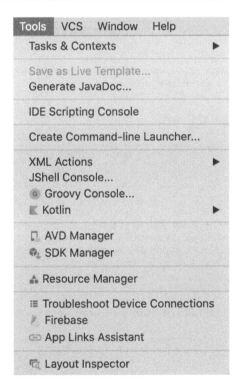

Figure 1.7: AVD Manager in the Tools menu

3. Click the button or toolbar option to open the **Your Virtual Devices** window:

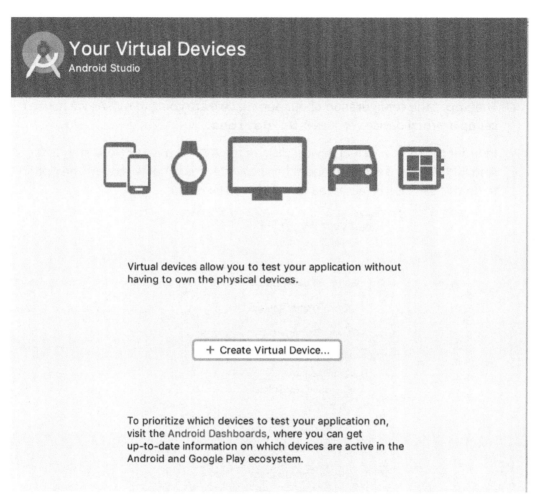

Virtual devices allow you to test your application without having to own the physical devices.

+ Create Virtual Device...

To prioritize which devices to test your application on, visit the Android Dashboards, where you can get up-to-date information on which devices are active in the Android and Google Play ecosystem.

Figure 1.8: The Your Virtual Devices window

4. Click the **Create Virtual Device...** button as shown in *Figure 1.8*:

Figure 1.9: Device definition creation

5. We are going to choose the **Pixel 3** device. The real (non-virtual device) Pixel range of devices are developed by Google and have access to the most up-to-date versions of the Android platform. Once selected, click the **Next** button:

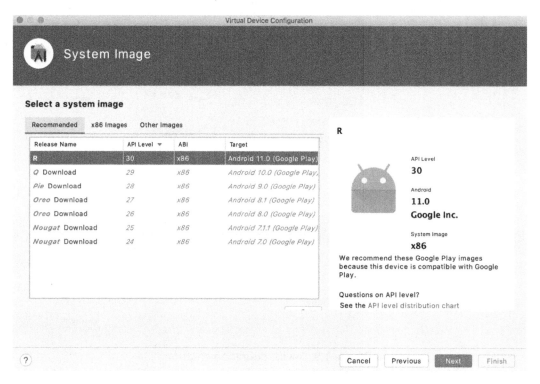

Figure 1.10: System Image

The **R** name displayed here is the initial code/release name for Android 11. Select the latest system image available. The **Target** column might also show **(Google Play)** or **(Google APIs)** in the name. Google APIs mean that the system image comes pre-installed with Google Play Services. This is a rich feature set of Google APIs and Google apps that your app can use and interact with. On first running the app, you will see apps such as Maps and Chrome instead of a plain emulator image. A Google Play system image means that, in addition to the Google APIs, the Google Play app will also be installed.

6. You should develop your app with the latest version of the Android platform to benefit from the latest features. On first creating a virtual device, you will have to download the system image. If a **Download** link is displayed next to **Release Name**, click on it and wait for the download to complete. Select the **Next** button to see the virtual device you have set up:

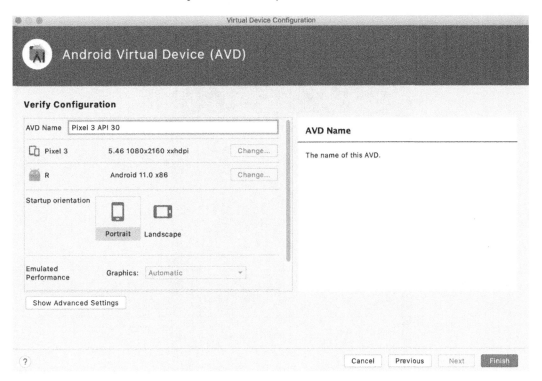

Figure 1.11: Virtual device configuration

You will then see a final configuration screen.

7. Click **Finish** and your virtual device will be created. You will then see your device highlighted:

Figure 1.12: Virtual devices listed

8. Press the right arrow button under the **Actions** column to run up the virtual device:

Figure 1.13: Virtual device launched

Now that you've created the virtual device and it's running, you can go back into Android Studio to run your app.

9. The virtual device you have set up and started will be selected. Press the green triangle/play button to launch your app:

Figure 1.14: App launch configuration

Figure 1.15: App running on a virtual device

In this exercise, you have gone through the steps to create a virtual device and run the app you created on it. The Android Virtual Device Manager, which you have used to do this, enables you to create the device (or range of devices) you would like to target your app for. Running your app on the virtual device allows a quick feedback cycle to verify how a new feature development behaves and that it displays the way you expect it to.

Next, you will explore the **AndroidManifest.xml** file of your project, which contains the information and configuration of your app.

THE ANDROID MANIFEST

The app you have just created, although simple, encompasses the core building blocks that you will use in all of the projects you create. The app is driven from the **AndroidManifest.xml** file, a manifest file that details the contents of your app. It has all the components, such as activities, content providers, services, receivers, and the list of permissions that the app requires to implement its features. For example, the camera permission is required to capture a photo in an app. You can find it in the Project view under **MyApplication | app | src | main**. Alternatively, if you are looking at the Android view, it is located at **app | manifests | AndroidManifest.xml**:

```xml
<?xml version="1.0" encoding="utf-8"?>
<manifest xmlns:android="http://schemas.android.com/apk/res/android"
    package="com.example.myapplication">

    <!--Permissions like camera go here-->

    <application
        android:allowBackup="true"
        android:icon="@mipmap/ic_launcher"
        android:label="@string/app_name"
        android:roundIcon="@mipmap/ic_launcher_round"
        android:supportsRtl="true"
        android:theme="@style/Theme.MyApplication">

        <activity android:name=".MainActivity"
          android:screenOrientation="portrait">
            <intent-filter>
                <action android:name="android.intent.action.MAIN" />
```

```
            <category android:name="android.intent.category.LAUNCHER" />
        </intent-filter>
    </activity>

</application>

</manifest>
```

A typical manifest file in general terms is a top-level file that describes the enclosed files or other data and associated metadata that forms a group or unit. The Android Manifest takes this concept and applies it to your Android app as an XML file. The distinguishing feature of the app specified is the package defined at the manifest XML root:

```
package="com.example.myapplication"
```

Every Android app has an application class that allows you to configure the app. By default, in version 4.1.1 of Android Studio, the following XML attributes and values are created in the application element:

- **android:allowBackup="true"**: This backs up a user's data from apps that target and run on Android 6.0 (API level 23) or later upon reinstall or switching devices.

- **android:icon="@mipmap/ic_launcher"**: The resources Android uses are referenced in XML preceded by the @ symbol and mipmap refers to the folder where launcher icons are stored.

- **android:label="@string/app_name"**: This is the name you specified when you created the app. It's also currently displayed in the toolbar of the app and will be shown as the name of the app on the user's device in the launcher. It is referenced by the @ symbol followed by a string reference to the name you specified when you created the app.

- **android:roundIcon="@mipmap/ic_launcher_round"**: Depending on the device the user has, the launcher icons may be square or round. **roundIcon** is used when the user's device displays round icons in the launcher.

- **android:supportsRtl="true"**: This specifies whether the app and its layout files support right-to-left language layouts.

- **android:theme="@style/Theme.MyApplication"**: This specifies the theme of your app in terms of text styles, colors, and other styles within your app.

After the **`<application>`** element opens, you define the components your app consists of. As we have just created our app, it only contains the first screen shown in the following code:

```
<activity android:name=".MainActivity">
```

The next child XML node specified is as follows:

```
<intent-filter>
```

Android uses intents as a mechanism for interacting with apps and system components. Intents get sent and the intent filter registers your app's capability to react to these intents. **`<android.intent.action.MAIN>`** is the main entry point into your app, which, as it appears in the enclosing XML of **`.MainActivity`**, specifies that this screen will be started when the app is launched. **`android.intent.category.LAUNCHER`** states that your app will appear in the launcher of your user's device.

As you have created your app from a template, it has a basic manifest that will launch the app and display an initial screen at startup through an **`Activity`** component. Depending on which other features you want to add to your app, you may need to add permissions in the Android Manifest file.

Permissions are grouped into three different categories: normal, signature, and dangerous.

- **Normal** permissions include accessing the network state, Wi-Fi, the internet, and Bluetooth. These are usually permitted without asking the user's consent at runtime.

- **Signature** permissions are those shared by the same group of apps that have to be signed with the same certificate. This means these apps can share data freely, but other apps can't get access.

- **Dangerous** permissions are centered around the user and their privacy, for example, sending SMS, access to accounts and location, and reading and writing to the filesystem and contacts.

These permissions have to be listed in the manifest, and, in the case of dangerous permissions from Android Marshmallow API 23 (Android 6 Marshmallow) onward, you must also ask the user to grant the permissions at runtime.

In the next exercise, we will configure the Android Manifest file.

EXERCISE 1.03: CONFIGURING THE ANDROID MANIFEST INTERNET PERMISSION

The key permission that most apps require is access to the internet. This is not added by default. In this exercise, we will fix that and, in the process, load a **WebView**, which enables the app to show web pages. This use case is a very common one in Android app development as most commercial apps will display a privacy policy, terms and conditions, etc. As these documents are likely to be common to all platforms, the usual way to display them is to load a web page. Perform the following steps:

1. Create a new Android Studio project as you did in *Exercise 1.01*, *Creating an Android Studio Project for Your App*.

2. Switch tabs to the **MainActivity** class. From the main project window, it's located in **MyApplication | app | src | main | java | com | example | myapplication**. This follows the package structure you defined when creating the app. Alternatively, if you are looking at the Android view within the project window, it is located at **app | java | com | example | myapplication**.

    You can change what the **Project** window displays by opening up the **Tool** window by selecting **View | Tool Windows | Project** - this will select **Project** view. The drop-down options on the top of the **Project** window allow you to change the way you view your project, with the most commonly used displays being **Project** and **Android**.

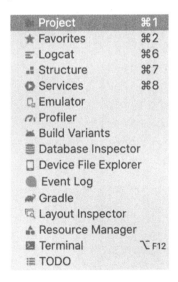

Figure 1.16 Tool Windows drop-down

On opening it, you'll see that it has the following content or similar:

```
package com.example.myapplication

import androidx.appcompat.app.AppCompatActivity
import android.os.Bundle

class MainActivity : AppCompatActivity() {

    override fun onCreate(savedInstanceState: Bundle?) {
        super.onCreate(savedInstanceState)
        setContentView(R.layout.Activity_main)
    }
}
```

You'll examine the contents of this file in more detail in the next section of this chapter, but for now, you just need to be aware that the **setContentView(R. layout.Activity_main)** statement sets the layout of the UI you saw when you first ran the app in the virtual device.

3. Use the following code to change this to the following:

```
package com.example.myapplication

import androidx.appcompat.app.AppCompatActivity
import android.os.Bundle
import android.webkit.WebView

class MainActivity : AppCompatActivity() {

    override fun onCreate(savedInstanceState: Bundle?) {
        super.onCreate(savedInstanceState)

        val webView = WebView(this)

        webView.settings.javaScriptEnabled = true
        setContentView(webView)
        webView.loadUrl("https://www.google.com")
    }
}
```

So, you are replacing the layout file with a **WebView**. The **val** keyword is a read-only property reference, which can't be changed once it has been set. JavaScript needs to be enabled in the WebView to execute JavaScript.

NOTE

We are not setting the type, but Kotlin has type inference, so it will infer the type if possible. So, specifying the type explicitly with `val webView: WebView = WebView(this)` is not necessary. Depending on which programming languages you have used in the past, the order of defining the parameter name and type may or may not be familiar. Kotlin follows Pascal notation, that is, name followed by type.

4. Now, run the app up and the text will appear as shown in the screenshot here:

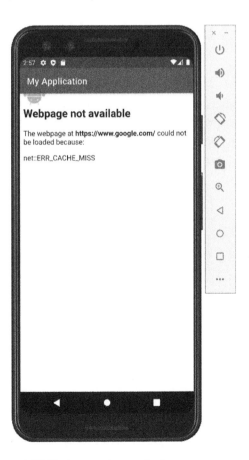

Figure 1.17 No internet permission error message

5. This error occurs because there is no **INTERNET** permission added in your **AndroidManifest.xml** file. (If you get the error **net::ERR_CLEARTEXT_ NOT_PERMITTED**, this is because the URL you are loading into the **WebView** is not HTTPS and non-HTTPS traffic is disabled from API level 28, Android 9.0 Pie and above.) Let's fix that by adding the internet permission to the manifest. Open up the Android Manifest and add the following to above the **<application>** tag:

```
<uses-permission android:name="android.permission.INTERNET" />
```

Your manifest file should now look like the following:

```
<?xml version="1.0" encoding="utf-8"?>
<manifest xmlns:android="http://schemas.android.com/apk/res/android"
    package="com.example.myapplication">

    <uses-permission android:name="android.permission.INTERNET" />

    <application
        android:allowBackup="true"
        android:icon="@mipmap/ic_launcher"
        android:label="@string/app_name"
        android:roundIcon="@mipmap/ic_launcher_round"
        android:supportsRtl="true"
        android:theme="@style/AppTheme">
        <activity android:name=".MainActivity">
            <intent-filter>
                <action android:name="android.intent.action.MAIN" />

                <category android:name=
                    "android.intent.category.LAUNCHER" />
            </intent-filter>
        </activity>
    </application>

</manifest>
```

Uninstall the app from the virtual device before running up the app again. You need to do this as app permissions can sometimes get cached. Do this by long pressing on the app icon and selecting the **App Info** option that appears and then pressing the Bin icon with **Uninstall** text below it. Alternatively, long press the app icon and then drag it to the Bin icon with **Uninstall** text beside it in the top-right corner of the screen.

6. Install the app again and see the web page appear in the **WebView**:

Figure 1.18 App displaying the WebView

In this example, you learned how to add a permission to the manifest. The Android Manifest can be thought of as a table of contents of your app. It lists all the components and permissions your app uses. As you have seen from starting the app from the launcher, it also provides the entry points into your app.

In the next section, you will explore the Android build system, which uses the Gradle build tool to get your app up and running.

USING GRADLE TO BUILD, CONFIGURE, AND MANAGE APP DEPENDENCIES

In the course of creating this project, you have principally used the Android platform SDK. The necessary Android libraries were downloaded when you installed Android Studio. These are not the only libraries, however, that are used to create your app. In order to configure and build your Android project or app, a build tool called Gradle is used. Gradle is a multi-purpose build tool that Android Studio uses to build your app. By default, in Android Studio, it uses Groovy, a dynamically typed JVM language, to configure the build process and allows easy dependency management so you can add libraries to your project and specify the versions. Android Studio can also be configured to use Kotlin to configure builds, but, as the default language is Groovy, you will be using this. The files that this build and configuration information is stored in are named **build.gradle**. When you first create your app, there are two **build.gradle** files, one at the root/top level of the project and one specific to your app in the app **module** folder.

PROJECT-LEVEL BUILD.GRADLE FILE

Let's now have a look at the project-level **build.gradle** file. This is where you add configuration options common to all sub-projects/modules, as shown in the following code:

```
buildscript {
    ext.kotlin_version = "1.4.21"
    repositories {
        google()
        jcenter()

    }
    dependencies {
```

```
            classpath "com.android.tools.build:gradle:4.4.1"
            classpath "org.jetbrains.kotlin:kotlin-gradle-plugin:
              $kotlin_version"
            // NOTE: Do not place your application dependencies here;
            //they belong in the individual module build.gradle files

    }
}


allprojects {
    repositories {
        google()
        jcenter()


    }
}


task clean(type: Delete) {
    delete rootProject.buildDir
}
```

The **buildscript** block has build and configuration information to actually create your project, whilst the **allprojects** block specifies the configuration for all of the app's modules. Groovy works on a plugin system, so you can write your own plugin that does a task or series of tasks and plug it into your build pipeline. The two plugins specified here are the Android tools plugin, which hooks into the **gradle** build toolkit and provides Android-specific settings and configuration to build your Android app, and the Kotlin **gradle** plugin, which takes care of compiling Kotlin code within the project. The dependencies themselves follow the Maven **Project Object Model (POM)** convention of **groupId**, **artifactId**, and **versionId** separated by ":" colons. So as an example, the Android tools plugin dependency above is shown as:

'com.android.tools.build:gradle:4.4.1'

The **groupId** is **com.android.tools.build**, the **artifactId** is **gradle**, and the **versionId** is **4.4.1**. In this way, the build system locates and downloads these dependencies by using the repositories referenced in the **repositories** block.

The specific versions of libraries can be specified directly (as is done with the Android **tools** plugin) in the dependency or added as variables. The **ext.** prefix on the variable means it is a Groovy extension property and can be used in the app **build. gradle** file as well.

> **NOTE**
>
> The dependency versions specified in the previous code section and in the following sections of this and other chapters are subject to change, and are updated over time so are likely to be higher when you create these projects.

APP-LEVEL BUILD.GRADLE

The **build.gradle** app is specific to your project configuration:

```
plugins {
    id 'com.android.application'
    id 'kotlin-android'
}

android {
    compileSdkVersion 30
    buildToolsVersion "30.0.3"

    defaultConfig {
        applicationId "com.example.myapplication"
        minSdkVersion 16
        targetSdkVersion 30
        versionCode 1
        versionName "1.0"
        testInstrumentationRunner
          "androidx.test.runner.AndroidJUnitRunner"

        buildTypes {
            release {
                minifyEnabled false
                proguardFiles getDefaultProguardFile(
                  'proguard-android-optimize.txt'), 'proguard-rules.pro'
            }
```

```
        }

        compileOptions {
            sourceCompatibility JavaVersion.VERSION_1_8
            targetCompatibility JavaVersion.VERSION_1_8
        }

        kotlinOptions {
            jvmTarget = '1.8'
        }
    }

    dependencies {
        implementation "org.jetbrains.kotlin:kotlin-stdlib:
          $kotlin_version"
        implementation 'androidx.core:core-ktx:1.3.2'
        implementation 'androidx.appcompat:appcompat:1.2.0'
        implementation 'com.google.android.material:material:1.2.1'
        implementation 'androidx.constraintlayout:constraintlayout:2.0.4'
        testImplementation 'junit:junit:4.+'
        androidTestImplementation 'androidx.test.ext:junit:1.1.2'
        androidTestImplementation 'androidx.test.espresso
          :espresso-core:3.3.0'
    }
}
```

The plugins for Android and Kotlin detailed in the preceding explanation are applied to your project here by id in the **plugins** lines.

The **android** block provided by the **com.android.application** plugin is where you configure your Android-specific configuration settings:

- **compileSdkVersion**: This is used to define the API level the app has been compiled with and the app can use the features of this API and lower.

- **buildToolsVersion**: The version of the build tools to build your app. (By default the **buildToolsVersion** line will be added to your project, but in order to always use the latest version of the build tools you can remove it).

- **defaultConfig**: This is the base configuration of your app.

- **applicationId**: This is set to the package of your app and is the app identifier that is used on Google Play to uniquely identify your app. It can be changed to be different from the package name if required.

- **minSdkVersion**: The minimum API level your app supports. This will filter out your app from being displayed in Google Play for devices that are lower than this.

- **targetSdkVersion**: The API level you are targeting. This is the API level your built app is intended to work with and has been tested with.

- **versionCode**: Specifies the version code of your app. Every time an update needs to be made to the app, the version code needs to be increased by 1 or more.

- **versionName**: A user-friendly version name that usually follows semantic versioning of X.Y.Z, where X is the major version, Y is the minor version, and Z is the patch version, for example, 1.0.3.

- **testInstrumentationRunner**: The test runner to use for your UI tests.

- **buildTypes**: Under **buildTypes**, a release is added that configures your app to create a **release** build. The **minifyEnabled** value, if set to **true**, will shrink your app size by removing any unused code, as well as obfuscate your app. This obfuscation step changes the name of the source code references to values such as **a.b.c()**. This makes your code less prone to reverse engineering and further reduces the size of the built app.

- **compileOptions**: Language level of the java source code (**sourceCompatibility**) and byte code (**targetCompatibility**)

- **kotlinOptions**: The **jvm** library the **kotlin gradle** plugin should use

The **dependencies** block specifies the libraries your app uses on top of the Android platform SDK, as shown here:

```
    dependencies {
//The version of Kotlin your app is being built with
        implementation "org.jetbrains.kotlin:kotlin-stdlib-jdk7:
          $kotlin_version"
//Kotlin extensions, jetpack
//component with Android Kotlin language features
        implementation 'androidx.core:core-ktx:1.3.2'
//Provides backwards compatible support libraries and jetpack components
        implementation 'androidx.appcompat:appcompat:1.2.0'
//Material design components to theme and style your app
        implementation 'com.google.android.material:material:1.2.1'
//The ConstraintLayout ViewGroup updated separately
//from main Android sources
```

```
        implementation 'androidx.constraintlayout:constraintlayout:2.0.4'

//Standard Test library for unit tests.
//The '+' is a gradle dynamic version which allows downloading the
//latest version. As this can lead to unpredictable builds if changes
//are introduced all projects will use fixed version '4.13.1'
        testImplementation 'junit:junit:4.+'
//UI Test runner
        androidTestImplementation 'androidx.test:runner:1.1.2'
//Library for creating Android UI tests
        androidTestImplementation
            'androidx.test.espresso:espresso-core:3.3.0'
    }
```

The **implementation** notation for adding these libraries means that their internal dependencies will not be exposed to your app, making compilation faster.

You will see here that the **androidx** components are added as dependencies, rather than in the Android platform source. This is so that they can be updated independently from Android versions. **androidx** is the repackaged support library and Jetpack components. In order to add or verify that your **gradle.properties** file has **androidx** enabled, you need to inspect the **gradle.properties** file at the root of your project and look for the **android.useAndroidX** and **android. enableJetifier** properties and ensure that they are set to **true**.

You can open up the **gradle.properties** file now, and you will see the following:

```
# Project-wide Gradle settings.
# IDE (e.g. Android Studio) users:
# Gradle settings configured through the IDE *will override*
# any settings specified in this file.
# For more details on how to configure your build environment visit
# http://www.gradle.org/docs/current/userguide/build_environment.html
# Specifies the JVM arguments used for the daemon process.
# The setting is particularly useful for tweaking memory settings.
org.gradle.jvmargs=-Xmx2048m -Dfile.encoding=UTF-8

# When configured, Gradle will run in incubating parallel mode.
# This option should only be used with decoupled projects.
# More details, visit
# http://www.gradle.org/docs/current/userguide/multi_project_builds
# .html#sec
#:decoupled_projects
```

```
# org.gradle.parallel=true
# AndroidX package structure to make it clearer which packages are
# bundled with #the Android operating system, and which are packaged
# with your app's APK
# https://developer.android.com/topic/libraries/support-library/
# androidx-rn
android.useAndroidX=true


# Automatically convert third-party libraries to use AndroidX
android.enableJetifier=true


# Kotlin code style for this project: "official" or "obsolete":
kotlin.code.style=official
```

As you created the project with an Android Studio template, it set these flags to **true**, as well as adding the relevant **androidx** dependencies the app uses into the **dependencies** block of the app's **build.gradle** file. In addition to the preceding commented explanation, the **android.useAndroidX=true** flag states that the project is using the **androidx** libraries rather than the older support libraries and **android.enableJetifier=true** will also convert any older versions of the support libraries used in third-party libraries into the AndroidX format. **kotlin.code.style=official** will set the code style to the official kotlin one rather than the default Android Studio one.

The final Gradle file to examine is **settings.gradle**. This file shows which modules your app uses. On first creating a project with Android Studio, there will only be one module, **app**, but when you add more features, you can add new modules that are dedicated to containing the source of this feature rather than packaging it in the main **app** module. These are called feature modules, and you can supplement them with other types of modules such as shared modules, which are used by all other modules like a networking module. The **settings.gradle** file will look like this:

```
include ':app'
rootProject.name='My Application'
```

EXERCISE 1.04: EXPLORING HOW MATERIAL DESIGN IS USED TO THEME AN APP

In this exercise, you will learn about Google's new design language, **Material Design**, and use it to load a **Material Design** themed app. **Material Design** is a design language created by Google that adds enriched UI elements based on real-world effects such as lighting, depth, shadows, and animations. Perform the following steps:

1. Create a new Android Studio project as you did in *Exercise 1.01*, *Creating an Android Studio Project for Your App*.

2. Firstly, look at the **dependencies** block and find the material design dependency

```
implementation 'com.google.android.material:material:1.2.1'
```

3. Next, open the **themes.xml** file located at **app | src | main | res | values | themes.xml**:

```xml
<resources xmlns:tools="http://schemas.android.com/tools">
    <!-- Base application theme. -->
    <style name="Theme.MyApplication"
      parent="Theme.MaterialComponents.DayNight.DarkActionBar">
        <!-- Primary brand color. -->
        <item name="colorPrimary">@color/purple_500</item>
        <item name="colorPrimaryVariant">@color/purple_700</item>
        <item name="colorOnPrimary">@color/white</item>
        <!-- Secondary brand color. -->
        <item name="colorSecondary">@color/teal_200</item>
        <item name="colorSecondaryVariant">@color/teal_700</item>
        <item name="colorOnSecondary">@color/black</item>
        <!-- Status bar color. -->
        <item name="android:statusBarColor"
          tools:targetApi="l">?attr/colorPrimaryVariant</item>
        <!-- Customize your theme here. -->
    </style>
</resources>
```

Notice that the parent of **Theme.MyApplication** is **Theme. MaterialComponents.DayNight.DarkActionBar**

The Material Design dependency added in the **dependencies** block is being used here to apply the theme of the app.

4. If you run the app now, you will see the default Material themed app as shown in *Figure 1.15*

In this exercise, you've learned how **Material Design** can be used to theme an app. As you are currently only displaying a **TextView** on the screen, it is not clear what benefits material design provides, but this will change when you start using Material UI design widgets more. Now that you've learned how the project is built and configured, in the next section, you'll explore the project structure in detail, learn how it has been created, and gain familiarity with the core areas of the development environment.

ANDROID APPLICATION STRUCTURE

Now that we have covered how the Gradle build tool works, we'll explore the rest of the project. The simplest way to do this is to examine the folder structure of the app. There is a tool window at the top left of Android Studio called **Project**, which allows you to browse the contents of your app. By default, it is **open/selected** when your Android project is first created. When you select it, you will see a view similar to the screenshot in *Figure 1.19*. (If you can't see any window bars on the left-hand side of the screen, then go to the top toolbar and select **View** | Appearance | **Tool Window Bars** and make sure it is ticked). There are many different options for how to browse your project, but **Android** will be pre-selected. This view neatly groups the **app** folder structure together, so let's take a look at it.

Here is an overview of these files with more detail about the most important ones. On opening it, you will see that it consists of the following folder structure:

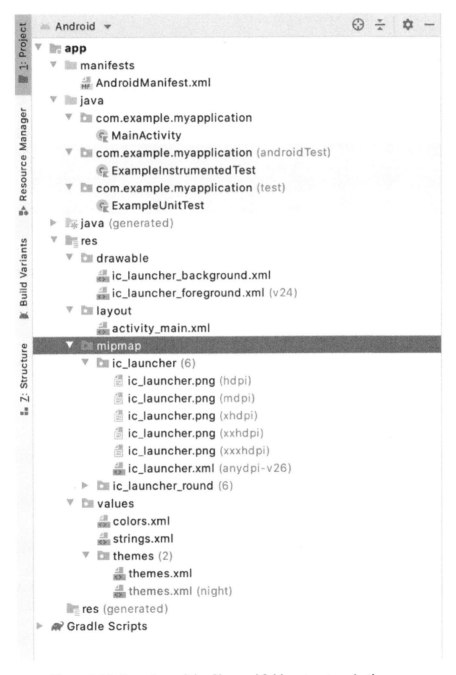

Figure 1.19: Overview of the files and folder structure in the app

The Kotlin file (**MainActivity**), which you've specified as running when the app starts, is as follows:

```
package com.example.myapplication

import androidx.appcompat.app.AppCompatActivity
import android.os.Bundle

class MainActivity : AppCompatActivity() {

    override fun onCreate(savedInstanceState: Bundle?) {
        super.onCreate(savedInstanceState)
        setContentView(R.layout.activity_main)
    }
}
```

The **import** statements include the libraries and the source of what this activity uses. The class header **class MainActivity : AppCompatActivity()** creates a class that extends **AppCompatActivity**. In Kotlin, the : colon character is used for both deriving from a class (also known as inheritance) and implementing an interface.

MainActivity derives from **androidx.appcompat.app.AppCompatActivity**, which is the backward-compatible activity designed to make your app work on older devices.

Android activities have many callback functions that you can override at different points of the activity's life. This is known as the **Activity Lifecycle**. For this activity, as you want to display a screen with a layout, you override the **onCreate** function as shown here:

```
override fun onCreate(savedInstanceState: Bundle?)
```

The **override** keyword in Kotlin specifies that you are providing a specific implementation for a function that is defined in the parent class. The **fun** keyword (as you may have guessed) stands for *function*. The **savedInstanceState: Bundle?** parameter is Android's mechanism for restoring previously saved state. For this simple activity, you haven't stored any state, so this value will be **null**. The question mark, **?**, that follows the type declares that this type can be **null**. The **super.onCreate(savedInstanceState)** line calls through to the overridden method of the base class, and finally, **setContentView(R.layout.Activity_main)** loads the layout we want to display in the activity; otherwise, it would be displayed as a blank screen as no layout has been defined.

Let's have a look at some other files (*Figure 1.19*) present in the folder structure:

- **ExampleInstrumentedTest**: This is an example UI test. You can check and verify the flow and structure of your app by running tests on the UI when the app is running.

- **ExampleUnitTest**: This is an example unit test. An essential part of creating an Android app is writing unit tests in order to verify that the source code works as expected.

- **ic_launcher_background.xml/ic_launcher_foreground.xml**: These two files together make up the launcher icon of your app in vector format, which will be used by the launcher icon file, **ic_launcher.xml**, in Android API 26 (Oreo) and above.

- **activity_main.xml**: This is the layout file that was created by Android Studio when we created the project. It is used by **MainActivity** to draw the initial screen content, which appears when the app runs:

```xml
<?xml version="1.0" encoding="utf-8"?>
<androidx.constraintlayout.widget.ConstraintLayout
    xmlns:android="http://schemas.android.com/apk/res/android"
    xmlns:app="http://schemas.android.com/apk/res-auto"
    xmlns:tools="http://schemas.android.com/tools"
    android:layout_width="match_parent"
    android:layout_height="match_parent"
    tools:context=".MainActivity">

    <TextView
        android:layout_width="wrap_content"
        android:layout_height="wrap_content"
        android:text="Hello World!"
        app:layout_constraintBottom_toBottomOf="parent"
        app:layout_constraintStart_toStartOf="parent"
        app:layout_constraintEnd_toEndOf="parent"
        app:layout_constraintTop_toTopOf="parent" />

</androidx.constraintlayout.widget.ConstraintLayout>
```

In order to support internationalization of your app and right-to-left (**rtl**) layouts, you should remove these attributes if they are present:

```
app:layout_constraintStart_toLeftOf="parent"
app:layout_constraintEnd_toRightOf="parent"
```

Replace them with the following:

```
app:layout_constraintStart_toStartOf="parent"
app:layout_constraintEnd_toEndOf="parent"
```

In this way, start and end are determined by the app language, whereas left and right mean start and end only in left-to-right languages.

Most screen displays in Android are created using XML layouts. The document starts with an XML header followed by a top-level **ViewGroup** (which here is **ConstraintLayout**) and then one or more nested **Views** and **ViewGroups**.

The **ConstraintLayout ViewGroup** allows very precise positioning of views on a screen constraining views with parent and sibling views, guidelines, and barriers.

TextView, which is currently the only child view of **ConstraintLayout**, displays text on the screen through the **android:text** attribute. The positioning of the view horizontally is done by constraining the view to both the start and end of the parent, which, as both constraints are applied, centers the view horizontally. (start and end in left-to-right languages (**ltr**) are left and right, but right-to-left in **non ltr** languages). The view is positioned vertically in the center by constraining the view to both the top and the bottom of its parent. The result of applying all four constraints centers **TextView** both horizontally and vertically within **ConstraintLayout**.

There are three XML namespaces in the **ConstraintLayout** tag:

- **xmlns:android** refers to the Android-specific namespace and it is used for all attributes and values within the main Android SDK.

- The **xmlns:app** namespace is for anything not in the Android SDK. So, in this case, **ConstraintLayout** is not part of the main Android SDK but is added as a library.

- **xmnls:tools** refers to a namespace used for adding metadata to the XML, which is used to indicate here where the layout is used (**tools:context=". MainActivity"**).

The two most important attributes of an Android XML layout file are **android:layout_width** and **android:layout_height**.

These can be set to absolute values, usually of density-independent pixels (known as **dip** or **dp**) that scale pixel sizes to be roughly equivalent on different density devices. More commonly, however, these attributes have the values of **wrap_content** or **match_parent** set for them. **wrap_content** will be as big as required to enclose its contents only. **match_parent** will be sized according to its parent.

There are other **ViewGroups** you can use to create layouts. **LinearLayout** lays out views vertically or horizontally, **FrameLayout** is usually used to display a single child view, and **RelativeLayout** is a simpler version of **ConstraintLayout**, which lays out views positioned relative to the parent and sibling views.

The **ic_launcher.png** files are **.png** launcher icons that have an icon for every different density of devices. As the minimum version of Android we are using is API 16: Android 4.1 (Jelly Bean), these **.png** images are included as support for the launcher vector format was not introduced until Android API 26 (Oreo).

The **ic_launcher.xml** file uses the vector files (**ic_launcher_background. xml/ic_launcher_foreground.xml**) to scale to different density devices in Android API 26 (Oreo) and above.

> **NOTE**
>
> In order to target different density devices on the Android platform, besides each one of the **ic_launcher.png** icons, you will see in brackets the density it targets. As devices vary widely in their pixel densities, Google created density buckets so that the correct image would be selected to be displayed depending on how many dots per inch the device has.

The different density qualifiers and their details are as follows:

- **nodpi**: Density-independent resources
- **ldpi**: Low-density screens of 120 dpi
- **mdpi**: Medium-density screens of 160 dpi (the baseline)
- **hdpi**: High-density screens of 240 dpi
- **xhdpi**: Extra-high-density screens of 320 dpi
- **xxhdpi**: Extra-extra-high-density screens of 480 dpi

- **xxxhdpi**: Extra-extra-extra-high-density screens of 640 dpi

- **tvdpi**: Resources for televisions (approx 213 dpi)

The baseline density bucket was created at **160** dots per inch for medium-density devices and is called **mdpi**. This represents a device where an inch of the screen is **160** dots/pixels, and the largest display bucket is **xxxhdpi**, which has **640** dots per inch. Android determines the appropriate image to display based on the individual device. So, the Pixel 3 emulator has a density of approximately **443dpi**, so it uses resources from the extra-extra-high-density bucket (xxhdpi), which is the closest match. Android has a preference for scaling down resources to best match density buckets, so a device with **400dpi**, which is halfway between the **xhdpi** and **xxhdpi** buckets, is likely to display the **480dpi** asset from the **xxhdpi** bucket.

To create alternative bitmap drawables for different densities, you should follow the **3:4:6:8:12:16** scaling ratio between the six primary densities. For example, if you have a bitmap drawable that's **48x48** pixels for medium-density screens, all the different sizes should be:

- **36x36** (**0.75x**) for low density (**ldpi**)

- **48x48** (**1.0x** baseline) for medium density (**mdpi**)

- **72x72** (**1.5x**) for high density (**hdpi**)

- **96x96** (**2.0x**) for extra-high density (**xhdpi**)

- **144x144** (**3.0x**) for extra-extra-high density (**xxhdpi**)

- **192x192** (**4.0x**) for extra-extra-extra-high density (**xxxhdpi**)

For a comparison of these physical launcher icons per density bucket, refer to the following table:

mdpe	hdpi	xhdpi	xxhdpi	xxxhdpi

Figure 1.20: Comparison of principal density bucket launcher image sizes

> **NOTE**
>
> Launcher icons are made slightly larger than normal images within your app as they will be used by the device's launcher. As some launchers can scale up the image, this is to ensure there is no pixelation and blurring of the image.

Now you are going to look at some of the resources the app uses. These are referenced in XML files and keep the display and formatting of your app consistent.

In the **colors.xml** file, you define the colors you would like to use in your app in hexadecimal format.

```xml
<?xml version="1.0" encoding="utf-8"?>
<resources>
    <color name="purple_200">#FFBB86FC</color>
    <color name="purple_500">#FF6200EE</color>
    <color name="purple_700">#FF3700B3</color>
    <color name="teal_200">#FF03DAC5</color>
    <color name="teal_700">#FF018786</color>
    <color name="black">#FF000000</color>
    <color name="white">#FFFFFFFF</color>
</resources>
```

The format is based on the RGB color space, so the first two characters are for red, the next two for green, and the last two for blue, where **#00** means none of the color is added to make up the composite color, and **#FF** means all of the color is added.

If you would like some transparency in the color, then precede it with two hexadecimal characters, from **#00** for completely transparent to **#FF** for completely opaque. So, to create blue and 50% transparent blue characters, here's the format:

```xml
    <color name="colorBlue">#0000FF</color>
    <color name="colorBlue50PercentTransparent">#770000FF</color>
```

The **strings.xml** file displays all the text displayed in the app:

```xml
<resources>
    <string name="app_name">My Application</string>
</resources>
```

You can use hardcoded strings in your app, but this leads to duplication and also means you cannot customize the text if you want to make the app multilingual. By adding strings as resources, you can also update the string in one place if it is used in different places in the app.

Common styles you would like to use throughout your app are added to the **themes.xml** file.

```
<resources xmlns:tools="http://schemas.android.com/tools">
    <!-- Base application theme. -->
    <style name="Theme.MyApplication"
      parent="Theme.MaterialComponents.DayNight.DarkActionBar">
        <!-- Primary brand color. -->
        <item name="colorPrimary">@color/purple_500</item>
        <item name="colorPrimaryVariant">@color/purple_700</item>
        <item name="colorOnPrimary">@color/white</item>
        <!-- Secondary brand color. -->
        <item name="colorSecondary">@color/teal_200</item>
        <item name="colorSecondaryVariant">@color/teal_700</item>
        <item name="colorOnSecondary">@color/black</item>
        <!-- Status bar color. -->
        <item name="android:statusBarColor"
          tools:targetApi="l">?attr/colorPrimaryVariant</item>
        <!-- Customize your theme here. -->
    </style>
</resources>
```

It is possible to apply style information directly to views by setting **android:textStyle="bold"** as an attribute on **TextView**. However, you would have to repeat this in multiple places for every **TextView** you wanted to display in bold. When you start to have multiple style attributes added to individual views, it adds a lot of duplication and can lead to errors when you want to make a change to all similar views and miss changing a style attribute on one view. If you define a style, you only have to change the style and it will update all the views that have that style applied to them. A top-level theme was applied to the application tag in the **AndroidManifest.xml** file when you created the project and is referred to as a theme that styles all views contained within the app. The colors you have defined in the **colors.xml** file are used here. In effect, if you change one of the colors defined in the **colors.xml** file, it will now propagate to style the app as well.

You've now explored the core areas of the app. You have added **TextView** views to display labels, headings, and blocks of text. In the next exercise, you will be introduced to UI elements that will allow the user to interact with your app.

EXERCISE 1.05: ADDING INTERACTIVE UI ELEMENTS TO DISPLAY A BESPOKE GREETING TO THE USER

The goal of this exercise is to add the capability of users to add and edit text and then submit this information to display a bespoke greeting with the entered data. You will need to add editable text views to achieve this. The **EditText** View is typically how this is done and can be added in an XML layout file like this:

```
<EditText
    android:id="@+id/full_name"
    style="@style/TextAppearance.AppCompat.Title"
    android:layout_width="wrap_content"
    android:layout_height="wrap_content"
    android:hint="@string/first_name" />
```

This uses an android style **TextAppearance.AppCompat.Title** to display a title as shown below:

First name:

Figure 1.21: EditText with hint

Although this is perfectly fine to enable the user to add/edit text, the material **TextInputEditText** and it's wrapper View **TextInputLayout** view gives some polish to the **EditText** display. Let's use the following code:

```
<com.google.android.material.textfield.TextInputLayout
    android:id="@+id/first_name_wrapper"
    style="@style/text_input_greeting"
    android:layout_width="match_parent"
    android:layout_height="wrap_content"
    android:hint="@string/first_name_text">

    <com.google.android.material.textfield.TextInputEditText
        android:id="@+id/first_name"
        android:layout_width="match_parent"
```

```
                android:layout_height="wrap_content" />

    </com.google.android.material.textfield.TextInputLayout>
```

The output is as follows:

Figure 1.22: Material TextInputLayout/TextInputEditText with hint

TextInputLayout allows us to create a label for the **TextInputEditText** view and does a nice animation when the **TextInputEditText** view is focused (moving to the top of the field) while still displaying the label. The label is specified with **android:hint**.

You are going to change the **Hello World** text in your app so a user can enter their first and last name and further display a greeting on pressing a button. Perform the following steps:

1. Create the labels and text you are going to use in your app by adding these entries to **app | src | main | res | values | strings.xml**:

```xml
<resources>
    <string name="app_name">My Application</string>
    <string name="first_name_text">First name:</string>
    <string name="last_name_text">Last name:</string>
    <string name="enter_button_text">Enter</string>
    <string name="welcome_to_the_app">Welcome to the app</string>
    <string name="please_enter_a_name">Please enter a full name!
    </string>
</resources>
```

2. Next, we are going to update our styles to use in the layout by adding the following styles to **app | src | main | res | themes.xml** after the Base application theme)

```xml
<resources xmlns:tools="http://schemas.android.com/tools">

    <!-- Base application theme. -->
    <style name="Theme.MyApplication"
      parent="Theme.MaterialComponents.DayNight.DarkActionBar">
        <!-- Primary brand color. -->
```

```xml
        <item name="colorPrimary">@color/purple_500</item>
        <item name="colorPrimaryVariant">@color/purple_700</item>
        <item name="colorOnPrimary">@color/white</item>
        <!-- Secondary brand color. -->
        <item name="colorSecondary">@color/teal_200</item>
        <item name="colorSecondaryVariant">@color/teal_700</item>
        <item name="colorOnSecondary">@color/black</item>
        <!-- Status bar color. -->
        <item name="android:statusBarColor"
          tools:targetApi="l">?attr/colorPrimaryVariant</item>
        <!-- Customize your theme here. -->
    </style>

    <style name="text_input_greeting"
      parent="Widget.MaterialComponents.TextInputLayout.OutlinedBox">
        <item name="android:layout_margin">8dp</item>
    </style>

    <style name="button_greeting">
        <item name="android:layout_margin">8dp</item>
        <item name="android:gravity">center</item>
    </style>

    <style name="greeting_display"
        parent="@style/TextAppearance.MaterialComponents.Body1">
        <item name="android:layout_margin">8dp</item>
        <item name="android:gravity">center</item>
        <item name="android:layout_height">40dp</item>
    </style>

    <style name="screen_layout_margin">
        <item name="android:layout_margin">12dp</item>
    </style>

</resources>
```

NOTE

The parents of some of the styles refer to material styles, so these styles will be applied directly to the views as well as the styles that are specified.

3. Now that we have added the styles we want to apply to views in the layout and the text, we can update the layout in **`activity_main.xml`** in **`app`** | **`src`** | **`main`** | **`res`** | **`layout`** folder. The code below is truncated for space, but you can view the full source code using the link below.

`activity_main.xml`

```
10    <com.google.android.material.textfield.TextInputLayout
11        android:id="@+id/first_name_wrapper"
12        style="@style/text_input_greeting"
13        android:layout_width="match_parent"
14        android:layout_height="wrap_content"
15        android:hint="@string/first_name_text"
16        app:layout_constraintTop_toTopOf="parent"
17        app:layout_constraintStart_toStartOf="parent">
18
19        <com.google.android.material.textfield.TextInputEditText
20            android:id="@+id/first_name"
21            android:layout_width="match_parent"
22            android:layout_height="wrap_content" />
23
24    </com.google.android.material.textfield.TextInputLayout>
25
26    <com.google.android.material.textfield.TextInputLayout
27        android:id="@+id/last_name_wrapper"
28        style="@style/text_input_greeting"
29        android:layout_width="match_parent"
30        android:layout_height="wrap_content"
31        android:hint="@string/last_name_text"
32        app:layout_constraintTop_toBottomOf="@id/first_name_wrapper"
33        app:layout_constraintStart_toStartOf="parent">
34
35        <com.google.android.material.textfield.TextInputEditText
36            android:id="@+id/last_name"
37            android:layout_width="match_parent"
38            android:layout_height="wrap_content" />
39
40    </com.google.android.material.textfield.TextInputLayout>
41
42    <com.google.android.material.button.MaterialButton
43        android:layout_width="match_parent"
44        android:layout_height="wrap_content"
45        style="@style/button_greeting"
46        android:id="@+id/enter_button"
47        android:text="@string/enter_button_text"
48        app:layout_constraintTop_toBottomOf="@id/last_name_wrapper"
49        app:layout_constraintStart_toStartOf="parent"/>
50
51    <TextView
52        android:id="@+id/greeting_display"
53        android:layout_width="match_parent"
54        style="@style/greeting_display"
55        app:layout_constraintTop_toBottomOf="@id/enter_button"
56        app:layout_constraintStart_toStartOf="parent" />
```

The complete code for this step can be found at http://packt.live/35T5IMN.

You have added IDs for all the views so they can be constrained against their siblings and also provided a way in the activity to get the values of the **TextInputEditText** views. The **style="@style.."** notation applies the style from the **themes.xml** file.

4. Run the app and see the look and feel. If you select one of the **TextInputEditText** views, you'll see the label animated and move to the top of the view:

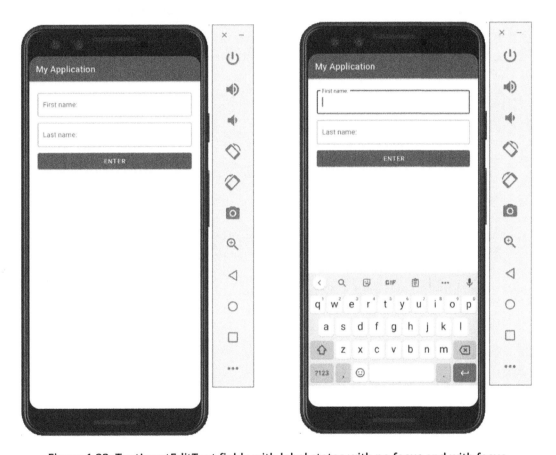

Figure 1.23: TextInputEditText fields with label states with no focus and with focus

5. Now, we have to add the interaction with the view in our activity. The layout by itself doesn't do anything other than allow the user to enter text into the **EditText** fields. Clicking the button at this stage will not do anything. You will accomplish this by capturing the entered text by using the IDs of the form fields when the button is pressed and then using the text to populate a **TextView** message.

6. Open **MainActivity** and complete the next steps to process the entered text and use this data to display a greeting and handle any form input errors.

7. In the **onCreate** function, set a click listener on the button so we can respond to the button click and retrieve the form data by updating **MainActivity** to what is displayed below:

```
package com.example.myapplication

import androidx.appcompat.app.AppCompatActivity
import android.os.Bundle
import android.view.Gravity
import android.widget.Button
import android.widget.TextView
import android.widget.Toast
import com.google.android.material.textfield.TextInputEditText

class MainActivity : AppCompatActivity() {
    override fun onCreate(savedInstanceState: Bundle?) {
        super.onCreate(savedInstanceState)
        setContentView(R.layout.activity_main)

        findViewById<Button>(R.id.enter_button)?.setOnClickListener {
            //Get the greeting display text
            val greetingDisplay =
                findViewById<TextView>(R.id.greeting_display)

            //Get the first name TextInputEditText value
            val firstName = findViewById<TextInputEditText>
                (R.id.first_name)?.text.toString().trim()
```

```
                 //Get the last name TextInputEditText value
                 val lastName = findViewById<TextInputEditText>
                   (R.id.last_name)?.text.toString().trim()


                 //Check names are not empty here:
             }

         }

     }
```

8. Then, check that the trimmed names are not empty and format the name using Kotlin's string templates:

```
if (firstName.isNotEmpty() && lastName.isNotEmpty()) {

    val nameToDisplay = firstName.plus(" ").plus(lastName)
    //Use Kotlin's string templates feature to display the name
    greetingDisplay?.text =
        " ${getString(R.string.welcome_to_the_app)}
${nameToDisplay}!"
}
```

9. Finally, show a message if the form fields have not been filled in correctly:

```
else {
    Toast.makeText(this, getString(R.string.please_enter_a_name),
      Toast.LENGTH_LONG).
    apply{
        setGravity(Gravity.CENTER, 0, 0)
        show()
    }
}
```

The **Toast** specified is a small text dialog that appears above the main layout for a short time to display a message to the user before disappearing.

10. Run up the app and enter text into the fields and verify that a greeting message is shown when both text fields are filled in, and a pop-up message appears with why the greeting hasn't been set if both fields are not filled in. You should see the following display for each one of these cases:

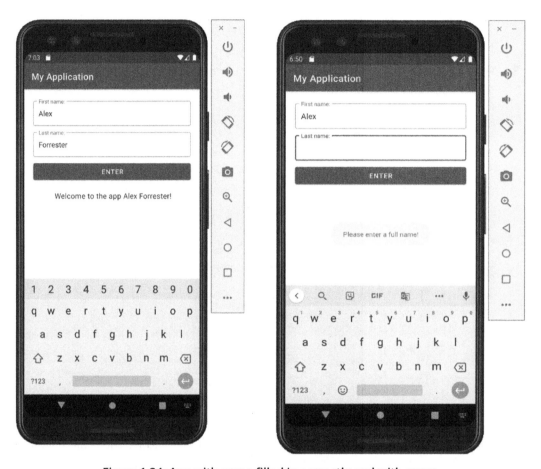

Figure 1.24: App with name filled in correctly and with error

The full exercise code can be viewed here: http://packt.live/39JyOzB.

The preceding exercise has introduced you to adding interactivity to your app with **EditText** fields that a user can fill in, adding a click listener to respond to button events and perform some validation.

ACCESSING VIEWS IN LAYOUT FILES

The established way to access Views in layout files is to use **findViewById** with the name of the View's id. So the **enter_button Button** is retrieved by the syntax **findViewById<Button>(R.id.enter_button)** after the layout has been set in **setContentView(R.layout.activity_main)** in the Activity. You will use this technique in this course. Google has also introduced ViewBinding to replace **findViewById** which creates a binding class to access Views and has the advantage of null and type safety. You can read about this here: https://developer.android.com/topic/libraries/view-binding.

FURTHER INPUT VALIDATION

Validating user input is a key concept in processing user data and you must have seen it in action many times when you've not entered a required field in a form. This is what the previous exercise was validating when it checked that the user had entered values into both the first name and last name field.

There are other validation options that are available directly within XML view elements. Let's say, for instance, you wanted to validate an IP address entered into a field. You know that an IP address can be four numbers separated by periods/dots where the maximum length of a number is 3. So, the maximum number of characters that can be entered into the field is 15, and only numbers and periods can be entered. There are two XML attributes that can help us with the validation:

- **android:digits="0123456789."**: Restricts the characters that can be entered into the field by listing all the permitted individual characters.

- **android:maxLength="15"**: Restricts the user from entering more than the maximum number of characters an IP address will consist of.

So, this is how you could display this in a form field:

```
<com.google.android.material.textfield.TextInputLayout
    style="@style/Widget.MaterialComponents.TextInputLayout.OutlinedBox"
    android:layout_width="match_parent"
    android:layout_height="wrap_content">

    <com.google.android.material.textfield.TextInputEditText
        android:id="@+id/ip_address"
        android:digits="0123456789."
```

```
        android:layout_width="match_parent"
        android:layout_height="wrap_content"
        android:maxLength="15" />
</com.google.android.material.textfield.TextInputLayout>
```

This validation restricts the characters that can be input and the maximum length. Additional validation would be required on the sequence of characters and whether they are periods/dots or numbers, as per the IP address format, but it is the first step to assist the user in entering the correct characters.

With the knowledge gained from the chapter, let's start with the following activity.

ACTIVITY 1.01: PRODUCING AN APP TO CREATE RGB COLORS

In this activity, we will look into a scenario that uses validation. Suppose you have been tasked with creating an app that shows how the RGB channels of Red, Green, and Blue are added to the RGB color space to create a color. Each of the RGB channels should be added as two hexadecimal characters, where each character can be a value of 0-9 or A-F. The values will then be combined to produce a 6-character hexadecimal string that is displayed as a color within the app.

The aim of this activity is to produce a form with editable fields in which the user can add two hexadecimal values for each color. After filling in all three fields, the user should click a button that takes the three values and concatenates them to create a valid hexadecimal color string. This should then be converted to a color and displayed in the UI of the app.

The following steps will help you to complete the activity:

1. Create a new project called **Colors**

2. Add a title to the layout constrained to the top of the layout.

3. Add a brief description to the user on how to complete the form.

4. Add three material **TextInputLayout** fields wrapping three **TextInputEditText** fields that appear under **Title**. These should be constrained so that each view is on top of the other (rather than to the side). Name the **TextInputEditText** fields **Red Channel**, **Green Channel**, and **Blue Channel**, respectively, and add a restriction to each field to only be able to enter two characters and add hexadecimal characters.

5. Add a button that takes the inputs from the three-color fields.

6. Add a view that will display the produced color in the layout.

7. Finally, display the RGB color created from the three channels in the layout.

The final output should look like this (the color will vary depending on the inputs):

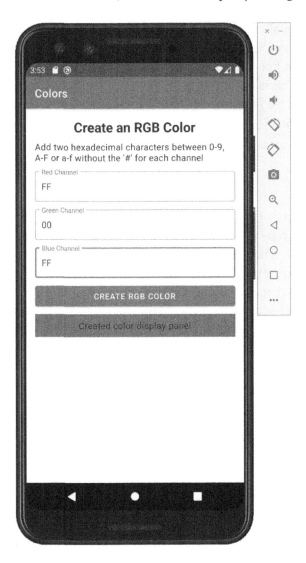

Figure 1.25: Output when the color is displayed

NOTE

The solution to this activity can be found at: http://packt.live/3sKj1cp.

The sources for all the exercises and the activity in this chapter are located here:
http://packt.live/2LLY9kb

> **NOTE**
>
> When loading all completed projects from the Github repository for this course into Android Studio for the first time, do *not* open the project using `File` | `Open` from the Top menu. Always use `File` | `New` | `Import Project`. This is needed to build the app correctly. When opening projects after the initial import, you can use `File` | `Open or File` | `Open Recent`.

SUMMARY

This chapter has covered a lot about the foundations of Android development. You started off with how to create Android projects using Android Studio and then created and ran apps on a virtual device. The chapter then progressed by exploring the **AndroidManifest** file, which details the contents of your app and the permission model, followed by an introduction to Gradle and the process of adding dependencies and building your app. This was then followed by going into the details of an Android application and the files and folder structure. Layouts and views were introduced, and exercises iterated on to illustrate how to construct UIs with an introduction to Google's Material Design. The next chapter will build on this knowledge by learning about the activity lifecycle, activity tasks, and launch modes, persisting and sharing data between screens, and how to create robust user journeys through your apps.

2

BUILDING USER SCREEN FLOWS

OVERVIEW

This chapter covers the Android activity lifecycle and explains how the Android system interacts with your app. By the end of this chapter, you'll have learned how to build user journeys through different screens. You'll also be able to use activity tasks and launch modes, save and restore the state of your activity, use logs to report on your application, and share data between screens.

INTRODUCTION

The previous chapter introduced you to the core elements of Android development, from configuring your app using the **AndroidManifest.xml** file, working with simple activities, and the Android resource structure, to building an app with **build. gradle** and running an app on a virtual device. In this chapter, you'll go further and learn how the Android system interacts with your app through the Android lifecycle, how you are notified of changes to your app's state, and how you can use the Android lifecycle to respond to these changes. You'll then progress to learning how to create user journeys through your app and how to share data between screens. You'll be introduced to different techniques to achieve these goals so that you'll be able to use them in your own apps and recognize them when you see them used in other apps.

THE ACTIVITY LIFECYCLE

In the previous chapter, we used the **onCreate(saveInstanceState: Bundle?)** method to display a layout in the UI of our screen. Now, we'll explore in more detail how the Android system interacts with your application to make this happen. As soon as an Activity is launched, it goes through a series of steps to take it through initialization and preparing it to be displayed to being partially displayed, and then fully displayed. There are also steps that correspond with your application being hidden, backgrounded, and then destroyed. This process is called the **Activity lifecycle**. For every one of these steps, there is a **callback** that your Activity can use to perform actions such as creating and changing the display and saving data when your app has been put into the background and then restoring that data after your app comes back into the foreground. You can consider these callbacks as hooks into how the system interacts with your activity/screen.

Every Activity has a parent Activity class that it extends. These callbacks are made on your Activity's parent, and it's up to you to decide whether you need to implement them in your own Activity to take any corresponding action. Every one of these callback functions has the **override** keyword. The **override** keyword in Kotlin means that either this function is providing an implementation of an interface or an abstract method, or, in the case of your Activity here, which is a subclass, it is providing the implementation that will override its parent.

Now that you know how the **Activity lifecycle** works in general, let's go into more detail about the principal callbacks you will work with in order, from creating an Activity to the Activity being destroyed:

- **override fun onCreate(savedInstanceState: Bundle?)**: This is the callback that you will use the most for activities that draw a full-sized screen. It's here where you prepare your Activity layout to be displayed. At this stage, after the method completes, it is still not displayed to the user, although it will appear that way if you don't implement any other callbacks. You usually set up the UI of your Activity here by calling the **setContentView** method **setContentView(R.layout.activity_main)** and carry out any initialization that is required. This method is only called once in its **lifecycle** unless the Activity is created again. This happens by default for some actions (such as rotating the phone from portrait to landscape orientation, for example). The **savedInstanceState** parameter of the **Bundle?** type (**?** means the type can be null) in its simplest form is a map of key-value pairs optimized to save and restore data. It will be null if this is the first time that the Activity has been run after the app has started or if the Activity is being created for the first time or recreated without any states being saved. It may contain a saved state if it has been saved in the **onSaveInstanceState(outState: Bundle?)** callback prior to the Activity being recreated.

- **override fun onRestart()**: When the Activity restarts, this is called immediately before **onStart()**. It is important to be clear about the difference between restarting an Activity and recreating an activity. When the Activity is backgrounded by pressing the home button—for instance, when it comes back into the foreground again—**onRestart()** will be called. Recreating an Activity is what happens when a configuration change happens, such as the device being rotated. The Activity is finished and then created again.

- **override fun onStart()**: This is the callback made when the Activity first comes into view. Also, after the app is backgrounded by pressing either the back, home, or the **recents/overview** hardware buttons, on selecting the app again from the **recents/overview** menu or the launcher, this function will be run. It is the first of the visible lifecycle methods.

- **override fun onRestoreInstanceState(savedInstanceState: Bundle?)**: If the state has been saved using **onSaveInstanceState(outState: Bundle?)** this is the method which the system calls after **onStart()** where you can retrieve the **Bundle** state instead of restoring the state during **onCreate(savedInstanceState: Bundle?)**

- **override fun onResume()**: This callback is run as the final stage of creating an Activity for the first time, and also when the app has been backgrounded and then is brought into the foreground. Upon the completion of this callback, the screen/activity is ready to be used, receive user events, and be responsive.

- **override fun onSaveInstanceState(outState: Bundle?)**: If you want to save the state of the activity, this function can do so. You add key-value pairs using one of the convenience functions depending on the data type. The data will then be available if your Activity is recreated in **onCreate(saveInstanceState: Bundle?)** and **onRestoreInstanceState(savedInstanceState: Bundle?)**.

- **override fun onPause()**: This function is called when the Activity starts to be backgrounded or another dialog or Activity comes into the foreground.

- **override fun onStop()**: This function is called when the Activity is hidden, either because it is being backgrounded or another Activity is being launched on top of it.

- **override fun onDestroy()**: This is called by the system to kill the Activity when system resources are low, when **finish()** is called explicitly on the Activity, or, more commonly, when the Activity is killed by the user closing the app from the recents/overview button.

Now that you understand what these common lifecycle callbacks do, let's implement them to see when they are called.

EXERCISE 2.01: LOGGING THE ACTIVITY CALLBACKS

Let's create an application called *Activity Callbacks* with an empty Activity, as you did previously in *Chapter 1, Creating Your First App*. The aim of this exercise is to log the Activity callbacks and the order that they occur for common operations:

1. After the application has been created, **MainActivity** will appear as follows:

```
package com.example.activitycallbacks

import androidx.appcompat.app.AppCompatActivity
import android.os.Bundle

class MainActivity : AppCompatActivity() {
```

```
        override fun onCreate(savedInstanceState: Bundle?) {
            super.onCreate(savedInstanceState)
            setContentView(R.layout.activity_main)
        }
    }
```

In order to verify the order of the callbacks, let's add a log statement at the end of each callback. To prepare the Activity for logging, import the Android log package by adding **import android.util.Log** to the **import** statements. Then, add a constant to the class to identify your Activity. Constants in Kotlin are identified by the **const** keyword and can be declared at the top level (outside the class) or in an object within the class. Top level constants are generally used if they are required to be public. For private constants, Kotlin provides a convenient way to add static functionality to classes by declaring a companion object. Add the following at the bottom of the class below **onCreate(savedInstanceState: Bundle?)**:

```
companion object {
    private const val TAG = "MainActivity"
}
```

Then add a log statement at the end of **onCreate(savedInstanceState: Bundle?)**:

```
Log.d(TAG, "onCreate")
```

Our Activity should now have the following code:

```
package com.example.activitycallbacks

import android.os.Bundle
import android.util.Log
import androidx.appcompat.app.AppCompatActivity

class MainActivity : AppCompatActivity() {

    override fun onCreate(savedInstanceState: Bundle?) {
        super.onCreate(savedInstanceState)
        setContentView(R.layout.activity_main)
        Log.d(TAG, "onCreate")
    }
```

```
companion object {
    private const val TAG = "MainActivity"
}
}
```

d in the preceding log statement refers to *debug*. There are six different log levels that can be used to output message information from the least to most important - **v** for *verbose*, **d** for *debug*, **i** for *info*, **w** for *warn*, **e** for *error*, and **wtf** for *what a terrible failure*. (This last log level highlights an exception that should never occur.)

```
Log.v(TAG, "verbose message")
Log.d(TAG, "debug message")
Log.i(TAG, "info message")
Log.w(TAG, "warning message")
Log.e(TAG, "error message")
Log.wtf(TAG, "what a terrible failure message")
```

2.   Now, let's see how the logs are displayed in Android Studio. Open the **Logcat** window. It can be accessed by clicking on the **Logcat** tab at the bottom of the screen and also from the toolbar by going to **View | Tool Windows | Logcat**.

3.   Run the app on the virtual device and examine the **Logcat** window output. You should see the log statement you have added formatted like the following line in *Figure 2.1*:

Figure 2.1: Log output in Logcat

4. Log statements can be quite difficult to interpret at first glance, so let's break down the following statement into its separate parts:

```
2020-03-03  20:36:12.308  21415-21415/com.example.activitycallbacks
D/MainActivity: onCreate
```

Let's examine the elements of the log statement in detail:

Fields	Values
Date	`2020-03-03`
Time	`20:36:12.308`
Process identifier and thread identifier (your app process ID and current thread ID)	`21415-21415`
Package name	`com.example.activitycallbacks`
Log level	`D (for Debug)`
Tag name	`MainActivity`
Log message	`onCreate`

Figure 2.2: Table explaining a log statement

You can examine the output of the different log levels by changing the log filter from **Debug** to other options in the drop-down menu. If you select **Verbose**, as the name implies, you will see a lot of output.

5. What's great about the **TAG** option of the log statement is that it enables you to filter the log statements that are reported in the **Logcat** window of Android Studio by typing in the text of the tag, as shown in *Figure 2.3*:

Figure 2.3: Filtering log statements by the TAG name

So, if you are debugging an issue in your Activity, you can type in the **TAG** name and add logs to your Activity to see the sequence of log statements. This is what you are going to do next by implementing the principal Activity callbacks and adding a log statement to each one to see when they are run.

6. Place your cursor on a new line after the closing brace of the **onCreate(savedInstanceState: Bundle?)** function and then add the **onRestart()** callback with a log statement. Make sure you call through to **super.onRestart()** so that the existing functionality of the Activity callback works as expected:

```
override fun onRestart() {
    super.onRestart()
    Log.d(TAG, "onRestart")
}
```

7. You will find that once you start typing the name of the function, Android Studio's autocomplete feature will suggest options for the name of the function you want to override.

> **NOTE**
>
> In Android Studio you can start typing the name of a function, and autocomplete options will pop up with suggestions for functions to override. Alternatively, if you go to the top menu and then **Code | Generate | Override methods**, you can select the methods to override.

Do this for all of the following callback functions:

```
onCreate(savedInstanceState: Bundle?)
onRestart()
onStart()
onRestoreInstanceState(savedInstanceState: Bundle?)
onResume()
onPause()
onStop()
onSaveInstanceStateoutState: Bundle?)
onDestroy()
```

8. Your Activity should now have the following code (truncated here). You can see the full code on GitHub at http://packt.live/38W7jU5

    The completed activity will now override the callbacks with your implementation, which adds a log message:

```
package com.example.activitycallbacks

import android.os.Bundle
import android.util.Log
import androidx.appcompat.app.AppCompatActivity

class MainActivity : AppCompatActivity() {

    override fun onCreate(savedInstanceState: Bundle?) {
        super.onCreate(savedInstanceState)
        setContentView(R.layout.activity_main)
        Log.d(TAG, "onCreate")
    }

    override fun onRestart() {
        super.onRestart()
        Log.d(TAG, "onRestart")
    }

    //Remaining callbacks follow: see github link above

    companion object {
        private const val TAG = "MainActivity"
    }
}
```

9. Run the app, and then once it has loaded, as in *Figure 2.4*, look at the **Logcat** output; you should see the following log statements (this is a shortened version):

```
D/MainActivity: onCreate
D/MainActivity: onStart
D/MainActivity: onResume
```

The Activity has been created, started, and then prepared for the user to interact with:

Figure 2.4: The app loaded and displaying MainActivity

10. Press the round home button in the center of the bottom navigation controls and background the app. You should now see the following Logcat output:

```
D/MainActivity: onPause
D/MainActivity: onStop
D/MainActivity: onSaveInstanceState
```

For apps which target below Android Pie (API 28) then **onSaveInstanceState(outState: Bundle?)** may also be called before **onPause()** or **onStop()**.

11. Now, bring the app back into the foreground by pressing the recents/overview button (usually a square or three vertical lines) on the right and selecting the app, or by going to the launcher and opening the app. You should now see the following:

```
D/MainActivity: onRestart
D/MainActivity: onStart
D/MainActivity: onResume
```

The Activity has been restarted. You might have noticed that the **onRestoreInstanceState(savedInstanceState: Bundle)** function was not called. This is because the Activity was not destroyed and recreated.

12. Press the triangle back button on the left of the bottom navigation controls (it may also be on the right) and you will see the Activity being destroyed. You can also do this by pressing the recents/overview button and then swiping the app upward to kill the activity. This is the output:

```
D/MainActivity: onPause
D/MainActivity: onStop
D/MainActivity: onDestroy
```

13. Launch your app again and then rotate the phone. You might find that the phone does not rotate and the display is sideways. If this happens drag down the status bar at the very top of the virtual device and select the auto-rotate button 2nd from the right in the settings.

Figure 2.5: Quick settings bar with Wi-Fi and Auto-rotate button selected

You should see the following callbacks:

```
D/MainActivity: onCreate
D/MainActivity: onStart
D/MainActivity: onResume

D/MainActivity: onPause
D/MainActivity: onStop
D/MainActivity: onSaveInstanceState
D/MainActivity: onDestroy

D/MainActivity: onCreate
D/MainActivity: onStart
D/MainActivity: onRestoreInstanceState
D/MainActivity: onResume
```

Please note that as stated in step 11, the order of the **onSaveInstanceState(outState: Bundle?)** callback may vary.

14. Configuration changes, such as rotating the phone, by default recreate the activity. You can choose not to handle certain configuration changes in the app, which will then not recreate the activity. To do this for rotation, add **android:configChanges="orientation|screenSize| screenLayout"** to **MainActivity** in the **AndroidManifest.xml** file. Launch the app and then rotate the phone, and these are the only callbacks that you have added to **MainActivity** that you will see:

```
D/MainActivity: onCreate
D/MainActivity: onStart
D/MainActivity: onResume
```

The **orientation** and **screenSize** values have the same function for different Android API levels for detecting screen orientation changes. The **screenLayout** value detects other layout changes which might occur on foldable phones. These are some of the config changes you can choose to handle yourself (another common one is **keyboardHidden** to react to changes in accessing the keyboard). The app will still be notified by the system of these changes through the following callback:

```
override fun onConfigurationChanged(newConfig: Configuration) {
    super.onConfigurationChanged(newConfig)
    Log.d(TAG, "onConfigurationChanged")
}
```

If you add this callback function to **MainActivity**, and you have added
**android:configChanges="orientation|screenSize|
screenLayout"** to **MainActivity** in the manifest, you will see it called
on rotation.

In this exercise, you have learned about the principal Activity callbacks and how they
run when a user carries out common operations with your app through the system's
interaction with **MainActivity**. In the next section, you will cover saving the state
and restoring it, as well as see more examples of how the Activity lifecycle works.

SAVING AND RESTORING THE ACTIVITY STATE

In this section, you'll explore how your Activity saves and restores the state. As you've
learned in the previous section, configuration changes, such as rotating the phone,
cause the Activity to be recreated. This can also happen if the system has to kill your
app in order to free up memory. In these scenarios, it is important to preserve the
state of the Activity and then restore it. In the next two exercises, you'll work through
an example ensuring that the user's data is restored when **TextView** is created and
populated from a user's data after filling in a form.

EXERCISE 2.02: SAVING AND RESTORING THE STATE IN LAYOUTS

In this exercise, firstly create an application called *Save and Restore* with an empty
activity. The app you are going to create will have a simple form that offers a discount
code for a user's favorite restaurant if they enter some personal details (no actual
information will be sent anywhere, so your data is safe):

1. Open up the **strings.xml** file (located in **app | src | main | res | values
   | strings.xml**) and create the following strings that you'll need for your app:

```
<resources>
    <string name="app_name">Save And Restore</string>
    <string name="header_text">Enter your name and email
      for a discount code at Your Favorite Restaurant!
        </string>
    <string name="first_name_label">First Name:</string>
    <string name="email_label">Email:</string>
    <string name="last_name_label">Last Name:</string>
    <string name="discount_code_button">GET DISCOUNT</string>
    <string name="discount_code_confirmation">Your
      discount code is below %s. Enjoy!</string>
</resources>
```

2. You are also going to specify some text sizes, layout margins, and padding directly, so create the **dimens.xml** file in the **app | src | main | res | values** folder and add the dimensions you'll need for the app (you can do this by right-clicking on the **res | values** folder within Android Studio and selecting **New values**):

```xml
<?xml version="1.0" encoding="utf-8"?>
<resources>
    <dimen name="grid_4">4dp</dimen>
    <dimen name="grid_8">8dp</dimen>
    <dimen name="grid_12">12dp</dimen>
    <dimen name="grid_16">16dp</dimen>
    <dimen name="grid_24">24dp</dimen>
    <dimen name="grid_32">32dp</dimen>
    <dimen name="default_text_size">20sp</dimen>
    <dimen name="discount_code_text_size">20sp</dimen>
</resources>
```

Here, you are specifying all the dimensions you need in the exercise. You will see here that **default_text_size** and **discount_code_text_size** are specified in **sp**. They represent the same values as density-independent pixels, which not only define the size measurement according to the density of the device that your app is being run on but also change the text size according to the user's preference, defined in **Settings | Display | Font style** (this might be **Font size and style** or something similar, depending on the exact device you are using).

3. In **R.layout.activity_main**, add the following XML, creating a containing layout file and adding header a **TextView** with the **Enter your name and email for a discount code at Your Favorite Restaurant!** text. This is done by adding the **android:text** attribute with the **@string/header_text** value:

```xml
<?xml version="1.0" encoding="utf-8"?>
<androidx.constraintlayout.widget.ConstraintLayout
    xmlns:android="http://schemas.android.com/apk/res/android"
    xmlns:app="http://schemas.android.com/apk/res-auto"
    xmlns:tools="http://schemas.android.com/tools"
    android:layout_width="match_parent"
    android:layout_height="match_parent"
    android:padding="@dimen/grid_4"
    android:layout_marginTop="@dimen/grid_4"
```

```
    tools:context=".MainActivity">

    <TextView
        android:id="@+id/header_text"
        android:gravity="center"
        android:textSize="@dimen/default_text_size"
        android:paddingStart="@dimen/grid_8"
        android:paddingEnd="@dimen/grid_8"
        android:layout_width="wrap_content"
        android:layout_height="wrap_content"
        android:text="@string/header_text"
        app:layout_constraintTop_toTopOf="parent"
        app:layout_constraintEnd_toEndOf="parent"
        app:layout_constraintStart_toStartOf="parent"/>
</androidx.constraintlayout.widget.ConstraintLayout>
```

You are using **ConstraintLayout** for constraining Views against the parent View and sibling Views.

Although you should normally specify the display of the View with styles, you can do this directly in the XML, as is done for some attributes here. The value of the **android:textSize** attribute is **@dimen/default_text_size**, defined in the previous code block, which you use to avoid repetition, and it enables you to change all the text size in one place. Using styles is the preferred option for setting text sizes as you will get sensible defaults and you can override the value in the style or, as you are doing here, on the individual Views.

Other attributes that affect positioning are also specified directly here in the Views. The most common ones are padding and margin. Padding is applied on the inside of Views and is the space between the text and the border. Margin is specified on the outside of Views and is the space from the outer edges of Views. For example, **android:padding** in **ConstraintLayout** sets the padding for the View with the specified value on all sides. Alternatively, you can specify the padding for one of the four sides of a View with **android:paddingTop**, **android:paddingBottom**, **android:paddingStart**, and **android:paddingEnd**. This pattern also exists to specify margins, so **android:layout_margin** specifies the margin value for all four sides of a View and **android:layoutMarginTop**, **android:layoutMarginBottom**, **android:layoutMarginStart**, and **android:layoutMarginEnd** allow setting the margin for individual sides.

For API levels less than 17 (and your app supports down to 16) you also have to add **android:layoutMarginLeft** if you use **android:layoutMarginStart** and **android:layoutMarginRight** if you use **android:layoutMarginEnd**. In order to have consistency and uniformity throughout the app, you define the margin and padding values as dimensions contained within the **dimens.xml** file.

To position the content within a View, you can specify **android:gravity**. The **center** value constrains the content both vertically and horizontally within the View.

4. Next, add three **EditText** views below the **header_text** for the user to add their first name, last name, and email:

```
<EditText
    android:id="@+id/first_name"
    android:textSize="@dimen/default_text_size"
    android:layout_marginStart="@dimen/grid_24"
    android:layout_marginLeft="@dimen/grid_24"
    android:layout_marginEnd="@dimen/grid_16"
    android:layout_marginRight="@dimen/grid_16"
    android:layout_width="wrap_content"
    android:layout_height="wrap_content"
    android:hint="@string/first_name_label"
    android:inputType="text"
    app:layout_constraintTop_toBottomOf="@id/header_text"
    app:layout_constraintStart_toStartOf="parent" />


<EditText
    android:textSize="@dimen/default_text_size"
    android:layout_marginEnd="@dimen/grid_24"
    android:layout_marginRight="@dimen/grid_24"
    android:layout_width="wrap_content"
    android:layout_height="wrap_content"
    android:hint="@string/last_name_label"
    android:inputType="text"
    app:layout_constraintTop_toBottomOf="@id/header_text"
    app:layout_constraintStart_toEndOf="@id/first_name"
    app:layout_constraintEnd_toEndOf="parent" />


<!-- android:inputType="textEmailAddress" is not enforced,
```

```
    but is a hint to the IME (Input Method Editor) usually a
    keyboard to configure the display for an email -
    typically by showing the '@' symbol -->
<EditText
    android:id="@+id/email"
    android:textSize="@dimen/default_text_size"
    android:layout_marginStart="@dimen/grid_24"
    android:layout_marginLeft="@dimen/grid_24"
    android:layout_marginEnd="@dimen/grid_32"
    android:layout_marginRight="@dimen/grid_32"
    android:layout_width="match_parent"
    android:layout_height="wrap_content"
    android:hint="@string/email_label"
    android:inputType="textEmailAddress"
    app:layout_constraintTop_toBottomOf="@id/first_name"
    app:layout_constraintEnd_toEndOf="parent"
    app:layout_constraintStart_toStartOf="parent" />
```

The **EditText** fields have an **inputType** attribute to specify the type of input that can be entered into the form field. Some values, such as **number** on **EditText**, restrict the input that can be entered into the field, and on selecting the field, suggest how the keyboard is displayed. Others, such as **android:inputType="textEmailAddress"**, will not enforce an @ symbol being added to the form field, but will give a hint to the keyboard to display it.

5. Finally, add a button for the user to press to generate a discount code, and display the discount code itself and a confirmation message:

```
<Button
    android:id="@+id/discount_button"
    android:textSize="@dimen/default_text_size"
    android:layout_marginTop="@dimen/grid_12"
    android:gravity="center"
    android:layout_width="wrap_content"
    android:layout_height="wrap_content"
    android:text="@string/discount_code_button"
    app:layout_constraintTop_toBottomOf="@id/email"
    app:layout_constraintEnd_toEndOf="parent"
    app:layout_constraintStart_toStartOf="parent"/>

<TextView
    android:id="@+id/discount_code_confirmation"
```

```
        android:gravity="center"
        android:textSize="@dimen/default_text_size"
        android:paddingStart="@dimen/grid_16"
        android:paddingEnd="@dimen/grid_16"
        android:layout_marginTop="@dimen/grid_8"
        android:layout_width="match_parent"
        android:layout_height="wrap_content"
        app:layout_constraintTop_toBottomOf="@id/discount_button"
        app:layout_constraintEnd_toEndOf="parent"
        app:layout_constraintStart_toStartOf="parent"
        tools:text="Hey John Smith! Here is your discount code" />


    <TextView
        android:id="@+id/discount_code"
        android:gravity="center"
        android:textSize="@dimen/discount_code_text_size"
        android:textStyle="bold"
        android:layout_marginTop="@dimen/grid_8"
        android:layout_width="match_parent"
        android:layout_height="wrap_content"
        app:layout_constraintTop_toBottomOf="@id/discount_code
          _confirmation"
        app:layout_constraintEnd_toEndOf="parent"
        app:layout_constraintStart_toStartOf="parent"
        tools:text="XHFG6H9O" />
```

There are also some attributes that you haven't seen before. The tools namespace **xmlns:tools="http://schemas.android.com/tools"** which was specified at the top of the xml layout file enables certain features that can be used when creating your app to assist with configuration and design. The attributes are removed when you build your app, so they don't contribute to the overall size of the app. You are using the **tools:text** attribute to show the text that will typically be displayed in the form fields. This helps when you switch to the **Design** view from viewing the XML in the **Code** view in Android Studio as you can see an approximation of how your layout displays on a device.

6. Run the app and you should see the output displayed in *Figure 2.6*:

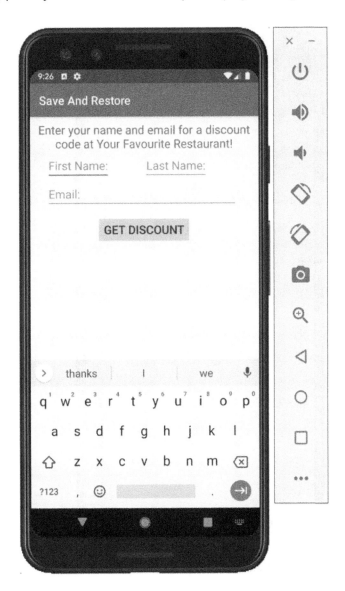

Figure 2.6: The Activity screen on the first launch

7. Enter some text into each of the form fields:

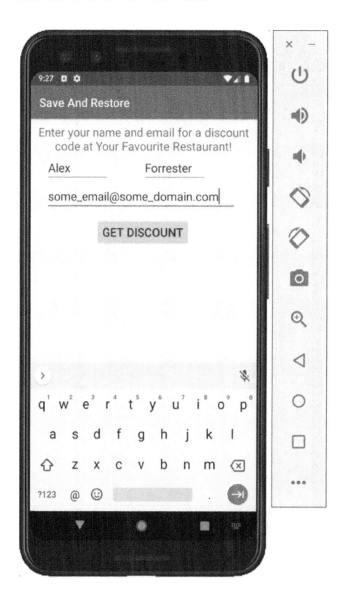

Figure 2.7: The EditText fields filled in

8. Now, use the second rotate button in the virtual device controls (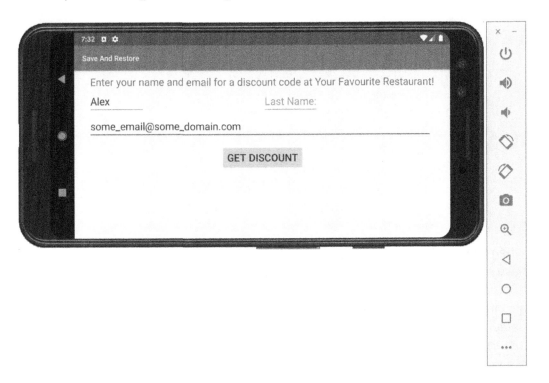) to rotate the phone 90 degrees to the right:

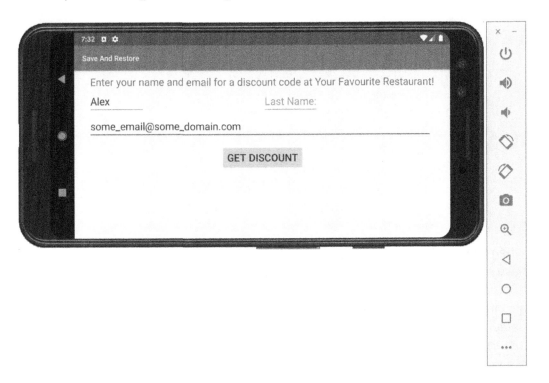

Figure 2.8: The virtual device turned to landscape orientation

Can you spot what has happened? The **Last Name** field value is no longer set. It has been lost in the process of recreating the activity. Why is this? Well, in the case of the **EditText** fields, the Android framework will preserve the state of the fields if they have an ID set on them.

9. Go back to the **activity_main.xml** layout file and add an ID for the **Last Name** value in the **EditText** field:

```
<EditText
    android:id="@+id/last_name"
    android:textSize="@dimen/default_text_size"
    android:layout_marginEnd="@dimen/grid_24"
    android:layout_width="wrap_content"
    android:layout_height="wrap_content"
    android:hint="@string/last_name_label"
    android:inputType="text"
    app:layout_constraintTop_toBottomOf="@id/header_text"
    app:layout_constraintStart_toEndOf="@id/first_name"
    app:layout_constraintEnd_toEndOf="parent"
    tools:text="Last Name:"/>
```

When you run up the app again and rotate the device, it will preserve the value you have entered. You've now seen that you need to set an ID on the **EditText** fields to preserve the state. For the **EditText** fields, it's common to retain the state on a configuration change when the user is entering details into a form so that it is the default behavior if the field has an ID. Obviously, you want to get the details of the **EditText** field once the user has entered some text, which is why you set an ID, but setting an ID for other field types, such as **TextView**, does not retain the state if you update them and you need to save the state yourself. Setting IDs for Views that enable scrolling, such as **RecyclerView**, is also important as it enables the scroll position to be maintained when the Activity is recreated.

Now, you have defined the layout for the screen, but you have not added any logic for creating and displaying the discount code. In the next exercise, we will work through this.

The layout created in this exercise is available at http://packt.live/35RSdgz.

You can find the code for the entire exercise at http://packt.live/3p1AZF3.

EXERCISE 2.03: SAVING AND RESTORING THE STATE WITH CALLBACKS

The aim of this exercise is to bring all the UI elements in the layout together to generate a discount code after the user has entered their data. In order to do this, you will have to add logic to the button to retrieve all the **EditText** fields and then display a confirmation to the user, as well as generate a discount code:

1. Open up **MainActivity.kt** and replace the default empty Activity from the project creation. A snippet of the code is shown here, but you'll need to use the link given below to find the full code block you need to add:

MainActivity.kt

```
14   class MainActivity : AppCompatActivity() {
15
16       private val discountButton: Button
17           get() = findViewById(R.id.discount_button)
18
19       private val firstName: EditText
20           get() = findViewById(R.id.first_name)
21
22       private val lastName: EditText
23           get() = findViewById(R.id.last_name)
24
25       private val email: EditText
26           get() = findViewById(R.id.email)
27
28       private val discountCodeConfirmation: TextView
29           get() = findViewById(R.id
30              .discount_code_confirmation)
31       private val discountCode: TextView
32           get() = findViewById(R.id.discount_code)
33
34       override fun onCreate(savedInstanceState: Bundle?) {
35           super.onCreate(savedInstanceState)
36           setContentView(R.layout.activity_main)
37           Log.d(TAG, "onCreate")
```

You can find the complete code here http://packt.live/38XcdQS.

The **get()** = ... is a custom accessor for a property.

Upon clicking the discount button, you retrieve the values from the **first_ name** and **last_name** fields, concatenate them with a space, and then use a string resource to format the discount code confirmation text. The string you reference in the **strings.xml** file is as follows:

```
<string name="discount_code_confirmation">Hey  %s! Here is
    your discount code</string>
```

The **%s** value specifies a string value to be replaced when the string resource is retrieved. This is done by passing in the full name when getting the string:

```
getString(R.string.discount_code_confirmation, fullName)
```

The code is generated by using the UUID (Universally Unique Identifier) library from the **java.util** package. This creates a unique id, and then the **take()** Kotlin function is used to get the first eight characters before setting these to uppercase. Finally, discount_code is set in the view, the keyboard is hidden, and all the form fields are set back to their initial values.

2. Run the app and enter some text into the name and email fields, and then click on **GET DISCOUNT**:

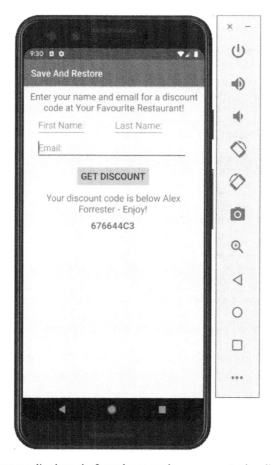

Figure 2.9: Screen displayed after the user has generated a discount code

The app behaves as expected, showing the confirmation.

3. Now, rotate the phone (pressing the fifth button down with the arrow on the right-hand side of the virtual device picture) and observe the result:

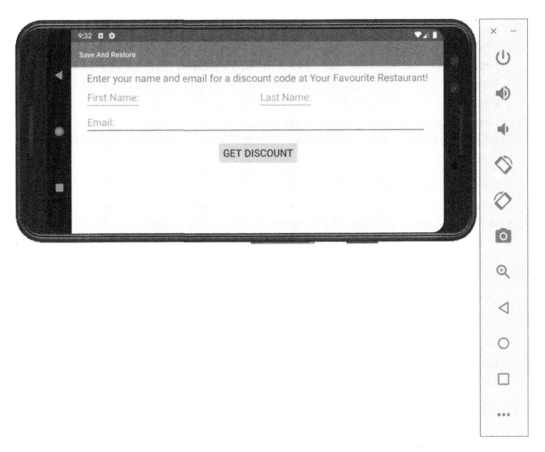

Figure 2.10: Discount code no longer displaying on the screen

Oh, no! The discount code has gone. The **TextView** fields do not retain the state, so you will have to save the state yourself.

4. Go back into **MainActivity.kt** and add the following Activity callbacks:

```
override fun onRestoreInstanceState(savedInstanceState:
  Bundle) {
    super.onRestoreInstanceState(savedInstanceState)
    Log.d(TAG, "onRestoreInstanceState")
}
```

```
override fun onSaveInstanceState(outState: Bundle) {
    super.onSaveInstanceState(outState)
    Log.d(TAG, "onSaveInstanceState")
}
```

These callbacks, as the names declare, enable you to save and restore the instance state. **onSaveInstanceState(outState: Bundle)** allows you to add key-value pairs from your Activity when it is being backgrounded or destroyed, which you can retrieve in either **onCreate(savedInstanceState: Bundle?)** or **onRestoreInstanceState(savedInstanceState: Bundle)**.

So, you have two callbacks to retrieve the state once it has been set. If you are doing a lot of initialization in **onCreate(savedInstanceState: Bundle)**, it might be better to use **onRestoreInstanceState(savedInstanceState: Bundle)** to retrieve this instance state when your Activity is being recreated. In this way, it's clear which state is being recreated. However, you might prefer to use **onCreate(savedInstanceState: Bundle)** if there is minimal setup required.

Whichever of the two callbacks you decide to use, you will have to get the state you set in the **onSaveInstanceState(outState: Bundle)** call. For the next step in the exercise, you will use **onRestoreInstanceState(savedInstanceState: Bundle)**.

5. Add two constants to the **MainActivity** companion object:

```
private const val DISCOUNT_CONFIRMATION_MESSAGE =
  "DISCOUNT_CONFIRMATION_MESSAGE"
private const val DISCOUNT_CODE = "DISCOUNT_CODE"
```

6. Now, add these constants as keys for the values you want to save and retrieve by making the following additions to the Activity:

```
override fun onRestoreInstanceState(
    savedInstanceState: Bundle) {
    super.onRestoreInstanceState(savedInstanceState)
    Log.d(TAG, "onRestoreInstanceState")

    //Get the discount code or an empty
      string if it hasn't been set
    discountCode.text = savedInstanceState
      .getString(DISCOUNT_CODE,"")
    //Get the discount confirmation message
      or an empty string if it hasn't been set
```

```
        discountCodeConfirmation.text =
          savedInstanceState.getString(
            DISCOUNT_CONFIRMATION_MESSAGE,"")
    }

    override fun onSaveInstanceState(outState: Bundle) {
        super.onSaveInstanceState(outState)
        Log.d(TAG, "onSaveInstanceState")

        outState.putString(DISCOUNT_CODE,
          discountCode.text.toString())
        outState.putString(DISCOUNT_CONFIRMATION_MESSAGE,
          discountCodeConfirmation.text.toString())
    }
```

7. Run the app, enter the values into the **EditText** fields, and then generate a discount code. Then, rotate the device and you will see that the discount code is restored in *Figure 2.11*:

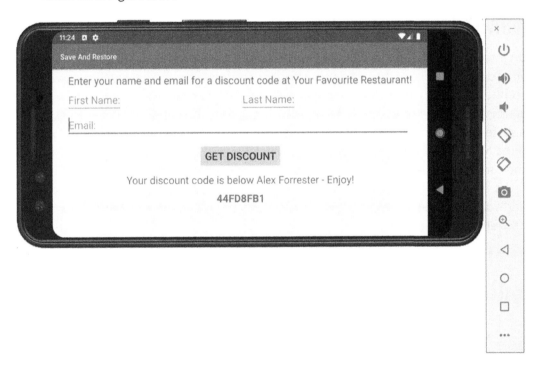

Figure 2.11: Discount code continues to be displayed on the screen

In this exercise, you first saw how the state of the **EditText** fields is maintained on configuration changes. You also saved and restored the instance state using the Activity lifecycle **onSaveInstanceState(outState: Bundle)** and **onCreate(savedInstanceState: Bundle?)/ onRestoreInstanceState(savedInstanceState: Bundle)** functions. These functions provide a way to save and restore simple data. The Android framework also provides **ViewModel**, an Android architecture component that is lifecycle-aware. The mechanisms of how to save and restore this state (with **ViewModel**) are managed by the framework, so you don't have to explicitly manage it as you have done in the preceding example. You will learn how to use this component in *Chapter 10, Android Architecture Components*.

So far, you have created a single-screen app. Although it is possible for simple apps to use one Activity, it is likely that you will want to organize your app into different activities that handle different functions. So, in the next section, you will add another Activity to an app and navigate between the activities.

ACTIVITY INTERACTION WITH INTENTS

An intent in Android is a communication mechanism between components. Within your own app, a lot of the time, you will want another specific Activity to start when some action happens in the current activity. Specifying exactly which Activity will start is called an **explicit intent**. On other occasions, you will want to get access to a system component, such as the camera. As you can't access these components directly, you will have to send an intent, which the system resolves in order to open the camera. These are called **implicit intents**. An intent filter has to be set up in order to register to respond to these events. Go to the **AndroidManifest.xml** file and you will see an example of two intent filters set within the **<intent-filter>** XML element:

```xml
<activity android:name=".MainActivity">
    <intent-filter>
        <action android:name="android.intent.action.MAIN" />
        <category android:name="android.intent.category.
          LAUNCHER" />
    </intent-filter>
</activity>
```

The one specified with **`<action android:name="android.intent.action.`** **`MAIN" />`** means that this is the main entry point into the app. Depending on which category is set, it governs which Activity first starts when the app is started. The other intent filter that is specified is **`<category android:name="android.`** **`intent.category.LAUNCHER" />`**, which defines that the app should appear in the launcher. When combined, the two intent filters define that when the app is started from the launcher, **`MainActivity`** should be started. Removing any one of these intent filters results in the **`"Error running 'app': Default`** **`Activity not found"`** message. As the app has not got a main entry point, it can't be launched, which is what also happens when you remove **`<action`** **`android:name="android.intent.action.MAIN". />`**. If you remove **`<category android:name="android.intent.category.LAUNCHER" />`** and don't specify a category, then there is nowhere that it can be launched from.

For the next exercise, you will see how intents work to navigate around your app.

EXERCISE 2.04: AN INTRODUCTION TO INTENTS

The goal of this exercise is to create a simple app that uses intents to display text to the user based on their input. Create a new project in Android Studio and select an empty Activity. Once you have set up the project, go to the toolbar and select **`File`** | **`New`** | **`Activity`** | **`Empty Activity`**. Call it **`WelcomeActivity`** and leave all the other defaults as they are. It will be added to the **`AndroidManifest.xml`** file, ready to use. The issue you have now that you've added **`WelcomeActivity`** is how do you do anything with it? **`MainActivity`** starts when you launch the app, but you need a way to launch **`WelcomeActivity`** and then, optionally, pass data to it, which is when you use intents:

1. In order to work through this example, add the following code to the **`strings.`** **`xml`** file. These are the strings you'll be using in the app:

```
<resources>
    <string name="app_name">Intents Introduction</string>
    <string name="header_text">Please enter your name and
        then we\'ll get started!</string>
    <string name="welcome_text">Hello %s, we hope you enjoy
        using the app!</string>
    <string name="full_name_label">Enter your full
        name:</string>
    <string name="submit_button_text">SUBMIT</string>
</resources>
```

2.   Next, update the styles in the **themes.xml** file adding the header style.

```
<style name="header" parent=
  "TextAppearance.AppCompat.Title">
    <item name="android:gravity">center</item>
    <item name="android:layout_marginStart">24dp</item>
    <item name="android:layout_marginEnd">24dp</item>
    <item name="android:layout_marginLeft">24dp</item>
    <item name="android:layout_marginRight">24dp</item>
    <item name="android:textSize">20sp</item>
</style>
<!-- continued below -->
```

Next, add the **fullname**, **button**, and **page** styles:

```
<style name="full_name" parent=
  "TextAppearance.AppCompat.Body1">
    <item name="android:layout_marginTop">16dp</item>
    <item name="android:layout_gravity">center</item>
    <item name="android:textSize">20sp</item>
    <item name="android:inputType">text</item>
</style>


<style name="button" parent=
  "TextAppearance.AppCompat.Button">
    <item name="android:layout_margin">16dp</item>
    <item name="android:gravity">center</item>
    <item name="android:textSize">20sp</item>
</style>


<style name="page">
    <item name="android:layout_margin">8dp</item>
    <item name="android:padding">8dp</item>
</style>
```

Normally, you wouldn't specify dimensions directly in the styles themselves. They should be referenced as **dimens** values so that they can be updated in one place, are more uniform, and can be labeled to represent what the dimension actually is. This is not done here for simplicity.

3. Next, change the **MainActivity** layout in **activity_main.xml** and add a **TextView** header:

```xml
<?xml version="1.0" encoding="utf-8"?>
<androidx.constraintlayout.widget.ConstraintLayout
    xmlns:android="http://schemas.android.com/apk/res/android"
    xmlns:app="http://schemas.android.com/apk/res-auto"
    xmlns:tools="http://schemas.android.com/tools"
    android:layout_width="match_parent"
    android:layout_height="match_parent"
    style="@style/page"
    tools:context=".MainActivity">

    <TextView
        android:id="@+id/header_text"
        style="@style/header"
        android:layout_width="wrap_content"
        android:layout_height="wrap_content"
        android:text="@string/header_text"
        app:layout_constraintTop_toTopOf="parent"
        app:layout_constraintEnd_toEndOf="parent"
        app:layout_constraintStart_toStartOf="parent"/>

</androidx.constraintlayout.widget.ConstraintLayout>
```

This should be the first View displayed, and as it's constrained using **ConstraintLayout** to the top of its parent, it displays at the top of the screen. As it's also constrained to both the start and end of its parent, it will be displayed in the middle when you run the app, as shown in *Figure 2.12*:

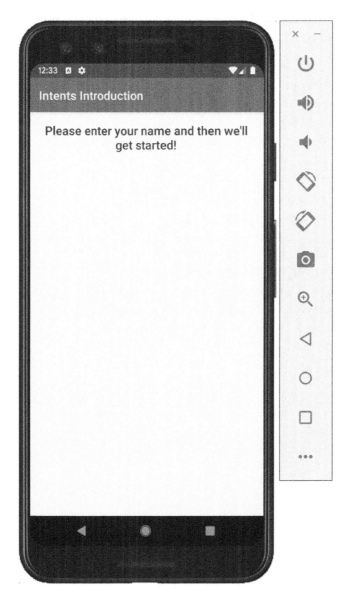

Figure 2.12: Initial app display after adding the TextView header

4. Now, add an **EditText** field for the full name and a **Button** field for the submit button in the **activity_main.xml** file below the **TextView** header:

```
<EditText
    android:id="@+id/full_name"
    style="@style/full_name"
    android:layout_width="wrap_content"
    android:layout_height="wrap_content"
    android:hint="@string/full_name_label"
    app:layout_constraintTop_toBottomOf="@id/header_text"
    app:layout_constraintStart_toStartOf="parent"
    app:layout_constraintEnd_toEndOf="parent"/>

<Button
    android:id="@+id/submit_button"
    style="@style/button"
    android:layout_width="wrap_content"
    android:layout_height="wrap_content"
    android:text="@string/submit_button_text"
    app:layout_constraintTop_toBottomOf="@id/full_name"
    app:layout_constraintEnd_toEndOf="parent"
    app:layout_constraintStart_toStartOf="parent"/>
```

The app, when run, looks as in *Figure 2.13*:

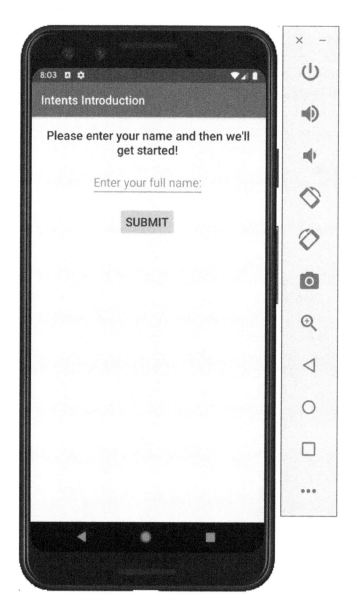

Figure 2.13: The app display after adding the EditText full name field and submit button

You now need to configure the button so that when it's clicked, it retrieves the user's full name from the **EditText** field and then sends it in an intent, which starts **WelcomeActivity**.

5. Update the **activity_welcome.xml** layout file to prepare to do this:

```xml
<?xml version="1.0" encoding="utf-8"?>
<androidx.constraintlayout.widget.ConstraintLayout
    xmlns:android="http://schemas.android.com/apk/res/android"
    xmlns:app="http://schemas.android.com/apk/res-auto"
    xmlns:tools="http://schemas.android.com/tools"
    android:layout_width="match_parent"
    android:layout_height="match_parent"
    style="@style/page"
    tools:context=".WelcomeActivity">

    <TextView
        android:id="@+id/welcome_text"
        style="@style/header"
        android:layout_width="wrap_content"
        android:layout_height="wrap_content"
        app:layout_constraintTop_toTopOf="parent"
        app:layout_constraintEnd_toEndOf="parent"
        app:layout_constraintStart_toStartOf="parent"
        app:layout_constraintBottom_toBottomOf="parent"
        tools:text="Welcome John Smith we hope you enjoy
          using the app!"/>

</androidx.constraintlayout.widget.ConstraintLayout>
```

You are adding a **TextView** field to display the full name of the user with a welcome message. The logic to create the full name and welcome message will be shown in the next step.

6. Now, open **MainActivity** and add a constant value above the class header and also update the imports:

```
package com.example.intentsintroduction


import android.content.Intent
import android.os.Bundle
import android.widget.Button
import android.widget.EditText
import android.widget.Toast
import androidx.appcompat.app.AppCompatActivity
```

```
const val FULL_NAME_KEY = "FULL_NAME_KEY"


class MainActivity : AppCompatActivity()...
```

You will use the constant to set the key to hold the full name of the user by setting it in the intent.

7. Then, add the following code to the bottom of **onCreate(savedInstanceState: Bundle?)**:

```
findViewById<Button>(R.id.submit_button).setOnClickListener {

    val fullName = findViewById<EditText>(R.id.full_name)
        .text.toString().trim()

    if (fullName.isNotEmpty()) {

        //Set the name of the Activity to launch
        Intent(this, WelcomeActivity::class.java)
            .also { welcomeIntent ->
            //Add the data
            welcomeIntent.putExtra(FULL_NAME_KEY, fullName)
            //Launch
            startActivity(welcomeIntent)
        }

    } else {
        Toast.makeText(this, getString(
            R.string.full_name_label),
            Toast.LENGTH_LONG).show()
    }
}
```

There is logic to retrieve the value of the full name and verify that the user has filled this in; otherwise, a pop-up toast message will be shown if it is blank. The main logic, however, takes the **fullName** value of the **EditText** field and creates an explicit intent to start **WelcomeActivity**. The **also** scope function allows you to carry on using the intent you've just created, **Intent(this, WelcomeActivity::class.java)**, and further operate on it by using something called a **lambda expression**. The lambda argument here has a default name of **it** but here for clarity we've called it **welcomeIntent**. Then, you use the lambda argument in the **welcomeIntent.putExtra(FULL_NAME_KEY, fullName)** line to add the **fullName** field, using **FULL_NAME_KEY** as the key and **fullName** as the value to the extras that the intent holds.

Then, you use the intent to start **WelcomeActivity**.

8. Now, run the app, enter your name, and press **SUBMIT**, as shown in *Figure 2.14*:

Figure 2.14: The default screen displayed when the intent extras data is not processed

Well, that's not very impressive. You've added the logic to send the user's name, but not to display it.

9. To enable this, please open **WelcomeActivity** and add the following to the bottom of the **onCreate(savedInstanceState: Bundle?)** callback:

```
//Get the intent which started this activity
intent?.let {

    //Set the welcome message
    val fullName = it.getStringExtra(FULL_NAME_KEY)
    findViewById<TextView>(R.id.welcome_text).text =
        getString(R.string.welcome_text, fullName)
}
```

We reference the intent that started the Activity with **intent?.let{}** **which** specifies that the **let** block will be run if the intent is not null, and **let** is a scope function in which you can reference the context object with a default lambda argument of **it**. This means you don't have to assign a variable before you can use it. You reference the intent with **it** and then retrieve the string value that was passed from the **MainActivity** intent by getting the string **FULL_NAME_KEY** extra key. You then format the **<string name="welcome_text">Hello %s, we hope you enjoy using the app!</string>** resource string by getting the string from the resources and passing in the **fullname** value retrieved from the intent. Finally, this is set as the text of **TextView**.

10. Run the app again, and a simple greeting will be displayed, as in *Figure 2.15*:

Figure 2.15: User welcome message displayed

This exercise, although very simple in terms of layouts and user interaction, allows the demonstration of some core principles of intents. You will use them to add navigation and create user flows from one section of your app to another. In the next section, you will see how you can use intents to launch an Activity and receive a result back from it.

EXERCISE 2.05: RETRIEVING A RESULT FROM AN ACTIVITY

For some user flows, you will only launch an Activity for the sole purpose of retrieving a result back from it. This pattern is often used to ask permission to use a particular feature, popping up a dialog with a question about whether the user gives their permission to access contacts, the calendar, and so on, and then reporting the result of yes or no back to the calling Activity. In this exercise, you will ask the user to pick their favorite color of the rainbow, and then once that is chosen, display the result in the calling activity:

1. Create a new project named **Activity Results** and add the following strings to the **strings.xml** file:

```
<string name="header_text_main">Please click the button
    below to choose your favorite color of the rainbow!
      </string>
<string name="header_text_picker">Rainbow Colors</string>
<string name="footer_text_picker">Click the button
   above which is your favorite color of the rainbow.
      </string>
<string name="color_chosen_message">%s is your favorite
    color!</string>
<string name="submit_button_text">CHOOSE COLOR</string>

<string name="red">RED</string>
<string name="orange">ORANGE</string>
<string name="yellow">YELLOW</string>
<string name="green">GREEN</string>
<string name="blue">BLUE</string>
<string name="indigo">INDIGO</string>
<string name="violet">VIOLET</string>

<string name="unexpected_color">Unexpected color</string>
```

2. Add the following colors to colors.xml

```
<!--Colors of the Rainbow -->
<color name="red">#FF0000</color>
<color name="orange">#FF7F00</color>
<color name="yellow">#FFFF00</color>
<color name="green">#00FF00</color>
<color name="blue">#0000FF</color>
<color name="indigo">#4B0082</color>
<color name="violet">#9400D3</color>
```

3. Add the relevant new styles to the **themes.xml** file. A snippet is shown below, but you'll need to follow the link given to see all the code that you need to add:

themes.xml

```
11    <!-- Style for page header on launch screen -->
12    <style name="header" parent=
        "TextAppearance.AppCompat.Title">
13        <item name="android:gravity">center</item>
14        <item name="android:layout_marginStart">24dp</item>
15        <item name="android:layout_marginEnd">24dp</item>
16        <item name="android:layout_marginLeft">24dp</item>
17        <item name="android:layout_marginRight">24dp</item>
18        <item name="android:textSize">20sp</item>
19    </style>
20
21    <!-- Style for page header on rainbow color
        selection screen -->
22    <style name="header.rainbows" parent="header">
23        <item name="android:textSize">22sp</item>
24        <item name="android:textAllCaps">true</item>
25    </style>
```

You can find the complete code here http://packt.live/39J0qES.

> **NOTE**
>
> Dimensions have not been added to **dimens.xml** for simplicity.

4. Now, you have to set up the Activity that will set the result you receive in **MainActivity**. Go to **File | New | Activity | EmptyActivity** and create an Activity called **RainbowColorPickerActivity**.

5. Update the **activity_main.xml** layout file to display a header, a button, and then a hidden **android:visibility="gone"** View, which will be made visible and set with the user's favorite color of the rainbow when the result is reported:

```
<?xml version="1.0" encoding="utf-8"?>
<androidx.constraintlayout.widget.ConstraintLayout
    xmlns:android="http://schemas.android.com/apk/res/android"
    xmlns:app="http://schemas.android.com/apk/res-auto"
    xmlns:tools="http://schemas.android.com/tools"
    android:layout_width="match_parent"
    android:layout_height="match_parent"
    style="@style/page"
    tools:context=".MainActivity">
```

```xml
    <TextView
        android:id="@+id/header_text"
        style="@style/header"
        android:layout_width="wrap_content"
        android:layout_height="wrap_content"
        android:text="@string/header_text_main"
        app:layout_constraintTop_toTopOf="parent"
        app:layout_constraintEnd_toEndOf="parent"
        app:layout_constraintStart_toStartOf="parent"/>

    <Button
        android:id="@+id/submit_button"
        style="@style/button"
        android:layout_width="wrap_content"
        android:layout_height="wrap_content"
        android:text="@string/submit_button_text"
        app:layout_constraintTop_toBottomOf="@id/header_text"
        app:layout_constraintEnd_toEndOf="parent"
        app:layout_constraintStart_toStartOf="parent"/>

    <TextView
        android:id="@+id/rainbow_color"
        style="@style/color_block"
        android:visibility="gone"
        app:layout_constraintTop_toBottomOf="@id/
          submit_button"
        app:layout_constraintStart_toStartOf="parent"
        app:layout_constraintEnd_toEndOf="parent"
        tools:text="This is your favorite color of the
          rainbow"/>

</androidx.constraintlayout.widget.ConstraintLayout>
```

6. You'll be using the **startActivityForResult(Intent intent, int requestCode)** function to get a result back from the Activity you launch. In order to ensure that the result you get back is from the operation you expected, you have to set **requestCode**. Add this constant for the request code, and two others to set keys for the values we want to use in the intent, as well as a default color above the class header in MainActivity so it is displayed as follows with the package name and imports:

```
package com.example.activityresults

import android.content.Intent
import androidx.appcompat.app.AppCompatActivity
import android.os.Bundle
import android.widget.Button
import android.widget.TextView

const val PICK_RAINBOW_COLOR_INTENT = 1  // The request code
// Key to return rainbow color name in intent
const val RAINBOW_COLOR_NAME = "RAINBOW_COLOR_NAME"
// Key to return rainbow color in intent
const val RAINBOW_COLOR = "RAINBOW_COLOR"
const val DEFAULT_COLOR = "#FFFFFF" // White

class MainActivity : AppCompatActivity()…
```

7. Then, at the bottom of **onCreate(savedInstanceState: Bundle?)** in **MainActivity** add the following:

```
findViewById<Button>(R.id.submit_button).setOnClickListener {
//Set the name of the Activity to launch passing
//in request code
    Intent(this, RainbowColorPickerActivity::class.java)
    .also { rainbowColorPickerIntent ->
        startActivityForResult(
            rainbowColorPickerIntent,
            PICK_RAINBOW_COLOR_INTENT
        )
    }
}
```

This uses the syntax you used previously with **also** to create an intent and use it with a named lambda parameter of the context object. In this case, you are using **rainbowColorPickerIntent** to refer to the intent you just created with **Intent(this, RainbowColorPickerActivity::class.java)**.

The key call is **startActivityForResult(rainbowColorPickerIntent, PICK_RAINBOW_COLOR_INTENT)**, which launches **RainbowColorPickerActivity** with a request code. So, when do we get this result back? You receive the result when it is set by overriding **onActivityResult(requestCode: Int, resultCode: Int, data: Intent?)**.

This call specifies the request code, which you can check to confirm that it is the same as the request code you sent. **resultCode** reports the status of the operation. You can set your own code, but it is usually set to **Activity. RESULT_OK** or **Activity.RESULT_CANCELED**, and the last parameter, **data**, is the intent that has been set by the activity started for the result, RainbowColorPickerActivity.

8. Add the following to **onActivityResult(requestCode: Int, resultCode: Int, data: Intent?)** callback in **MainActivity**:

```
override fun onActivityResult(requestCode: Int, resultCode:
  Int, data: Intent?) {
    super.onActivityResult(requestCode, resultCode, data)


    if (requestCode == PICK_RAINBOW_COLOR_INTENT &&
      resultCode == Activity.RESULT_OK) {


        val backgroundColor = data?.getIntExtra(RAINBOW_COLOR,
          Color.parseColor(DEFAULT_COLOR)) ?:
            Color.parseColor(DEFAULT_COLOR)
        val colorName = data?.getStringExtra
          (RAINBOW_COLOR_NAME) ?: ""
        val colorMessage = getString
          (R.string.color_chosen_message, colorName)


        val rainbowColor = findViewById
          <TextView>(R.id.rainbow_color)

    rainbowColor.setBackgroundColor(ContextCompat.getColor(this,
      backgroundColor))
        rainbowColor.text = colorMessage
        rainbowColor.isVisible = true
```

```
        }
    }
```

9. So, you check that the request code and response code values are what is expected, and then proceed to query the intent data for the values you are expecting. For this exercise, you want to get the background color name (**colorName**) and the hexadecimal value of the color (**backgroundColor**) so that we can display it. The **?** operator checks whether the value is null (that is, not set in the intent), and if so, the Elvis operator (**? :**) sets the default value. The color message uses String formatting to set a message replacing the placeholder in the resource value with the color name. Now that you've got the colors, you can make the **rainbow_color TextView** field visible and set the background color of the View to **backgroundColor** and add text displaying the name of the user's favorite color of the rainbow.

10. For the layout of the **RainbowColorPickerActivity** activity, you are going to display a button with a background color and color name for each of the seven colors of the rainbow: **RED**, **ORANGE**, **YELLOW**, **GREEN**, **BLUE**, **INDIGO**, and **VIOLET**. These will be displayed in a **LinearLayout** vertical list. For most of the layout files in the course, you will be using **ConstrainLayout**, as it provides fine-grained positioning of individual Views. For situations where you need to display a vertical or horizontal list of a small number of items, **LinearLayout** is also a good choice. If you need to display a large number of items, then **RecyclerView** is a better option as it can cache layouts for individual rows and recycle views that are no longer displayed on the screen. You will learn about **RecyclerView** in *Chapter 5, RecyclerView*.

11. The first thing you need to do in **RainbowColorPickerActivity** is create the layout. This will be where you present the user with the option to choose their favorite color of the rainbow.

12. Open **activity_rainbow_color_picker.xml** and replace the layout, inserting the following:

```
<?xml version="1.0" encoding="utf-8"?>
<ScrollView
    xmlns:android="http://schemas.android.com/apk/res/android"
    xmlns:app="http://schemas.android.com/apk/res-auto"
    xmlns:tools="http://schemas.android.com/tools"
    android:layout_width="match_parent"
    android:layout_height="wrap_content">

</ScrollView>
```

We are adding **ScrollView** to allow the contents to scroll if the screen height cannot display all of the items. **ScrollView** can only take one child View, which is the layout to scroll.

13. Next, add **LinearLayout** within **ScrollView** to display the contained views in the order that they are added with a header and a footer. The first child View is a header with the title of the page and the last View that is added is a footer with instructions to the user to pick their favorite color:

```
<LinearLayout
    style="@style/page"
    android:layout_width="match_parent"
    android:layout_height="wrap_content"
    android:gravity="center_horizontal"
    android:orientation="vertical"
    tools:context=".RainbowColorPickerActivity">

<TextView
    android:id="@+id/header_text"
    style="@style/header.rainbows"
    android:layout_width="wrap_content"
    android:layout_height="wrap_content"
    android:text="@string/header_text_picker"
    app:layout_constraintEnd_toEndOf="parent"
    app:layout_constraintStart_toStartOf="parent"
    app:layout_constraintTop_toTopOf="parent"/>

<TextView
    style="@style/body"
    android:layout_width="wrap_content"
    android:layout_height="wrap_content"
    android:text="@string/footer_text_picker"
    app:layout_constraintEnd_toEndOf="parent"
    app:layout_constraintStart_toStartOf="parent"
    app:layout_constraintTop_toTopOf="parent"/>
</LinearLayout>
```

The layout should now look as in *Figure 2.16* in the app:

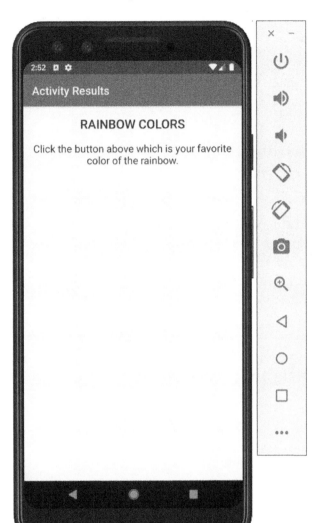

Figure 2.16: Rainbow colors screen with a header and footer

14. Now, finally, add the button views between the header and the footer to select a color of the rainbow, and then run the app:

```
<Button
    android:id="@+id/red_button"
    style="@style/button"
    android:layout_width="wrap_content"
    android:layout_height="wrap_content"
```

```
        android:background="@color/red"
        android:text="@string/red"/>

    <Button
        .......
        android:text="@string/orange"/>

    <Button
        .......
        android:text="@string/yellow"/>

    <Button
        .......
        android:text="@string/green"/>

    <Button
        .......
        android:text="@string/blue"/>

    <Button
        .......
        android:text="@string/indigo"/>

    <Button
        .......
        android:text="@string/violet"/>
```

The preceding layout created is available at the following link:
http://packt.live/2M7okBX

These Views are buttons that are displayed in the order of the colors of the
rainbow. Although there is a button label for the color and the background color,
which is filled in with the appropriate color, the most important XML attribute
is **id**. This is what you will use in the Activity to prepare the result of what is
returned to the calling activity.

15. Now, open **RainbowColorPickerActivity** and replace the content with the following:

```
package com.example.activityresults

import android.app.Activity
import android.content.Intent
import androidx.appcompat.app.AppCompatActivity
import android.os.Bundle
import android.view.View
import android.widget.Toast

class RainbowColorPickerActivity : AppCompatActivity() {
    override fun onCreate(savedInstanceState: Bundle?) {
        super.onCreate(savedInstanceState)
        setContentView(R.layout.activity_rainbow_color_picker)
    }

    private fun setRainbowColor(colorName: String, color: Int) {

        Intent().let { pickedColorIntent ->
            pickedColorIntent.putExtra(RAINBOW_COLOR_NAME,
                colorName)
            pickedColorIntent.putExtra(RAINBOW_COLOR, color)

            setResult(Activity.RESULT_OK, pickedColorIntent)
            finish()
        }
    }
}
```

This is the function that creates an intent and puts the relevant String extras holding the rainbow color name and the rainbow color **hex** value. The result is then returned to the calling Activity, and as you have no further use of this Activity, you call **finish()** so that the calling Activity is displayed. The way that you retrieve the rainbow color that the user has chosen is done by adding a listener for all the buttons in the layout.

16. Now, add the following to the bottom of **onCreate(savedInstanceState: Bundle?)**:

```
val colorPickerClickListener = View.OnClickListener { view ->

    when (view.id) {
        R.id.red_button -> setRainbowColor(
            getString(R.string.red), R.color.red)
        R.id.orange_button -> setRainbowColor(
            getString(R.string.orange), R.color.orange)
        R.id.yellow_button -> setRainbowColor(
            getString(R.string.yellow), R.color.yellow)
        R.id.green_button -> setRainbowColor(
            getString(R.string.green), R.color.green)
        R.id.blue_button -> setRainbowColor(
            getString(R.string.blue), R.color.blue)
        R.id.indigo_button -> setRainbowColor(
            getString(R.string.indigo), R.color.indigo)
        R.id.violet_button -> setRainbowColor(
            getString(R.string.violet), R.color.violet)
        else -> {
            Toast.makeText(this, getString(
                R.string.unexpected_color), Toast.LENGTH_LONG)
                .show()
        }
    }
}
```

The **colorPickerClickListener** click listener added in the preceding code determines which colors to set for the **setRainbowColor(colorName: String, color: Int)** function by using a **when** statement. The **when** statement is the equivalent of the **switch** statement in Java and languages based on C. It allows multiple conditions to be satisfied with one branch and is more concise. In the preceding example, **view.id** is matched against the IDs of the rainbow layout buttons and when found, executes the branch, setting the color name and hex value from the string resources to pass into **setRainbowColor(colorName: String, color: Int)**.

17. Now, add this click listener to the buttons from the layout:

```
findViewById<View>(R.id.red_button).setOnClickListener(
    colorPickerClickListener)
findViewById<View>(R.id.orange_button).setOnClickListener(
    colorPickerClickListener)
findViewById<View>(R.id.yellow_button).setOnClickListener(
    colorPickerClickListener)
findViewById<View>(R.id.green_button).setOnClickListener(
    colorPickerClickListener)
```

```
findViewById<View>(R.id.blue_button).setOnClickListener(
    colorPickerClickListener)
findViewById<View>(R.id.indigo_button).setOnClickListener(
    colorPickerClickListener)
findViewById<View>(R.id.violet_button).setOnClickListener(
    colorPickerClickListener)
```

Every button has a **ClickListener** interface attached, and as the operation is the same, they have the same **ClickListener** interface attached. Then, when the button is pressed, it sets the result of the color that the user has chosen and returns it to the calling activity.

18. Now, run the app and press the **CHOOSE COLOR** button, as shown in *Figure 2.17*:

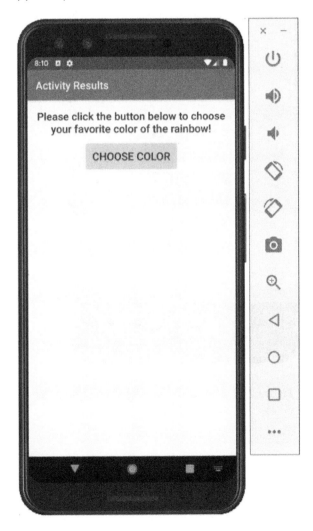

Figure 2.17: The rainbow colors app start screen

19. Now, select your favorite color of the rainbow:

Figure 2.18: The rainbow colors selection screen

20. Once you've chosen your favorite color, a screen with your favorite color will be displayed, as shown in *Figure 2.19*:

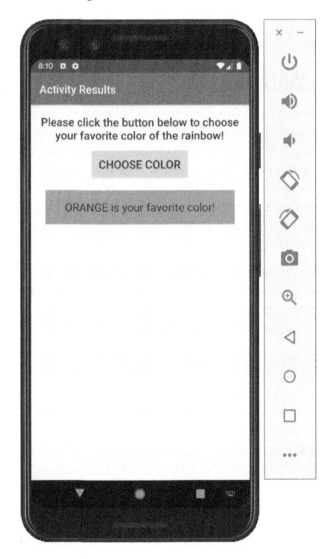

Figure 2.19: The app displaying the selected color

As you can see, the app displays the color that you've selected as your favorite color in *Figure 2.19*.

This exercise introduced you to another way of creating user flows using **startActivityForResult**. This can be very useful for carrying out a dedicated Task where you need a result before proceeding with the user's flow through the app. Next, you will explore launch modes and how they impact the flow of user journeys when building apps.

INTENTS, TASKS, AND LAUNCH MODES

Up until now, you have been using the standard behavior for creating Activities and moving from one Activity to the next. The flow you have been using is the default, and in most cases, this will be the one you choose to use. When you open the app from the launcher with the default behavior, it creates its own Task, and each Activity you create is added to a back stack, so when you open three Activities one after the other as part of your user's journey, pressing the back button three times will move the user back through the previous screens/Activities and then go back to the device's home screen, while still keeping the app open.

The launch mode for this type of Activity is called **Standard**; it is the default and doesn't need specifying in the Activity element of **AndroidManifest.xml**. Even if you launch the same Activity three times, one after the other, there will be three instances of the same activity that exhibit the behavior described previously.

For some apps, you may want to change this behavior. The scenario most commonly used that doesn't conform to this pattern is when you want to relaunch an Activity without creating a new separate instance. A common use case for this is when you have a home screen with a main menu and different news stories that the user can read. Once the user has gone through to an individual news story and then presses another news story title from the menu, when the user presses the back button, they will expect to return to the home screen and not the previous news story. The launch mode that can help here is called **singleTop**. If a **singleTop** Activity is at the top of the Task (*top*, in this context, means most recently added), when the same **singleTop** Activity is launched, then instead of creating a new Activity, it uses the same Activity and runs the **onNewIntent** callback. In the preceding scenario, this could then use the same activity to display a different news story. In this callback, you receive an intent, and you can then process this intent as you have done previously in **onCreate**.

There are two other launch modes to be aware of, called **SingleTask** and **SingleInstance**. These are not for general use and are only used for special scenarios. For both of these launch modes, only one Activity of this type can exist in the application and it is always at the root of its Task. If you launch an Activity with this launch mode, it will create a new Task. If it already exists, then it will route the intent through the **onNewIntent** call and not create another instance. The only difference between **SingleTask** and **SingleInstance** is that **SingleInstance** is the one and only Activity of its Task. No new Activities can be launched into its Task. In contrast, **SingleTask** does allow other Activities to be launched into its Task, but the **SingleTask** Activity is always at the root.

These launch modes can be added to the XML of **AndroidManifest.xml** or created programmatically by adding intent flags. The most common ones used are the following:

- **FLAG_ACTIVITY_NEW_TASK**: Launches the Activity into a new Task.

- **FLAG_ACTIVITY_CLEAR_TASK**: Clears the current Task, so finishes all Activities and launches the Activity at the root of the current Task.

- **FLAG_ACTIVITY_SINGLE_TOP**: Replicates the launch mode of the **launchMode="singleTop"** XML.

- **FLAG_ACTIVITY_CLEAR_TOP**: Removes all Activities that are above any other instances of the same activity. If this is launched on a standard launch mode Activity, then it will clear the Task down to the first existing instance of the same Activity, and then launch another instance of the same Activity. This will probably not be what you want, and you can launch this flag with the **FLAG_ACTIVITY_SINGLE_TOP** flag to clear all the activities down to the same instance of the Activity you are launching and not create a new instance, but instead route a new intent to the existing Activity. To create an Activity using these two **intent** flags, you would do the following:

```
val intent = Intent(this, MainActivity::class.java).apply {
    flags = Intent.FLAG_ACTIVITY_CLEAR_TOP or
    Intent.FLAG_ACTIVITY_SINGLE_TOP
}
startActivity(intent)
```

If an intent launches an Activity with one or more of the intent flags specified in the preceding code block, then the launch mode specified overrides the one that is set in the **AndroidManifest.xml** file.

Intent flags can be combined in multiple ways. For more information, see the official documentation at https://developer.android.com/reference/android/content/Intent.

You'll explore the differences in the behavior of these two launch modes in the next exercise.

EXERCISE 2.06: SETTING THE LAUNCH MODE OF AN ACTIVITY

This exercise has many different layout files and Activities to illustrate the two most commonly used launch modes. Please download the code from http://packt.live/2LFWo8t and then we will go through the exercise at http://packt.live/2XUo3Vk:

1. Open up the **activity_main.xml** file and examine it.

    This illustrates a new concept when using layout files. If you have a layout file and you would like to include it in another layout, you can use the **\<include>** XML element (have a look at the following snippet of the layout file):

```
<include layout="@layout/letters"
    android:id="@+id/letters_layout"
    android:layout_width="wrap_content"
    android:layout_height="wrap_content"
    app:layout_constraintLeft_toLeftOf="parent"
    app:layout_constraintRight_toRightOf="parent"
    app:layout_constraintTop_toBottomOf="@id/
      launch_mode_standard"/>

<include layout="@layout/numbers"
    android:layout_width="wrap_content"
    android:layout_height="wrap_content"
    app:layout_constraintLeft_toLeftOf="parent"
    app:layout_constraintRight_toRightOf="parent"
    app:layout_constraintTop_toBottomOf="@id/
      launch_mode_single_top"/>
```

    The preceding layout uses the **include** XML element to include the two layout files: **letters.xml** and **numbers.xml**.

2. Open up and inspect the **letters.xml** and **numbers.xml** files found in the **res | layout** folder. These are very similar and are only differentiated from the buttons they contain by the ID of the buttons themselves and the text label they display.

3. Run the app and you will see the following screen:

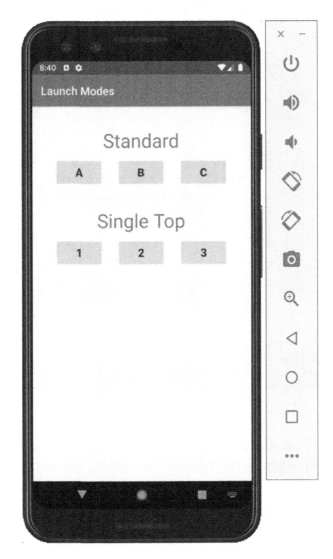

Figure 2.20: App displaying both the standard and single top modes

In order to demonstrate/illustrate the difference between **standard** and **singleTop** activity launch modes, you have to launch two or three activities one after the other.

4. Open up **MainActivity** and examine the contents of the code block in **onCreate(savedInstanceState: Bundle?)** after the signature:

```
val buttonClickListener = View.OnClickListener { view ->

    when (view.id) {
        R.id.letterA -> startActivity(Intent(this,
            ActivityA::class.java))
        //Other letters and numbers follow the same pattern/flow
        else -> {
            Toast.makeText(
                this,
                getString(R.string.unexpected_button_pressed),
                Toast.LENGTH_LONG
            )
            .show()
        }
    }
}

findViewById<View>(R.id.letterA).
setOnClickListener(buttonClickListener)
    //The buttonClickListener is set on all the number and letter
views
}
```

The logic contained in the main Activity and the other activities is basically the same. It displays an Activity and allows the user to press a button to launch another Activity using the same logic of creating a ClickListener and setting it on the button you saw in Exercise 2.05, *Retrieving a Result from an Activity*.

5. Open the **AndroidManifest.xml** file and you will see the following:

```
<?xml version="1.0" encoding="utf-8"?>
<manifest xmlns:android="http://schemas.android.com/apk/res/android"
    package="com.example.launchmodes">

    <application
        android:allowBackup="true"
        android:icon="@mipmap/ic_launcher"
        android:label="@string/app_name"
```

```
        android:roundIcon="@mipmap/ic_launcher_round"
        android:supportsRtl="true"
        android:theme="@style/Theme.LaunchModes">

        <activity android:name=".ActivityA"
          android:launchMode="standard"/>
        <activity android:name=".ActivityB"
          android:launchMode="standard"/>
        <activity android:name=".ActivityC"
          android:launchMode="standard"/>

        <activity android:name=".ActivityOne"
          android:launchMode="singleTop"/>
        <activity android:name=".ActivityTwo"
          android:launchMode="singleTop"/>
        <activity android:name=".ActivityThree"
          android:launchMode="singleTop"/>

        <activity android:name=".MainActivity">
            <intent-filter>
                <action android:name=
                  "android.intent.action.MAIN" />

                <category android:name=
                  "android.intent.category.LAUNCHER" />
            </intent-filter>
        </activity>
    </application>

</manifest>
```

You launch an Activity based on a button pressed on the main screen, but the letter and number activities have a different launch mode, which you can see specified in the **AndroidManifest.xml** file.

The **standard** launch mode is specified here to illustrate the difference between **standard** and **singleTop**, but **standard** is the default and would be how the Activity is launched if the **android:launchMode** XML attribute was not present.

6. Press one of the letters under the **Standard** heading and you will see the following screen (with **A** or letters **C** or **B**):

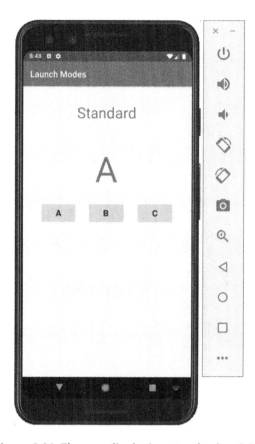

Figure 2.21: The app displaying standard activity

7. Keep on pressing any of the letter buttons, which will launch another Activity. Logs have been added to show this sequence of launching activities. Here is the log after pressing 10 letter Activities randomly:

```
2019-10-23 20:50:51.097 15281-15281/com.example.launchmodes D/
MainActivity: onCreate
2019-10-23 20:51:16.182 15281-15281/com.example.launchmodes D/
Activity B: onCreate
2019-10-23 20:51:18.821 15281-15281/com.example.launchmodes D/
Activity B: onCreate
2019-10-23 20:51:19.353 15281-15281/com.example.launchmodes D/
Activity C: onCreate
2019-10-23 20:51:20.334 15281-15281/com.example.launchmodes D/
Activity A: onCreate
2019-10-23 20:51:20.980 15281-15281/com.example.launchmodes D/
Activity B: onCreate
```

```
2019-10-23 20:51:21.853 15281-15281/com.example.launchmodes D/
Activity B: onCreate
2019-10-23 20:51:23.007 15281-15281/com.example.launchmodes D/
Activity C: onCreate
2019-10-23 20:51:23.887 15281-15281/com.example.launchmodes D/
Activity B: onCreate
2019-10-23 20:51:24.349 15281-15281/com.example.launchmodes D/
Activity C: onCreate
```

If you observe the preceding log, every time the user presses a character button in launch mode, a new instance of the character Activity is launched and added to the back stack.

8. Close the app, making sure it is not backgrounded (or in the recents/overview menu) but is actually closed, and then open the app again and press one of the number buttons under the `Single Top` heading:

Figure 2.22: The app displaying the Single Top activity

9. Press the number buttons 10 times, but make sure you press the same number button at least twice sequentially before pressing another number button.

    The logs you should see in the **Logcat** window (**View | Tool Windows | Logcat**) should be similar to the following:

```
2019-10-23 21:04:50.201 15549-15549/com.example.launchmodes D/
MainActivity: onCreate
2019-10-23 21:05:04.503 15549-15549/com.example.launchmodes D/
Activity 2: onCreate
2019-10-23 21:05:08.262 15549-15549/com.example.launchmodes D/
Activity 3: onCreate
2019-10-23 21:05:09.133 15549-15549/com.example.launchmodes D/
Activity 3: onNewIntent
2019-10-23 21:05:10.684 15549-15549/com.example.launchmodes D/
Activity 1: onCreate
2019-10-23 21:05:12.069 15549-15549/com.example.launchmodes D/
Activity 2: onNewIntent
2019-10-23 21:05:13.604 15549-15549/com.example.launchmodes D/
Activity 3: onCreate
2019-10-23 21:05:14.671 15549-15549/com.example.launchmodes D/
Activity 1: onCreate
2019-10-23 21:05:27.542 15549-15549/com.example.launchmodes D/
Activity 3: onNewIntent
2019-10-23 21:05:31.593 15549-15549/com.example.launchmodes D/
Activity 3: onNewIntent
2019-10-23 21:05:38.124 15549-15549/com.example.launchmodes D/
Activity 1: onCreate
```

You'll notice that instead of calling **onCreate** when you pressed the same button again, the Activity is not created, but a call is made to **onNewIntent**. If you press the back button, you'll notice that it will take you less than 10 clicks to back out of the app and return to the home screen, reflecting the fact that 10 activities have not been created.

ACTIVITY 2.01: CREATING A LOGIN FORM

The aim of this activity is to create a login form with username and password fields. Once the values in these fields are submitted, check these entered values against hardcoded values and display a welcome message if they match, or an error message if they don't, and return the user to the login form. The steps needed to achieve this are the following:

1. Create a form with username and password **EditText** Views and a **LOGIN** button.

2. Add a **ClickListener** interface to the button to react to a button press event.

3. Validate that the form fields are filled in.

4. Check the submitted username and password fields against the hardcoded values.

5. Display a welcome message with the username if successful and hide the form.

6. Display an error message if not successful and redirect the user back to the form.

There are a few possible ways that you could go about trying to complete this activity. Here are three ideas for approaches you could adopt:

- Use a **singleTop** Activity and send an intent to route to the same Activity to validate the credentials.

- Use a **standard** Activity to pass a username and password to another Activity and validate the credentials.

- Use **startActivityForResult** to carry out the validation in another Activity and then return the result.

The completed app, upon its first loading, should look as in *Figure 2.23*:

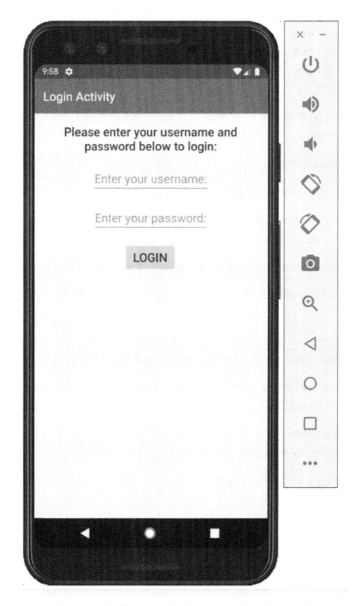

Figure 2.23: The app display when first loaded

NOTE

The solution to this activity can be found at: http://packt.live/3sKj1cp.

The source code for all the exercises and the activity in this chapter is located at http://packt.live/3o12sp4.

SUMMARY

In this chapter, you have covered a lot of the groundwork of how your application interacts with the Android framework, from the Activity lifecycle callbacks to retaining the state in your activities, navigating from one screen to another, and how intents and launch modes make this happen. These are core concepts that you need to understand in order to move on to more advanced topics.

In the next chapter, you will be introduced to fragments and how they fit into the architecture of your application, as well as exploring more of the Android resources framework.

3

DEVELOPING THE UI WITH FRAGMENTS

OVERVIEW

This chapter covers fragments and the fragment lifecycle. It demonstrates how to use them to build efficient and dynamic layouts that respond to different screen sizes and configurations, and allow you to divide your UI into different sections. By the end of this chapter, you will be able to create static and dynamic fragments, pass data to and from fragments and activities, and use the Jetpack Navigation component to detail how fragments fit together.

INTRODUCTION

In the previous chapter, we explored the Android **Activity Lifecycle** and looked into how it is used in apps to navigate between screens. We also analyzed various types of launch modes that defined how transitioning between screens happened. In this chapter, you'll explore **fragments**. A fragment is a section, portion, or, as the name implies, fragment of an Android activity.

Throughout the chapter, you'll learn how to use fragments, see how they can exist in more than one activity, and discover how multiple fragments can be used in one activity. You'll start by adding simple fragments to an activity and then progress to learning about the difference between static and dynamic fragments. Fragments can be used to simplify creating layouts for Android tablets that have larger form factors using dual-pane layouts. For example, if you have an average-sized phone screen and you want to include a list of news stories, you might only have enough space to display the list. If you viewed the same list of stories on a tablet, you'd have more space available so you could display the same list and also a story itself to the right of the list. Each of these different areas of the screen can use a fragment. You can then use the same fragment on both the phone and the tablet. You benefit from reusing and simplifying the layouts and don't have to repeat creating similar functionality.

Once you've explored how fragments are created and used, you'll then learn how to organize your user journeys with fragments. You'll apply some established practices for using fragments in this way. Finally, you'll learn how to simplify fragment use by creating a navigation graph with the Android Jetpack Navigation component, which allows you to specify linking fragments together with destinations.

Let's get started with the fragment lifecycle.

THE FRAGMENT LIFECYCLE

A fragment is a component with its own lifecycle. Understanding the **fragment lifecycle** is critical as it provides callbacks at certain stages of fragment creation, running state, and destruction where you can configure the initialization, display, and cleanup. Fragments run in an activity, and the fragment's lifecycle is bound to the activity's lifecycle.

In many ways, the fragment lifecycle is very similar to the activity lifecycle, and at first glance, it appears that the former replicates the latter. There are as many callbacks that are the same or similar in the fragment lifecycle as there are in the activity lifecycle, such as `onCreate(savedInstanceState: Bundle?)`.

The fragment lifecycle is tied to the activity lifecycle, so wherever fragments are used, the fragment callbacks are interleaved with the activity callbacks.

> **NOTE**
>
> The full sequence of the interaction between fragments and activities is illustrated in the official docs: https://developer.android.com/guide/fragments/lifecycle.

The same steps are gone through to initialize the fragment and prepare for it to be displayed to the user before being available for the user to interact with. The same teardown steps that an activity goes through happen to the fragment as well when the app is backgrounded, hidden, and exited. Fragments, like activities, have to extend/derive from a parent **Fragment** class, and you can choose which callbacks to override depending on your use case. Let's now explore these callbacks, the order they appear in, and what they do.

ONATTACH

`override fun onAttach(context: Context)`: This is the point where your fragment becomes linked to the activity it is used in. It allows you to reference the activity, although at this stage neither the fragment nor the activity has been fully created.

ONCREATE

`override fun onCreate(savedInstanceState: Bundle?)`: This is where you do any initialization of your fragment. This is not where you set the layout of your fragment, as at this stage, there is no UI available to display and no `setContentView` available as there is in an activity. As is the same in the activity's `onCreate()` function, you can use the `savedInstanceState` parameter to restore the state of the fragment when it is being re-created.

ONCREATEVIEW

`override fun onCreateView(inflater: LayoutInflater, container: ViewGroup?, savedInstanceState: Bundle?): View?`: Now, this is where you get to create the layout of your fragment. The most important thing to remember here is that instead of setting the layout (as is the case with an activity), the fragment will actually return the layout **View?** from this function. The views you have in your layout are available to refer to here, but there are a few caveats. You need to create the layout before you can reference the views contained within it, which is why it's preferred to do view manipulation in **onViewCreated**.

ONVIEWCREATED

`override fun onViewCreated(view View, savedInstanceState: Bundle?)`: This callback is the one in between your fragment being fully created and being visible to the user. It's where you'll typically set up your views and add any functionality and interactivity to these views. This might be adding a **click listener** to a button and then calling a function when it's clicked.

ONACTIVITYCREATED

`override fun onActivityCreated(context: Context)`: Called immediately after the activity's **onCreate** has been run. Most of the initialization of the view state of the fragment will have been done, and this is the place to do the final setup if required.

ONSTART

`override fun onStart()`: This is called when the fragment is about to become visible to the user but is not yet available for the user to interact with.

ONRESUME

`override fun onResume()`: At the end of this call, your fragment is available for the user to interact with. Normally, there is minimal setup or functionality defined in this callback as when the app goes into the background and then comes back into the foreground, this callback will always be called. Therefore, you don't want to have to needlessly repeat the setup of the fragment when this could be done with a callback that isn't run when the fragment becomes visible.

ONPAUSE

override fun onPause(): Like its counterpart, **onPause()** in an activity signals that your app is going into the background or has been partially covered by something else on the screen. Use this to save any changes to the fragment state.

ONSTOP

override fun onStop(): The fragment is no longer visible at the end of this call and goes into the background.

ONDESTROYVIEW

override fun onDestroyView(): This is usually called for doing final clean-up before the fragment is destroyed. You should use this callback if it is necessary to clean-up any resources. If the fragment is pushed to the back stack and retained then it can also be called without destroying the fragment. On completion of this callback, the fragment's layout view is removed.

ONDESTROY

override fun onDestroy(): The fragment is being destroyed. This can occur because the app is being killed or because this fragment is being replaced by another fragment.

ONDETACH

override fun onDetach(): This is called when the fragment has been detached from its activity.

There are more fragment callbacks, but these are the ones you will use for the majority of cases. Typically, you'll only use a subset of these callbacks: **onAttach()** to associate an activity with the fragment, **onCreate** to initialize the fragment, **onCreateView** to set the layout, and then **onViewCreated/ onActivityCreated** to do further initialization, and perhaps **onPause()** to do some cleanup.

> **NOTE**
>
> Further details of these callbacks can be found in the official documentation at https://developer.android.com/guide/fragments.

Now that we've gone through some of the theory of the fragment lifecycle and how it is affected by the host activity's lifecycle, let's see those callbacks being run in action.

EXERCISE 3.01: ADDING A BASIC FRAGMENT AND THE FRAGMENT LIFECYCLE

In this exercise, we will create and add a basic fragment to an app. The aim of this exercise is to gain familiarity with how fragments are added to an activity and the layout they display. To do this, you will create a new blank fragment with a layout in Android Studio. You will then add the fragment to the activity and verify the fragment has been added by the display of the fragment layout. Perform the following steps:

1. Create an application in Android Studio with an empty activity called **Fragment Lifecycle** with package name 'com.example.fragmentlifecyle'.

2. Next, create a new fragment by going to **File | New | Fragment (Blank)**. You just want to create a plain vanilla fragment at this stage, so you use the **Fragment (Blank)** option. When you've selected this option, you will be presented with the screen shown in *Figure 3.1*:

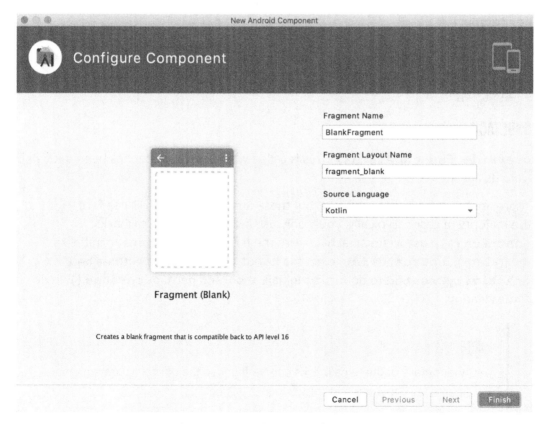

Figure 3.1: Creating a new fragment

3. Rename the fragment to **MainFragment** and the layout to **fragment_main**. Then, press **Finish** and the Fragment class will be created and opened. There is one function which has been added **onCreateView** (displayed below) which inflates the layout file used for the fragment.

```
override fun onCreateView(
    inflater: LayoutInflater, container: ViewGroup?,
    savedInstanceState: Bundle?
): View? {
    // Inflate the layout for this fragment
    return inflater.inflate(R.layout.fragment_main,
        container, false)
}
```

4. When you open up **fragment_main.xml** layout file, you'll see the following code:

```
<?xml version="1.0" encoding="utf-8"?>
<FrameLayout
  xmlns:android="http://schemas.android.com/apk/res/android"
    xmlns:tools="http://schemas.android.com/tools"
      android:layout_width="match_parent"
        android:layout_height="match_parent"
          tools:context=".MainFragment">
    <!-- TODO: Update blank fragment layout -->
    <TextView
        android:layout_width="match_parent"
        android:layout_height="match_parent"
        android:text="@string/hello_blank_fragment" />
</FrameLayout>
```

A simple layout has been added with a **TextView** and some example text using **@string/hello_blank_fragment**. This string resource has the text **hello blank fragment**. As the **layout_width** and **layout_height** are specified as **match_parent**, the **TextView** will occupy the whole of the screen. The text itself, however, will be added at the top left of the view with the default position.

5. Add the **android:gravity="center"** attribute and value to the **TextView** so that the text appears in the center of the screen:

```
<TextView
    android:layout_width="match_parent"
    android:layout_height="match_parent"
    android:gravity="center"
    android:text="@string/hello_blank_fragment" />
```

If you run up the UI now, you'll see the "Hello World!" display in *Figure 3.2*:

Figure 3.2: Initial app layout display without a fragment added

Well, you can see some **Hello World!** text, but not the **hello blank fragment** text you might have been expecting. The fragment and its layout do not automatically get added to an activity when you create it. This is a manual process.

6. Open the **activity_main.xml** file and replace the contents with the following:

```xml
<?xml version="1.0" encoding="utf-8"?>
<androidx.constraintlayout.widget.ConstraintLayout
    xmlns:android="http://schemas.android.com/apk/res/android"
    xmlns:tools="http://schemas.android.com/tools"
    android:layout_width="match_parent"
    android:layout_height="match_parent"
    tools:context=".MainActivity">

    <fragment
        android:id="@+id/main_fragment"
        android:name="com.example.fragmentlifecycle.MainFragment"
        android:layout_width="match_parent"
        android:layout_height="match_parent" />

</androidx.constraintlayout.widget.ConstraintLayout>
```

Just as there are view declarations you can add to layouts in XML, there is also a **fragment** element. You've added the fragment to the **ConstraintLayout** with constraints of **match_parent** for the **layout_width** and **layout_height** so it will occupy the whole of the screen. The most important **xml** attribute to examine here is **android:name**. It's here where you specify the fully qualified name of the package and **Fragment** class that you are going to add to the layout with **com.example.fragmentlifecycle. MainFragment**.

7. Now run the app, and you will see the output shown in *Figure 3.3*:

Figure 3.3: App layout display with a fragment added

This proves that your fragment with the text **Hello blank fragment** has been added to the activity and the layout you defined is being displayed. Next, you'll examine the callback methods between the activity and the fragment and how this happened.

8. Open up the **MainFragment** class and add a **TAG** constant to the companion object with the value **"MainFragment"** to identify the class. Then add/update the functions with appropriate log statements. You will need to add the imports for the 'Log' statement and the 'context' to the imports at the top of the class. The code snippet below is truncated. Follow the link shown to see the full code block you need to use:

MainFragment.kt

```
3     import android.content.Context
4     import android.util.Log

27        override fun onAttach(context: Context) {
28            super.onAttach(context)
29            Log.d(TAG, "onAttach")
30        }
31
32        override fun onCreate(savedInstanceState: Bundle?) {
33            super.onCreate(savedInstanceState)
34            Log.d(TAG, "onCreate")
35            arguments?.let {
36                param1 = it.getString(ARG_PARAM1)
37                param2 = it.getString(ARG_PARAM2)
38            }
39        }
40
41        override fun onCreateView(
42            inflater: LayoutInflater, container: ViewGroup?,
43            savedInstanceState: Bundle?
44        ): View? {
45            Log.d(TAG, "onCreateView")
46
47            // Inflate the layout for this fragment
48            return inflater.inflate(R.layout.fragment_main,
                  container, false)
49        }
```

You can find the complete code for this step at http://packt.live/3bYaNY6.

You will need to add **Log.d(TAG, "onCreateView")** to the **onCreateView** callback and **Log.d(TAG, "onCreate")** to the **onCreate** callback which already exist.

9. Next, open the **MainActivity** class and add the common callback methods **onStart** and **onResume**. Then add a companion object with a **TAG** constant with the value **"MainActivity"** as shown below and also add the Log import to the top of the class:

```
import android.util.log
override fun onCreate(savedInstanceState: Bundle?) {
    super.onCreate(savedInstanceState)
    setContentView(R.layout.activity_main)
    Log.d(TAG, "onCreate")
}

override fun onStart() {
    super.onStart()
    Log.d(TAG, "onStart")
}
```

```
override fun onResume() {
    super.onResume()
    Log.d(TAG, "onResume")
}


companion object {
    private const val TAG = "MainActivity"
}
```

You'll see that you also have to add the **onCreate** log statement **Log.d(TAG, "onCreate")** as this callback was already there when you added the activity in the project.

You learned in *Chapter 2, Building User Screen Flows*, how to view log statements, and you are going to open the **Logcat** window in Android Studio to examine the logs and the order they are called when you run the app. In *Chapter 2, Building User Screen Flows*, you were viewing logs from a single activity so you could see the order they were called in. Now you'll examine the order in which the **MainActivity** and **MainFragment** callbacks happen.

10. Open up the **Logcat** window. (Just to remind you, it can be accessed by clicking the **Logcat** tab at the bottom of the screen and also from the toolbar with **View | Tool Windows | Logcat**). As both **MainActivity** and **MainFragment** start with the text **Main**, you can type **Main** in the search box to filter the logs to only show statements with this text. Run the app, and you should see the following:

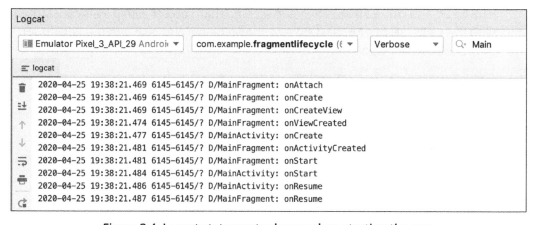

Figure 3.4: Logcat statements shown when starting the app

What's interesting here is that the first few callbacks are from the fragment. It is linked to the activity it has been placed in with the **onAttach** callback. The fragment is initialized and its view is displayed in **onCreate** and **onCreateView**, before another callback, **onViewCreated**, is called, confirming that the fragment UI is ready to be displayed. This is before the activity's **onCreate** method is called. This makes sense as the activity creates its UI based on what it contains. As this is a fragment that defines its own layout, the activity needs to know how to measure, lay out, and draw the fragment as it does in the **onCreate** method. Then, the fragment receives confirmation that this has been done with the **onActivityCreated** callback before both the fragment and activity start to display the UI in **onStart** before preparing the user to interact with it after their respective **onResume** callbacks have finished.

> **NOTE**
>
> The interaction between the activity and fragment lifecycles detailed previously is for the case when static fragments, which are those defined in the layout of an activity, are created. For dynamic fragments, which can be added when the activity is already running, the interaction can differ.

So, now that the fragment and the containing activity are shown, what happens when the app is backgrounded or closed? The callbacks are still interleaved when the fragment and activity are paused, stopped, and finished.

11. Add the following callbacks to the **MainFragment** class:

```
override fun onPause() {
    super.onPause()
    Log.d(TAG, "onPause")
}

override fun onStop() {
    super.onStop()
    Log.d(TAG, "onStop")
}

override fun onDestroyView() {
    super.onDestroyView()
    Log.d(TAG, "onDestroyView")
}
```

```kotlin
override fun onDestroy() {
    super.onDestroy()
    Log.d(TAG, "onDestroy")
}

override fun onDetach() {
    super.onDetach()
    Log.d(TAG, "onDetach")

}
```

12. Then add these callbacks to **MainActivity**:

```kotlin
override fun onPause() {
    super.onPause()
    Log.d(TAG, "onPause")
}

override fun onStop() {
    super.onStop()
    Log.d(TAG, "onStop")
}

override fun onDestroy() {
    super.onDestroy()
    Log.d(TAG, "onDestroy")
}
```

13. Build the app up, and once it is running, you'll see the callbacks from before starting both the fragment and activity. You can use the dustbin icon at the top left of the **Logcat** window to clear the statements. Then close the app and review the output log statements:

Figure 3.5: Logcat statements shown when closing the app

The **onPause** and **onStop** statements are as you might expect in that the fragment gets notified of these callbacks first as it is contained within the activity. You can think of this as being inwards to outwards in that the child elements are notified before the containing parent, so the parent knows how to respond. The fragment is then torn down, removed from the activity, and then destroyed with the **onDestroyView**, **onDestroy**, and **onDetach** functions before the activity itself is destroyed after any final clean-up is done in **onDestroy**. It doesn't make sense for the activity to finish until all the component parts that make up the activity are themselves removed.

The full fragment lifecycle callbacks and how they relate to the activity callbacks is a complicated area of Android because which callbacks are applied in which situation can differ quite substantially. To view a more detailed overview, see the official documentation at https://developer.android.com/guide/fragments.

For the majority of situations, you will only use the preceding fragment callbacks. This example demonstrates both how self-contained fragments are in their creation, display, and destruction, and also their interdependence on the containing Activity. Through the **onAttach** and **onActivityCreated** callbacks, they can access both the containing activity and its state, which will be demonstrated in the following example.

Now that we've gone through a basic example of adding a fragment to an activity and examining the interaction between the fragment and the activity, let's see a more detailed example of how you add two fragments to an activity.

EXERCISE 3.02: ADDING FRAGMENTS STATICALLY TO AN ACTIVITY

This exercise will demonstrate how to add two fragments to an activity with their own UI and separate functionality. You'll create a simple counter class that increments and decrements a number and a styling class that changes the style applied programmatically to some **Hello World** text. Perform the following steps:

1. Create an application in Android Studio with an empty activity called **Fragment Intro**. Then replace the content with the following strings required for the exercise in the **res | values | strings.xml** file:

```
<resources>
    <string name="app_name">Fragment Intro</string>

    <string name="hello_world">Hello World</string>
    <string name="bold_text">Bold</string>
    <string name="italic_text">Italic</string>
    <string name="reset">Reset</string>

    <string name="zero">0</string>
    <string name="plus">+</string>
    <string name="minus">-</string>
    <string name="counter_text">Counter</string>

</resources>
```

These strings are used in both the counter fragment as well as the style fragment, which you will create next.

2. Add a new blank fragment by going to **File | New | Fragment (Blank)** called **CounterFragment** with layout name **fragment_counter**

3. Now make changes to the **fragment_counter.xml** file. To add the fields, you'll need to create the **counter** in the **Fragment** class. The code below is truncated for space. Follow the link shown for the full code you need to use:

fragment_counter.xml

```
9     <TextView
10        android:id="@+id/counter_text"
11        android:layout_width="wrap_content"
12        android:layout_height="wrap_content"
13        android:text="@string/counter_text"
14        android:paddingTop="10dp"
15        android:textSize="44sp"
16        app:layout_constraintEnd_toEndOf="parent"
17        app:layout_constraintStart_toStartOf="parent"
18        app:layout_constraintTop_toTopOf="parent"/>
19
20    <TextView
21        android:id="@+id/counter"
22        android:layout_width="wrap_content"
23        android:layout_height="wrap_content"
24        android:text="@string/zero"
25        android:textSize="54sp"
26        android:textStyle="bold"
27        app:layout_constraintEnd_toEndOf="parent"
28        app:layout_constraintStart_toStartOf="parent"
29        app:layout_constraintTop_toBottomOf="@id/counter_text"
30        app:layout_constraintBottom_toTopOf="@id/plus"/>
```

You can find the complete code for this step at http://packt.live/2LFCJpa.

We are using a simple **ConstraintLayout** file that has **TextViews** set up for the header **@+id/counter_text** and the value of the **android:id="@+id/counter"** (with a default of **@string/zero**), which will be changed by the **android:id="@+id/plus"** and **android:id="@+id/minus"** buttons.

> **NOTE**
>
> For a simple example like this, you are not going to set individual styles on the views with **style="@some_style"** notation, which would be best practice to avoid repeating these values on each view.

4. Now open the **CounterFragment** and override the **onViewCreated** function. You will also need to add the following imports:

```
import android.widget.Button
import android.widget.TextView
override fun onViewCreated(view: View, savedInstanceState: Bundle?) {
    super.onViewCreated(view, savedInstanceState)
    val counter = view.findViewById<TextView>(R.id.counter)
    view.findViewById<Button>(R.id.plus).setOnClickListener {
        var counterValue = counter.text.toString().toInt()
        counter.text = (++counterValue).toString()
    }
    view.findViewById<Button>(R.id.minus).setOnClickListener {
        var counterValue = counter.text.toString().toInt()
        if (counterValue > 0) counter.text
          = (--counterValue).toString()
    }
}
```

We've added **onViewCreated**, which is the callback run when the layout has been applied to your fragment. The **onCreateView** callback, which creates the view, was run when the fragment itself was created. The buttons you've specified in the preceding fragment have **click listeners** set up on them to increment and decrement the value of the **counter** view.

5. Firstly, with this line, you are retrieving the current value of the counter as an integer:

```
var counterValue = counter.text.toString().toInt()
```

6. Then with the following line, you are incrementing the value by **1** with the **++** notation:

```
counter.text = (++counterValue).toString()
```

As this is done by adding the **++** before the **counterValue**, it increments the integer value before it is cast to a string. If you didn't do it this way, but instead did a post increment with **counter++**, the value would only be available the next time you used this value in a statement, which would reset the counter to the same value.

7. The line within the minus button **click listener** does a similar thing to the add **click listener** but decrements the value by **1**:

```
if (counterValue > 0) counter.text = (--counterValue).toString()
```

You only do the operation if the value is greater than **0** so that no negative numbers are set.

8. You have not added the fragment to the **MainActivity** layout. To do this, go into the **activity_main.xml** and add the following code:

```
<?xml version="1.0" encoding="utf-8"?>
<LinearLayout xmlns:android="http://schemas.android.com/apk/res/
    android"
    xmlns:tools="http://schemas.android.com/tools"
    android:layout_width="match_parent"
    android:layout_height="match_parent"
    android:orientation="vertical"
    tools:context=".MainActivity">

    <fragment
        android:id="@+id/counter_fragment"
        android:name="com.example.fragmentintro.CounterFragment"
        android:layout_width="match_parent"
        android:layout_height="match_parent"/>

</LinearLayout>
```

You are going to change the layout from a **FrameLayout** to a **LinearLayout** as you will need this to put one fragment above the other when you add the next fragment. You specify the fragment to be used within the **fragment** XML element by the **name** attribute with the fully qualified package name used for the class: **android:name="com.example.fragmentintro. CounterFragment**. If you used a different package name when you created the app, then this must refer to the **CounterFragment** you created. The important thing to grasp here is that you have added a fragment to your main activity layout and the fragment also has a layout. This shows some of the power of using fragments as you can encapsulate the functionality of one feature of your app, complete with a layout file and fragment class, and add it to multiple activities.

Once you've done this, run the fragment in the virtual device as in *Figure 3.6*:

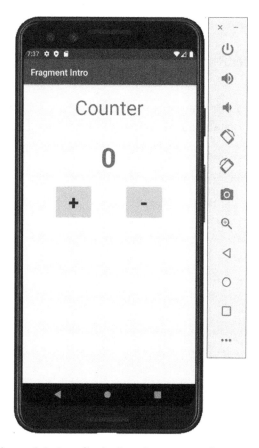

Figure 3.6: App displaying the counter fragment

You have created a simple counter. The basic functionality works as expected, incrementing and decrementing a counter value.

9. In the next step, you are going to add another fragment to the bottom half of the screen. This demonstrates the versatility of fragments. You can have encapsulated pieces of UI with functionality and features in different areas of the screen.

10. Now create a new fragment using the earlier steps for creating the **CounterFragment** called **StyleFragment** with layout name **fragment_style**.

11. Next, open up the **fragment_style.xml** file that has been created and replace the contents with the code at the link below. The snippet shown below is truncated – see the link for the full code:

fragment_style.xml

```
10    <TextView
11        android:id="@+id/hello_world"
12        android:layout_width="wrap_content"
13        android:layout_height="0dp"
14        android:textSize="34sp"
15        android:paddingBottom="12dp"
16        android:text="@string/hello_world"
17        app:layout_constraintEnd_toEndOf="parent"
18        app:layout_constraintStart_toStartOf="parent"
19        app:layout_constraintTop_toTopOf="parent" />
20
21    <Button
22        android:id="@+id/bold_button"
23        android:layout_width="wrap_content"
24        android:layout_height="0dp"
25        android:textSize="24sp"
26        android:text="@string/bold_text"
27        app:layout_constraintEnd_toStartOf="@+id/italic_button"
28        app:layout_constraintStart_toStartOf="parent"
29        app:layout_constraintTop_toBottomOf="@id/hello_world" />
```

You can find the complete code for this step at http://packt.live/2KykTDS.

The layout adds a **TextView** with three buttons. The **TextView** text and the text for all the buttons are set as string resources **(@string)**.

12. Next, go into the **activity_main.xml** file and add the **StyleFragment** below the **CounterFragment** inside the **LinearLayout**:

```
<?xml version="1.0" encoding="utf-8"?>
<LinearLayout xmlns:android="http://schemas.android.com/apk/res/
    android"
    xmlns:tools="http://schemas.android.com/tools"
    android:layout_width="match_parent"
    android:layout_height="match_parent"
    android:orientation="vertical"
    tools:context=".MainActivity">

    <fragment
        android:id="@+id/counter_fragment"
        android:name="com.example.fragmentintro.CounterFragment"
        android:layout_width="match_parent"
        android:layout_height="match_parent"/>

    <fragment
```

```
        android:id="@+id/style_fragment"
        android:name="com.example.fragmentintro.StyleFragment"
        android:layout_width="match_parent"
        android:layout_height="match_parent"/>

</LinearLayout>
```

When you run the app, you will see that the **StyleFragment** is not visible, as
in *Figure 3.7*:

Figure 3.7: App shown without the StyleFragment displayed

You've included the **StyleFragment** in the layout, but because the
CounterFragment has its width and height set to match its parent
(**android:layout_width="match_parent android:layout_
height="match_parent"**) and it is the first view in the layout, it takes up all
the space.

What you need is some way to specify the proportion of the height that each fragment should occupy. The **LinearLayout** orientation is set to vertical so the fragments will appear one on top of the other when the **layout_height** is not set to **match_parent**. In order to define the proportion of this height, you need to add another attribute **layout_weight** to each fragment in the **activity_main.xml** layout file. When you use **layout_weight** to determine this proportional height, the fragments should occupy you set the **layout_height** of the fragments to **0dp**.

13. Update the **activity_main.xml** layout with the following changes setting the **layout_height** of both fragments to **0dp** and adding the **layout_weight** attributes with the values below:

```xml
<?xml version="1.0" encoding="utf-8"?>
<LinearLayout xmlns:android="http://schemas.android.com/apk/res/
  android"
    xmlns:tools="http://schemas.android.com/tools"
    android:layout_width="match_parent"
    android:layout_height="match_parent"
    android:orientation="vertical"
    tools:context=".MainActivity">

    <fragment
        android:id="@+id/counter_fragment"
        android:name="com.example.fragmentintro.CounterFragment"
        android:layout_width="match_parent"
        android:layout_height="0dp"
        android:layout_weight="2"/>

    <fragment
        android:id="@+id/style_fragment"
        android:name="com.example.fragmentintro.StyleFragment"
        android:layout_width="match_parent"
        android:layout_height="0dp"
        android:layout_weight="1"/>

</LinearLayout>
```

These changes make the **CounterFragment** occupy twice the height of the **StyleFragment**, as shown in *Figure 3.8*:

Figure 3.8: CounterFragment with twice the amount of vertical space allocated

You can experiment by changing the weight values to see the differences you can make to the display of the layout.

14. At this point, pressing the styling buttons **Bold** and **Italic** will have no effect on the text **Hello World**. The button actions have not been specified. The next step involves adding interactivity to the buttons to make changes to the style of the **Hello World** text. Add the following **onViewCreated** function, which overrides its parent to add behavior to the fragment after the layout view has been set up. You will also need to add the following widgets and the typeface import to change the style for the text:

```
import android.widget.Button
import android.widget.TextView
import android.graphics.Typeface
```

```
override fun onViewCreated(view: View, savedInstanceState: Bundle?) {
    super.onViewCreated(view, savedInstanceState)
    val boldButton = view.findViewById<Button>(R.id.bold_button)
    val italicButton = view.findViewById<Button>(R.id.italic_button)
    val resetButton = view.findViewById<Button>(R.id.reset_button)
    val helloWorldTextView = view.findViewById<TextView>
      (R.id.hello_world)
    boldButton.setOnClickListener {
        if (helloWorldTextView.typeface?.isItalic == true)
          helloWorldTextView.setTypeface(helloWorldTextView.typeface,
          Typeface.BOLD_ITALIC)
        else helloWorldTextView.setTypeface(null, Typeface.BOLD)
    }

    italicButton.setOnClickListener {
        if (helloWorldTextView.typeface?.isBold == true)
          helloWorldTextView.setTypeface(helloWorldTextView.typeface,
            Typeface.BOLD_ITALIC)
        else helloWorldTextView.setTypeface(null, Typeface.ITALIC)
    }

    resetButton.setOnClickListener {
        helloWorldTextView.setTypeface(null, Typeface.NORMAL)
    }
}
```

Here, you are adding **click listeners** to each button defined in the layout and setting the **Hello World** text to the desired **Typeface**. (In this context, **Typeface** refers to the style which will be applied to the text and not a font). The conditional statement for the **bold_button** checks whether the italic **Typeface** is set and if it is, to make the text bold and italic, and if not, just make the text bold. This logic works the opposite way for the **italic_button**, checking the state of the **Typeface** and making the corresponding changes to the **Typeface**, initially setting it to italic if no **TypeFace** is defined.

15. Finally, the **reset_button** clears the **Typeface** and sets it back to normal. Run the app up and click the **ITALIC** and **BOLD** buttons. You should see a display as in *Figure 3.9*:

Figure 3.9: StyleFragment setting text to bold and italic

This exercise, although simple, has demonstrated some fundamental concepts of using fragments. The features of your app that the user can interact with can be developed independently and not rely on bundling two or more features into one layout and activity. This makes fragments reusable and means you can focus your attention when developing your app on adding well-defined UI, logic, and features into a single fragment.

STATIC FRAGMENTS AND DUAL-PANE LAYOUTS

The previous exercise introduced you to static fragments, those that can be defined in the activity XML layout file. One of the advantages of the Android development environment is the ability to create different layouts and resources for different screen sizes. This is used for deciding which resources to display depending on whether the device is a phone or a tablet. The space for laying out UI elements can increase substantially with the larger size of a tablet. Android allows specifying different resources depending on many different form factors. The qualifier frequently used to define a tablet in the **res** (resources) folder is **sw600dp**. This states that if the **shortest width** (**sw**) of the device is over 600 dp, then use these resources. This qualifier is used for 7" tablets and larger. Tablets facilitate what is known as dual-pane layouts. A pane represents a self-contained part of the user interface. If the screen is large enough, then two panes (dual-pane) layouts can be supported. This also provides the opportunity for one pane to interact with another to update content.

EXERCISE 3.03: DUAL-PANE LAYOUTS WITH STATIC FRAGMENTS

In this exercise, you are going to create a simple app that displays a list of star signs and specific information about each star sign. It will use different displays for phones and tablets. The phone will display a list and then open the selected list item's content in another screen whilst the tablet will display the same list in one pane and open the list item's content in another pane on the same screen in a dual-pane layout. In order to do this, you have to create another layout that will only be used for 7" tablets and above. Perform the following steps:

1. Firstly, create a new Android Studio project with an **Empty Activity** with the name **Dual Pane Layouts**. Once created, go to the layout file that has been created, **res | layout | activity_main.xml**.

2. Once you've selected this in the top toolbar of the design view, select the orientation layout button.

3. In this dropdown, you can select **Create Tablet Variation** for the app. This creates a new folder in the **main | res** folder named **'layout-sw600dp'** with the layout file **activity_main.xml** added:

Figure 3.10: Design View orientation button dropdown

At the moment, it is a duplicate of the **activity_main.xml** file added when you created the app, but you will change it to customize the screen display for tablets.

In order to demonstrate the use of dual-pane layouts, you are going to create a list of star signs that, when a list item is selected, will display some basic information about the star sign.

4. Go to the top toolbar and select **File | New | Fragment | Fragment (Blank)**. Call it **ListFragment**.

For this exercise, you need to update the **strings.xml** and **themes.xml** files adding the entries below:

strings.xml

```
<string name="star_signs">Star Signs</string>

<string name="symbol">Symbol: %s</string>
<string name="date_range">Date Range: %s</string>

<string name="aquarius">Aquarius</string>
<string name="pisces">Pisces</string>
<string name="aries">Aries</string>
<string name="taurus">Taurus</string>
<string name="gemini">Gemini</string>
<string name="cancer">Cancer</string>
<string name="leo">Leo</string>
```

```xml
    <string name="virgo">Virgo</string>
    <string name="libra">Libra</string>
    <string name="scorpio">Scorpio</string>
    <string name="sagittarius">Sagittarius</string>
    <string name="capricorn">Capricorn</string>
    <string name="unknown_star_sign">Unknown Star Sign</string>
```

themes.xml

```xml
    <style name="StarSignTextView"
      parent="Base.TextAppearance.AppCompat.Large" >
        <item name="android:padding">18dp</item>
    </style>


    <style name="StarSignTextViewHeader"
      parent="Base.TextAppearance.AppCompat.Display1" >
        <item name="android:padding">18dp</item>
    </style>
```

Open the **main | res | layout | fragment_list.xml** file and replace the default contents with the following:

```xml
<?xml version="1.0" encoding="utf-8"?>
<ScrollView xmlns:android="http://schemas.android.com/apk/res/
  android"
    xmlns:tools="http://schemas.android.com/tools"

    android:layout_width="match_parent"
    android:layout_height="wrap_content"
    tools:context=".ListFragment">

    <LinearLayout
        android:layout_width="match_parent"
        android:layout_height="wrap_content"
        android:orientation="vertical">

        <TextView
            android:layout_width="match_parent"
            android:layout_height="wrap_content"
            android:gravity="center"
            android:textSize="24sp"
            android:textStyle="bold"
            style="@style/StarSignTextView"
```

```
                    android:text="@string/star_signs" />

        <View
                android:layout_width="match_parent"
                android:layout_height="1dp"
                android:background="?android:attr/dividerVertical" />

        <TextView
                android:id="@+id/aquarius"
                style="@style/StarSignTextView"
                android:layout_width="match_parent"
                android:layout_height="wrap_content"
                android:text="@string/aquarius" />

    </LinearLayout>

</ScrollView>
```

You will see that the first **xml** element is a **ScrollView**. A **ScrollView** is a **ViewGroup** that allows the contents to scroll, and as you will be adding 12 star signs into the **LinearLayout** it contains, this is likely to occupy more vertical space than is available on the screen.

Adding the **ScrollView** prevents the contents from cutting off vertically when there is no more room to display them and scrolls the layout. A **ScrollView** can only contain one child view. Here, it's a **LinearLayout** and as the contents will be displayed vertically, the orientation is set to vertical (**android:orientation="vertical"**). Below the first title **TextView** you have added a divider **View** and a **TextView** for the first star sign Aquarius.

5. Add the other 11 star signs with the same format, adding first the divider and then the **TextView**. The name of the string resource and the **id** should be the same for each **TextView**. The names of the star signs you will create a view from are specified in the **strings.xml** file.

> **NOTE**
>
> The technique used to lay out a list is fine for an example, but in a real-world app, you would create a **RecyclerView** dedicated to displaying lists that can scroll, with the data bound to the list by an adapter. You will cover this in a later chapter.

6. Next create the StarSignListener and make the MainActivity implement it by adding the following:

```
interface StarSignListener {
    fun onSelected(id: Int)
}


class MainActivity : AppCompatActivity(), StarSignListener {
    ...
    override fun onSelected(id: Int) {
        TODO("not implemented yet")
    }
}
```

This is how the fragments will communicate back to the activity when a user selects a star sign from the **ListFragment** and logic will be added depending on whether a dual pane is available or not.

7. Once you've created the layout file, go into the **ListFragment** class and update it with the contents below, keeping **onCreateView()** in place. You can see in the fragment in the **onAttach()** callback you are stating that the activity implements the **StarSignListener** interface so it can be notified when the user clicks an item in the list: Add the import for the **Context** required for **onAttach** with the other imports at the top of the file:

```
import android.content.Context


class ListFragment : Fragment(), View.OnClickListener {

    private lateinit var starSignListener: StarSignListener

        override fun onAttach(context: Context) {
        super.onAttach(context)
        if (context is StarSignListener) {
            starSignListener = context
        } else {
            throw RuntimeException("Must implement StarSignListener")
        }
    }


    override fun onCreateView(...)
```

```kotlin
    override fun onViewCreated(view: View,
        savedInstanceState:Bundle?) {
        super.onViewCreated(view, savedInstanceState)
        val starSigns = listOf<View>(
            view.findViewById(R.id.aquarius),
            view.findViewById(R.id.pisces),
            view.findViewById(R.id.aries),
            view.findViewById(R.id.taurus),
            view.findViewById(R.id.gemini),
            view.findViewById(R.id.cancer),
            view.findViewById(R.id.leo),
            view.findViewById(R.id.virgo),
            view.findViewById(R.id.libra),
            view.findViewById(R.id.scorpio),
            view.findViewById(R.id.sagittarius),
            view.findViewById(R.id.capricorn)
        )

        starSigns.forEach {
            it.setOnClickListener(this)
        }
    }


    override fun onClick(v: View?) {
        v?.let { starSign ->
            starSignListener.onSelected(starSign.id)
        }
    }
}
```

The remaining callbacks are similar to what you have seen in the previous exercises. You create the fragment view with **onCreateView**. You set up the buttons with a **click listener** in **onViewCreated** and then you handle clicks in **onClick**.

The **listOf** syntax in **onViewCreated** is a way of creating a **readonly** list with the specified elements, which in this case are your star sign **TextViews**. Then, in the following code, you loop over these **TextViews**, setting the **click listener** for each of the individual **TextViews** by iterating over the **TextView** list with the **forEach** statement. The **it** syntax here refers to the element of the list that is being operated on, which will be one of the 12 star sign **TextViews**.

8. Finally, the **onClick** statement communicates back to the activity through the **StarSignListener** when one of the star signs in the list has been clicked:

```
v?.let { starSign ->
    starSignListener.onSelected(starSign.id)
}
```

You check whether the View specified as **v** is null with the **?** and then only operate upon it with the **let** scope function if it isn't, before passing the **id** of the star sign to the **Activity/StarSignListener**.

> **NOTE**
>
> Listeners are a common way to react to changes. By specifying a **Listener** interface, you are specifying a contract to be fulfilled. The implementing class is then notified of the results of the listener operation.

9. Next create the **DetailFragment**, which will display the star sign details. Create a fragment as you have done before and call it **DetailFragment**. Replace the **fragment_detail** layout file contents with the following XML file:

```xml
<?xml version="1.0" encoding="utf-8"?>
<LinearLayout xmlns:android="http://schemas.android.com/apk/res/
  android"
    xmlns:tools="http://schemas.android.com/tools"
    android:layout_width="match_parent"
    android:layout_height="match_parent"
    android:orientation="vertical"
    tools:context=".DetailFragment">

    <TextView
        android:id="@+id/star_sign"
        style="@style/StarSignTextViewHeader"
        android:textStyle="bold"
        android:gravity="center"
        android:layout_width="match_parent"
        android:layout_height="wrap_content"
        tools:text="Aquarius"/>

    <TextView
        android:id="@+id/symbol"
```

```
        style="@style/StarSignTextView"
        android:layout_width="match_parent"
        android:layout_height="wrap_content"
        tools:text="Water Carrier"/>

    <TextView
        android:id="@+id/date_range"
        style="@style/StarSignTextView"
        android:layout_width="match_parent"
        android:layout_height="wrap_content"
        tools:text="Date Range: January 20 - February 18" />

</LinearLayout>
```

Here, you create a simple **LinearLayout**, which will display the star sign name, the symbol of the star sign, and the date range. You'll set these values in the **DetailFragment**.

10. Open the **DetailFragment** and update the contents with the following text and also add widget imports to the imports list:

```kotlin
import android.widget.TextView
import android.widget.Toast

class DetailFragment : Fragment() {

    private val starSign: TextView?
        get() = view?.findViewById(R.id.star_sign)

    private val symbol: TextView?
        get() = view?.findViewById(R.id.symbol)

    private val dateRange: TextView?
        get() = view?.findViewById(R.id.date_range)

    override fun onCreateView(
        inflater: LayoutInflater, container: ViewGroup?,
            savedInstanceState: Bundle?): View? {

        // Inflate the layout for this fragment
        return inflater.inflate(R.layout.fragment_detail,
            container, false)
```

```
    }

    fun setStarSignData(starSignId: Int) {

        when (starSignId) {
            R.id.aquarius -> {
                starSign?.text = getString(R.string.aquarius)
                symbol?.text = getString(R.string.symbol,
                    "Water Carrier")
                dateRange?.text = getString(R.string.date_range,
                    "January 20 - February 18")
            }
        }
    }
}
```

The **onCreateView** inflates the layout as normal. The **setStarSignData()** function is what populates the data from the passed in **starSignId**. The **when** expression is used to determine the ID of the star sign and set the appropriate contents.

The **setStarSignData** function above formats text passed with the **getString** function – **getString(R.string.symbol,"Water Carrier")**, for example, passes the text **Water Carrier** into the **symbol** string, **<string name="symbol">Symbol: %s</string>**, and replaces the **%s** with the passed-in value. You can see what other string formatting options there are in the official docs: https://developer.android.com/guide/topics/resources/string-resource.

Following the pattern introduced by the star sign **aquarius**, add the other 11 star signs below the **aquarius** block. For simplicity, all of the detailed text of the star sign has not been added into the **strings.xml** file. Consult the example here for the completed class file:

http://packt.live/35Vynkx

Right now, you have added both **ListFragment** and **DetailFragment**. Currently, however, they have not been synced together, so selecting the star sign item in the **ListFragment** does not load contents into the **DetailFragment**. Let's look at how you can change that.

11. Firstly, you need to change the layout of **activity_main.xml** in both the **layout** folder and the **layout-sw600dp**.

12. Open up **res | layout | activity_main.xml** if in the Project View. In the default Android View open up **res | layout | activity_main.xml** and select the top **activity_main.xml** file without (sw600dp). Replace the contents with the following:

```xml
<?xml version="1.0" encoding="utf-8"?>
<androidx.constraintlayout.widget.ConstraintLayout
  xmlns:android="http://schemas.android.com/apk/res/android"
    xmlns:tools="http://schemas.android.com/tools"
    android:layout_width="match_parent"
    android:layout_height="match_parent"
    tools:context=".MainActivity">

    <fragment
        android:id="@+id/star_sign_list"
        android:name="com.example.staticfragments.ListFragment"
        android:layout_height="match_parent"
        android:layout_width="match_parent"/>


</androidx.constraintlayout.widget.ConstraintLayout>
```

13. Then open up **res | layout-sw600dp | activity_main.xml** if in the Project View. In the default Android View open up **res | layout | activity_main.xml (sw600dp)**. Replace the contents with the following:

```xml
<?xml version="1.0" encoding="utf-8"?>
<LinearLayout xmlns:android="http://schemas.android.com/apk/res/
  android"
    xmlns:tools="http://schemas.android.com/tools"
    android:layout_width="match_parent"
    android:layout_height="match_parent"
    android:orientation="horizontal"
    tools:context=".MainActivity">

    <fragment
        android:id="@+id/star_sign_list"
        android:name="com.example.staticfragments.ListFragment"
        android:layout_height="match_parent"
```

```
        android:layout_width="0dp"
        android:layout_weight="1"/>

    <View
        android:layout_width="1dp"
        android:layout_height="match_parent"
        android:background="?android:attr/dividerVertical" />

    <fragment
        android:id="@+id/star_sign_detail"
        android:name="com.example.staticfragments.DetailFragment"
        android:layout_height="match_parent"
        android:layout_width="0dp"
        android:layout_weight="2"/>

</LinearLayout>
```

You are adding a **LinearLayout**, which will by default lay out its content horizontally.

You add the **ListFragment**, a divider, and then the **DetailFragment** and assign the fragments appropriate IDs. Notice also that you are using the concept of weights to assign the space available for each fragment. When you do this, you specify **android:layout_width="0dp"**. The **layout_weight** then sets the proportion of the width available by the weight measurements as the **LinearLayout** is set to layout the fragments horizontally. The **ListFragment** is specified as **android:layout_weight="1"** and the **DetailFragment** is specified as **android:layout_weight="2"**, which tells the system to assign the **DetailFragment** twice the width of the **ListFragment**. In this case, where there are three views including the divider, which is a fixed dp width, this will result roughly in the **ListFragment** occupying one-third of the width and the **DetailFragment** occupying two-thirds.

14. To see the app, create a new virtual device as shown in *Chapter 1, Create Your First App*, and select **Category | Tablet | Nexus 7**.

15. This will create a 7" tablet. Then launch the virtual device and run the app. This is the initial view you will see when you launch the tablet in portrait mode:

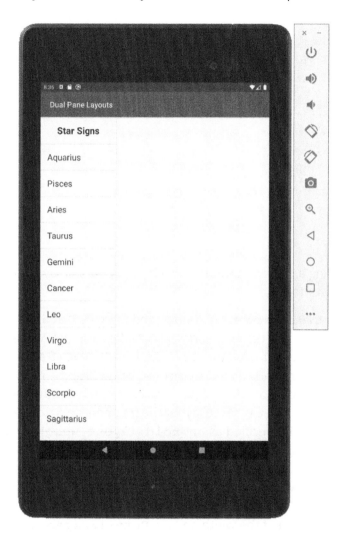

Figure 3.11: Initial star sign app UI display

You can see that the list takes up about a third of the screen and the blank space two-thirds of the screen.

16. Click the ◈ bottom rotate button on the virtual device to turn the virtual device through 90 degrees clockwise.

17. Once you've done that, the virtual device will go into landscape mode. It will not, however, change the screen orientation to landscape.

18. In order to do this, click on the 🔲 rotate button in the bottom-left corner of the virtual device. You can also select the status bar at the top of the virtual device, hold and drag down to display the quick settings bar where you can turn on auto-rotation by selecting the rotate button.

Figure 3.12: Quick settings bar with auto rotate selected

19. This will then change the tablet layout to landscape:

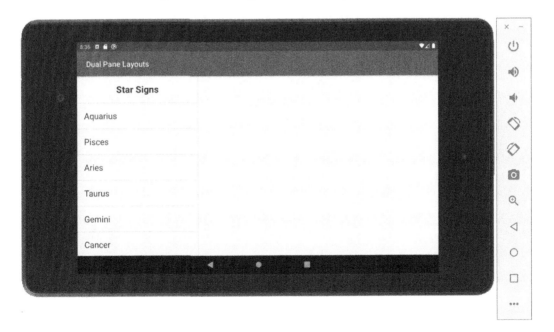

Figure 3.13: Initial star sign app UI display in landscape on a tablet

20. The next thing to do is enable selecting a list item to load contents into the **Detail** pane of the screen. For that, we need to make changes in the **MainActivity**. Update the following code to retrieve fragments by their ID in the pattern of retrieving views by their IDs:

```
package com.example.dualpanelayouts

import android.content.Intent
import android.os.Bundle
import android.view.View
import androidx.appcompat.app.AppCompatActivity
const val STAR_SIGN_ID = "STAR_SIGN_ID"

interface StarSignListener {
    fun onSelected(id: Int)
}

class MainActivity : AppCompatActivity(), StarSignListener {

    var isDualPane: Boolean = false

    override fun onCreate(savedInstanceState: Bundle?) {
        super.onCreate(savedInstanceState)
        setContentView(R.layout.activity_main)

        isDualPane = findViewById<View>(R.id.star_sign_detail) != null
    }

    override fun onSelected(id: Int) {

        if (isDualPane) {
```

```
            val detailFragment = supportFragmentManager
              .findFragmentById(R.id.star_sign_detail) as DetailFragment
            detailFragment.setStarSignData(id)
        } else {
            val detailIntent = Intent(this,
              DetailActivity::class.java).apply {
                putExtra(STAR_SIGN_ID, id)
            }
            startActivity(detailIntent)
        }
    }
}
```

> **NOTE**
>
> This example and those that follow use **supportFragmentManager.
> findFragmentById**.

You can also, however, retrieve fragments by **Tag** if you add a tag to the
fragment XML by using **android:tag="MyFragmentTag"**.

21. You can then retrieve the fragment by using **supportFragmentManager.
findFragmentByTag("MyFragmentTag")**.

22. In order to retrieve data from the fragment, the activity needs to implement the **StarSignListener**. This completes the contract set in the fragment to pass back details to the implementing class. The **onCreate** function sets the layout and then checks whether **DetailFragment** is in the activity's inflated layout by checking whether id **R.id.star_sign_detail** exists. From the Project View the **res | layout | activity_main.xml** file only contains the **ListFragment**, but you've added the code in the **res | layout-sw600dp | activity_main.xml** file to contain the **DetailFragment** with **android:id="@+id/star_sign_detail"**. This will be used for the layout of the Nexus 7 tablet. In the default Android View open up **res | layout | activity_main.xml** and select the top **activity_main.xml** file without (sw600dp) and then select **activity_main.xml (sw600dp)** to see these differences.

23. So now we can retrieve the star sign ID passed from the **ListFragment** back to the **MainActivity** by the **StarSignListener** and pass it into the **DetailFragment**. This is achieved by checking the **isDualPane** Boolean, and if that evaluates to **true**, you know you can pass the star sign ID to the **DetailFragment** with this code:

```
val detailFragment = supportFragmentManager .findFragmentById
   (R.id.star_sign_detail) as DetailFragment
detailFragment.setStarSignData(id)
```

24. You cast the fragment from the **id** to the **DetailFragment** and call the following:

```
detailFragment.setStarSignData(id)
```

25. As you've implemented this function in the fragment and are checking by the **id** which contents to display, the UI is updated:

Figure 3.14: Star sign app dual-pane display in landscape on a tablet

26. Now clicking on a list item works as intended, showing the dual-pane layout with the contents set correctly.

27. If the device is not a tablet, however, even when a list item is clicked, nothing will happen as there is not an **else** branch condition to do anything if the device is not a tablet, which is defined by **isDualPane** Boolean. The display will be as in *Figure 3.15* and won't change when items are selected:

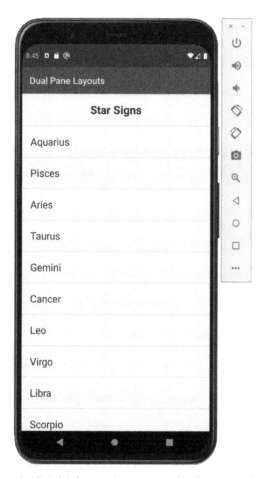

Figure 3.15: Initial star sign app UI display on a phone

28. You are going to display the star sign detail in another activity. Create a new **DetailActivity** by going to **File | New | Activity | Empty Activity**. Once created, update the **activity_detail.xml** with this layout:

```
<?xml version="1.0" encoding="utf-8"?>
<androidx.constraintlayout.widget.ConstraintLayout
  xmlns:android="http://schemas.android.com/apk/res/android"
    xmlns:app="http://schemas.android.com/apk/res-auto"
    xmlns:tools="http://schemas.android.com/tools"
    android:layout_width="match_parent"
```

```
    android:layout_height="match_parent"
    tools:context=".DetailActivity">
    <fragment
        android:id="@+id/star_sign_detail"
        android:name="com.example.staticfragments.DetailFragment"
        android:layout_height="match_parent"
        android:layout_width="match_parent"/>

</androidx.constraintlayout.widget.ConstraintLayout>
```

29. This adds the **DetailFragment** as the only fragment in the layout. Now update the **DetailActivity** with the following contents:

```
override fun onCreate(savedInstanceState: Bundle?) {
    super.onCreate(savedInstanceState)
    setContentView(R.layout.activity_detail)

    val starSignId = intent.extras?.getInt(STAR_SIGN_ID, 0) ?: 0

    val detailFragment = supportFragmentManager
        .findFragmentById(R.id.star_sign_detail) as DetailFragment
    detailFragment.setStarSignData(starSignId)
}
```

30. The star sign **id** is expected to be passed from another activity to this one through setting a key in the intent's extras (also called a **Bundle**). We covered intents in *Chapter 2, Building User Screen Flows,* but as a reminder, they enable communication between different components and also can send data. In this case, the intent that opened this activity has set a star sign ID. It will use **id** to set the star sign ID in the **DetailFragment**. Next, you need to implement the **else** branch of the **isDualPane** check to launch the **DetailActivity** passing through the star sign ID in the intent. Update the **MainActivity** to do this below. You will also need to add the **Intent** import to the list of imports:

```
import android.content.Intent
override fun onSelected(id: Int) {

    if (isDualPane) {

        val detailFragment = supportFragmentManager
            .findFragmentById(R.id.star_sign_detail)
            as DetailFragment
        detailFragment.setStarSignData(id)
```

```
        } else {

        val detailIntent = Intent(this, DetailActivity::class.java)
          .apply {
            putExtra(STAR_SIGN_ID, id)
          }
        startActivity(detailIntent)
      }
    }
```

31. Once you click on one of the star sign names on a phone display, it shows the contents in the **DetailActivity** occupying the whole of the screen without the list:

Figure 3.16: Single-pane star sign detail screen on a phone

This exercise has demonstrated the flexibility of fragments. They can encapsulate the logic and display of different features of your app that can be integrated in different ways depending on the form factor of the device. They can be arranged onscreen in a variety of ways, which are constrained by the layout they are included in, therefore they can feature as a part of dual-pane layouts or all or part of a single-pane layout. This exercise showed fragments being laid out side by side on a tablet, but they can also be laid out on top of each other and in a variety of other ways. The next topic illustrates how the configuration of fragments used in your app doesn't have to be specified statically in XML, but can also be done dynamically.

DYNAMIC FRAGMENTS

So far, you've only seen fragments added in XML at compile time. Although this can satisfy many use cases, you might want to add fragments dynamically at runtime to respond to the user's actions. This can be achieved by adding a **ViewGroup** as a container for fragments and then adding, replacing, and removing fragments from the **ViewGroup**. This technique is more flexible as the fragments can be active until they are no longer needed and then removed instead of always being inflated in XML layouts as you have seen with static fragments. If 3 or 4 more fragments are required to fulfill separate user journeys in one activity, then the preferred option is to react to the user's interaction in the UI by adding/replacing fragments dynamically. Using static fragments works better when the user's interaction with the UI is fixed at compile time and you know in advance how many fragments you need. For example, this would be the case for selecting items from a list to display the contents.

EXERCISE 3.04: ADDING FRAGMENTS DYNAMICALLY TO AN ACTIVITY

In this exercise, we will build the same star sign app as before but will demonstrate how the list and detail fragments can be added to screen layouts dynamically and not directly within an XML layout. You can also pass arguments into a fragment. For simplicity, you are going to create the same configuration for both phones and tablets. Perform the following steps:

1. Create a new project with an **Empty Activity** with the name **Dynamic Fragments**.

2. Once you have done that, add the following dependency you need to use the **FragmentContainerView**, an optimized ViewGroup to handle Fragment Transactions to **app/build.gradle** within the **dependences{ }** block:

```
implementation 'androidx.fragment:fragment-ktx:1.2.5'
```

3. Copy the contents of the following XML resource files from *Exercise 3.03, Dual-Pane Layouts with Static Fragments*, and add them to the corresponding files in this exercise: **strings.xml** (changing the **app_name** string from **Static Fragments** to **Dynamic Fragments**), **fragment_detail.xml**, and **fragment_list.xml**. All of these files exist in the project created in the previous exercise and you are simply adding the contents to this new project. Then copy **DetailFragment** and **ListFragment** to the new project. You will have to change the package name from **package com.example. staticfragments** to **package com.example.dynamicfragments** in these two files. Finally add the styles defined below the base application style in themes.xml from the last exercise to the themes.xml in this project.

4. You now have the same fragments set up as in the previous exercise. Now open the **activity_main.xml** layout and replace the contents with this:

```xml
<?xml version="1.0" encoding="utf-8"?>
<androidx.fragment.app.FragmentContainerView
    xmlns:android="http://schemas.android.com/apk/res/android"
        android:id="@+id/fragment_container"
        android:layout_width="match_parent"
        android:layout_height="match_parent" />
```

This is the **FragmentContainerView** you will add the fragments to. You'll notice that there are no fragments added in the layout XML as these will be added dynamically.

5. Go into the **MainActivity** and replace the content with the following:

```kotlin
package com.example.dynamicfragments

import androidx.appcompat.app.AppCompatActivity
import android.os.Bundle
import androidx.fragment.app.FragmentContainerView
class MainActivity : AppCompatActivity() {

    override fun onCreate(savedInstanceState: Bundle?) {
        super.onCreate(savedInstanceState)
        setContentView(R.layout.activity_main)

        if (savedInstanceState == null) {
            findViewById<FragmentContainerView>
                (R.id.fragment_container)?.let { frameLayout ->
```

```
                    val listFragment = ListFragment()

            supportFragmentManager.beginTransaction()
                .add(frameLayout.id, listFragment).commit()
        }
    }
  }
}
```

You are getting a reference to the **FrameLayout** specified in **activity_main.xml**, creating a new **ListFragment** and then adding this fragment to the **ViewGroup FrameLayout** with the ID of the **fragment_container**. The fragment transaction specified is **add** as you are adding a fragment to the **FrameLayout** for the first time. You call **commit()** to execute the transaction immediately. There is a null check with **savedInstanceState** to only add this **ListFragment** if there is no state to restore, which there would be if a fragment had been previously added.

6. Next make the **MainActivity** implement the **StarSignListener** by adding the following and also add a constant to pass the star sign from the ListFragment to the DetailFragment:

```
class MainActivity : AppCompatActivity(), StarSignListener {
...
override fun onSelected(id: Int) {


    }
}
```

7. Now if you run the app, you will see the Star sign list being displayed on mobile and tablet.

The problem you now come to is how to pass the star sign ID to the **DetailFragment** now that it's not in an XML layout.

One option would be to use the same technique as in the last example by creating a new activity and passing the star sign ID in an intent, but you shouldn't have to create a new activity to add a new fragment, otherwise you might as well dispense with fragments and just use activities. You are going to replace the **ListFragment** in the **FrameLayout** with the **DetailFragment**, but first, you need to find a way to pass the star sign ID into the **DetailFragment**. You do this by passing this **id** as an argument when you create the fragment. The standard way to do this is by using a **Factory** method in a fragment.

8. Add the following code to the bottom of the **DetailFragment**: (A sample factory method will have been added when you created the fragment using the template/wizard which you can update here)

```
companion object {

    private const val STAR_SIGN_ID = "STAR_SIGN_ID"

    fun newInstance(starSignId: Int) = DetailFragment().apply {
        arguments = Bundle().apply {
            putInt(STAR_SIGN_ID, starSignId)
        }
    }
}
```

A **companion** object allows you to add Java's equivalent of static members into your class. Here, you are instantiating a new **DetailFragment** and setting arguments passed into the fragment. The arguments of the fragment are stored in a **Bundle()**, so in the same way as an activity's intent extras (which is also a bundle), you add the values as key pairs. In this case, you are adding the key **STAR_SIGN_ID** with the value **starSignId**.

9. The next thing to do is override one of the **DetailFragment** lifecycle functions to use the passed-in argument:

```
override fun onViewCreated(view: View, savedInstanceState: Bundle?) {

    val starSignId = arguments?.getInt(STAR_SIGN_ID, 0) ?: 0
    setStarSignData(starSignId)
}
```

10. You do this in **onViewCreated** as at this stage the layout of the fragment has been done and you can access the view hierarchy (whereas if you accessed the arguments in **onCreate**, the fragment layout would not be available as this is done in **onCreateView**):

```
val starSignId = arguments?.getInt(STAR_SIGN_ID, 0) ?: 0
```

11. This line gets the star sign ID from the passed in fragment arguments, setting a default of **0** if the **STAR_SIGN_ID** key cannot be found. Then you call **setStarSignData(starSignId)** to display the star sign contents.

12. Now you just need to implement the **StarSignListener** interface in the **MainActivity** to retrieve the star sign ID from the **ListFragment**:

```
class MainActivity : AppCompatActivity(), StarSignListener {

    override fun onCreate(savedInstanceState: Bundle?) {
        super.onCreate(savedInstanceState)
        setContentView(R.layout.activity_main)

        if (savedInstanceState == null) {
            findViewById<FragmentContainerView>
                (R.id.fragment_container)?.let { frameLayout ->

                val listFragment = ListFragment()

                supportFragmentManager.beginTransaction()
                    .add(frameLayout.id, listFragment).commit()
            }
        }
    }


    override fun onSelected(starSignId: Int) {

        findViewById<FragmentContainerView>(R.id.fragment_container)
            ?.let {frameLayout ->

        val detailFragment = DetailFragment.newInstance(starSignId)

            supportFragmentManager.beginTransaction()
                .replace(frameLayout.id, detailFragment)
                .addToBackStack(null)
                .commit()
        }
    }
}
```

You create the **DetailFragment** as explained earlier with the factory method passing in the star sign ID: **DetailFragment.newInstance(starSignId)**.

At this stage, the **ListFragment** is still the fragment that has been added to the activity **FrameLayout**. You need to replace it with the **DetailFragment**, which requires another transaction. This time, however, you use the **replace** function to replace the **ListFragment** with the **DetailFragment**. Before you commit the transaction, you call **.addToBackStack(null)** so the app does not exit when the back button is pressed but instead goes back to the **ListFragment** by popping the **DetailFragment** off the fragment stack.

This exercise has introduced adding fragments dynamically to your activity. The next topic introduces a more well-defined structure of creating fragments, called a navigation graph.

JETPACK NAVIGATION

Using dynamic and static fragments, although very flexible, introduces a lot of boilerplate code into your app and can become quite complicated when user journeys require adding, removing, and replacing multiple fragments while managing the back stack. Google introduced the Jetpack components, as you learned in *Chapter 1, Creating Your First App*, to use established best practices in your code. The **Navigation** component within the suite of Jetpack components enables you to reduce boilerplate code and simplify navigation within your app. We are going to use it now to update the *Star Sign* app to use this component.

EXERCISE 3.05: ADDING A JETPACK NAVIGATION GRAPH

In this exercise, we are going to reuse most of the classes and resources from the last exercise. We will first create an empty project and copy the resources. Next, we will add the dependencies and create a navigation graph. Using a step-by-step approach, we will configure the navigation graph and add destinations to navigate between fragments. Perform the following steps:

1. Create a new project with an **Empty Activity** called **Jetpack Fragments**.

2. Copy **strings.xml**, **fragment_detail.xml**, **fragment_list. xml**, **DetailFragment**, and **ListFragment** from the previous exercise, remembering to change the **app_name** string in **strings.xml** and the package name for the fragment classes. Finally add the styles defined below the base application style in themes.xml from the last exercise to the themes. xml in this project. You will also need to add the constant property **const val STAR_SIGN_ID = "STAR_SIGN_ID"** above the class header in the **MainActivity**.

3. Once you have done that, add the following dependencies you need to use the **Navigation** component into **app/build.gradle** within the **dependences{ }** block:

```
implementation "androidx.navigation:navigation-fragment-ktx:2.3.2"
implementation "androidx.navigation:navigation-ui-ktx:2.3.2"
```

4. It will prompt you to **sync now** in the top-right hand corner of the screen to update the dependencies. Click the button, and after they've updated, make sure the 'app' module is selected and go to **File | New | Android Resource** file:

Figure 3.17: Menu option to create Android Resource File

5. Once this dialog appears, change the **Resource type** to **Navigation** and then name the file **nav_graph**:

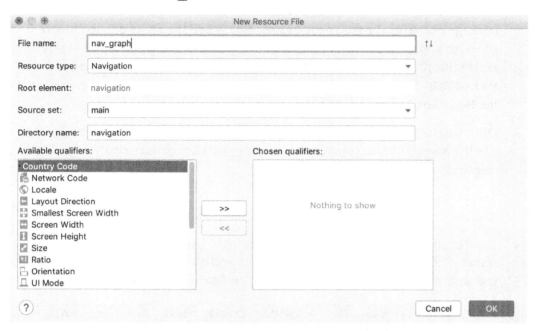

Figure 3.18: New Resource File dialog

Click OK to proceed. This creates a new folder in the **res** folder called **Navigation** with **nav_graph.xml** inside it.

6. Opening the file, you see the following code:

```
<?xml version="1.0" encoding="utf-8"?>
<navigation xmlns:android="http://schemas.android.com/apk/res/
  android"
    xmlns:app="http://schemas.android.com/apk/res-auto"
    android:id="@+id/nav_graph">

</navigation>
```

As it's not being used anywhere, you might see a warning with the **** element underlined in red:

```xml
<?xml version="1.0" encoding="utf-8"?>
<navigation xmlns:android="http://schemas.android.com/apk/res/android"
    xmlns:app="http://schemas.android.com/apk/res-auto" android:id="@+id/nav_graph">

</navigation>
```

Figure 3.19: Navigation not used warning underline

Ignore this for now.

7. Update the **nav_graph.xml** navigation file with the following code:

```xml
<?xml version="1.0" encoding="utf-8"?>
<navigation xmlns:android="http://schemas.android.com/apk/res/
  android"
    xmlns:app="http://schemas.android.com/apk/res-auto"
    xmlns:tools="http://schemas.android.com/tools"
    android:id="@+id/nav_graph"
    app:startDestination="@id/starSignList">
    <fragment
        android:id="@+id/starSignList"
        android:name="com.example.jetpackfragments.ListFragment"
        android:label="List"
        tools:layout="@layout/fragment_list">
        <action
            android:id="@+id/star_sign_id_action"
            app:destination="@id/starSign">
        </action>
    </fragment>
    <fragment
        android:id="@+id/starSign"
        android:name="com.example.jetpackfragments.DetailFragment"
        android:label="Detail"
        tools:layout="@layout/fragment_detail" />
</navigation>
```

The preceding file is a working **Navigation** graph. Although the syntax is unfamiliar, it is quite straightforward to understand:

a. The **ListFragment** and **DetailFragment** are present as they would be if you were adding static fragments.

b. There is an **id** to identify the graph at the root **** element and IDs on the fragments themselves. Navigation graphs introduce the concept of destinations, so at the root **navigation** level, there is the **app:startDestination**, which has the ID of **starSignList**, which is the **ListFragment**, then within the **<fragment>** tag, there is the **<action>** element.

c. Actions are what link the destinations within the navigation graph together. The destination action here has an ID so you can refer to it in code and has a destination, which, when used, it will direct to.

Now that you've added the navigation graph, you need to use it to link the activity and fragments together.

8. Open up **activity_main.xml** and replace the **TextView** inside the **ConstraintLayout** with the following **FragmentContainerView**:

```xml
<?xml version="1.0" encoding="utf-8"?>
<androidx.fragment.app.FragmentContainerView
  xmlns:android="http://schemas.android.com/apk/res/android"
    xmlns:app="http://schemas.android.com/apk/res-auto"
    android:id="@+id/nav_host_fragment"
    android:name="androidx.navigation.fragment.NavHostFragment"
    android:layout_width="match_parent"
    android:layout_height="match_parent"
    app:defaultNavHost="true"
    app:navGraph="@navigation/nav_graph" />
```

A **FragmentContainerView** has been added with name **android:name="androidx.navigation.fragment. NavHostFragment"**. It will host the fragments from the **app:navGraph="@ navigation/nav_graph"** that you have just created. The **app:defaultNavHost** states that it is the app's default navigation graph. It also controls the back navigation when one fragment replaces another. You can have more than one **NavHostFragment** in a layout for controlling two or more areas of the screen that manage their own fragments, which you might use for dual-pane layouts in tablets, but there can only be one default.

There are a few changes you need to make to make the app work as expected in the **ListFragment**.

9. Firstly, remove the class file header and references to the **StarSignListener**. So, the following will be replaced:

```
interface StarSignListener {
    fun onSelected(starSignId: Int)
}


class ListFragment : Fragment(), View.OnClickListener {

    private lateinit var starSignListener: StarSignListener

    override fun onAttach(context: Context) {
        super.onAttach(context)
        if (context is StarSignListener) {
            starSignListener = context
        } else {
            throw RuntimeException("Must implement StarSignListener")
        }
    }
}
```

And it will be replaced with the following line of code:

```
class ListFragment : Fragment() {
```

10. Next, at the bottom of the class, remove the **onClick** overridden method as you are not implementing the **View.OnClicklistener**:

```
override fun onClick(v: View?) {

    v?.let { starSign ->
        starSignListener.onSelected(starSign.id)
    }
}
```

11. In the **onViewCreated** method, replace the **forEach** statement that loops over the star sign views:

```
starSigns.forEach {
    it.setOnClickListener(this)
}
```

Replace it with the following code below and add the Navigation import to the imports list:

```
import androidx.navigation.Navigation
starSigns.forEach { starSign ->
    val fragmentBundle = Bundle()
    fragmentBundle.putInt(STAR_SIGN_ID, starSign.id)
    starSign.setOnClickListener(
        Navigation.createNavigateOnClickListener(
            R.id.star_sign_id_action,
            fragmentBundle
        )
    )
}
```

Here, you are creating a bundle to pass the **STAR_SIGN_ID** with the view ID of the selected star sign to a **NavigationClickListener**. It uses the ID of the **R.id.star_sign_id_action** action to load the **DetailFragment** when clicked as that is the destination for the action. The **DetailFragment** does not need any changes and uses the passed-in fragment argument to load the details of the selected star sign ID.

12. Run up the app, and you'll see that the app behaves as it did before.

Now you've been able to remove a significant amount of boilerplate code and documented the navigation within the app in the navigation graph. In addition, you have offloaded more of the management of the **fragment lifecycle** to the Android framework, saving more time to work on features. Jetpack Navigation is a powerful **androidx** component and enables you to map your whole app and the relationships between fragments, activities, and so on. You can also use it selectively to manage different areas of your app that have a defined user flow, such as the startup of your app and guiding the user through a series of welcome screens, or some wizard layout user journey, for example.

With this knowledge, let's try completing an activity using the techniques learned from all these exercises.

ACTIVITY 3.01: CREATING A QUIZ ON THE PLANETS

For this activity, you will create a quiz where users have to answer one of three questions on the planets of the Solar System. The number of fragments you choose to use is up to you. However, considering this chapter's content, which is separating UI and logic into separate fragment components, it is likely you will use two fragments or more to achieve this. The screenshots that follow show one way this could be done, but there are multiple ways to create this app. You can use one of the approaches detailed in this chapter, such as static fragments, dynamic fragments, the Jetpack Navigation component, or something custom that uses a combination of these and other approaches.

The content of the quiz is as follows. In the UI, you need to ask the user these three questions:

- What is the largest planet?

- Which planet has the most moons?

- Which planet spins on its side?

Then you need to provide a list of planets where the user can choose a planet that they believe is the answer to the question:

- MERCURY

- VENUS

- EARTH

- MARS

- JUPITER

- SATURN

- URANUS

- NEPTUNE

Once they have given their answer, you need to show them whether they are correct or wrong. The correct answer should be accompanied by some text that gives more detail about the question's answer.

```
Jupiter is the largest planet and is 2.5 times the mass of all the other
planets put together.
Saturn has the most moons and has 82 moons.
Uranus spins on its side with its axis at nearly a right angle to the
sun.
```

Following are some screenshots of how the UI might look to achieve the requirements of the app you need to build:

Questions Screen

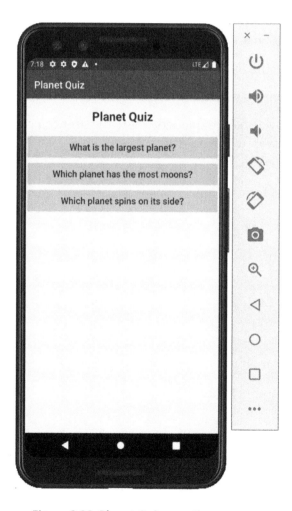

Figure 3.20: Planet Quiz questions screen

Answers Options Screen

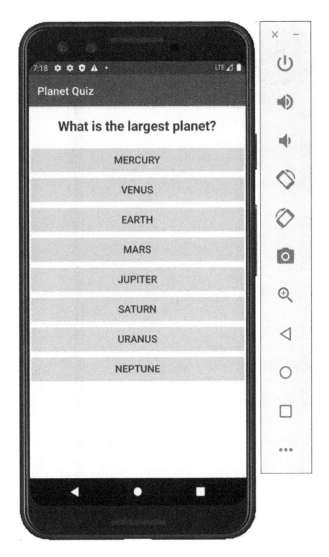

Figure 3.21: Planet Quiz multiple choice answers screen

Answer Screen

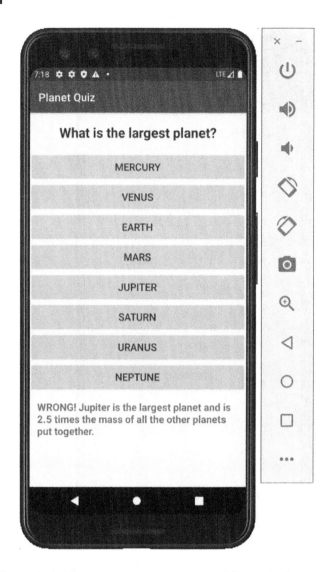

Figure 3.22: Planet Quiz Answer screen with detailed answer

The following steps will help to complete the activity:

1. Create an Android project with an **Empty Activity**

2. Update the **strings.xml** file with entries you need for the project.

3. Amend the **themes.xml** file with styles for the project.

4. Create a **QuestionsFragment**, update the layout with the questions, and add interaction with buttons and click listeners.

5. Optionally, create a multiple choice fragment and add answer options and button click handling (this can also be done by adding the possible answer options to the **QuestionsFragment**).

6. Create an **AnswersFragment** that displays the relevant question's answer and also displays more details about the answer itself.

> **NOTE**
>
> The solution to this activity can be found at: http://packt.live/3sKj1cp

The sources for all the exercises and the activity in this chapter are located at http://packt.live/3qw0nms.

SUMMARY

This chapter has covered fragments in depth, starting with learning the **fragment lifecycle** and the key functions to override in your own fragments. We then moved on to adding simple fragments statically to an app in XML and demonstrating how UI display and logic can be self-contained in individual fragments. Other options for how to add fragments to an app using a **ViewGroup** and dynamically adding and replacing fragments were then covered. We then finished with how this can be simplified by using the Jetpack Navigation component.

Fragments are one of the fundamental building blocks of Android development. The concepts you have learned here will allow you to build upon and progress to creating increasingly more advanced apps. Fragments are at the core of building effective navigation into your app in order to bind features and functionality that is simple and easy to use. The next chapter will explore this area in detail by using established UI patterns to build clear and consistent navigation and illustrate how fragments are used to enable this.

4

BUILDING APP NAVIGATION

OVERVIEW

In this chapter, you will build user-friendly app navigation through three primary patterns: bottom navigation, the navigation drawer, and tabbed navigation. Through guided theory and practice, you will learn how each of these patterns works so that users can easily access your app's content. This chapter will also focus on making the user aware of where they are in the app and which level of your app's hierarchy they can navigate to.

By the end of this chapter, you will know how to use these three primary navigation patterns and understand how they work with the app bar to support navigation.

INTRODUCTION

In the previous chapter, you explored fragments and the **fragment lifecycle**, and employed Jetpack navigation to simplify their use in your apps. In this chapter, you will learn how to add different types of navigation to your app while continuing to use Jetpack navigation. You will start off by learning about the navigation drawer, the earliest widely adopted navigational pattern used in Android apps, before exploring bottom navigation and tab navigation. You'll learn about the Android navigation user flow, how it is built around destinations, and how they govern navigation within the app. The difference between primary and secondary destinations will be explained, as well as which one of the three primary navigation patterns is more suitable, depending on your app's use case.

Let's get started with a navigation overview.

NAVIGATION OVERVIEW

The Android navigation user flow is built around what are called *destinations* within your app. There are primary destinations that are available at the top level of your app and, subsequently, are always displayed in the main app navigation and secondary destinations. A guiding principle of each of the three navigation patterns is to contextually provide information about the main section of the app the user is in at any point in time.

This can take the form of a label in the top app bar of the destination the user is in, optionally displaying an arrow hint that the user is not at the top level, and/or providing highlighted text and icons in the UI that indicate the section the user is in. Navigation in your app should be fluid and natural, intuitively guiding the user while also providing some context of where they are at any given point in time. Each of the three navigation patterns you are about to explore accomplishes this goal in varying ways. Some of these navigational patterns are more suitable for use with a higher number of top-level primary destinations to display, and others are suitable for less.

NAVIGATION DRAWER

The navigation drawer is one of the most common navigation patterns used in Android apps and was certainly the first pattern to be widely adopted. The following is a screenshot of the culmination of the next exercise, which shows a simple navigation drawer in its closed state:

Figure 4.1: App with the navigation drawer closed

The navigation drawer is accessed through what has become commonly known as the hamburger menu, which is the icon with three horizontal lines at the top left of *Figure 4.1*. The navigation options are not visible on the screen, but contextual information about the screen you are on is displayed in the top app bar. This can also be accompanied by an overflow menu on the right-hand side of the screen, through which other contextually relevant navigation options can be accessed. The following screenshot is of a navigation drawer in the open state, showing all the navigation options:

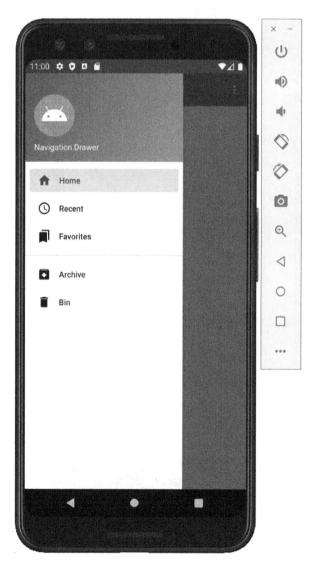

Figure 4.2: App with the navigation drawer open

Upon selecting the hamburger menu, the navigation drawer slides out from the left with the current section highlighted. This can be displayed with or without an icon. Due to the nature of the navigation occupying the height of the screen, it is best suited to five or more top-level destinations. The destinations can also be grouped together to indicate multiple hierarchies of primary destinations (shown by the dividing line in the preceding screenshot), and these hierarchies can also have labels. In addition, the drawer content is also scrollable. In summary, the navigation drawer is a very convenient way to provide quick access to many different destinations of the app. A weakness of the navigation drawer is that it requires the user to select the hamburger menu for the destinations to become visible. Tabs and bottom navigation (with fixed tabs), in contrast, are always visible. This is conversely also a strength of the navigation drawer as more screen space can be used for the app's content.

Let's get started with the first exercise of this chapter and create a navigation drawer so that we can access all the sections of an app.

EXERCISE 4.01: CREATING AN APP WITH A NAVIGATION DRAWER

In this exercise, you will create a new app in Android Studio named **Navigation Drawer** using the Empty Activity project template, while leaving all the other defaults as they are. There are wizard options where you can create a new project with all the navigation patterns you are going to produce in the exercises within this chapter, but we are going to build the apps incrementally to guide you through the steps. You are going to build an app that often uses a navigation drawer, such as a news or mail app. The sections we will be adding are **Home**, **Favorites**, **Recents**, **Archive**, **Bin**, and **Settings**.

Perform the following steps to complete this exercise:

1. Create a new project with an Empty Activity called Navigation Drawer. Do not use the **Navigation Drawer Activity** project template as we are going to use incremental steps to build the app.

2. Add the Gradle dependencies you will require to **app/build.gradle**:

```
implementation
  'androidx.navigation:navigation-fragment-ktx:2.3.2'
implementation 'androidx.navigation:navigation-ui-ktx:2.3.2'
```

3. Then, add/update all the resource files you will need in the app. Start by adding the **dimens.xml** file to the **res/values** folder:

dimens.xml

```xml
<?xml version="1.0" encoding="utf-8"?>
<resources>
    <dimen name="activity_horizontal_padding">16dp</dimen>
    <dimen name="activity_vertical_padding">16dp</dimen>
    <dimen name="nav_header_vertical_spacing">8dp</dimen>
    <dimen name="nav_header_height">176dp</dimen>
</resources>
```

4. Update **strings.xml** and replace **themes.xml** in the **res/values** folder with the following content:

strings.xml

```xml
<string name="nav_header_desc">Navigation header</string>

<string name="home">Home</string>
<string name="settings">Settings</string>
<string name="content">Content</string>
<string name="archive">Archive</string>
<string name="recent">Recent</string>
<string name="favorites">Favorites</string>
<string name="bin">Bin</string>

<string name="home_fragment">Home Fragment</string>
<string name="settings_fragment">
  Settings Fragment</string>
<string name="content_fragment">Content Fragment</string>
<string name="archive_fragment">Archive Fragment</string>
<string name="recent_fragment">Recent Fragment</string>
<string name="favorites_fragment">
  Favorites Fragment</string>
<string name="bin_fragment">Bin Fragment</string>

<string name="link_to_content_button">
  Link to Content Button</string>
```

themes.xml

```xml
<resources xmlns:tools="http://schemas.android.com/tools">
    <!-- Base application theme. -->
    <style name="Theme.NavigationDrawer" parent=
      "Theme.MaterialComponents.DayNight.DarkActionBar">
        <!-- Primary brand color. -->
        <item name="colorPrimary">@color/purple_500</item>
        <item name="colorPrimaryVariant">
          @color/purple_700</item>
        <item name="colorOnPrimary">@color/white</item>
        <!-- Secondary brand color. -->
        <item name="colorSecondary">@color/teal_200</item>
        <item name="colorSecondaryVariant">
          @color/teal_700</item>
        <item name="colorOnSecondary">@color/black</item>
        <!-- Status bar color. -->
        <item name="windowActionBar">false</item>
        <item name="windowNoTitle">true</item>
        <!-- Customize your theme here. -->
    </style>


    <style name="Theme.NavigationDrawer.NoActionBar">
        <item name="windowActionBar">false</item>
        <item name="windowNoTitle">true</item>
    </style>


    <style name="Theme.NavigationDrawer.AppBarOverlay"
      parent="ThemeOverlay.AppCompat.Dark.ActionBar" />


    <style name="Theme.NavigationDrawer.PopupOverlay"
        parent="ThemeOverlay.AppCompat.Light" />


    <style name="button_card" parent=
        "Widget.MaterialComponents.Button.OutlinedButton">
        <item name="strokeColor">@color/purple_700</item>
        <item name="strokeWidth">2dp</item>
    </style>


</resources>
```

5. Create the following Fragments **(File | New | Fragment | Fragment (Blank)** from the Toolbar:

- **HomeFragment**

- **FavoritesFragment**

- **RecentFragment**

- **ArchiveFragment**

- **SettingsFragment**

- **BinFragment**

- **ContentFragment**

6. Change each of these fragment layouts to use the following content:

```xml
<?xml version="1.0" encoding="utf-8"?>
<androidx.constraintlayout.widget.ConstraintLayout
    xmlns:android="http://schemas.android.com/apk/res/android"
        xmlns:app="http://schemas.android.com/apk/res-auto"
        android:layout_width="match_parent"
        android:layout_height="match_parent">

        <TextView
            android:layout_width="match_parent"
            android:layout_height="wrap_content"
            android:layout_marginStart="8dp"
            android:layout_marginTop="8dp"
            android:layout_marginBottom="8dp"
            android:layout_marginEnd="8dp"
            android:text="@string/archive_fragment"
            android:textAlignment="center"
            android:layout_gravity="center_horizontal"
            android:textSize="20sp"
            app:layout_constraintBottom_toBottomOf="parent"
            app:layout_constraintEnd_toEndOf="parent"
            app:layout_constraintStart_toStartOf="parent"
            app:layout_constraintTop_toTopOf="parent" />

</androidx.constraintlayout.widget.ConstraintLayout>
```

The only difference is the **android:text** attribute, which will have the corresponding string from the **strings.xml** file. So, create these fragments with the correct string, indicating which fragment the user is viewing. This may seem a bit repetitive, and one single fragment could be updated with this text, but it demonstrates how you would separate different sections in a real-world app.

7. Update the **fragment_home.xml** layout adding a button to it (this is the body content you can see in *Figure 4.1*, with the closed navigation drawer):

```xml
<?xml version="1.0" encoding="utf-8"?>
<androidx.constraintlayout.widget.ConstraintLayout
    xmlns:android="http://schemas.android.com/apk/res/android"
    xmlns:app="http://schemas.android.com/apk/res-auto"
    android:layout_width="match_parent"
    android:layout_height="match_parent">

    <TextView
        android:id="@+id/text_home"
        android:layout_width="match_parent"
        android:layout_height="wrap_content"
        android:layout_marginStart="8dp"
        android:layout_marginEnd="8dp"
        android:layout_marginBottom="8dp"
        android:text="@string/home_fragment"
        android:textAlignment="center"
        android:layout_gravity="center_horizontal"
        android:textSize="20sp"
        app:layout_constraintBottom_toBottomOf="parent"
        app:layout_constraintEnd_toEndOf="parent"
        app:layout_constraintStart_toStartOf="parent"
        app:layout_constraintTop_toTopOf="parent" />

    <com.google.android.material.button.MaterialButton
        android:id="@+id/button_home"
        style="@style/button_card"
        android:layout_width="140dp"
        android:layout_height="140dp"
        android:layout_marginTop="16dp"
        android:text="@string/link_to_content_button"
        app:layout_constraintEnd_toEndOf="parent"
```

```
app:layout_constraintStart_toStartOf="parent"
app:layout_constraintTop_toBottomOf="@+id/text_home" />
```

```
</androidx.constraintlayout.widget.ConstraintLayout>
```

TextView is the same as what's specified in the other fragment layouts, except it has an ID (**id**) with which it constrains the button below it.

8. Create the navigation graph that will be used in the app.

    Select **File | New | Android Resource File** (making sure the res folder is selected in the project window so you see this option) or alternatively right click on the res folder to see this option. Select **Navigation** as the resource type and name it **mobile_navigation.xml**.

    This creates the navigation graph:

Figure 4.3: Android Studio New Resource File dialog

9. Open the **mobile_navigation.xml** file in the **res/navigation** folder and update it with the code from the file in the link below. A truncated version of the code is shown here. See the link for the entire code block you need to use:

mobile_navigation.xml

```
8    <fragment
9        android:id="@+id/nav_home"
10       android:name="com.example.navigationdrawer
                        .HomeFragment"
11       android:label="@string/home"
12       tools:layout="@layout/fragment_home">
13       <action
14           android:id="@+id/nav_home_to_content"
15           app:destination="@id/nav_content"
16           app:popUpTo="@id/nav_home" />
17   </fragment>
18
19   <fragment
20       android:id="@+id/nav_content"
21       android:name="com.example.navigationdrawer
                        .ContentFragment"
22       android:label="@string/content"
23       tools:layout="@layout/fragment_content" />
```

Th complete code for this step can be found at http://packt.live/38W9maC.

This creates all the destinations in your app. However, it doesn't specify whether these are primary or secondary destinations. This should be familiar from the fragment Jetpack navigation exercise from the previous chapter. The most important point to note here is **app:startDestination="@+id/nav_ home**, which specifies what will be displayed to start with when the navigation loads, and that there is an action available from within **HomeFragment** to move to the **nav_content** destination in the graph:

```
<action
    android:id="@+id/nav_home_to_content"
    app:destination="@id/nav_content"
    app:popUpTo="@id/nav_home" />
```

You are now going to see how this is set up in **HomeFragment** and its layout.

10. Open the fragment_home.xml layout file. Then open the layout file in design view by selecting the **Design** option in the top-right-hand corner:

≡ Code   ≣ Split   ▣ Design

Figure 4.4: Android Studio Design view header

You will see that the display renders as a square, sometimes called a **card** display. If you look at the style of the button, you'll see it inherits from a material component. **Material** styles make theming your app with basic interactive elements quite simple. In this case, you are adding a style with a stroke (border) around the button, and when you run the app, you will see a button animation when you select it in the **user interface** (**UI**):

```
<style name="button_card"
  parent="Widget.MaterialComponents.Button.OutlinedButton">
    <item name="strokeColor">@color/colorPrimary</item>
    <item name="strokeWidth">2dp</item>
</style>
```

11. **Open HomeFragment** and update **onCreateView** to set up the button:

HomeFragment

```
package com.example.navigationdrawer
import android.os.Bundle
import android.view.LayoutInflater
import android.view.View
import android.view.ViewGroup
import android.widget.Button
import androidx.fragment.app.Fragment
import androidx.navigation.Navigation
class HomeFragment : Fragment() {
    override fun onCreateView(
        inflater: LayoutInflater,
        container: ViewGroup?,
        savedInstanceState: Bundle?
    ): View? {
        val view = inflater.inflate(R.layout.fragment_home,
          container, false)
        view.findViewById<Button>
          (R.id.button_home)?.setOnClickListener(
            Navigation.createNavigateOnClickListener
              (R.id.nav_home_to_content, null)
        )
        return view
    }
}
```

This uses the navigation click listener to complete the **R.id.nav_home_to_content** action when the **button_home** is clicked.

These changes will not, however, do anything yet as you still need to set up the navigation host for your app and add all the other layout files, along with the navigation drawer.

12. Create a **Nav** host fragment by creating a new file in the layout folder called **content_main.xml**. This can be done by right-clicking on the **layout** folder in the **res** directory and then going to **File | New | Layout Resource File**. Once created, update it with the **FragmentContainerView**:

```xml
<?xml version="1.0" encoding="utf-8"?>
<androidx.fragment.app.FragmentContainerView
    xmlns:android="http://schemas.android.com/apk/res/android"
    xmlns:app="http://schemas.android.com/apk/res-auto"
    android:id="@+id/nav_host_fragment"
    android:name="androidx.navigation.fragment
      .NavHostFragment"
    android:layout_width="match_parent"
    android:layout_height="match_parent"
    app:defaultNavHost="true"
    app:navGraph="@navigation/mobile_navigation" />
```

13. You'll notice that the navigation graph is set to the graph you just created:

```xml
app:navGraph="@navigation/mobile_navigation"
```

14. With that, the body of the app and its destination have been set up. Now, you need to set up the UI navigation. Create another layout resource file called **nav_header_main.xml** and add the following content:

```xml
<?xml version="1.0" encoding="utf-8"?>
<LinearLayout
  xmlns:android="http://schemas.android.com/apk/res/android"
    xmlns:app="http://schemas.android.com/apk/res-auto"
    android:layout_width="match_parent"
    android:layout_height="@dimen/nav_header_height"
    android:background="@color/teal_700"
    android:gravity="bottom"
    android:orientation="vertical"
    android:paddingLeft="@dimen/activity_horizontal_margin"
    android:paddingTop="@dimen/activity_vertical_margin"
    android:paddingRight="@dimen/activity_horizontal_margin"
    android:paddingBottom="@dimen/activity_vertical_margin"
    android:theme="@style/ThemeOverlay.AppCompat.Dark">
```

```xml
    <ImageView
        android:id="@+id/imageView"
        android:layout_width="wrap_content"
        android:layout_height="wrap_content"
        android:contentDescription="@string/nav_header_desc"
        android:paddingTop=
          "@dimen/nav_header_vertical_spacing"
        app:srcCompat="@mipmap/ic_launcher_round" />

    <TextView
        android:layout_width="match_parent"
        android:layout_height="wrap_content"
        android:paddingTop=
          "@dimen/nav_header_vertical_spacing"
        android:text="@string/app_name"
        android:textAppearance=
          "@style/TextAppearance.AppCompat.Body1" />

</LinearLayout>
```

This is the layout that's displayed in the header of the navigation drawer.

15. Create the app bar with a toolbar layout file, called **app_bar_main.xml**, and include the following content:

```xml
<?xml version="1.0" encoding="utf-8"?>
<androidx.coordinatorlayout.widget.CoordinatorLayout
  xmlns:android="http://schemas.android.com/apk/res/android"
    xmlns:app="http://schemas.android.com/apk/res-auto"
    xmlns:tools="http://schemas.android.com/tools"
    android:layout_width="match_parent"
    android:layout_height="match_parent"
    tools:context=".MainActivity">

    <com.google.android.material.appbar.AppBarLayout
        android:layout_width="match_parent"
        android:layout_height="wrap_content"
        android:theme=
          "@style/Theme.NavigationDrawer.AppBarOverlay">
```

```
<androidx.appcompat.widget.Toolbar
    android:id="@+id/toolbar"
    android:layout_width="match_parent"
    android:layout_height="?attr/actionBarSize"
    android:background="?attr/colorPrimary"
    app:popupTheme=
        "@style/Theme.NavigationDrawer.PopupOverlay" />

</com.google.android.material.appbar.AppBarLayout>
<include layout="@layout/content_main" />

</androidx.coordinatorlayout.widget.CoordinatorLayout>
```

This integrates the main body layout of the app with the app bar that appears above it. The remaining part is to create the items that will appear in the navigation drawer and create and populate the navigation drawer with these items.

16. To use icons with these menu items you need to copy the vector assets in the drawable folder of the completed exercise to the drawable folder of your project. Vector assets use coordinates for points, lines and curves to layout images with associated color information. They are significantly smaller when compared to png and jpg images and vectors can be resized to different sizes without loss of quality. You can find them here: http://packt.live/2XQnY5a

Copy the following drawables:

- **favorites.xml**
- **archive.xml**
- **recent.xml**
- **home.xml**
- **bin.xml**

17. These icons are going to be used for the menu items. To create your own icon, import a **.svg** file into Android Studio or select one of the stock images that come bundled with Android Studio. To see this in action, go to **File | New | Vector Asset** and make sure you have the **res** folder selected so that these menu options appear. An example of one of these assets is below (You can select the 'Clip Art' icon to see others):

Figure 4.5: Configuring a Vector Asset

18. Use the local file option to import a **.svg** or **.psd** file or select clipart to add one of the Android Studio icons.

19. Create a menu with these items. To do this, go to **File | New | Android Resource File**, select **Menu** as the resource type, call it **activity_main_drawer**, and then populate it with the following content:

```
<?xml version="1.0" encoding="utf-8"?>
<menu
    xmlns:android="http://schemas.android.com/apk/res/android"
        xmlns:tools="http://schemas.android.com/tools"
```

```
    tools:showIn="navigation_view">
    <group
        android:id="@+id/menu_top"
        android:checkableBehavior="single">
        <item
            android:id="@+id/nav_home"
            android:icon="@drawable/home"
            android:title="@string/home" />
        <item
            android:id="@+id/nav_recent"
            android:icon="@drawable/recent"
            android:title="@string/recent" />
        <item
            android:id="@+id/nav_favorites"
            android:icon="@drawable/favorites"
            android:title="@string/favorites" />
    </group>

    <group
        android:id="@+id/menu_bottom"
        android:checkableBehavior="single">
        <item
            android:id="@+id/nav_archive"
            android:icon="@drawable/archive"
            android:title="@string/archive" />
        <item
            android:id="@+id/nav_bin"
            android:icon="@drawable/bin"
            android:title="@string/bin" />
    </group>
</menu>
```

This sets up the menu items that will appear in the navigation drawer itself. The magic that ties up the menu items to the destinations within the navigation graph is the name of the IDs. If the IDs of the menu items (in **activity_main_ drawer.xml**) exactly match the IDs of the destinations in the navigation graph (which, in this case, are fragments within **mobile_navigation.xml**), then the destination is automatically loaded into the navigation host.

20. The layout for **MainActivity** ties the navigation drawer to all the layouts specified previously. Open **activity_main.xml** and update it with the following content:

```xml
<?xml version="1.0" encoding="utf-8"?>
<androidx.drawerlayout.widget.DrawerLayout
    xmlns:android="http://schemas.android.com/apk/res/android"
    xmlns:app="http://schemas.android.com/apk/res-auto"
    xmlns:tools="http://schemas.android.com/tools"
    android:id="@+id/drawer_layout"
    android:layout_width="match_parent"
    android:layout_height="match_parent"
    android:fitsSystemWindows="true"
    tools:openDrawer="start">

    <include
        layout="@layout/app_bar_main"
        android:layout_width="match_parent"
        android:layout_height="match_parent" />

    <com.google.android.material.navigation.NavigationView
        android:id="@+id/nav_view"
        android:layout_width="wrap_content"
        android:layout_height="match_parent"
        android:layout_gravity="start"
        android:fitsSystemWindows="true"
        app:headerLayout="@layout/nav_header_main"
        app:menu="@menu/activity_main_drawer" />

</androidx.drawerlayout.widget.DrawerLayout>
```

21. As you can see, there is an **include** that's used to add **app_bar_main.xml**. The **<include>** element allows you to add layouts that will be replaced at compile time with the actual layout itself. They allow us to encapsulate different layouts as they can be reused in multiple layout files within the app. **NavigationView** (which is the class that creates the navigation drawer) specifies the layout files you have just created to configure its header and menu items:

```xml
app:headerLayout="@layout/nav_header_main"
app:menu="@menu/activity_main_drawer"
```

22. Now that you have specified all the layout files, update **MainActivity** by adding the following interaction logic:

```kotlin
package com.example.navigationdrawer
import android.os.Bundle
import androidx.appcompat.app.AppCompatActivity
import androidx.navigation.findNavController
import androidx.navigation.fragment.NavHostFragment
import androidx.navigation.ui.*
import com.google.android.material.navigation.NavigationView
class MainActivity : AppCompatActivity() {
    private lateinit var appBarConfiguration:
      AppBarConfiguration
    override fun onCreate(savedInstanceState: Bundle?) {
        super.onCreate(savedInstanceState)
        setContentView(R.layout.activity_main)
        setSupportActionBar(findViewById(R.id.toolbar))
        val navHostFragment = supportFragmentManager
          .findFragmentById(R.id.nav_host_fragment) as
            NavHostFragment
        val navController = navHostFragment.navController
        //Creating top level destinations
        //and adding them to the draw
        appBarConfiguration = AppBarConfiguration(
            setOf(
                R.id.nav_home, R.id.nav_recent,
                  R.id.nav_favorites, R.id.nav_archive,
                    R.id.nav_bin
            ), findViewById(R.id.drawer_layout)
        )
        setupActionBarWithNavController(navController,
          appBarConfiguration)
        findViewById<NavigationView>(R.id.nav_view)
          ?.setupWithNavController(navController)
    }
    override fun onSupportNavigateUp(): Boolean {
        val navController =
          findNavController(R.id.nav_host_fragment)
        return navController.navigateUp(appBarConfiguration)
          || super.onSupportNavigateUp()
    }
}
```

Now, let's go through the preceding code.
setSupportActionBar(toolbar) configures the toolbar used in the app by referencing it from the layout and setting it. Retrieving the **NavHostFragment** is done with the code below:

```
val navHostFragment = supportFragmentManager
    .findFragmentById(R.id.nav_host_fragment) as
        NavHostFragment
val navController = navHostFragment.navController
```

Next you add the menu items you want to display in the navigation drawer:

```
appBarConfiguration = AppBarConfiguration(
    setOf(
        R.id.nav_home, R.id.nav_recent, R.id.nav_favorites,
            R.id.nav_archive, R.id.nav_bin
    ), findViewById(R.id.drawer_layout)
)
```

drawer_layout is the container for **nav_view**, the main app bar, and its included content.

This may seem like you are doing this twice as these items are displayed in the **activity_main_drawer.xml** menu for the navigation drawer. However, the function of setting these in **AppBarConfiguration** is that these primary destinations will not display an up arrow when they are selected as they are at the top level. It also adds **drawer_layout** as the last parameter to specify which layout should be used when the hamburger menu is selected to display in the navigation drawer.

The next line is as follows:

```
setupActionBarWithNavController(navController,
    appBarConfiguration)
```

This sets up the app bar with the navigation graph so that any changes that are made to the destinations are reflected in the app bar:

```
findViewById<NavigationView>
    (R.id.nav_view)?.setupWithNavController(navController)
```

This is the last statement in **onCreate** and it specifies the item within the navigation drawer that should be highlighted when the user clicks on it.

The next function in the class handles pressing the up button for the secondary destination, ensuring that it goes back to its parent primary destination:

```
override fun onSupportNavigateUp(): Boolean {
    val navController =
      findNavController(R.id.nav_host_fragment)
    return navController.navigateUp(appBarConfiguration) ||
      super.onSupportNavigateUp()
}
```

The app bar can also display other menu items through the overflow menu, which when configured is displayed as three vertical dots at the top on the right-hand side. Take a look at the **menu/main.xml** file:

```
<?xml version="1.0" encoding="utf-8"?>
<menu
  xmlns:android="http://schemas.android.com/apk/res/android"
    xmlns:app="http://schemas.android.com/apk/res-auto">

    <item
        android:id="@+id/nav_settings"
        android:title="@string/settings"
        app:showAsAction="never" />
</menu>
```

This configuration shows one item: **Settings**. Since it specifies the same ID as the **SettingsFragment** destination in the navigation graph, **android:id="@+id/nav_settings"** it will open the **SettingsFragment**. The attribute being set to **app:showAsAction="never"** ensures it will stay as a menu option within the three dots overflow menu and will not appear on the app bar itself. There are other values for **app:showAsAction** which set menu options to appear on the app bar always and if there is room. See the full list here: https://developer. android.com/guide/topics/resources/menu-resource.

23. To add the overflow menu to the app bar, add the following to the **MainActivity** class:

```
override fun onCreateOptionsMenu(menu: Menu): Boolean {
    menuInflater.inflate(R.menu.main, menu)
    return true
}
```

```
override fun onOptionsItemSelected(item: MenuItem): Boolean {
    return item.onNavDestinationSelected(findNavController
        (R.id.nav_host_fragment))
}
```

You will also need to add the following imports:

```
import android.view.Menu
import android.view.MenuItem
```

The **onCreateOptionsMenu** function selects the menu to add to the app bar, while **onOptionsItemSelected** handles what to do when the item is selected using the **item.onNavDestinationSelected(findNavController(R. id.nav_host_fragment))** navigation function. This is used to navigate to the destination within the navigation graph.

24. Run the app and navigate to a top-level destination by using the navigation drawer. The following screenshot shows an example of navigating to the **Recent** destination:

Figure 4.6: Recent menu item opened from the navigation drawer

25. When you select the navigation drawer again to toggle it out, you will see that the **Recent** menu item is selected:

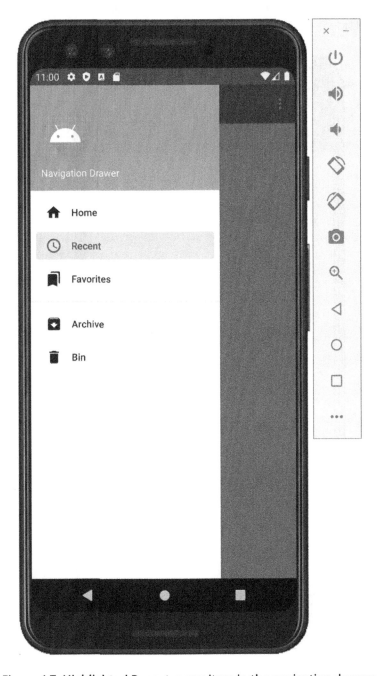

Figure 4.7: Highlighted Recent menu item in the navigation drawer

26. Select the **Home** menu item again. This screen shows a link in the material-themed button that goes to a secondary content destination. When you select the button, a nice material animation will emanate from the center of the button to the outside:

Figure 4.8: Home screen with a button to the secondary destination

27. Click this button to go to the secondary destination. You will see an up arrow being displayed:

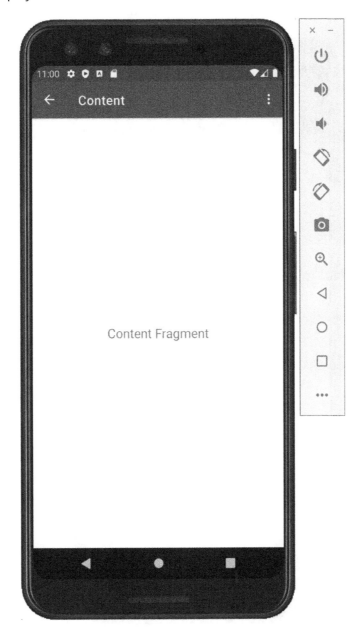

Figure 4.9: Secondary destination with an up arrow displayed

In all the preceding screenshots the overflow menu is displayed. After selecting it, you will see a **Settings** option appear. Upon pressing it, you will be taken to **SettingsFragment**, with the up arrow displayed:

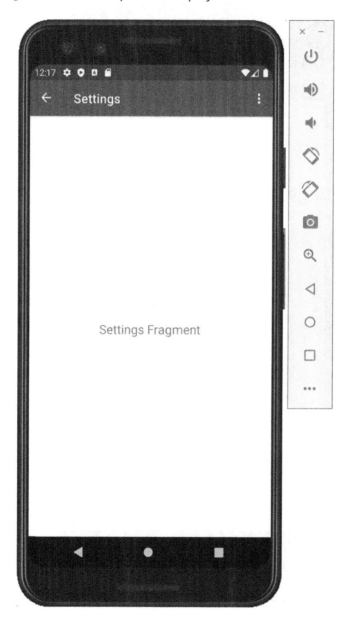

Figure 4.10: Settings fragment

Although there are quite a few steps to go through to set up an app with a navigation drawer, once created, it is very configurable. By adding a menu item entry to the drawer menu and a destination to the navigation graph, a new fragment can be created and set up for use straight away. This removes a lot of the boilerplate code you needed to use fragments in the previous chapter. The next navigational pattern you'll explore is bottom navigation. This has become the most popular navigational pattern in Android, largely because it makes the main sections of the app easily accessible.

BOTTOM NAVIGATION

Bottom navigation is used when there are a limited number of top-level destinations, and these can range from three to five primary destinations that are not related to each other. Each item on the bottom navigation bar displays an icon and an optional text label. This navigation allows quick access as the items are always available, no matter which secondary destination of the app the user navigates to.

EXERCISE 4.02: ADDING BOTTOM NAVIGATION TO YOUR APP

Create a new app in Android Studio named **Bottom Navigation** using the **Empty Activity** project template, leaving all the other defaults as they are. Do not use the **Bottom Navigation Activity** project template as we are going to use incremental steps to build the app. You are going to build a loyalty app that provides offers, rewards, and so on for customers who have signed up to use it. Bottom navigation is quite common for this kind of app because, typically, there will be limited top-level destinations. Let's get started:

1. Many of the steps are very similar to the previous exercise as you will be using Jetpack navigation and defining destinations in a navigation graph and a corresponding menu.

2. Create a new project with an Empty Activity called Navigation Drawer.

3. Add the Gradle dependencies you will require to **app/build.gradle**:

```
implementation 'androidx.navigation:navigation-fragment-
  ktx:2.3.2'
implementation 'androidx.navigation:navigation-ui-ktx:2.3.2'
```

4. Replace **colors.xml** with the following:

```xml
<?xml version="1.0" encoding="utf-8"?>
<resources>
    <color name="colorPrimary">#6200EE</color>
    <color name="colorPrimaryDark">#3700B3</color>
    <color name="colorAccent">#03DAC5</color>
</resources>
```

5. Append **strings.xml** and **themes.xml** in the **res/values** folder with the values below:

strings.xml

```xml
<!-- Bottom Navigation -->
<string name="home">Home</string>
<string name="tickets">Tickets</string>
<string name="offers">Offers</string>
<string name="rewards">Rewards</string>


<!-- Action Bar -->
<string name="settings">Settings</string>
<string name="cart">Shopping Cart</string>


<string name="content">Content</string>


<string name="home_fragment">Home Fragment</string>
<string name="tickets_fragment">Tickets Fragment</string>
<string name="offers_fragment">Offers Fragment</string>
<string name="rewards_fragment">Rewards Fragment</string>


<string name="settings_fragment">
    Settings Fragment</string>
<string name="cart_fragment">
    Shopping Cart Fragment</string>


<string name="content_fragment">Content Fragment</string>
<string name="link_to_content_button">
    Link to Content Button</string>
```

themes.xml

```
<style name="button_card" parent=
  "Widget.MaterialComponents.Button.OutlinedButton">
    <item name="strokeColor">@color/colorPrimary</item>
    <item name="strokeWidth">2dp</item>
    <item name="android:textColor">
      @color/colorPrimary</item>
</style>
```

You're using the same material style here that you used in the previous exercise to create the buttons for the home screen.

6. Create eight fragments with the following names:

- **HomeFragment**

- **ContentFragment**

- **OffersFragment**

- **RewardsFragment**

- **SettingsFragment**

- **TicketsFragment**

- **CartFragment**

7. Apply the same layout that you applied in the previous exercise for all the fragments adding the corresponding string resource except for **fragment_ home.xml**. For this layout, use the same layout file that you used in the previous exercise.

8. Create the navigation graph as you did in the previous exercise and call it **mobile_navigation**. Update it with the code from the file linked below. A truncated snippet of the code is shown here. Follow the link to see the full code you need to use:

mobile_navigation.xml

```
8    <fragment
9        android:id="@+id/nav_home"
10       android:name="com.example.bottomnavigation
                          .HomeFragment"
11       android:label="@string/home"
12       tools:layout="@layout/fragment_home">
13
```

```
14          <action
15              android:id="@+id/nav_home_to_content"
16              app:destination="@id/nav_content"
17              app:popUpTo="@id/nav_home" />
18      </fragment>
19
20      <fragment
21          android:id="@+id/nav_content"
22          android:name="com.example.bottomnavigation
                            .ContentFragment"
23          android:label="@string/content"
24          tools:layout="@layout/fragment_content" />
```

The complete code for this step can be found at http://packt.live/2KrgcLV.

9. Update the **onCreateView** function in **HomeFragment** to use the destination
    in the navigation graph to navigate to the **ContentFragment**. You will also
    need to add the following imports:

```
import android.widget.Button
import androidx.navigation.Navigation
    override fun onCreateView(
    inflater: LayoutInflater,
    container: ViewGroup?,
    savedInstanceState: Bundle?
): View? {
    val view = inflater.inflate(R.layout.fragment_home,
      container, false)
    view.findViewById<Button>(R.id.button_home)
      ?.setOnClickListener(
        Navigation.createNavigateOnClickListener
          (R.id.nav_home_to_content, null)
    )
    return view

}
```

10. Now that the destinations have been defined in the navigation graph, create
    the menu in the bottom navigation to reference these destinations. First,
    however, you need to gather the icons that will be used in this exercise.
    Go to the completed exercise on GitHub and find the vector assets in the
    drawable folder:

    http://packt.live/3qvUzJQ

Copy the following drawables:

- **cart.xml**
- **home.xml**
- **offers.xml**
- **rewards.xml**
- **tickets.xml**

11. Create a **bottom_nav_menu** (Right click on the **res** folder and select **Android Resource File** and select **Menu** using all of these icons except the **cart.xml** vector asset which will be used for the top toolbar. Notice that the IDs of the items match the IDs in the navigation graph.

bottom_nav_menu.xml

```xml
<?xml version="1.0" encoding="utf-8"?>
<menu
    xmlns:android="http://schemas.android.com/apk/res/android">

    <item
        android:id="@+id/nav_home"
        android:icon="@drawable/home"
        android:title="@string/home" />

    <item
        android:id="@+id/nav_tickets"
        android:icon="@drawable/tickets"
        android:title="@string/tickets"/>

    <item
        android:id="@+id/nav_offers"
        android:icon="@drawable/offers"
        android:title="@string/offers" />

    <item
        android:id="@+id/nav_rewards"
        android:icon="@drawable/rewards"
        android:title="@string/rewards"/>

</menu>
```

12. Update the **`activity_main.xml`** file with the following content:

activity_main.xml

```xml
<?xml version="1.0" encoding="utf-8"?>
<androidx.constraintlayout.widget.ConstraintLayout
  xmlns:android="http://schemas.android.com/apk/res/android"
    xmlns:app="http://schemas.android.com/apk/res-auto"
    android:id="@+id/container"
    android:layout_width="match_parent"
    android:layout_height="match_parent"
    android:paddingTop="?attr/actionBarSize">

    <com.google.android.material.bottomnavigation
      .BottomNavigationView
        android:id="@+id/nav_view"
        android:layout_width="0dp"
        android:layout_height="wrap_content"
        android:layout_marginStart="0dp"
        android:layout_marginEnd="0dp"
        android:background="?android:attr/windowBackground"
        app:layout_constraintBottom_toBottomOf="parent"
        app:layout_constraintLeft_toLeftOf="parent"
        app:layout_constraintRight_toRightOf="parent"
        app:menu="@menu/bottom_nav_menu"
        app:labelVisibilityMode="labeled"/>

    <androidx.fragment.app.FragmentContainerView
        android:id="@+id/nav_host_fragment"
        app:layout_constraintStart_toStartOf="parent"
        app:layout_constraintEnd_toEndOf="parent"
        app:layout_constraintLeft_toLeftOf="parent"
        app:layout_constraintRight_toRightOf="parent"
        app:layout_constraintTop_toTopOf="parent"
        android:name
          ="androidx.navigation.fragment.NavHostFragment"
        android:layout_width="match_parent"
        android:layout_height="match_parent"
        app:defaultNavHost="true"
        app:navGraph="@navigation/mobile_navigation" />

</androidx.constraintlayout.widget.ConstraintLayout>
```

The **BottomNavigation** view is configured with the menu you created previously, that is, **app:menu="@menu/bottom_nav_menu"**, while **NavHostFragment** is configured with **app:navGraph="@navigation/mobile_navigation"**. As the bottom navigation in the app is not connected directly to the app bar, there are fewer layout files to set up. This differs from the navigation drawer, which has the hamburger menu to toggle the navigation drawer in the app bar.

13. Update **MainActivity** with the following content:

```
package com.example.bottomnavigation

import android.os.Bundle
import androidx.appcompat.app.AppCompatActivity
import androidx.navigation.findNavController
import androidx.navigation.fragment.NavHostFragment
import androidx.navigation.ui.*
import com.google.android.material.bottomnavigation
  .BottomNavigationView
class MainActivity : AppCompatActivity() {

    private lateinit var appBarConfiguration:
      AppBarConfiguration

    override fun onCreate(savedInstanceState: Bundle?) {
        super.onCreate(savedInstanceState)
        setContentView(R.layout.activity_main)

    val navHostFragment =
      supportFragmentManager.findFragmentById
        (R.id.nav_host_fragment) as NavHostFragment
    val navController = navHostFragment.navController

        //Creating top level destinations
        //and adding them to bottom navigation
        appBarConfiguration = AppBarConfiguration(setOf(
            R.id.nav_home, R.id.nav_tickets, R.id.nav_offers,
            R.id.nav_rewards))
        setupActionBarWithNavController(navController,
          appBarConfiguration)
        findViewById<BottomNavigationView>(R.id.nav_view)
          ?.setupWithNavController(navController)
    }
```

```
override fun onSupportNavigateUp(): Boolean {
    val navController
        = findNavController(R.id.nav_host_fragment)
    return navController.navigateUp(appBarConfiguration)
        || super.onSupportNavigateUp()
    }
}
```

The preceding code should be very familiar because it was explained in the previous exercise. The main change here is that instead of a **NavigationView** that holds the main UI navigation for the navigation drawer, it is now replaced with **BottomNavigationView**. The configuration after this is the same.

14. Run the app. You should see the following output:

Figure 4.11: Bottom navigation with Home selected

15. The display shows the four menu items you set up, with the **Home** item selected as the start destination. Click the square button to be taken to the secondary destination within **Home**:

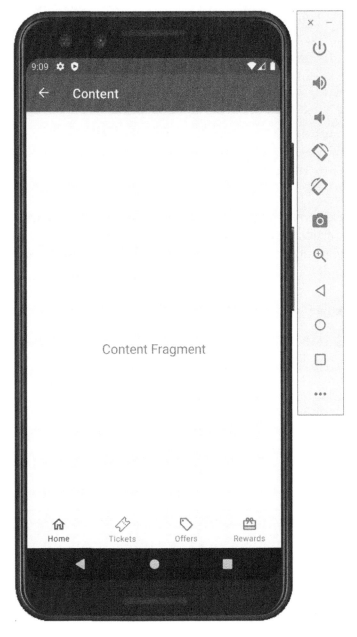

Figure 4.12: Secondary destination within Home

16. The action that makes this possible is specified in the navigation graph:

mobile_navigation.xml (snippet)

```xml
<fragment
    android:id="@+id/nav_home"
    android:name="com.example.bottomnavigation.HomeFragment"
    android:label="@string/home"
    tools:layout="@layout/fragment_home">

    <action
        android:id="@+id/nav_home_to_content"
        app:destination="@id/nav_content"
        app:popUpTo="@id/nav_home" />
</fragment>
```

17. Since there is no hamburger menu available in the bottom navigation UI, sometimes, action items (those that have a dedicated icon) are added to the app bar. Create another menu called **Main** and add the following content:

main.xml

```xml
<?xml version="1.0" encoding="utf-8"?>
<menu
  xmlns:android="http://schemas.android.com/apk/res/android"
    xmlns:app="http://schemas.android.com/apk/res-auto">

    <item
        android:id="@+id/nav_cart"
        android:title="@string/cart"
        android:icon="@drawable/cart"
        app:showAsAction="always" />
```

```
    <item
        android:id="@+id/nav_settings"
        android:title="@string/settings"
        app:showAsAction="never" />
</menu>
```

18. This menu will be used in the overflow menu in the app bar. The overflow menu will be available when you click on the three dots. A **cart** vector asset will also be displayed on the top app bar because the **app:showAsAction** attribute is set to **always**. Configure the overflow menu within **MainActivity** by adding the following:

Add these two imports at the top of the file:

```
import android.view.Menu
import android.view.MenuItem
```

And then these two functions:

```
override fun onCreateOptionsMenu(menu: Menu): Boolean {
    menuInflater.inflate(R.menu.main, menu)
    return true
}


override fun onOptionsItemSelected(item: MenuItem): Boolean {
    super.onOptionsItemSelected(item)
    return item.onNavDestinationSelected(findNavController
      (R.id.nav_host_fragment))
}
```

19. This will now display the main menu in the app bar. Run the app again, and you'll see the following:

Figure 4.13: Bottom navigation with the overflow menu

Selecting the shopping cart takes you to the secondary destination we configured in the navigation graph:

Figure 4.14: Bottom navigation with the Overflow menu in the secondary destination

As you've seen in this exercise, setting up bottom navigation is quite straightforward. The navigation graph and the menu setup make linking the menu items to the fragments simple. Additionally, integrating the action bar and the overflow menu are also small steps to implement. If you are developing an app that has very well-defined top-level destinations and switching between them is important, then the visibility of these destinations makes bottom navigation an ideal choice. The final primary navigation pattern to explore is tabbed navigation. This is a versatile pattern as it can be used as an app's primary navigation, but can also be used as secondary navigation with the other navigation patterns we've studied.

TABBED NAVIGATION

Tabbed navigation is mostly used when you want to display related items. It is common to have fixed tabs if there's only a few of them (typically between two and five tabs) and scrolling horizontal tabs if you have more than five tabs. They are used mostly for grouping destinations that are at the same hierarchical level.

This can be the primary navigation if the destinations are related. This might be the case if the app you developed is in a narrow or specific subject field where the primary destinations are related, such as a news app. More commonly, it is used with bottom navigation to present secondary navigation that's available within a primary destination. The following exercise demonstrates using tabbed navigation for displaying related items.

EXERCISE 4.03: USING TABS FOR APP NAVIGATION

Create a new app in Android Studio with an empty activity named **Tab Navigation**. You are going to build a skeleton movies app that displays the genres of movies. Let's get started:

1. Replace **strings.xml** content and update **themes.xml** in the **res/values** folder:

    strings.xml

```
<resources>
    <string name="app_name">Tab Navigation</string>

    <string name="action">Action</string>
    <string name="comedy">Comedy</string>
    <string name="drama">Drama</string>
    <string name="sci_fi">Sci-Fi</string>
    <string name="family">Family</string>
```

```xml
    <string name="crime">Crime</string>
    <string name="history">History</string>


<string name="dummy_text">
    Lorem ipsum dolor sit amet, consectetuer adipiscing
    elit. Aenean commodo ligula eget dolor. Aenean massa.
    Cum sociis natoque penatibus et magnis dis parturient
    montes, nascetur ridiculus mus. Donec quam felis,
    ultricies nec, pellentesque eu, pretium quis, sem.
    Nulla consequat massa quis enim. Donec pede justo,
    fringilla vel, aliquet nec, vulputate eget, arcu. In
    enim justo, rhoncus ut, imperdiet a, venenatis vitae,
    justo. Nullam dictum felis eu pede mollis pretium.
    Integer tincidunt. Cras dapibus. Vivamus elementum
    semper nisi. Aenean vulputate eleifend tellus. Aenean
    leo ligula, porttitor eu, consequat vitae, eleifend
    ac, enim. Aliquam lorem ante, dapibus in, viverra
    quis, feugiat a, tellus. Phasellus viverra nulla ut
    metus varius laoreet. Quisque rutrum. Aenean
    imperdiet. Etiam ultricies nisi vel augue. Curabitur
    ullamcorper ultricies nisi.

</string>


</resources>
```

The **`<string name="dummy_text">`** file specified provides some body text for each movie genre:

themes.xml

```xml
<resources xmlns:tools="http://schemas.android.com/tools">
    <!-- Base application theme. -->
    <style name="Theme.TabNavigation"
      parent="Theme.AppCompat.DayNight.DarkActionBar">
        <!-- Primary brand color. -->
        <item name="colorPrimary">@color/purple_500</item>
        <item name="colorPrimaryVariant">
          @color/purple_700</item>
        <item name="colorOnPrimary">@color/white</item>
        <!-- Secondary brand color. -->
        <item name="colorSecondary">@color/teal_200</item>
        <item name="colorSecondaryVariant">
          @color/teal_700</item>
        <item name="colorOnSecondary">@color/black</item>
        <!-- Customize your theme here. -->
        <item name="windowActionBar">false</item>
        <item name="windowNoTitle">true</item>
        <!-- Status bar color. -->
```

```xml
            <item name="android:statusBarColor"
                tools:targetApi="l">?attr/colorPrimaryVariant</item>
        </style>


        <style name="Theme.TabNavigation.AppBarOverlay"
            parent="ThemeOverlay.AppCompat.Dark.ActionBar" />


        <style name="Theme.TabNavigation.PopupOverlay"
            parent="ThemeOverlay.AppCompat.Light" />


        <style name="title" >
            <item name="android:textSize">24sp</item>
            <item name="android:textStyle">bold</item>
        </style>


        <style name="body" >
            <item name="android:textSize">16sp</item>
        </style>
    </resources>
```

2. Create a single **MoviesFragment** which displays the title of a movie genre and some dummy text. The title will be updated dynamically. Then update the movie fragment layout:

fragment_movies.xml

```xml
<?xml version="1.0" encoding="utf-8"?>
<androidx.constraintlayout.widget.ConstraintLayout
    xmlns:android="http://schemas.android.com/apk/res/android"
    xmlns:app="http://schemas.android.com/apk/res-auto"
    xmlns:tools="http://schemas.android.com/tools"
    android:layout_width="match_parent"
    android:layout_height="match_parent"
    tools:context=".MoviesFragment">
    <TextView
        android:id="@+id/movie_genre"
        android:layout_width="wrap_content"
        android:layout_height="wrap_content"
        android:paddingTop="8dp"
        style="@style/title"
        android:layout_margin="16dp"
        app:layout_constraintStart_toStartOf="parent"
        app:layout_constraintTop_toTopOf="parent" />
    <TextView
```

```
            android:layout_width="wrap_content"
            android:layout_height="wrap_content"
            style="@style/body"
            android:text="@string/dummy_text"
            android:padding="16dp"
            app:layout_constraintStart_toStartOf="parent"
            app:layout_constraintTop_toBottomOf="@id/movie_genre"
            />
</androidx.constraintlayout.widget.ConstraintLayout>
```

In the **fragment_movies** layout, the **TextView** label with an ID of **movie_type** will be updated dynamically with a title. The dummy text you added into the **strings.xml** file will be displayed below it.

3. Update **MoviesFragment** with the following content:

MoviesFragment

```
package com.example.tabnavigation
import android.os.Bundle
import android.view.LayoutInflater
import android.view.View
import android.view.ViewGroup
import android.widget.TextView
import androidx.fragment.app.Fragment
class MoviesFragment : Fragment() {
    override fun onCreateView(
        inflater: LayoutInflater, container: ViewGroup?,
        savedInstanceState: Bundle?
    ): View? {
        val root = inflater.inflate
          (R.layout.fragment_movies, container, false)
        root.findViewById<TextView>(R.id.movie_genre)?.text
          = arguments?.getString(MOVIE_GENRE)
            ?: "Undefined Genre"
        return root
    }
    companion object {
        private const val MOVIE_GENRE = "MOVIE_TYPE"
        @JvmStatic
        fun newInstance(movieGenre: String): MoviesFragment {
            return MoviesFragment().apply {
                arguments = Bundle().apply {
```

```
                    putString(MOVIE_GENRE, movieGenre)
            }
        }
    }
  }
}
```

There are a couple of points to highlight here. First, note that a factory method is being used to create **MoviesFragment**. Since this is done from a companion object, it can be referenced directly from another class with static syntax such as **MoviesFragment.newInstance(movieGenre)**. The second point is that the factory method sets the **MOVIE_GENRE** key as a **Bundle** argument with the **movieGenre** string so that it can be retrieved from **MoviesFragment** at a later date.

4. Update the **activity_main.xml** file with the following content:

```
<?xml version="1.0" encoding="utf-8"?>
<androidx.coordinatorlayout.widget.CoordinatorLayout
  xmlns:android="http://schemas.android.com/apk/res/android"
    xmlns:app="http://schemas.android.com/apk/res-auto"
    xmlns:tools="http://schemas.android.com/tools"
    android:layout_width="match_parent"
    android:layout_height="match_parent"
    tools:context=".MainActivity">


    <com.google.android.material.appbar.AppBarLayout
        android:layout_width="match_parent"
        android:layout_height="wrap_content"
        android:theme
          ="@style/Theme.TabNavigation.AppBarOverlay">

        <androidx.appcompat.widget.Toolbar
            android:id="@+id/toolbar"
            android:layout_width="match_parent"
            android:layout_height="?attr/actionBarSize"
            android:background="?attr/colorPrimary"
            app:popupTheme
              ="@style/Theme.TabNavigation.PopupOverlay"/>
```

```
        <com.google.android.material.tabs.TabLayout
            android:id="@+id/tabs"
            android:layout_width="match_parent"
            android:layout_height="wrap_content"
            app:tabIndicatorHeight="4dp"
            app:tabIndicatorColor="@color/teal_200"
            app:tabRippleColor="@android:color/transparent"
            android:background="?attr/colorPrimary" />

    </com.google.android.material.appbar.AppBarLayout>

    <androidx.viewpager.widget.ViewPager
        android:id="@+id/view_pager"
        android:layout_width="match_parent"
        android:layout_height="match_parent"
        app:layout_behavior="@string/appbar_scrolling_view_behavior"
/>

</androidx.coordinatorlayout.widget.CoordinatorLayout>
```

The **AppBarLayout** label and the toolbar contained within it are familiar from
the previous exercises. Below the toolbar, a **TabLayout** label is displayed,
which will contain the movie tabs. There are various attributes you can use
to style the tabs. Here you are setting the tabs' height, color and the material
ripple effect to transparent to not show the normal material style button. To
display the required content, you are going to use **ViewPager**. **ViewPager**
is a swipeable layout that allows you to add multiple views or fragments so
that when a user swipes to change one of the tabs, the body content displays
the corresponding view or fragment. For this exercise, you are going to swipe
between movie fragments. The component that provides the data that's used in
the **ViewPager** is called an adapter.

5. Create a simple adapter that will be used to display our movies. Call it **MovieGenresPagerAdapter**:

```
package com.example.tabnavigation
import android.content.Context
import androidx.fragment.app.Fragment
import androidx.fragment.app.FragmentManager
import androidx.fragment.app.FragmentPagerAdapter
    private val TAB_GENRES_SCROLLABLE = listOf(
        R.string.action,
        R.string.comedy,
        R.string.drama,
        R.string.sci_fi,
        R.string.family,
        R.string.crime,
        R.string.history
)
private val TAB_GENRES_FIXED = listOf(
    R.string.action,
    R.string.comedy,
    R.string.drama
)
class MovieGenresPagerAdapter(private val context: Context,
  fm: FragmentManager)
: FragmentPagerAdapter(fm,
  BEHAVIOR_RESUME_ONLY_CURRENT_FRAGMENT) {
    override fun getItem(position: Int): Fragment {
        return MoviesFragment.newInstance(context.resources
          .getString(TAB_GENRES_FIXED[position]))
    }
    override fun getPageTitle(position: Int): CharSequence? {
        return context.resources
          .getString(TAB_GENRES_FIXED[position])
    }
    override fun getCount(): Int {
        // Show total pages.
        return TAB_GENRES_FIXED.size
    }
}
```

First, look at the **MovieGenresPagerAdapter** class header. It extends from **FragmentPagerAdapter**, which is an adapter used specifically for swiping. This is also called paging through fragments. **FragmentPagerAdapter** is used when you have a defined number of fragments that isn't too large. Since you are using it for a set of tabs, this is ideal.

Since **FragmentPagerAdapter** keeps the fragments in memory when it's not on the screen, it is not suitable for a large number of fragments. In this case, you would use a **FragmentStatePagerAdpater**, which can recycle the fragments when they are not on screen.

When creating **FragmentPagerAdapter**, you pass in a **FragmentManager**, which is responsible for managing the fragments used in the activity. The **BEHAVIOR_RESUME_ONLY_CURRENT_FRAGMENT** flag only keeps the current fragment in a state where it's available for the user to interact with (**RESUMED**). The other fragments are in the **STARTED** state, which means they can be visible when swiping, for instance, but not active.

The callback method's functions are as follows:

- **getCount()**: This method returns the total number of items to be displayed.

- **getPageTitle(position: Int): CharSequence?**: This retrieves the genre title at the specified position in the list by using a specific position.

- **getItem(position: Int): Fragment**: This gets **MoviesFragment** at this position in the list (or creates a new **MoviesFragment** if it's being accessed for the first time) by passing in the genre title you want to display in the fragment. Once created, **MoviesFragment** will be kept in memory.

Tabs can be either fixed or scrollable. The first example you'll see is with fixed tabs. As **TAB_GENRES_FIXED** is being used in all these methods, only three tabs will be displayed. This does not, however, set **TabLayout** as fixed or scrollable. This needs to be done in the Activity.

6. Update **MainActivity** so that it uses tabs with **ViewPager**:

```
package com.example.tabnavigation
import android.os.Bundle
import androidx.appcompat.app.AppCompatActivity
import androidx.viewpager.widget.ViewPager
import com.google.android.material.tabs.TabLayout
class MainActivity : AppCompatActivity() {
    override fun onCreate(savedInstanceState: Bundle?) {
        super.onCreate(savedInstanceState)
        setContentView(R.layout.activity_main)
        setSupportActionBar(findViewById(R.id.toolbar))
        val viewPager = findViewById<ViewPager>
          (R.id.view_pager)
        val tabs = findViewById<TabLayout>(R.id.tabs)
        viewPager.adapter = MovieGenresPagerAdapter(this,
          supportFragmentManager)
        tabs?.tabMode = TabLayout.MODE_FIXED
        tabs?.setupWithViewPager(viewPager)
    }
}
```

7. In the **onCreate** method, after setting the layout, set up the app bar so that it uses the toolbar:

```
setSupportActionBar(toolbar)
```

8. Set up the data to be displayed in the swipeable **ViewPager** so that it comes from **MovieGenresPagerAdapter**:

```
view_pager.adapter = MovieGenresPagerAdapter(this,
  supportFragmentManager)
```

9. Set **TabLayout** up so that it displays the configured **ViewPager**:

```
tabs?.tabMode = TabLayout.MODE_FIXED
tabs?.setupWithViewPager(viewPager)
```

10. This takes care of settings the tab titles and making the tab body content swipeable. **tabMode** has been set to **FIXED** (**tabs.tabMode = TabLayout.MODE_FIXED**) so that the tabs will be laid out uniformly with a width that's equal to the width of the screen. Now, run the app. You should see the following:

Figure 4.15: Tab layout with fixed tabs

You can swipe left and right in the body of the page to go to each of the three tabs, and you can also select one of the respective tabs to perform the same action. Now, let's change the tab data that's being displayed and set the tabs so that they can be scrolled through.

11. First, change **MovieGenresPagerAdapter** so that it uses a few extra genres:

```
class MovieGenresPagerAdapter(private val context: Context,
  fm: FragmentManager)
: FragmentPagerAdapter(fm,
  BEHAVIOR_RESUME_ONLY_CURRENT_FRAGMENT) {

    override fun getItem(position: Int): Fragment {
        return MoviesFragment.newInstance(context.resources
          .getString(TAB_GENRES_SCROLLABLE[position]))
    }

    override fun getPageTitle(position: Int): CharSequence? {
        return context.resources
          .getString(TAB_GENRES_SCROLLABLE[position])
    }

    override fun getCount(): Int {
        // Show total pages.
        return TAB_GENRES_SCROLLABLE.size
    }

}
```

12. In **MainActivity**, set **tabMode** so that it's scrollable:

```
tabs.tabMode = TabLayout.MODE_SCROLLABLE
```

13. Run the app. You should see the following:

Figure 4.16: Tab layout with scrollable tabs

The list of tabs continues to display off the screen. The tabs can be swiped and selected, and the body content can also be swiped so that you can go left and right through the tab pages.

With this exercise, you've learned how versatile tabs are when it comes to providing navigation in an app. Fixed width tabs can be used for both primary and secondary navigation, while scrollable tabs can be used to group related items together for secondary navigation. Scrollable tabs act as secondary navigation, so you need to add primary navigation to the app as well. In this example, the primary navigation has been omitted for simplicity, but for more real world and complex apps you can either add a navigation drawer or bottom navigation.

ACTIVITY 4.01: BUILDING PRIMARY AND SECONDARY APP NAVIGATION

You have been tasked with creating a sports app. It can have three or more top-level destinations. One of the primary destinations, however, must be called **My Sports** and should link to one or more secondary destinations, which are sports. You can use any one of the navigation patterns we have explored in this chapter, or a combination of them, and you can also introduce any customizations that you feel are appropriate. Each destination the user is currently in should be displayed in the **App** bar.

There are different ways of attempting this activity. One approach would be to use bottom navigation and add the individual secondary sports destinations to the navigation graph so that it can link to these destinations. It is fairly simple and delegates to the navigation graph using actions. Here is what the home screen should look like after using this approach:

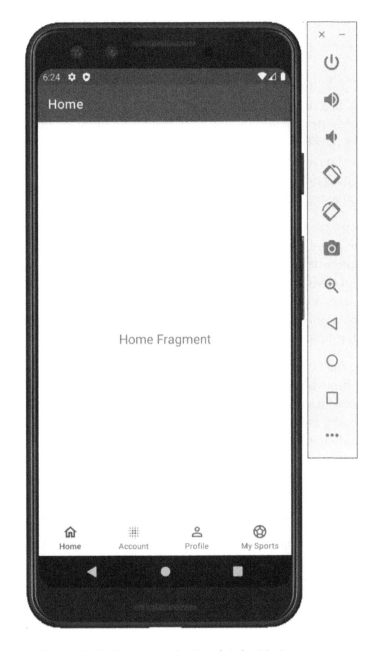

Figure 4.17: Bottom navigation for the My Sports app

NOTE

The solution to this activity can be found at: http://packt.live/3sKj1cp

The sources for all the exercises and the activity in this chapter are located here: http://packt.live/39IAjxL

SUMMARY

This chapter has covered the most important navigation techniques you need to know about in order to create clear and consistent navigation in your apps. You started off by learning how to create an Android Studio project with a navigation drawer to connect navigation menu items to individual fragments using Jetpack navigation. You then progressed to actions within Jetpack navigation to navigate to other secondary destinations in your app within the navigation graph.

The next exercise then used bottom navigation to display primary navigation destinations that are always visible on the screen. We followed this by looking at tabbed navigation, where you learned how to display both fixed and scrollable tabs. For each different navigational pattern, you were shown when it might be more suitable to use, depending on the type of app you were building. We finished this chapter by building our own app using one or more of these navigational patterns and adding both primary and secondary destinations.

This chapter has built upon the comprehensive introduction we provided to Android with Android Studio in *Chapter 1, Creating Your First App*, as well as what you learned about activities and fragments in *Chapter 2, Building User Screen Flows*, and *Chapter 3, Developing the UI with Fragments*. These chapters covered the knowledge, practice, and fundamental Android components you need to create apps. This chapter has tied these previous chapters together by guiding you through the primary navigational patterns available to make your apps stand out and be easy to use.

The next chapter will build on these concepts and introduce you to more advanced ways of displaying app content. You will start off by learning about binding data with lists using `RecyclerView`. After that, you will explore the different mechanisms you can use to retrieve and populate content within apps.

5

ESSENTIAL LIBRARIES: RETROFIT, MOSHI, AND GLIDE

OVERVIEW

In this chapter, we will cover the steps needed to present app users with dynamic content fetched from remote servers. You will be introduced to the different libraries required to retrieve and handle this dynamic data.

By the end of this chapter, you will be able to fetch data from a network endpoint using Retrofit, parse JSON payloads into Kotlin data objects using Moshi, and load images into **ImageViews** using Glide.

INTRODUCTION

In the previous chapter, we learned how to implement navigation in our app. In this chapter, we will learn how to present dynamic content to the user as they navigate around our app.

Data presented to users can come from different sources. It can be hardcoded into the app, but that comes with limitations. To change hardcoded data, we have to publish an update to our app. Some data cannot be hardcoded by its nature, such as currency exchange rates, the real-time availability of assets, and the current weather, to name a few. Other data may become outdated, such as the terms of use of an app.

In such cases, you would usually fetch the relevant data from a server. One of the most common architectures for serving such data is the **representational state transfer** (**REST**) architecture. The REST architecture is defined by a set of six constraints: the client-server architecture, statelessness, cacheability, a layered system, code on demand (optional), and a uniform interface. To read more about REST, visit https://medium.com/extend/what-is-rest-a-simple-explanation-for-beginners-part-1-introduction-b4a072f8740f.

When applied to a web service **application programming interface** (**API**), we get a **HyperText Transfer Protocol** (**HTTP**)-based RESTful API. The HTTP protocol is the foundation of data communication for the World Wide Web, also known as the internet. It is the protocol used by servers all around the world to serve websites to users in the form of HTML documents, images, style sheets, and so forth. An interesting article on this topic for further information can be found at https://developer.mozilla.org/en-US/docs/Web/HTTP/Overview.

RESTful APIs rely on the standard HTTP methods—**GET**, **POST**, **PUT**, **DELETE**, and **PATCH**—to fetch and transform data. These methods allow us to fetch, store, delete, and update data entities on remote servers.

To execute these HTTP methods, we can rely on the built-in Java `HttpURLConnection` class or use a library such as **OkHttp**, which offers additional features such as gzipping, redirects, retries, and both synchronous and asynchronous calls. Interestingly, from Android 4.4, `HttpURLConnection` is just a wrapper around **OkHttp**. If we choose **OkHttp**, we might as well go for **Retrofit**, as we will in this chapter, to benefit from its type safety, which is better suited for handling REST calls.

Most commonly, data is represented by **JavaScript Object Notation (JSON)**. JSON is a text-based data transfer format. As the name implies, it was derived from JavaScript. However, it has since become one of the most popular standards for data transfer, and its most modern programming languages have libraries that encode or decode data to or from JSON. A simple JSON payload may look something like this:

```
{"employees":[
    {"name": "James", "email": "james.notmyemail@gmail.com"},
    {"name": "Lea", "email": "lea.dontemailme@gmail.com"},
    {"name": "Steve", "email": "steve.notreally@gmail.com"}
]}
```

Another common data structure used by RESTful services is **Extensible Markup Language** (**XML**), which encodes documents in a format that is human- and machine-readable. XML is considerably more verbose than JSON. The same data structure as the previous in XML would look something like this:

```
<employees>
    <employee>
        <name>James</name>
        <email>james.notmyemail@gmail.com</email>
    </employee>
    <employee>
        <name>Lea</name>
        <email>lea.dontemailme@gmail.com</email>
    </employee>
    <employee>
        <name>Steve</name>
        <email>steve.notreally@gmail.com</email>
    </employee>
</employees>
```

In this chapter, we will focus on JSON.

When obtaining a JSON payload, we are essentially receiving a string. To convert that string into a data object, we have a few options—the most popular ones being libraries such as **GSON**, **Jackson**, and **Moshi**, as well as the built-in `org.json` package. For its lightweight nature, we will focus on Moshi.

Finally, we will look into loading images from the web. Doing so will allow us not only to provide up-to-date images but also to load the right images for the user's device. It will also let us only load the images when we need them, thus keeping our APK size smaller.

FETCHING DATA FROM A NETWORK ENDPOINT

For the purpose of this section, we will use TheCatAPI (https://thecatapi.com/). This RESTful API offers us vast data about, well... cats.

To get started, we will create a new project. We then have to grant our app internet access permission. This is done by adding the following code to your **AndroidManifest.xml** file, right before the **Application** tag:

```
<uses-permission android:name="android.permission.INTERNET" />
```

Next, we need to set up our app to include Retrofit. **Retrofit** is a type-safe library provided by Square that is built on top of the **OkHttp** HTTP client. Retrofit helps us generate **Uniform Resource Locators** (**URLs**), which are the addresses of the server endpoints we want to access. It also makes the decoding of JSON payloads easier by providing integration with several parsing libraries. Sending data to the server is also easier with Retrofit, as it helps with encoding the requests. You can read more about Retrofit here: https://square.github.io/retrofit/.

To add Retrofit to our project, we need to add the following code to the **dependencies** block of the **build.gradle** file of our app:

```
implementation 'com.squareup.retrofit2:retrofit:(insert latest version)'
```

> **NOTE**
>
> You can find the latest version here: https://github.com/square/retrofit.

With Retrofit included in our project, we can proceed to set it up.

First, to access an HTTP(S) endpoint, we start by defining the contract with that endpoint. A contract to access the **https://api.thecatapi.com/v1/images/search** endpoint looks like this:

```
interface TheCatApiService {
    @GET("images/search")
    fun searchImages(
        @Query("limit") limit: Int,
        @Query("size") format: String
    ): Call<String>
}
```

There are a few things to note here. First, you will notice that the contract is implemented as an interface. This is how you define contracts for Retrofit. Next, you will notice that the name of the interface implies that this interface can, eventually, cover all calls made to the TheCatAPI service. It is a bit unfortunate that Square chose **Service** as the conventional suffix for these contracts, as the term service has a different meaning in the Android world, as you will see in *Chapter 8, Services, Broadcast Receivers, and Notifications*. Nevertheless, this is the convention.

To define our endpoint, we start by stating the method with which the call will be made using the appropriate annotation—in our case, **@GET**. The parameter passed to the annotation is the path of the endpoint to access. You'll notice that **https://api.thecatapi.com/v1/** is stripped from that path. That is because this is the common address for all of the endpoints of TheCatAPI, and so will be passed to our Retrofit instance at construction time instead. Next, we choose a meaningful name for our function—in this case, we'll be calling the image search endpoint, and so **searchImages** seems appropriate. The parameters of the **searchImages** function define the values we can pass to the API when we make the calls.

There are different ways in which we can transfer data to the API. **@Query** allows us to define values added to the query of our request URL (that's the optional part of the URL that comes after the question mark). It takes a key value pair (in our case, we have **limit** and **size**) and a data type. If the data type is not a string, the value of that type will be transformed into a string. Any value passed will be URL-encoded for us.

Another such way is using **@Path**. This annotation can be used to replace a token in our path wrapped in curly brackets with a provided value. The **@Header**, **@Headers**, and **@HeaderMap** annotations will allow us to add or remove HTTP headers from the request. **@Body** can be used to pass content in the body of **POST/PUT** requests.

Lastly, we have a return type. To keep things simple at this stage, we will accept the response as a string. We wrapped our string in a **Call** interface. **Call** is Retrofit's mechanism for executing network requests synchronously (via **execute()**) or asynchronously (via **enqueue(Callback)**). When using RxJava (the Java implementation of ReactiveX, or Reactive Extensions; you can read more about ReactiveX at **https://reactivex.io/**), we can wrap our result in an **Observable** class (a class that emits data) or a **Single** class (a class that emits data once) as appropriate instead (see *Chapter 13, RxJava and Coroutines*, for more information on RxJava).

With our contract defined, we can get Retrofit to implement our service interface:

```
val retrofit = Retrofit.Builder()
    .baseUrl("https://api.thecatapi.com/v1/")
    .build()


val theCatApiService = retrofit.create(TheCatApiService::class.java)
```

If we try to run our app with this code, our app will crash with
IllegalArgumentException. This is because Retrofit needs us to tell the app
how to process the server response to a string. This processing is done with what
Retrofit calls **converters**. To set a **ConverterFactory** instance to our **retrofit**
instance, we need to add the following:

```
val retrofit = Retrofit.Builder()
    .baseUrl("https://api.thecatapi.com/v1/")
    .addConverterFactory(ScalarsConverterFactory.create())
    .build()
```

For our project to recognize **ScalarsConverterFactory**, we need to update our
app's **build.gradle** file by adding another dependency:

```
implementation 'com.squareup.retrofit2:converter-scalars:(insert latest
version)'
```

Now, we can obtain a **Call** instance by calling **val call =
theCatApiService.searchImages(1, "full")**. With the instance
obtained in this fashion, we can execute an async request by calling **call.
enqueue(Callback)**.

Our **Callback** implementation will have two methods: **onFailure(Call,
Throwable)** and **onResponse(Call, Response)**. Note that we are not
guaranteed to have a successful response if **onResponse** was called. **onResponse**
is called whenever we successfully receive any response from the server and no
unexpected exception occurred. So, to confirm that the response is a success
response, we should check the **response.isSuccessful** property. The
onFailure function will be called in the case of a network error or an unexpected
exception somewhere along the way.

So, where should we implement the Retrofit code? In clean architecture, data is provided by repositories. Repositories, in turn, have data sources. One such data source can be a network data source. This is where we would be implementing our network calls. Our ViewModels (in the case of **Model-View-ViewModel** (**MVVM**), the ViewModel is an abstraction of the view that exposes properties and commands) will then request data from repositories via use cases.

For our implementation, we will simplify the process by instantiating Retrofit and the service in the Activity. This is not good practice. Do not do this in a production app. It does not scale well and is very difficult to test. Instead, adopt an architecture that decouples your views from your business logic and your data. See *Chapter 14, Architecture Patterns*, for some ideas.

EXERCISE 5.01: READING DATA FROM AN API

In the following chapters, we will be developing an app for an imaginary secret agency with a worldwide network of agents saving the world from countless dangers. The secret agency in question is quite unique: it operates secret cat agents. In this exercise, we will create an app that presents us with one random secret cat agent from TheCatAPI. Before you can present data from an API to your user, you first have to fetch that data. Let's start:

1. Start by creating a new **Empty Activity** project (**File | New | New Project | Empty Activity**). Click **Next**.

2. Name your application **Cat Agent Profile**.

3. Make sure your package name is **com.example.catagentprofile**.

4. Set the save location to where you want to save your project.

5. Leave everything else at its default values and click **Finish**.

6. Make sure you are on the **Android** view in your **Project** pane:

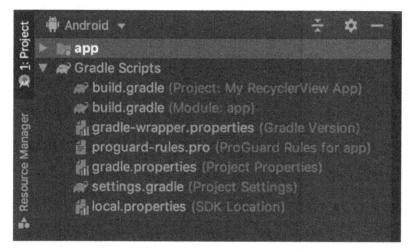

Figure 5.1: Android view in the Project pane

7. Open your **AndroidManifest.xml** file. Add internet permission to your app like so:

```
<manifest xmlns:android="http://schemas.android.com/apk/res/android"
    package="com.example.catagentprofile">

    <uses-permission android:name="android.permission.INTERNET" />

    <application ...>
        ...
    </application>

</manifest>
```

8. To add Retrofit and the scalars converter to your app, open the app module, **build.gradle** (**Gradle Scripts | build.gradle (Module: app)**), and add the following lines anywhere inside the **dependencies** block:

```
dependencies {
    ...
    implementation 'com.squareup.retrofit2:retrofit:2.9.0'
    implementation 'com.squareup.retrofit2:converter-scalars:2.9.0'
    ...
}
```

Your **dependencies** block should now look something like this:

```
dependencies {
    implementation "org.jetbrains.kotlin:kotlin-stdlib
      :$kotlin_version"
    implementation 'androidx.core:core-ktx:1.3.2'
    implementation 'androidx.appcompat:appcompat:1.2.0'
    implementation 'com.google.android.material:material:1.2.1'
    implementation 'androidx.constraintlayout:constraintlayout:2.0.4'
    implementation 'androidx.navigation:navigation-fragment
      -ktx:2.2.2'
    implementation 'androidx.navigation:navigation-ui-ktx:2.2.2'
    implementation 'com.squareup.retrofit2:retrofit:2.9.0'
    implementation 'com.squareup.retrofit2:converter-scalars:2.9.0'
    testImplementation 'junit:junit:4.+'
    androidTestImplementation 'androidx.test.ext:junit:1.1.2'
    androidTestImplementation 'androidx.test.espresso:espresso-core
      :3.3.0'
}
```

Between the time of writing and when you carry out this exercise, some dependencies may have changed. You should still only add the lines in bold from the preceding code block. These will add Retrofit and support for reading server responses as single strings.

> **NOTE**
>
> It is worth noting that Retrofit now requires, as a minimum, Android API 21 or Java 8.

9. Click the **Sync Project with Gradle Files** button in Android Studio.

10. Open your **activity_main.xml** file in **Text** mode.

11. To be able to use your label to present the latest server response, you need to assign an ID to it:

```
<TextView
    android:id="@+id/main_server_response"
    android:layout_width="wrap_content"
    android:layout_height="wrap_content"
    android:text="Hello World!"
```

```
        app:layout_constraintBottom_toBottomOf="parent"
        app:layout_constraintLeft_toLeftOf="parent"
        app:layout_constraintRight_toRightOf="parent"
        app:layout_constraintTop_toTopOf="parent" />
```

12. In the **Project** pane on the left, right-click on your app package (**com. example.catagentprofile**), then select **New | Package**.

13. Name your package **api**.

14. Now, right-click on the newly created package (**com.example. catagentprofile.api**), then select **New | Kotlin File/Class**.

15. Name your new file **TheCatApiService**. For **Kind**, choose **Interface**.

16. Add the following into the **interface** block:

```
interface TheCatApiService {
    @GET("images/search")
    fun searchImages(
        @Query("limit") limit: Int,
        @Query("size") format: String
    ) : Call<String>
}
```

This defines the image search endpoint. Make sure to import all the required Retrofit dependencies.

17. Open your **MainActivity** file.

18. At the top of the **MainActivity** class block, add the following:

```
class MainActivity : AppCompatActivity() {
    private val retrofit by lazy {
        Retrofit.Builder()
            .baseUrl("https://api.thecatapi.com/v1/")
            .addConverterFactory(ScalarsConverterFactory.create())
            .build()
    }

    private val theCatApiService
        by lazy { retrofit.create(TheCatApiService::class.java) }

    ...
}
```

This will instantiate Retrofit and the API service. We use **lazy** to make sure the instances are only created when needed.

19. Add **serverResponseView** as a field:

```
class MainActivity : AppCompatActivity() {
    private val serverResponseView: TextView
            by lazy { findViewById(R.id.main_server_response) }
```

This will look up the view with the **main_server_response** ID the first time **serverRespnseView** is accessed and then keep a reference to it.

20. Now, add the **getCatImageResponse()** function after the **onCreate(Bundle?)** function:

```
override fun onCreate(savedInstanceState: Bundle?) {
    ...
}


private fun getCatImageResponse() {
    val call = theCatApiService.searchImages(1, "full")
    call.enqueue(object : Callback<String> {
        override fun onFailure(call: Call<String>, t: Throwable) {
            Log.e("MainActivity", "Failed to get search results", t)
        }

        override fun onResponse(
            call: Call<String>,
            response: Response<String>
        ) {
            if (response.isSuccessful) {
                serverResponseView.text = response.body()
            } else {
                Log.e(
                    "MainActivity",
                    "Failed to get search results\n
                     ${response.errorBody()?.string() ?: ""}"
                )
            }
        }
    })
}
```

This function will fire off the search request and handle the possible outcomes—a successful response, an error response, and any other thrown exception.

21. Invoke a call to **getCatImageResponse()** in **onCreate()**. This will trigger the call as soon as the activity is created:

```
override fun onCreate(savedInstanceState: Bundle?) {
    ...
    getCatImageResponse()
}
```

22. Add the missing imports.

23. Run your app by clicking the **Run 'app'** button or pressing *Ctrl + R*. On the emulator, it should look like this:

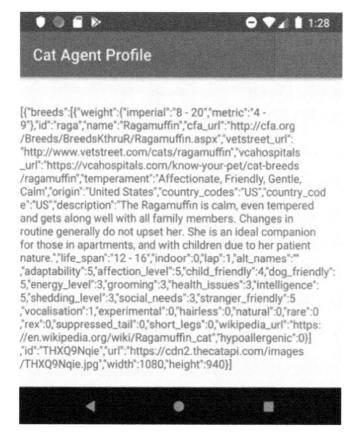

Figure 5.2: The app presenting the server response JSON

Because every time you run your app a new call is made and a random response is returned, your result will likely differ. However, whatever your result, if successful, it should be a JSON payload. Next, we will learn how to parse that JSON payload and extract the data we want from it.

PARSING A JSON RESPONSE

Now that we have successfully retrieved a JSON response from an API, it is time to learn how to use the data we have obtained. To do so, we need to parse the JSON payload. This is because the payload is a plain string representing the data object, and we are interested in specific properties of that object. If you look closely at *Figure 5.2*, you may notice that the JSON contains breed information, an image URL, and some other bits of information. However, for our code to use that information, first we have to extract it.

As mentioned in the introduction, multiple libraries exist that will parse a JSON payload for us. The most popular ones are Google's GSON (https://github.com/google/gson) and, more recently, Square's Moshi (https://github.com/square/moshi). Moshi is very lightweight, which is why we have chosen to use it in this chapter.

What do JSON libraries do? Basically, they help us convert data classes into JSON strings (serialization) and vice versa (deserialization). This helps us communicate with servers that understand JSON strings while allowing us to use meaningful data structures in our code.

To use Moshi with Retrofit, we need to add the Moshi Retrofit converter to our project. This is done by adding the following line to the **dependencies** block of our app's **build.gradle** file:

```
implementation 'com.squareup.retrofit2:converter-moshi:2.9.0'
```

Since we will no longer be accepting the responses as strings, we can go ahead and remove the scalars Retrofit converter.

Next, we need to create a data class to map the server JSON response to. One convention is to suffix the names of API response data classes with **Data**—so we'll call our data class **ImageResultData**. Another common suffix is **Entity**.

When we design our server response data classes, we need to take two factors into account: the structure of the JSON response and our data requirements. The first will affect our data types and field names, while the second will allow us to omit fields we do not currently need. JSON libraries know that they should ignore data in fields we have not defined in our data classes.

One more thing JSON libraries do for us is automatically map JSON data to fields if they happen to have the exact same name. While this is a nice feature, it is also problematic. If we rely solely on it, our data classes (and the code accessing them) will be tightly coupled to the API naming. Because not all APIs are designed well, you might end up with meaningless field names, such as **fn** or **last**, or inconsistent naming. Luckily, there is a solution to this problem. Moshi provides us with an @ **field:Json** annotation. It can be used to map a JSON field name to a meaningful field name:

```
data class UserData(
    @field:Json(name = "fn") val firstName: String,
    @field:Json(name = "last") val lastName: String
)
```

Some consider it better practice to include the annotation even when the API name is the same as the field name for the sake of consistency. We prefer the conciseness of direct conversion when the field name is clear enough. This approach can be challenged when obfuscating our code. If we do, we have to either exclude our data classes or make sure to annotate all fields.

While we are not always lucky enough to have properly documented APIs, when we do, it is best to consult the documentation when designing our model. Our model would be a data class into which the JSON data from all calls we make will be decoded. The documentation for the image search endpoint of TheCatAPI can be found at https://docs.thecatapi.com/api-reference/images/images-search. You will often find documentation to be partial or inaccurate. If this happens to be the case, the best thing you can do is contact the owners of the API and request that they update the documentation. You may have to resort to experimenting with an endpoint, unfortunately. This is risky because undocumented fields or structures are not guaranteed to remain the same, so when possible, try and get the documentation updated.

Based on the response schema obtained from the preceding link, we can define our model as follows:

```
data class ImageResultData(
    @field:Json(name = "url") val imageUrl: String,
    val breeds: List<CatBreedData>
)
```

```
data class CatBreedData(
    val name: String,
    val temperament: String
)
```

Note that the response structure is actually that of a list of results. This means we need our responses mapped to **List<ImageResultData>**, not simply **ImageResultData**.

Now, we need to update **TheCatApiService**. Instead of **Call<String>**, we can now have **Call<List<ImageResultData>>**.

Next, we need to update the construction of our Retrofit instance. Instead of **ScalarsConverterFactory**, we will now have **MoshiConverterFactory**.

Lastly, we need to update our callback, since it should no longer be handing string calls, but **List<ImageResultData>** instead:

```
@GET("images/search")
fun searchImages(
    @Query("limit") limit: Int,
    @Query("size") format: String
) : Call<List<ImageResultData>>
```

EXERCISE 5.02: EXTRACTING THE IMAGE URL FROM THE API RESPONSE

So, we have a server response as a string. Now, we want to extract the image URL from that string and present only that URL on the screen:

1. Open the app's **build.gradle** file and replace the scalars converter implementation with a Moshi converter one:

    ```
    implementation 'com.squareup.retrofit2:retrofit:2.9.0'
    implementation 'com.squareup.retrofit2:converter-moshi:2.9.0'
    testImplementation 'junit:junit:4.12'
    ```

2. Click the **Sync Project with Gradle Files** button.

3. Under your app package (**com.example.catagentprofile**), create a **model** package.

4. Within the **com.example.catagentprofile.model** package, create a new Kotlin file named **CatBreedData**.

5. Populate the newly created file with the following:

```
package com.example.catagentprofile.model

data class CatBreedData(
    val name: String,
    val temperament: String
)
```

6. Next, create **ImageResultData** under the same package.

7. Set its contents to the following:

```
package com.example.catagentprofile.model

import com.squareup.moshi.Json

data class ImageResultData(
    @field:Json(name = "url") val imageUrl: String,
    val breeds: List<CatBreedData>
)
```

8. Open the **TheCatApiService** file and update the **searchImages** return type:

```
@GET("images/search")
fun searchImages(
    @Query("limit") limit: Int,
    @Query("size") format: String
) : Call<List<ImageResultData>>
```

9. Lastly, open **MainActivity**.

10. Update the Retrofit initialization block to use the Moshi converter to deserialize JSON:

```
private val retrofit by lazy {
    Retrofit.Builder()
        .baseUrl("https://api.thecatapi.com/v1/")
        .addConverterFactory(MoshiConverterFactory.create())
        .build()
}
```

11. Update the **getCatImageResponse()** function to handle **List<ImageResultData>** requests and responses:

```
private fun getCatImageResponse() {
    val call = theCatApiService.searchImages(1, "full")
    call.enqueue(object : Callback<List<ImageResultData>> {
        override fun onFailure(call: Call<List<ImageResultData>>,
          t: Throwable) {
            Log.e("MainActivity", "Failed to get search results",
              t)
        }

        override fun onResponse(
            call: Call<List<ImageResultData>>,
            response: Response<List<ImageResultData>>
        ) {
            if (response.isSuccessful) {
                val imageResults = response.body()
                val firstImageUrl = imageResults?.firstOrNull()
                  ?.imageUrl ?: "No URL"
                serverResponseView.text = "Image URL:
                  $firstImageUrl"
            } else {
                Log.e(
                    "MainActivity",
                    "Failed to get search
                      results\n${response.errorBody()?.string()
                        ?: ""}"
                )
            }
        }
    })
}
```

12. Now, you need to check not only for a successful response but also that there is at least one **ImageResultData** instance. You can then read the **imageUrl** property of that instance and present it to the user.

13. Run your app. It should now look something like the following:

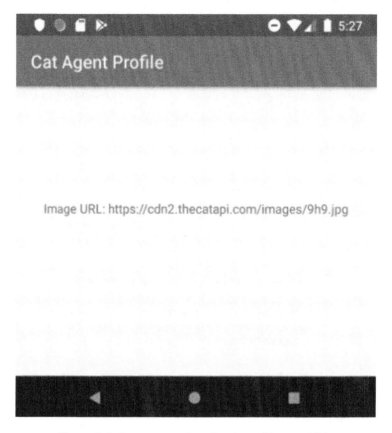

Figure 5.3: App presenting the parsed image URL

14. Again, due to the random nature of the API responses, your URL will likely be different.

You have now successfully extracted a specific property from an API response. Next, we will learn how to load the image from the URL provided to us by the API.

LOADING IMAGES FROM A REMOTE URL

We just learned how to extract particular data from an API response. Quite often, that data will include URLs to images we want to present to the user. There is quite a bit of work involved in achieving that. First, you have to fetch the image as a binary stream from the URL. Then, you need to transform that binary stream into an image (it could be a GIF, JPEG, or one of a few other image formats). Then, you need to convert it into a bitmap instance, potentially resizing it to use less memory.

You may also want to apply other transformations to it at that point. Then, you need to set it to an **ImageView**. Sounds like a lot of work, doesn't it? Well, luckily for us, there are a few libraries that do all of that (and more) for us. The most commonly used libraries are Square's **Picasso** (https://square.github.io/picasso/) and **Glide** by Bump Technologies (https://github.com/bumptech/glide). Facebook's **Fresco** (https://frescolib.org/) is somewhat less popular. We will proceed with Glide because it is consistently the faster of the two for loading images, whether it is from the internet or from the cache. It's worth noting that Picasso is more lightweight, so it is a trade-off, and both libraries are quite useful.

To include Glide in your project, add it to the **dependencies** block of your app's **build.gradle** file:

```
dependencies {
    implementation 'com.github.bumptech.glide:glide:4.10.0'
    ...
}
```

In fact, because we might change our minds at a later point, this is a great opportunity to abstract away the concrete library to have a simpler interface of our own. So, let's start by defining our **ImageLoader** interface:

```
interface ImageLoader {
    fun loadImage(imageUrl: String, imageView: ImageView)
}
```

This is a naïve implementation. In a production implementation, you might want to add arguments (or multiple functions) to support options such as different cropping strategies or having loading states.

Our implementation of the interface will rely on Glide, and so will look something like this:

```
class GlideImageLoader(private val context: Context) : ImageLoader {
    override fun loadImage(imageUrl: String, imageView: ImageView) {
        Glide.with(context)
            .load(imageUrl)
            .centerCrop()
            .into(imageView)
    }
}
```

We prefix our class name with **Glide** to differentiate it from other potential implementations. Constructing **GlideImageLoader** with **context** allows us to implement the clean **loadImage(String, ImageView)** interface without having to worry about the context, which is required by Glide for image loading. In fact, Glide is smart about the Android context. That means we could have separate implementations for **Activity** and **Fragment** scopes, and Glide would know when an image-loading request went beyond the scope.

Since we haven't yet added an **ImageView** to our layout, let's do that now:

```
<TextView
    ...
    app:layout_constraintBottom_toTopOf="@+id/main_profile_image"
    ... />

<ImageView
    android:id="@+id/main_profile_image"
    android:layout_width="150dp"
    android:layout_height="150dp"
    app:layout_constraintBottom_toBottomOf="parent"
    app:layout_constraintEnd_toEndOf="parent"
    app:layout_constraintStart_toStartOf="parent"
    app:layout_constraintTop_toBottomOf="@+id/main_server_response" />
```

This will add an **ImageView** with an ID of **main_profile_image** below our **TextView**.

We can now create an instance of **GlideImageLoader** in **MainActivity**:

```
private val imageLoader: ImageLoader by lazy { GlideImageLoader(this) }
```

Again, in a production app, you would be injecting the dependency, rather than creating it inline.

Next, we tell our Glide loader to load the image and, once loaded, center-crop it inside the provided **ImageView**. This means the image will be scaled up or down to fully fill the **ImageView**, with any excess content cut off (cropped). Since we already obtained an image URL before, all we need to do is make the call:

```
val firstImageUrl = imageResults?.firstOrNull()?.imageUrl ?: ""
if (!firstImageUrl.isBlank()) {
    imageLoader.loadImage(firstImageUrl, profileImageView)
} else {
    Log.d("MainActivity", "Missing image URL")
}
```

We have to make sure the result contains a string that is not empty or made of spaces (**isBlank()** in the preceding code block). Then, we can safely load the URL into our **ImageView**. And we're done. If we run our app now, we should see something similar to the following:

Image URL: https://cdn2.thecatapi.com/images/7mc.gif

Figure 5.4: Server response image URL with the actual image

Remember that the API returns random results, so the actual image is likely to be different. If we're lucky, we might even get an animated GIF, which we would then see animating.

EXERCISE 5.03: LOADING THE IMAGE FROM THE OBTAINED URL

In the previous exercise, we extracted the image URL from the API response. Now, we will use that URL to fetch an image from the web and display it in our app:

1. Open the app's **build.gradle** file and add the Glide dependency:

```
dependencies {
    ...
    implementation 'com.squareup.retrofit2:converter-moshi:2.9.0'
    implementation 'com.github.bumptech.glide:glide:4.11.0'
    testImplementation 'junit:junit:4.12'
    ...
}
```

Synchronize your project with the Gradle files.

2. On the left **Project** panel, right-click on your project package name (**com.example.catagentprofile**) and select **New | Kotlin File/Class**.

3. Fill in **ImageLoader** in the **Name** field. For **Kind**, choose **Interface**.

4. Open the newly created **ImageLoader.kt** file and update it like so:

```
interface ImageLoader {
    fun loadImage(imageUrl: String, imageView: ImageView)
}
```

This will be your interface for any image loader in the app.

5. Right-click on the project package name again, and again select **New | Kotlin File/Class**.

6. Name the new file **GlideImageLoader**, and select **Class** for **Kind**.

7. Update the newly created file:

```
class GlideImageLoader(private val context: Context) : ImageLoader {
    override fun loadImage(imageUrl: String, imageView: ImageView) {
        Glide.with(context)
            .load(imageUrl)
            .centerCrop()
```

```
            .into(imageView)
    }
}
```

8. Open **activity_main.xml**.

   Update it like so:

```xml
<?xml version="1.0" encoding="utf-8"?>
<androidx.constraintlayout.widget.ConstraintLayout
    xmlns:android="http://schemas.android.com/apk/res/android"
    xmlns:app="http://schemas.android.com/apk/res-auto"
    xmlns:tools="http://schemas.android.com/tools"
    android:layout_width="match_parent"
    android:layout_height="match_parent"
    tools:context=".MainActivity">

    <TextView
        android:id="@+id/main_server_response"
        android:layout_width="wrap_content"
        android:layout_height="wrap_content"
        android:text="Hello World!"
        app:layout_constraintBottom_toTopOf="@+id/main_profile_image"
        app:layout_constraintLeft_toLeftOf="parent"
        app:layout_constraintRight_toRightOf="parent"
        app:layout_constraintTop_toTopOf="parent" />

    <ImageView
        android:id="@+id/main_profile_image"
        android:layout_width="150dp"
        android:layout_height="150dp"
        app:layout_constraintBottom_toBottomOf="parent"
        app:layout_constraintEnd_toEndOf="parent"
        app:layout_constraintStart_toStartOf="parent"
        app:layout_constraintTop_toBottomOf=
          "@+id/main_server_response" />

</androidx.constraintlayout.widget.ConstraintLayout>
```

   This will add an **ImageView** named **main_profile_image** below
   your **TextView**.

9. Open the **MainActivity.kt** file.

10. Add a field for your newly added **ImageView** at the top of your class:

```
private val serverResponseView: TextView
    by lazy { findViewById(R.id.main_server_response) }
private val profileImageView: ImageView
    by lazy { findViewById(R.id.main_profile_image) }
```

11. Define **ImageLoader** just above the **onCreate(Bundle?)** function:

```
private val imageLoader: ImageLoader by lazy { GlideImageLoader(this)
}

override fun onCreate(savedInstanceState: Bundle?) {
```

12. Update your **getCatImageResponse()** function like so:

```
private fun getCatImageResponse() {
    val call = theCatApiService.searchImages(1, "full")
    call.enqueue(object : Callback<List<ImageResultData>> {
        override fun onFailure(call: Call<List<ImageResultData>>,
          t: Throwable) {
            Log.e("MainActivity", "Failed to get search results", t)
        }

        override fun onResponse(
            call: Call<List<ImageResultData>>,
            response: Response<List<ImageResultData>>
        ) {
            if (response.isSuccessful) {
                val imageResults = response.body()
                val firstImageUrl =
                    imageResults?.firstOrNull()?.imageUrl ?: ""
                if (firstImageUrl.isNotBlank()) {
                    imageLoader.loadImage(firstImageUrl,
                        profileImageView)
                } else {
                    Log.d("MainActivity", "Missing image URL")
                }
                serverResponseView.text = "Image URL: $firstImageUrl"
            } else {
                Log.e(
                    "MainActivity",
```

```
                        "Failed to get search results\n
                            ${response.errorBody()?.string() ?: ""}"
                    )
                }
            }
        })
    }
```

13. Now, once you have a non-blank URL, it will be loaded into **profileImageView**.

14. Run the app:

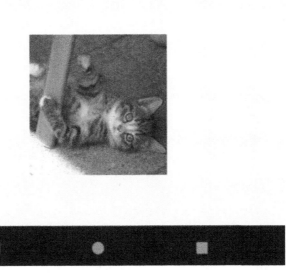

Figure 5.5: Exercise outcome – showing a random image and its source URL

The following are bonus steps.

15. Update your layout like so:

```xml
<?xml version="1.0" encoding="utf-8"?>
<androidx.constraintlayout.widget.ConstraintLayout
    xmlns:android="http://schemas.android.com/apk/res/android"
    xmlns:app="http://schemas.android.com/apk/res-auto"
    xmlns:tools="http://schemas.android.com/tools"
    android:layout_width="match_parent"
    android:layout_height="match_parent"
    tools:context=".MainActivity">

    <TextView
        android:id="@+id/main_agent_breed_label"
        android:layout_width="wrap_content"
        android:layout_height="wrap_content"
        android:padding="16dp"
        android:text="Agent breed:"
        app:layout_constraintStart_toStartOf="parent"
        app:layout_constraintTop_toTopOf="parent" />

    <TextView
        android:id="@+id/main_agent_breed_value"
        android:layout_width="wrap_content"
        android:layout_height="wrap_content"
        android:paddingTop="16dp"
        app:layout_constraintStart_toEndOf=
          "@+id/main_agent_breed_label"
        app:layout_constraintTop_toTopOf=
          "@+id/main_agent_breed_label" />

    <ImageView
        android:id="@+id/main_profile_image"
        android:layout_width="150dp"
        android:layout_height="150dp"
        android:layout_margin="16dp"
        app:layout_constraintStart_toStartOf="parent"
        app:layout_constraintTop_toBottomOf=
```

```
        "@+id/main_agent_breed_label" />

    </androidx.constraintlayout.widget.ConstraintLayout>
```

This will add an **Agent breed** label and tidy up the view layout. Now, your layout looks a bit more like a proper cat agent profile app.

16. In **MainActivity.kt**, locate the following lines:

```
private val serverResponseView: TextView
    by lazy { findViewById(R.id.main_server_response) }
```

Replace that line with the following to look up the new name field:

```
private val agentBreedView: TextView
    by lazy { findViewById(R.id.main_agent_breed_value) }
```

17. Update **getCatImageResponse()** like so:

```
private fun getCatImageResponse() {
    val call = theCatApiService.searchImages(1, "full")
    call.enqueue(object : Callback<List<ImageResultData>> {
        override fun onFailure(call: Call<List<ImageResultData>>,
            t: Throwable) {
            Log.e("MainActivity", "Failed to get search results", t)
        }

        override fun onResponse(
            call: Call<List<ImageResultData>>,
            response: Response<List<ImageResultData>>
        ) {
            if (response.isSuccessful) {
                val imageResults = response.body()
                val firstImageUrl =
                    imageResults?.firstOrNull()?.imageUrl ?: ""
                if (!firstImageUrl.isBlank()) {
                    imageLoader.loadImage(firstImageUrl,
                        profileImageView)
                } else {
                    Log.d("MainActivity", "Missing image URL")
                }
                agentBreedView.text =
                    imageResults?.firstOrNull()?.breeds?
                        .firstOrNull()?.name ?: "Unknown"
            } else {
```

```
        Log.e(
          "MainActivity",
          "Failed to get search results\n
            ${response.errorBody()?.string() ?:""}"
        )
      }
    }
  })
}
```

This is done to load the first breed returned from the API into **agentNameView**, with a fallback to **Unknown**.

18. At the time of writing, not many pictures in TheCatAPI have breed data. However, if you run your app enough times, you will end up seeing something like this:

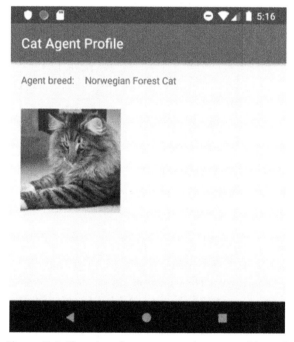

Figure 5.6: Showing the cat agent image and breed

In this chapter, we learned how to fetch data from a remote API. We then learned how to process that data and extract the information we need from it. Lastly, we learned how to present an image on the screen when given an image URL.

In the following activity, we will apply our knowledge to develop an app that tells the user the current weather in New York, presenting the user with a relevant weather icon, too.

ACTIVITY 5.01: DISPLAYING THE CURRENT WEATHER

Let's say we want to build an app that shows the current weather in New York. Furthermore, we also want to display an icon that represents the current weather.

This activity aims to create an app that polls an API endpoint for the current weather in JSON format, transforms that data into a local model, and uses that model to present the current weather. It also extracts the URL to an icon representing the current weather and fetches that icon to be displayed on the screen.

We will use the free OpenWeatherMap.org API for the purpose of this activity. Documentation can be found at https://www.metaweather.com/api/. To sign up for an API token, please go to https://home.openweathermap.org/users/sign_up. You can find your keys and generate new ones as needed at https://home.openweathermap.org/api_keys.

The steps are as follows:

1. Create a new app.

2. Grant internet permissions to the app in order to be able to make API and image requests.

3. Add Retrofit, the Moshi converter, and Glide to the app.

4. Update the app layout to support the presentation of the weather in a textual form (short and long description) as well as a weather icon image.

5. Define the model. Create classes that will contain the server response.

6. Add the Retrofit service for the OpenWeatherMap API, https://api.openweathermap.org/data/2.5/weather.

7. Create a Retrofit instance with a Moshi converter.

8. Call the API service.

9. Handle the successful server response.

10. Handle the different failure scenarios.

The expected output is shown here:

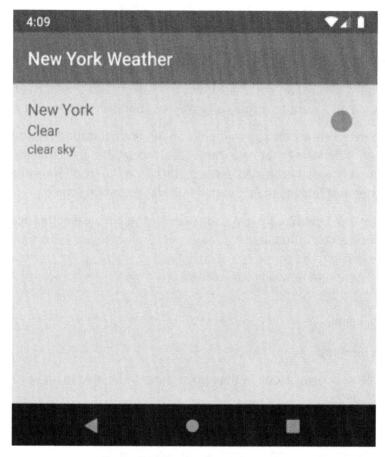

Figure 5.7: The final weather app

NOTE

The solution to this activity can be found at: http://packt.live/3sKj1cp

SUMMARY

In this chapter, we learned how to fetch data from an API using Retrofit. We then learned how to handle JSON responses using Moshi, as well as plain text responses. We also saw how different error scenarios can be handled.

We later learned how to load images from URLs using Glide and how to present them to the user via `ImageView`.

There are quite a few popular libraries for fetching data from APIs as well as for loading images. We only covered some of the most popular ones. You might want to try out some of the other libraries to find out which ones fit your purpose best.

In the next chapter, we will be introduced to `RecyclerView`, which is a powerful UI component that we can use to present our users with lists of items.

6

RECYCLERVIEW

OVERVIEW

In this chapter, you will learn how to add lists and grids of items to your apps and effectively leverage the recycling power of **RecyclerView**. You'll also learn how to handle user interaction with the item views on the screen and support different item view types—for example, for titles. Later in the chapter, you'll add and remove items dynamically.

By the end of the chapter, you will have the skills required to present your users with interactive lists of rich items.

INTRODUCTION

In the previous chapter, we learned how to fetch data, including lists of items and image URLs, from APIs, and how to load images from URLs. Combining that knowledge with the ability to display lists of items is the goal of this chapter.

Quite often, you will want to present your users with a list of items. For example, you might want to show them a list of pictures on their device, or let them select their country from a list of all countries. To do that, you would need to populate multiple views, all sharing the same layout but presenting different content.

Historically, this was achieved by using **ListView** or **GridView**. While both are still viable options, they do not offer the robustness and flexibility of **RecyclerView**. For example, they do not support large datasets well, they do not support horizontal scrolling, and they do not offer rich divider customization. Customizing the divider between items in **RecyclerView** can be easily achieved using **RecyclerView.ItemDecorator**.

So, what does **RecyclerView** do? **RecyclerView** orchestrates the creation, population, and reuse (hence the name) of views representing lists of items. To use **RecyclerView**, you need to familiarize yourself with two of its dependencies: the adapter (and through it, the view holder) and the layout manager. These dependencies provide our **RecyclerView** with the content to show, as well as telling it how to present that content and how to lay it out on the screen.

The adapter provides **RecyclerView** with child views (nested Android views within **RecyclerView** used to represent individual data items) to draw on the screen, binds those views to data (via **ViewHolder** instances), and reports user interaction with those views. The layout manager tells **RecyclerView** how to lay its children out. We are provided with three layout types by default: linear, grid, and staggered grid—managed by **LinearLayoutManager**, **GridLayoutManager**, and **StaggeredGridLayoutManager**, respectively.

In this chapter, we will develop an app that lists secret agents and whether they are currently active or sleeping (and thus unavailable). The app will then allow us to add new agents or delete existing ones by swiping them away. There is a twist, though—as you saw in Chapter 5, *Essential Libraries: Retrofit, Moshi, and Glide*, all our agents will be cats.

ADDING RECYCLERVIEW TO OUR LAYOUT

In *Chapter 3*, *Screens and UI*, we saw how we can add views to our layouts to be inflated by activities, fragments, or custom views. **RecyclerView** is just another such view. To add it to our layout, we need to add the following tag to our layout:

```
<androidx.recyclerview.widget.RecyclerView
    android:id="@+id/recycler_view"
    android:layout_width="match_parent"
    android:layout_height="wrap_content"
    tools:listitem="@layout/item_sample" />
```

You should already be able to recognize the **android:id** attribute, as well as the **android:layout_width** and **android:layout_height** ones.

We can use the optional **tools:listitem** attribute to tell Android Studio which layout to inflate as a list item in our preview toolbar. This will give us an idea of how **RecyclerView** might look in our app.

Adding a **RecyclerView** tag to our layout means we now have an empty container to hold the child views representing our list items. Once populated, it will handle the presenting, scrolling, and recycling of child views for us.

EXERCISE 6.01: ADDING AN EMPTY RECYCLERVIEW TO YOUR MAIN ACTIVITY

To use **RecyclerView** in your app, you first need to add it to one of your layouts. Let's add it to the layout inflated by our main activity:

1. Start by creating a new empty activity project (**File | New | New Project | Empty Activity**). Name your application **My RecyclerView App**. Make sure your package name is **com.example.myrecyclerviewapp**.

2. Set the save location to where you want to save your project. Leave everything else at its default values and click **Finish**. Make sure you are on the **Android** view in your **Project** pane:

Figure 6.1: Android view in the Project pane

3. Open your **activity_main.xml** file in **Text** mode.

4. To turn your label into a title at the top of the screen under which you can add your **RecyclerView**, add an ID to **TextView** and align it to the top, like so:

```
<TextView
    android:id="@+id/hello_label"
    android:layout_width="wrap_content"
    android:layout_height="wrap_content"
    android:text="Hello World!"
    app:layout_constraintLeft_toLeftOf="parent"
    app:layout_constraintRight_toRightOf="parent"
    app:layout_constraintTop_toTopOf="parent" />
```

5. Add the following after **TextView** tag to add an empty **RecyclerView** element to our layout, constrained below your **hello_label TextView** title:

```
<androidx.recyclerview.widget.RecyclerView
    android:id="@+id/recycler_view"
    android:layout_width="match_parent"
    android:layout_height="wrap_content"
    app:layout_constraintTop_toBottomOf="@+id/hello_label" />
```

Your layout file should now look something like this:

```xml
<?xml version="1.0" encoding="utf-8"?>
<androidx.constraintlayout.widget.ConstraintLayout
xmlns:android="http://schemas.android.com/apk/res/android"
    xmlns:app="http://schemas.android.com/apk/res-auto"
    xmlns:tools="http://schemas.android.com/tools"
    android:layout_width="match_parent"
    android:layout_height="match_parent"
    tools:context=".MainActivity">

    <TextView
        android:id="@+id/hello_label"
        android:layout_width="wrap_content"
        android:layout_height="wrap_content"
        android:text="Hello World!"
        app:layout_constraintLeft_toLeftOf="parent"
        app:layout_constraintRight_toRightOf="parent"
        app:layout_constraintTop_toTopOf="parent" />

    <androidx.recyclerview.widget.RecyclerView
        android:id="@+id/recycler_view"
        android:layout_width="match_parent"
        android:layout_height="wrap_content"
        app:layout_constraintTop_toBottomOf="@+id/hello_label" />

</androidx.constraintlayout.widget.ConstraintLayout>
```

6. Run your app by clicking the **Run app** button or pressing *Ctrl + R* (*Shift + F10* on Windows). On the emulator, it should look like this:

Figure 6.2: App with an empty RecyclerView (image cropped for space)

As you can see, our app runs and our layout is presented on the screen. However, we do not see our **RecyclerView**. Why is that? At this stage, our **RecyclerView** has no content. **RecyclerView** with no content does not render by default—so, while our **RecyclerView** is indeed on the screen, it is not visible. This brings us to the next step—populating **RecyclerView** with content that we can actually see.

POPULATING THE RECYCLERVIEW

So, we added **RecyclerView** to our layout. For us to benefit from **RecyclerView**, we need to add content to it. Let's see how we go about doing that.

As we mentioned before, to add content to our **RecyclerView**, we would need to implement an adapter. An adapter binds our data to child views. In simpler terms, this means it tells **RecyclerView** how to plug data into views designed to present that data.

For example, let's say we want to present a list of employees.

First, we need to design our UI model. This will be a data object holding all the information needed by our view to present a single employee. Because this is a UI model, one convention is to suffix its name with **UiModel**:

```
data class EmployeeUiModel(
    val name: String,
    val biography: String,
    val role: EmployeeRole,
    val gender: Gender,
    val imageUrl: String
)
```

We will define **EmployeeRole** and **Gender** as follows:

```
enum class EmployeeRole {
    HumanResources,
    Management,
    Technology
}

enum class Gender {
    Female,
    Male,
    Unknown
}
```

The values are provided as an example, of course. Feel free to add more of your own!

Figure 6.3: The model's hierarchy

Now we know what data to expect when binding to a view—so, we can design our view to present this data (this is a simplified version of the actual layout, which we'll save as **item_employee.xml**). We'll start with the **ImageView**:

```xml
<?xml version="1.0" encoding="utf-8"?>
<androidx.constraintlayout.widget.ConstraintLayout
  xmlns:android="http://schemas.android.com/apk/res/android"
    xmlns:app="http://schemas.android.com/apk/res-auto"
    xmlns:tools="http://schemas.android.com/tools"
    android:layout_width="match_parent"
    android:layout_height="wrap_content"
    android:orientation="vertical"
    android:padding="8dp">

    <ImageView
        android:id="@+id/item_employee_photo"
        android:layout_width="60dp"
        android:layout_height="60dp"
        android:contentDescription="@string/item_employee_photo"
        app:layout_constraintStart_toStartOf="parent"
        app:layout_constraintTop_toTopOf="parent"
        tools:background="@color/colorPrimary" />
```

And then add each **TextView**:

```xml
    <TextView
        android:id="@+id/item_employee_name"
        android:layout_width="wrap_content"
        android:layout_height="wrap_content"
        android:layout_marginStart="16dp"
        android:layout_marginLeft="16dp"
        android:textStyle="bold"
        app:layout_constraintStart_toEndOf="@+id/item_employee_photo"
        app:layout_constraintTop_toTopOf="parent"
        tools:text="Oliver" />

    <TextView
        android:id="@+id/item_employee_role"
        android:layout_width="wrap_content"
        android:layout_height="wrap_content"
        android:textColor="@color/colorAccent"
        app:layout_constraintStart_toStartOf="@+id/item_employee_name"
```

```
            app:layout_constraintTop_toBottomOf="@+id/item_employee_name"
            tools:text="Exotic Shorthair" />


    <TextView
            android:id="@+id/item_employee_biography"
            android:layout_width="wrap_content"
            android:layout_height="wrap_content"
            app:layout_constraintStart_toStartOf="@+id/item_employee_role"
            app:layout_constraintTop_toBottomOf="@+id/item_employee_role"
            tools:text="Stealthy and witty. Better avoid in dark alleys." />


    <TextView
            android:id="@+id/item_employee_gender"
            android:layout_width="wrap_content"
            android:layout_height="wrap_content"
            android:textSize="30sp"
            app:layout_constraintEnd_toEndOf="parent"
            app:layout_constraintTop_toTopOf="parent"
            tools:text="&#9794;" />


</androidx.constraintlayout.widget.ConstraintLayout>
```

So far, there is nothing new. You should be able to recognize all of the different view types from *Chapter 2, Building User Screen Flows*:

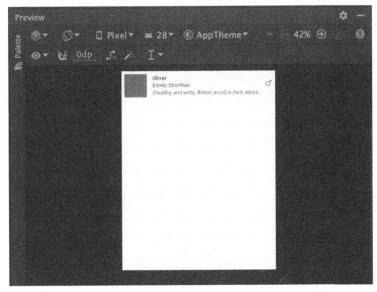

Figure 6.4: Preview of the item_cat.xml layout file

With a data model and a layout, we now have everything we need to bind our data to the view. To do that, we will implement a view holder. Usually, a view holder has two responsibilities: it holds a reference to a view (as its name implies), but it also binds data to that view. We will implement our view holder as follows:

```
private val FEMALE_SYMBOL by lazy {
    HtmlCompat.fromHtml("&#9793;", HtmlCompat.FROM_HTML_MODE_LEGACY)
}
private val MALE_SYMBOL by lazy {
    HtmlCompat.fromHtml("&#9794;", HtmlCompat.FROM_HTML_MODE_LEGACY)
}
private const val UNKNOWN_SYMBOL = "?"

class EmployeeViewHolder(
    containerView: View,
    private val imageLoader: ImageLoader
) : ViewHolder(containerView) {
    private val employeeNameView: TextView
        by lazy { containerView.findViewById(R.id.item_employee_name) }
    private val employeeRoleView: TextView
        by lazy { containerView.findViewById(R.id.item_employee_role) }
    private val employeeBioView: TextView
        by lazy { containerView.findViewById(R.id.item_employee_bio) }
    private val employeeGenderView: TextView
        by lazy { containerView.findViewById(R.id.item_employee_gender) }

    fun bindData(employeeData: EmployeeUiModel) {
        imageLoader.loadImage(employeeData.imageUrl, employeePhotoView)
        employeeNameView.text = employeeData.name
        employeeRoleView.text = when (employeeData.role) {
            EmployeeRole.HumanResources -> "Human Resources"
            EmployeeRole.Management -> "Management"
            EmployeeRole.Technology -> "Technology"
        }
        employeeBioView.text = employeeData.biography
        employeeGenderView.text = when (employeeData.gender) {
            Gender.Female -> FEMALE_SYMBOL
            Gender.Male -> MALE_SYMBOL
```

```
                else -> UNKNOWN_SYMBOL
        }
    }
}
```

There are a few things worth noting in the preceding code. First, by convention, we suffixed the name of our view holder with **ViewHolder**. Second, note that **EmployeeViewHolder** needs to implement the abstract **RecyclerView. ViewHolder** class. This is required so that the generic type of our adapter can be our view holder. Lastly, we lazily keep references to the views we are interested in. The first time **bindData(EmployeeUiModel)** is called, we will find these views in the layout and keep references to them.

Next, we introduced a **bindData(EmployeeUiModel)** function. This function will be called by our adapter to bind the data to the view held by the view holder. The last but most important thing to note is that we always make sure to set a state for all modified views for any possible input.

With our view holder set up, we can proceed to implement our adapter. We will start by implementing the minimum required functions, plus a function to set the data. Our adapter will look something like this:

```
class EmployeesAdapter(
    private val layoutInflater: LayoutInflater,
    private val imageLoader: ImageLoader
) : RecyclerView.Adapter<EmployeeViewHolder>() {
    private val employeesData = mutableListOf<EmployeeUiModel>()

    fun setData(employeesData: List<EmployeeUiModel>) {
        this.employeesData.clear()
        this.employeesData.addAll(employeesData)
        notifyDataSetChanged()
    }

    override fun onCreateViewHolder(parent: ViewGroup, viewType: Int):
      EmployeeViewHolder {
        val view = layoutInflater.inflate(R.layout.item_employee,
          parent, false)
        return EmployeeViewHolder(view, imageLoader)
    }

    override fun getItemCount() = employeesData.size
```

```
    override fun onBindViewHolder(holder: EmployeeViewHolder,
        position:Int) {
        holder.bindData(employeesData[position])
    }
}
```

Let's go over this implementation. First, we inject our dependencies to the adapter via its constructor. This will make testing our adapter much easier—but will also allow us to change some of its behavior (for example, replace the image loading library) painlessly. In fact, we would not need to change the adapter at all in that case.

Then, we define a private mutable list of **EmployeeUiModel** to store the data currently provided by the adapter to **RecyclerView**. We also introduce a method to set that list. Note that we keep a local list and set its contents, rather than allowing **employeesData** to be set directly. This is mainly because Kotlin, just like Java, passes variables by reference. Passing variables by reference means changes to the content of the list passed into the adapter would change the list held by the adapter. So, for example, if an item was removed from outside the adapter, the adapter would have that item removed as well. This becomes a problem because the adapter would not be aware of that change, and so would not be able to notify **RecyclerView**. There are other risks around the list being modified from outside the adapter, but covering them is beyond the scope of this book.

Another benefit of encapsulating the modification of the data in a function is that we avoid the risk of forgetting to notify **RecyclerView** that the dataset has changed, which we do by calling **notifyDataSetChanged()**.

We proceed to implement the adapter's **onCreateViewHolder(ViewGroup, Int)** function. This function is called when the **RecyclerView** needs a new **ViewHolder** to render data on the screen. It provides us with a container **ViewGroup** and a view type (we'll look into view types later in this chapter). The function then expects us to return a view holder initialized with a view (in our case, an inflated one). So, we inflate the view we designed earlier, passing it to a new **EmployeeViewHolder** instance. Note that the last argument to the inflated function is **false**. This makes sure we do not attach the newly inflated view to the parent. Attaching and detaching views will be managed by the layout manager. Setting it to **true** or omitting it would result in **IllegalStateException** being thrown. Finally, we return the newly created **EmployeeViewHolder**.

To implement **getItemCount()**, we simply return the size of our **employeesData** list.

Lastly, we implement **onBindViewHolder(EmployeeViewHolder, Int)**. This is done by passing **EmployeeUiModel**, stored in **catsData**, at the given position to the **bindData(EmployeeUiModel)** function of our view holder. Our adapter is now ready.

If we tried to plug our adapter into our **RecyclerView** at this point and run our app, we would still see no content. This is because we are still missing two small steps: setting data to our adapter and assigning a layout manager to our **RecyclerView**. The complete working code would look like this:

```
class MainActivity : AppCompatActivity() {
    private val employeesAdapter by lazy {
        EmployeesAdapter(layoutInflater, GlideImageLoader(this)) }
    private val recyclerView: RecyclerView by lazy
        { findViewById(R.id.main_recycler_view) }

    override fun onCreate(savedInstanceState: Bundle?) {
        super.onCreate(savedInstanceState)
        setContentView(R.layout.activity_main)
        recyclerView.adapter = employeesAdapter
        recyclerView.layoutManager =
            LinearLayoutManager(this, LinearLayoutManager.VERTICAL,
                false)
        employeesAdapter.setData(
            listOf(
                EmployeeUiModel(
                    "Robert",
                    "Rose quickly through the organization",
                    EmployeeRole.Management,
                    Gender.Male,
                    "https://images.pexels.com/photos/220453
                        /pexels-photo-220453.jpeg?auto
                            =compress&cs=tinysrgb&h=650&w=940"
                ),
                EmployeeUiModel(
                    "Wilma",
                    "A talented developer",
                    EmployeeRole.Technology,
                    Gender.Female,
```

```
                    "https://images.pexels.com/photos/3189024
                        /pexels-photo-3189024.jpeg?auto=compress&cs
                            =tinysrgb&h=650&w=940"
            ),
            EmployeeUiModel(
                "Curious George",
                "Excellent at retention",
                EmployeeRole.HumanResources,
                Gender.Unknown,
                "https://images.pexels.com/photos/771742
                    /pexels-photo-771742.jpeg?auto
                        =compress&cs=tinysrgb&h=750&w=1260"
            )
        )
    )
}
}
```

Running our app now, we would see a list of our employees.

Note that we hardcoded the list of employees. In a production app, following a **Model-View-View-Model** (**MVVM**) pattern (we will cover this pattern in *Chapter 14, Architecture Patterns*), you would be provided with data to present by your **ViewModel**. It is also important to note that we kept a reference to **employeesAdapter**. This is so that we could indeed, at a later time, set the data to different values. Some implementations rely on reading the adapter from **RecyclerView** itself—this can potentially result in unnecessary casting operations and unexpected states where the adapter is not yet assigned to **RecyclerView**, and so this is generally not a recommended approach.

Lastly, note that we chose to use **LinearLayoutManager**, providing it with the activity for context, a **VERTICAL** orientation flag, and **false** to tell it that we do not want the order of the items in the list reversed.

EXERCISE 6.02: POPULATING YOUR RECYCLERVIEW

RecyclerView is not very interesting without any content. It is time you populate **RecyclerView** by adding your secret cat agents to it.

A quick recap before you dive in: in the previous exercise, we introduced an empty list designed to hold a list of secret cat agents that the users have at their disposal. In this exercise, you will be populating that list to present the users with the available secret cat agents in the agency:

1. To keep our file structure tidy, we will start by creating a model package. Right-click on the package name of our app, then select **New | Package**:

Figure 6.5: Creating a new package

2. Name the new package **model**. Click **OK** to create the package.

3. To create our first model data class, right-click on the newly created model package, then select **New | Kotlin File/Class**.

4. Under **name**, fill in **CatUiModel**. Leave **kind** as **File** and click on **OK**. This will be the class holding the data we have about every individual cat agent.

5. Add the following to the newly created **CatUiModel.kt** file to define the data class with all the relevant properties of a cat agent:

```
data class CatUiModel(
    val gender: Gender,
    val breed: CatBreed,
    val name: String,
    val biography: String,
    val imageUrl: String
)
```

For each cat agent, other than their name and photo, we want to know the gender, breed, and biography. This will help us choose the right agent for a mission.

6. Again, right-click on the model package, then navigate to **New | Kotlin File/Class**.

7. This time, name the new file **CatBreed** and set **kind** to the **Enum** class. This class will hold our different cat breeds.

8. Update your newly created enum with some initial values, as follows:

```
enum class CatBreed {
    AmericanCurl,

    BalineseJavanese,

    ExoticShorthair
}
```

9. Repeat *steps 6* and *7*, only this time call your file **Gender**. This will hold the accepted values for a cat agent's gender.

10. Update the **Gender** enum like so:

```
enum class Gender {
    Female,

    Male,

    Unknown
}
```

11. Now, to define the layout of the view holding the data about each cat agent, create a new layout resource file by right-clicking on **layout** and then selecting **New | Layout resource file**:

Figure 6.6: Creating a new layout resource file

12. Name your resource **item_cat**. Leave all the other fields as they are and click **OK**.

13. Update the contents of the newly created **item_cat.xml** file. (The following code block has been truncated for space. Use the link below to see the full code that you need to add.)

item_cat.xml

```
10    <ImageView
11        android:id="@+id/item_cat_photo"
12        android:layout_width="60dp"
13        android:layout_height="60dp"
14        android:contentDescription="@string/item_cat_photo"
15        app:layout_constraintStart_toStartOf="parent"
16        app:layout_constraintTop_toTopOf="parent"
17        tools:background="@color/colorPrimary" />
18
19    <TextView
20        android:id="@+id/item_cat_name"
21        android:layout_width="wrap_content"
22        android:layout_height="wrap_content"
23        android:layout_marginStart="16dp"
24        android:layout_marginLeft="16dp"
25        android:textStyle="bold"
26        app:layout_constraintStart_toEndOf="@+id/item_cat_photo"
27        app:layout_constraintTop_toTopOf="parent"
28        tools:text="Oliver" />
```

The complete code for this step can be found at http://packt.live/3sopUjo.

This will create a layout with an image and text fields for a name, breed, and biography to be used in our list.

14. You will notice that *line 14* is highlighted in red. This is because you haven't declared **item_cat_photo** in **strings.xml** under the **res/values** folder yet. Do so now by placing the text cursor over **item_cat_photo** and pressing *Alt + Enter* (*Option + Enter* on Mac), then select **Create string value resource 'item_cat_photo'**:

Figure 6.7: A string resource is not yet defined

15. Under **Resource value**, fill in **Photo**. Press **OK**.

16. You will need a copy of **ImageLoader.kt**, introduced in *Chapter 5, Essential Libraries: Retrofit, Moshi, and Glide*, so right-click on the package name of your app, navigate to **New | Kotlin File/Class**, and then set the name to **ImageLoader** and **kind** to **Interface**, and click **OK**.

17. Similar to *Chapter 5, Essential Libraries: Retrofit, Moshi, and Glide*, you only need to add one function here:

```
interface ImageLoader {
    fun loadImage(imageUrl: String, imageView: ImageView)
}
```

Make sure to import **ImageView**.

18. Right-click on the package name of your app again, then select **New | Kotlin File/Class**.

19. Call the new file **CatViewHolder**. Click **OK**.

20. To implement **CatViewHolder**, which will bind the cat agent data to your views, replace the contents of the **CatViewHolder.kt** file with the following:

```
private val FEMALE_SYMBOL by lazy {
    HtmlCompat.fromHtml("&#9793;", HtmlCompat.FROM_HTML_MODE_LEGACY)
}
private val MALE_SYMBOL by lazy {
    HtmlCompat.fromHtml("&#9794;", HtmlCompat.FROM_HTML_MODE_LEGACY)
}
private const val UNKNOWN_SYMBOL = "?"

class CatViewHolder(
    containerView: View,
    private val imageLoader: ImageLoader
) : ViewHolder(containerView) {
    private val catBiographyView: TextView
        by lazy { containerView.findViewById(R.id.item_cat_biography)
}
    private val catBreedView: TextView
        by lazy { containerView.findViewById(R.id.item_cat_breed) }
    private val catGenderView: TextView
        by lazy { containerView.findViewById(R.id.item_cat_gender) }
    private val catNameView: TextView
        by lazy { containerView.findViewById(R.id.item_cat_name) }
    private val catPhotoView: ImageView
        by lazy { containerView.findViewById(R.id.item_cat_photo) }

    fun bindData(catData: CatUiModel) {
        imageLoader.loadImage(catData.imageUrl, catPhotoView)
```

```
            catNameView.text = catData.name
            catBreedView.text = when (catData.breed) {
                CatBreed.AmericanCurl -> "American Curl"
                CatBreed.BalineseJavanese -> "Balinese-Javanese"
                CatBreed.ExoticShorthair -> "Exotic Shorthair"
            }
            catBiographyView.text = catData.biography
            catGenderView.text = when (catData.gender) {
                Gender.Female -> FEMALE_SYMBOL
                Gender.Male -> MALE_SYMBOL
                else -> UNKNOWN_SYMBOL
            }
        }
    }
}
```

21. Still under our app package name, create a new Kotlin file named
    CatsAdapter.

22. To implement **CatsAdapter**, which is responsible for storing the data for
    RecyclerView, as well as creating instances of your view holder and using
    them to bind data to views, replace the contents of the **CatsAdapter.kt** file
    with this:

```
package com.example.myrecyclerviewapp

import android.view.LayoutInflater
import android.view.ViewGroup
import androidx.recyclerview.widget.RecyclerView
import com.example.myrecyclerviewapp.model.CatUiModel

class CatsAdapter(
    private val layoutInflater: LayoutInflater,
    private val imageLoader: ImageLoader
) : RecyclerView.Adapter<CatViewHolder>() {
    private val catsData = mutableListOf<CatUiModel>()

    fun setData(catsData: List<CatUiModel>) {
        this.catsData.clear()
        this.catsData.addAll(catsData)
        notifyDataSetChanged()
    }
```

```
override fun onCreateViewHolder(parent: ViewGroup,
    viewType: Int): CatViewHolder {
        val view = layoutInflater.inflate(R.layout.item_cat,
    parent, false)
        return CatViewHolder(view, imageLoader)
    }
    override fun getItemCount() = catsData.size
    override fun onBindViewHolder(holder: CatViewHolder,
        position: Int) {
        holder.bindData(catsData[position])
    }
}
```

23. At this point, you need to include Glide in your project. Start by adding the following line of code to the **dependencies** block inside your app's **gradle.build** file:

```
implementation 'com.github.bumptech.glide:glide:4.11.0'
```

24. Create a **GlideImageLoader** class in your app package path, containing the following:

```
package com.example.myrecyclerviewapp

import android.content.Context
import android.widget.ImageView
import com.bumptech.glide.Glide

class GlideImageLoader(private val context: Context) : ImageLoader {
    override fun loadImage(imageUrl: String, imageView: ImageView) {
        Glide.with(context)
            .load(imageUrl)
            .centerCrop()
            .into(imageView)
    }
}
```

This is a simple implementation assuming the loaded image should always be center-cropped.

25. Update your **MainActivity** file:

```kotlin
class MainActivity : AppCompatActivity() {
    private val recyclerView: RecyclerView
        by lazy { findViewById(R.id.recycler_view) }
    private val catsAdapter by lazy { CatsAdapter(layoutInflater,
        GlideImageLoader(this)) }

    override fun onCreate(savedInstanceState: Bundle?) {
        super.onCreate(savedInstanceState)
        setContentView(R.layout.activity_main)
        recyclerView.adapter = catsAdapter
        recyclerView.layoutManager = LinearLayoutManager(this,
            LinearLayoutManager.VERTICAL, false)
        catsAdapter.setData(
            listOf(
                CatUiModel(
                    Gender.Male,
                    CatBreed.BalineseJavanese,
                    "Fred",
                    "Silent and deadly",
                    "https://cdn2.thecatapi.com/images/DBmIBhhyv.jpg"
                ),
                CatUiModel(
                    Gender.Female,
                    CatBreed.ExoticShorthair,
                    "Wilma",
                    "Cuddly assassin",
                    "https://cdn2.thecatapi.com/images/KJF8fB_20.jpg"
                ),
                CatUiModel(
                    Gender.Unknown,
                    CatBreed.AmericanCurl,
                    "Curious George",
                    "Award winning investigator",
```

```
                        "https://cdn2.thecatapi.com/images/vJB8rwfdX.jpg"
                    )
                )
            )
        }
    }
```

This will define your adapter, attach it to **RecyclerView**, and populate it with some hardcoded data.

26. In your **AndroidManifest.xml** file, add the following in the **manifest** tag before the application tag:

```
<uses-permission android:name="android.permission.INTERNET" />
```

This will allow your app to download images off the internet.

27. For some final touches, such as giving our title view a proper name and text, update your **activity_main.xml** file like so:

```
<?xml version="1.0" encoding="utf-8"?>
<androidx.constraintlayout.widget.ConstraintLayout
  xmlns:android="http://schemas.android.com/apk/res/android"
    xmlns:app="http://schemas.android.com/apk/res-auto"
    xmlns:tools="http://schemas.android.com/tools"
    android:layout_width="match_parent"
    android:layout_height="match_parent"
    tools:context=".MainActivity">

    <TextView
        android:id="@+id/main_label"
        android:layout_width="wrap_content"
        android:layout_height="wrap_content"
        android:text="@string/main_title"
        android:textSize="24sp"
        app:layout_constraintLeft_toLeftOf="parent"
        app:layout_constraintRight_toRightOf="parent"
        app:layout_constraintTop_toTopOf="parent" />

    <androidx.recyclerview.widget.RecyclerView
        android:id="@+id/recycler_view"
        android:layout_width="match_parent"
```

```
          android:layout_height="wrap_content"
          app:layout_constraintTop_toBottomOf="@+id/main_label" />


</androidx.constraintlayout.widget.ConstraintLayout>
```

28. Also, update your **strings.xml** file to give your app a proper name and title:

```
<resources>
    <string name="app_name">SCA - Secret Cat Agents</string>
    <string name="item_cat_photo">Cat photo</string>
    <string name="main_title">Our Agents</string>
</resources>
```

29. Run your app. It should look like this:

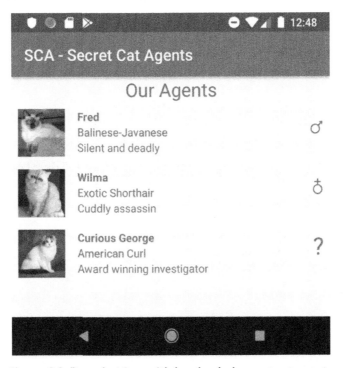

Figure 6.8: RecyclerView with hardcoded secret cat agents

As you can see, **RecyclerView** now has content, and your app is starting to take shape. Note how the same layout is used to present different items based on the data bound to each instance. As you would expect, if you added enough items for them to go off-screen, scrolling works. Next, we'll look into allowing the user to interact with the items inside our **RecyclerView**.

RESPONDING TO CLICKS IN RECYCLERVIEW

What if we want to let our users select an item from the presented list? To achieve that, we need to communicate clicks back to our app.

The first step in implementing click interaction is to capture clicks on items at the **ViewHolder** level.

To maintain separation between our view holder and the adapter, we define a nested **OnClickListener** interface in our view holder. We choose to define the interface within the view holder because they are tightly coupled. The interface will, in our case, have only one function. The purpose of this function is to inform the owner of the view holder about the clicks. The owner of a view holder is usually a Fragment or an Activity. Since we know that a view holder can be reused, we know that it can be challenging to define it at construction time in a way that would tell us which item was clicked (since that item will change over time with reuse). We work around that by passing the currently presented item back to the owner of the view holder on clicking. This means our interface would look like this:

```
interface OnClickListener {
    fun onClick(catData: CatUiModel)
}
```

We will also add this listener as a parameter to our **ViewHolder** constructor:

```
class CatViewHolder(
    containerView: View,
    private val imageLoader: ImageLoader,
    private val onClickListener: OnClickListener
) : ViewHolder(containerView) {
    .
    .
    .
}
```

It will be used like this:

```
containerView.setOnClickListener { onClickListener.onClick(catData) }
```

Now, we want our adapter to pass in a listener. In turn, that listener will be responsible for informing the owner of the adapter of the click. This means our adapter, too, would need a nested listener interface, quite similar to the one we implemented in our view holder.

While this seems like duplication that can be avoided by reusing the same listener, that is not a great idea, as it leads to tight coupling between the view holder and the adapter through the listener. What happens when you want your adapter to also report other events through the listener? You would have to handle those events coming from the view holder, even though they would not actually be implemented in the view holder.

Finally, to handle the click event and show a dialog, we define a listener in our activity and pass it to our adapter. We set that listener to show a dialog on clicking. In an MVVM implementation, you would be notifying **ViewModel** of the click at this point instead. **ViewModel** would then update its state, telling the view (our activity) that it should display the dialog.

EXERCISE 6.03: RESPONDING TO CLICKS

Your app already shows the user a list of secret cat agents. It is time to allow your user to choose a secret cat agent by clicking on its view. Click events are delegates from the view holder to the adapter to the activity, as shown in *Figure 6.9*:

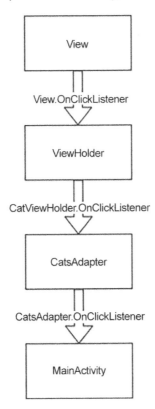

Figure 6.9: The flow of click events

The following are the steps that you need to follow to complete this exercise:

1. Open your **CatViewHolder.kt** file. Add a nested interface to it right before the final closing curly bracket:

```
interface OnClickListener {
    fun onClick(catData: CatUiModel)
}
```

This will be the interface a listener would have to implement in order to register for click events on individual cat items.

2. Update the **CatViewHolder** constructor to accept **OnClickListener** and make containerView accessible:

```
class CatViewHolder(
    private val containerView: View,
    private val imageLoader: ImageLoader,
    private val onClickListener: OnClickListener
) : ViewHolder(containerView) {
```

Now, when constructing a **CatViewHolder** constructor, you also register for clicks on item views.

3. At the top of your **bindData(CatUiModel)** function, add the following to intercept clicks and report them to the provided listener:

```
containerView.setOnClickListener { onClickListener.onClick(catData) }
```

4. Now, open your **CatsAdapter.kt** file. Add this nested interface right before the final closing curly bracket:

```
interface OnClickListener {
    fun onItemClick(catData: CatUiModel)
}
```

This defines the interface that listeners would have to implement to receive item click events from the adapter.

5. Update the **CatsAdapter** constructor to accept a call implementing the **OnClickListener** adapter you just defined:

```
class CatsAdapter(
    private val layoutInflater: LayoutInflater,
    private val imageLoader: ImageLoader,
```

```
        private val onClickListener: OnClickListener
) : RecyclerView.Adapter<CatViewHolder>() {
```

6. In **onCreateViewHolder(ViewGroup, Int)**, update the creation of the view holder, as follows:

```
        return CatViewHolder(view, imageLoader, object :
            CatViewHolder.OnClickListener {
                override fun onClick(catData: CatUiModel) =
                    onClickListener.onItemClick(catData)
        })
```

This will add an anonymous class that delegates **ViewHolder** click events to the adapter listener.

7. Finally, open your **MainActivity.kt** file. Update your **catsAdapter** construction as follows to provide the required dependencies to the adapter in the form of an anonymous listener handling click events by showing a dialog:

```
private val catsAdapter by lazy {
    CatsAdapter(
        layoutInflater,
        GlideImageLoader(this),
        object : CatsAdapter.OnClickListener {
        override fun onClick(catData: CatUiModel) =
            onClickListener.onItemClick(catData)
        }
    )
}
```

8. Add the following function right before the final closing curly bracket:

```
private fun showSelectionDialog(catData: CatUiModel) {
    AlertDialog.Builder(this)
        .setTitle("Agent Selected")
        .setMessage("You have selected agent ${catData.name}")
        .setPositiveButton("OK") { _, _ -> }
        .show()
}
```

This function will show a dialog with the name of the cat whose data was passed in.

9. Make sure to import the right version of **AlertDialog**, which is **androidx. appcompat.app.AlertDialog**, not **android.app.AlertDialog**. This is usually a better choice to support backward compatibility.

10. Run your app. Clicking on one of the cats should now show a dialog:

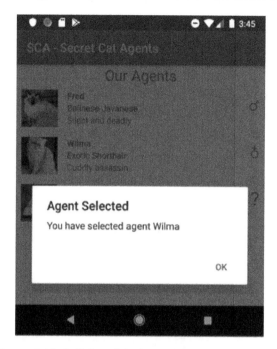

Figure 6.10: A dialog showing an agent was selected

Try clicking the different items and note the different messages presented. You now know how to respond to users clicking on items inside your **RecyclerView**. Next, we will look at how we can support different item types in our lists.

SUPPORTING DIFFERENT ITEM TYPES

In the previous sections, we learned how to handle a list of items of a single type (in our case, all our items were **CatUiModel**). What happens if you want to support more than one type of item? A good example of this would be having group titles within our list.

Let's say that instead of getting a list of cats, we instead get a list containing happy cats and sad cats. Each of the two groups of cats is preceded by a title of the corresponding group. Instead of a list of **CatUiModel** instances, our list would now contain **ListItem** instances. **ListItem** might look like this:

```
sealed class ListItem {
    data class Group(val name: String) : ListItem()
    data class Cat(val data: CatUiModel) : ListItem()
}
```

Our list of items may look like this:

```
listOf(
    ListItem.Group("Happy Cats"),
    ListItem.Cat(
        CatUiModel(
            Gender.Female,
            CatBreed.AmericanCurl,
            "Kitty",
            "Kitty is warm and fuzzy.",
            "https://cdn2.thecatapi.com/images/..."
        )
    ),
    ListItem.Cat(
        CatUiModel(
            Gender.Male,
            CatBreed.ExoticShorthair,
            "Joey",
            "Loves to cuddle.",
            "https://cdn2.thecatapi.com/images/..."
        )
    ),
    ListItem.Group("Sad Cats"),
    ListItem.Cat(
        CatUiModel(
            Gender.Unknown,
            CatBreed.AmericanCurl,
            "Ginger",
            "Just not in the mood.",
            "https://cdn2.thecatapi.com/images/..."
        )
    ),
    ListItem.Cat(
        CatUiModel(
            Gender.Female,
            CatBreed.ExoticShorthair,
            "Butters",
            "Sleeps most of the time.",
```

```
                        "https://cdn2.thecatapi.com/images/..."
            )
        )
    )
```

In this case, having just one layout type will not do. Luckily, as you may have noticed in our earlier exercises, **RecyclerView.Adapter** provides us with a mechanism to handle this (remember the **viewType** parameter used in the **onCreateViewHolder(ViewGroup, Int)** function?).

To help the adapter determine which view type is needed for each item, we override its **getItemViewType(Int)** function. An example of an implementation that would do the trick for us is the following:

```
override fun getItemViewType(position: Int) = when (listData[position]) {
    is ListItem.Group -> VIEW_TYPE_GROUP
    is ListItem.Cat -> VIEW_TYPE_CAT
}
```

Here, **VIEW_TYPE_GROUP** and **VIEW_TYPE_CAT** are defined as follows:

```
private const val VIEW_TYPE_GROUP = 0
private const val VIEW_TYPE_CAT = 1
```

This implementation maps the data type at a given position to a constant value representing one of our known layout types. In our case, we know of titles and cats, thus the two types. The values we use can be any integer values, as they're passed back to us as is in the **onCreateViewHolder(ViewGroup, Int)** function. All we need to do is make sure not to repeat the same value more than once.

Now that we have told the adapter which view types are needed and where, we also need to tell it which view holder to use for each view type. This is done by implementing the **onCreateViewHolder(ViewGroup, Int)** function:

```
override fun onCreateViewHolder(parent: ViewGroup, viewType: Int) =
    when (viewType) {
        VIEW_TYPE_GROUP -> {
            val view = layoutInflater.inflate(R.layout.item_title,
                parent, false)
            GroupViewHolder(view)
        }
        VIEW_TYPE_CAT -> {
            val view = layoutInflater.inflate(R.layout.item_cat, parent, false)
            CatViewHolder(view, imageLoader, object :
```

```
            CatViewHolder.OnClickListener {
                override fun onClick(catData: CatUiModel) =
                    onClickListener.onItemClick(catData)
        })
    }
    else -> throw IllegalArgumentException("Unknown view type requested:
        $viewType")
}
```

Unlike the earlier implementations of this function, we now take the value of **viewType** into account.

As we now know, **viewType** is expected to be one of the values we returned from **getItemViewType(Int)**.

For each of these values (**VIEW_TYPE_GROUP** and **VIEW_TYPE_CAT**), we inflate the corresponding layout and construct a suitable view holder. Note that we never expect to receive any other value, and so throw an exception if such a value is encountered. Depending on your needs, you could instead return a default view holder with a layout showing an error or nothing at all. It may also be a good idea to log such values to allow you to investigate why you received them and decide how to handle them.

For our title layout, a simple **TextView** may be sufficient. The **item_cat.xml** layout can remain as is.

Now onto the view holder. We need to create a view holder for the title. This means we will now have two different view holders. However, our adapter only supports one adapter type. The easiest solution is to define a common view holder that both **GroupViewHolder** and **CatViewHolder** will extend. Let's call it **ListItemViewHolder**. The **ListItemViewHolder** class can be abstract, as we never intend to use it directly. To make it easy to bind data, we can also introduce a function in our abstract view holder—**abstract fun bindData(listItem: ListItemUiModel)**. Our concrete implementations can expect to receive a specific type, and so we can add the following lines to both **GroupViewHolder** and **CatViewHolder**, respectively:

```
require(listItem is ListItemUiModel.Cat) {
    "Expected ListItemUiModel.Cat"
}
```

We can also add the following:

```
require(listItem is ListItemUiModel.Cat) { "Expected ListItemUiModel.Cat"
}
```

Specifically, in **CatViewHolder**, thanks to some Kotlin magic, we can then use **define val catData = listItem.data** and leave the rest of the class unchanged.

Having made those changes, we can now expect to see the **Happy Cats** and **Sad Cats** group titles, each followed by the relevant cats.

EXERCISE 6.04: ADDING TITLES TO RECYCLERVIEW

We now want to be able to present our secret cat agents in two groups: active agents that are available for us to deploy to the field, and sleeper agents, which cannot currently be deployed. We will do that by adding a title above the active agents and another above the sleeper agents:

1. Under **com.example.myrecyclerviewapp.model**, create a new Kotlin file called **ListItemUiModel**.

2. Add the following to the **ListItemUiModel.kt** file, defining our two data types—titles and cats:

```
sealed class ListItemUiModel {
    data class Title(val title: String) : ListItemUiModel()
    data class Cat(val data: CatUiModel) : ListItemUiModel()
}
```

3. Create a new Kotlin file in **com.example.myrecyclerviewapp** named **ListItemViewHolder**. This will be our base view holder.

4. Populate the **ListItemViewHolder.kt** file with the following:

```
abstract class ListItemViewHolder(
    containerView: View
) : RecyclerView.ViewHolder(containerView) {
    abstract fun bindData(listItem: ListItemUiModel)
}
```

5. Open the **CatViewHolder.kt** file.

6. Make **CatViewHolder** extend **ListItemViewHolder**:

```
class CatViewHolder(
   ...
) : ListItemViewHolder(containerView) {
```

7. Replace the **bindData(CatUiModel)** parameter with **ListItemUiModel** and make it override the **ListItemViewHolder** abstract function:

```
override fun bindData(listItem: ListItemUiModel)
```

8. Add the following two lines to the top of the **bindData(ListItemUiModel)** function to enforce casting **ListItemUiModel** to **ListItemUiModel.Cat** and to fetch the cat data from it:

```
require(listItem is ListItemUiModel.Cat) {
   "Expected ListItemUiModel.Cat" }
val catData = listItem.data
```

Leave the rest of the file untouched.

9. Create a new layout file. Name your layout **item_title**.

10. Replace the default content of the newly created **item_title.xml** file with the following:

```
<?xml version="1.0" encoding="utf-8"?>
<TextView xmlns:android="http://schemas.android.com/apk/res/android"
    xmlns:app="http://schemas.android.com/apk/res-auto"
    xmlns:tools="http://schemas.android.com/tools"
    android:id="@+id/item_title_title"
    android:layout_width="match_parent"
    android:layout_height="wrap_content"
    android:padding="8dp"
    android:textSize="16sp"
    android:textStyle="bold"
    app:layout_constraintStart_toStartOf="parent"
    app:layout_constraintTop_toTopOf="parent"
    tools:text="Sleeper Agents" />
```

This new layout, containing only a **TextView** with a 16sp-sized bold font, will host our titles:

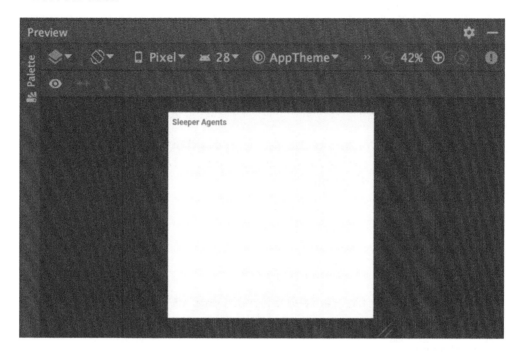

Figure 6.11: Preview of the item_title.xml layout

11. Implement **TitleViewHolder** in a new file with the same name under **com. example.myrecyclerviewapp**:

```
class TitleViewHolder(
    containerView: View
) : ListItemViewHolder(containerView) {
    private val titleView: TextView
        by lazy { containerView
            .findViewById(R.id.item_title_title) }

    override fun bindData(listItem: ListItemUiModel) {
        require(listItem is ListItemUiModel.Title) {
            "Expected ListItemUiModel.Title"
        }
        titleView.text = listItem.title
    }
}
```

This is very similar to **CatViewHolder**, but since we only set the text on **TextView**, it is also much simpler.

12. Now, to make things tidier, select **CatViewHolder**, **ListItemViewHolder**, and **TitleViewHolder**.

13. Move all the files to a new namespace: right-click on one of the files, and then select **Refactor | Move** (or press *F6*).

14. Append **/viewholder** to the prefilled **To directory** field. Leave **Search references** and **Update package directive (Kotlin files)** checked and **Open moved files in editor** unchecked. Click **OK**.

15. Open the **CatsAdapter.kt** file.

16. Now, rename **CatsAdapter** to **ListItemsAdapter**. It is important to maintain the naming of variables, functions, and classes to reflect their actual usage to avoid future confusion. Right-click on the **CatsAdapter** class name in the code window, then select **Refactor | Rename** (or *Shift + F6*).

17. When **CatsAdapter** is highlighted, type **ListItemsAdapter** and press *Enter*.

18. Change the adapter generic type to **ListItemViewHolder**:

```
class ListItemsAdapter(
    ...
) : RecyclerView.Adapter<ListItemViewHolder>() {
```

19. Update **listData** and **setData(List<CatUiModel>)** to handle **ListItemUiModel** instead:

```
private val listData = mutableListOf<ListItemUiModel>()

fun setData(listData: List<ListItemUiModel>) {
    this.listData.clear()
    this.listData.addAll(listData)
    notifyDataSetChanged()
}
```

20. Update **onBindViewHolder(CatViewHolder)** to comply with the adapter contract change:

```
override fun onBindViewHolder(holder: ListItemViewHolder,
    position: Int) {
        holder.bindData(listData[position])
}
```

21. At the top of the file, after the imports and before the class definition, add the view type constants:

```
private const val VIEW_TYPE_TITLE = 0
private const val VIEW_TYPE_CAT = 1
```

22. Implement **getItemViewType(Int)** like so:

```
override fun getItemViewType(position: Int) =
    when (listData[position]) {
        is ListItemUiModel.Title -> VIEW_TYPE_TITLE
        is ListItemUiModel.Cat -> VIEW_TYPE_CAT
    }
```

23. Lastly, change your **onCreateViewHolder(ViewGroup, Int)** implementation, as follows:

```
override fun onCreateViewHolder(parent: ViewGroup,
    viewType: Int) = when (viewType) {
    VIEW_TYPE_TITLE -> {
        val view = layoutInflater.inflate(R.layout.item_title,
            parent, false)
        TitleViewHolder(view)
    }
    VIEW_TYPE_CAT -> {
        val view = layoutInflater.inflate(R.layout.item_cat,
            parent, false)
        CatViewHolder(
            view,
            imageLoader,
            object : CatViewHolder.OnClickListener {
                override fun onClick(catData: CatUiModel) =
                    onClickListener.onItemClick(catData)
```

```
                    })
              }
              else -> throw IllegalArgumentException("Unknown view type
                  requested: $viewType")
         }
```

24. Update **MainActivity** to populate the adapter with appropriate data, replacing the previous **catsAdapter.setData(List<CatUiModel>)** call. (Please note that the code below has been truncated for space. Refer to the link below to access the full code that you need to add.)

MainActivity.kt

```
32      listItemsAdapter.setData(
33          listOf(
34              ListItemUiModel.Title("Sleeper Agents"),
35              ListItemUiModel.Cat(
36                  CatUiModel(
37                      Gender.Male,
38                      CatBreed.ExoticShorthair,
39                      "Garvey",
40                      "Garvey is as a lazy, fat, and cynical orange cat.",
41                      "https://cdn2.thecatapi.com/images/FZpeiLi4n.jpg"
42                  )
43              ),
44              ListItemUiModel.Cat(
45                  CatUiModel(
46                      Gender.Unknown,
47                      CatBreed.AmericanCurl,
48                      "Curious George",
49                      "Award winning investigator",
50                      "https://cdn2.thecatapi.com/images/vJB8rwfdX.jpg"
51                  )
52              ),
53              ListItemUiModel.Title("Active Agents"),
```

The complete code for this step can be found at http://packt.live/3icCrSt.

25. Since **catsAdapter** is no longer holding **CatsAdapter** but **ListItemsAdapter**, rename it accordingly. Name it **listItemsAdapter**.

26. Run the app. You should see something similar to the following:

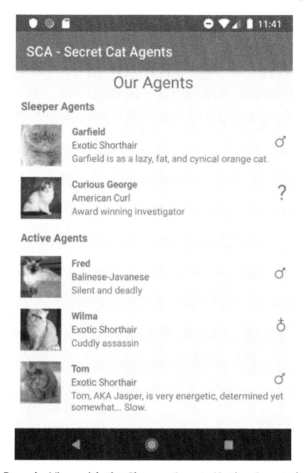

Figure 6.12: RecyclerView with the Sleeper Agents/Active Agents header views

As you can see, we now have titles above our two agent groups. Unlike the **Our Agents** title, these titles will scroll with our content. Next, we will learn how to swipe an item to remove it from **RecyclerView**.

SWIPING TO REMOVE ITEMS

In the previous sections, we learned how to present different view types. However, up until now, we have worked with a fixed list of items. What if you want to be able to remove items from the list? There are a few common mechanisms to achieve that—fixed delete buttons, swipe to delete, and long-click to select then a "click to delete" button, to name a few. In this section, we will focus on the "swipe to delete" approach.

Let's start by adding the deletion functionality to our adapter. To tell the adapter to remove an item, we need to indicate which item we want to remove. The simplest way to achieve this is by providing the position of the item. In our implementation, this will directly correlate to the position of the item in our **listData** list. So, our **removeItem(Int)** function should look like this:

```
fun removeItem(position: Int) {
    listData.removeAt(position)
    notifyItemRemoved(position)
}
```

> **NOTE**
>
> Just like when setting data, we need to notify **RecyclerView** that the dataset has changed—in this case, an item was removed.

Next, we need to define the swipe gesture detection. This is done by utilizing **ItemTouchHelper**. Now, **ItemTouchHelper** handles certain touch events, namely dragging and swiping, by reporting them to us via a callback. We handle these callbacks by implementing **ItemTouchHelper.Callback**. Also, **RecyclerView** provides **ItemTouchHelper.SimpleCallback**, which takes away the writing of a lot of boilerplate code.

We want to respond to swipe gestures but ignore move gestures. More specifically, we want to respond to swipes to the right. Moving is used to reorder items, which is beyond the scope of this chapter. So, our implementation of **SwipToDeleteCallback** will look as follows:

```
inner class SwipeToDeleteCallback :
    ItemTouchHelper.SimpleCallback(0, ItemTouchHelper.RIGHT) {
    override fun onMove(
        recyclerView: RecyclerView,
        viewHolder: RecyclerView.ViewHolder,
        target: RecyclerView.ViewHolder
    ): Boolean = false

    override fun getMovementFlags(
        recyclerView: RecyclerView,
        viewHolder: RecyclerView.ViewHolder
    ) = if (viewHolder is CatViewHolder) {
```

```
        makeMovementFlags(
            ItemTouchHelper.ACTION_STATE_IDLE,
            ItemTouchHelper.RIGHT
        ) or makeMovementFlags(
            ItemTouchHelper.ACTION_STATE_SWIPE,
            ItemTouchHelper.RIGHT
        )
    } else {
        0
    }
}

override fun onSwiped(viewHolder: RecyclerView.ViewHolder,
    direction: Int) {
    val position = viewHolder.adapterPosition
    removeItem(position)
}
}
```

Because our implementation is tightly coupled to our adapter and its view types, we can comfortably define it as an inner class. The benefit we gain is the ability to directly call methods on the adapter.

As you can see, we return **false** from the **onMove(RecyclerView, ViewHolder, ViewHolder)** function. This means we ignore move events.

Next, we need to tell **ItemTouchHelper** which items can be swiped. We achieve this by overriding **getMovementFlags(RecyclerView, ViewHolder)**. This function is called when a user is about to start a drag or swipe gesture. **ItemTouchHelper** expects us to return the valid gestures for the provided view holder. We check the **ViewHolder** class, and if it is **CatViewHolder**, we want to allow swiping—otherwise, we do not. We use **makeMovementFlags(Int, Int)**, which is a helper function used to construct flags in a way that **ItemTouchHelper** can decipher them. Note that we define rules for **ACTION_STATE_IDLE**, which is the starting state of a gesture, thus allowing a gesture to start from the left or the right. We then combine it (using **or**) with the **ACTION_STATE_SWIPE** flags, allowing the ongoing gesture to swipe left or right. Returning **0** means neither swiping nor moving will occur for the provided view holder.

Once a swipe action is completed, **onSwiped(ViewHolder, Int)** is called. We then obtain the position from the passed-in view holder by calling **adapterPosition**. Now, **adapterPosition** is important because it is the only reliable way to obtain the real position of the item presented by the view holder.

With the correct position, we can remove the item by calling **removeItem(Int)** on the adapter.

To expose our newly created **SwipeToDeleteCallback** implementation, we define a read-only variable within our adapter, namely **swipeToDeleteCallback**, and set it to a new instance of **SwipeToDeleteCallback**.

Finally, to plug our **callback** mechanism to **RecyclerView**, we need to construct a new **ItemTouchHelper** and attach it to our **RecyclerView**. We should do this when setting up our **RecyclerView**, which we do in the **onCreate(Bundle?)** function of our main activity. This is how the creation and attaching will look:

```
val itemTouchHelper = ItemTouchHelper(listItemsAdapter.
swipeToDeleteCallback)
itemTouchHelper.attachToRecyclerView(recyclerView)
```

We can now swipe items to remove them from the list. Note how our titles cannot be swiped, just as we intended.

You may have noticed a small glitch: the last item is cut off as it animates up. This is happening because **RecyclerView** shrinks to accommodate the new (smaller) number of items before the animation starts. A quick fix to this would be to fix the height of our **RecyclerView** by confining its bottom to the bottom of its parent.

EXERCISE 6.05: ADDING SWIPE TO DELETE FUNCTIONALITY

We previously added **RecyclerView** to our app and then added items of different types to it. We will now allow users to delete some items (we want to let the users remove secret cat agents, but not titles) by swiping them left or right:

1. To add item removal functionality to our adapter, add the following function to **ListItemsAdapter** right after the **setData(List<ListItemUiModel>)** function:

```
fun removeItem(position: Int) {
    listData.removeAt(position)
    notifyItemRemoved(position)
}
```

2. Next, right before the closing curly bracket of your **ListItemsAdapter** class, add the following **callback** implementation to handle the user swiping a cat agent left or right:

```
inner class SwipeToDeleteCallback :
    ItemTouchHelper.SimpleCallback(0, ItemTouchHelper.LEFT or
        ItemTouchHelper.RIGHT) {
    override fun onMove(
        recyclerView: RecyclerView,
        viewHolder: RecyclerView.ViewHolder,
        target: RecyclerView.ViewHolder
    ): Boolean = false

    override fun getMovementFlags(
        recyclerView: RecyclerView,
        viewHolder: RecyclerView.ViewHolder
    ) = if (viewHolder is CatViewHolder) {
        makeMovementFlags(
            ItemTouchHelper.ACTION_STATE_IDLE,
            ItemTouchHelper.LEFT or ItemTouchHelper.RIGHT
        ) or makeMovementFlags(
            ItemTouchHelper.ACTION_STATE_SWIPE,
            ItemTouchHelper.LEFT or ItemTouchHelper.RIGHT
        )
    } else {
        0
    }

    override fun onSwiped(viewHolder: RecyclerView.ViewHolder,
        direction: Int) {
        val position = viewHolder.adapterPosition
        removeItem(position)
    }
}
```

We have implemented an **ItemTouchHelper.SimpleCallback** instance, passing in the directions we were interested in—**LEFT** and **RIGHT**. Joining the values is achieved by using the **or** Boolean operator.

We have overridden the **getMovementFlags** function to make sure we have only handled swiping on a cat agent view, not a title. Creating flags for both **ItemTouchHelper.ACTION_STATE_SWIPE** and **ItemTouchHelper. ACTION_STATE_IDLE** allows us to intercept both swipe and release events, respectively.

Once a swipe is completed (the user has lifted their finger from the screen), **onSwiped** will be called, and in response, we remove the item at the position provided by the dragged view holder.

3. At the top of your adapter, expose an instance of the **SwipeToDeleteCallback** class you just created:

```
class ListItemsAdapter(

    ...

) : RecyclerView.Adapter<ListItemViewHolder>() {
    val swipeToDeleteCallback = SwipeToDeleteCallback()
```

4. Lastly, tie it all together by implementing **ItemViewHelper** and attaching it to our **RecyclerView**. Add the following code to the **onCreate(Bundle?)** function of your **MainActivity** file right after assigning the layout manager to your adapter:

```
recyclerView.layoutManager = ...
val itemTouchHelper = ItemTouchHelper(listItemsAdapter
    .swipeToDeleteCallback)
itemTouchHelper.attachToRecyclerView(recyclerView)
```

5. To address the small visual glitch you would get when items are removed, scale **RecyclerView** to fit the screen by updating the code in **activity_main. xml**, as follows. The changes are in **RecyclerView** tag, right before the **app:layout_constraintTop_toBottomOf** attribute:

```
android:layout_height="0dp"
app:layout_constraintBottom_toBottomOf="parent"
app:layout_constraintTop_toBottomOf="@+id/main_label" />
```

Note that there are two changes: we added a constraint of the bottom of the view to the bottom of the parent, and we set the layout height to **0dp**. The latter change tells our app to calculate the height of **RecyclerView** based on its constraints:

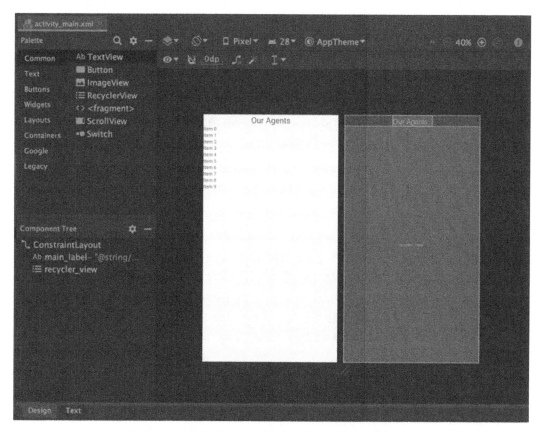

Figure 6.13: RecyclerView taking the full height of the layout

6. Run your app. You should now be able to swipe secret cat agents left or right to remove them from the list. Note that **RecyclerView** handles the collapsing animation for us:

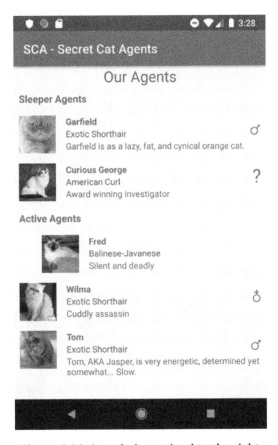

Figure 6.14: A cat being swiped to the right

Note how even though titles are item views, they cannot be swiped. You have implemented a callback for swiping gestures that distinguishes between different item types and responds to a swipe by deleting the swiped item. Now we know how to remove items interactively. Next, we will learn how to add new items as well.

ADDING ITEMS INTERACTIVELY

We have just learned how to remove items interactively. What about adding new items? Let's look into it.

Similar to the way we implemented the removal of items, we start by adding a function to our adapter:

```
fun addItem(position: Int, item: ListItemUiModel) {
    listData.add(position, item)
    notifyItemInserted(position)
}
```

You will notice that the implementation is very similar to the **removeItem(Int)** function we implemented earlier. This time, we also receive an item to add and a position to add it. We then add it to our **listData** list and notify **RecyclerView** that we added an item in the requested position.

To trigger a call to **addItem(Int, ListItemUiModel)**, we could add a button to our main activity layout. This button could be as follows:

```
<Button
    android:id="@+id/main_add_item_button"
    android:layout_width="match_parent"
    android:layout_height="wrap_content"
    android:text="Add A Cat"
    app:layout_constraintBottom_toBottomOf="parent" />
```

The app will now look like this:

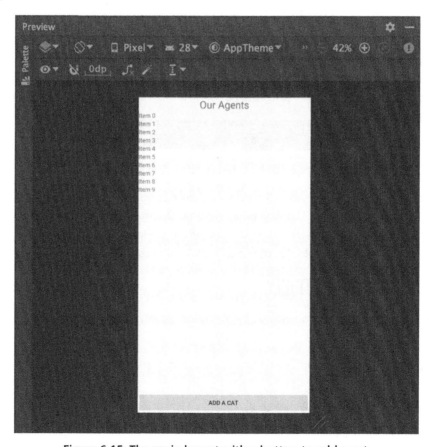

Figure 6.15: The main layout with a button to add a cat

Don't forget to update your **RecyclerView** so that its bottom will be constrained to the top of this button. Otherwise, the button and **RecyclerView** will overlap.

In a production app, you could add a rationale around what a new item would be. For example, you could have a form for the user to fill in different details. For the sake of simplicity, in our example, we will always add the same dummy item—an anonymous female secret cat agent.

To add the item, we set **OnClickListener** on our button:

```
addItemButton.setOnClickListener {
    listItemsAdapter.addItem(
        1,
        ListItemUiModel.Cat(
            CatUiModel(
                Gender.Female,
                CatBreed.BalineseJavanese,
                "Anonymous",
                "Unknown",
                "https://cdn2.thecatapi.com/images/zJkeHza2K.jpg"
            )
        )
    )
}
```

And that is it. We add the item at position 1 so that it is added right below our first title, which is the item at position 0. In a production app, you could have logic to determine the correct place to insert an item. It could be below the relevant title or always be added at the top, bottom, or in the correct place to preserve some existing order.

We can now run the app. We will now have a new **Add A Cat** button. Every time we click the button, an anonymous secret cat agent will be added to **RecyclerView**. The newly added cats can be swiped away to be removed, just like the hardcoded cats before them.

EXERCISE 6.06: IMPLEMENTING AN "ADD A CAT" BUTTON

Having implemented a mechanism to remove items, it is time we implemented a mechanism to add items:

1. Add a function to **ListItemsAdapter** to support adding items. Add it below the **removeItem(Int)** function:

```
fun addItem(position: Int, item: ListItemUiModel) {
    listData.add(position, item)
    notifyItemInserted(position)
}
```

2. Add a button to **activity_main.xml**, right after **RecyclerView** tag:

```
<Button
    android:id="@+id/main_add_item_button"
    android:layout_width="match_parent"
    android:layout_height="wrap_content"
    android:text="Add A Cat"
    app:layout_constraintBottom_toBottomOf="parent" />
```

3. You will notice that **android:text="Add A Cat"** is highlighted. If you hover your mouse over it, you will see that this is because of the hardcoded string. Click on the **Add** word to place the editor cursor over it.

4. Press *Option + Enter* (iOS) or *Alt + Enter* (Windows) to show the context menu, then *Enter* again to show the **Extract Resource** dialog.

5. Name the resource **add_button_label**. Press **OK**.

6. To change the bottom constraint on **RecyclerView** so that the button and **RecyclerView** do not overlap, within your **RecyclerView** tag, locate the following:

```
app:layout_constraintBottom_toBottomOf="parent"
```

Replace it with the following line of code:

```
app:layout_constraintBottom_toTopOf="@+id/main_add_item_button"
```

7. Add a lazy field holding a reference to the button at the top of the class, right after the definition of **recyclerView**:

```
private val addItemButton: View
    by lazy { findViewById(R.id.main_add_item_button) }
```

Notice **addItemButton** is defined as a View. This is because in our code we don't need to know the type of View to add a click listener to it. Choosing the more abstract type allows us to later change the type of the view in the layout without having to modify this code.

8. Lastly, update **MainActivity** to handle the click. Find the line that says the following:

```
itemTouchHelper.attachToRecyclerView(recyclerView)
```

Right after it, add the following:

```
addItemButton.setOnClickListener {
    listItemsAdapter.addItem(
        1,
        ListItemUiModel.Cat(
            CatUiModel(
                Gender.Female,
                CatBreed.BalineseJavanese,
                "Anonymous",
                "Unknown",
                "https://cdn2.thecatapi.com/images/zJkeHza2K.jpg"
            )
        )
    )
}
```

This will add a new item to **RecyclerView** every time the button is clicked.

9. Run the app. You should see a new button at the bottom of your app:

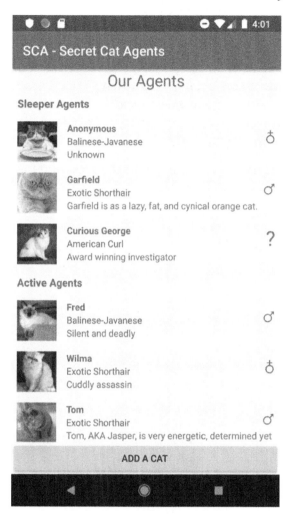

Figure 6.16: An anonymous cat is added with the click of a button

10. Try clicking it a few times. Every time you click it, a new anonymous secret cat agent is added to your **RecyclerView**. You can swipe away the newly added cats just like you could the hardcoded ones.

In this exercise, you added new items to **RecyclerView** in response to user interaction. You now know how to change the contents of **RecyclerView** at runtime. It is useful to know how to update lists at runtime because quite often, the data you are presenting to your users changes while the app is running, and you want to present your users with a fresh, up-to-date state.

ACTIVITY 6.01: MANAGING A LIST OF ITEMS

Imagine you want to develop a recipe management app. Your app would support sweet and savory recipes. Users of your app could add new sweet or savory recipes, scroll through the list of added recipes—grouped by flavor (sweet or savory)—click a recipe to get information about it, and finally, they could delete recipes by swiping them aside.

The aim of this activity is to create an app with **RecyclerView** that lists the title of recipes, grouped by flavor. **RecyclerView** will support user interaction. Each recipe will have a title, a description, and a flavor. Interactions will include clicks and swipes. A click will present the user with a dialog showing the description of the recipe. A swipe will remove the swiped recipe from the app. Finally, with two **EditText** fields (see *Chapter 3, Screens and UI*) and two buttons, the user can add a new sweet or savory recipe, respectively, with the title and description set to the values set in the **EditText** fields.

The steps to complete are as follows:

1. Create a new empty activity app.

2. Add **RecyclerView** support to the app's **build.gradle** file.

3. Add **RecyclerView**, two **EditText** fields, and two buttons to the main layout. Your layout should look something like this:

Figure 6.17: Layout with RecyclerView, two EditText fields, and two buttons

4. Add models for flavor titles and recipes, and an enum for flavor.

5. Add a layout for flavor titles.

6. Add a layout for recipe titles.

7. Add view holders for flavor titles and recipe titles, as well as an adapter.

8. Add click listeners to show a dialog with recipe descriptions.

9. Update **MainActivity** to construct the new adapter and hook up the buttons for adding new savory and sweet recipes. Make sure the form is cleared after the recipe is added.

10. Add a swipe helper to remove items.

The final output will be as follows:

Figure 6.18: The Recipe Book app

> **NOTE**
>
> The solution to this activity can be found at: http://packt.live/3sKj1cp

SUMMARY

In this chapter, we learned how to add **RecyclerView** to our project. We also learned how to add it to our layout and how to populate it with items. We went through adding different item types, which is particularly useful for titles. We covered interaction with **RecyclerView**: responding to clicks on individual items and responding to swipe gestures. Lastly, we learned how to dynamically add and remove items to and from **RecyclerView**. The world of **RecyclerView** is very rich, and we have only scratched the surface. Going further would be beyond the scope of this book. However, it is strongly recommended that you investigate it on your own so that you can have carousels, designed dividers, and fancier swipe effects in your apps. You could start your exploration here: https://awesomeopensource.com/projects/recyclerview-adapter.

In the next chapter, we will look into requesting special permissions on behalf of our app to enable performing certain tasks, such as accessing the user's contacts list or their microphone. We will also look into using Google's Maps API and accessing the user's physical location.

7

ANDROID PERMISSIONS AND GOOGLE MAPS

OVERVIEW

This chapter will provide you with knowledge of how to request and obtain app permissions in Android. You will gain a solid understanding of how to include local and global interactive maps in your app, as well as how to request permissions to use device features that provide richer functionality by using the Google Maps API.

By the end of the chapter, you will be able to create permission requests for your app and handle missing permissions.

INTRODUCTION

In the previous chapter, we learned how to present data in lists using `RecyclerView`. We used that knowledge to present the user with a list of Secret Cat Agents. In this chapter, we will learn how to find the user's location on the map, and how to deploy cat agents to the field by selecting locations on the map.

First, we will look into the Android permissions system. Many Android features are not immediately available to us. To protect the user, these features are gated behind a permission system. For us to access those features, we have to ask the user to allow us to do so. Some such features include, but are not limited to, obtaining the user's location, accessing the user's contacts, accessing their camera, and establishing a Bluetooth connection. Different Android versions enforce different permission rules. When Android 6 (Marshmallow) was introduced in 2015, for example, a number of permissions were deemed insecure (those you could silently obtain on installation) and became runtime permissions.

We will then look at the Google Maps API. This API allows us to present the user with a map of any desired location, add data to that map, and let the user interact with the map. It also lets you show points of interest and render a street view of supported locations, though we will not go into these features in this book.

REQUESTING PERMISSIONS FROM THE USER

Our app might want to implement certain features that are deemed to be dangerous by Google. This usually means access to those features could risk the user's privacy. Those permissions may, for example, allow you to read users' messages or determine their current location.

Depending on the particular permission and the target Android API level we are developing, we may need to request that permission from the user. If the device is running on Android 6 (Marshmallow, or API level 23), and the target API of our app is 23 or higher, which it almost certainly will be, as most devices by now will run newer versions of Android, there will be no user notifications alerting the user of any permissions requested by the app at install time. Instead, our app must ask the user to grant it those permissions at runtime.

When we request a permission, the user sees a dialog much like the one shown in the following screenshot:

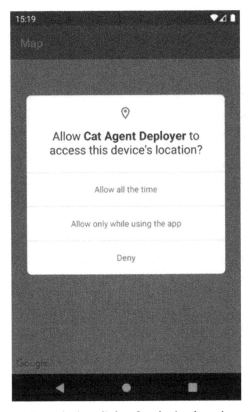

Figure 7.1 Permission dialog for device location access

> **NOTE**
>
> For a full list of permissions and their protection level, see here:
> https://developer.android.com/reference/android/Manifest.permission

When we intend to use a permission, we must include that permission in our manifest file. A manifest with the **SEND_SMS** permission would look something like the following snippet:

```
<manifest xmlns:android="http://schemas.android.com/apk/res/android"
        package="com.example.snazzyapp">
    <uses-permission android:name="android.permission.SEND_SMS"/>
    <application ...>
...
    </application>
</manifest>
```

Safe permissions (or normal permissions, as Google refers to them) would get automatically granted to the user. Dangerous ones, however, would only be granted if explicitly approved by the user. If we fail to request permission from the user and try to execute an action that requires that permission, the result would be the action not running at best, and our app crashing at worst.

To ask the user for permission, we should first check whether the user has already granted us that permission.

If the user has not yet granted us permission, we may need to check whether a rationale dialog should be shown prior to the permission request. This depends on how obvious the justification for the request would be to the user. For example, if a camera app requests permission to access the camera, we can safely assume the reason would be clear to the user. However, some cases may not be as clear to the user, especially if the user is not tech-savvy. In those cases, we may have to justify the request to the user. Google provides us with a function called **shouldShowRequestPermissionRationale(Activity, String)** for this purpose. Under the hood, this function checks whether the user has previously denied the permission, but also whether the user has selected **Don't ask again** in the permission request dialog. The idea is to give us an opportunity to justify our request to the user for permission prior to requesting it, thus increasing the likelihood of them approving it.

Once we determine whether a permission rationale should be presented to the user, or whether the user should accept our rationale or no rationale was required, we can proceed to request the permission.

Let's see how we can request a permission.

The **Activity** class from which we request the permission must implement the **OnRequestPermissionsResultCallback** interface. This is because once the user is granted (or denied) the permission, the **onRequestPermissionsResult(Int, Array<String>, IntArray)** function will be called. The **FragmentActivity** class, which **AppCompatActivity** extends, already implements this interface, so we only have to override the **onRequestPermissionsResult** function to process the response of the user to the permission request. The following is an example of an **Activity** class requesting the **Location** permission:

```
private const val PERMISSION_CODE_REQUEST_LOCATION = 1

class MainActivity : AppCompatActivity() {
    override fun onResume() {
```

```
        . . .
        val hasLocationPermissions = getHasLocationPermission()
    }
```

When our **Activity** class resumes, we check whether we have
the location permission (**ACCESS_FINE_LOCATION**) by calling
getHasLocationPermissions():

```
    private fun getHasLocationPermission() = if (
        ContextCompat.checkSelfPermission(
            this, Manifest.permission.ACCESS_FINE_LOCATION
        ) == PackageManager.PERMISSION_GRANTED
    ) {
        true
    } else {
        if (ActivityCompat.shouldShowRequestPermissionRationale(
                this, Manifest.permission.ACCESS_FINE_LOCATION
            )
        ) {
            showPermissionRationale { requestLocationPermission() }
        } else {
            requestLocationPermission()
        }
        false
    }
```

This function first checks whether the user has already granted us the
requested permissions by calling **checkSelfPermission(Context,
String)** with the requested permission. If the user hasn't, we call
shouldShowRequestPermissionRationale(Activity, String), which
we mentioned earlier, to check whether a rationale dialog should be presented to
the user.

If showing our rationale is needed, we call **showPermissionRationale(()
-> Unit)**, passing in a lambda that will call **requestLocationPermission()**
after the user dismisses our rationale dialog. If no rationale is needed, we call
requestLocationPermission() directly:

```
    private fun showPermissionRationale(positiveAction: () -> Unit) {
        AlertDialog.Builder(this)
            .setTitle("Location permission")
```

```
        .setMessage("We need your permission to find
          your current position")
        .setPositiveButton(
            "OK"
        ) { _, _ -> positiveAction() }
        .create()
        .show()
    }
```

Our **showPermissionRationale** function simply presents the user with a dialog with a brief explanation about why we need their permission. The confirmation button will execute the positive action provided:

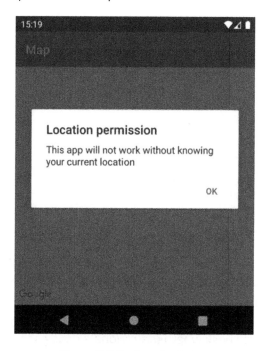

Figure 7.2 Rationale dialog

```
    private fun requestLocationPermission() {
        ActivityCompat.requestPermissions(
            this,
            arrayOf(
                Manifest.permission.ACCESS_FINE_LOCATION
            ),
            PERMISSION_CODE_REQUEST_LOCATION
        )
    }
```

Lastly, our **requestLocationPermission()** function calls
requestPermissions(Activity, Array<out String>, Int), passing
our activity an array containing the requested permission and our unique request
code. We will use this code to later identify the response as belonging to this request.

If we've requested the location permission from the user, we now need to process the
response. This is done by overriding the **onRequestPermissionsResult(Int,
Array<out String>, IntArray)** function, as shown in the following code:

```
override fun onRequestPermissionsResult(
    requestCode: Int,
    permissions: Array<out String>,
    grantResults: IntArray
) {
    super.onRequestPermissionsResult(requestCode, permissions,
      grantResults)

    when (requestCode) {
        PERMISSION_CODE_REQUEST_LOCATION -> getLastLocation()
    }
}
```

When **onRequestPermissionsResult** gets called, three values are passed in.
The first is the request code, which will be the same request code we provided when
calling **requestPermissions**. The second is the array of requested permissions.
The third is an array of results for our request. For each permission requested,
this array will contain either **PackageManager.PERMISSION_GRANTED**
or **PackageManager.PERMISSION_DENIED**.

This chapter will take us through the development of an app that shows us our
current location on a map and allows us to place a marker where we want to deploy
our Secret Cat Agent. Let's start with our first exercise.

EXERCISE 7.01: REQUESTING THE LOCATION PERMISSION

In this exercise, we will request that the user provides the location permission. We will first create a Google Maps Activity project. We will define the permission required in the manifest file. To get started, let's implement the code required to request permission from the user to access their location:

1. Start by creating a new Google Maps Activity project (**File** | **New** | **New Project** | **Google Maps Activity**). We're not using Google Maps in this exercise. However, the Google Maps Activity is still a good choice in this case. It will save you a lot of boilerplate coding in the next exercise (*Exercise 7.02*). Don't worry; it will have no impact on your current exercise. Click **Next**, as shown in the following screenshot:

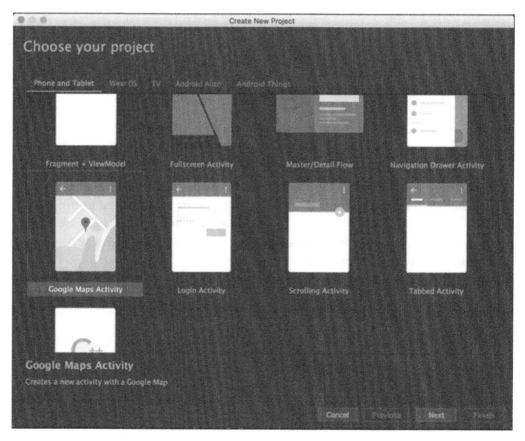

Figure 7.3: Choose your project

2. Name your application **Cat Agent Deployer**.

3. Make sure your package name is **com.example.catagentdeployer**.

4. Set the save location to where you want to save your project.

5. Leave everything else at its default values and click **Finish**.

6. Make sure you are on the **Android** view in your **Project** pane:

Figure 7.4: Android view

7. Open your **AndroidManifest.xml** file. Make sure the location permission was already added to your app:

```
<manifest xmlns:android="http://schemas.android.com/apk/res/android"
    package="com.example.catagentdeployer">


    <uses-permission
      android:name="android.permission.ACCESS_FINE_LOCATION" />


    <application ...>

        ...

    </application>


</manifest>
```

ACCESS_FINE_LOCATION is the permission you will need to obtain the user's location based on GPS in addition to the less accurate Wi-Fi and mobile data-based location information you could obtain by using the **ACCESS_COARSE_LOCATION** permission.

8. Open your **MapsActivity.kt** file. At the bottom of the **MapsActivity** class block, add an empty **getLastLocation()** function:

```
class MapsActivity : AppCompatActivity(), OnMapReadyCallback {
    ...
    private fun getLastLocation() {
        Log.d("MapsActivity", "getLastLocation() called.")
    }
}
```

This will be the function you will call when you have made sure the user has granted you the location permission.

9. Next, add the request code constant to the top of the file, between the imports and the class definition:

```
...
import com.google.android.gms.maps.model.MarkerOptions

private const val PERMISSION_CODE_REQUEST_LOCATION = 1

class MapsActivity : AppCompatActivity(), OnMapReadyCallback {
```

This will be the code we pass when we request the location permission. Whatever value we define here will be returned to us when the user has finished interacting with the request dialog by granting or denying us the permission.

10. Now add the **requestLocationPermission()** function right before the **getLastLocation()** function:

```
private fun requestLocationPermission() {
    ActivityCompat.requestPermissions(
        this,
        arrayOf(Manifest.permission.ACCESS_FINE_LOCATION),
        PERMISSION_CODE_REQUEST_LOCATION
    )
}

private fun getLastLocation() {
    ...
}
```

This function will present a standard permission request dialog to the user (as shown in the following figure), asking them to allow the app to access their location. We pass the activity, which will receive the callback (**this**), an array of the requested permissions you want the user to grant your app (**Manifest. permission.ACCESS_FINE_LOCATION**), and the **PERMISSION_CODE_ REQUEST_LOCATION** constant you defined a moment ago to associate it with the permission request:

Figure 7.5: Permission dialog

11. Override the **onRequestPermissionsResult(Int, Array<String>, IntArray)** function of your **MapsActivity** class:

```
override fun onRequestPermissionsResult(
    requestCode: Int, permissions: Array<out String>,
      grantResults: IntArray) {
        super.onRequestPermissionsResult(requestCode,
          permissions,grantResults)

    when (requestCode) {
            PERMISSION_CODE_REQUEST_LOCATION -> if (
                grantResults[0] == PackageManager.PERMISSION_GRANTED
            ) {
                getLastLocation()
            }
        }
    }
```

You should first call the super implementation (this should already be done for you as soon as you override the function). This will handle the delegation of permission response processing to child fragments where relevant.

Then, you can check the **requestCode** parameter and see if it matches the **requestCode** parameter you passed to the **requestPermissions(Activity, Array<out String>, Int)** function (**PERMISSION_CODE_REQUEST_LOCATION**). If it does, since you know you only requested one permission, you can check the first **grantResults** value. If it equals **PackageManager.PERMISSION_GRANTED**, the user has granted your app permission, and you can proceed to get their last location by calling **getLastLocation()**.

12. If the user denied your app the requested permission, you can present them with the rationale for the request. Implement the **showPermissionRationale(() -> Unit)** function right before the **requestLocationPermission()** function:

```
private fun showPermissionRationale(positiveAction: () -> Unit) {
    AlertDialog.Builder(this)
        .setTitle("Location permission")
        .setMessage("This app will not work without knowing your
            current location")
        .setPositiveButton(
            "OK"
        ) { _, _ -> positiveAction() }
        .create()
        .show()
}
```

This function will present the user with a simple alert dialog explaining the app would not work without knowing their current location, as shown in the following screenshot. Clicking **OK** will execute the provided **positiveAction** lambda:

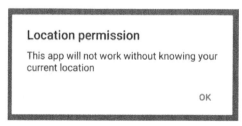

Location permission

This app will not work without knowing your current location

OK

Figure 7.6: Rationale dialog

13. Add the logic required to determine whether to show the permission request dialog or the rationale one. Create the **requestPermissionWithRationaleIfNeeded()** function right before the **showPermissionRationale(() -> Unit)** function:

```
private fun requestPermissionWithRationaleIfNeeded() = if (
    ActivityCompat.shouldShowRequestPermissionRationale(
        this, Manifest.permission.ACCESS_FINE_LOCATION
    )
) {
    showPermissionRationale {
        requestLocationPermission()
    }
} else {
    requestLocationPermission()
}
```

This function checks whether your app should display the rationale dialog. If it should, it calls **showPermissionRationale(() -> Unit)**, passing in a lambda that will request the location permission by calling **requestLocationPermission()**. Otherwise, it requests the location permission by calling the **requestLocationPermission()** function directly.

14. To determine whether or not your app already has the location permission, introduce the **hasLocationPermission()** function shown here right before the **requestPermissionWithRationaleIfNeeded()** function:

```
private fun hasLocationPermission() =
    ContextCompat.checkSelfPermission(
        this, Manifest.permission.ACCESS_FINE_LOCATION
    ) == PackageManager.PERMISSION_GRANTED
```

15. Finally, update the **onMapReady()** function of your **MapsActivity** class to request permission or get the user's current location as soon as the map is ready:

```
override fun onMapReady(googleMap: GoogleMap) {
    mMap = googleMap

    if (hasLocationPermission()) {
        getLastLocation()
    } else {
        requestPermissionWithRationaleIfNeeded()
    }
}
```

16. To make sure you present the rationale when the user denies the permission, update **onRequestPermissionsResult(Int, Array<String>, IntArray)** with an **else** condition:

```
override fun onRequestPermissionsResult(
    requestCode: Int,
    permissions: Array<out String>,
    grantResults: IntArray
) {
    super.onRequestPermissionsResult(requestCode, permissions,
      grantResults)

    when (requestCode) {
        PERMISSION_CODE_REQUEST_LOCATION -> if (
            grantResults[0] == PackageManager.PERMISSION_GRANTED
        ) {
            getLastLocation()
        } else {
            requestPermissionWithRationaleIfNeeded()
        }
    }
}
```

17. Run your app. You should now see a system permission dialog requesting you to allow the app to access the location of the device:

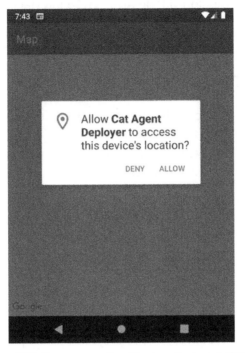

Figure 7.7: App requesting the location permission

If you deny the permission, the rationale dialog will appear, followed by another system permission dialog requesting permission, as shown in the following screenshot. This time, the user has the option to choose not to let the app ask for permission again. Every time the user chooses to deny the permission, the rationale dialog will be presented to them again, until they choose to allow the permission or tick the **Don't ask again** option:

Figure 7.8: Don't ask again

Once the user has allowed or permanently denied the permission, the dialog will never show again. To reset the state of your app permissions, you would have to manually grant it the permission via the **App Info** interface.

Now that we can get the location permission, we will now look into obtaining the user's current location.

SHOWING A MAP OF THE USER'S LOCATION

Having successfully obtained permission from the user to access their location, we can now ask the user's device to provide us with its last known location, which would also usually be the user's current location. We will then use this location to present the user with a map of their current location.

To obtain the user's last known location, Google has provided us with the Google Play Location service, and more specifically, with the **FusedLocationProviderClient** class. The **FusedLocationProviderClient** class helps us interact with Google's Fused Location Provider API, which is a location API that intelligently combines different signals from multiple device sensors to provide us with device location information.

To access the **FusedLocationProviderClient** class, we must first include the Google Play Location service library in our project. This simply means adding the following code snippet to the **dependencies** block of our app **build.gradle**:

```
implementation "com.google.android.gms:play-services-location:17.1.0"
```

With the location service imported, we can now obtain an instance of the **FusedLocationProviderClient** class by calling **LocationServices.getFusedLocationProviderClient(this@MainActivity)**.

Once we have a fused location client, given that we have already received the location permission from the user, we can obtain the user's last location by calling **fusedLocationClient.lastLocation**. Since this is an asynchronous call, we should also provide a success listener at a minimum. If we wanted to, we could also add listeners for cancellation, failure, and the completion of requests. The **getLastLocation()** call (**lastLocation** for short in Kotlin) returns a **Task<Location>**. A Task is a Google API abstract class whose implementations perform async operations. In this case, that operation is returning a location. So adding listeners is simply a matter of chaining. We will add the following code snippet to our call:

```
.addOnSuccessListener { location: Location? ->
}
```

Note that the **location** parameter could be **null** if the client failed to obtain the user's current location. This is not very common but could happen if, for example, the user disabled their location services during the call.

Once the code inside our success listener block is executed and **location** is not null, we have the user's current location in the form of a **Location** instance.

A **Location** instance holds a single coordinate on Earth, expressed using longitude and latitude. For our purpose, it is sufficient to know that each point on the surface of the Earth is mapped to a single pair of longitude (abbreviation: Lng) and latitude (abbreviation: Lat) values.

This is where it gets really exciting. Google lets us present any location on an interactive map by using a **SupportMapFragment** class. All it takes is signing up for a free API key. When you create your application with a Google Maps Activity, Google generates an extra file for us, named **google_maps_api.xml**, which can be found under **res/values**. That file is required for our **SupportMapFragment** class to work, as it contains our API key. It also contains clear instructions on how to obtain a new API key. Conveniently, it also contains a link that will prefill much of the required sign-up data for us. The link looks something like **https://console. developers.google.com/flows/enableapi?apiid=....** Copy it from the **google_maps_api.xml** file to your browser (or *CMD* + *click* on the link), follow the directions on the page once the page loads, and click **Create**. Once you have a key, replace the **YOUR_KEY_HERE** string at the bottom of the file with your newly obtained key.

At this point, if you run your app, you will already see an interactive map on your screen:

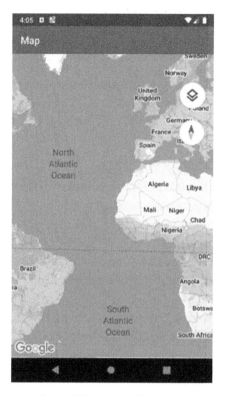

Figure 7.9: Interactive map

To position the map based on our current location, we create a **LatLng** instance with the coordinates from our **Location** instance, and call **moveCamera(CameraUpdate)** on the **GoogleMap** instance. To satisfy the **CameraUpdate** requirement, we call **CameraUpdateFactory. newLatLng(LatLng)**, passing in the **LatLng** parameter created earlier. The call would look something like this:

```
mMap.moveCamera(CameraUpdateFactory.newLatLng(latLng))
```

We could also call **newLatLngZoom(LatLng, Float)** to modify the zoom-in and zoom-out feature of the map.

> **NOTE**
>
> Valid zoom values range between **2.0** (farthest) and **21.0** (closest). Values outside of that range are capped.

Some areas may not have tiles to render the closest zoom values. To discover the rest of the available **CameraUpdateFactory** options, visit https://developers.google.com/android/reference/com/google/android/gms/maps/CameraUpdateFactory.html.

To add a pin (called a marker in Google's Map APIs) at the user's coordinate, we call **addMarker(MarkerOptions)** on the **GoogleMap** instance. **MarkerOptions** parameters are configured by chaining calls to a **MarkerOptions()** instance. For a simple marker at our desired position, we could call **position(LatLng)** and **title(String)**. The call would look similar to the following:

```
mMap.addMarker(MarkerOptions().position(latLng).title("Pin Label"))
```

The order in which we chain the calls does not matter.

Let's practice this in the following exercise.

EXERCISE 7.02: OBTAINING THE USER'S CURRENT LOCATION

Now that your app can be granted location permission, you can proceed to utilize the location permission to get the user's current location. You will then display the map and update it to zoom into the user's current location and show a pin at that location. Perform the following steps:

1. First, add the Google Play location service to your **build.gradle** file. You should add it within the **dependencies** block:

```
dependencies {
    implementation "com.google.android.gms:play-services-
      location:17.1.0"
    implementation "org.jetbrains.kotlin:kotlin-
      stdlib:$kotlin_version"
    implementation 'androidx.core:core-ktx:1.3.2'
    implementation 'androidx.appcompat:appcompat:1.2.0'
    implementation 'com.google.android.material:material:1.2.1'
    implementation 'com.google.android.gms:play-services-maps:17.0.0'
    implementation 'androidx.constraintlayout:constraintlayout:2.0.4'
    testImplementation 'junit:junit:4.+'
    androidTestImplementation 'androidx.test.ext:junit:1.1.2'
    androidTestImplementation 'androidx.test
      .espresso:espresso-core:3.3.0'
}
```

2. Click the **Sync Project with Gradle Files** button in Android Studio for Gradle to fetch the newly added dependency.

3. Obtain an API key: start by opening the generated **google_maps_api.xml** file (**app/src/debug/res/values/google_maps_api.xml**) and *CMD + click* the link that starts with **https://console.developers.google.com/ flows/enableapi?apiid=**.

4. Follow the instructions on the website until you have generated a new API key.

5. Update your **google_maps_api.xml** file by replacing **YOUR_KEY_HERE** with your new API key in the following line:

```
<string name="google_maps_key" templateMergeStrategy="preserve"
    translatable="false">YOUR_KEY_HERE</string>
```

6. Open your **MapsActivity.kt** file. At the top of your **MapsActivity** class, define a lazily initialized fused location provider client:

```
class MapsActivity : AppCompatActivity(), OnMapReadyCallback {
    private val fusedLocationProviderClient by lazy {
        LocationServices.getFusedLocationProviderClient(this)
    }

    override fun onCreate(savedInstanceState: Bundle?) {
        ...
    }
    ...
}
```

By making **fusedLocationProviderClient** initialize lazily, you are making sure it is only initialized when needed, which essentially guarantees the **Activity** class will have been created before initialization.

7. Introduce an **updateMapLocation(LatLng)** function and an **addMarkerAtLocation(LatLng, String)** function immediately after the **getLastLocation()** function to zoom the map at a given location and add a marker at that location, respectively:

```
private fun updateMapLocation(location: LatLng) {
    mMap.moveCamera(CameraUpdateFactory.newLatLngZoom(location, 7f))
}


private fun addMarkerAtLocation(location: LatLng, title: String) {
    mMap.addMarker(MarkerOptions().title(title).position(location))
}
```

8. Now update your **getLastLocation()** function to retrieve the user's location:

```
private fun getLastLocation() {
    fusedLocationProviderClient.lastLocation
        .addOnSuccessListener { location: Location? ->
            location?.let {
                val userLocation = LatLng(location.latitude,
                    location.longitude)
                updateMapLocation(userLocation)
                addMarkerAtLocation(userLocation, "You")

            }

        }

}
```

Your code requests the last location in a Kotlin concise way by calling **lastLocation**, and then attaches a **lambda** function as an **OnSuccessListener** interface. Once a location is obtained, the **lambda** function is executed, updating the map location and adding a marker at that location with the title **You** if a non-null location was returned.

9. Run your app:

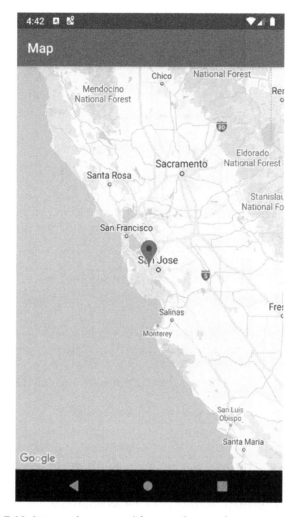

Figure 7.10: Interactive map with a marker at the current location

Once the app has been granted permission, it can request the user's last location from the Google Play location service via the fused location provider client. This gives you an easy and concise way to fetch the user's current location. Remember to turn on location on your device for the app to work.

With the user's location, your app can tell the map where to zoom and where to place a pin. If the user clicks on the pin, they will see the title you assigned to it (**You** in the exercise).

In the next section, we will learn how to respond to clicks on the map and how to move markers.

MAP CLICKS AND CUSTOM MARKERS

With a map showing the user's current location by zooming in at the right location and placing a pin there, we have rudimentary knowledge of how to render the desired map, as well as knowledge of how to obtain the required permissions and the user's current location.

In this section, we will learn how to respond to a user interacting with the map, and how to use markers more extensively. We will learn how to move markers on the map and how to replace the default pin with custom icons. When we know how to let the user place a marker anywhere on the map, we can let them choose where to deploy the Secret Cat Agent.

To listen for clicks on the map, we need to add a listener to the **GoogleMap** instance. Looking at our **MapsActivity.kt** file, the best place to do so would be in **onMapReady(GoogleMap)**. A naïve implementation would look like this:

```
override fun onMapReady(googleMap: GoogleMap) {
    mMap = googleMap.apply {
        setOnMapClickListener { latLng ->
            addMarkerAtLocation(latLng, "Deploy here")
        }
    }
    ...
}
```

However, if we ran this code, we'd find that for every click on the map, a new marker is added. This is not our desired behavior.

To control a marker on the map, we need to keep a reference to that marker. That is achieved easily enough by keeping a reference to the output of **GoogleMap.addMarker(MarkerOptions)**. The **addMarker** function returns a **Marker** instance. To move a marker on the map, we simply assign a new value by calling its **position** setter.

To replace the default pin icon with a custom icon, we need to provide **BitmapDescriptor** to the marker or the **MarkerOptions()** instance. **BitmapDescriptor** wrappers work around Bitmaps used by **GoogleMap** to render markers (and ground overlays, but we won't cover that in this book). We obtain **BitmapDescriptor** by using **BitmapDescriptorFactory**. The factory will require an asset, which can be provided in a number of ways. You can provide it with the name of a bitmap in the **assets** directory, a **Bitmap**, a filename of a file in the internal storage, or a resource ID. The factory can also create default markers of different colors. We are interested in the **Bitmap** option because we intend to use a vector drawable, and those are not directly supported by the factory. In addition, when converting the drawable to a **Bitmap**, we can manipulate it to suit our needs (for example, we could change its color).

Android Studio offers us quite a wide range of free vector **Drawables** out of the box. For this example, we want the **paw** drawable. To do this, right-click anywhere in the left Android pane, and select **New | Vector Asset**.

Now, click the Android icon next to the **Clip Art** label for the list of icons:

Figure 7.11: Asset Studio

We'll now access a window in which we can choose from the offered pool of clip art:

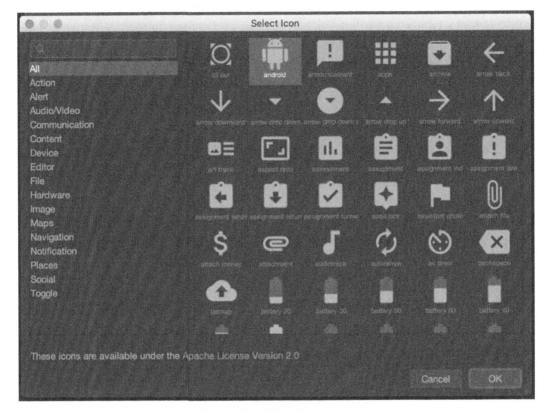

Figure 7.12: Selecting an icon

Once we choose an icon, we can name it, and it will be created for us as a vector drawable XML file. We will name it **target_icon**.

To use the created asset, we must first get it as a **Drawable** instance. This is done by calling **ContextCompat.getDrawable(Context, Int)**, passing in the activity and **R.drawable.target_icon** as a reference to our asset. Next, we need to define bounds for the **Drawable** instance to draw in. Calling **Drawable. setBound(Int, Int, Int, Int)** with (0, 0, **drawable.intrinsicWidth**, **drawable.intrinsicHeight**) will tell it to draw within its intrinsic size.

To change the color of our icon, we have to tint it. To tint a **Drawable** instance in a way that is supported by devices running APIs older than **21**, we must first wrap our **Drawable** instance with **DrawableCompat** by calling **DrawableCompat. wrap(Drawable)**. The returned **Drawable** can then be tinted using **DrawableCompat.setTint(Drawable, Int)**.

Next, we need to create a **Bitmap** to hold our icon. Its dimensions can match those of the **Drawable** bounds, and we want its **Config** to be **Bitmap.Config.ARGB_8888** – which means full red, green, blue, and alpha channels. We then create a **Canvas** for the **Bitmap**, allowing us to draw our **Drawable** instance by calling... you guessed it, **Drawable.draw(Canvas)**:

```kotlin
private fun getBitmapDescriptorFromVector(@DrawableRes
    vectorDrawableResourceId: Int): BitmapDescriptor? {
    val bitmap =
        ContextCompat.getDrawable(this, vectorDrawableResourceId)?.let {
          vectorDrawable ->
            vectorDrawable
                .setBounds(0, 0, vectorDrawable.intrinsicWidth,
                    vectorDrawable.intrinsicHeight)

            val drawableWithTint = DrawableCompat.wrap(vectorDrawable)
            DrawableCompat.setTint(drawableWithTint, Color.RED)

            val bitmap = Bitmap.createBitmap(
                vectorDrawable.intrinsicWidth,
                vectorDrawable.intrinsicHeight,
                Bitmap.Config.ARGB_8888
            )
            val canvas = Canvas(bitmap)
            drawableWithTint.draw(canvas)
            bitmap
        }

    return BitmapDescriptorFactory.fromBitmap(bitmap)
        .also {
            bitmap?.recycle()
        }
}
```

With the **Bitmap** containing our icon, we are now ready to obtain a **BitmapDescriptor** instance from **BitmapDescriptorFactory**. Don't forget to recycle your **Bitmap** afterward. This will avoid a memory leak.

You learned how to present the user with a meaningful map by centering it on their current location and showing their current location using a pin marker.

EXERCISE 7.03: ADDING A CUSTOM MARKER WHERE THE MAP WAS CLICKED

In this exercise, you will respond to a user's map click by placing a red paw-shaped marker at the location on the map the user clicked:

1. In **MapsActivity.kt** (found under **app/src/main/java/com/example/catagentdeployer**), right below the definition of the **mMap** variable, define a nullable **Marker** variable to hold a reference to the paw marker on the map:

```
private lateinit var mMap: GoogleMap
private var marker: Marker? = null
```

2. Update **addMarkerAtLocation(LatLng, String)** to also accept a nullable **BitmapDescriptor** with a default value of **null**:

```
private fun addMarkerAtLocation(
    location: LatLng,
    title: String,
    markerIcon: BitmapDescriptor? = null
) = mMap.addMarker(
        MarkerOptions()
            .title(title)
            .position(location)
            .apply {
                markerIcon?.let { icon(markerIcon) }
            }
    )
```

If the **markerIcon** provided is not null, the app sets it to **MarkerOptions**. The function now returns the marker it added to the map.

3. Create a **getBitmapDescriptorFromVector(Int): BitmapDescriptor?** function below your **addMarkerAtLocation(LatLng, String, BitmapDescriptor?): Marker** function to provide **BitmapDescriptor** given a **Drawable** resource ID:

```
private fun getBitmapDescriptorFromVector(@DrawableRes
  vectorDrawableResourceId: Int): BitmapDescriptor? {
    val bitmap =
        ContextCompat.getDrawable(this,
          vectorDrawableResourceId)?.let { vectorDrawable ->
            vectorDrawable
                .setBounds(0, 0, vectorDrawable.intrinsicWidth,
                    vectorDrawable.intrinsicHeight)

            val drawableWithTint = DrawableCompat
              .wrap(vectorDrawable)
            DrawableCompat.setTint(drawableWithTint, Color.RED)

            val bitmap = Bitmap.createBitmap(
                vectorDrawable.intrinsicWidth,
                vectorDrawable.intrinsicHeight,
                Bitmap.Config.ARGB_8888
            )
            val canvas = Canvas(bitmap)
            drawableWithTint.draw(canvas)
            bitmap
        }
    return BitmapDescriptorFactory.fromBitmap(bitmap).also {
        bitmap?.recycle()
    }
}
```

This function first obtains a drawable using **ContextCompat** by passing in the provided resource ID. It then sets the drawing bounds for the drawable, wraps it in **DrawableCompat**, and sets its tint to red.

Then, it creates a **Bitmap** and a **Canvas** for that **Bitmap**, upon which it draws the tinted drawable. The bitmap is then returned to be used by **BitmapDescriptorFactory** to build **BitmapDescriptor**. Lastly, **Bitmap** is recycled to avoid a memory leak.

4. Before you can use the **Drawable** instance, you must first create it. Right-click on the Android pane, and then select **New | Vector Asset**.

5. In the window that opens, click on the Android icon next to the **Clip Art** label to select a different icon:

Figure 7.13: Asset Studio

6. From the list of icons, select the **pets** icon. You can type **pets** into the search field if you can't find the icon. Once you select the **pets** icon, click **OK**:

Figure 7.14: Selecting an icon

7. Name your icon **target_icon**. Click **Next** and **Finish**.

8. Define an **addOrMoveSelectedPositionMarker(LatLng)** function to create a new marker or, if one has already been created, move it to the provided location. Add it after the **getBitmapDescriptorFromVector(Int)** function:

```
private fun addOrMoveSelectedPositionMarker(latLng: LatLng) {
    if (marker == null) {
        marker = addMarkerAtLocation(
            latLng, "Deploy here",
                getBitmapDescriptorFromVector(R.drawable.target_icon)
        )
    } else {
        marker?.apply {
            position = latLng
        }
    }
}
```

9. Update your **onMapReady(GoogleMap)** function to set an **OnMapClickListener** event on **mMap**, which will add a marker to the clicked location or move the existing marker to the clicked location:

```
override fun onMapReady(googleMap: GoogleMap) {
    mMap = googleMap.apply {
        setOnMapClickListener { latLng ->
            addOrMoveSelectedPositionMarker(latLng)
        }
    }

    if (hasLocationPermission()) {
        getLastLocation()
    } else {
        requestPermissionWithRationaleIfNeeded()
    }
}
```

10. Run your app:

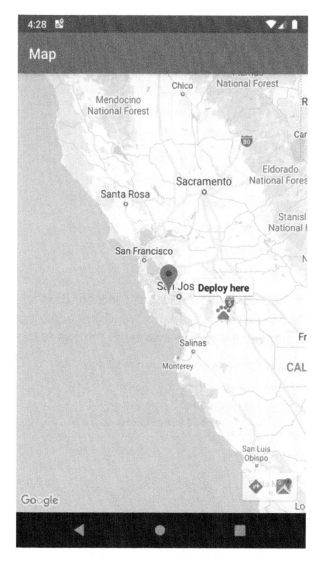

Figure 7.15: The complete app

Clicking anywhere on the map will now move the paw icon to that location. Clicking the paw icon will show the **Deploy here** label. Note that the location of the paw is a geographical one, not a screen one. That means if you drag your map or zoom in, the paw will move with the map and remain in the same geographical location. You now know how to respond to user clicks on the map and how to add and move markers around. You also know how to customize the appearance of markers.

ACTIVITY 7.01: CREATING AN APP TO FIND THE LOCATION OF A PARKED CAR

Some people often forget where it was that they parked their car. Let's say you want to help these individuals by developing an app that lets the user store the last place they parked. When the user launches the app, it will show a pin at the last place the user told the app about the car's location. The user can click an **I'm parked here** button to update the pin location to the current location the next time they park.

Your goal in this activity is to develop an app that shows the user a map with the current location. It will first have to ask the user for permission to access their location. Make sure to also provide a rationale dialog if needed, according to the SDK. The app will show a car icon where the user last told it the car was. The user can click a button labeled **I'm parked here** to move the car icon to the current location. When the user relaunches the app, it will show the user's current location and the car icon where the car was last parked.

As a bonus feature of your app, you can choose to add functionality that stores the car's location so that it can be restored after the user has killed and then re-opened the app. This bonus functionality relies on using **SharedPreferences**; a concept that will be covered in *Chapter 11, Persisting Data*. As such, steps 9 and 10 below will give you the required implementation.

The following steps will help you complete the activity:

1. Create a Google Maps Activity app.

2. Obtain an API key for the app and update your **google_maps_api.xml** file with that key.

3. Show a button at the bottom with an **I'm parked here** label.

4. Include the location service in your app.

5. Request the user's permission to access their location.

6. Obtain the user's location and place a pin on the map at that location.

7. Add a car icon to your project.

8. Add functionality to move the car icon to the user's current location.

9. Store the selected location in **SharedPreferences**. This function, placed in your activity, will help:

```
private fun saveLocation(latLng: LatLng) =
    getPreferences(MODE_PRIVATE)?.edit()?.apply {
        putString("latitude", latLng.latitude.toString())
        putString("longitude", latLng.longitude.toString())
        apply()
    }
```

10. Restore any saved location from **SharedPreferences**. You can use the following function:

```
val latitude = sharedPreferences.getString("latitude", null)
    ?.toDoubleOrNull() ?: return null
val longitude = sharedPreferences.getString("longitude",
    null)?.toDoubleOrNull()
    ?: return null
```

> **NOTE**
>
> The solution to this activity can be found at: http://packt.live/3sKj1cp

SUMMARY

In this chapter, we have learned about Android permissions. We touched on the reasons for having them and saw how we could request the user's permission to perform certain tasks. We also learned how to use Google's Maps API and how to present the user with an interactive map. Lastly, we leveraged our knowledge of presenting a map and requesting permissions to find out the user's current location and present it on the map. There is a lot more that can be done with the Google Maps API, and you could explore a lot more possibilities with certain permissions. You should now have enough understanding of the foundations of both to explore further. To read more about permissions, visit https://developer.android.com/reference/android/Manifest.permission. To read more about the Maps API, visit https://developers.google.com/maps/documentation/android-sdk/intro.

In the next chapter, we will learn how to perform background tasks using **Services** and **WorkManager**. We will also learn how to present the user with notifications, even when the app is not running. These are powerful tools to have in your arsenal as a mobile developer.

8

SERVICES, WORKMANAGER, AND NOTIFICATIONS

OVERVIEW

This chapter will introduce you to the concepts of managing long-running tasks in the background of an app. By the end of this chapter, you will be able to trigger a background task, create a notification for the user when a background task is complete, and launch an application from a notification. This chapter will give you a solid understanding of how to manage background tasks and keep the user informed about the progress of these tasks.

INTRODUCTION

In the previous chapter, we learned how to request permissions from the user and use Google's Maps API. With that knowledge, we obtained the user's location and allowed them to deploy an agent on a local map. In this chapter, we will learn how to track a long-running process and report its progress to the user.

We will build an example app where we will assume that **Secret Cat Agents (SCAs)** get deployed in a record time of 15 seconds. That way, we'll avoid having to wait for very long before our background task completes. When a cat successfully deploys, we will notify the user and let them launch the app, presenting them with a successful deployment message.

Ongoing background tasks are quite common in the mobile world. Background tasks run even when an application is not active. Examples of long-running background tasks include the downloading of files, resource cleanup jobs, playing music, and tracking the user's location. Historically, Google offered Android developers multiple ways of executing such tasks: services, **JobScheduler**, and Firebase's **JobDispatcher** and **AlarmManager**. With the fragmentation in the Android world, it was quite a mess to cope with. Luckily for us, since March 2019 we have had a better (more stable) option. With the introduction of **WorkManager**, Google has abstracted the logic of choosing a background executing mechanism based on the API version away for us. We still use a foreground service, which is a special kind of service, for certain tasks that should be known to the user while running—such as playing music or tracking the location of the user in a running app.

Before we proceed, a quick step back. We have mentioned services, and we will be focusing on foreground services, but we haven't quite explained what services are. Services are application components designed to run in the background, even when an app is not running. With the exception of foreground services, which are tied to a notification, services have no user interface. It is important to note that services run on the main thread of their hosting process. This means that their operations can block the app. It is up to us to start a separate thread from within a service to avoid that.

Let's get started and look at the implementation of the multiple approaches available in Android for managing a background task.

STARTING A BACKGROUND TASK USING WORKMANAGER

The first question we will address here is, Should we opt for **WorkManager** or a foreground service? To answer that, a good rule of thumb is to ask; do you need the action to be tracked by the user in real time? If the answer is yes (for example, if you have a task such as responding to the user's location or playing music in the background), then you should use a foreground service, with its attached notification to give the user a real-time indication of state. When the background task can be delayed or does not require user interaction (for example, downloading a large file), use **WorkManager**.

> **NOTE**
>
> Starting with version 2.3.0-alpha02 of the **WorkManager**, you can launch a foreground service via the **WorkManager** by calling **setForegroundAsync(ForegroundInfo)**. Our control over that foreground service is quite limited. It does allow you to attach a (pre-defined) notification to the work, which is why it is worth mentioning.

In our example, in our app, we will track the SCAs' preparation for deployment. Before an agent can head out, they need to stretch, groom their fur, visit the litter box, and suit up. Each one of these tasks takes some time. Because you can't rush a cat, the agent will finish each step in its own time. All we can do is wait (and let the user know when the task is done). **WorkManager** is perfect for such a scenario.

To use **WorkManager**, we need to familiarize ourselves with its four main classes:

- The first is **WorkManager** itself. **WorkManager** receives work and enqueues it based on provided arguments and constraints (such as internet connectivity and the device charging).

- The second is **Worker**. Now, **Worker** is a wrapper around the work that needs doing. It has one function, **doWork()**, which we override to implement the background work code. **doWork()** will be executed in a background thread.

- The third class is **WorkRequest**. This class binds a **Worker** class to arguments and constraints. There are two types of **WorkRequest**: **OneTimeWorkRequest**, which runs the work once, and **PeriodicWorkRequest**, which can be used to schedule work to run at a fixed interval.

- The fourth class is **ListenableWorker.Result**. You probably guessed it, but this is the class holding the result of the executed work. The result can be one of **Success**, **Failure**, or **Retry**.

Other than these four classes, we also have the **Data** class, which holds data passed to and from the worker.

Let's get back to our example. We want to define four tasks that need to occur in sequential order: the cat needs to stretch, then it needs to groom its fur, then visit the litter box, and finally, it needs to suit up.

Before we can start using **WorkManager**, we have to first include its dependency in our app **build.gradle** file:

```
implementation "androidx.work:work-runtime:2.4.0"
```

With **WorkManager** included in our project, we'll go ahead and create our workers. The first worker will look something like this:

```
class CatStretchingWorker(
    context: Context,
    workerParameters: WorkerParameters
) : Worker(context, workerParameters) {
    override fun doWork(): Result {
        val catAgentId = inputData.getString(INPUT_DATA_CAT_AGENT_ID)
        Thread.sleep(3000L)
        val outputData = Data.Builder()
            .putString(OUTPUT_DATA_CAT_AGENT_ID, catAgentId)
            .build()
        return Result.success(outputData)
    }

    companion object {
        const val INPUT_DATA_CAT_AGENT_ID = "id"
        const val OUTPUT_DATA_CAT_AGENT_ID = "id"
    }
}
```

We start by extending **Worker** and overriding its **doWork()** function. We then read the SCA ID from the input data. Then, because we have no real sensors to track the progress of the cat stretching, we fake our wait by introducing a 3-second (3,000-millisecond) **Thread.sleep(Long)** call. Finally, we construct an output data class with the ID we received in our input and return it with the successful result.

Starting a Background Task Using WorkManager | 369

Once we've created workers for all our tasks (**CatStretchingWorker**, **CatFurGroomingWorker**, **CatLitterBoxSittingWorker**, and **CatSuitUpWorker**), similarly to how we created the first one, we can call **WorkManager** to chain them. Let's also assume we can't tell the progress of the agent unless we're connected to the internet. Our call would look something like this:

```
val catStretchingInputData = Data.Builder()
  .putString(CatStretchingWorker.INPUT_DATA_CAT_AGENT_ID,
    "catAgentId").build()
val catStretchingRequest = OneTimeWorkRequest
  .Builder(CatStretchingWorker::class.java)
val catStretchingRequest =
  OneTimeWorkRequest.Builder(CatStretchingWorker::class.java)
    .setConstraints(networkConstraints)
    .setInputData(catStretchingInputData)
    .build()
...
WorkManager.getInstance(this).beginWith(catStretchingRequest)
    .then(catFurGroomingRequest)
    .then(catLitterBoxSittingRequest)
    .then(catSuitUpRequest)
    .enqueue()
```

In the preceding code, we first construct a **Constraints** instance declaring we need to be connected to the internet for the work to execute. We then define our input data, setting it to the SCA ID. Next, we bind the constraints and input data to our **Worker** class by constructing **OneTimeWorkRequest**. The construction of the other **WorkRequest** instances has been left out, but they are pretty much identical to the one shown here. We can now chain all the requests and enqueue them on the **WorkManager** class. You can enqueue a single **WorkRequest** instance by passing it directly to the **WorkManager enqueue()** function, or you can also have multiple **WorkRequest** instances run in parallel by passing them all to the **WorkManager enqueue()** function as a list.

Our tasks will be executed by **WorkManager** when the constraints are met.

Each **Request** instance has a unique identifier. **WorkManager** exposes a **LiveData** property for each request, allowing us to track the progress of its work by passing its unique identifier as shown in the following code:

```
workManager.getWorkInfoByIdLiveData(catStretchingRequest.id)
    .observe(this, Observer { info ->
        if (info.state.isFinished) {
```

```
        doSomething()
    }
})
```

The state of work can be **BLOCKED** (there is a chain of requests, and it is not next in the chain), **ENQUEUED** (there is a chain of requests, and this work is next), **RUNNING** (the work in **doWork()** is executing), and **SUCCEEDED**. Work can also be canceled, leading to a **CANCELLED** state, or it can fail, leading to a **FAILED** state.

Finally, there's **Result.retry**. Returning this result tells the **WorkManager** class to enqueue the work again. The policy governing when to run the work again is defined by a **backoff** criteria set on **WorkRequest Builder**. The default **backoff** policy is exponential, but we can set it to be linear instead. We can also define the initial **backoff** time.

Let's put into practice the knowledge gained so far in the following exercise.

In this section, we will track our SCA from the moment we fire off the command to deploy it to the field to the moment it arrives at its destination.

EXERCISE 8.01: EXECUTING BACKGROUND WORK WITH THE WORKMANAGER CLASS

In this first exercise, we will track the SCA as it prepares to head out by enqueuing chained **WorkRequest** classes:

1. Start by creating a new **Empty Activity** project (**File -> New -> New Project -> Empty Activity**). Click **Next**.

2. Name your application **Cat Agent Tracker**.

3. Make sure your package name is **com.example.catagenttracker**.

4. Set the save location to where you want to save your project.

5. Leave everything else at its default values and click **Finish**.

6. Make sure you are on the Android view in your **Project** pane.

7. Open your app's **build.gradle** file. In the **dependencies** block, add the **WorkManager** dependency:

```
dependencies {
    implementation "org.jetbrains.kotlin:kotlin-stdlib:$kotlin_
version"
    ...
```

```
        implementation "androidx.work:work-runtime:2.4.0"

        ...
    }
```

This will allow you to use **WorkManager** and its dependencies in your code.

8. Create a new package under your app package (right-click on **com.example.catagenttracker**, then **New | Package**). Name the new package **com.example.catagenttracker.worker**.

9. Create a new class under **com.example.catagenttracker.worker** named **CatStretchingWorker** (right-click on **worker**, then **New | New Kotlin File/Class**). Under **Kind**, choose **Class**.

10. To define a **Worker** instance that will sleep for **3** seconds, update the new class like so:

```
package com.example.catagenttracker.worker

import android.content.Context
import androidx.work.Data
import androidx.work.Worker
import androidx.work.WorkerParameters

class CatStretchingWorker(
    context: Context,
    workerParameters: WorkerParameters
) : Worker(context, workerParameters) {
    override fun doWork(): Result {
        val catAgentId = inputData.getString(INPUT_DATA_CAT_AGENT_ID)
        Thread.sleep(3000L)
        val outputData = Data.Builder()
            .putString(OUTPUT_DATA_CAT_AGENT_ID, catAgentId)
            .build()
        return Result.success(outputData)
    }

    companion object {
        const val INPUT_DATA_CAT_AGENT_ID = "inId"
        const val OUTPUT_DATA_CAT_AGENT_ID = "outId"
    }
}
```

This will add the required dependencies for a **Worker** implementation and then extend the **Worker** class. To implement the actual work, you will override **doWork(): Result**, making it read the Cat Agent ID from the input, sleep for **3** seconds (**3000** milliseconds), construct an output data instance with the Cat Agent ID, and pass it inside a **Result.success** value.

11. Repeat steps 9 and 10 to create three more identical workers named **CatFurGroomingWorker**, **CatLitterBoxSittingWorker**, and **CatSuitUpWorker**.

12. Open **MainActivity**. Right before the end of the class, add the following:

```
private fun getCatAgentIdInputData(catAgentIdKey: String,
  catAgentIdValue: String) =
    Data.Builder().putString(catAgentIdKey, catAgentIdValue)
        .build()
```

This helper function constructs an input **Data** instance for you with the Cat Agent ID.

13. Add the following to the **onCreate(Bundle?)** function:

```
override fun onCreate(savedInstanceState: Bundle?) {
    super.onCreate(savedInstanceState)
    setContentView(R.layout.activity_main)

    val networkConstraints =
        Constraints.Builder()
            .setRequiredNetworkType(NetworkType.CONNECTED).build()

    val catAgentId = "CatAgent1"
    val catStretchingRequest =
      OneTimeWorkRequest.Builder
          (CatLitterBoxSittingWorker::class.java)
        .setConstraints(networkConstraints)
        .setInputData(
            getCatAgentIdInputData(CatStretchingWorker
                .INPUT_DATA_CAT_AGENT_ID, catAgentId)
        ).build()
    val catFurGroomingRequest =
      OneTimeWorkRequest.Builder(CatFurGroomingWorker::class.java)
        .setConstraints(networkConstraints)
        .setInputData(
            getCatAgentIdInputData(CatFurGroomingWorker
                .INPUT_DATA_CAT_AGENT_ID, catAgentId)
        ).build()
```

```
        val catLitterBoxSittingRequest =
            OneTimeWorkRequest.Builder
                (CatLitterBoxSittingWorker::class.java)
                    .setConstraints(networkConstraints)
                    .setInputData(
                        getCatAgentIdInputData(
                            CatLitterBoxSittingWorker
                                .INPUT_DATA_CAT_AGENT_ID,
                            catAgentId
                        )
                    ).build()
        val catSuitUpRequest =
            OneTimeWorkRequest.Builder(CatSuitUpWorker::class.java)
                .setConstraints(networkConstraints)
                .setInputData(
                    getCatAgentIdInputData(CatSuitUpWorker
                        .INPUT_DATA_CAT_AGENT_ID, catAgentId)
            ).build()
    }
```

The first line added defines a network constraint. It tells the **WorkManager** class
to wait for an internet connection before executing work. Then, you define your
Cat Agent ID. Finally, you define four requests, passing in your **Worker** classes,
the network constraints, and the Cat Agent ID in the form of input data.

14. At the top of the class, define your **WorkManager**:

```
private val workManager = WorkManager.getInstance(this)
```

15. Add a chained **enqueue** request right below the code you just added, still within
the **onCreate** function:

```
val catSuitUpRequest =
    OneTimeWorkRequest.Builder(CatSuitUpWorker::class.java)
        .setConstraints(networkConstraints)
        .setInputData(
            getCatAgentIdInputData(CatSuitUpWorker
                .INPUT_DATA_CAT_AGENT_ID, catAgentId)
        ).build()

workManager.beginWith(catStretchingRequest)
    .then(catFurGroomingRequest)
    .then(catLitterBoxSittingRequest)
    .then(catSuitUpRequest)
    .enqueue()
```

Your **WorkRequests** are now enqueued to be executed in sequence when their constraints are met and the **WorkManager** class is ready to execute them.

16. Define a function to show a toast with a provided message. It should look like this:

```
private fun showResult(message: String) {
    Toast.makeText(this, message, LENGTH_SHORT).show()
}
```

17. To track the progress of the enqueued **WorkRequest** instances, add the following after the **enqueue** call:

```
workManager.beginWith(catStretchingRequest)
    .then(catFurGroomingRequest)
    .then(catLitterBoxSittingRequest)
    .then(catSuitUpRequest)
    .enqueue()


workManager.getWorkInfoByIdLiveData(catStretchingRequest.id)
    .observe(this, Observer { info ->
        if (info.state.isFinished) {
            showResult("Agent done stretching")
        }
    })


workManager.getWorkInfoByIdLiveData(catFurGroomingRequest.id)
    .observe(this, Observer { info ->
        if (info.state.isFinished) {
            showResult("Agent done grooming its fur")
        }
    })


workManager.getWorkInfoByIdLiveData(catLitterBoxSittingRequest.id)
    .observe(this, Observer { info ->
        if (info.state.isFinished) {
            showResult("Agent done sitting in litter box")
        }
    })


workManager.getWorkInfoByIdLiveData(catSuitUpRequest.id)
    .observe(this, Observer { info ->
```

```
        if (info.state.isFinished) {
            showResult("Agent done suiting up. Ready to go!")
        }
    })
```

The preceding code observes a **WorkInfo** observable provided by the **WorkManager** class for each **WorkRequest**. When each request is finished, a toast is shown with a relevant message.

18. Run your app:

Figure 8.1: Toasts showing in order

You should now see a simple **Hello World!** screen. However, if you wait a few seconds, you will start seeing toasts informing you of the progress of your SCA preparing to deploy to the field. You will notice that the toasts follow the order in which you enqueued the requests and execute their delays sequentially.

BACKGROUND OPERATIONS NOTICEABLE TO THE USER – USING A FOREGROUND SERVICE

With our SCA all suited up, they are now ready to get to the assigned destination. To track the SCA, we will periodically poll the location of the SCA using a foreground service and update the sticky notification (a notification that cannot be dismissed by the user) attached to that service with the new location. For the sake of simplicity, we will fake the location. Following what you learned in *Chapter 7*, *Android Permissions and Google Maps*, you could later replace this implementation with a real one that uses a map.

Foreground services are another way of performing background operations. The name may be a bit counter-intuitive. It is meant to differentiate these services from the base Android (background) services. The former are tied to a notification, while the latter run in the background with no user-facing representation built in. Another important difference between foreground services and background services is that the latter are candidates for termination when the system is low on memory, while the former are not.

As of Android 9 (Pie, or API level 28), we have to request the **FOREGROUND_SERVICE** permission to use foreground services. Since it is a normal permission, it will be granted to our app automatically.

Before we can launch a foreground service, we must first create one. A foreground service is a subclass of the Android abstract **Service** class. If we do not intend to bind to the service, and in our example, we indeed do not, we can simply override **onBind(Intent)** so that it returns **null**. As a side note, binding is one of the ways for interested clients to communicate with a Service. We will not focus on this approach in this book, as there are other, easier approaches, as you will discover below.

A foreground service must be tied to a notification. On Android 8 (Oreo, or API level 26) and above, if a foreground service is not tied to one within the **Application Not Responding** (**ANR**) time window (around 5 seconds), the service is stopped, and the app is declared as not responding. Because of this requirement, it is best if we tie the service to a notification as soon as we can. The best place to do that would be in the `onCreate()` function of the service. A quick implementation would look something like this:

```
private fun onCreate() {
    val channelId = if (Build.VERSION.SDK_INT >= Build.VERSION_CODES.O) {
        val newChannelId = "ChannelId"
        val channelName = "My Background Service"
        val channel =
            NotificationChannel(newChannelId, channelName,
                NotificationManager.IMPORTANCE_DEFAULT)
        val service = getSystemService(Context.NOTIFICATION_SERVICE) as
            NotificationManager
        service.createNotificationChannel(channel)

        newChannelId
    } else {
        ""

    }

    val pendingIntent = Intent(this, MainActivity::class.java).let {
        notificationIntent ->
        PendingIntent.getActivity(this, 0, notificationIntent, 0)
    }

    val notification = NotificationCompat.Builder(this, channelId)
        .setContentTitle("Content title")
        .setContentText("Content text")
        .setSmallIcon(R.drawable.notification_icon)
        .setContentIntent(pendingIntent)
        .setTicker("Ticker message")
        .build()

    startForeground(NOTIFICATION_ID, notificationBuilder.build())
}
```

Let's break this down.

We start by defining the channel ID. This is only required for Android Oreo or above and is ignored in earlier versions of Android. In Android Oreo, Google introduced the concept of channels. Channels are used to group notifications and allow users to filter out unwanted notifications:

```
val channelId = if (Build.VERSION.SDK_INT >= Build.VERSION_CODES.O) {
    val newChannelId = "ChannelId"
    val channelName = "My Background Service"
    val channel =
        NotificationChannel(newChannelId, channelName,
            NotificationManager.IMPORTANCE_DEFAULT)
    val service = getSystemService(Context.NOTIFICATION_SERVICE) as
        NotificationManager
    service.createNotificationChannel(channel)
    newChannelId
} else {
    ""

}
```

Next, we define **pendingIntent**. This will be the intent launched if the user taps on the notification. In this example, the main activity would be launched:

```
val pendingIntent = Intent(this, MainActivity::class.java).let {
    notificationIntent ->
    PendingIntent.getActivity(this, 0, notificationIntent, 0)
}
```

With the channel ID and **pendingIntent**, we can construct our notification. We use **NotificationCompat**, which takes away some of the boilerplate around supporting older API levels. We pass in the service as the context and the channel ID. We define the title, text, small icon, intent, and ticker message and build the notification:

```
val notification = NotificationCompat.Builder(this, channelId)
    .setContentTitle("Content title")
    .setContentText("Content text")
    .setSmallIcon(R.drawable.notification_icon)
    .setContentIntent(pendingIntent)
    .setTicker("Ticker message")
    .build()
```

To start a service in the foreground, attaching the notification to it, we call it **startForeground(Int, Notification)** function, passing in a notification ID (any unique int value to identify this service, which must not be 0) and a notification, which must have its priority set to **PRIORITY_LOW** or higher. In our case, we have not specified the priority, which sets it to **PRIORITY_DEFAULT**:

```
startForeground(NOTIFICATION_ID, notificationBuilder.build())
```

If launched, our service will now show a sticky notification. Clicking on the notification would launch our main activity. However, our service won't be doing anything useful. To add some functionality to it, we need to override **onStartCommand(Intent?, Int, Int)**. This function gets called when the service is launched via an intent, which also gives us the opportunity to read any extra data passed via that intent. It also provides us with flags (which may be set to **START_FLAG_REDELIVERY** or **START_FLAG_RETRY**) and a unique request ID. We will get to reading the extra data later in this chapter. You don't need to worry about the flags or the request ID in a simple implementation.

It is important to note that **onStartCommand(Intent?, Int, Int)** gets called on the UI thread, so don't perform any long-running operations here, or your app will freeze, giving the user a poor experience. Instead, we could create a new handler using a new **HandlerThread** (a thread with a looper, a class used to run a message loop for a thread) and post our work to it. This means we'll have an infinite loop running, waiting for us to post to it via a **Handler**. When we receive a start command, we can post the work we want done to it. That work will then be executed on that thread.

When our long-running work is done, there are a few things we may want to happen. First, we may want to inform whoever is interested (our main activity, if it is running, for example) that we are done. Then, we probably want to stop running in the foreground. Lastly, if we do not expect to require the service again, we could stop it.

An app has several ways to communicate with a service—binding, using broadcast receivers, using a bus architecture, or using a result receiver, to name a few. For our example, we will use Google's **LiveData**.

> Before we proceed, it is worth touching on broadcast receivers. Broadcast receivers allow our app to send and receive messages using a pattern much like the *publish-subscribe design pattern*.

The system broadcasts events such as the device booting up or charging having started. Our services can broadcast status updates as well. For example, they can broadcast a long calculation result on completion.

If our app registers to receive a certain message, the system will inform it when that message is broadcast.

This used to be a common way to communicate with services, but the **LocalBroadcastManager** class is now deprecated as it was an application-wide event bus that encouraged anti-patterns.

Having said that, broadcast receivers are still useful for system-wide events. We first define a class overriding the **BroadcastReceiver** abstract class:

```
class ToastBroadcastReceiver : BroadcastReceiver() {
    override fun onReceive(context: Context, intent: Intent) {
        StringBuilder().apply {
            append("Action: ${intent.action}\n")
            append("URI: ${intent.toUri(Intent.URI_INTENT_SCHEME)}\n")
            toString().let { eventText ->
                Toast.makeText(context, eventText,
                    Toast.LENGTH_LONG).show()
            }
        }
    }
}
```

When an event is received by **ToastBroadcastReceiver**, it will show a toast showing the action and URI of the event.

We can register our receiver via the **Manifest.xml** file:

```
<receiver android:name=".ToastBroadcastReceiver" android:exported="true">
    <intent-filter>
        <action android:name=
            "android.intent.action.ACTION_POWER_CONNECTED" />
    </intent-filter>
</receiver>
```

Specifying **android:exported="true"** tells the system that this receiver can receive messages from outside of the application. The action defines the message we are interested in. We can specify multiple actions. In this example, we listen for when the device starts charging. Keep in mind that setting this value to "true" allows other apps, including malicious ones, to activate this receiver.

We can also register for messages in code:

```
val filter = IntentFilter(ConnectivityManager.CONNECTIVITY_ACTION).apply {
    addAction(Intent.ACTION_POWER_CONNECTED)
}
registerReceiver(ToastBroadcastReceiver(), filter)
```

Adding this code to an activity or in our custom application class would register a new instance of our receiver as well. This receiver will live so long as the context (activity or application) is valid. So, correspondingly, if the activity or application is destroyed, our receiver will be freed to be garbage collected.

Now back to our implementation. To use **LiveData** in our app, we must add a dependency in our **app/build.gradle** file:

```
Dependencies {
    ...
    implementation "androidx.lifecycle:lifecycle-livedata-ktx:2.2.0"
    ...
}
```

We can then define a **LiveData** instance in the companion object of the service, like so:

```
companion object {
    private val mutableWorkCompletion = MutableLiveData<String>()
    val workCompletion: LiveData<String> = mutableWorkCompletion
}
```

Note that we hide the **MutableLiveData** instance behind a **LiveData** interface. This is so that consumers can only read the data. We can now use the **mutableWorkCompletion** instance to report completion by assigning it a value. However, we must remember that values can only be assigned to **LiveData** instances on the main thread. This means once our work is done, we must switch back to the main thread. We can easily achieve that—all we need is a new handler with the main **Looper** (obtained by calling **Looper.getMainLooper()**) to which we can post our update.

Now that our service is ready to do some work, we can finally launch it. Before we do, we must make sure we added the service to our **AndroidManifest.xml** file within the **<application></application>** block as shown in the following code:

```
<application ...>


    <service android:name=".ForegroundService" />


</application>
```

To launch the service we just added to our manifest, we create **Intent**, passing in any extra data required as shown in the following code:

```
val serviceIntent = Intent(this, ForegroundService::class.java).apply {
    putExtra("ExtraData", "Extra value")
}
```

And then we call **ContextCompat.startForegroundService(Context, Intent)** to fire off **Intent** and launch the service.

EXERCISE 8.02: TRACKING YOUR SCA'S WORK WITH A FOREGROUND SERVICE

In the first exercise, you tracked the SCA as it was preparing to head out using the **WorkManager** class. In this exercise, you will track the SCA as it deploys to the field and moves toward the assigned target by showing a sticky notification counting down the time to arrival at the destination. This notification will be driven by a foreground service, which will present and continuously update it. Clicking the notification at any time will launch your main activity if it's not already running and will always bring it to the foreground:

1. Start by adding the **LiveData** dependency to your project by updating your app's **build.gradle** file:

```
implementation "androidx.work:work-runtime:2.4.0"
implementation "androidx.lifecycle:lifecycle-livedata-ktx:2.2.0"
```

2. Then, create a new class called **RouteTrackingService**, extending the abstract **Service** class:

```
class RouteTrackingService : Service() {
    override fun onBind(intent: Intent): IBinder? = null
}
```

You will not rely on binding in this exercise, so it is safe to simply return **null** in the **onBind(Intent)** implementation.

3. In the newly created service, define some constants that you will later need, as well as the **LiveData** instance used to observe progress:

```
companion object {
    const val NOTIFICATION_ID = 0xCA7
    const val EXTRA_SECRET_CAT_AGENT_ID = "scaId"

    private val mutableTrackingCompletion = MutableLiveData<String>()
    val trackingCompletion: LiveData<String> =
mutableTrackingCompletion
}
```

NOTIFICATION_ID has to be a unique identifier for the notification owned by this service and must not be **0**. Now, **EXTRA_SECRET_CAT_AGENT_ID** is the constant you would use to pass data to the service. **mutableTrackingCompletion** is private and is used to allow you to post completion updates internally via **LiveData** without exposing the mutability outside of the service. **trackingCompletion** is then used to expose the **LiveData** instance for observation in an immutable fashion.

4. Add a function to your **RouteTrackingService** class to provide **PendingIntent** to your sticky notification:

```
private fun getPendingIntent() =
    PendingIntent.getActivity(this, 0, Intent(this,
      MainActivity::class.java), 0)
```

This will launch **MainActivity** whenever the user clicks on **Notification**. You call **PendingIntent.getActivity()**, passing a context, no request code (**0**), **Intent** that will launch **MainActivity**, and no flags (**0**) to it. You get back **PendingIntent**, which will launch that activity.

5. Add another function to create **NotificationChannel** for devices running Android Oreo or newer:

```
@RequiresApi(Build.VERSION_CODES.O)
private fun createNotificationChannel(): String {
    val channelId = "routeTracking"
    val channelName = "Route Tracking"
    val channel =
        NotificationChannel(channelId, channelName,
          NotificationManager.IMPORTANCE_DEFAULT)
    val service = getSystemService(Context.NOTIFICATION_SERVICE) as
      NotificationManager
```

```
        service.createNotificationChannel(channel)
        return channelId
}
```

You start by defining the channel ID. This needs to be unique to a package. Next, you define a channel name that will be visible to the user. This can (and should) be localized. We skipped that part for the sake of simplicity. A **NotificationChannel** instance is then created with importance set to **IMPORTANCE_DEFAULT**. The importance dictates how disruptive the notifications posted to this channel are. Lastly, a channel is created using **Notification Service** with the data provided in the **NotificationChannel** instance. The function returns the channel ID so that it can be used to construct **Notification**.

6. Create a function to provide you with **Notification.Builder**:

```
private fun getNotificationBuilder(pendingIntent: PendingIntent,
channelId: String) =
    NotificationCompat.Builder(this, channelId)
        .setContentTitle("Agent approaching destination")
        .setContentText("Agent dispatched")
        .setSmallIcon(R.drawable.ic_launcher_foreground)
        .setContentIntent(pendingIntent)
        .setTicker("Agent dispatched, tracking movement")
```

This function takes the **pendingIntent** and **channelId** instances generated from the functions you created earlier and constructs a **NotificationCompat.Builder** class. The builder lets you define a title (the first row), text (the second row), a small icon (size differs based on the device) to use, the intent to be triggered when the user clicks on **Notification**, and a ticker (used for accessibility; before Android Lollipop, this showed before the notification was presented). You can set other properties, too. Explore the **NotificationCompat.Builder** class. In a real project, remember to use string resources from strings.xml rather than hardcoded strings.

7. Implement the following code to introduce a function to start the foreground service:

```
private fun startForegroundService(): NotificationCompat.Builder {
    val pendingIntent = getPendingIntent()
```

```
      val channelId =
        if (Build.VERSION.SDK_INT >= Build.VERSION_CODES.O) {
          createNotificationChannel()
      } else {
          ""

      }
      val notificationBuilder = getNotificationBuilder(pendingIntent,
        channelId)
      startForeground(NOTIFICATION_ID, notificationBuilder.build())
      return notificationBuilder
}
```

You first get **PendingIntent** using the function you introduced earlier. Then, depending on the API level of the device, you create a notification channel and get its ID or set an empty ID. You pass **pendingIntent** and **channelId** to the function that constructs **NotificationCompat.Builder**, and start the service as a foreground service, providing it with **NOTIFICATION_ID** and a notification built using the builder. The function returns **NotificationCompat.Builder**, to be used later to update the notification.

8. Define two fields in your service—one to hold a reusable **NotificationCompat.Builder** class, and another to hold a reference to **Handler**, which you will later use to post work in the background:

```
private lateinit var notificationBuilder: NotificationCompat.Builder
private lateinit var serviceHandler: Handler
```

9. Next, override **onCreate()** to start the service as a foreground service, keep a reference to the **Notification.Builder**, and create **serviceHandler**:

```
override fun onCreate() {
    super.onCreate()
    notificationBuilder = startForegroundService()
    val handlerThread = HandlerThread("RouteTracking").apply {
        start()
    }
    serviceHandler = Handler(handlerThread.looper)
}
```

Note that to create the **Handler** instance, you must first define and start **HandlerThread**.

10. Define a call that tracks your deployed SCA as it approaches its designated destination:

```
private fun trackToDestination(notificationBuilder:
  NotificationCompat.Builder) {
    for (i in 10 downTo 0) {
        Thread.sleep(1000L)
        notificationBuilder
          .setContentText("$i seconds to destination")
        startForeground(NOTIFICATION_ID,
          notificationBuilder.build())
    }
}
```

This will count down from **10** to **1**, sleeping for 1 second between updates and then updating the notification with the remaining time.

11. Add a function to notify observers of completion on the main thread:

```
private fun notifyCompletion(agentId: String) {
    Handler(Looper.getMainLooper()).post {
        mutableTrackingCompletion.value = agentId
    }
}
```

By posting on a handler using the main **Looper**, you make sure that updates occur on the main (UI) app thread. When setting the value to the agent ID, you are notifying all observers that that agent ID has reached its destination.

12. Override **onStartCommand(Intent?, Int, Int)** like so:

```
override fun onStartCommand(intent: Intent?, flags: Int,
  startId: Int): Int {
    val returnValue = super.onStartCommand(intent, flags, startId)
    val agentId =
      intent?.getStringExtra(EXTRA_SECRET_CAT_AGENT_ID)
        ?: throw IllegalStateException("Agent ID must be provided")
    serviceHandler.post {
        trackToDestination(notificationBuilder)
        notifyCompletion(agentId)
        stopForeground(true)
        stopSelf()
    }
    return returnValue
}
```

You first delegate the call to **super**, which internally calls **onStart()** and returns a backward-compatible state you could return. You store this returned value. Next, you obtain the SCA ID from the extras passed via the intent. This service would not work without an agent ID, so you throw an exception if one is not provided. Next, you switch to the background thread defined in **onCreate** to track the agent to its destination in a blocking way. When tracking is done, you notify observers that the task is complete, stop the foreground service (removing the notification by passing **true**), and stop the service itself, as you don't expect to require it again soon. You then return the earlier stored return value from **super**.

13. Update your **AndroidManifest.xml** to request the **FOREGROUND_SERVICE** permission and introduce the service:

```
<manifest ...>

    <uses-permission android:name=
      "android.permission.FOREGROUND_SERVICE"/>

    <application ...>

        <service
            android:name=".RouteTrackingService"
            android:enabled="true"
            android:exported="true" />

        <activity ...>
```

First, we declare that our app would require the **FOREGROUND_ SERVICE** permission. Unless we do so, the system will block our app from using foreground services. Next, we declare the service. Setting **android:enabled="true"** tells the system it can instantiate the service. The default is **"true"**, so this is optional. Defining the service with **android:exported="true"** tells the system that other applications could start the service. In our case, we don't need this extra functionality, but we have added it just so that you are aware of this capability.

14. Back to your **MainActivity**. Introduce a function to launch **RouteTrackingService**:

```
private fun launchTrackingService() {
    RouteTrackingService.trackingCompletion.observe(this, Observer {
        agentId ->
        showResult("Agent $agentId arrived!")
    })
    val serviceIntent = Intent(this,
        RouteTrackingService::class.java).apply {
        putExtra(EXTRA_SECRET_CAT_AGENT_ID, "007")
    }
    ContextCompat.startForegroundService(this, serviceIntent)
}
```

This function first observes **LiveData** for completion updates, showing a result on completion. Then, it defines **Intent** for launching the service, setting the SCA ID as an extra parameter for that **Intent**. It then launches the service as a foreground service using **ContextCompat**, which hides away compatibility-related logic for you.

15. Lastly, update **onCreate()** to start tracking the SCA as soon as it is suited up and ready to go:

```
workManager.getWorkInfoByIdLiveData(catSuitUpRequest.id)
    .observe(this, Observer { info ->
        if (info.state.isFinished) {
            showResult("Agent done suiting up. Ready to go!")
            launchTrackingService()
        }
    })
```

16. Launch the app:

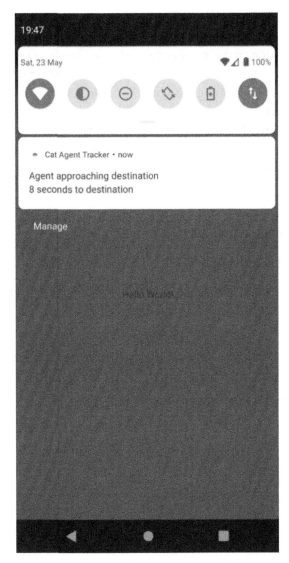

Figure 8.2: Notification counting down

After the notifications informing you of the SCA's preparation steps, you should see a notification in your status bar. That notification should then count down from 10 to 0, disappear, and be replaced by a toast informing you that the agent arrived at its destination. Seeing that last toast tells you that you managed to communicate the SCA ID to the service as well as getting it back on completion of the background task.

With all the knowledge gained from this chapter, let's complete the following activity.

ACTIVITY 8.01: REMINDER TO DRINK WATER

The average human loses about 2,500 ml of water per day (see https://en.wikipedia. org/wiki/Fluid_balance#Output). To stay healthy, we need to consume as much water as we lose. However, due to the busy nature of modern life, a lot of us forget to stay hydrated regularly. Suppose you wanted to develop an app that keeps track of your water loss (statistically) and gives you a constant update of your fluid balance. Starting from a balanced state, the app would gradually decrease the user's tracked water level. The user could tell the app when they drank a glass of water, and it would update the water level accordingly. The continuous updating of the water level will leverage your knowledge of running a background task, and you will also utilize your knowledge of communicating with a service to update a balance in response to user interaction.

The following steps will help you complete the activity:

1. Create an empty activity project and name your app **My Water Tracker**.

2. Add a foreground service permission to your **AndriodManifest.xml** file.

3. Create a new service.

4. Define a variable in your service to track the water level.

5. Define constants for a notification ID and for an extra intent data key.

6. Set up the creation of the notification from the service.

7. Add functions to start the foreground service and to update the water level.

8. Set the water level to decrease every 5 seconds.

9. Handle the addition of fluids from outside the service.

10. Make sure the service cleans up callbacks and messages when destroyed.

11. Register the service in the **Manifest.xml** file.

12. Start the service from **MainActivity** when the activity is created.

13. Add a button to the main activity layout.

14. When the user clicks the button, notify the service that it needs to increment the water level.

> **NOTE**
>
> The solution to this activity can be found at: http://packt.live/3sKj1cp.

SUMMARY

In this chapter, we learned how to execute long-running background tasks using **WorkManager** and foreground services. We discussed how to communicate progress to the user, and how to get the user back into an app once a task is finished executing. All the topics covered in this chapter are quite broad, and you could explore communicating with services, building notifications, and using the **WorkManager** class further. Hopefully, for most common scenarios, you now have the tools you need. Common use cases include background downloads, the background cleaning up of cached assets, playing music while the app is not running in the foreground, and, combined with the knowledge we gained from *Chapter 7, Android Permissions and Google Maps*, tracking the user's location over time.

In the next chapter, we will look into making our apps more robust and maintainable by writing unit tests and integration tests. This is particularly helpful when the code you write runs in the background and it is not immediately evident when something goes wrong.

9

UNIT TESTS AND INTEGRATION TESTS WITH JUNIT, MOCKITO, AND ESPRESSO

OVERVIEW

In this chapter, you will learn about testing on the Android platform and how to create unit tests, integration tests, and UI tests. You will see how to create each of these types of tests, analyze how it runs, and work with frameworks such as JUnit, Mockito, Robolectric, and Espresso. You will also learn about test-driven development, a software development practice that prioritizes tests over implementation. By the end of this chapter, you will be able to combine your new testing skills to work on a realistic project.

INTRODUCTION

In previous chapters, you learned about how to load background data and display it in the UI and how to set up API calls to retrieve data. But how can you be sure that things work well? What if you're in a situation where you have to fix a bug in a project that you haven't interacted much with in the past? How can you know that the fix you are applying won't trigger another bug? The answer to these questions is through tests.

In this chapter, we will analyze the types of tests developers can write and we will look at available testing tools to ease the testing experience. The first issue that arises is the fact that desktops or laptops, which have different operating systems, are used to develop mobile applications. This implies that the tests also have to be run on the device or emulator, which will slow the tests down. In order to solve this issue, we are presented with two types of tests: **local tests**, which are located in the `test` folder and will run on your machine, and **instrumented tests**, which are located in the `androidTest` folder and will run on the device or emulator.

Both of these tests rely on the Java **JUnit** library, which helps developers set up their tests and group them in different categories. It also provides different configuration options, as well as extensions that other libraries can build upon. We will also look into the testing pyramid, which helps guide developers as to how to structure their tests. We will start at the bottom of the pyramid, which is represented by **unit tests**, move upward through **integration tests**, and finally reach the top, which is represented by **end-to-end tests** (UI tests). You'll have the opportunity to learn about the tools that aid in writing each of these types of tests:

- **Mockito** and **mockito-kotlin**, which help mainly in unit tests and are useful for creating mocks or test double in which we can manipulate inputs so that we can assert different scenarios. (A mock or test double is an object that mimics the implementation of another object. Every time a test interacts with mocks, you can specify the behavior of these interactions.)

- **Robolectric**, an open source library that brings the Android framework onto your machine, allowing you to test activities and fragments locally and not on the emulator. This can be used for both unit tests and integration tests.

- **Espresso**, which allows developers to create interactions (clicking buttons, inserting text in `EditText` components, and so on) and assertions (verifying that views display certain text, are currently being displayed to the user, are enabled, and so on) on an app's UI in an instrumented test.

In this chapter, we will also take a look at **test-driven development** (**TDD**). This is a software development process where tests take priority. A simple way of describing it is as writing the test first. We will analyze how this approach is taken when developing features for Android applications. One of the things to keep in mind is that in order for an application to be properly tested, its classes must be properly written. One way to do this is by clearly defining the boundaries between your classes and splitting them based on the tasks you want them to accomplish. Once you have achieved this, you can also rely on the **dependency inversion** and **dependency injection** principles when writing your classes. When these principles are applied properly, you should be able to inject fake objects into the subjects of your tests and manipulate the inputs to suit your testing scenario. Dependency injection also helps when writing instrumented tests to help you swap modules that make network calls with local data in order to make your tests independent of external factors, such as networks. Instrumented tests are tests that run on a device or an emulator. The "instrument" keyword comes from the instrumentation framework, which assembles these tests and then executes them on the device.

Ideally, each application should have three types of tests:

- **Unit tests**: These are local tests that validate individual classes and methods. They should represent the majority of your tests and they should be fast, easy to debug, and easy to maintain. They are also known as small tests.

- **Integration tests**: These are either local tests with Robolectric, or instrumented tests that validate interactions between your app's modules and components. These are slower and more complex than unit tests. The increase in complexity is due to the interaction between the components. These are also known as medium tests.

- **UI tests (end-to-end tests)**: These are instrumented tests that verify complete user journeys and scenarios. This makes them more complex and harder to maintain; they should represent the smallest number of your total test number. These are also known as large tests.

In the following figure, you can observe the **testing pyramid**. The recommendation from Google is to keep a ratio of 70:20:10 (unit tests: integration tests: UI tests) for your tests:

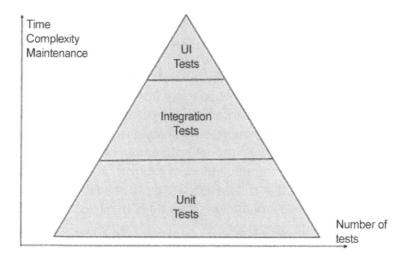

Figure 9.1: Testing pyramid

As mentioned in the previous section, a unit test is a test that verifies a small portion of your code, and the majority of your tests should be unit tests that should cover all sorts of scenarios (success, errors, limits, and more). Ideally, these tests should be local, but there are a few exceptions where you can make them instrumented. Those cases are rare and should be limited to when you want to interact with specific hardware of the device.

JUNIT

JUnit is a framework for writing unit tests both in Java and in Android. It is responsible for how tests are executed, allowing developers to configure their tests. It offers a multitude of features, such as the following:

- **Setup and teardown**: These are called before and after each test method is executed, allowing developers to set up relevant data for the test and clear it once the test is executed. They are represented by the @**Before** and @**After** annotations.

- **Assertions**: These are used to verify the result of an operation against an expected value.

- **Rules**: These allow developers to set up inputs that are common for multiple tests.

- **Runners**: Using these, you can specify how the tests can be executed.
- **Parameters**: These allow a test method to be executed with multiple inputs.
- **Orderings**: These specify in which order the tests should be executed.
- **Matchers**: These allow you to define patterns that can then be used to validate the results of the subject of your tests, or help you control the behavior of mocks.

In Android Studio, when a new project is created, the **app** module comes with the JUnit library in Gradle. This should be visible in **app/build.gradle**:

```
testImplementation 'junit:junit:4.13.1'
```

Let's look at the following class that we need to test:

```
class MyClass {

    fun factorial(n: Int): Int {
        return IntArray(n) {
            it+1
        }.reduce { acc, i ->
            acc * i
        }
    }
}
```

This method should return the factorial of the number **n**. We can start with a simple test that checks the value. In order to create a new unit test, you will need to create a new class in the **test** directory of your project. The typical convention most developers follow is to add the **Test** suffix to your class name and place it under the same package in the **test** directory. For example, **com.mypackage.ClassA** will have the test in **com.mypackage.ClassATest**:

```
import org.junit.Assert.assertEquals
import org.junit.Test
class MyClassTest {

    private val myClass = MyClass()

    @Test
    fun computesFactorial() {
        val n = 3
```

```
        val result = myClass.factorial(n)
        assertEquals(6, result)

    }

}
```

In this test, you can see that we initialize the class under test, and the test method itself is annotated with the @**Test** annotation. The test method itself will assert that **(3!)==6**. The assertion is done using the **assertEquals** method from the JUnit library. A common practice in development is to split the test into three areas, also known as AAA (Arrange-Act-Assert):

- Arrange - Where the inputs are initialized

- Act - Where the method under test is called

- Assert - Where the verification is done

We can write another test to make sure that the value is correct, but that would mean that we end up duplicating the code. We can now attempt to write a parameterized test. In order to do this, we will need to use the parameterized test runner. The preceding test has its own built-in runner provided by JUnit. The parameterized runner will run the test repeatedly for different values that we provide, and it will look like the following. (Please note that import statements have been removed for brevity.)

```
@RunWith(Parameterized::class)
class MyClassTest(
    private val input: Int,
    private val expected: Int
) {
    companion object {
        @Parameterized.Parameters
        @JvmStatic
        fun getData(): Collection<Array<Int>> = listOf(
            arrayOf(0, 1),
            arrayOf(1, 1),
            arrayOf(2, 2),
            arrayOf(3, 6),
            arrayOf(4, 24),
            arrayOf(5, 120)
        )
    }
```

```
    private val myClass = MyClass()

    @Test
    fun computesFactorial() {
        val result = myClass.factorial(input)

        assertEquals(expected, result)
    }
}
```

This will actually run six tests. The usage of the @**Parameterized** annotation tells JUnit that this is a test with multiple parameters, and also allows us to add a constructor for the test that will represent the input value for our factorial function and the output. We then defined a collection of parameters with the use of the @ **Parameterized.Parameters** annotation. Each parameter for this test is a separate list containing the input and the expected output. When JUnit runs this test, it will run a new instance for each parameter and then execute the test method. This will produce five successes and one failure for when we test *0!*, meaning that we have found a bug. We never accounted for a situation when *n = 0*. Now, we can go back to our code to fix the failure. We can do this by replacing the **reduce** function, which doesn't allow us to specify an initial value with a **fold** function, which allows us to give the initial value of **1**:

```
fun factorial(n: Int): Int {
    return IntArray(n) {
        it + 1
    }.fold(1, { acc, i -> acc * i })
}
```

Running the tests now, they will all pass. But that doesn't mean we are done here. There are many things that can go wrong. What happens if **n** is a negative number? Since we are dealing with factorials, we may get really large numbers. We are working with integers in our examples, which means that the integer will overflow after *12!*. Normally, we would create new test methods in the **MyClassTest** class, but since the parametrized runner is used, all of our new methods will be run multiple times, which will cost us time, so we will create a new test class to check our errors:

```
class MyClassTest2 {

    private val myClass = MyClass()

    @Test(expected = MyClass.FactorialNotFoundException::class)
```

```kotlin
fun computeNegatives() {
    myClass.factorial(-10)
}
}
```

This would lead to the following change in the class that was tested:

```kotlin
class MyClass {

    @Throws(FactorialNotFoundException::class)
    fun factorial(n: Int): Int {
        if (n < 0) {
            throw FactorialNotFoundException
        }
        return IntArray(n) {
            it + 1
        }.fold(1, { acc, i -> acc * i })
    }

    object FactorialNotFoundException : Throwable()
}
```

Let's solve the issue with very large factorials. We can use the **BigInteger** class, which is capable of holding large numbers. We can update the test as follows (import statements not shown):

```kotlin
@RunWith(Parameterized::class)
class MyClassTest(
    private val input: Int,
    private val expected: BigInteger
) {
    companion object {
        @Parameterized.Parameters
        @JvmStatic
        fun getData(): Collection<Array<Any>> = listOf(
            arrayOf(0, BigInteger.ONE),
            arrayOf(1, BigInteger.ONE),
            arrayOf(2, BigInteger.valueOf(2)),
            arrayOf(3, BigInteger.valueOf(6)),
            arrayOf(4, BigInteger.valueOf(24)),
            arrayOf(5, BigInteger.valueOf(120)),
            arrayOf(13, BigInteger("6227020800")),
```

```
            arrayOf(25, BigInteger("15511210043330985984000000"))

    )
}

private val myClass = MyClass()

@Test
fun computesFactorial() {
    val result = myClass.factorial(input)

    assertEquals(expected, result)
}
}
```

The class under test now looks like this:

```
@Throws(FactorialNotFoundException::class)
fun factorial(n: Int): BigInteger {
    if (n < 0) {
        throw FactorialNotFoundException
    }
    return IntArray(n) {
        it + 1
    }.fold(BigInteger.ONE, { acc, i -> acc * i.toBigInteger() })
}
```

In the preceding example, we have implemented the factorial with the help of
IntArray. This implementation is based more on Kotlin's ability to chain methods
together, but it has one drawback: the fact that it uses memory for the array when
it doesn't need to. We only care about the factorial and not storing all the numbers
from 1 to *n*. We can change the implementation to a simple **for** loop and use the
tests to guide us during the refactoring process. We can observe here two benefits of
having tests in your application:

- They serve as updated documentation of how the features should
  be implemented.

- They guide us when refactoring code by maintaining the same assertion and
  detecting whether new changes to the code broke it.

Let's update the code to get rid of **IntArray**:

```
@Throws(FactorialNotFoundException::class)
fun factorial(n: Int): BigInteger {
    if (n < 0) {
        throw FactorialNotFoundException
    }
    var result = BigInteger.ONE
    for (i in 1..n){
        result = result.times(i.toBigInteger())
    }
    return result
}
```

If we modify the **factorial** function, as in the preceding example, and run the tests, we should see them all passing.

In certain situations, your tests will use a resource that is common to the test or the application (databases, files, and so on). Ideally, this shouldn't happen for unit tests, but there can always be exceptions to this. Let's analyze that scenario and see how JUnit can aid us with it. We will add a **companion** object, which will store the result, in order to simulate this behavior:

```
companion object {

    var result: BigInteger = BigInteger.ONE
}


@Throws(FactorialNotFoundException::class)
fun factorial(n: Int): BigInteger {
    if (n < 0) {
        throw FactorialNotFoundException
    }
    for (i in 1..n) {
        result = result.times(i.toBigInteger())
    }
    return result
}
```

If we execute the tests for the preceding code, we will start seeing that some will fail. That's because after the first tests execute the **factorial** function, the result will have the value of the executed tests, and when a new test is executed, the result of the factorial will be multiplied by the previous value of the result. Normally, this would be good because the tests tell us that we are doing something wrong and we should remedy this, but for this example, we will address the issue directly in the tests:

```
@Before
fun setUp(){
    MyClass.result = BigInteger.ONE
}


@After
fun tearDown(){
    MyClass.result = BigInteger.ONE
}


@Test
fun computesFactorial() {
    val result = myClass.factorial(input)

    assertEquals(expected, result)
}
```

In the tests, we've added two methods with the @**Before** and @**After** annotations. When these methods are introduced, JUnit will change the execution flow as follows: all methods with the @**Before** annotation will be executed, a method with the @ **Test** annotation will be executed, and then all methods with the @**After** annotation will be executed. This process will repeat for every @**Test** method in your class.

If you find yourself repeating the same statements in your @**Before** method, you can consider using @**Rule** in order to remove the repetition. We can set up a test rule for the preceding example. Test rules should be in the **test** or **androidTest** packages, because their usage is only limited to testing. They tend to be used in multiple tests, so you can place your rules in a **rules** package (import statements not shown):

```
class ResultRule : TestRule {

    override fun apply(
        base: Statement,
        description: Description?
```

```
    ): Statement? {

        return object : Statement() {

            @Throws(Throwable::class)
            override fun evaluate() {
                MyClass.result = BigInteger.ONE
                try {
                    base.evaluate()
                } finally {
                    MyClass.result = BigInteger.ONE
                }
            }
        }
    }
}
```

In the preceding example, we can see that the rule will implement **TestRule**, which in turn comes with the **apply()** method. We then create a new **Statement** object that will execute the base statement (the test itself) and reset the value of the result before and after the statement. We can now modify the test as follows:

```
@JvmField
@Rule
val resultRule = ResultRule()
private val myClass = MyClass()

@Test
fun computesFactorial() {
    val result = myClass.factorial(input)

    assertEquals(expected, result)
}
```

In order to add the rule to the test, we use the **@Rule** annotation. Since the test is written in Kotlin, we are using **@JvmField** to avoid generating getters and setters because **@Rule** requires a public field and not a method.

ANDROID STUDIO TESTING TIPS

Android Studio comes with a good set of shortcuts and visual tools to help with testing. If you want to create a new test for your class or go to existing tests for your class, you can use the *Ctrl + Shift + T* (Windows) or *Command + Shift + T* (Mac) shortcut. In order to run tests, there are multiple options: right-click your file or the package and select the `Run Tests in...` option, or if you want to run a test independently, you can go to the particular test method and select the green icon either to the top of the class, which will execute all the tests in the class; or, for an individual test, you can click the green icon next to the `@Test` annotated methods. This will trigger the test execution, which will be displayed in the **Run** tab, as shown in the following screenshot. When the tests are completed, they will become either red or green, depending on their success state:

Figure 9.2: Test output in Android Studio

Another important feature that can be found in tests is the debug one. This is important because you can debug both the test and the method under test, so if you find problems in fixing an issue, you can use this to view what the test was using as input and how your code handles the input. The third feature you can find in the green icon next to a test is the `Run With Coverage` option.

This helps developers identify what lines of code are covered by the test and which ones are skipped. The higher the coverage, the higher the chances of finding crashes and bugs:

Element	Class, %	Method, %	Line, %
BuildConfig	0% (0/1)	0% (0/1)	0% (0/1)
MyClass	50% (1/2)	66% (2/3)	75% (6/8)

Coverage: MyClassTest ×

25% classes, 60% lines covered in package 'com.android.testable.myapplication'

Figure 9.3: Test coverage in Android Studio

In the preceding figure, you can see the coverage of our class broken down into the number of classes under test, the number of methods under test, and the number of lines under test.

Another way to run tests for your Android app is through the command line. This is usually handy in situations where your project has **continuous integration** set up, meaning that every time you upload your code to a repository in the cloud, a set of scripts will be triggered to test it and ensure functionality. Since this is done in the cloud, there is no need for Android Studio to be installed. For simplicity, we will be using the **Terminal** tab in Android Studio to emulate that behavior. The **Terminal** tab is usually located in the bottom bar in Android Studio near the **Logcat** tab. In every Android Studio project, a file called **gradlew** is present. This is an executable file that allows developers to execute Gradle commands. In order to run your local unit tests, you can use the following:

- **gradlew.bat test** (for Windows)

- **./gradlew test** (for Mac and Linux)

Once that command is executed, the app will be built and tested. You can find a variety of commands that you can input in **Terminal** in the **Gradle** tab located on the right-hand side in Android Studio. The outputs of the tests, when executed from either **Terminal** or the **Gradle** tab, can be found in the **app/build/reports** folder:

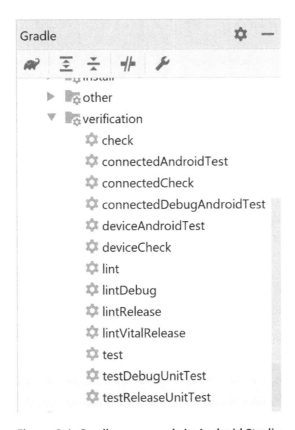

Figure 9.4: Gradle commands in Android Studio

MOCKITO

In the preceding examples, we looked at how to set up a unit test and how to use assertions to verify the result of an operation. What if we want to verify whether a certain method was called? Or what if we want to manipulate the test input in order to test a specific scenario? In these types of situations, we can use **Mockito**. This is a library that helps developers set up dummy objects that can be injected into the objects under test and allows them to verify method calls, set up inputs, and even monitor the test objects themselves.

The library should be added to your **test** Gradle setup, as follows:

```
testImplementation 'org.mockito:mockito-core:3.6.0'
```

Now, let's look at the following code example (please note that, for brevity, import statements have been removed from the following code snippets):

```
class StringConcatenator(private val context: Context) {

    fun concatenate(@StringRes stringRes1: Int,
        @StringRes stringRes2: Int): String {
        return context.getString(stringRes1).plus(context
            .getString(stringRes2))
    }

}
```

Here, we have the **Context** object, which normally cannot be unit tested because it's part of the Android framework. We can use **mockito** to create a test double and inject it into the **StringConcatenator** object. Then, we can manipulate the call to **getString()** to return whatever input we chose. This process is referred to as mocking.

```
class StringConcatenatorTest {

    private val context = Mockito.mock(Context::class.java)
    private val stringConcatenator = StringConcatenator(context)

    @Test
    fun concatenate() {
        val stringRes1 = 1
        val stringRes2 = 2
        val string1 = "string1"
        val string2 = "string2"
        Mockito.`when`(context.getString(stringRes1)).thenReturn(string1)
        Mockito.`when`(context.getString(stringRes2)).thenReturn(string2)

        val result = stringConcatenator.concatenate(stringRes1,
            stringRes2)

        assertEquals(string1.plus(string2), result)
    }

}
```

> **NOTE**
>
> ` is an escape character present in Kotlin and should not be confused with a quote mark. It allows the developer to give methods any name that they want, including special characters or reserved words.

In the test, we have created a **mock** context. When the **concatenate** method was tested, we used Mockito to return a specific string when the **getString()** method was called with a particular input. This allowed us to then assert the final result.

Mockito is not limited to mocking Android Framework classes only. We can create a **SpecificStringConcatenator** class that will use **StringConcatenator** to concatenate two specific strings from **strings.xml**:

```kotlin
class SpecificStringConcatenator(private val stringConcatenator:
  StringConcatenator) {

    fun concatenateSpecificStrings(): String {
        return stringConcatenator.concatenate(R.string.string_1,
          R.string.string_2)
    }
}
```

We can write the test for it as follows:

```kotlin
class SpecificStringConcatenatorTest {

    private val stringConcatenator = Mockito
      .mock(StringConcatenator::class.java)
    private val specificStringConcatenator =
      SpecificStringConcatenator(stringConcatenator)

    @Test
    fun concatenateSpecificStrings() {
        val expected = "expected"
        Mockito.'when'(stringConcatenator.concatenate(R.string.string_1,
          R.string.string_2))
            .thenReturn(expected)

        val result = specificStringConcatenator
          .concatenateSpecificStrings()
```

```
            assertEquals(expected, result)
    }
}
```

Here, we are mocking the previous **StringConcatenator** and instructing the mock to return a specific result. If we run the test, it will fail because Mockito is limited to mocking final classes. Here, it encounters a conflict with Kotlin that makes all classes *final* unless we specify them as *open*. Luckily, there is a configuration we can apply that solves this dilemma without making the classes under test *open*:

1. Create a folder named **resources** in the **test** package.

2. In **resources**, create a folder named **mockito-extensions**.

3. In the **mockito-extensions** folder, create a file named **org.mockito. plugins.MockMaker**.

4. Inside the file, add the following line:

```
mock-maker-inline
```

In situations where you have callbacks or asynchronous work and cannot use the JUnit assertions, you can use **mockito** to verify the invocation on the callback or lambdas:

```
class SpecificStringConcatenator(private val stringConcatenator:
  StringConcatenator) {

    fun concatenateSpecificStrings(): String {
        return stringConcatenator.concatenate(R.string.string_1,
          R.string.string_2)
    }

    fun concatenateWithCallback(callback: Callback) {
        callback.onStringReady(concatenateSpecificStrings())
    }

    interface Callback {

        fun onStringReady(input: String)
    }
}
```

In the preceding example, we have added the **concatenateWithCallback**
method, which will invoke the callback with the result of the
concatenateSpecificStrings method. The test for this method would look
something like this:

```
@Test
fun concatenateWithCallback() {
    val expected = "expected"
    Mockito.`when`(stringConcatenator.concatenate(R.string.string_1,
        R.string.string_2))
        .thenReturn(expected)
    val callback =
        Mockito.mock(SpecificStringConcatenator.Callback::class.java)

    specificStringConcatenator.concatenateWithCallback(callback)

    Mockito.verify(callback).onStringReady(expected)
}
```

Here, we are creating a mock **Callback** object, which we can then verify at
the end with the expected result. Notice that we had to duplicate the setup
of the **concatenateSpecificStrings** method in order to test the
concatenateWithCallback method. You should never mock the objects
you are testing; however, you can use **spy** to change their behavior. We can
spy the **stringConcatenator** object in order to change the outcome of the
concatenateSpecificStrings method:

```
@Test
fun concatenateWithCallback() {
    val expected = "expected"
    val spy = Mockito.spy(specificStringConcatenator)

    Mockito.`when`(spy.concatenateSpecificStrings())
        .thenReturn(expected)
    val callback
        = Mockito.mock(SpecificStringConcatenator.Callback::class.java)

    specificStringConcatenator.concatenateWithCallback(callback)

    Mockito.verify(callback).onStringReady(expected)
}
```

Mockito also relies on dependency injection to initialize class variables and has a custom build JUnit test runner. This can simplify the initialization of our variables, as follows:

```
@RunWith(MockitoJUnitRunner::class)
class SpecificStringConcatenatorTest {

    @Mock
    lateinit var stringConcatenator: StringConcatenator
    @InjectMocks
    lateinit var specificStringConcatenator: SpecificStringConcatenator

}
```

In the preceding example, **MockitoRunner** will inject the variables with the **@Mock** annotation with mocks. Next, it will create a new non-mocked instance of the field with the **@InjectionMocks** annotation. When this instance is created, Mockito will try to inject the mock objects that will match the signature of the constructor of that object.

MOCKITO-KOTLIN

You may have noticed, in the preceding example, that the **when** method from Mockito has escaped. This is because of a conflict with the Kotlin programming language. Mockito is built mainly for Java, and when Kotlin was created, it introduced this keyword. Conflicts like this are escaped using the ` character. This, along with some other minor issues, causes some inconvenience when using Mockito in Kotlin. A few libraries were introduced to wrap Mockito and provide a nicer experience when using it. One of those is **mockito-kotlin**. You can add this library to your module using the following command:

```
testImplementation "com.nhaarman.mockitokotlin2:mockito-kotlin:2.2.0"
```

A big visible change this library adds is replacing the **when** method with **whenever**. Another useful change is replacing the **mock** method to rely on generics, rather than class objects. The rest of the syntax is similar to the Mockito syntax.

We can now update the previous tests with the new library, starting with **StringConcatenatorTest** (import statements have been removed for brevity):

```
class StringConcatenatorTest {

    private val context = mock<Context>()
```

```
    private val stringConcatenator = StringConcatenator(context)

    @Test
    fun concatenate() {
        val stringRes1 = 1
        val stringRes2 = 2
        val string1 = "string1"
        val string2 = "string2"
        whenever(context.getString(stringRes1)).thenReturn(string1)
        whenever(context.getString(stringRes2)).thenReturn(string2)

        val result =
            stringConcatenator.concatenate(stringRes1, stringRes2)

        assertEquals(string1.plus(string2), result)
    }
}
```

As you can observe, the ` character has disappeared, and our mock initialization for the **Context** object has been simplified. We can apply the same thing for the **SpecificConcatenatorTest** class (import statements have been removed for brevity):

```
@RunWith(MockitoJUnitRunner::class)
class SpecificStringConcatenatorTest {

    @Mock
    lateinit var stringConcatenator: StringConcatenator
    @InjectMocks
    lateinit var specificStringConcatenator: SpecificStringConcatenator

    @Test
    fun concatenateSpecificStrings() {
        val expected = "expected"
        whenever(stringConcatenator.concatenate(R.string.string_1,
            R.string.string_2))
            .thenReturn(expected)

        val result =
            specificStringConcatenator.concatenateSpecificStrings()

        assertEquals(expected, result)
```

```
    }

    @Test
    fun concatenateWithCallback() {
        val expected = "expected"
        val spy = spy(specificStringConcatenator)

        whenever(spy.concatenateSpecificStrings()).thenReturn(expected)
        val callback = mock<SpecificStringConcatenator.Callback>()

        specificStringConcatenator.concatenateWithCallback(callback)

        verify(callback).onStringReady(expected)
    }
}
```

EXERCISE 9.01: TESTING THE SUM OF NUMBERS

Using JUnit, Mockito, and **mockito-kotlin**, write a set of tests for the following class that should cover the following scenarios:

- Assert the values for **0**, **1**, **5**, **20**, and **Int.MAX_VALUE**.

- Assert the outcome for a negative number.

- Fix the code and replace the sum of numbers with the formula $n*(n+1)/2$.

> **NOTE**
>
> Throughout this exercise, import statements are not shown. To see full code files, refer to http://packt.live/35TW8JI):

The code to test is as follows.

```
class NumberAdder {

    @Throws(InvalidNumberException::class)
    fun sum(n: Int, callback: (BigInteger) -> Unit) {
        if (n < 0) {
            throw InvalidNumberException
        }
        var result = BigInteger.ZERO
```

```
        for (i in 1..n){
          result = result.plus(i.toBigInteger())
        }
        callback(result)


    }


    object InvalidNumberException : Throwable()
}
```

Perform the following steps to complete this exercise:

1. Let's make sure the necessary libraries are added to the **app/build. gradle** file:

```
testImplementation 'junit:junit:4.13.1'
testImplementation 'org.mockito:mockito-core:3.6.0'
testImplementation 'com.nhaarman.mockitokotlin2:mockito-kotlin:2.2.0'
```

2. Create a class named **NumberAdder** and copy the preceding code inside it.

3. Move the cursor inside the newly created class and, with *Command + Shift + T* or *Ctrl + Shift + T*, create a test class called **NumberAdderParameterTest**.

4. Create a parametrized test inside this class that will assert the outcomes for the **0**, **1**, **5**, **20**, and **Int.MAX_VALUE** values:

```
@RunWith(Parameterized::class)
class NumberAdderParameterTest(
    private val input: Int,
    private val expected: BigInteger
) {

    companion object {
        @Parameterized.Parameters
        @JvmStatic
        fun getData(): List<Array<out Any>> = listOf(
            arrayOf(0, BigInteger.ZERO),
            arrayOf(1, BigInteger.ONE),
            arrayOf(5, 15.toBigInteger()),
            arrayOf(20, 210.toBigInteger()),
            arrayOf(Int.MAX_VALUE, BigInteger("2305843008139952128"))
        )
```

```
    }

        private val numberAdder = NumberAdder()


        @Test
        fun sum() {
            val callback = mock<(BigInteger) -> Unit>()

            numberAdder.sum(input, callback)

            verify(callback).invoke(expected)
        }
    }
```

5. Create a separate test class that handles the exception thrown when there are negative numbers, named **NumberAdderErrorHandlingTest**:

```
@RunWith(MockitoJUnitRunner::class)
class NumberAdderErrorHandlingTest {

    @InjectMocks
    lateinit var numberAdder: NumberAdder

    @Test(expected = NumberAdder.InvalidNumberException::class)
    fun sum() {
        val input = -1
        val callback = mock<(BigInteger) -> Unit>()

        numberAdder.sum(input, callback)
    }
}
```

6. Since $1 + 2 + ...n = n * (n + 1) / 2$, we can use the formula in the code and this would make the execution of the method run faster:

```
class NumberAdder {

    @Throws(InvalidNumberException::class)
    fun sum(n: Int, callback: (BigInteger) -> Unit) {
        if (n < 0) {
            throw InvalidNumberException
```

```
        }
        callback(n.toBigInteger().times((n.toBigInteger() +
            1.toBigInteger())).divide(2.toBigInteger()))
    }

    object InvalidNumberException : Throwable()
}
```

Run the tests by right-clicking the package in which the tests are located and selecting **Run all in [package_name]**. An output similar to the following will appear, signifying that the tests have passed:

Figure 9.5: Output of Exercise 9.01

By completing this exercise, we have taken the first steps into unit testing, managed to create multiple test cases for a single operation, taken the first steps into understanding Mockito, and used tests to guide us on how to refactor code without introducing any new issues.

INTEGRATION TESTS

Let's assume your project is covered by unit tests where a lot of your logic is held. You now have to add these tested classes to an activity or a fragment and require them to update your UI. How can you be certain that these classes will work well with each other? The answer to that question is through integration testing. The idea behind this type of testing is to ensure that different components within your application integrate well with each other. Some examples include the following:

- Ensuring that your API-related components parse the data well and interact well with your storage components.

- The storage components are capable of storing and retrieving the data correctly.

- The UI components load and display the appropriate data.

- The transition between different screens in your application.

To aid with integration testing, the requirements are sometimes written in the format **Given - When - Then**. These usually represent acceptance criteria for a user story. Take the following example:

```
Given I am not logged in
And I open the application
When I enter my credentials
And click Login
Then I see the Main screen
```

We can use these steps to approach how we can write the integration tests for the feature we are developing.

On the Android platform, integration testing can be achieved with two libraries:

- **Robolectric**: This library gives developers the ability to test Android components as unit tests; that is, executing integration tests without an actual device or emulator.

- **Espresso**: This library is helpful in instrumentation tests on an Android device or emulator.

We'll have a look at these libraries in detail in the next sections.

ROBOLECTRIC

Robolectric started as an open source library that was meant to give users the ability to unit test classes from the Android framework as part of their local tests instead of the instrumented tests. Recently, it has been endorsed by Google and has been integrated with AndroidX Jetpack components. One of the main benefits of this library is the simplicity of testing activities and fragments. This is a benefit when it comes to integration tests because we can use this feature to make sure that our components integrate well with each other. Some of Robolectric's features are as follows:

- The possibility to instantiate and test the activity and fragment life cycle

- The possibility to test view inflation

- The possibility to provide configurations for different Android APIs, orientations, screen size, layout direction, and so on

- The possibility to change the **Application** class, which then helps to change the modules to permit data mocks to be inserted

In order to add Robolectric, along with the AndroidX integration, we will need the following libraries:

```
testImplementation 'org.robolectric:robolectric:4.3'
testImplementation 'androidx.test.ext:junit:1.1.1'
```

The second library will bring a set of **utility** methods and classes required for testing Android components.

Let's assume we have to deliver a feature in which we display the text **Result x**, where **x** is the factorial function for a number that the user will insert in the **EditText** element. In order to achieve this, we have two classes, one that computes the factorial and another that concatenates the word **Result** with the factorial if the number is positive, or it will return the text **Error** if the number is negative. The factorial class will look something like this (throughout this example, import statements have been removed for brevity):

```
class FactorialGenerator {

    @Throws(FactorialNotFoundException::class)
    fun factorial(n: Int): BigInteger {
        if (n < 0) {
            throw FactorialNotFoundException
        }
        var result = BigInteger.ONE
        for (i in 1..n) {
            result = result.times(i.toBigInteger())
        }
        return result
    }

    object FactorialNotFoundException : Throwable()
}
```

The **TextFormatter** class will look like this:

```
class TextFormatter(
    private val factorialGenerator: FactorialGenerator,
    private val context: Context
) {


    fun getFactorialResult(n: Int): String {
        return try {
            context.getString(R.string.result,
                factorialGenerator.factorial(n).toString())
        } catch (e: FactorialGenerator.FactorialNotFoundException) {
            context.getString(R.string.error)
        }
    }
}
```

We can combine these two components in our activity and have something similar to this:

```
class MainActivity : AppCompatActivity() {

    private lateinit var textFormatter: TextFormatter

    override fun onCreate(savedInstanceState: Bundle?) {
        super.onCreate(savedInstanceState)
        setContentView(R.layout.activity_main)
        ttextFormatter = TextFormatter(FactorialGenerator(),
            applicationContext)
        findViewById<Button>(R.id.button).setOnClickListener {
            findViewById<TextView>(R.id.text_view).text
                = textFormatter.getFactorialResult(findViewById<EditText>
                (R.id.edit_text).text.toString().toInt())
        }
    }
}
```

We can observe three components interacting with each other in this case. We can use Robolectric to test our activity. By testing the activity that creates the components, we can also test the interaction between all three of the components. We can write a test that looks like this:

```
@RunWith(AndroidJUnit4::class)
class MainActivityTest {

    private val context = getApplicationContext<Application>()

    @Test
    fun `show factorial result in text view`() {
        val scenario = launch<MainActivity>(MainActivity::class.java)

        scenario.moveToState(Lifecycle.State.RESUMED)

        scenario.onActivity { activity ->
            activity.edit_text.setText(5.toString())
            activity.button.performClick()
            assertEquals(context.getString(R.string.result,
                "120"),activity.text_view.text)
        }
    }
}
```

In the preceding example, we can see the AndroidX support for the activity test. The **AndroidJUnit4** test runner will set up Robolectric and create the necessary configurations, while the `launch` method will return a `scenario` object, which we can then play with in order to achieve the necessary conditions for the test.

If we want to add configurations for the test, we can use the @**Config** annotation both on the class and on each of the test methods:

```
@Config(
    sdk = [Build.VERSION_CODES.P],
    minSdk = Build.VERSION_CODES.KITKAT,
    maxSdk = Build.VERSION_CODES.Q,
    application = Application::class,
    assetDir = "/assetDir/"
)
@RunWith(AndroidJUnit4::class)
class MainActivityTest
```

We can also specify global configurations in the **test/resources** folder in the **robolectric.properties** file, like so:

```
sdk=28
minSdk = 14
maxSdk = 29
```

Another important feature that has recently been added to Robolectric is support for the Espresso library. This allows developers to use the syntax from Espresso in order to interact with views and make assertions on the views. Another library that can be used in combination with Robolectric is **FragmentScenario**, which allows the possibility to test fragments. These libraries can be added in Gradle using the following:

```
testImplementation 'androidx.fragment:fragment-testing:1.1.0'
testImplementation 'androidx.test.espresso:espresso-core:3.2.0'
```

Testing fragments is similar to activities using the **scenario** setup:

```
val scenario = launchFragmentInContainer<MainFragment>()
scenario.moveToState(Lifecycle.State.CREATED)
```

ESPRESSO

Espresso is a library designed to perform interactions and assertions in a concise way. It was initially designed to be used in instrumented tests and now it has migrated to be used with Robolectric as well. The typical usage for performing an action is as follows:

```
onView(Matcher<View>).perform(ViewAction)
```

For verification, we can use the following:

```
onView(Matcher<View>).check(ViewAssertion)
```

We can provide custom **ViewMatchers** if none can be found in the **ViewMatchers** class. Some of the most common ones are **withId** and **withText**. These two allow us to identify views based on their **R.id.myId** identifier or the text identifier. Ideally, the first one should be used to identify a particular view. Another interesting aspect of Espresso is the reliance on the **Hamcrest** library for matchers. This is a Java library that aims to improve testing. This allows multiple matchers to be combined if necessary. Let's say that the same ID is present in different views on your UI. You can narrow your search for a specific view using the following expression:

```
onView(allOf(withId(R.id.edit_text), withParent(withId(R.id.root))))
```

The **allOf** expression will evaluate all of the other operators and will pass only if all of the operators inside will pass. The preceding expressions will translate to "Find the view with **id=edit_text** that has the parent with **id=R.id.root**." Other **Hamcrest** operators may include **anyOf**, **both**, **either**, **is**, **isA**, **hasItem**, **equalTo**, **any**, **instanceOf**, **not**, **null**, and **notNull**.

ViewActions have a similar approach to **ViewMatchers**. We can find common ones in the **ViewActions** class. Common ones include **typeText**, **click**, **scrollTo**, **clearText**, **swipeLeft**, **swipeRight**, **swipeUp**, **swipeDown**, **closeSoftKeyboard**, **pressBack**, **pressKey**, **doubleClick**, and **longClick**. If you have custom views and certain actions are required, then you can implement your own **ViewAction** element by implementing the **ViewAction** interface.

Similar to the preceding examples, **ViewAssertions** have their own class. Typically, the **matches** method is used where you can then use **ViewMatchers** and **Hamcrest** matchers to validate the result:

```
onView(withId(R.id.text_view)).check(matches(withText("My text"))))
```

The preceding example will verify that the view with the **text_view** ID will contain the text **My text**:

```
onView(withId(R.id.button)).perform(click())
```

This will click the view with the ID button.

We can now rewrite the Robolectric test and add Espresso, which will give us this (import statement not shown):

```
@RunWith(AndroidJUnit4::class)
class MainActivityTest {

    @Test
    fun `show factorial result in text view`() {
        val scenario = launch<MainActivity>(MainActivity::class.java)

        scenario.moveToState(Lifecycle.State.RESUMED)

        scenario.onActivity { activity ->
            onView(withId(R.id.edit_text)).perform(typeText("5"))
            onView(withId(R.id.button)).perform(click())
            onView(withId(R.id.text_view))
                .check(matches(withText(activity
                    .getString(R.string.result, "120")))))
```

```
            }
        }
    }
```

In the preceding code sample, we can observe how, using Espresso, we input the number **5** in **EditText**, then click on the button, and then assert the text displayed in **TextView** with the help of the **onView()** method to obtain a reference to the view, and then execute actions using **perform()** or make assertions using **check()**.

> **NOTE**
>
> For the following exercise, you will need an emulator or a physical device with USB debugging enabled. You can do so by selecting **Tools | AVD Manager** in Android Studio. Then, you can create one with the **Create Virtual Device** option by selecting the type of emulator, clicking **Next**, and then selecting an x86 image. Any image larger than Lollipop should be alright for this exercise. Next, you can give your image a name and click **Finish**.

EXERCISE 9.02: DOUBLE INTEGRATION

Develop an application that observes the following requirements:

```
Given I open the application
And I insert the number n
When I press the Calculate button
Then I should see the text "The sum of numbers from 1 to n is [result]"

Given I open the application
And I insert the number -n
When I press the Calculate button
Then I should see the text "Error: Invalid number"
```

You should implement both unit tests and integration tests using Robolectric and Espresso, and migrate the integration tests to become instrumentation tests.

> **NOTE**
>
> Throughout this exercise, import statements are not shown. To see full code files, refer to http://packt.live/2M1MtcY):

Implement the following steps to complete this exercise:

1. Let's start by adding the necessary test libraries to **app/build.gradle**:

```
testImplementation 'junit:junit:4.13.1'
testImplementation 'org.mockito:mockito-core:3.6.0'
testImplementation 'com.nhaarman.mockitokotlin2
   :mockito-kotlin:2.2.0'
testImplementation 'org.robolectric:robolectric:4.4'
testImplementation 'androidx.test.ext:junit:1.1.2'
testImplementation 'androidx.test.espresso:espresso-core:3.3.0'
androidTestImplementation 'androidx.test.ext:junit:1.1.2'
androidTestImplementation 'androidx.test
   .espresso:espresso-core:3.3.0'
androidTestImplementation 'androidx.test:rules:1.3.0'
```

2. For Robolectric, we will need to add extra configurations, the first of which is to add the following line to **app/build.gradle** in the **android** closure:

```
testOptions.unitTests.includeAndroidResources = true
```

3. Create a **resources** directory in the **test** package.

4. Add the **robolectric.properties** file and add the following configuration to that file:

```
sdk=28
```

5. Create a folder named **resources** in the test package.

6. In **resources**, create a folder named **mockito-extensions**.

7. In the **mockito-extensions** folder, create a file named **org.mockito. plugins.MockMaker**, and inside the file, add the following line:

```
mock-maker-inline
```

8. Create the **NumberAdder** class. This is similar to the one in *Exercise 9.01*:

```
import java.math.BigInteger
class NumberAdder {

    @Throws(InvalidNumberException::class)
    fun sum(n: Int, callback: (BigInteger) -> Unit) {
        if (n < 0) {
            throw InvalidNumberException
        }
        callback(n.toBigInteger().times((n.toLong()
            + 1).toBigInteger()).divide(2.toBigInteger()))
    }

    object InvalidNumberException : Throwable()
}
```

9. Create the tests for **NumberAdder** in the **test** folder. First, create
NumberAdderParameterTest:

```
@RunWith(Parameterized::class)
class NumberAdderParameterTest(
    private val input: Int,
    private val expected: BigInteger
) {

    companion object {
        @Parameterized.Parameters
        @JvmStatic
        fun getData(): List<Array<out Any>> = listOf(
            arrayOf(0, BigInteger.ZERO),
            arrayOf(1, BigInteger.ONE),
            arrayOf(5, 15.toBigInteger()),
            arrayOf(20, 210.toBigInteger()),
            arrayOf(Int.MAX_VALUE, BigInteger("2305843008139952128"))
        )
    }

    private val numberAdder = NumberAdder()


    @Test
```

```
        fun sum() {
            val callback = mock<(BigInteger) -> Unit>()

            numberAdder.sum(input, callback)

            verify(callback).invoke(expected)
        }
    }
```

10. Then, create the **NumberAdderErrorHandlingTest** test:

```
@RunWith(MockitoJUnitRunner::class)
class NumberAdderErrorHandlingTest {

    @InjectMocks
    lateinit var numberAdder: NumberAdder

    @Test(expected = NumberAdder.InvalidNumberException::class)
    fun sum() {
        val input = -1
        val callback = mock<(BigInteger) -> Unit>()

        numberAdder.sum(input, callback)

    }
}
```

11. Create a class that will format the sum and concatenate it with the necessary strings:

```
class TextFormatter(
    private val numberAdder: NumberAdder,
    private val context: Context
) {

    fun getSumResult(n: Int, callback: (String) -> Unit) {
        try {
            numberAdder.sum(n) {
                callback(
                    context.getString(
                        R.string.the_sum_of_numbers_from_1_to_is,
                        n,
                        it.toString()
```

```
                    )
                )
            }
        } catch (e: NumberAdder.InvalidNumberException) {
            callback(context.getString
              (R.string.error_invalid_number))
        }
    }
}
```

12. Unit test this class for both the success and error scenarios. Start with the success scenario:

```
@RunWith(MockitoJUnitRunner::class)
class TextFormatterTest {

    @InjectMocks
    lateinit var textFormatter: TextFormatter
    @Mock
    lateinit var numberAdder: NumberAdder
    @Mock
    lateinit var context: Context

    @Test
    fun getSumResult_success() {
        val n = 10
        val sumResult = BigInteger.TEN
        val expected = "expected"
        whenever(numberAdder.sum(eq(n), any())).thenAnswer {
            (it.arguments[1] as (BigInteger)->Unit)
                .invoke(sumResult)
        }
        whenever(context.getString
          (R.string.the_sum_of_numbers_from_1_to_is, n,
            sumResult.toString())).thenReturn(expected)
        val callback = mock<(String)->Unit>()

        textFormatter.getSumResult(n, callback)

        verify(callback).invoke(expected)
    }
```

Then, create the test for the error scenario:

```
@Test
fun getSumResult_error() {
    val n = 10
    val expected = "expected"
    whenever(numberAdder.sum(eq(n),
        any())).thenThrow(NumberAdder.InvalidNumberException)
    whenever(context.getString(R.string.error_invalid_number))
        .thenReturn(expected)
    val callback = mock<(String)->Unit>()

    textFormatter.getSumResult(n, callback)

    verify(callback).invoke(expected)
}
}
```

13. Create the layout for **activity_main.xml**:

```
<?xml version="1.0" encoding="utf-8"?>
<LinearLayout xmlns:android="http://schemas.android.com/apk/res/
android"
    android:id="@+id/root"
    android:layout_width="match_parent"
    android:layout_height="match_parent"
    android:orientation="vertical">

    <EditText
        android:id="@+id/edit_text"
        android:layout_width="match_parent"
        android:layout_height="wrap_content"
        android:inputType="number" />

    <Button
        android:id="@+id/button"
        android:layout_width="wrap_content"
        android:layout_height="wrap_content"
        android:layout_gravity="center_horizontal"
        android:text="@string/calculate" />

    <TextView
        android:id="@+id/text_view"
```

```
            android:layout_width="wrap_content"
            android:layout_height="wrap_content"
            android:layout_gravity="center_horizontal" />
    </LinearLayout>
```

14. Create the **MainActivity** class, which will contain all the other components:

```
class MainActivity : AppCompatActivity() {

    private lateinit var textFormatter: TextFormatter

    override fun onCreate(savedInstanceState: Bundle?) {
        super.onCreate(savedInstanceState)
        setContentView(R.layout.activity_main)
        textFormatter = TextFormatter(NumberAdder(),
applicationContext)
        findViewById<Button>(R.id.button).setOnClickListener {
            textFormatter.getSumResult(findViewById<EditText>
                (R.id.edit_text).text.toString().toIntOrNull() ?: 0) {
                findViewById<TextView>(R.id.text_view).text = it
            }
        }
    }
}
```

15. Create a test for **MainActivity** and place it in the **test** directory. It will contain two test methods, one for success and one for error:

```
@RunWith(AndroidJUnit4::class)
class MainActivityTest {

    @Test
    fun `show sum result in text view`() {
        val scenario = launch<MainActivity>(MainActivity::class.java)

        scenario.moveToState(Lifecycle.State.RESUMED)

        scenario.onActivity { activity ->
            onView(withId(R.id.edit_text)).perform(replaceText("5"))
            onView(withId(R.id.button)).perform(click())
            onView(withId(R.id.text_view)).check(matches(withText
              (activity.getString
                (R.string.the_sum_of_numbers_from_1_to_is, 5, "15"))))
```

```
        }
    }

    @Test
    fun `show error in text view`() {
        val scenario = launch<MainActivity>(MainActivity::class.java)

        scenario.moveToState(Lifecycle.State.RESUMED)

        scenario.onActivity { activity ->
            onView(withId(R.id.edit_text))
                .perform(replaceText("-5"))
            onView(withId(R.id.button)).perform(click())
            onView(withId(R.id.text_view)).check(
                matches(withText(activity.getString(
                R.string.error_invalid_number))))
        }
    }
}
```

If you run the tests by right-clicking the package in which the tests are located and select **Run all in [package_name]**, then an output similar to the following will appear:

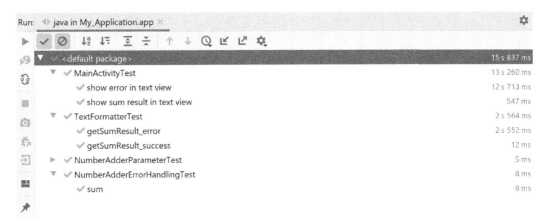

Figure 9.6: Result of executing the tests in the test folder for Exercise 9.02

If you execute the preceding tests, you should see an output similar to *Figure 9.6*. The Robolectric test is executed in the same way as a regular unit test; however, there is an increase in the execution time.

16. Let's now migrate the preceding test to an instrumented integration test. In order to do this, we will copy the preceding test from the **test** package into the **androidTest** package and remove the code related to scenarios from our tests. After copying the file, we will use **ActivityTestRule**, which will launch our activity before every test is executed. We will also need to rename the class to avoid duplicates and rename the test methods because the syntax is not supported for instrumented tests:

```
@RunWith(AndroidJUnit4::class)
class MainActivityUiTest {

    @JvmField
    @Rule
    var activityRule: ActivityTestRule<MainActivity> =
      ActivityTestRule(MainActivity::class.java)

    @Test
    fun showSumResultInTextView() {

        activityRule.activity.let { activity ->
            onView(withId(R.id.edit_text)).perform(replaceText("5"))
            onView(withId(R.id.button)).perform(click())
            onView(withId(R.id.text_view)).check(matches
              (withText(activity.getString
                (R.string.the_sum_of_numbers_from_1_to_is, 5, "15"))))
        }
    }


    @Test
    fun showErrorInTextView() {
        activityRule.activity.let { activity ->
            onView(withId(R.id.edit_text)).perform(replaceText("-5"))
            onView(withId(R.id.button)).perform(click())
            onView(withId(R.id.text_view)).check(matches
              (withText(activity.getString
                (R.string.error_invalid_number))))
        }
    }
}
```

If you run the tests by right-clicking the package in which the tests are located and select **Run all in [package_name]**, then an output similar to the following will appear:

Figure 9.7: Result of executing the tests in the androidTest folder for Exercise 9.02

In *Figure 9.7*, we can see what Android Studio displays as an output for the result. If you pay attention to the emulator while the tests are executing, you can see that for each test, your activity will be opened, the input will be set in the field, and the button will be clicked. Both of our integration tests (on the workstation and the emulator) try to match the accepted criteria of the requirement. The integration tests verify the same behavior, the only difference being that one checks it locally and the other checks it on an Android device or emulator. The main benefit here is the fact that Espresso was able to bridge the gap between them, making integration tests easier to set up and execute.

UI TESTS

UI tests are instrumented tests where developers can simulate user journeys and verify the interactions between different modules of the application. They are also referred to as end-to-end tests. For small applications, you can have one test suite, but for larger applications, you should split your test suites to cover particular user journeys (logging in, creating an account, setting up flows, and so on). Because they are executed on the device, you will need to write them in the **androidTest** package, which means they will run with the **Instrumentation** framework. Instrumentation works as follows:

- The app is built and installed on the device.

- A testing app will also be installed on the device that will monitor your app.

- The testing app will execute the tests on your app and record the results.

One of the drawbacks of this is the fact that the tests will share persisted data, so if a test stores data on the device, then the second test can have access to that data, which means that there is a risk of failure. Another drawback is that if a test comes across a crash, this will stop the entire testing because the application under test is stopped. These issues were solved in the Jetpack updates with the introduction of the **orchestrator** framework. Orchestrators give you the ability to clear the data after each test is executed, sparing developers the need to make any adjustments. The orchestrator is represented by another application that will manage how the testing app will coordinate the tests and the data between the tests. In order to add it to your project, you need a configuration similar to this in the **app/build.gradle** file:

```
android {
    ...
    defaultConfig {
        ...
        testInstrumentationRunner
          "androidx.test.runner.AndroidJUnitRunner"
        testInstrumentationRunnerArguments clearPackageData: 'true'
    }
    testOptions {
        execution 'ANDROIDX_TEST_ORCHESTRATOR'
    }
}

dependencies {
    ...
    androidTestUtil 'androidx.test:orchestrator:1.3.0'
}
```

You can execute the orchestrator test on a connected device using Gradle's **connectedCheck** command, either from **Terminal** or from the list of Gradle commands.

In the configuration, you will notice the following line: **testInstrumentationRunner**. This allows us to create a custom configuration for the test, which gives us the opportunity to inject mock data into the modules:

```
testInstrumentationRunner "com.android.CustomTestRunner"
```

CustomTestRunner looks like this (import statements not shown in following code snippets):

```
class CustomTestRunner: AndroidJUnitRunner() {

    @Throws(Exception::class)
    override fun newApplication(
        cl: ClassLoader?,
        className: String?,
        context: Context?
    ): Application? {
        return super.newApplication(cl,
            MyApplication::class.java.name, context)
    }

}
```

The test classes themselves can be written by applying the JUnit4 syntax with the help of the **androidx.test.ext.junit.runners.AndroidJUnit4** test runner:

```
@RunWith(AndroidJUnit4::class)
class MainActivityUiTest {
}
```

Another important feature that comes from the AndroidX testing support is the activity rule. When this rule is used with the default constructor, the activity will be launched before each test and will be ready for interactions and assertions:

```
@JvmField
@Rule
var activityRule: ActivityTestRule<MainActivity>
    = ActivityTestRule(MainActivity::class.java)
```

You can also use the rule to avoid starting the activity and customize the intent used to start it in your test:

```
@JvmField
@Rule
var activityRule: ActivityTestRule<MainActivity> =
    ActivityTestRule(MainActivity::class.java, false ,false)
```

```
@Test
fun myTestMethod() {
    val myIntent = Intent()
    activityRule.launchActivity(myIntent)
}
```

The **@Test** methods themselves run in a dedicated test thread, which is why a library such as Espresso is helpful. Espresso will automatically move every interaction with a view on the UI thread. Espresso can be used for UI tests in a similar way as it is used with Robolectric tests:

```
@Test
fun myTest() {
    onView(withId(R.id.edit_text)).perform(replaceText("5"))
    onView(withId(R.id.button)).perform(click())
    onView(withId(R.id.text_view))
      .check(matches(withText("my test")))
}
```

Typically, in UI tests, you will find interactions and assertions that may get repetitive. In order to avoid duplicating multiple scenarios in your code, you can apply a pattern called **Robot**. Each screen will have an associated **Robot** class in which the interactions and assertions can be grouped into specific methods. Your test code will use the robots and assert them. A typical robot will look something like this:

```
class MyScreenRobot {

    fun setText(): MyScreenRobot {
        onView(ViewMatchers.withId(R.id.edit_text))
          .perform(ViewActions.replaceText("5"))
        return this
    }

    fun pressButton(): MyScreenRobot {
        onView(ViewMatchers.withId(R.id.button))
          .perform(ViewActions.click())
        return this
    }

    fun assertText(): MyScreenRobot {
        onView(ViewMatchers.withId(R.id.text_view))
          .check(ViewAssertions.matches(ViewMatchers
          .withText("my test")))
```

```
        return this
    }
}
```

The test will look like this:

```
@Test
fun myTest() {
    MyScreenRobot()
        .setText()
        .pressButton()
        .assertText()
}
```

Because apps can be multithreaded and sometimes it takes a while to load data from various sources (internet, files, local storage, and so on), the UI tests will have to know when the UI is available for interactions. One way to implement this is through the usage of idling resources. These are objects that can be registered to Espresso before the test and injected into your application's components where multithreaded work is done. The apps will mark them as non-idle when the work is in progress and idle when the work is done. It is at this point where Espresso will then start executing the test. One of the most commonly used ones is **CountingIdlingResource**. This specific implementation uses a counter that should be incremented when you want Espresso to wait for your code to complete its execution and decremented when you want to let Espresso verify your code. When the counter reaches **0**, Espresso will resume testing. An example of a component with an idling resource looks something like this:

```
class MyHeavyliftingComponent(private val
    countingIdlingResource:CountingIdlingResource) {

    fun doHeavyWork() {
        countingIdlingResource.increment()
        // do work
        countingIdlingResource.decrement()
    }
}
```

The **Application** class can be used to inject the idling resource, like this:

```
class MyApplication : Application(){

    val countingIdlingResource = CountingIdlingResource("My heavy work")
    val myHeavyliftingComponent =
      MyHeavyliftingComponent(countingIdlingResource)
}
```

Then, in the test, we can access the **Application** class and register the resource to Espresso:

```
@RunWith(AndroidJUnit4::class)
class MyTest {

    @Before
    fun setUp() {
        val myApplication = getApplicationContext<MyApplication>()
        IdlingRegistry.getInstance()
           .register(myApplication.countingIdlingResource)
    }

}
```

Espresso comes with a set of extensions that can be used to assert different Android components. One extension is intents testing. This is useful when you want to test an activity in isolation (more appropriate for integration tests). In order to use this, you need to add the library to Gradle:

```
androidTestImplementation 'androidx.test.espresso:espresso-intents:3.3.0'
```

After you add the library, you need to use **IntentsTestRule** in order to set up the necessary intent monitoring. This rule is a subclass of **ActivityTestRule**:

```
    @JvmField
    @Rule
    var intentsRule: IntentsTestRule<MainActivity>
       = IntentsTestRule(MainActivity::class.java)
```

In order to assert the values of the intent, you need to trigger the appropriate action and then use the **intended** method:

```
onView(withId(R.id.button)).perform(click())
intended(allOf(
    hasComponent(hasShortClassName(".MainActivity")),
    hasExtra(MainActivity.MY_EXTRA, "myExtraValue")))
```

The **intended** method works in a similar way to the **onView** method. It requires a matcher that can be combined with a **Hamcrest** matcher. The intent-related matchers can be found in the **IntentMatchers** class. This class contains methods to assert different methods of the **Intent** class: extras, data, components, bundles, and so on.

Another important extension library comes to the aid of **RecyclerView**. The **onData** method from Espresso is only capable of testing **AdapterViews** such as **ListView** and isn't capable of asserting **RecyclerView**. In order to use the extension, you need to add the following library to your project:

```
androidTestImplementation
    'com.android.support.test.espresso:espresso-contrib:3.0.2'
```

This library provides a **RecyclerViewActions** class, which contains a set of methods that allow you to perform actions on items inside **RecyclerView**:

```
onView(withId(R.id.recycler_view))
    .perform(RecyclerViewActions.actionOnItemAtPosition(0, click()))
```

The preceding statement will click the item at position **0**:

```
onView(withId(R.id.recycler_view)).perform(RecyclerViewActions
    .scrollToPosition<RecyclerView.ViewHolder>(10))
```

This will scroll to the tenth item in the list:

```
onView(withText("myText")).check(matches(isDisplayed()))
```

The preceding code will check whether a view with the **myText** text is displayed, which will also apply to **RecyclerView** items.

EXERCISE 9.03: RANDOM WAITING TIMES

Write an application that will have two screens. The first screen will have a button. When the user presses the button, it will wait a random time between 1 and 5 seconds and then launch the second screen, which will display the text **Opened after x seconds**, where **x** is the number of seconds that passed. Write a UI test that will cover this scenario with the following features adjusted for the test:

- The **random** function will return the value **1** when the test is run.

- **CountingIdlingResource** will be used to indicate when the timer has stopped.

> **NOTE**
>
> Throughout this exercise, import statements are not shown. To see full code files, refer to http://packt.live/38V7krh.

Take the following steps to complete this exercise:

1. Add the following libraries to **app/build.gradle**:

```
implementation 'androidx.test.espresso:espresso-core:3.3.0'
testImplementation 'junit:junit:4.13.1'
androidTestImplementation 'androidx.test.ext:junit:1.1.2'
androidTestImplementation 'androidx.test:rules:1.3.0'
```

2. Then, start with a **Randomizer** class:

```
class Randomizer(private val random: Random) {

    fun getTimeToWait(): Int {
        return random.nextInt(5) + 1
    }
}
```

3. Next, create a **Synchronizer** class, which will use **Randomizer** and **Timer** to wait for the random time interval. It will also use **CountingIdlingResource** to mark the start of the task and the end of the task:

```
class Synchronizer(
    private val randomizer: Randomizer,
    private val timer: Timer,
```

```
        private val countingIdlingResource: CountingIdlingResource
) {

    fun executeAfterDelay(callback: (Int) -> Unit) {
        val timeToWait = randomizer.getTimeToWait()
        countingIdlingResource.increment()
        timer.schedule(CallbackTask(callback, timeToWait),
          timeToWait * 1000L)
    }


    inner class CallbackTask(
        private val callback: (Int) -> Unit,
        private val time: Int
    ) : TimerTask() {
        override fun run() {
            callback(time)
            countingIdlingResource.decrement()

        }


    }
}
```

4. Now create an **Application** class that will be responsible for creating all the instances of the preceding classes:

```
class MyApplication : Application() {

    val countingIdlingResource =
      CountingIdlingResource("Timer resource")
    val randomizer = Randomizer(Random())
    val synchronizer = Synchronizer(randomizer, Timer(),
      countingIdlingResource)
}
```

5. Add the **MyApplication** class to **AndroidManifest** in the **application** tag with the **android:name** attribute.

6. Create an **activity_1** layout file, which will contain a parent layout and a button:

```
<?xml version="1.0" encoding="utf-8"?>
<LinearLayout xmlns:android="http://schemas.android.com/apk/res/
android"
    android:layout_width="match_parent"
```

```
        android:layout_height="match_parent"
        android:orientation="vertical">

    <Button
        android:id="@+id/activity_1_button"
        android:layout_width="wrap_content"
        android:layout_height="wrap_content"
        android:layout_gravity="center"
        android:text="@string/press_me" />
</LinearLayout>
```

7. Create an **activity_2** layout file, which will contain a parent layout
   and **TextView**:

```
<?xml version="1.0" encoding="utf-8"?>
<LinearLayout xmlns:android="http://schemas.android.com/apk/res/
android"
    android:layout_width="match_parent"
    android:layout_height="match_parent"
    android:orientation="vertical">

    <TextView
        android:id="@+id/activity_2_text_view"
        android:layout_width="wrap_content"
        android:layout_height="wrap_content"
        android:layout_gravity="center" />
</LinearLayout>
```

8. Create the **Activity1** class, which will implement the logic for the button click:

```
class Activity1 : AppCompatActivity() {

    override fun onCreate(savedInstanceState: Bundle?) {
        super.onCreate(savedInstanceState)
        setContentView(R.layout.activity_1)
        findViewById<Button>(R.id.activity_1_button)
            .setOnClickListener {
                (application as MyApplication).synchronizer
                    .executeAfterDelay {
                        startActivity(Activity2.newIntent(this, it))
                    }
            }
    }
```

```
        }
    }
```

9. Create the **Activity2** class, which will display the received data through the intent:

```
class Activity2 : AppCompatActivity() {

    companion object {

        private const val EXTRA_SECONDS = "extra_seconds"

        fun newIntent(context: Context, seconds: Int) =
            Intent(context, Activity2::class.java).putExtra(
                EXTRA_SECONDS, seconds
            )

    }

    override fun onCreate(savedInstanceState: Bundle?) {
        super.onCreate(savedInstanceState)
        setContentView(R.layout.activity_2)
        findViewById<TextView>(R.id.activity_2_text_view).text =
            getString(R.string.opened_after_x_seconds,
                intent.getIntExtra(EXTRA_SECONDS, 0))
    }
}
```

10. Create a **FlowTest** class in the **androidTest** directory, which will register **IdlingResource** from the **MyApplication** object and will assert the outcome of the click:

```
@RunWith(AndroidJUnit4::class)
@LargeTest
class FlowTest {

    @JvmField
    @Rule
    var activityRule: ActivityTestRule<Activity1> =
        ActivityTestRule(Activity1::class.java)
    private val myApplication = getApplicationContext<MyApplication>()

    @Before
```

```
    fun setUp() {
        IdlingRegistry.getInstance().register(myApplication
            .countingIdlingResource)
    }


    @Test
    fun verifyFlow() {
        onView(withId(R.id.activity_1_button)).perform(click())
        onView(withId(R.id.activity_2_text_view))
            .check(matches(withText(myApplication
                .getString(R.string.opened_after_x_seconds, 1))))

    }
}
```

11. Run the test multiple times and check the test results. Notice that the test will have a 20% chance of success, but it will wait until the button is clicked. This means that the idling resource is working. Another thing to observe is that there is an element of randomness here.

12. Tests don't like randomness, so we need to eliminate it by making the **Randomizer** class open and create a sub-class in the **androidTest** directory. We can do the same for the **MyApplication** class and provide a different randomizer called **TestRandomizer**:

```
class TestRandomizer(random: Random) : Randomizer(random) {

    override fun getTimeToWait(): Int {
        return 1
    }
}
```

13. Now, modify the **MyApplication** class in a way in which we can override the randomizer from a subclass:

```
open class MyApplication : Application() {

    val countingIdlingResource =
        CountingIdlingResource("Timer resource")
    lateinit var synchronizer: Synchronizer

    override fun onCreate() {
        super.onCreate()
        synchronizer = Synchronizer(createRandomizer(), Timer(),
            countingIdlingResource)
```

```
        }

        open fun createRandomizer() = Randomizer(Random())
    }
```

14. In the **androidTest** directory, create **TestMyApplication**, which will extend **MyApplication** and override the **createRandomizer** method:

```
class TestMyApplication : MyApplication() {

    override fun createRandomizer(): Randomizer {
        return TestRandomizer(Random())
    }

}
```

15. Finally, create an instrumentation test runner that will use this new **Application** class inside the test:

```
class MyApplicationTestRunner : AndroidJUnitRunner() {

    @Throws(Exception::class)
    override fun newApplication(
        cl: ClassLoader?,
        className: String?,
        context: Context?
    ): Application? {
        return super.newApplication(cl,
           TestMyApplication::class.java.name, context)
    }
}
```

16. Add the new test runner to the Gradle configuration:

```
android {
    ...
    defaultConfig {
        ...
        testInstrumentationRunner
            "com.android.testable.myapplication
            .MyApplicationTestRunner"
    }
}
```

By running the test now, everything should pass similar to *Figure 9.8*:

Figure 9.8: Output of Exercise 9.03

This type of exercise shows how to avoid randomness in a test and provide concrete and repeatable inputs to make our tests reliable. Similar approaches are taken with dependency injection frameworks where entire modules can be replaced in the test suite in order to ensure the test's reliability. One of the most common things to be replaced is API communication. Another issue this approach solves is the decrease in waiting time. If this type of scenario were to have been repeated across your tests, then the execution time of them would have increased as a result of this.

TEST-DRIVEN DEVELOPMENT

Let's assume that you are tasked with building an activity that displays a calculator with the add, subtract, multiply, and divide options. You must also write tests for your implementation. Typically, you would build your UI and your activity and a separate `Calculator` class. Then, you would write the unit tests for your `Calculator` class and then your activity class.

Under the **Android TDD** process, you would have to write your UI test with your scenarios first. In order to achieve this, you can create a skeleton UI to avoid compile-time errors. After your UI test, you would need to write your `Calculator` test. Here, you would also need to create the necessary methods in the `Calculator` class to avoid compile-time errors.

If you run your tests in this phase, they would fail. This would force you to implement your code until the tests pass. Once your `Calculator` tests pass, you can connect your calculator to your UI until your UI tests pass. While this seems like a counter-intuitive approach, it solves two issues once the process is mastered:

- Less time will be spent writing code because you will ensure that your code is testable, and you need to write only the amount of code necessary for the test to pass.

- Fewer bugs will be introduced because developers will be able to analyze different outcomes.

Have a look at the following diagram, which shows the TDD cycle:

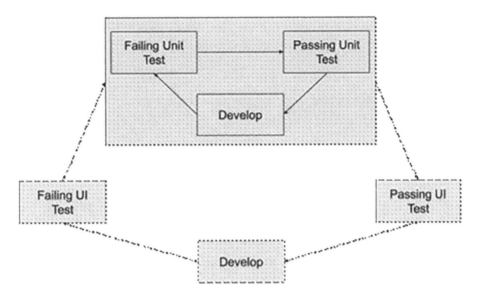

Figure 9.9: TDD cycle

In the preceding figure, we can see the development cycle in a TDD process. You should start from a point where your tests are failing. Implement changes in order for the tests to pass. When you update or add new features, you can repeat the process.

Going back to our factorial examples, we started with a factorial function that didn't cover all our scenarios and had to keep updating the function every time a new test was added. TDD is built with that idea in mind. You start with an empty function. You start defining your testing scenarios: What are the conditions for success? What's the minimum? What's the maximum? Are there any exceptions from the main rule? What are they? These questions can help developers define their test cases. Then, these cases can be written. Let's now see how this can be done practically through the next exercise.

EXERCISE 9.04: USING TDD TO CALCULATE THE SUM OF NUMBERS

Write a function that will take as input the integer *n* and will return the sum of numbers from 1 to *n*. The function should be written with a TDD approach, and the following criteria should be satisfied:

- For *n<=0*, the function will return the value **−1**.

- The function should be able to return the correct value for **Int.MAX_VALUE**.

- The function should be quick, even for **Int.MAX_VALUE**.

> **NOTE**
>
> Throughout this exercise, import statements are not shown. To see full code files, refer to http://packt.live/3a0jJd9.

Perform the following steps to complete this exercise:

1. Make sure that the following library is added to **app/build.gradle**:

```
testImplementation 'junit:junit:4.13.1'
```

2. Create an **Adder** class with the **sum** method, which will return **0**, to satisfy the compiler:

```
class Adder {

    fun sum(n: Int): Int = 0

}
```

3. Create an **AdderTest** class in the test directory and define our test cases. We will have the following test cases: *n=1, n=2, n=0, n=-1, n=10, n=20*, and *n=Int. MAX_VALUE*. We can split the successful scenarios into one method and the unsuccessful ones into a separate method:

```
class AdderTest {

    private val adder = Adder()

    @Test
    fun sumSuccess() {
        assertEquals(1, adder.sum(1))
        assertEquals(3, adder.sum(2))
```

```
        assertEquals(55, adder.sum(10))
        assertEquals(210, adder.sum(20))
        assertEquals(2305843008139952128L, adder.sum(Int.MAX_VALUE))
    }


    @Test
    fun sumError(){
        assertEquals(-1, adder.sum(0))
        assertEquals(-1, adder.sum(-1))
    }

}
```

4. If we run the tests for the **AdderTest** class, we will see an output similar to the following figure, meaning that all our tests failed:

Figure 9.10: Initial test status for Exercise 9.04

5. Let's first address the success scenarios by implementing the sum in a loop from 1 to *n*:

```
class Adder {

    fun sum(n: Int): Long {
        var result = 0L
        for (i in 1..n) {
            result += i
        }
        return result
    }

}
```

6. If we run the tests now, you will see that one will pass and the other will fail, similar to the following figure:

Figure 9.11: Test status after resolving the success scenario for Exercise 9.04

7. If we take a look at the time it took to execute the successful test, it seems a bit long. This can add up when thousands of unit tests are present in one project. We can now optimize our code to deal with the issue by applying the *n(n+1)/2* formula:

```
class Adder {

    fun sum(n: Int): Long {
        return (n * (n.toLong() + 1)) / 2
    }
}
```

Running the tests now will drastically reduce the speed to a few milliseconds.

8. Now, let's focus on solving our failure scenarios. We can do this by adding a condition for when *n* is smaller than or equal to **0**:

```
class Adder {

    fun sum(n: Int): Long {
        return if (n > 0) (n * (n.toLong() + 1)) / 2 else -1
    }
}
```

9. If we run the tests now, we should see them all passing, similar to the following figure:

Figure 9.12: Passing tests for Exercise 9.04

In this exercise, we have applied the concept of TDD to a very small example to demonstrate how the technique can be used. We have observed how starting from skeleton code, we can create a suite of tests to verify our conditions, and how by constantly running tests, we improved the code until a point where all the tests pass. As you have probably noticed, the concept isn't an intuitive one. Some developers find it hard to define how big skeleton code should be in order to start creating the test cases, while others, out of habit, focus on writing the code first and then developing the test. In either case, developers will need a lot of practice with the technique until it's properly mastered.

ACTIVITY 9.01: DEVELOPING WITH TDD

Using the TDD approach, develop an application that contains three activities and works as follows:

- In activity 1, you will display a numeric **EditText** element and a button. When the button is clicked, the number in **EditText** will be passed to activity 2.

- Activity 2 will generate a list of items asynchronously. The number of items will be represented by the number passed from activity 1. You can use the **Timer** class with a delay of 1 second. Each item in the list will display the text **Item x**. **x** is the position in the list. When an item is clicked, you should pass the clicked item to activity 3.

- Activity 3 will display the text **You clicked y. y** is the text of the item the user has clicked.

The tests the app will have will be the following:

- Unit tests with Mockito and **mockito-kotlin** annotated with @**SmallTest**
- Integration tests with Robolectric and Espresso annotated with @**MediumTest**
- UI tests with Espresso annotated with @**LargeTest** and using the Robot pattern

Run the test commands from the command line.

In order to complete this activity, you need to take the following steps:

1. You will need Android Studio 4.1.1 or higher with Kotlin 1.4.21 or higher for the Parcelize Kotlin plugin

2. Create the three activities and the UI for each of them.

3. In the **androidTest** folder, create three robots, one for each activity:

- Robot 1 will contain the interaction with **EditText** and the button.
- Robot 2 will assert the number of items on the screen and interaction with an item in the list.
- Robot 3 will assert the text displayed in **TextView**.

4. Create an instrumented test class that will have one test method using the preceding robots.

5. Create an **Application** class that will hold instances to all the classes that will be unit tested.

6. Create three classes representing integration tests, one for each of the activities. Each of these classes will contain one test method for the interactions and data loading. Each integration test will assert the intents passed between the activities.

7. Create a class that will provide the text required for the UI. It will have a reference to a **Context** object and will contain two methods that will provide the text for the UI, which will return an empty string.

8. Create the test for the preceding class in which the two methods are tested.

9. Implement the class in order for the preceding tests to pass.

10. Create a class that will be responsible for loading the list in **Activity2** and provide an empty method for loading. The class will have a reference to the timer and the idling resource. Here, you should also create a data class that will represent the model for **RecyclerView**.

11. Create a unit test for the preceding class.

12. Create the implementation for the preceding class and run the unit tests until they pass.

13. In the **Application** class, instantiate the classes that were unit tested and start using them in your activities. Do this until your integration tests pass.

14. Provide **IntegrationTestApplication**, which will return a new implementation of the class responsible for loading. This is to avoid making your integration test for activity 2 wait until loading is complete.

15. Provide **UiTestApplication**, which will again reduce the loading time of your models and connect the idling resource to Espresso. Implement the remaining work in order for the UI test to pass.

> **NOTE**
>
> The solution to this activity can be found at: http://packt.live/3sKj1cp.

SUMMARY

In this chapter, we looked at the different types of testing and the frameworks available for implementing these tests. We also took a look at the testing environment and how to structure it for each environment, as well as structuring your code in multiple components that can be individually unit tested. We analyzed different ways to test code, how we should approach testing, and how, by looking at different test results, we can improve our code. With TDD, we learned that by starting with testing, we can write our code faster and ensure it is less error-prone. The activity is where all these concepts came together into building a simple Android application, and we can observe how, by adding tests, the development time increases, but this pays off in the long term by eliminating possible bugs that appear when the code is modified.

The frameworks we have studied are some of the most common ones, but there are others that build on top of these and are used by developers in their projects, including mockk (a mocking library designed for Kotlin that takes advantage of a lot of the features of the language), Barista (written on top of Espresso and simplifies the syntax of UI tests), screenshot tests (which take screenshots of your UI tests and compare them to verify no bugs were introduced), UIAutomator, and monkeyrunner (which executes UI tests without requiring access to the application's code, but are written on top of it), Spoon (allows UI tests to be executed in parallel on multiple emulators to reduce time on testing), and Firebase Test Lab (allows tests to be executed in the cloud).

Think of all the concepts presented here as building blocks that fit into two processes present in the software engineering world: Automation and continuous integration. Automation takes redundant and repetitive work out of the hands of developers and puts it into the hands of machines. Instead of having a team of quality assurance people testing your application to make sure the requirements are met, you can instruct a machine through a variety of tests and test cases to test the application instead and just have one person reviewing the results of the tests. Continuous integration builds on the concept of automation in order to verify your code the moment you submit it for review from other developers. A project with continuous integration would have a setup along the following lines: A developer submits work for review in a source control repository such as GitHub.

A machine in the cloud would then start executing the tests for the entire project, making sure that nothing was broken and the developer can move on to a new task. If the tests pass, then the rest of the developers can review the code, and when it is correct, it can be merged and a new build can be created in the cloud and distributed to the rest of the team and the testers. All of this takes place while the initial developer can safely work on something else. If anything fails in the process, then they can pause the new task and go and address any issues in their work. The continuous integration process can then be expanded into continuous delivery, where similar automation can be set up when preparing a submission into Google Play that can be handled almost entirely by machines with minor involvement from developers. In the chapters that follow, you will learn about how to organize your code when building more complex applications that use the storage capabilities of the device and connect to the cloud to request data. Each of those components can be individually unit tested and you can apply integration tests to assert a successful integration of multiple components.

10

ANDROID ARCHITECTURE COMPONENTS

OVERVIEW

In this chapter, you will learn about the key components of the Android Jetpack libraries and what benefits they bring to the standard Android framework. You will also learn how to structure your code and give different responsibilities to your classes with the help of Jetpack components. Finally, you'll improve the test coverage of your code.

By the end of this chapter, you'll be able to create applications that handle the life cycles of activities and fragments with ease. You'll also know more about how to persist data on an Android device using Room, as well as how to use ViewModels to separate your logic from your Views.

INTRODUCTION

In the previous chapters, you learned how to write unit tests. The question is: what can you unit test? Can you unit test activities and fragments? They are pretty hard to unit test on your machine because of the way they are built. Testing would be easier if you could move the code away from activities and fragments.

Also, consider the situation where you are building an application that supports different orientations, such as landscape and portrait, and supports multiple languages. What tends to happen in these scenarios by default is that when the user rotates the screen, the activities and fragments are recreated for the new display orientation. Now, imagine that happens while your application is in the middle of processing data. You have to keep track of the data you are processing, you have to keep track of what the user was doing to interact with your screens, and you have to avoid causing a context leak.

> **NOTE**
>
> A context leak occurs when your destroyed activity cannot be garbage collected because it is referenced in a component with a longer life cycle – like a thread that is currently processing your data.

In many situations, you would have to resort to using **onSaveInstanceState** in order to save the current state of your activity/fragment, and then in **onCreate** or **onRestoreInstanceState**, you would need to restore the state of your activity/fragment. This would add extra complexity to your code and would also make it repetitive, especially if the processing code is going to be part of your activity or fragment.

These scenarios are where **ViewModel** and **LiveData** come in. **ViewModels** are components built with the express goal of holding data in case of life cycle changes. They also separate the logic from the Views, which makes them very easy to unit test. **LiveData** is a component used to hold data and notify observers when changes occur while taking their life cycle into account. In simpler terms, the fragment only deals with the Views, **ViewModel** does the heavy lifting, and **LiveData** deals with delivering the results to the fragment, but only when the fragment is there and ready.

If you've ever used WhatsApp or a similar messaging app and you've turned off the internet, you'll have noticed that you are still able to use the application. The reason for this is because the messages are stored locally on your device. This is achieved through the use of a database file called **SQLite** in most cases. The Android Framework already allows you to use this feature for your application. This requires a lot of boilerplate code in order to read and write data. Every time you want to interact with the local storage, you must write a SQL query. When you read the SQLite data, you must convert it into a Java/Kotlin object. All of this requires a lot of code, time, and unit testing. What if someone else handles the SQLite connection and all you have to do is focus on the code part? This is where **Room** comes in. This is a library that is a wrapper over SQLite. All you need to do is define how your data should be saved and let the library take care of the rest.

Let's say you want your activity to know when there is an internet connection and when the internet drops. You can use something called **BroadcastReceiver** for this. A slight problem with this is that every time you register a **BroadcastReceiver** in an activity, you have to unregister it when the activity is destroyed. You can use **Lifecycle** to observe the state of your activity, thereby allowing your receiver to be registered in the desired state and unregistered in the complementary one (for example, **RESUMED-PAUSED**, **STARTED-STOPPED**, or **CREATED-DESTROYED**).

ViewModels, **LiveData**, and **Room** are all part of the Android architecture components, which are part of the Android Jetpack libraries. The architecture components are designed to help developers structure their code, write testable components, and help reduce boilerplate code. Other architecture components include **Databinding** (which binds views with models or **ViewModels**, allowing the data to be directly set in the Views), **WorkManager** (which allows developers to handle background work with ease), **Navigation** (which allows developers to create visual navigation graphs and specify relationships between activities and fragments), and **Paging** (which allows developers to load paginated data, which helps in situations where infinite scrolling is required).

VIEWMODEL AND LIVEDATA

Both **ViewModel** and **LiveData** represent specialized implementations of the life cycle mechanisms. They come in handy in situations where you want to keep your data saved when the screen rotates and when you want your data to be displayed only when the Views are available, thus avoiding one of the most common issues developers face – a **NullPointerException** – when trying to update a View. A good use of this is when you want to display the live score of your favorite team's game and the current minute of the game.

VIEWMODEL

The **ViewModel** component is responsible for holding and processing data required by the UI. It has the benefit of surviving configuration changes that destroy and recreate fragments and activities, which allows it to retain the data that can then be used to re-populate the UI. It will be eventually destroyed when the activity or fragment will be destroyed without being recreated or when the application process is terminated. This allows **ViewModel** to serve its responsibility and to be garbage collected when it is no longer necessary. The only method **ViewModel** has is the **onCleared()** method, which is called when **ViewModel** terminates. You can overwrite this method to terminate ongoing tasks and deallocate resources that will no longer be required.

Migrating data processing from the activities into the **ViewModel**s helps in creating better and faster unit tests. Testing an activity requires an Android test that will be executed on a device. Activities also have states, which means that your test should get the activity into the proper state for the assertions to work. A **ViewModel** can be unit tested locally on your development machine and can be stateless, which means that your data processing logic can be tested individually.

One of the most important features of ViewModels is that they allow communication between fragments. To communicate between fragments without a **ViewModel**, you would have to make your fragment communicate with the activity, which will then call the fragment you wish to communicate with. To achieve this with ViewModels, you can just attach them to the parent activity and use the same **ViewModel** in the fragment you wish to communicate with. This will reduce the boilerplate code that was required previously.

In the following diagram, you can see that a **ViewModel** can be created at any point in an activity's life cycle (in practice they are normally initialized in the **onCreate** for Activities and **onCreateView** or **onViewCreated** for Fragments because these represent the points where the views are created and ready to be updated), and that once created, it will live as long as the activity does:

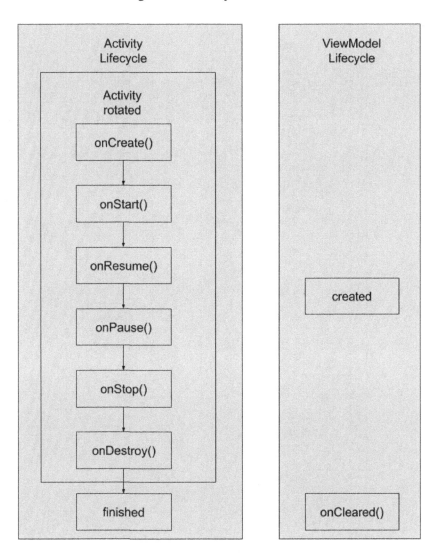

Figure 10.1: The life cycle of an activity compared to the ViewModel life cycle

The following diagram shows how **ViewModel** connects to a fragment:

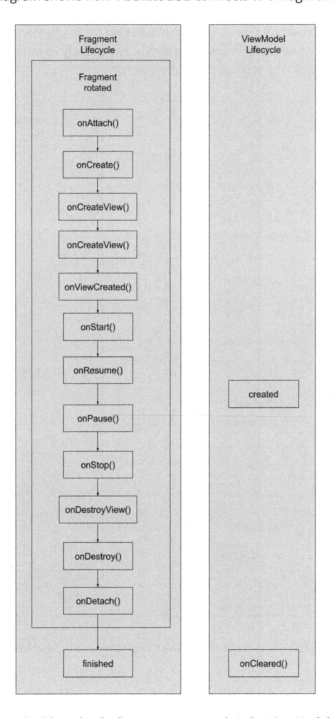

Figure 10.2: The life cycle of a fragment compared to the ViewModel life cycle

LIVEDATA

LiveData is a life cycle-aware component that permits updates to your UI, but only if the UI is in an active state (for example, if the activity or fragment is in the **STARTED** or **RESUMED** state). To monitor changes on your **LiveData**, you need an observer combined with a **LifecycleOwner**. When the activity is set to an active state, the observers will be notified when changes occur. If the activity is recreated, then the observer will be destroyed and a new one will be reattached. Once this happens, the last value of **LiveData** will be emitted to allow us to restore the state. Activities and fragments are **LifecycleOwners**, but fragments have a separate **LifecycleOwner** for the View states. Fragments have this particular **LifecycleOwner** due to their behavior in the fragment **BackStack**. When fragments are replaced within the back stack, they are not fully destroyed; only their Views are. Some of the common callbacks that developers use to trigger processing logic are **onViewCreated()**, **onActivityResumed()**, and **onCreateView()**. If we were to register observers on **LiveData** in these methods, we might end up with scenarios where multiple observers will be created every time our fragment pops back onto the screen.

When updating a **LiveData** model, we are presented with two options: **setValue()** and **postValue()**. **setValue()** will deliver the result immediately and is meant to be called only on the UI thread. On the other hand, **postValue()** can be called on any thread. When **postValue()** is called, **LiveData** will schedule an update of the value on the UI thread and update the value when the UI thread becomes free.

In the **LiveData** class, these methods are protected, which means that there are subclasses that allow us to change the data. **MutableLiveData** makes the methods public, which gives us a simple solution for observing data in most cases. **MediatorLiveData** is a specialized implementation of **LiveData** that allows us to merge multiple **LiveData** objects into one (this is useful in situations where our data is kept in different repositories and we want to show a combined result). **TransformLiveData** is another specialized implementation that allows us to convert from one object into another (this helps us in situations where we're grabbing data from one repository and we want to request data from another repository that depends on the previous data, as well as in situations where we want to apply extra logic to a result from a repository). **Custom LiveData** allows us to create our own **LiveData** implementations (usually when we periodically receive updates, such as the odds in a sports betting app, stock market updates, and Facebook and Twitter feeds).

> **NOTE**
>
> It is a common practice to use **LiveData** in a **ViewModel**. Holding **LiveData** in the fragment or activity will cause losses in data when configuration changes occur.

The following diagram shows how **LiveData** is connected to the life cycle of a **LifecycleOwner**:

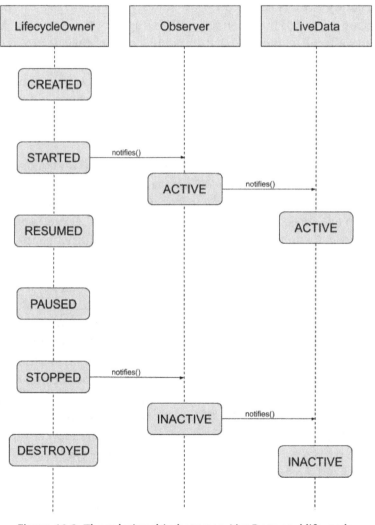

Figure 10.3: The relationship between LiveData and life cycle
observers with LifecycleOwners

> **NOTE**
>
> We can register multiple observers on a **LiveData** and each observer can be registered for a different **LifecycleOwner**. In this situation, a **LiveData** will become inactive, but only when all the observers are inactive.

EXERCISE 10.01: CREATING A LAYOUT WITH CONFIGURATION CHANGES

You have been tasked with building an app that has one screen that is split into two vertically when in portrait mode and horizontally when in landscape mode. The first half contains some text and below it is a button. The second half contains only text. When the screen is opened, the text in both halves displays **Total: 0**. When the button is clicked, the text will change to **Total: 1**. When clicked again, the text will change to **Total: 2**, and so on. When the device is rotated, the last total will be displayed on the new orientation.

In order to solve this task, we will define the following:

- An activity that will hold two fragments – one layout for portrait and another layout for landscape.

- One fragment with one layout containing **TextView** and a button.

- One fragment with one layout containing **TextView**.

- One **ViewModel** that will be shared between the two fragments.

- One **LiveData** that will hold the total.

Let's begin by setting up our configurations:

1. Create a new project called **ViewModelLiveData** and add an empty activity called **SplitActivity**.

2. In the root **build.gradle** file, add the **google()** repository:

```
allprojects {
    repositories {
        google()
        jcenter()
    }
}
```

This will allow Gradle (the build system) to know where to locate the Android Jetpack libraries, which are developed by Google.

3. Let's add the **ViewModel** and **LiveData** libraries to **app/build.gradle**:

```
dependencies {
    ...
    def lifecycle_version = "2.2.0"
    implementation "androidx.lifecycle:lifecycle-
        extensions:$lifecycle_version"
    ...
}
```

This will bring both the **ViewModel** and **LiveData** code into our project.

4. Create and define **SplitFragmentOne**:

```
class SplitFragmentOne : Fragment() {
    override fun onCreateView(
        inflater: LayoutInflater,
        container: ViewGroup?,
        savedInstanceState: Bundle?
    ): View? {
        return inflater.inflate(R.layout.fragment_split_one,
            container, false)
    }
    override fun onViewCreated(view: View, savedInstanceState:
      Bundle?) {
        super.onViewCreated(view, savedInstanceState)
        view.findViewById<TextView>
            (R.id.fragment_split_one_text_view).text =
            getString(R.string.total, 0)
    }
}
```

5. Add the **fragment_split_one.xml** file to the **res/layout** folder:

```
<?xml version="1.0" encoding="utf-8"?>
<LinearLayout xmlns:android=
  "http://schemas.android.com/apk/res/android"
    android:layout_width="match_parent"
    android:layout_height="match_parent"
    android:gravity="center"
    android:orientation="vertical">

    <TextView
```

```
        android:id="@+id/fragment_split_one_text_view"
        android:layout_width="wrap_content"
        android:layout_height="wrap_content" />


    <Button
        android:id="@+id/fragment_split_one_button"
        android:layout_width="wrap_content"
        android:layout_height="wrap_content"
        android:text="@string/press_me" />


</LinearLayout>
```

6. Now, let's create and define **SplitFragmentTwo**:

```
class SplitFragmentTwo : Fragment() {

    override fun onCreateView(
        inflater: LayoutInflater,
        container: ViewGroup?,
        savedInstanceState: Bundle?
    ): View? {
        return inflater.inflate(R.layout.fragment_split_two,
            container, false)
    }


    override fun onViewCreated(view: View, savedInstanceState:
        Bundle?) {
        super.onViewCreated(view, savedInstanceState)
        view.findViewById<TextView>
          (R.id.fragment_split_two_text_view).text =
            getString(R.string.total, 0)
    }

}
```

7. Add the **fragment_split_two.xml** file to the **res/layout** folder:

```
<?xml version="1.0" encoding="utf-8"?>
<LinearLayout xmlns:android
  ="http://schemas.android.com/apk/res/android"
    android:layout_width="match_parent"
    android:layout_height="match_parent"
    android:gravity="center"
    android:orientation="vertical">
```

```
    <TextView
        android:id="@+id/fragment_split_two_text_view"
        android:layout_width="wrap_content"
        android:layout_height="wrap_content" />
</LinearLayout>
```

8. Define **SplitActivity**:

```
class SplitActivity : AppCompatActivity() {

    override fun onCreate(savedInstanceState: Bundle?) {
        super.onCreate(savedInstanceState)
        setContentView(R.layout.activity_split)
    }

}
```

9. Create the **activity_split.xml** file in the **res/layout** folder:

```
<?xml version="1.0" encoding="utf-8"?>
<LinearLayout xmlns:android
  ="http://schemas.android.com/apk/res/android"
    xmlns:tools="http://schemas.android.com/tools"
    android:layout_width="match_parent"
    android:layout_height="match_parent"
    android:orientation="vertical"
    tools:context=".SplitActivity">

    <androidx.fragment.app.FragmentContainerView
        android:id="@+id/activity_fragment_split_1"
        android:name="com.android
          .testable.viewmodellivedata.SplitFragmentOne"
        android:layout_width="match_parent"
        android:layout_height="0dp"
        android:layout_weight="1" />

    <androidx.fragment.app.FragmentContainerView
        android:id="@+id/activity_fragment_split_2"
        android:name="com.android
          .testable.viewmodellivedata.SplitFragmentTwo"
        android:layout_width="match_parent"
```

```
    android:layout_height="0dp"
    android:layout_weight="1" />


</LinearLayout>
```

10. Next, let's create a **layout-land** folder in the **res** folder. Then, in the **layout-land** folder, we'll create an **activity_split.xml** file with the following layout:

```
<?xml version="1.0" encoding="utf-8"?>
<LinearLayout xmlns:android=
  "http://schemas.android.com/apk/res/android"
    xmlns:tools="http://schemas.android.com/tools"
    android:layout_width="match_parent"
    android:layout_height="match_parent"
    android:baselineAligned="false"
    android:orientation="horizontal"
    tools:context=".SplitActivity">

    <androidx.fragment.app.FragmentContainerView
        android:id="@+id/activity_fragment_split_1"
        android:name="com.android
          .testable.viewmodellivedata.SplitFragmentOne"
        android:layout_width="0dp"
        android:layout_height="match_parent"
        android:layout_weight="1" />


    <androidx.fragment.app.FragmentContainerView
        android:id="@+id/activity_fragment_split_2"
        android:name="com.android
          .testable.viewmodellivedata.SplitFragmentTwo"
        android:layout_width="0dp"
        android:layout_height="match_parent"
        android:layout_weight="1" />


</LinearLayout>
```

Notice the **android:id** attribute in both **activity_split.xml** files. This allows the operating system to correctly save and restore the state of the fragment during rotation.

> **NOTE**
>
> Make sure to properly point to your fragments with the right package declaration in the **android:name** attribute in the **FragmentContainerView** tag in both **activity_split.xml** files. Also, the **id** attribute is a must in the **FragmentContainerView** tag, so make sure it's present; otherwise, the app will crash.

11. The following strings should be added to **res/strings.xml**:

```
<string name="press_me">Press Me</string>
<string name="total">Total %d</string>
```

12. Make sure that **ActivitySplit** is present in the **AndroidManifest.xml** file:

```
<activity android:name=".SplitActivity">
```

> **NOTE**
>
> If this is the only activity in your manifest, then make sure to add the launcher **intent-filter** tags so that the system knows which activity it should open when your app is installed:
>
> ```
> <intent-filter>
>         <action android:name="android.intent.action.MAIN" />
>         <category android:name="android.intent.category.LAUNCHER" />
> </intent-filter>
> ```

Now, let's run the project. After it's run, you can rotate the device and see that the screens are oriented according to the specifications. The **Total** is set to 0 and clicking on the button will do nothing:

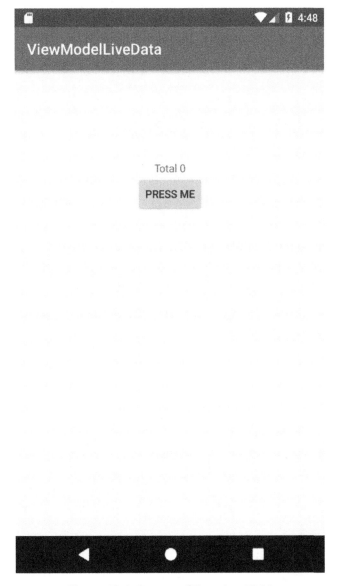

Figure 10.4: Output of Exercise 10.01

We will need to build the logic required for adding 1 every time the button is clicked. That logic will need to be testable as well. We can build a **ViewModel** and attach it to each fragment. This will make the logic testable and it will also solve the issues with the life cycle.

EXERCISE 10.02: ADDING A VIEWMODEL

We now need to implement the logic for connecting our **ViewModel** to the button click and ensuring that the value is kept across configuration changes, such as rotations. Let's get started:

1. Create a **TotalsViewModel** that looks like this:

```
class TotalsViewModel : ViewModel() {

    var total = 0

    fun increaseTotal(): Int {
        total++
        return total
    }

}
```

Notice that we extended from the **ViewModel** class, which is part of the life cycle library. In the **ViewModel** class, we defined one method that increases the value of the total and returns the updated value.

2. Now, add the **updateText** and **prepareViewModel** methods to the **SplitFragment1** fragment:

```
class SplitFragmentOne : Fragment() {

    override fun onCreateView(
        inflater: LayoutInflater,
        container: ViewGroup?,
        savedInstanceState: Bundle?
    ): View? {
        return inflater.inflate(R.layout.fragment_split_one,
            container, false)
    }

    override fun onViewCreated(view: View, savedInstanceState:
        Bundle?) {
        super.onViewCreated(view, savedInstanceState)
        prepareViewModel()
    }

    private fun prepareViewModel() {
}
```

```
        private fun updateText(total: Int) {
          view?.findViewById<TextView>
            (R.id.fragment_split_one_text_view)?.text =
              getString(R.string.total, total)

        }

      }
```

3. In the **prepareViewModel()** function, let's start adding our **ViewModel**:

```
private fun prepareViewModel() {
    val totalsViewModel
      = ViewModelProvider(this).get(TotalsViewModel::class.java)
}
```

This is how the **ViewModel** instance is accessed.
ViewModelProvider(this) will make **TotalsViewModel** be bound to
the life cycle of the fragment. **.get(TotalsViewModel::class.java)** will
retrieve the instance of **TotalsViewModel** that we defined previously. If the
fragment is being created for the first time, it will produce a new instance, while
if the fragment is recreated after a rotation, it will provide the previously created
instance. The reason we pass the class as an argument is because a fragment or
activity can have multiple ViewModels and the class serves as an identifier for
the type of **ViewModel** we want.

4. Now, set the last known value on the view:

```
private fun prepareViewModel() {
    val totalsViewModel
      = ViewModelProvider(this).get(TotalsViewModel::class.java)
    updateText(totalsViewModel.total)
}
```

The second line will help during device rotation. It will set the last total that was
computed. If we remove this line and rebuild, then we will see **Total 0** every
time we rotate, and after every click we will see the previously computed total
plus 1.

5. Update the View when the button is clicked:

```
private fun prepareViewModel() {
    val totalsViewModel
      = ViewModelProvider(this).get(TotalsViewModel::class.java)
    updateText(totalsViewModel.total)
    view?.findViewById<Button>
      (R.id.fragment_split_one_button)?.setOnClickListener {
        updateText(totalsViewModel.increaseTotal())
```

```
        }
    }
```

The last few lines indicate that when a click is performed on the button, we tell **ViewModel** to recompute the total and set the new value.

6. Now, run the app, press the button, and rotate the screen to see what happens:

Figure 10.5: Output of Exercise 10.02

As you press the button, you will see the total increase, and when you rotate the display, the value is kept constant. If you press the back button and reopen the activity, you will notice that the total is set to 0. We will need to notify the other fragment that the value has changed. We can do this by using an interface and letting the activity know so that the activity can alert **SplitFragmentOne**. Alternatively, we can attach our **ViewModel** to the activity, which will allow us to share it between fragments.

EXERCISE 10.03: SHARING OUR VIEWMODEL BETWEEN THE FRAGMENTS

We need to access **TotalsViewModel** in **SplitFragmentOne** and attach our
ViewModel to the activity. Let's get started:

1. Add the same **ViewModel** we used previously to our **SplitFragmentTwo**:

```
class SplitFragmentTwo : Fragment() {

    override fun onCreateView(
        inflater: LayoutInflater,
        container: ViewGroup?,
        savedInstanceState: Bundle?
    ): View? {
        return inflater.inflate(R.layout.fragment_split_two,
          container, false)
    }

    override fun onViewCreated(view: View, savedInstanceState:
      Bundle?) {
        super.onViewCreated(view, savedInstanceState)
        val totalsViewModel = ViewModelProvider(this)
          .get(TotalsViewModel::class.java)
        updateText(totalsViewModel.total)
    }

    private fun updateText(total: Int) {
        view?.findViewById<TextView>
          (R.id.fragment_split_one_text_view)?.text =
            getString(R.string.total, total)

    }

}
```

If we run the app now, we'll see that nothing has changed. The first fragment
works as before but the second fragment doesn't get any of the updates. This
is because even though we defined one **ViewModel**, we actually have two
instances of that **ViewModel** for each of our fragments. We will need to limit
the number of instances to one per fragment. We can achieve this by attaching
our **ViewModel** to the **SplitActivity** life cycle using a method called
requireActiviy.

2. Let's modify our fragments. In both fragments, we need to find and change the following code:

```
val totalsViewModel =
  ViewModelProvider(this).get(TotalsViewModel::class.java)
```

We will change it to the following:

```
val totalsViewModel =
  ViewModelProvider(requireActivity())
    .get(TotalsViewModel::class.java)
```

3. Now, let's run the application:

Figure 10.6: Output of Exercise 10.03

Again, here, we can observe something interesting. When the button is clicked, we don't see any changes in our second fragment, but we do see the total. This means that the fragments communicate, but not in real time. We can solve this through **LiveData**. By observing **LiveData** in both fragments, we can update each of the fragments' **TextView** classes when the value changes.

> **NOTE**
>
> Using ViewModels to communicate between fragments will only work when the fragments are placed in the same activity.

EXERCISE 10.04: ADDING LIVEDATA

Now, we need to ensure that our fragments communicate in real time with each other. We can use **LiveData** to achieve this. This way, every time one fragment makes a change, the other fragment will be notified about the change and will make the necessary adjustments.

Perform the following steps to achieve this:

1. Our **TotalsViewModel** should be modified so that it supports **LiveData**:

```
class TotalsViewModel : ViewModel() {

    private val total = MutableLiveData<Int>()

    init {
        total.postValue(0)
    }

    fun increaseTotal() {
        total.postValue((total.value ?: 0) + 1)
    }

    fun getTotal(): LiveData<Int> {
        return total
    }
}
```

Here, we created a **MutableLiveData**, a subclass of **LiveData** that allows us to change the value of the data. When **ViewModel** is created, we set the default value of **0**, and then when we increase the total, we post the previous value plus 1. We also created the **getTotal()** method, which returns a **LiveData** class that can be observed but not modified from the fragment.

2. Now, we need to modify our fragments so that they adjust to the new **ViewModel**. For **SplitFragmentOne**, we do the following:

```
override fun onViewCreated(view: View, savedInstanceState:
  Bundle?) {
    super.onViewCreated(view, savedInstanceState)

    val totalsViewModel =
      ViewModelProvider(requireActivity())
        .get(TotalsViewModel::class.java)

    totalsViewModel.getTotal().observe(viewLifecycleOwner,
      Observer {
        updateText(it)
    })

    view.findViewById<Button>
      (R.id.fragment_split_one_button).setOnClickListener {
        totalsViewModel.increaseTotal()

    }

}


private fun updateText(total: Int) {

    view?.findViewById<TextView>
      (R.id.fragment_split_one_text_view)?.text
        = getString(R.string.total, total)

}
```

For **SplitFragmentTwo**, we do the following:

```
override fun onViewCreated(view: View, savedInstanceState:
  Bundle?) {
    super.onViewCreated(view, savedInstanceState)

    val totalsViewModel =
      ViewModelProvider(requireActivity())
        .get(TotalsViewModel::class.java)

    totalsViewModel.getTotal().observe(viewLifecycleOwner,
      Observer {
        updateText(it)
    })

}


private fun updateText(total: Int) {
```

```
        view?.findViewById<TextView>
          (R.id.fragment_split_two_text_view)?.text =
            getString(R.string.total, total)

}
```

NOTE

Let's look at this line from the preceding snippet:

totalsViewModel.getTotal().
observe(viewLifecycleOwner, Observer {
  updateText(it)
})

The **LifecycleOwner** parameter for the **observe** method is called
viewLifecycleOwner. This is inherited from the **fragment**
class and it helps when we are observing data while the View that
the fragment manages is being rendered. In our example, swapping
viewLifecycleOwner with **this** would've caused no impact. But if our
fragment would've been part of a back stack feature, then there would've
been the risk of creating multiple observers, which would've lead to being
notified multiple times for the same dataset.

3. Now, let's write a test for our new **ViewModel**. We will name it
   TotalsViewModelTest and place it in the **test** package, not
   androidTest. This is because we want this test to execute on our
   workstation, not the device:

```
class TotalsViewModelTest {

    private val totalsViewModel = TotalsViewModel()

    @Before
    fun setUp() {
        assertEquals(0, totalsViewModel.getTotal().value)
    }

    @Test
    fun increaseTotal() {
        val total = 5
        for (i in 0 until total) {
            totalsViewModel.increaseTotal()
```

```
        }
            assertEquals(4, totalsViewModel.getTotal().value)
        }
    }
```

4. In the preceding test, before testing begins, we assert that the initial value of
    LiveData is set to 0. Then, we write a small test in which we increase the
    total five times and we assert that the final value is **5**. Let's run the test and see
    what happens:

```
java.lang.RuntimeException: Method getMainLooper in
    android.os.Looper not mocked.
```

5. A message similar to the preceding one will appear. This is because of how
    LiveData is implemented. Internally, it uses Handlers and Loopers, which
    are part of the Android framework, thus preventing us from executing the test.
    Luckily, there is a way around this. We will need the following configuration in
    our Gradle file for our test:

```
testImplementation 'android.arch.core:core-testing:2.1.0'
```

6. This adds a testing library to our testing code, not our application code.
    Now, let's add the following line to our code, above the instantiation of the
    ViewModel class:

```
class TotalsViewModelTest {

    @get:Rule
    val rule = InstantTaskExecutorRule()
    private val totalsViewModel = TotalsViewModel()
```

7. What we have done here is added a **TestRule** that says that every time a
    LiveData has its value changed, it will make the change instantly and will
    avoid using the Android Framework components. Every test we will write in this
    class will be impacted by this rule, thus giving us the freedom to play with the
    LiveData class for each new test method. If we run the test again, we will see
    the following:

```
java.lang.RuntimeException: Method getMainLooper
```

8. Does this mean that our new rule didn't work? Not exactly. If you look in your **TotalsViewModels** class, you'll see this:

```
init {
        total.postValue(0)

}
```

9. This means that because we created the **ViewModel** class outside of the scope of the rule, the rule will not apply. We can do two things to avoid this scenario: we can change our code to handle a null value that will be sent when we first subscribe to the **LiveData** class, or we can adjust our test so that we put the **ViewModel** class in the scope of the rule. Let's go with the second approach and change how we create our **ViewModel** class in the test. It should look something like this:

```
@get:Rule
val rule = InstantTaskExecutorRule()
private lateinit var totalsViewModel: TotalsViewModel

@Before
fun setUp() {
    totalsViewModel = TotalsViewModel()
    assertEquals(0, totalsViewModel.getTotal().value)
}
```

10. Let's run the test again and see what happens:

```
java.lang.AssertionError:
Expected :4
Actual   :5
```

See if you can spot where the error in the test is, fix it, and then rerun it:

Figure 10.7: Output of Exercise 10.04

The same output in landscape mode will look as follows:

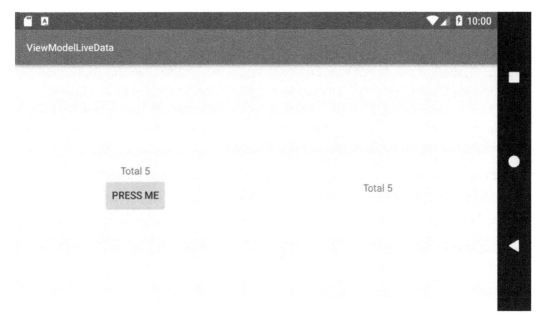

Figure 10.8: Output of Exercise 10.04 in landscape mode

By looking at the preceding example, we can see how using a combination of the **LiveData** and **ViewModel** approaches helped us solve our problem while taking into account the particularities of the Android operating system:

- **ViewModel** helped us hold the data across device orientation change and it solved the issue of communicating between fragments.

- **LiveData** helped us retrieve the most up-to-date information that we've processed while taking into account the fragment's life cycle.

- The combination of the two helped us delegate our processing logic in an efficient way, allowing us to unit test this processing logic.

ROOM

The Room persistence library acts as a wrapper between your application code and the SQLite storage. You can think of SQLite as a database that runs without its own server and saves all the application data in an internal file that's only accessible by your application (if the device is not rooted). Room will sit between the application code and the SQLite Android Framework, and it will handle the necessary Create, Read, Update, and Delete (CRUD) operations while exposing an abstraction that your application can use to define the data and how you want the data to be handled. This abstraction comes in the form of the following objects:

- **Entities**: You can specify how you want your data to be stored and the relationships between your data.

- **Data Access Object** (**DAO**): The operations that can be done on your data.

- **Database**: You can specify the configurations that your database should have (the name of the database and migration scenarios).

These can be seen in the following diagram:

Figure 10.9: Relationship between your application and Room components

In the preceding diagram, we can see how the Room components interact with each other. It's easier to visualize this with an example. Let's assume you want to make a messaging app and store each message in your local storage. In this case, **Entity** would be a **Message** object that will have an ID, and will contain the contents of the message, the sender, the time, status, and so on. In order to access messages from the local storage, you will need a **MessageDao**, which will contain methods such as **insertMessage()**, **getMessagesFromUser()**, **deleteMessage()**, and **updateMessage()**. Since it's a messaging application, you will need a **Contact** entity to hold information about the senders and receivers of a message. The **Contact** entity would contain information such as name, last online time, phone number, email, and so on. In order to access the contact information, you would need a **ContactDao** interface, which will contain **createUser()**, **updateUser()**, **deleteUser()**, and **getAllUsers()**. Both entities will create a matching table in SQLite that contains the fields we defined inside the entity classes as columns. In order to achieve this, we'll have to create a **MessagingDatabase** in which we will reference both of these entities.

In a world without Room or similar DAO libraries, we would need to use the Android Framework's SQLite components. This typically involves code when setting up our database, such as a query to create a table and applying similar queries for every table we would have. Every time we would query a table for data, we would need to convert the resulting object into a Java or Kotlin one. Then, for every object we updated or created, we would need to perform a conversion in the other direction and invoke the appropriate method. Room removes all this boilerplate code, allowing us to focus on our app's requirements.

By default, Room does not allow any operations on the UI thread to enforce the Android standards related to input-output operations. In order to make asynchronous calls to access data, Room is compatible with a number of libraries and frameworks, such as Kotlin coroutines, RxJava, and **LiveData**, on top of its default definitions.

ENTITIES

Entities serve two purposes: to define the structure of tables and to hold the data from a table row. Let's use our scenario of the messaging app and define two entities: one for the user and one for the message. The **User** entity will contain information about who sent the messages, while the **Message** entity will contain information about the contents of a message, the time it was sent, and a reference to the sender of the message. The following code snippet provides an example of how entities are defined with Room:

```
@Entity(tableName = "messages")
data class Message(
    @PrimaryKey(autoGenerate = true) @ColumnInfo(name = "message_id")
        val id: Long,
    @ColumnInfo(name = "text", defaultValue = "") val text: String,
    @ColumnInfo(name = "time") val time: Long,
    @ColumnInfo(name = "user") val userId: Long,
)


@Entity(tableName = "users")
data class User(
    @PrimaryKey @ColumnInfo(name = "user_id") val id: Long,
    @ColumnInfo(name = "first_name") val firstName: String,
    @ColumnInfo(name = "last_name") val lastName: String,
    @ColumnInfo(name = "last_online") val lastOnline: Long
)
```

As you can see, entities are just *data classes* with annotations that will tell Room how the tables should be built in SQLite. The annotations we used are as follows:

- The @**Entity** annotation defines the table. By default, the table name will be the name of the class. We can change the name of the table through the **tableName** method in the **Entity** annotation. This is useful in situations where we want our code obfuscated but wish to keep the consistency of the SQLite structure.

- @**ColumnInfo** defines configurations for a certain column. The most common one is the name of the column. We can also specify a default value, the SQLite type of the field, and whether the field should be indexed.

- @**PrimaryKey** indicates what in our entity will make it unique. Every entity should have at least one primary key. If your primary key is an integer or a long, then we can add the **autogenerate** field. This means that every entity that gets inserted into the **Primary Key** field is automatically generated by SQLite. Usually, this is done by incrementing the previous ID. If you wish to define multiple fields as primary keys, then you can adjust the @**Entity** annotation to accommodate this; such as the following:

```
@Entity(tableName = "messages", primaryKeys = ["id", "time"])
```

Let's assume that our messaging application wants to send locations. Locations have latitude, longitude, and name. We can add them to the **Message** class, but that would increase the complexity of the class. What we can do is create another entity and reference the ID in our class. The problem with this approach is that we would then query the **Location** entity every time we query the **Message** entity. Room has a third approach through the @**Embedded** annotation. Now, let's look at the updated **Message** entity:

```
@Entity(tableName = "messages")
data class Message(
    @PrimaryKey(autoGenerate = true) @ColumnInfo(name = "message_id")
        val id: Long,
    @ColumnInfo(name = "text", defaultValue = "") val text: String,
    @ColumnInfo(name = "time") val time: Long,
    @ColumnInfo(name = "user") val userId: Long,
    @Embedded val location: Location?
)

data class Location(
    @ColumnInfo(name = "lat") val lat: Double,
    @ColumnInfo(name = "long") val log: Double,
    @ColumnInfo(name = "location_name") val name: String
)
```

What this code does is add three columns (**lat**, **long**, and **location_name**) to the messages table. This allows us to avoid having objects with a large number of fields while keeping the consistency of our tables.

If we look at our entities, we'll see that they exist independent of each other. The **Message** entity has a **userId** field, but there's nothing preventing us from adding messages from invalid users. This may lead to situations where we collect data without any purpose. If we want to delete a particular user, along with their messages, then we have to do so manually. Room provides us with a way to define this relationship through a **ForeignKey**:

```
@Entity(
    tableName = "messages",
    foreignKeys = [ForeignKey(
        entity = User::class,
        parentColumns = ["user_id"],
        childColumns = ["user"],
        onDelete = ForeignKey.CASCADE
    )]
)
data class Message(
    @PrimaryKey(autoGenerate = true) @ColumnInfo(name = "message_id")
      val id: Long,
    @ColumnInfo(name = "text", defaultValue = "") val text: String,
    @ColumnInfo(name = "time") val time: Long,
    @ColumnInfo(name = "user") val userId: Long,
    @Embedded val location: Location?
)
```

In the preceding example, we added the **foreignKeys** field and created a new **ForeignKey** to the **User** entity, while for the parent column, we defined the **user_id** field in the **User** class and for the child column, the **user** field in the **Message** class. Every time we add a message to the table, there needs to be a **User** entry in the **users** table. If we try to delete a user and there are any messages from that user that still exist, then, by default, this will not work because of the dependencies. However, we can tell Room to do a cascade delete, which will erase the user and the associated messages.

DAO

If entities specify how we define and hold our data, then DAOs specify what to do with that data. A DAO class is a place where we define our CRUD operations. Ideally, each entity should have a corresponding DAO, but there are situations where crossovers occur (usually, this happens when we have to deal with JOINs between two tables).

Continuing with our previous example, let's build some corresponding DAOs for our entity:

```kotlin
@Dao
interface MessageDao {

    @Insert(onConflict = OnConflictStrategy.REPLACE)
    fun insertMessages(vararg messages: Message)

    @Update
    fun updateMessages(vararg messages: Message)

    @Delete
    fun deleteMessages(vararg messages: Message)

    @Query("SELECT * FROM messages")
    fun loadAllMessages(): List<Message>

    @Query("SELECT * FROM messages WHERE user=:userId AND
        time>=:time")
    fun loadMessagesFromUserAfterTime(userId: String, time: Long):
        List<Message>
}

@Dao
interface UserDao {

    @Insert(onConflict = OnConflictStrategy.REPLACE)
    fun insertUser(user: User)

    @Update
    fun updateUser(user: User)

    @Delete
    fun deleteUser(user: User)

    @Query("SELECT * FROM users")
    fun loadAllUsers(): List<User>
}
```

In the case of our messages, we have defined the following functions: insert one or more messages, update one or more messages, delete one or more messages, and retrieve all the messages from a certain user that are older than a particular time. For our users, we can insert one user, update one user, delete one user, and retrieve all the users.

If you look at our **Insert** methods, you'll see we have defined that in the case of a conflict (when we try to insert something with an ID that already exists), it will replace the existing entry. The **Update** field has a similar configuration, but in our case, we have chosen the default. This means that nothing will happen if the update cannot occur.

The @**Query** annotation stands out from all the others. This is where we use SQLite code to define how our read operations work. **SELECT** * means we want to read all the data for every row in the table, which will populate all our entities' fields. The **WHERE** clause indicates a restriction that we want to apply to our query. We can also define a method like this:

```
@Query("SELECT * FROM messages WHERE user IN (:userIds) AND
    time>=:time")
fun loadMessagesFromUserAfterTime(userIds: List<String>, time: Long):
    List<Message>
```

This allows us to filter messages from multiple users.

We can define a new class like this:

```
data class TextWithTime(
    @ColumnInfo(name = "text") val text: String,
    @ColumnInfo(name = "time") val time: Long
)
```

Now, we can define the following query:

```
@Query("SELECT text,time FROM messages")
fun loadTextsAndTimes(): List<TextWithTime>
```

This will allow us to extract information from certain columns at a time, not the entire row.

Now, let's say that you want to add the user information of the sender to every message. Here, we'll need to use a similar approach to the one we used previously:

```
data class MessageWithUser(
    @Embedded val message: Message,
```

```
    @Embedded val user: User
)
```

By using the new data class, we can define this query:

```
@Query("SELECT * FROM messages INNER JOIN users on
  users.user_id=messages.user")
fun loadMessagesAndUsers(): List<MessageWithUser>
```

Now, we have the user information for every message we want to display. This will come in handy in scenarios such as group chats, where we should display the name of the sender of every message.

SETTING UP THE DATABASE

What we have so far is a bunch of DAOs and entities. Now, it's time to put them together. First, let's define our database:

```
@Database(entities = [User::class, Message::class], version = 1)
abstract class ChatDatabase : RoomDatabase() {

    companion object {

        private lateinit var chatDatabase: ChatDatabase

        fun getDatabase(applicationContext: Context): ChatDatabase {
            if (!(::chatDatabase.isInitialized)) {
                chatDatabase =
                    Room.databaseBuilder(applicationContext,
                        chatDatabase::class.java, "chat-db")
                        .build()
            }
            return chatDatabase
        }
    }

    abstract fun userDao(): UserDao

    abstract fun messageDao(): MessageDao
}
```

In the @**Database** annotation, we specify what entities go in our database, and we also specify our version. Then, for every DAO, we define an abstract method in our **RoomDatabase**. This allows the build system to build a subclass of our class in which it provides the implementations for these methods. The build system will also create the tables related to our entities.

The **getDatabase** method in the companion object is used to illustrate how we create an instance of the **ChatDatabase** class. Ideally, there should be one instance of the database for our application due to the complexity involved in building a new database object. This can be better achieved through a dependency injection framework.

Let's assume you've released your chat application. Your database is currently version 1, but your users are complaining that the message status feature is missing. You decide to add this feature in the next release. This involves changing the structure of the database, which can impact databases that have already built their structures. Luckily, Room offers something called a migration. In the migration, we can define how our database changed between versions 1 and 2. So, let's look at our example:

```
data class Message(
    @PrimaryKey(autoGenerate = true) @ColumnInfo(name = "message_id")
        val id: Long,
    @ColumnInfo(name = "text", defaultValue = "") val text: String,
    @ColumnInfo(name = "time") val time: Long,
    @ColumnInfo(name = "user") val userId: Long,
    @ColumnInfo(name = "status") val status: Int,
    @Embedded val location: Location?
)
```

Here, we added the status flag to the **Message** entity.

Now, let's look at our **ChatDatabase**:

```
Database(entities = [User::class, Message::class], version = 2)
abstract class ChatDatabase : RoomDatabase() {

    companion object {

        private lateinit var chatDatabase: ChatDatabase

        private val MIGRATION_1_2 = object : Migration(1, 2) {
```

```kotlin
        override fun migrate(database: SupportSQLiteDatabase) {
            database.execSQL("ALTER TABLE messages ADD COLUMN
                status INTEGER")
        }



    }

    fun getDatabase(applicationContext: Context): ChatDatabase {
        if (!(::chatDatabase.isInitialized)) {
            chatDatabase =
                Room.databaseBuilder(applicationContext,
                    chatDatabase::class.java, "chat-db")
                    .addMigrations(MIGRATION_1_2)
                    .build()
        }
        return chatDatabase
    }


}


    abstract fun userDao(): UserDao

    abstract fun messageDao(): MessageDao
}
```

In our database, we've increased the version to 2 and added a migration between versions 1 and 2. Here, we added the status column to the table. We'll add this migration when we build the database. Once we've released the new code, when the updated app is opened and the code to build the database is executed, it will compare the version on the stored data with the one specified in our class and it will notice a difference. Then, it will execute the migrations we specified until it reaches the latest version. This allows us to maintain an application for years without impacting the user's experience.

If you look at our **Message** class, you may have noticed that we defined the time as a Long. In Java and Kotlin, we have the **Date** object, which may be more useful than the timestamp of the message. Luckily, Room has a solution for this in the form of TypeConverters. The following table shows what data types we can use in our code and the SQLite equivalent. Complex data types need to be brought down to these levels using TypeConverters:

Java/Kotlin	SQLite
String	TEXT
Byte, Short, Integer, Long, Boolean	INTEGER
Double, Float	REAL
Array<Byte>	BLOB

Figure 10.10: Relationship between Kotlin/Java data types and the SQLite data types

Here, we've modified the **lastOnline** field so that it's of the **Date** type:

```
data class User(
    @PrimaryKey @ColumnInfo(name = "user_id") val id: Long,
    @ColumnInfo(name = "first_name") val firstName: String,
    @ColumnInfo(name = "last_name") val lastName: String,
    @ColumnInfo(name = "last_online") val lastOnline: Date
)
```

Here, we've defined a couple of methods that convert a **Date** object into a **Long** and vice versa. The **@TypeConverter** annotation helps Room identify where the conversion takes place:

```
class DateConverter {
    @TypeConverter
    fun from(value: Long?): Date? {
        return value?.let { Date(it) }
    }

    @TypeConverter
    fun to(date: Date?): Long? {
        return date?.time
    }
}
```

Finally, we'll add our converter to Room through the @**TypeConverters** annotation:

```
@Database(entities = [User::class, Message::class], version = 2)
@TypeConverters(DateConverter::class)
abstract class ChatDatabase : RoomDatabase() {
```

In the next section, we will look at some third-party frameworks.

THIRD-PARTY FRAMEWORKS

Room works well with third-party frameworks such as LiveData, RxJava, and coroutines. This solves two issues: multi-threading and observing data changes.

LiveData will make the @**Query** annotated methods in your DAOs reactive, which means that if new data is added, **LiveData** will notify the observers of this:

```
@Query("SELECT * FROM users")
fun loadAllUsers(): LiveData<List<User>>
```

Kotlin coroutines complement **LiveData** by making the @**Insert**, @**Delete**, and @**Update** methods asynchronous:

```
@Insert(onConflict = OnConflictStrategy.REPLACE)
suspend fun insertUser(user: User)
@Update
suspend fun updateUser(user: User)
@Delete
suspend fun deleteUser(user: User)
```

RxJava solves both issues: making the @**Query** methods reactive through components such as **Publisher**, **Observable**, or **Flowable** and making the rest of the methods asynchronous through **Completable**, **Single**, or **Maybe**:

```
@Insert(onConflict = OnConflictStrategy.REPLACE)
fun insertUser(user: User) : Completable
@Update
fun updateUser(user: User) : Completable
@Delete
fun deleteUser(user: User) : Completable
@Query("SELECT * FROM users")
fun loadAllUsers(): Flowable<List<User>>
```

Executors and threads come with the Java framework and can be a useful solution to solve threading issues with Room if none of the aforementioned third-party integrations are part of your project. Your DAO classes will not suffer from any modifications; however, you will need the components that access your DAOs to adjust and use either an executor or a thread:

```
@Query("SELECT * FROM users")
fun loadAllUsers(): List<User>
@Insert(onConflict = OnConflictStrategy.REPLACE)
fun insertUser(user: User)
@Update
fun updateUser(user: User)
@Delete
fun deleteUser(user: User)
```

An example of accessing the DAO is as follows:

```
fun getUsers(usersCallback:()->List<User>){
    Thread(Runnable {
        usersCallback.invoke(userDao.loadUsers())
    }).start()
}
```

The preceding example will create a new thread and start it every time we want to retrieve the list of users. There are two major issues with this code:

- Thread creation is an expensive operation

- The code is hard to test

The solution to the first issue can be solved with **ThreadPools** and **Executors**. The Java framework offers a robust set of options when it comes to **ThreadPools**. A thread pool is a component that is responsible for thread creation and destruction and allows the developer to specify the number of threads in the pool. Multiple threads in a thread pool will ensure that multiple tasks can be executed concurrently.

We can rewrite the preceding code as follows:

```
private val executor:Executor =
    Executors.newSingleThreadExecutor()
fun getUsers(usersCallback:(List<User>)->Unit){
    executor.execute {
        usersCallback.invoke(userDao.loadUsers())
    }
}
```

In the preceding example, we defined an executor that will use a pool of 1 thread. When we want to access the list of users, we move the query inside the executor, and when the data is loaded, our callback lambda will be invoked.

EXERCISE 10.05: MAKING A LITTLE ROOM

You have been hired by a news agency to build a news application. The application will display a list of articles written by journalists. An article can be written by one or more journalists, and each journalist can write one or more articles. The data information for each article includes the article's title, content, and date. The journalist's information includes their first name, last name, and job title. You will need to build a Room database that holds this information so it can be tested.

Before we start, let's look at the relationship between the entities. In the chat application example, we defined the rule that one user can send one or multiple messages. This relationship is known as a one-to-many relationship. That relationship is implemented as a reference between one entity to another (the user was defined in the message table in order to be connected to the sender). In this case, we have a many-to-many relationship. In order to implement a many-to-many relationship, we need to create an entity that's holding references that will link the other two entities. Let's get started:

1. Let's start by adding the annotation processing plugin to **app/build.gradle**. This will read the annotations used by Room and generate the code necessary for interacting with the database:

    ```
    apply plugin: 'kotlin-kapt'
    ```

2. Next, let's add the Room libraries in **app/build.gradle**:

    ```
    def room_version = "2.2.5"
    implementation "androidx.room:room-runtime:$room_version"
    kapt "androidx.room:room-compiler:$room_version"
    ```

    The first line defines the library version, the second line brings in the Room library for Java and Kotlin, and the last line is for the Kotlin annotation processor. This allows the build system to generate boilerplate code from the Room annotations.

3. Let's define our entities:

    ```
    @Entity(tableName = "article")
    data class Article(
        @PrimaryKey(autoGenerate = true)
        @ColumnInfo(name = "id") val id: Long = 0,
    ```

```
    @ColumnInfo(name = "title") val title: String,
    @ColumnInfo(name = "content") val content: String,
    @ColumnInfo(name = "time") val time: Long
)

@Entity(tableName = "journalist")
data class Journalist(
    @PrimaryKey(autoGenerate = true)
      @ColumnInfo(name = "id") val id: Long = 0,
    @ColumnInfo(name = "first_name") val firstName: String,
    @ColumnInfo(name = "last_name") val lastName: String,
    @ColumnInfo(name = "job_title") val jobTitle: String
)
```

4. Now, define the entity that connects the journalist to the article and the appropriate constraints:

```
@Entity(
    tableName = "joined_article_journalist",
    primaryKeys = ["article_id", "journalist_id"],
    foreignKeys = [ForeignKey(
        entity = Article::class,
        parentColumns = arrayOf("id"),
        childColumns = arrayOf("article_id"),
        onDelete = ForeignKey.CASCADE
    ), ForeignKey(
        entity = Journalist::class,
        parentColumns = arrayOf("id"),
        childColumns = arrayOf("journalist_id"),
        onDelete = ForeignKey.CASCADE
    )]
)
data class JoinedArticleJournalist(
    @ColumnInfo(name = "article_id") val articleId: Long,
    @ColumnInfo(name = "journalist_id") val journalistId: Long
)
```

In the preceding code, we defined our connecting entity. As you can see, we haven't defined an ID for uniqueness, but both the article and the journalist, when used together, will be unique. We also defined foreign keys for each of the other entities referred to by our entity.

5. Create the **ArticleDao** DAO:

```
@Dao
interface ArticleDao {

    @Insert(onConflict = OnConflictStrategy.REPLACE)
    fun insertArticle(article: Article)

    @Update
    fun updateArticle(article: Article)

    @Delete
    fun deleteArticle(article: Article)

    @Query("SELECT * FROM article")
    fun loadAllArticles(): List<Article>

    @Query("SELECT * FROM article INNER JOIN
      joined_article_journalist ON
        article.id=joined_article_journalist.article_id WHERE
          joined_article_journalist.journalist_id=:journalistId")
    fun loadArticlesForAuthor(journalistId: Long): List<Article>
}
```

6. Now, create the **JournalistDao** data access object:

```
@Dao
interface JournalistDao {

    @Insert(onConflict = OnConflictStrategy.REPLACE)
    fun insertJournalist(journalist: Journalist)

    @Update
    fun updateJournalist(journalist: Journalist)

    @Delete
    fun deleteJournalist(journalist: Journalist)

    @Query("SELECT * FROM journalist")
    fun loadAllJournalists(): List<Journalist>

    @Query("SELECT * FROM journalist INNER JOIN
      joined_article_journalist ON
```

```
          journalist.id=joined_article_journalist.journalist_id
            WHERE joined_article_journalist.article_id=:articleId")
    fun getAuthorsForArticle(articleId: Long): List<Journalist>
}
```

7. Create the **JoinedArticleJournalistDao** DAO:

```
@Dao
interface JoinedArticleJournalistDao {

    @Insert(onConflict = OnConflictStrategy.REPLACE)
    fun insertArticleJournalist(joinedArticleJournalist:
        JoinedArticleJournalist)

    @Delete
    fun deleteArticleJournalist(joinedArticleJournalist:
        JoinedArticleJournalist)
}
```

Let's analyze our code a little bit. For the articles and journalists, we have the ability to add, insert, delete, and update queries. For articles, we have the ability to extract all of the articles but also extract articles from a certain author. We also have the option to extract all the journalists that wrote an article. This is done through a JOIN with our intermediary entity. For that entity, we define the options to insert (which will link an article to a journalist) and delete (which will remove that link).

8. Finally, let's define our **Database** class:

```
@Database(
    entities = [Article::class, Journalist::class,
        JoinedArticleJournalist::class],
    version = 1
)
abstract class NewsDatabase : RoomDatabase() {

    abstract fun articleDao(): ArticleDao

    abstract fun journalistDao(): JournalistDao

    abstract fun joinedArticleJournalistDao():
        JoinedArticleJournalistDao
}
```

We avoided defining the **getInstance** method here because we won't be calling the database anywhere. But if we don't do that, how will we know if it works? The answer to this is that we'll test it. This won't be a test that will run on your machine but one that will run on the device. This means that we will create it in the **androidTest** folder.

9. Let's start by setting up the test data. Here, we will add some articles and journalists to the database:

NewsDatabaseTest.kt

```
15 @RunWith(AndroidJUnit4::class)
16 class NewsDatabaseTest {
17
18    private lateinit var db: NewsDatabase
19    private lateinit var articleDao: ArticleDao
20    private lateinit var journalistDao: JournalistDao
21    private lateinit var joinedArticleJournalistDao:
         JoinedArticleJournalistDao
22
23    @Before
24    fun setUp() {
25       val context =
            ApplicationProvider.getApplicationContext<Context>()
26       db = Room.inMemoryDatabaseBuilder(context,
            NewsDatabase::class.java).build()
27       articleDao = db.articleDao()
28       journalistDao = db.journalistDao()
29       joinedArticleJournalistDao =
            db.joinedArticleJournalistDao()
30       initData()
31    }
```

The complete code for this step can be found at http://packt.live/3oWok6a.

10. Let's test whether the data is updated:

```
@Test
fun updateArticle() {
    val article = articleDao.loadAllArticles()[0]
    articleDao.updateArticle(article.copy(title =
      "new title"))

    assertEquals("new title",
      articleDao.loadAllArticles()[0].title)
}


@Test
fun updateJournalist() {
    val journalist = journalistDao.loadAllJournalists()[0]
    journalistDao.updateJournalist(journalist.copy(jobTitle
      = "new job title"))
```

```
        assertEquals("new job title",
            journalistDao.loadAllJournalists()[0].jobTitle)
    }
```

11. Next, let's test clearing the data:

```
    @Test
    fun deleteArticle() {
        val article = articleDao.loadAllArticles()[0]
        assertEquals(2,
            journalistDao.getAuthorsForArticle(article.id).size)
        articleDao.deleteArticle(article)

        assertEquals(4, articleDao.loadAllArticles().size)
        assertEquals(0,
            journalistDao.getAuthorsForArticle(article.id).size)
    }
```

Here, we have defined a few examples of how to test a Room database. What's interesting is how we build the database. Our database is an in-memory database. This means that all the data will be kept as long as the test is run and will be discarded afterward. This allows us to start with a clean slate for each new state and avoids the consequences of each of our testing sessions affecting each other. In our test, we've set up five articles and ten journalists. The first article was written by the top two journalists, while the second article was written by the first journalist. The rest of the articles have no authors. By doing this, we can test our update and delete methods. For the delete method, we can test our foreign key relationship as well. In the test, we can see that if we delete article 1, it will delete the relationship between the article and the journalists that wrote it. When testing your database, you should add the scenarios that your app will use. Feel free to add other testing scenarios and improve the preceding tests in your own database.

CUSTOMIZING LIFE CYCLES

Previously, we discussed **LiveData** and how it can be observed through a **LifecycleOwner**. We can use LifecycleOwners to subscribe to a **LifecycleObserver** so that it will monitor when the state of an owner changes. This is useful in situations where you would want to trigger certain functions when certain life cycle callbacks are invoked; for example, requesting locations, starting/stopping videos, and monitoring connectivity changes from your activity/fragment. We can achieve this with the use of a **LifecycleObserver**:

```
class ToastyLifecycleObserver(val onStarted: () -> Unit) :
    LifecycleObserver {
```

```
@OnLifecycleEvent(Lifecycle.Event.ON_START)
fun onStarted() {
    onStarted.invoke()
}
}
```

In the preceding code, we have defined a class that implements the **LifecycleObserver** interface and defined a method that will be called when the life cycle goes into the **ON_START** event. The **@OnLifecycleEvent** annotation will be used by the build system to generate boilerplate code that will invoke the annotation it is used for.

What we need to do next is register our observer in the activity/fragment:

```
lifecycle.addObserver(ToastyLifecycleObserver {
    Toast.makeText(this, "Started", Toast.LENGTH_LONG).show()
})
```

In the preceding code, we registered the observer on a **Lifecycle** object. The **Lifecycle** object is inherited from the parent activity class through the **getLifecycle()** method.

> **NOTE**
>
> **LiveData** are specialized uses of this principle. In the **LiveData** scenario, you would have multiple LifecycleOwners subscribing to a single **LiveData**. Here, you can just subscribe new owners for the same **LifecycleOwner**.

EXERCISE 10.06: REINVENTING THE WHEEL

In this exercise, we will implement a custom **LifecycleOwner** that triggers the **Lifecycle.Event.ON_START** event in **ToastyLifecycleObserver** when the activity starts. Let's get started by creating a new Android Studio Project with an empty activity named SplitActivity:

1. Let's start by adding the observer to our activity:

```
class SplitActivity : AppCompatActivity() {

    override fun onCreate(savedInstanceState: Bundle?) {
```

```
            super.onCreate(savedInstanceState)
            lifecycle.addObserver(ToastyLifecycleObserver {
                Toast.makeText(this, "Started",
                   Toast.LENGTH_LONG).show()
            })
        }
    }
```

If you run the code and open the activity, rotate the device, put the app in the background, and resume the app, you will see the **Started** toast.

2. Now, define a new activity that will reinvent the wheel and make it worse:

```
class LifecycleActivity : Activity(), LifecycleOwner {

    private val lifecycleRegistry: LifecycleRegistry =
        LifecycleRegistry(this)

    override fun onCreate(savedInstanceState: Bundle?) {
        super.onCreate(savedInstanceState)
        lifecycleRegistry.currentState = Lifecycle.State.CREATED

        lifecycleRegistry.addObserver(ToastyLifecycleObserver {
            Toast.makeText(applicationContext, "Started",
               Toast.LENGTH_LONG).show()
        })
    }

    override fun getLifecycle(): Lifecycle {
        return lifecycleRegistry
    }

    override fun onStop() {
        super.onStop()
        lifecycleRegistry.currentState = Lifecycle.State.STARTED
    }
}
```

3. In the **AndroidManifest.xml** file you can replace the SplitActivity with LifecycleActivity and it will look something like this

```
<activity android:name=".LifecycleActivity" >
    <intent-filter>
        <action android:name="android.intent.action.MAIN"
            />
```

```
        <category android:name=
            "android.intent.category.LAUNCHER" />
    </intent-filter>
</activity>
```

If we run the preceding code, we will see that a toast will appear every time an activity is started.

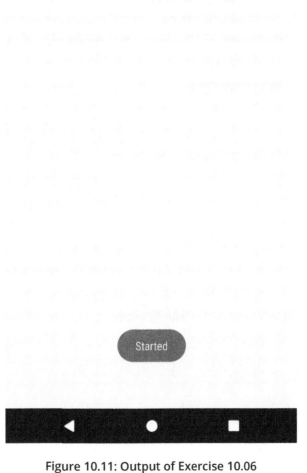

Figure 10.11: Output of Exercise 10.06

Notice that this is triggered without overriding the `onStart()` method from the `Activity` class. You can further experiment with the `LifecycleObserver` class to trigger the toast in other states of the `Activity` class.

Now, let's analyze the code for our new activity. Notice that we've extended the activity and not the `AppCompatActivity` class. This is because the `AppCompatActivity` class already contains the `LifecycleRegistry` logic. In our new activity, we defined a `LifecycleRegistry`, which will be responsible for adding our observers and changing the states. Then, we implemented the `LifecycleOwner` interface and in the `getLifecycle()` method, we return `LifecycleRegistry`. Then, for each of our callbacks, we can change the state of the registry. In the `onCreate()` method, we set the registry in the **CREATED** state (which will trigger the **ON_CREATE** event on the LifecycleObservers) and then we registered our `LifecycleObserver`. In order to achieve our task, we sent the **STARTED** event in the `onStop()` method. If we run the preceding example and minimize our activity, we should see our `Started` toast.

ACTIVITY 10.01: SHOPPING NOTES APP

You want to keep track of your shopping items, so you decide to build an app in which you can save the items you wish to buy during your next trip to the store. The requirements for this are as follows:

- The UI will be split into two: top/bottom in portrait mode and left/ right in landscape mode. The UI will look similar to what is shown in the following screenshot.

- The first half will display the number of notes, a text field, and a button. Every time the button is pressed, a note will be added with the text that was placed in the text field.

- The second half will display the list of notes.

- For each half, you will have a View model that will hold the relevant data.

- You should define a repository that will be used on top of the Room database to access your data.

- You should also define a Room database that will hold your notes.

- The note entity will have the following attributes: id, text:

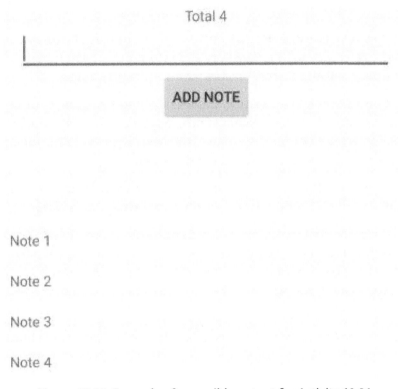

Figure 10.12: Example of a possible output for Activity 10.01

Perform the following steps to complete this activity:

1. Start with Room integration by creating the **Entity**, **Dao**, and **Database** methods. For **Dao**, the @**Query** annotated methods can directly return a **LiveData** object so that if the data changes, the observers can be directly notified.

2. Define a template of our repository in the form of an interface.

3. Implement the repository. The repository will have one reference to the **Dao** object we defined previously. The code for inserting the data will need to be moved to a separate thread. Create the **NotesApplication** class to provide one instance of the repository that will be used across the application. Make sure to update the **<application>** tag in the **AndroidManifest.xml** file to add your new application class.

4. Unit test the repository and define **ViewModels**, as follows:

- Define **NoteListViewModel** and the associated test. This will have a reference to the repository and return the list of notes.

- Define **CountNotesViewModel** and the associated test. **CountViewModel** will have a reference to the repository and return the total number of notes as a **LiveData**. It will also be responsible for inserting new notes.

- Define **CountNotesFragment** and the associated **fragment_count_notes.xml** layout. In the layout, define a **TextView** that will display the total number, an **EditText** for the name of the new notes, and a button that will insert the note that was introduced in **EditText**.

- Define an adapter for the list of notes called **NoteListAdapter** and an associated layout file for the rows called **view_note_item.xml**.

- Define the associated layout file, called **fragment_note_list.xml**, which will contain a **RecyclerView**. The layout will be used by **NoteListFragment**, which will connect **NoteListAdapter** to **RecyclerView**. It will also observe the data from **NoteListViewModel** and update the adapter.

- Define **NotesActivity** with an associated layout for landscape mode and portrait mode.

5. Make sure you have all the necessary data in **strings.xml**.

> **NOTE**
>
> The solution to this activity can be found at: http://packt.live/3sKj1cp.

SUMMARY

In this chapter, we analyzed the building blocks required to build a maintainable application. We also looked into one of the most common issues that developers come across when using the Android Framework, which is maintaining the states of objects during life cycle changes.

We started by analyzing **ViewModels** and how they solve the issue of holding data during orientation changes. We added **LiveData** to **ViewModels** to show how the two complement each other.

We then moved on to Room to show how we can persist data with minimal effort and without a lot of SQLite boilerplate code. We also explored one-to-many and many-to-many relationships, as well as how to migrate data and break down complex objects into primitives for storage.

After that, we reinvented the **Lifecycle** wheel in order to show how **LifecycleOwners** and **LifecycleObservers** interact.

We also built our first repository, which we will expand upon in the following chapters when other data sources are added into the mix.

The activity we completed in this chapter serves as an example of what direction Android apps are heading in. However, this was not a complete example due to the numerous frameworks and libraries that you will discover that give developers the flexibility to go in different directions.

The information you've learned about in this chapter will serve you well for the next one, which will expand on the concept of repositories. This will allow you to save data that's been obtained from a server into a room database. The concept of persisting data will also be expanded on as you will explore other ways to persist data, such as through **SharedPreferences** and files. Our focus will be on certain types of files: media files obtained from the camera of the device.

11

PERSISTING DATA

OVERVIEW

This chapter goes in depth about data persistence in Android, as well as exploring the repository pattern. By the end of the chapter, you will be able to build a repository that can connect to multiple data sources, and then use this repository to download files from an API and save them on a device. You will know multiple ways to store (persist) data directly on a device and the frameworks accessible to do this. When dealing with a filesystem, you will learn how it's partitioned and how you can read and write files in different locations and using different frameworks.

INTRODUCTION

In the previous chapter, you learned how to structure your code and how to save data. In the activity, you also had the opportunity to build a repository and use it to access data and save data through Room. You probably asked the question: Why do you need this repository? This chapter will seek to answer that. With the repository pattern, you will be able to retrieve data from a server and store it locally in a centralized way. The pattern is useful in situations where the same data is required in multiple places, thereby avoiding code duplication while also keeping ViewModels clean of any unnecessary extra logic.

If you look into the Settings app on your device, or the Settings feature of many apps, you will see some similarities. A list of items with toggles that can be on or off. This is achieved through **SharedPreferences** and **PreferenceFragments**. **SharedPreferences** is a way that allows you to store values in a file in key-value pairs. It has specialized mechanisms for reading and writing, thereby removing the concerns regarding threading. It's useful for small amounts of data and eliminates the need for something such as Room.

In this chapter, you will also learn about the Android filesystem and how it's structured into external and internal memory. You'll also develop your understanding of read and write permissions, how to create **FileProvider** class in order to offer other apps access to your files, and how you can save those files without requesting permissions on the external drives. You'll also see how to download files from the internet and save them on the filesystem.

Another concept that will be explored in this chapter is using the *Camera* application to take photos and videos on your application's behalf and save them to external storage using FileProviders.

REPOSITORY

Repository is a pattern that helps developers keep code for data sources separate from activities and ViewModels. It offers centralized access to data that can then be unit tested:

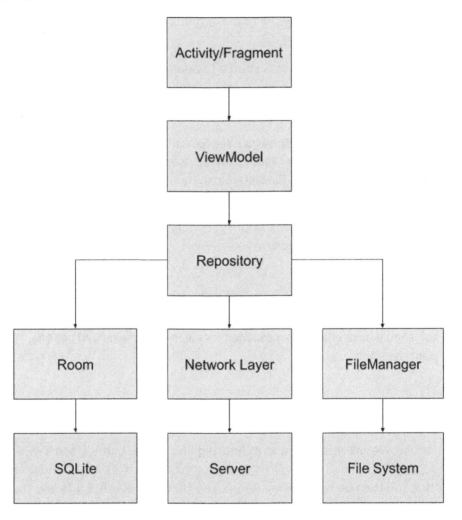

Figure 11.1: Diagram of repository architecture

In the preceding diagram, you can see the central role the repository plays in an application's code. Its responsibilities include:

- Keeping all the data sources (SQLite, Network, File System) required by your activity or the application

- Combining and transforming the data from multiple sources into a single output required at your activity level

- Transferring data from one data source to another (saving the result of a network call to Room)

- Refreshing expired data (if necessary)

Room, network layer, and **FileManager** represent the different types of data sources your repository can have. Room may be used to save large amounts of data from the network, while the filesystem can be used to store small amounts (**SharedPreferences**) or whole files.

ViewModel will have a reference to your repository and will deliver the results to the activity, which will display the result.

> **NOTE**
>
> Repositories should be organized based on domains, which means your app should have different repositories for different domains and not one giant repository.

EXERCISE 11.01: CREATING A REPOSITORY

In this exercise, we will create an app in Android Studio that connects to the API located at https://jsonplaceholder.typicode.com/posts using Retrofit and retrieves a list of posts that will then be saved using Room. The UI will display the title and the body of each post in **RecyclerView**. We will implement this using the repository pattern with **ViewModel**.

In order to complete this exercise, we will need to build the following:

- A network component responsible for downloading and parsing the JSON file

- A Room database responsible for storing the data with one entity

- A repository that manages the data between the components built previously

- A **ViewModel** that accesses the repository

- An activity with **RecyclerView** model that displays the data

Perform the following steps to complete this exercise:

1. Let's begin by adding the **required libraries** to the **app/build.gradle** folder:

```
implementation "androidx.constraintlayout
  :constraintlayout:2.0.4"
implementation 'androidx.recyclerview:recyclerview:1.1.0'

def lifecycle_version = "2.2.0"
implementation "androidx.lifecycle:lifecycle-extensions
  :$lifecycle_version"

def room_version = "2.2.5"
  implementation "androidx.room:room-runtime:$room_version"
kapt "androidx.room:room-compiler:$room_version"

implementation 'com.squareup.retrofit2:retrofit:2.6.2'
implementation 'com.squareup.retrofit2:converter-gson:2.6.2'
implementation 'com.google.code.gson:gson:2.8.6'

testImplementation 'junit:junit:4.12'
testImplementation 'android.arch.core:core-testing:2.1.0'
testImplementation 'org.mockito:mockito-core:2.23.0'
androidTestImplementation 'androidx.test.ext:junit:1.1.2'
androidTestImplementation 'androidx.test.espresso:espresso-
  core:3.3.0
```

2. We will need to group the classes that will deal with the API communication. We will do this by creating an **api** package that will contain the classes required for networking.

3. Next, we define a **Post** class, which will map the data in the JSON file. Each field in the JSON file representing a post will be defined in our new model:

```
data class Post(
    @SerializedName("id") val id: Long,
    @SerializedName("userId") val userId: Long,
    @SerializedName("title") val title: String,
    @SerializedName("body") val body: String
)
```

4. Next, we create a **PostService** interface, which will be responsible for loading the data from the server through Retrofit. The class will have one method for retrieving the list of posts and will perform an **HTTP GET** call to retrieve the data:

```
interface PostService {

    @GET("posts")
    fun getPosts(): Call<List<Post>>

}
```

5. Next, let's set up our Room database, which will contain one entity and one data access object. Let's define a **db** package for this.

6. The **PostEntity** class will have similar fields to the **Post** class:

```
@Entity(tableName = "posts")
data class PostEntity(
    @PrimaryKey(autoGenerate = true) @ColumnInfo(name = "id")
        val id: Long,
    @ColumnInfo(name = "userId") val userId: Long,
    @ColumnInfo(name = "title") val title: String,
    @ColumnInfo(name = "body") val body: String
)
```

7. **PostDao** should contain methods for storing a list of posts and retrieving the list of posts:

```
@Dao
interface PostDao {

    @Insert(onConflict = OnConflictStrategy.REPLACE)
    fun insertPosts(posts: List<PostEntity>)

    @Query("SELECT * FROM posts")
    fun loadPosts(): LiveData<List<PostEntity>>

}
```

8. And finally, in the case of the Room configuration, the **Post** database should look like this:

```
@Database(
    entities = [PostEntity::class],
    version = 1
)
abstract class PostDatabase : RoomDatabase() {

    abstract fun postDao(): PostDao
}
```

It's time to move into the **Repository** territory. So, let's create a repository package.

9. Previously, we defined two types of **Post**, one modeled on the JSON and one entity. Let's define a **PostMapper** class that converts from one to the other:

```
class PostMapper {

    fun serviceToEntity(post: Post): PostEntity {
        return PostEntity(post.id, post.userId, post.title,
            post.body)
    }
}
```

10. Let's now define a repository interface that will be responsible for loading the data. The repository will load the data from the API and store it using Room and will then provide **LiveData** with the **Room** entity that the UI layer will then consume:

```
interface PostRepository {

    fun getPosts(): LiveData<List<PostEntity>>

}
```

11. Now, let's provide the implementation for this:

```
class PostRepositoryImpl(
    private val postService: PostService,
    private val postDao: PostDao,
    private val postMapper: PostMapper,
    private val executor: Executor
```

```
) : PostRepository {
    override fun getPosts(): LiveData<List<PostEntity>> {
        postService.getPosts().enqueue(object :
            Callback<List<Post>> {

            override fun onFailure(call: Call<List<Post>>, t:
                Throwable) {

            }

            override fun onResponse(call: Call<List<Post>>,
                response: Response<List<Post>>) {
                response.body()?.let { posts ->
                    executor.execute {
                        postDao.insertPosts(posts.map { post ->
                            postMapper.serviceToEntity(post)
                        })
                    }
                }
            }

        })
        return postDao.loadPosts()
    }
}
```

If you look at the preceding code, you can see that when the posts are loaded, we will make an asynchronous call to the network to load the posts. When the call finishes, we update Room with a new list of posts on a separate thread. The method will always return what Room returns. This is because when the data eventually changes in Room, it will be propagated to the observers.

12. Let's now set up our dependencies. Because we have no dependency injection framework, we will have to rely on the **Application** class, which means we will need a **RepositoryApplication** class in which we will initialize all the services that the repository will require and then create the repository:

```
class RepositoryApplication : Application() {

    lateinit var postRepository: PostRepository

    override fun onCreate() {
```

```
            super.onCreate()
        val retrofit = Retrofit.Builder()
            .baseUrl("https://jsonplaceholder.typicode.com/")
            .addConverterFactory(GsonConverterFactory.create())
            .build()
        val postService =
            retrofit.create<PostService>(PostService::class.java)

        val notesDatabase =
            Room.databaseBuilder(applicationContext,
                PostDatabase::class.java, "post-db")
                .build()

        postRepository = PostRepositoryImpl(
            postService,
            notesDatabase.postDao(),
            PostMapper(),
            Executors.newSingleThreadExecutor()
        )
    }
}
```

13. Add **RepositoryApplication** to **android:name** in the **<application>** tag in **AndroidManifest.xml**.

14. Add internet permission to the **AndroidManifest.xml** file:

```
<uses-permission android:name="android.permission.INTERNET" />
```

15. Let's now define our **ViewModel**:

```
class PostViewModel(private val postRepository: PostRepository) :
    ViewModel() {

    fun getPosts() = postRepository.getPosts()
}
```

16. The **view_post_row.xml** layout file for each row will be as follows:

```
<?xml version="1.0" encoding="utf-8"?>
<androidx.constraintlayout.widget.ConstraintLayout
    xmlns:android="http://schemas.android.com/apk/res/android"
    xmlns:app="http://schemas.android.com/apk/res-auto"
    android:layout_width="match_parent"
    android:layout_height="wrap_content"
```

```
            android:padding="10dp">

        <TextView
            android:id="@+id/view_post_row_title"
            android:layout_width="wrap_content"
            android:layout_height="wrap_content"
            app:layout_constraintStart_toStartOf="parent"
            app:layout_constraintTop_toTopOf="parent" />

        <TextView
            android:id="@+id/view_post_row_body"
            android:layout_width="wrap_content"
            android:layout_height="wrap_content"
            android:layout_marginTop="5dp"
            app:layout_constraintStart_toStartOf="parent"
            app:layout_constraintTop_toBottomOf
              ="@id/view_post_row_title" />

    </androidx.constraintlayout.widget.ConstraintLayout>
```

17. The **activity_main.xml** layout file for our activity will be as follows:

```
<?xml version="1.0" encoding="utf-8"?>
<androidx.constraintlayout.widget.ConstraintLayout
    xmlns:android="http://schemas.android.com/apk/res/android"
    xmlns:app="http://schemas.android.com/apk/res-auto"
    xmlns:tools="http://schemas.android.com/tools"
    android:layout_width="match_parent"
    android:layout_height="match_parent"
    tools:context=".MainActivity">

    <androidx.recyclerview.widget.RecyclerView
        android:id="@+id/activity_main_recycler_view"
        android:layout_width="0dp"
        android:layout_height="0dp"
        app:layout_constraintBottom_toBottomOf="parent"
        app:layout_constraintLeft_toLeftOf="parent"
        app:layout_constraintRight_toRightOf="parent"
        app:layout_constraintTop_toTopOf="parent" />

</androidx.constraintlayout.widget.ConstraintLayout>
```

18. The **PostAdapter** class for the rows will be as follows:

```kotlin
class PostAdapter(private val layoutInflater: LayoutInflater) :
    RecyclerView.Adapter<PostAdapter.PostViewHolder>() {

    private val posts = mutableListOf<PostEntity>()

    override fun onCreateViewHolder(parent: ViewGroup, viewType:
      Int): PostViewHolder =
        PostViewHolder(layoutInflater.inflate
          (R.layout.view_post_row, parent, false))

    override fun getItemCount() = posts.size

    override fun onBindViewHolder(holder: PostViewHolder,
      position: Int) {
        holder.bind(posts[position])
    }

    fun updatePosts(posts: List<PostEntity>) {
        this.posts.clear()
        this.posts.addAll(posts)
        this.notifyDataSetChanged()
    }

    inner class PostViewHolder(containerView: View) :
      RecyclerView.ViewHolder(containerView) {

        private val titleTextView: TextView =
          containerView.findViewById<TextView>
            (R.id.view_post_row_title)
        private val bodyTextView: TextView =
          containerView.findViewById<TextView>
            (R.id.view_post_row_body)

        fun bind(postEntity: PostEntity) {
            bodyTextView.text = postEntity.body
            titleTextView.text = postEntity.title
        }
    }
}
```

19. And finally, the **MainActivity** file will be as follows:

```
class MainActivity : AppCompatActivity() {

    private lateinit var postAdapter: PostAdapter

    override fun onCreate(savedInstanceState: Bundle?) {
        super.onCreate(savedInstanceState)
        setContentView(R.layout.activity_main)

        postAdapter = PostAdapter(LayoutInflater.from(this))
        val recyclerView = findViewById<RecyclerView>
          (R.id.activity_main_recycler_view)
        recyclerView.adapter = postAdapter
        recyclerView.layoutManager = LinearLayoutManager(this)

        val postRepository = (application as
          RepositoryApplication).postRepository
        val postViewModel = ViewModelProvider(this, object :
          ViewModelProvider.Factory {
            override fun <T : ViewModel?> create(modelClass:
              Class<T>): T {
                return PostViewModel(postRepository) as T
            }

        }).get(PostViewModel::class.java)
        postViewModel.getPosts().observe(this, Observer {
            postAdapter.updatePosts(it)
        })
    }
}
```

If you run the preceding code, you will see the following output:

Figure 11.2: Output of Exercise 11.01

You can now turn the internet on and off and close and re-open the app to see that the data that was initially persisted will continue to be displayed. In the current implementation, the error handling is left empty for now. This means that in case something goes wrong when retrieving the list of posts, the user will not be informed of this. This may become a problem and make users frustrated. Most applications have some error message or other displayed on their user interface, with one of the most common error messages being **Something went wrong. Please try again**, which is used as a generic placeholder when the error is not properly identified.

EXERCISE 11.02: ADDING ERROR HANDLING

In this exercise, we will modify the previous exercise. In the case of an internet error, we will ensure that it will display a toast with the message *Something went wrong*. In the process of adding error handling, we will also need to remove the dependency between the UI and the entity classes by creating a new model class that will hold the relevant data.

In order to handle the error, we will need to build the following:

- A new model class containing just the body and text

- A sealed class containing three inner classes for success, error, and loading

- A mapping function between our new model and the network post

Perform the following steps to complete this exercise:

1. Let's start with our new model. This type of model is common when combined with the repository pattern and the reason for this is simple. The new models may contain data that is specific for this screen that requires some extra logic (let's say you have a user that has **firstName** and **lastName**, but your UI requires you to display both in the same **TextView**. By creating a new model with a name field, you can solve this issue and also unit test the conversion and avoid moving that concatenation on your UI layer):

```
data class UiPost(
    val title: String,
    val body: String
)
```

2. And now to our new sealed class. The subclasses of this sealed class contain all the states of the data loading. The **Loading** state will be emitted when the repository starts loading the data, the **Success** state will be emitted when the repository has successfully loaded the data and contains the list of posts, and the **Error** state will be emitted when an error occurs:

```
sealed class Result {
    object Loading : Result()
    class Success(val uiPosts: List<UiPost>) : Result()
    class Error(val throwable: Throwable) : Result()
}
```

3. The mapping method in **PostMapper** will look like this. It has an extra method that will convert the data extract from the API to the UI model, which will only have the fields necessary for the UI to be properly displayed:

```
class PostMapper {
    fun serviceToEntity(post: Post): PostEntity {
        return PostEntity(post.id, post.userId, post.title,
            post.body)
    }

    fun serviceToUi(post: Post): UiPost {
        return UiPost(post.title, post.body)
    }
}
```

4. Now, let's modify **PostRepository**:

```
interface PostRepository {
    fun getPosts(): LiveData<Result>


}
```

5. And now let's modify **PostRepositoryImpl**. Our result will be **MutableLiveData** that will begin with the **Loading** value and, based on the status of the HTTP request, it will either send a **Success** message with a list of items or an **Error** message with the error **Retrofit encountered**. This approach will no longer rely on showing the stored values at all times. When the request is successful, the output from the HTTP call will be passed instead of the output from Room:

```
override fun getPosts(): LiveData<Result> {
        val result = MutableLiveData<Result>()
```

```
                result.postValue(Result.Loading)
            postService.getPosts().enqueue(object :
                Callback<List<Post>> {

                override fun onFailure(call: Call<List<Post>>, t:
                    Throwable) {
                        result.postValue(Result.Error(t))
                }


                override fun onResponse(call: Call<List<Post>>,
                    response: Response<List<Post>>) {
                    if (response.isSuccessful) {

                        response.body()?.let { posts ->

                            executor.execute {

                                postDao.insertPosts(posts.map
                                    { post ->
                                        postMapper.serviceToEntity(post)

                                })

                                result.postValue(Result
                                    .Success(posts.map { post ->
                                        postMapper.serviceToUi(post)

                                }))

                            }

                        }

                    } else {

                        result.postValue(Result.Error
                            (RuntimeException("Unexpected error")))

                    }

                }

            })

            return result

        }
```

6. In the activity where you observe the live data, the following changes need to
    be implemented. Here, we will check each state and update the UI accordingly.
    If there is an error, we show an error message; if successful, we show the list of
    items; and when it is loading, we show a progress bar, indicating to the user that
    work is being done in the background:

```
            postViewModel.getPosts().observe(this,
                Observer { result ->
                    when (result) {

                        is Result.Error -> {

                            Toast.makeText(applicationContext,
                                R.string.error_message, Toast.LENGTH_LONG)
```

```
                      .show()
                  result.throwable.printStackTrace()
              }
              is Result.Loading -> {
                  // TODO show loading spinner
              }
              is Result.Success -> {
                  postAdapter.updatePosts(result.uiPosts)
              }
          }
      }
  })
```

7. And finally, your adapter should be as follows:

```kotlin
class PostAdapter(private val layoutInflater: LayoutInflater) :
    RecyclerView.Adapter<PostAdapter.PostViewHolder>() {

    private val posts = mutableListOf<UiPost>()

    override fun onCreateViewHolder(parent: ViewGroup, viewType:
      Int): PostViewHolder =
        PostViewHolder(layoutInflater
          .inflate(R.layout.view_post_row, parent, false))

    override fun getItemCount(): Int = posts.size

    override fun onBindViewHolder(holder: PostViewHolder,
      position: Int) {
        holder.bind(posts[position])
    }

    fun updatePosts(posts: List<UiPost>) {
        this.posts.clear()
        this.posts.addAll(posts)
        this.notifyDataSetChanged()
    }

    inner class PostViewHolder(containerView: View) :
      RecyclerView.ViewHolder(containerView) {

        private val titleTextView: TextView =
        containerView.findViewById<TextView>
          (R.id.view_post_row_title)
        private val bodyTextView: TextView =
```

```
        containerView.findViewById<TextView>
           (R.id.view_post_row_body)

    fun bind(post: UiPost) {
        bodyTextView.text = post.body
        titleTextView.text = post.title
    }

    }
}
```

When you run the preceding code, you should see the screen presented in *Figure 11.3*:

Figure 11.3: Output of Exercise 11.02

From this point on, the repository can be expanded in multiple ways:

- Adding algorithms that will request the data only after a certain time has passed

- Defining a more complex result class that will be able to store the cached data as well as an error message

- Adding in-memory caching

- Adding swipe-to-refresh functionality that will refresh the data when **RecyclerView** is swiped down and connecting the loading widget to the **Loading** state

PREFERENCES

Imagine you are tasked with integrating a third-party API that uses something such as OAuth to implement logging in with Facebook, Google, and suchlike. The way these mechanisms work is as follows: they give you a token that you have to store locally and that can then be used to send other requests to access user data. The questions you're faced with are: How can you store that token? Do you use Room just for one token? Do you save the token in a separate file and implement methods for writing the file? What if that file has to be accessed in multiple places at the same time? **SharedPreferences** is an answer to these questions. **SharedPreferences** is a functionality that allows you to save Booleans, integers, floats, longs, strings, and sets of strings into an XML file. When you want to save new values, you specify what values you want to save for the associated keys, and when you are done, you commit the change, which will trigger the save to the XML file in an asynchronous way. The **SharedPreferences** mappings are also kept in memory, so that when you want to read these values it's instantaneous, thereby removing the need for an asynchronous call to read the XML file.

The standard way of accessing **SharedPreferences** data is through the **SharedPreferences** objects and the more recent **EncryptedSharedPreferences** option (if you wish to keep your data encrypted). There is also a specialized implementation through **PreferenceFragments**. These are useful in situations where you want to implement a settings-like screen where you want to store different configuration data that the user wishes to adjust.

SHAREDPREFERENCES

The way to access the **SharedPreference** object is through the **Context** object:

```
val prefs = getSharedPreferences("my-prefs-file",
    Context.MODE_PRIVATE)
```

The first parameter is where you specify the name of your preferences, and the second is how you want to expose the file to other apps. Currently, the best mode is the private one. All of the others present potential security risks.

There is a specialized implementation for accessing the default **SharedPreferences** file, which is used by **PreferenceFragment**:

```
PreferenceManager.getDefaultSharedPreferences(context)
```

If you want to write data into your preferences file, you first need to get access to the Preferences editor. The editor will give you access to writing the data. You can then write your data in the editor. Once you finish writing, you will have to apply the changes that will trigger persistence to the XML file and will change the in-memory values as well. You have two choices for applying the changes on your preference file: **apply** or **commit**. **apply** will save your changes in memory instantly, but then the writing to the disk will be asynchronous, which is good if you want to call this from your app's main thread. **commit** does everything synchronously and gives you a boolean result informing you if the operation was successful. In practice, **apply** tends to be favored over **commit**.

```
val editor = prefs.edit()
editor.putBoolean("my_key_1", true)
editor.putString("my_key_2", "my string")
editor.putLong("my_key_3", 1L)
editor.apply()
```

Now, you want to clear your entire data. The same principle will apply; you'll need the **editor**, **clear**, and **apply**:

```
val editor = prefs.edit()
editor.clear()
editor.apply()
```

If you want to read the values you previously saved, you can use the
SharedPreferences object to read the stored values. In case there is no saved
value, you can opt for a default value to be returned instead.

```
prefs.getBoolean("my_key_1", false)
prefs.getString("my_key_2", "")
prefs.getLong("my_key_3", 0L)
```

EXERCISE 11.03: WRAPPING SHAREDPREFERENCES

We're going to build an application that displays **TextView**, **EditText**, and a
button. **TextView** will display the previous saved value in **SharedPreferences**.
The user can type new text, and when the button is clicked, the text will be saved in
SharedPreferences and **TextView** will display the updated text. We will need to
use **ViewModel** and **LiveData** in order to make the code more testable.

In order to complete this exercise, we will need to create a **Wrapper** class, which
will be responsible for saving the text. This class will return the value of the text
as **LiveData**. This will be injected into our **ViewModel**, which will be bound to
the activity:

1. Let's begin by adding the appropriate libraries to **app/build.gradle**:

```
implementation
  "androidx.constraintlayout:constraintlayout:2.0.4"

def lifecycle_version = "2.2.0"
implementation "androidx.lifecycle:lifecycle-
  extensions:$lifecycle_version"

testImplementation 'junit:junit:4.12'
testImplementation 'android.arch.core:core-testing:2.1.0'
testImplementation 'org.mockito:mockito-core:2.23.0'
androidTestImplementation 'androidx.test.ext:junit:1.1.2'
androidTestImplementation
  'androidx.test.espresso:espresso-core:3.3.0'
```

2. Let's make our **Wrapper** class, which will listen for changes in **SharedPreferences** and update the value of **LiveData** when the preferences change. The class will contain methods to save the new text and to retrieve **LiveData**:

```
const val KEY_TEXT = "keyText"

class PreferenceWrapper(private val sharedPreferences:
    SharedPreferences) {

    private val textLiveData = MutableLiveData<String>()

    init {
        sharedPreferences
            .registerOnSharedPreferenceChangeListener { _, key ->
                when (key) {
                    KEY_TEXT -> {
                        textLiveData.postValue(sharedPreferences
                            .getString(KEY_TEXT, ""))
                    }
                }
            }
    }

    fun saveText(text: String) {
        sharedPreferences.edit()
            .putString(KEY_TEXT, text)
            .apply()
    }

    fun getText(): LiveData<String> {
        textLiveData.postValue(sharedPreferences
            .getString(KEY_TEXT, ""))
        return textLiveData
    }
}
```

Notice the top of the file. We've added a listener so that when our **SharedPreferences** values change, we can look up the new value and update our **LiveData** model. This will allow us to observe the **LiveData** for any changes and just update the UI. The **saveText** method will open the editor, set the new value, and apply the changes. The **getText** method will read the last saved value, set it in **LiveData**, and return the **LiveData** object. This is helpful in scenarios where the app is opened and we want to access the last value prior to the app closing.

3. Now, let's set up the **Application** class with the instance of the preferences:

```kotlin
class PreferenceApplication : Application() {

    lateinit var preferenceWrapper: PreferenceWrapper

    override fun onCreate() {
        super.onCreate()
        preferenceWrapper =
            PreferenceWrapper(getSharedPreferences("prefs",
                Context.MODE_PRIVATE))
    }
}
```

4. Now, let's add the appropriate attributes in the **application** tag to **AndroidManifest.xml**:

```xml
android:name=".PreferenceApplication"
```

5. And now, let's build the **ViewModel** component:

```kotlin
class PreferenceViewModel(private val preferenceWrapper:
  PreferenceWrapper) : ViewModel() {

    fun saveText(text: String) {
        preferenceWrapper.saveText(text)
    }

    fun getText(): LiveData<String> {
        return preferenceWrapper.getText()
    }
}
```

6. Finally, let's define our **activity_main.xml** layout file:

activity_main.xml

```
9    <TextView
10       android:id="@+id/activity_main_text_view"
11       android:layout_width="wrap_content"
12       android:layout_height="wrap_content"
13       android:layout_marginTop="50dp"
14       app:layout_constraintLeft_toLeftOf="parent"
15       app:layout_constraintRight_toRightOf="parent"
16       app:layout_constraintTop_toTopOf="parent" />
17
18   <EditText
19       android:id="@+id/activity_main_edit_text"
20       android:layout_width="200dp"
21       android:layout_height="wrap_content"
22       android:inputType="none"
23       app:layout_constraintLeft_toLeftOf="parent"
24       app:layout_constraintRight_toRightOf="parent"
25       app:layout_constraintTop_toBottomOf=
            "@id/activity_main_text_view" />
26
27   <Button
28       android:id="@+id/activity_main_button"
29       android:layout_width="wrap_content"
30       android:layout_height="wrap_content"
31       android:inputType="none"
32       android:text="@android:string/ok"
33       app:layout_constraintLeft_toLeftOf="parent"
34       app:layout_constraintRight_toRightOf="parent"
35       app:layout_constraintTop_toBottomOf=
            "@id/activity_main_edit_text" />
```

The complete code for this step can be found at http://packt.live/39RhIj0.

7. And finally, in **MainActivity**, perform the following steps:

```
class MainActivity : AppCompatActivity() {

    override fun onCreate(savedInstanceState: Bundle?) {
        super.onCreate(savedInstanceState)
        setContentView(R.layout.activity_main)

        val preferenceWrapper = (application as
        PreferenceApplication).preferenceWrapper
        val preferenceViewModel = ViewModelProvider(this, object
          : ViewModelProvider.Factory {
            override fun <T : ViewModel?> create(modelClass:
              Class<T>): T {
                return PreferenceViewModel(preferenceWrapper)
                  as T
            }

        }).get(PreferenceViewModel::class.java)
```

```
preferenceViewModel.getText().observe(this, Observer {
findViewById<TextView>(R.id.activity_main_text_view)
    .text = it
})


findViewById<Button>(R.id.activity_main_button)
    .setOnClickListener {
preferenceViewModel.saveText(findViewById<EditText>
    (R.id.activity_main_edit_text).text.toString())
}

    }

}
```

The preceding code will produce the output presented in *Figure 11.4*:

Figure 11.4: Output of Exercise 11.03

Once you insert a value, try closing the application and re-opening it. The app will display the last persisted value.

PREFERENCEFRAGMENT

As mentioned previously, **PreferenceFragment** is a specialized implementation of a fragment that relies on **SharedPreferences** in order to store user settings. Its features include storing Booleans based on on/off toggles, storing text based on dialogs displayed to the user, storing string sets based on single and multi-choice dialogs, storing integers based on **SeekBars**, and categorizing the sections and linking to other **PreferenceFragment** classes.

While **PreferenceFragment** classes are part of the Android framework, they are marked as deprecated, which means that the recommended approach for fragments is to rely on the Jetpack Preference library, which introduces **PreferenceFragmentCompat**. **PreferenceFragmentCompat** is useful for ensuring backward compatibility between newer Android frameworks and older ones.

In order to build a **PreferenceFragment** class, two things are required:

- A resource in the **res/xml** folder, where the structure of your preferences will be structured

- A class extending **PreferenceFragment**, which will link the XML file with the fragment

If you want to access the values that your **PreferenceFragment** stored from non-**PreferenceFragment** resources, you can access the **SharedPreference** object using the **PreferenceManager.getDefaultSharedPreferences(context)** method. The keys to accessing the values are the keys you defined in the XML file.

An example of a preference XML file named settings_preference.xml would look something like this:

```
<?xml version="1.0" encoding="utf-8"?>
<PreferenceScreen xmlns:app="http://schemas.android.com/apk/res-auto">

    <PreferenceCategory app:title="Primary settings">
        <SwitchPreferenceCompat
            app:key="work_offline"
            app:title="Work offline" />

        <Preference
```

```
            app:icon="@mipmap/ic_launcher"
            app:key="my_key"
            app:summary="Summary"
            app:title="Title" />
    </PreferenceCategory>
</PreferenceScreen>
```

For every preference, you have the ability to show icons, a title, a summary, a current value, and whether it's selectable. An important thing is the key and how to link it to your Kotlin code. You can use the **strings.xml** file to declare non-translatable strings, which you can then extract in your Kotlin code.

Your **PreferenceFragment** will look similar to this:

```
class MyPreferenceFragment : PreferenceFragmentCompat() {
    override fun onCreatePreferences(savedInstanceState: Bundle?,
      rootKey: String?) {
        setPreferencesFromResource(R.xml.settings_preferences,
          rootKey)
    }
}
```

The **onCreatePreferences** method is abstract, and you will need to implement it in order to specify the XML resource for your preferences through the **setPreferencesFromResource** method.

You can also access the preferences programmatically using the **findPreference** method:

```
findPreference<>(key)
```

This will return an object that will extend from **Preference**. The nature of the object should match the type declared in the XML for that particular key. You can modify the **Preference** object programmatically and change the desired fields.

You can also build a Settings screen programmatically using **createPreferenceScreen(Context)** on the **PreferenceManager** class that's inherited in **PreferenceFragment**:

```
val preferenceScreen =
  preferenceManager.createPreferenceScreen(context)
```

You can use the **addPreference(Preference)** method on the **PreferenceScreen** container to add a new **Preference** object:

```
val editTextPreference = EditTextPreference(context)
editTextPreference.key = "key"
editTextPreference.title = "title"
val preferenceScreen = preferenceManager.createPreferenceScreen(context)
preferenceScreen.addPreference(editTextPreference)
setPreferenceScreen(preferenceScreen)
```

Let's now move on to the next exercise to customize your settings.

EXERCISE 11.04: CUSTOMIZED SETTINGS

In this exercise, we're going to build the settings for a VPN app. The product requirements for the settings page are as follows:

- **Connectivity**: Network scan – Toggle; Frequency – **SeekBar**

- **Configuration**: IP address – Text; Domain – Text

- **More**: This will open a new screen containing one option named **Use mobile data**, with a toggle and a non-selectable option below containing the text **Manage your mobile data wisely**.

Perform the following steps to complete this exercise:

1. Let's start by adding the Jetpack Preference library:

```
implementation 'androidx.preference:preference-ktx:1.1.1'
```

2. In **res/values**, create a file named **preference_keys.xml** and let's define the key for the **More preferences** screen:

```xml
<?xml version="1.0" encoding="utf-8"?>
<resources>
    <string name="key_mobile_data"
        translatable="false">mobile_data</string>
</resources>
```

3. Create the **xml** folder in **res** if it's not available.

4. Create the **preferences_more.xml** file in the **res/xml** folder.

5. In the **preferences_more.xml** file, add the following preferences:

```xml
<?xml version="1.0" encoding="utf-8"?>
<PreferenceScreen xmlns:app=
  "http://schemas.android.com/apk/res-auto">

    <SwitchPreferenceCompat
        app:key="@string/key_mobile_data"
        app:title="@string/mobile_data" />

    <Preference
        app:selectable="false"
        app:summary="@string/manage_data_wisely" />

</PreferenceScreen>
```

6. In **strings.xml**, add the following strings:

```xml
<string name="mobile_data">Mobile data</string>
<string name="manage_data_wisely">Manage your data
  wisely</string>
```

7. Create a **PreferenceFragment** class called **MorePreferenceFragment**:

```kotlin
class MorePreferenceFragment : PreferenceFragmentCompat() {
    override fun onCreatePreferences(savedInstanceState: Bundle?,
      rootKey: String?) {
        setPreferencesFromResource(R.xml.preferences_more,
          rootKey)
    }
}
```

We are done with the **More** section. Let's now create the main section.

8. Let's create the keys for the main preference section. In **preference_keys.xml**, add the following:

```xml
<string name="key_network_scan"
  translatable="false">network_scan</string>
<string name="key_frequency"
  translatable="false">frequency</string>
<string name="key_ip_address"
  translatable="false">ip_address</string>
<string name="key_domain" translatable="false">domain</string>
```

9. In **res/xml**, create the **preferences_settings.xml** file.

10. Now, define your preferences according to the specs:

```xml
<?xml version="1.0" encoding="utf-8"?>
<PreferenceScreen xmlns:app=
  "http://schemas.android.com/apk/res-auto">

    <PreferenceCategory app:title="@string/connectivity">
        <SwitchPreferenceCompat
            app:key="@string/key_network_scan"
            app:title="@string/network_scan" />

        <SeekBarPreference
            app:key="@string/key_frequency"
            app:title="@string/frequency" />

    </PreferenceCategory>

    <PreferenceCategory app:title="@string/configuration">
        <EditTextPreference
            app:key="@string/key_ip_address"
            app:title="@string/ip_address" />

        <EditTextPreference
            app:key="@string/key_domain"
            app:title="@string/domain" />

    </PreferenceCategory>

    <Preference
        app:fragment="com.android.testable.preferencefragments
        .MorePreferenceFragment"
        app:title="@string/more" />

</PreferenceScreen>
```

Notice the last part. That is how we establish the link between one **PreferenceFragment** and another. By default, the system will do the transition for us, but there is a way to override this behavior in case we want to update our UI.

11. In **strings.xml**, make sure you have the following values:

```xml
<string name="connectivity">Connectivity</string>
<string name="network_scan">Network scan</string>
<string name="frequency">Frequency</string>
<string name="configuration">Configuration</string>
<string name="ip_address">IP Address</string>
<string name="domain">Domain</string>
<string name="more">More</string>
```

12. Create a fragment called **SettingsPreferenceFragment**.

13. Add the following setup:

```kotlin
class SettingsPreferenceFragment : PreferenceFragmentCompat() {
    override fun onCreatePreferences(savedInstanceState: Bundle?,
      rootKey: String?) {
        setPreferencesFromResource(R.xml.preferences_settings,
          rootKey)
    }
}
```

14. Now, let's add **Fragments** to our activity.

15. In **activity_main.xml**, define a **FrameLayout** tag to contain the fragments:

```xml
<?xml version="1.0" encoding="utf-8"?>
<FrameLayout
  xmlns:android="http://schemas.android.com/apk/res/android"
    xmlns:tools="http://schemas.android.com/tools"
    android:layout_width="match_parent"
    android:layout_height="match_parent"
    tools:context=".MainActivity"
    android:id="@+id/fragment_container"/>
```

16. And finally, in **MainActivity**, perform the following steps:

```kotlin
class MainActivity : AppCompatActivity(),
    PreferenceFragmentCompat.OnPreferenceStartFragmentCallback {


    override fun onCreate(savedInstanceState: Bundle?) {
        super.onCreate(savedInstanceState)
        setContentView(R.layout.activity_main)
        if (savedInstanceState == null) {
```

```
                    supportFragmentManager.beginTransaction()
                        .replace(R.id.fragment_container,
                            SettingsPreferenceFragment())
                        .commit()
            }
        }


    override fun onPreferenceStartFragment(
        caller: PreferenceFragmentCompat?,
        pref: Preference
    ): Boolean {
        val args = pref.extras
        val fragment =
            supportFragmentManager.fragmentFactory.instantiate(
                classLoader,
                pref.fragment
            )
        fragment.arguments = args
        fragment.setTargetFragment(caller, 0)

        supportFragmentManager.beginTransaction()
            .replace(R.id.fragment_container, fragment)
            .addToBackStack(null)
            .commit()
        return true
    }
}
```

Look at **onPreferenceStartFragment**
from the **PreferenceFragmentCompat.**
OnPreferenceStartFragmentCallback interface. This allows us to
intercept the switch between fragments and add our own behavior. The
first half of the method will use the inputs of the method to create a new
instance of **MorePreferenceFragment**, while the second half performs
the fragment transaction. Then, we return **true** because we have handled the
transition ourselves.

17. Running the preceding code will produce the following output:

Figure 11.5: Output of Exercise 11.04

We can now monitor the changes to preferences and display them in the UI. We can apply this functionality to the IP address and domain sections to display what the user typed as a summary.

18. Let's now modify **SettingsPreferenceFragment** to programmatically set a listener for when values change, which will display the new value in the summary. We will also need to set the saved values when the screen is first opened. We will need to locate preferences we want to modify using **findPreference(key)**. This allows us to programmatically modify a preference. We can also register listeners on the preference, which will give us access to the new value. In our case, we can register a listener for when the IP address changes, so we can update the summary of the field based on what was introduced in **EditText** by the user:

```
class SettingsPreferenceFragment : PreferenceFragmentCompat() {

    override fun onCreatePreferences(savedInstanceState: Bundle?,
        rootKey: String?) {
        setPreferencesFromResource(R.xml.preferences_settings,
            rootKey)
        val ipAddressPref =
            findPreference<EditTextPreference>(getString
                (R.string.key_ip_address))
        ipAddressPref?.setOnPreferenceChangeListener {
            preference, newValue ->
                preference.summary = newValue.toString()

                true

        }
        val domainPref = findPreference<EditTextPreference>
            (getString(R.string.key_domain))
        domainPref?.setOnPreferenceChangeListener { preference,
            newValue ->
                preference.summary = newValue.toString()

                true

        }


        val sharedPrefs = PreferenceManager
            .getDefaultSharedPreferences(requireContext())
        ipAddressPref?.summary = sharedPrefs
            .getString(getString(R.string.key_ip_address), "")
        domainPref?.summary = sharedPrefs
            .getString(getString(R.string.key_domain), "")
    }
}
```

PreferenceFragment is a good way of building settings-like functionality for any application. Its integration with **SharedPreferences** and built-in UI components allow developers to build elements quicker than usual and solve many issues with regard to handling the clicks and elements inserted for each setting element.

FILES

We've discussed Room and **SharedPreferences** and specified how the data they store is written to files. You may ask yourself, where are these files stored? These particular files are stored in internal storage. Internal storage is a dedicated space for every app that other apps are unable to access (unless the device is rooted). There is no limit to the amount of storage your app uses. However, users have the ability to delete your app's files from the Settings menu. Internal storage occupies a smaller part of the total available space, which means that you should be careful when it comes to storing files in internal storage. There is also external storage. The files your app stores are accessible to other apps and the files from other apps are accessible to your app:

> ## NOTE
>
> In Android Studio, you can use the Device File Explorer tool to navigate through the files on the device or emulator. Internal storage is located in **/data/data/{packageName}**. If you have access to this folder, this means that the device is rooted. Using this, you can visualize the database files and the **SharedPreferences** files.

Figure 11.6: Android Device File Explorer

INTERNAL STORAGE

Internal storage requires no permissions from the user. To access the internal storage directories, you can use one of the following methods from the **Context** object:

- **getDataDir()**: Returns the root folder of your application sandbox.

- **getFilesDir()**: A dedicated folder for application files; recommended for usage.

- **getCacheDir()**: A dedicated folder where files can be cached. Storing files here does not guarantee that you can retrieve them later because the system may decide to delete this directory to free memory. This folder is linked to the **Clear Cache** option in **Settings**.

- **getDir(name, mode)**: Returns a folder that will be created if it does not exist based on the name specified.

When users use the **Clear Data** option from **Settings**, most of these folders will be deleted, bringing the app to a similar state as a fresh install. When the app is uninstalled, then these files will be deleted as well.

A typical example of reading a cache file is as follows:

```
val cacheDir = context.cacheDir
val fileToReadFrom = File(cacheDir, "my-file.txt")
val size = fileToReadFrom.length().toInt()
val bytes = ByteArray(size)
val tmpBuff = ByteArray(size)
val fis = FileInputStream(fileToReadFrom)
try {

    var read = fis.read(bytes, 0, size)
    if (read < size) {
        var remain = size - read
        while (remain > 0) {
            read = fis.read(tmpBuff, 0, remain)
            System.arraycopy(tmpBuff, 0, bytes,
                             size - remain, read)
            remain -= read
        }
    }
} catch (e: IOException) {
    throw e
```

```
    } finally {
        fis.close()
    }
```

The preceding example will read from **my-file.txt**, located in the **Cache** directory, and will create **FileInputStream** for that file. Then, a buffer will be used that will collect the bytes from the file. The collected bytes will be placed in the **bytes** byte array, which will contain all of the data read from that file. Reading will stop when the entire length of the file has been read.

Writing to the **my-file.txt** file will look something like this:

```
val bytesToWrite = ByteArray(100)
val cacheDir = context.cacheDir
val fileToWriteIn = File(cacheDir, "my-file.txt")
try {
    if (!fileToWriteIn.exists()) {
        fileToWriteIn.createNewFile()
    }
    val fos = FileOutputStream(fileToWriteIn)
    fos.write(bytesToWrite)
    fos.close()
} catch (e: Exception) {
    e.printStackTrace()
}
```

What the preceding example does is take the byte array you want to write, create a new **File** object, create the file if it doesn't exist, and write the bytes into the file through **FileOutputStream**.

> **NOTE**
>
> There are many alternatives to dealing with files. The readers (**StreamReader**, **StreamWriter**, and so on) are better equipped for character-based data. There are also third-party libraries that help with disk I/O operations. One of the most common third parties that help with I/O operations is called Okio. It started life as part of the **OkHttp** library, which is used in combination with Retrofit to make API calls. The methods provided by Okio are the same methods it uses to write and read data in HTTP communications.

EXTERNAL STORAGE

Reading and writing in external storage requires user permissions for reading and writing. If write permission is granted, then your app has the ability to read the external storage. Once these permissions are granted, then your app can do whatever it pleases on the external storage. That may present a problem because users may not choose to grant these permissions. However, there are specialized methods that offer you the possibility to write on the external storage in folders dedicated to your application.

Some of the most common ways of accessing external storage are from the **Context** and **Environment** objects:

- **Context.getExternalFilesDir(mode)**: This method will return the path to the directory on the external storage dedicated to your application. Specifying different modes (pictures, movies, and so on) will create different subfolders depending on how you want your files saved. This method *does not require permissions*.

- **Context.getExternalCacheDir()**: This will point toward the application's cache directory on the external storage. The same considerations should be applied to this **cache** folder as to the internal storage option. This method *does not require permissions*.

- The **Environment** class has access to paths of some of the most common folders on the device. However, on newer devices, apps may not have access to those files and folders.

> **NOTE**
>
> Avoid using hardcoded paths to files and folders. The Android operating system may shift the location of folders around depending on the device or operating system.

FILEPROVIDER

This represents a specialized implementation of **ContentProviders** that is useful in organizing the file and folder structure of your application. It allows you to specify an XML file in which you define how your files should be split between internal and external storage if you choose to do so. It also gives you the ability to grant access to other apps to your files by hiding the path and generating a unique URI to identify and query your file.

FileProvider gives you the choice to pick between six different folders where you can set up your folder hierarchies:

- **Context.getFilesDir()** (files-path)

- **Context.getCacheDir()** (cache-path)

- **Environment.getExternalStorageDirectory()** (external-path)

- **Context.getExternalFilesDir(null)** (external-files-path)

- **Context.getExternalCacheDir()** (external-cache-path)

- First result of **Context.getExternalMediaDirs()** (external-media-path)

The main benefits of **FileProvider** are the abstractions it provides in organizing your files since leaving the developer to define the paths in an XML file and, more importantly, if you chose to use it to store files on the external storage, you do not have to ask for permissions from the user. Another benefit is the fact that it makes sharing of internal files easier while giving the developer control of what files other apps can access without exposing their real location.

Let us understand better through the following example:

```
<paths xmlns:android="http://schemas.android.com/apk/res/android">
    <files-path name="my-visible-name" path="/my-folder-name" />
</paths>
```

The preceding example will make **FileProvider** use the internal **files** directory and create a folder named **my-folder-name**. When the path is converted to a URI, then the URI will use **my-visible-name**.

STORAGE ACCESS FRAMEWORK (SAF)

The SAF is a file picker introduced in Android KitKat that apps can use for their users to pick files with a view to being processed or uploaded. You can use it in your app for the following scenarios:

1. Your app requires the user to process a file saved on the device by another app (photos and videos).

2. You want to save a file on the device and give the user the choice of where they want the file to be saved and the name of the file.

3. You want to offer the files your application uses to other apps for scenarios similar to scenario number 1.

This is again useful because your app will avoid read and write permissions and still write and access external storage. The way this works is based on intents. You can start an activity for a result with **Intent.ACTION_OPEN_DOCUMENT** or **Intent. ACTION_CREATE_DOCUMENT**. Then, in **onActivityResult**, the system will give you a URI that grants you temporary permissions to that file, allowing you to read and write.

Another benefit of the SAF is the fact that the files don't have to be on a device. Apps such as Google Drive expose their content in the SAF and when a Google Drive file is selected, it will be downloaded to the device and the URI will be sent as a result. Another important thing to mention is the SAF's support for virtual files, meaning that it will expose Google docs, which have their own format, but when those docs are downloaded through the SAF, their formats will be converted to a common format such as PDF.

ASSET FILES

Asset files are files you can package as part of your APK. If you've used apps that played certain videos or GIFs when the app is launched or as part of a tutorial, odds are that the videos were bundled with the APK. To add files to your assets, you need the **assets** folder inside your project. You can then group your files inside your assets using folders.

You can access these files at runtime through the **AssetManager** class, which itself can be accessed through the context object. **AssetManager** offers you the ability to look up the files and read them, but it does not permit any write operations:

```
val assetManager = context.assets
val root = ""
```

```
val files = assetManager.list(root)
files?.forEach {
    val inputStream = assetManager.open(root + it)
}
```

The preceding example lists all files inside the root of the **assets** folder. The **open** function returns **inputStream**, which can be used to read the file information if necessary.

One common usage of the **assets** folder is for custom fonts. If your application uses custom fonts, then you can use the **assets** folder to store font files.

EXERCISE 11.05: COPYING FILES

> **NOTE**
>
> For this exercise, you will need an emulator. You can do so by selecting the **Tools | AVD Manager** in Android Studio. Then, you can create one with the **Create Virtual Device** option, selecting the type of emulator, clicking **Next**, and then selecting an x86 image. Any image larger than Lollipop should be acceptable for this exercise. Next, you can give your image a name and click **Finish**.

Let's create an app that will keep a file named **my-app-file.txt** in the **assets** directory. The app will display two buttons called **FileProvider** and **SAF**. When the **FileProvider** button is clicked, the file will be saved on the external storage inside the app's external storage dedicated area (**Context. getExternalFilesDir(null)**). The **SAF** button will open the SAF and allow the user to indicate where the file should be saved.

In order to implement this exercise, the following approach will be adopted:

- Define a file provider that will use the **Context. getExternalFilesDir(null)** location.

- Copy **my-app-file.txt** to the preceding location when the **FileProvider** button is clicked.

- Use **Intent.ACTION_CREATE_DOCUMENT** when the **SAF** button is clicked and copy the file to the location provided.

- Use a separate thread for the file copy to comply with the Android guidelines.

- Use the Apache IO library to help with the file copy functionality, by providing methods that allow us to copy data from an InputStream to an OutputStream.

The steps for completion are as follows:

1. Let's start with our Gradle configuration:

```
implementation 'commons-io:commons-io:2.6'
testImplementation 'org.mockito:mockito-core:2.23.0'
```

2. Create the **my-app-file.txt** file in the **main/assets** folder. Feel free to fill it up with the text you want to be read. If the **main/assets** folder doesn't exist, then you can create it. In order to create the **assets** folder, you can right-click on the **main** folder and select **New** and then select **Directory** and name it **assets**. This folder will now be recognized by the build system and any file inside it will also be installed on the device along with the app.

3. We can also define a class that will wrap **AssetManager** and define a method to access this particular file:

```
class AssetFileManager(private val assetManager: AssetManager) {

    fun getMyAppFileInputStream() =
      assetManager.open("my-app-file.txt")
}
```

4. Now, let's work on the **FileProvider** aspect. Create the **xml** folder in the **res** folder. Define **file_provider_paths.xml** inside the new folder. We will define **external-files-path**, name it **docs**, and place it in the **docs/** folder:

```
<?xml version="1.0" encoding="utf-8"?>
<paths>
    <external-files-path name="docs" path="docs/"/>
</paths>
```

5. Next, we need to add **FileProvider** to the **AndroidManifest.xml** file and link it with the new path we defined:

```
<provider
        android:name="androidx.core.content.FileProvider"
        android:authorities="com.android.testable.files"
        android:exported="false"
        android:grantUriPermissions="true">
```

```
        <meta-data
            android:name="android.support
                        .FILE_PROVIDER_PATHS"
            android:resource="@xml/file_provider_paths" />
    </provider>
```

The name will point to the **FileProvider** path that's part of the Android Support library. The authorities field represents the domain your application has (usually the package name of the application). The exported field indicates if we wish to share our provider with other apps, and **grantUriPermissions** indicates if we wish to grant other applications access to certain files through the URI. The meta-data links the XML file we defined previously with **FileProvider**.

6. Define the **ProviderFileManager** class, which is responsible for accessing the **docs** folder and writing data into the file:

```
class ProviderFileManager(
    private val context: Context,
    private val fileToUriMapper: FileToUriMapper,
    private val executor: Executor
) {

    private fun getDocsFolder(): File {
        val folder = File(context.getExternalFilesDir(null),
          "docs")
        if (!folder.exists()) {
            folder.mkdirs()
        }
        return folder
    }

    fun writeStream(name: String, inputStream: InputStream) {
        executor.execute {
            val fileToSave = File(getDocsFolder(), name)
            val outputStream =
              context.contentResolver.openOutputStream(
                fileToUriMapper.getUriFromFile(
                    context,
                    fileToSave
                ), "rw"
            )
            IOUtils.copy(inputStream, outputStream)
```

```
                }
            }
        }
```

getDocsFolder will return the path to the **docs** folder we defined in the XML. If the folder does not exist, then it will be created. The **writeStream** method will extract the URI for the file we wish to save and, using the Android **ContentResolver** class, will give us access to the **OutputStream** class of the file we will be saving into. Notice that **FileToUriMapper** doesn't exist yet. The code is moved into a separate class in order to make this class testable.

7. The **FileToUriMapper** class looks like this:

```
class FileToUriMapper {

    fun getUriFromFile(context: Context, file: File): Uri {
        return FileProvider.getUriForFile(context,
            "com.android.testable.files", file)
    }
}
```

The **getUriForFile** method is part of the **FileProvider** class and its role is to convert the path of a file into a URI that can be used by **ContentProviders/ContentResolvers** to access data. Because the method is static, it prevents us from testing properly.

Notice the test rule we used. This comes in handy when testing files. What it does is supply the test with the necessary files and folders and when the test finishes, it will remove all the files and folders.

8. Let's now move on to defining our UI for the **activity_main.xml** file:

activity_main.xml

```
9    <Button
10       android:id="@+id/activity_main_file_provider"
11       android:layout_width="wrap_content"
12       android:layout_height="wrap_content"
13       android:layout_marginTop="200dp"
14       android:text="@string/file_provider"
15       app:layout_constraintEnd_toEndOf="parent"
16       app:layout_constraintStart_toStartOf="parent"
17       app:layout_constraintTop_toTopOf="parent" />
18
19    <Button
20       android:id="@+id/activity_main_saf"
21       android:layout_width="wrap_content"
22       android:layout_height="wrap_content"
23       android:layout_marginTop="50dp"
24       android:text="@string/saf"
25       app:layout_constraintEnd_toEndOf="parent"
```

```
26        app:layout_constraintStart_toStartOf="parent"
27        app:layout_constraintTop_toBottomOf=
            "@id/activity_main_file_provider" />
```

The complete code for this step can be found at http://packt.live/3bTNmz4.

9. Now, let's define our **MainActivity** class:

```
class MainActivity : AppCompatActivity() {

    private val assetFileManager: AssetFileManager by lazy {
        AssetFileManager(applicationContext.assets)
    }
    private val providerFileManager: ProviderFileManager by lazy {
        ProviderFileManager(
            applicationContext,
            FileToUriMapper(),
            Executors.newSingleThreadExecutor()
        )
    }



    override fun onCreate(savedInstanceState: Bundle?) {
        super.onCreate(savedInstanceState)
        setContentView(R.layout.activity_main)
        findViewById<Button>(R.id.activity_main_file_provider)
          .setOnClickListener {
            val newFileName = "Copied.txt"

            providerFileManager.writeStream(newFileName,
              assetFileManager.getMyAppFileInputStream())
        }
    }
}
```

For this example, we chose **MainActivity** to create our objects and inject data into the different classes we have. If we execute this code and click the **FileProvider** button, we don't see an output on the UI. However, if we look with Android Device File Explorer, we can locate where the file was saved. The path may be different on different devices and operating systems. The paths could be as follows:

- **mnt/sdcard/Android/data/<package_name>/files/docs**

- **sdcard/Android/data/<package_name>/files/docs**

- **storage/emulated/0/Android/data/<package_name>/files/docs**

The output will be as follows:

Figure 11.7: Output of copy through FileProvider

10. Let's add the logic for the **SAF** button. We will need to start an activity pointing toward the **SAF** with the **CREATE_DOCUMENT** intent in which we specify that we want to create a text file. We will then need the result of the **SAF** so we can copy the file to the location selected by the user. In **MainActivity** in **onCreateMethod**, we can add the following:

```
findViewById<Button>(R.id.activity_main_saf)
    .setOnClickListener {
        if (Build.VERSION.SDK_INT >=
            Build.VERSION_CODES.KITKAT) {
            val intent =
                Intent(Intent.ACTION_CREATE_DOCUMENT).apply {
                    addCategory(Intent.CATEGORY_OPENABLE)
                    type = "text/plain"
                    putExtra(Intent.EXTRA_TITLE, "Copied.txt")
                }
```

```
                    startActivityForResult(intent,
                        REQUEST_CODE_CREATE_DOC)
            }
        }
```

What the preceding code will do is to create an intent to create a document with the name of **Copied.txt** and the **text/plain** MIME (Multipurpose Internet Mail Extensions) type (which is suitable for text files). This code will only run in Android versions bigger than KitKat.

11. Let's now tell the activity how to handle the result of the document creation. We will receive a URI object with an empty file selected by the user. We can now copy our file to that location. In **MainActivity**, we add **onActivityResult**, which will look like this:

```
override fun onActivityResult(requestCode: Int, resultCode:
    Int, data: Intent?) {
      if (requestCode == REQUEST_CODE_CREATE_DOC
        && resultCode == Activity.RESULT_OK) {
        data?.data?.let { uri ->

        }
      } else {
        super.onActivityResult(requestCode, resultCode, data)
      }
}
```

12. We now have the URI. We can add a method to **ProviderFileManager** that will copy our file to a location given by **uri**:

```
fun writeStreamFromUri(name: String, inputStream:
    InputStream, uri:Uri){
      executor.execute {

        val outputStream =
          context.contentResolver.openOutputStream(uri, "rw")
        IOUtils.copy(inputStream, outputStream)

      }
}
```

13. And we can invoke this method from the **onActivityResult** method of **MainActivity** like this:

```
if (requestCode == REQUEST_CODE_CREATE_DOC
    && resultCode == Activity.RESULT_OK) {
    data?.data?.let { uri ->
        val newFileName = "Copied.txt"
        providerFileManager.writeStreamFromUri(
            newFileName,
```

```
                                assetFileManager.getMyAppFileInputStream(),
                                uri
                )
        }
}
```

If we run the preceding code and click on the **SAF** button, we will see the output presented in *Figure 11.8*:

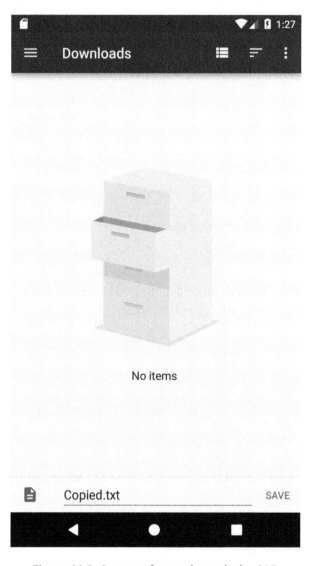

Figure 11.8: Output of copy through the SAF

If you choose to save the file, the SAF will be closed and our activity's **onActivityResult** method will be called, which will trigger the file copy. Afterward, you can navigate the Android Device File Manager tool to see whether the file was saved properly.

SCOPED STORAGE

Since Android 10 and with further updates in Android 11, the notion of Scoped Storage was introduced. The main idea behind this is to allow apps to gain more control of their files on the external storage and prevent other apps from accessing these files. The consequences of this mean that **READ_EXTERNAL_STORAGE** and **WRITE_EXTERNAL_STORAGE** will only apply for files the user interacts with (like media files). This discourages apps to create their own directories on the external storage and instead stick with the one already provided to them through the **Context.getExternalFilesDir**.

FileProviders and Storage Access Framework are a good way of keeping your app's compliance with the scoped storage practices because one allows the app to use the **Context.getExternalFilesDir** and the other uses the built-in File Explorer app which will now avoid files from other applications in the **Android/data** and **Android/obb** folders on the external storage.

CAMERA AND MEDIA STORAGE

Android offers a variety of ways to interact with media on an Android device, from building your own camera application and controlling how users take photos and videos to using the existing camera application and instructing it on how to take photos and videos. Android also comes with a **MediaStore** content provider, allowing applications to extract information about media files that are set on the device and shared between applications. This is useful in situations where you want a custom display for media files that exist on the device (such as a photo or music player application) and in situations where you use the **MediaStore.ACTION_PICK** intent to select a photo from the device and want to extract the information about the selected media image (this is usually the case for older applications where the SAF cannot be used).

In order to use an existing camera application, you will need to use the **MediaStore.ACTION_IMAGE_CAPTURE** intent to start a camera application for a result and pass the URI of the image you wish to save. The user will then go to the camera activity, take the photo, and then you handle the result of the operation:

```
val intent = Intent(MediaStore.ACTION_IMAGE_CAPTURE)
intent.putExtra(MediaStore.EXTRA_OUTPUT, photoUri)
startActivityForResult(intent, REQUEST_IMAGE_CAPTURE)
```

The **photoUri** parameter will represent the location of where you want your photo to be saved. It should point to an empty file with a JPEG extension. You can build this file in two ways:

- Create a file on the external storage using the **File** object (this requires the **WRITE_EXTERNAL_STORAGE** permission) and then use the **Uri.fromFile()** method to convert it into a **URI** - no longer applicable on Android 10 and above

- Create a file in a **FileProvider** location using the **File** object and then use the **FileProvider.getUriForFile()** method to obtain the URI and grant it permissions if necessary. - the recommended approach for when your app targets Android 10 and Android 11

> **NOTE**
>
> The same mechanism can be applied to videos using **MediaStore.ACTION_VIDEO_CAPTURE**.

If your application relies heavily on the camera features, then you can exclude the application from users whose devices don't have cameras by adding the **<uses-feature>** tag to the **AndroidManifest.xml** file. You can also specify the camera as non-required and query whether the camera is available using the **Context.hasSystemFeature(PackageManager.FEATURE_CAMERA_ANY)** method.

If you wish to have your file saved in **MediaStore**, there are multiple ways to achieve this:

- Send an **ACTION_MEDIA_SCANNER_SCAN_FILE** broadcast with the URI of your media:

```
val intent =
    Intent(Intent.ACTION_MEDIA_SCANNER_SCAN_FILE)
intent.data = photoUri
sendBroadcast(intent)
```

- Use the media scanner to scan files directly:

```
val paths = arrayOf("path1", "path2")
val mimeTypes= arrayOf("type1", "type2")
MediaScannerConnection.scanFile(context,paths,
   mimeTypes) { path, uri ->
}
```

- Insert the media into **ContentProvider** directly using **ContentResolver**:

```
val contentValues = ContentValues()
contentValues.put(MediaStore.Images.ImageColumns.TITLE,
   "my title")
   contentValues.put(MediaStore.Images.ImageColumns
     .DATE_ADDED, timeInMillis)
   contentValues.put(MediaStore.Images.ImageColumns
     .MIME_TYPE, "image/*")
   contentValues.put(MediaStore.Images.ImageColumns
     .DATA, "my-path")
   val newUri = contentResolver.insert(MediaStore.Video
     .Media.EXTERNAL_CONTENT_URI, contentValues)
      newUri?.let {
   val outputStream = contentResolver
     .openOutputStream(newUri)
     // Copy content in outputstream

}
```

NOTE

The **MediaScanner** functionality no longer adds files from **Context. getExternalFilesDir** in Android 10 and above. Apps should rely on the **insert** method instead if they chose to share their media files with the rest of the apps.

EXERCISE 11.06: TAKING PHOTOS

We're going to build an application that has two buttons: the first button will open the camera app to take a photo, and the second button will open the camera app to record a video. We will use **FileProvider** to save the photos to the external storage (external-path) in two folders: **pictures** and **movies**. The photos will be saved using **img_{timestamp}.jpg**, and the videos will be saved using **video_{timestamp}.mp4**. After a photo and video have been saved, you will copy the file from the **FileProvider** into the **MediaStore** so it will be visible for other apps:

1. Let's add the libraries in **app/build.gradle**:

```
implementation 'commons-io:commons-io:2.6'
testImplementation 'org.mockito:mockito-core:2.23.0'
```

2. We will be targeting Android 11 which means that we need the following configuration in **app/build.gradle**

```
...
compileSdkVersion 30
    defaultConfig {
        ...
        targetSdkVersion 30
        ...
    }
...
```

3. We will need to request the WRITE_EXTERNAL_STORAGE permission for devices that have less than Android 10, which means we need the following in **AndroidManifest.xml**:

```
<uses-permission
        android:name="android.permission.WRITE_EXTERNAL_STORAGE"
        android:maxSdkVersion="28" />
```

4. Let's define a **FileHelper** class, which will contain methods that are harder to test in the **test** package:

```
class FileHelper(private val context: Context) {

    fun getUriFromFile(file: File): Uri {
        return FileProvider.getUriForFile(context,
            "com.android.testable.camera", file)
    }
}
```

```kotlin
    fun getPicturesFolder(): String =
      Environment.DIRECTORY_PICTURES


    fun getVideosFolder(): String = Environment.DIRECTORY_MOVIES

}
```

5. Let's define our **FileProvider** paths in **res/xml/file_provider_paths.xml**. Make sure to include the appropriate package name for your application in **FileProvider**:

```xml
<?xml version="1.0" encoding="utf-8"?>
<paths>
    <external-path name="photos" path="Android/data
      /com.android.testable.camera/files/Pictures"/>
    <external-path name="videos" path="Android/data
      /com.android.testable.camera/files/Movies"/>
</paths>
```

6. Let's add the file provider paths to the **AndroidManifest.xml** file:

```xml
        <provider
            android:name="androidx.core.content.FileProvider"
            android:authorities="com.android.testable.camera"
            android:exported="false"
            android:grantUriPermissions="true">
            <meta-data
                android:name="android.support
                  .FILE_PROVIDER_PATHS"
                android:resource="@xml/file_provider_paths" />
        </provider>
```

7. Let's now define a model that will hold both the **Uri** and the associated path for a file:

```kotlin
data class FileInfo(
    val uri: Uri,
    val file: File,
    val name: String,
    val relativePath:String,
    val mimeType:String
)
```

8. Let's create a **ContentHelper** class which will provide us with data required for the **ContentResolver**. We will define two methods for accessing the Photo and Video content Uri and two methods that will create the **ContentValues**. We do this because of the static methods required to obtain Uris and the **ContentValues** creation which makes this functionality hard to test. The code below is truncated for space. The full code you need to add can be found via the link below.

MediaContentHelper.kt

```
7    class MediaContentHelper {
8
9        fun getImageContentUri(): Uri =
10           if (android.os.Build.VERSION.SDK_INT >=
                 android.os.Build.VERSION_CODES.Q) {
11               MediaStore.Images.Media.getContentUri
                   (MediaStore.VOLUME_EXTERNAL_PRIMARY)
12           } else {
13               MediaStore.Images.Media.EXTERNAL_CONTENT_URI
14           }
15
16       fun generateImageContentValues(fileInfo: FileInfo)
           = ContentValues().apply {
17           this.put(MediaStore.Images.Media
               .DISPLAY_NAME, fileInfo.name)
18       if (android.os.Build.VERSION.SDK_INT >=
             android.os.Build.VERSION_CODES.Q) {
19               this.put(MediaStore.Images.Media
                   .RELATIVE_PATH, fileInfo.relativePath)
20           }
21           this.put(MediaStore.Images.Media
               .MIME_TYPE, fileInfo.mimeType)
22   }
```

The complete code for this step can be found at http://packt.live/3ivwekp.

9. Now, let's create the **ProviderFileManager** class, where we will define methods to generate files for photos and videos that will then be used by the camera and the methods that will save to the media store. Again, the code has been truncated for brevity. Please see the link below for the full code that you need to use:

ProviderFileManager.kt

```
12   class ProviderFileManager(
13       private val context: Context,
14       private val fileHelper: FileHelper,
15       private val contentResolver: ContentResolver,
16       private val executor: Executor,
17       private val mediaContentHelper: MediaContentHelper
18   ) {
19
20       fun generatePhotoUri(time: Long): FileInfo {
21           val name = "img_$time.jpg"
22           val file = File(
```

```
23                   context.getExternalFilesDir(fileHelper
                        .getPicturesFolder()),
24                   name
25               )
26         return FileInfo(
27              fileHelper.getUriFromFile(file),
28              file,
29              name,
30              fileHelper.getPicturesFolder(),
31              "image/jpeg"
32          )
33      }
```

The complete code for this step can be found at http://packt.live/2XXB9Bu.

Notice how we defined the root folders as **context.
getExternalFilesDir(Environment.DIRECTORY_PICTURES)**
and **context.getExternalFilesDir(Environment.DIRECTORY_
MOVIES)**. This connects to **file_provider_paths.xml** and it will create
a set of folders called **Movies** and **Pictures** in the application's dedicated
folder on the external storage. The **insertToStore** method is where the files
will be then copied to the **MediaStore**. First we will create an entry into that
store which will give us a Uri for that entry. Next we copy the contents of our
files from the Uri generated by the **FileProvider** into the **OutputStream**
pointing to the **MediaStore** entry.

10. Let's define the layout for our activity in **res/layout/activity_main.xml**:

activity_main.xml

```
10      <Button
11          android:id="@+id/photo_button"
12          android:layout_width="wrap_content"
13          android:layout_height="wrap_content"
14          android:text="@string/photo" />
15
16      <Button
17          android:id="@+id/video_button"
18          android:layout_width="wrap_content"
19          android:layout_height="wrap_content"
20          android:layout_marginTop="5dp"
21          android:text="@string/video" />
```

The complete code for this step can be found at http://packt.live/3qDSyLU.

11. Let's create the **MainActivity** class where we will check if we need to request the WRITE_STORAGE_PERMISSION, request it if we need to and after it was granted open the camera to take a photo or a video. As above, code has been truncated for brevity. You can access the full code using the link shown:

MainActivity.kt

```
14    class MainActivity : AppCompatActivity() {
15
16        companion object {
17
18            private const val REQUEST_IMAGE_CAPTURE = 1
19            private const val REQUEST_VIDEO_CAPTURE = 2
20            private const val REQUEST_EXTERNAL_STORAGE = 3
21        }
22
23        private lateinit var providerFileManager:
              ProviderFileManager
24        private var photoInfo: FileInfo? = null
25        private var videoInfo: FileInfo? = null
26        private var isCapturingVideo = false
27
28        override fun onCreate(savedInstanceState: Bundle?) {
29            super.onCreate(savedInstanceState)
30            setContentView(R.layout.activity_main)
31            providerFileManager =
32                ProviderFileManager(
33                    applicationContext,
34                    FileHelper(applicationContext),
35                    contentResolver,
36                    Executors.newSingleThreadExecutor(),
37                    MediaContentHelper()
38                )
```

The complete code for this step can be found at http://packt.live/3ivUTpm.

If we execute the preceding code, we will see the following:

Figure 11.9: Output of Exercise 11.06

12. By clicking on either of the buttons, you will be redirected to the camera application where you can take a photo or a video if you are running the example on Android 10 and above. If you're running on lower Android versions then the permissions will be asked first. Once you have taken your photo and confirmed it, you will be taken back to the application. The photo will be saved in the location you defined in **FileProvider**:

Device File Explorer				⚙ —

Emulator Nexus_5X_API_25 Android 7.1.1, API 25			▼

Name	Pe...	Date	Size
▼ ▣ storage	drwxı	2019-12-01 17:57	100 B
▶ ▣ 1B11-2206	drwxı	1970-01-01 01:00	512 B
▼ ▣ emulated	drwx	2019-12-01 11:57	4 KB
▼ ▣ 0	drwxı	2020-01-20 19:45	4 KB
▶ ▣ Alarms	drwxı	2019-12-01 11:57	4 KB
▼ ▣ Android	drwxı	2019-12-01 11:58	4 KB
▼ ▣ data	drwxı	2019-12-16 21:53	4 KB
▶ ▣ com.android.gallery3d	drwxı	2019-12-01 17:59	4 KB
▼ ▣ com.android.testable.camerɑ	drwxı	2019-12-16 21:53	4 KB
▼ ▣ files	drwxı	2019-12-16 22:09	4 KB
▼ ▣ Movies	drwxı	2019-12-16 22:27	4 KB
▣ video_157653503€	-rw-r	2019-12-16 22:24	439.3 KE
▣ video_1576535264	-rw-r	2019-12-16 22:27	465 KB
▼ ▣ Pictures	drwxı	2019-12-16 22:26	4 KB
▣ img_15765334510	-rw-r	2019-12-16 21:57	47.8 KB
▣ img_15765341612	-rw-r	2019-12-16 22:09	46.3 KB
▣ img_15765349972	-rw-r	2019-12-16 22:23	33.1 KB
▣ img_15765352149	-rw-r	2019-12-16 22:26	33.3 KB
▶ ▣ com.android.testable.files	drwxı	2019-12-01 11:57	4 KB
▶ ▣ com.android.testable.remote	drwxı	2019-12-01 22:07	4 KB

Figure 11.10: The location of the captured files through the camera app

In the preceding screenshot, you can see where the files are located with the help of the Android Studio Device File Explorer.

13. Modify **MainActivity** and add the **onActivityResult** method to trigger the save of the files to the MediaStore:

```
override fun onActivityResult(requestCode: Int,
    resultCode: Int, data: Intent?) {
    when (requestCode) {
        REQUEST_IMAGE_CAPTURE -> {
            providerFileManager.insertImageToStore(photoInfo)
        }
```

```
REQUEST_VIDEO_CAPTURE -> {
    providerFileManager.insertVideoToStore(videoInfo)
}
else -> {
    super.onActivityResult(requestCode,
        resultCode, data)
}
}
}
```

If you open any file exploring app like the "Files" app or the Gallery or Google Photos app, you will be able to see the videos and pictures taken.

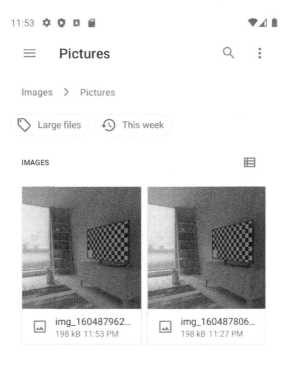

Figure 11.11: The files from the app present in the File Explorer app

ACTIVITY 11.01: DOG DOWNLOADER

You are tasked with building an application that will target Android versions above API 21 that will display a list of URLs for dog photos. The URL you will connect to is **https://dog.ceo/api/breed/hound/images/random/{number}**, where **number** will be controlled through a Settings screen where the user can choose the number of URLs they want to be displayed. The Settings screen will be opened through an option presented on the home screen. When the user clicks on a URL, the image will be downloaded locally in the application's external cache path. While the image is being downloaded, the user will see an indeterminate progress bar. The list of URLs will be persisted locally using Room.

The technologies that will be used are the following:

- Retrofit for retrieving the list of URLs and for downloading files

- Room for persisting the list of URLs

- **SharedPreferences** and **PreferencesFragment** for storing the number of URLs to retrieve

- **FileProvider** for storing the files in the cache

- Apache IO for writing the files

- Repository for combining all the data sources

- **LiveData** and **ViewModel** for handling the logic from the user

- **RecyclerView** for the list of Items

The response JSON will look similar to this:

```
{
    "message": [
        "https://images.dog.ceo/breeds/hound-
            afghan/n02088094_4837.jpg",
        "https://images.dog.ceo/breeds/hound-
            basset/n02088238_13908.jpg",
        "https://images.dog.ceo/breeds/hound-
            ibizan/n02091244_3939.jpg"
    ],
    "status": "success"
}
```

Perform the following steps to complete this activity:

1. Create an **api** package that will contain the network-related classes.

2. Create a data class that will model the response JSON.

3. Create a Retrofit **Service** class that will contain two methods. The first method will represent the API call to return a list of breeds, and the second method will represent the API call to download the file.

4. Create a **storage** package and, inside the **storage** package, create a **room** package.

5. Create the **Dog** entity, which will contain an autogenerated ID and a URL.

6. Create the **DogDao** class, which will contain methods to insert a list of **Dogs**, delete all the **Dogs**, and query all **Dogs**. The **delete** method is required because the API model does not have any unique identifiers.

7. Inside the **storage** package, create a **preference** package.

8. Inside the **preference** package, create a wrapper class around **SharedPreferences** that will return the number of URLs we need to use. The default will be **10**.

9. In **res/xml**, define your folder structure for **FileProvider**. The files should be saved in the root folder of the **external-cache-path** tag.

10. Inside the **storage** package, create a **filesystem** package.

11. Inside the **filesystem** package, define a class that will be responsible for writing **InputStream** into a file in **FileProvider**, using **Context.externalCacheDir**.

12. Create a **repository** package.

13. Inside the **repository** package, create a sealed class that will hold the result of an API call. The subclasses of the sealed class will be **Success, Error,** and **Loading**.

14. Define a **Repository** interface that will contain two methods, one to load the list of URLs, and the other to download a file.

15. Define a **DogUi** model class that will be used in the UI layer of your application and that will be created in your repository.

16. Define a mapper class that will convert your API models into entities and entities into UI models.

17. Define an implementation for **Repository** that will implement the preceding two methods. The repository will hold references to **DogDao**, the Retrofit **Service** class, the **Preferences** wrapper class, the class managing the files, the **Dog** mapping class, and an **Executor** class for multithreading. When downloading the files, we will be using the filename extracted from the URL.

18. Create a class that will extend **Application**, which will initialize the repository.

19. Define the **ViewModel** used by your UI, which will have a reference to **Repository** and will call **Repository** to load the URL list and download the images.

20. Define your UI, which will be composed of two activities:

- The activity displays the list of URLs and will have the click action to start the downloads. This activity will have a progress bar, which will be displayed when the download takes place. The screen will also have a **Settings** option, which will open the Settings screen.

- The Settings activity, which will display one setting indicating the number of URLs to load.

> **NOTE**
>
> The solution to this activity can be found at: http://packt.live/3sKj1cp.

SUMMARY

In this chapter, we've analyzed the different ways of persisting data in Android and how to centralize them through the repository pattern. We've started with a look at the pattern itself to see how we can organize the data sources by combining Room and Retrofit.

Then, we moved on to analyze alternatives to Room when it comes to persisting data. We looked first at **SharedPreferences** and how they constitute a handy solution for data persistence when it's in a key-value format and the amount of data is small. We then looked at how you can use **SharedPreferences** to save data directly on the device, and then we examined **PreferenceFragments** and how they can be used to take in user input and store it locally.

Next, we looked over something that was in continuous change when it comes to the Android framework. That is the evolution of the abstractions regarding the filesystem. We started with an overview of the types of storage Android has and then took a more in-depth look at two of the abstractions: **FileProvider**, which your app can use to store files on the device and share them with others if there is a need to do so, and the SAF, which can be used to save files on the device in a location selected by the user.

We also used the benefits of **FileProvider** to generate URIs for files in order to use the camera applications to take photos and record videos and save them in the application's files, while also adding them to **MediaStore**.

The activity performed in this chapter combines all the elements discussed above to illustrate the point that even though you have to balance multiple sources inside an application, you can do it in a more readable way.

Note that for the activity and the exercises in this chapter and the previous one, we kept having to use the application class to instantiate the data sources. In the next chapter, you will learn how to overcome this through dependency injection and see how it can benefit an Android application.

12

DEPENDENCY INJECTION WITH DAGGER AND KOIN

OVERVIEW

This chapter covers the concept of dependency injection and the benefits it provides to an Android application. We will look at how we can perform dependency injection manually with the help of container classes. We will also cover some of the frameworks available for Android, Java, and Kotlin that can help developers when it comes to applying this concept. By the end of this chapter, you will be able to use Dagger and Koin to manage your app's dependencies, and you will know how to organize them efficiently.

INTRODUCTION

In the previous chapter, we looked at how to structure code into different components, including ViewModels, repositories, API components, and persistence components. One of the difficulties that always emerged was the dependencies between all of these components, especially when it came to how we approached the unit tests for them.

We have constantly used the **Application** class to create instances of these components and pass them in the constructors of the components one layer above (we created the API and Room instances, then the Repository instances, and so on). What we were doing was a simplistic version of dependency injection.

Dependency injection (**DI**) is a software technique in which one object (application) supplies the dependencies of another object (repositories, **ViewModels**). The reason for this is to increase the reusability and testability of the code and to shift the responsibility for creating instances from our components to the **Application** class. One of the benefits of DI comes with regard to how objects are created across the code base. DI separates the creation of an object from its usage. In other words, one object shouldn't care how another object is created; it should only be concerned with the interaction with the other object.

In this chapter, we will analyze three ways of how we can inject dependencies in Android: manual DI, Dagger, and Koin.

Manual DI is a technique in which developers handle DI manually by creating container classes. In this chapter, we will look over how we can do this in Android. By studying how we manually manage dependencies, we will get some insight into how other DI frameworks operate and get a basis for how we can integrate these frameworks.

Dagger is a DI framework developed for Java. It allows you to group your dependencies in different **modules**. You can also define **components**, where the modules are added in order to create the dependency graph, and which Dagger automatically implements in order to perform the injection. It relies on annotation processors to generate the necessary code in order to perform the injection.

Koin is a lightweight DI library developed for Kotlin. It doesn't rely on annotation processors; it relies on Kotlin's mechanisms to perform the injection. Here we can also split dependencies into **modules**.

In what follows, we will explore how both these libraries work and the steps required to add them to a simple Android application.

MANUAL DI

In order to understand how DI works, we can first analyze how we can manually inject dependencies into different objects across an Android application. This can be achieved by creating container objects that will contain the dependencies required across the app. You can also create multiple containers representing different scopes that are required across the application. Here, you can define dependencies that will only be required as long as a particular screen is displayed, and when the screen is destroyed, the instances can also be garbage collected.

A sample of a container that will hold instances as long as an application lives is shown here:

```
class AppContainer(applicationContext:Context) {

    val myRepository: MyRepository
    init {
        val retrofit =
          Retrofit.Builder().baseUrl("https://google.com/").build()
        val myService=
          retrofit.create<MyService>(MyService::class.java)
        val database = Room.databaseBuilder(applicationContext,
          MyDatabase::class.java, "db").build()
        myRepository = MyRepositoryImpl(myService, database.myDao())
    }

}
```

An **Application** class using that container looks something like the following:

```
class MyApplication : Application() {

    lateinit var appContainer: AppContainer

    override fun onCreate() {
        super.onCreate()
        appContainer = AppContainer(this)
    }
}
```

As you can see in the preceding example, the responsibility for creating the dependencies shifted from the **Application** class to the **Container** class. Activities across the code base can still access the dependencies using the following command:

```
override fun onCreate(savedInstanceState: Bundle?) {
    ....
    val myRepository = (application as
        MyApplication).appContainer. myRepository
    ...
}
```

Modules with a limited scope could be used for something such as creating **ViewModel** factories, which, in turn, are used by the framework to create **ViewModel**:

```
class MyContainer(private val myRepository: MyRepository) {

    fun geMyViewModelFactory(): ViewModelProvider.Factory {
        return object : ViewModelProvider.Factory {
            override fun <T : ViewModel?> create(modelClass:
                Class<T>): T {
                return MyViewModel(myRepository) as T
            }
        }
    }
}
```

This particular container can be used by an activity or fragment to initialize **ViewModel**:

```
class MyActivity : AppCompatActivity() {

    private lateinit var myViewModel: MyViewModel
    private lateinit var myContainer: MyContainer

    override fun onCreate(savedInstanceState: Bundle?) {
        super.onCreate(savedInstanceState)
        ....
        val myRepository = (application as
            MyApplication).appContainer. myRepository
        myContainer = MyContainer (myRepository)

        myViewModel = ViewModelProvider(this,
            myContainer.geMyViewModelFactory())
```

```
                .get(MyViewModel::class.java)
        }
    }
```

Again, we see here that the responsibility of creating the **Factory** class was shifted from the **Activity** class to the **Container** class. **MyContainer** could be expanded to provide instances required by **MyActivity** in situations where the life cycle of those instances should be the same as the activity, or the constructor could be expanded to provide instances with a different life cycle.

Now, let's apply some of these examples to an exercise.

EXERCISE 12.01: MANUAL INJECTION

In this exercise, we will write an Android application that will apply the concept of manual DI. The application will have a Repository, which will generate a random number and a **ViewModel** object with a **LiveData** object responsible for retrieving the number generated by the Repository and publishing it in the **LiveData** object. In order to do so, we will need to create two containers that will manage the following dependencies:

- Repository

- A **ViewModel** factory responsible for creating **ViewModel**

The app itself will display the randomly generated number each time a button is clicked:

1. Let's start by adding the **ViewModel** and **LiveData** library to the **app/build.gradle** file:

```
implementation "androidx.lifecycle:lifecycle-
    extensions:2.2.0"
```

2. Next, let's write a **NumberRepository** interface, which will contain a method to retrieve an integer:

```
interface NumberRepository {
    fun generateNextNumber(): Int
}
```

3. Now, we will provide the implementation for this. We can use the **java.util. Random** class to generate a random number:

```
class NumberRepositoryImpl(private val random: Random) :
  NumberRepository {
    override fun generateNextNumber(): Int {
```

```
        return random.nextInt()
    }
}
```

4. We will now move on to the **MainViewModel** class, which will contain a **LiveData** object containing each generated number from the repository:

```
class MainViewModel(private val numberRepository:
  NumberRepository) : ViewModel() {
    private val numberLiveData = MutableLiveData<Int>()
    fun getLiveData(): LiveData<Int> = numberLiveData
    fun generateNextNumber() {
        numberLiveData.postValue(numberRepository
           .generateNextNumber())
    }
}
```

5. Next, let's move on to create our UI containing **TextView** for displaying the number and **Button** for generating the next random number. This will be part of the **res/layout/activity_main.xml** file:

```xml
<?xml version="1.0" encoding="utf-8"?>
<LinearLayout xmlns:android="http://schemas.android.com/apk/res/
android"
    android:layout_width="match_parent"
    android:layout_height="match_parent"
    android:gravity="center"
    android:orientation="vertical">
    <TextView
        android:id="@+id/activity_main_text_view"
        android:layout_width="wrap_content"
        android:layout_height="wrap_content" />

    <Button
        android:id="@+id/activity_main_button"
        android:layout_width="wrap_content"
        android:layout_height="wrap_content"
        android:text="@string/randomize" />
</LinearLayout>
```

6. Make sure to add the string for the button to the **res/values/strings. xml** file:

```xml
    <string name="randomize">Randomize</string>
```

7. And now let's create the **MainActivity** class responsible for rendering the preceding UI:

```
class MainActivity : AppCompatActivity() {
    override fun onCreate(savedInstanceState: Bundle?) {
        super.onCreate(savedInstanceState)
        setContentView(R.layout.activity_main)
    }
}
```

8. Now, let's create our **Application** class:

```
class RandomApplication : Application() {
    override fun onCreate() {
        super.onCreate()
    }
}
```

9. Let's also add the **Application** class to the **AndroidManifest.xml** file in the **application** tag:

```
    <application
        ...
        android:name=".RandomApplication"
.../>
```

10. Now, let's create our first container responsible for managing the **NumberRepository** dependency:

```
class ApplicationContainer {
    val numberRepository: NumberRepository =
      NumberRepositoryImpl(Random())
}
```

11. Let's add this container to the **RandomApplication** class:

```
class RandomApplication : Application() {
    val applicationContainer = ApplicationContainer()
    override fun onCreate() {
        super.onCreate()
    }
}
```

12. We now move on to creating **MainContainer**, which will need a reference to the **NumberRepository** dependency and will provide a dependency to the **ViewModel** factory required to create **MainViewModel**:

```
class MainContainer(private val numberRepository:
    NumberRepository) {
    fun getMainViewModelFactory(): ViewModelProvider.Factory {
        return object : ViewModelProvider.Factory {
            override fun <T : ViewModel?> create(modelClass:
                Class<T>): T {
                return MainViewModel(numberRepository) as T
            }
        }
    }
}
```

13. Finally, we can modify **MainActivity** to inject our dependencies from our containers and connect the UI elements in order to display the output:

```
class MainActivity : AppCompatActivity() {

    override fun onCreate(savedInstanceState: Bundle?) {
        super.onCreate(savedInstanceState)
        setContentView(R.layout.activity_main)
        val mainContainer = MainContainer((application as
            RandomApplication).applicationContainer
            .numberRepository)

        val viewModel = ViewModelProvider(this,
            mainContainer.getMainViewModelFactory())
            .get(MainViewModel::class.java)

        viewModel.getLiveData().observe(this, Observer {
            findViewById<TextView>
                (R.id.activity_main_text_view).text = it.toString()
        }
        )

        findViewById<TextView>(R.id.activity_main_button)
            .setOnClickListener {
            viewModel.generateNextNumber()
        }
    }
}
```

14. In the highlighted code, we can see that we are using the repository defined in **ApplicationContainer** and injecting it into **MainContainer**, which will then inject it into **ViewModel** through **ViewModelProvider.Factory**. The preceding example should render the output presented in *Figure 12.1*:

Figure 12.1: Emulator output of Exercise 12.01 displaying a randomly generated number

Manual DI is an easy way to set up your dependencies in situations where the app is small, but it can become extremely difficult as the app grows. Imagine if, in *Exercise 12.01, Manual Injection*, we had two classes that extended from `NumberRepository`. How would we handle such a scenario? How would developers know which one went in what activity? These types of questions become very common in most of the well-known apps on Google Play, which is why manual DI is rarely used. When used, it will probably take the form of a DI framework similar to the ones we will look over next.

DAGGER

Dagger offers a comprehensive way to organize your application's dependencies. It has the advantage of being adopted first on Android by the developer community before Kotlin was introduced. This is one of the reasons that many Android applications use Dagger as their DI framework. Another advantage the framework holds is for Android projects written in Java, because the library is developed in the same language. The framework was initially developed by Square (Dagger 1) and later transitioned to Google (Dagger 2). We will cover Dagger 2 in this chapter and describe its benefits. Some of the key functionalities Dagger 2 provides are the following:

- Injection

- Dependencies grouped in modules

- Components used to generate dependency graphs

- Qualifiers

- Scopes

- Subcomponents

Annotations are the key elements when dealing with Dagger, because it generates the code required to perform the DI through an annotation processor. The main annotations can be grouped as follows:

- **Provider**: Classes that are annotated with `@Module` are responsible for providing an object (dependent object) that can be injected.

- **Consumer**: The `@Inject` annotation is used to define a dependency.

- **Connector**: A `@Component`-annotated interface defines the connection between the provider and the consumer.

In order to add Dagger to your project, in the **app/build.gradle** file, you will
need the following dependencies:

```
implementation 'com.google.dagger:dagger:2.29.1'
kapt 'com.google.dagger:dagger-compiler:2.29.1'
```

Since we are dealing with annotation processors, in the same **build.gradle** file,
you will need to add the plugin for them:

```
apply plugin: 'com.android.application'
apply plugin: 'kotlin-android'
apply plugin: 'kotlin-kapt'
```

CONSUMERS

Dagger uses **javax.inject.Inject** to identify objects that require injection.
There are multiple ways to inject dependencies, but the recommended ways are
through constructor injection and field injection. Constructor injection looks similar to
the following code:

```
import javax.inject.Inject

class ClassA @Inject constructor()

class ClassB @Inject constructor(private val classA: ClassA)
```

When constructors are annotated with @**Inject**, Dagger will generate **Factory**
classes that will be responsible for instantiating the objects. In the example of
ClassB, Dagger will try to find the appropriate dependencies that fit the signature of
the constructor, which, in this example, is **ClassA**, which Dagger already created an
instance for.

If you do not want Dagger to manage the instantiation of **ClassB** but still have the
dependency to **ClassA** injected, you can use field injection and it will look something
like this:

```
import javax.inject.Inject

class ClassA @Inject constructor()

class ClassB {
```

```
@Inject
lateinit var classA: ClassA
}
```

In this case, Dagger will generate the necessary code just to inject the dependency between **ClassB** and **ClassA**.

PROVIDERS

You will find yourself in situations where your application uses external dependencies. That means that you will not be able to provide instances through constructor injections. Another situation where constructor injection is not possible is when interfaces or abstract classes are used. In this situation, Dagger offers the possibility to provide the instance using the @**Provides** annotation. You will then need to group the methods where instances are provided into modules annotated with @**Module**:

```
import dagger.Module
import dagger.Provides


class ClassA
class ClassB(private val classA: ClassA)

@Module
object MyModule {

    @Provides
    fun provideClassA(): ClassA = ClassA()

    @Provides
    fun provideClassB(classA: ClassA): ClassB = ClassB(classA)
}
```

As you can see in the preceding example, **ClassA** and **ClassB** don't have any Dagger annotations. A module was created that will provide the instance for **ClassA**, which will then be used to provide the instance for **ClassB**. In this case, Dagger will generate a **Factory** class for each of the @**Provides** annotated methods.

CONNECTORS

Assuming we will have multiple modules, we will need to combine them in a graph of dependencies that can be used across the application. Dagger offers the @ **Component** annotation. This is usually used for an interface or an abstract class that will be implemented by Dagger. Along with assembling the dependency graph, components also offer the functionality to add methods to inject dependencies into a certain object's members. In components, you can specify provision methods that return dependencies provided in the modules:

```
import dagger.Component

@Component(modules = [MyModule::class])
interface MyComponent {

    fun inject(myApplication: MyApplication)
}
```

For the preceding **Component**, Dagger will generate a **DaggerMyComponent** class and we can build it as described in the following code:

```
import android.app.Application
import javax.inject.Inject

class MyApplication : Application() {

    @Inject
    lateinit var classB: ClassB

    override fun onCreate() {
        super.onCreate()
        val component = DaggerMyComponent.create()
        //needs to build the project once to generate
        //DaggerMyComponent.class
        component.inject(this)
    }
}
```

The **Application** class will create the Dagger dependency graph and component. The **inject** method in **Component** allows us to perform DI on the variables in the **Application** class annotated with @**Inject**, giving us access to the **ClassB** object defined in the module.

QUALIFIERS

If you want to provide multiple instances of the same class (such as injecting different Strings or Integers across an application), you can use qualifiers. These are annotations that can help you identify instances. One of the most common ones is the **@Named** qualifier, as described in the following code:

```
@Module
object MyModule {

    @Named("classA1")
    @Provides
    fun provideClassA1(): ClassA = ClassA()

    @Named("classA2")
    @Provides
    fun provideClassA2(): ClassA = ClassA()

    @Provides
    fun provideClassB(@Named("classA1") classA: ClassA): ClassB =
        ClassB(classA)
}
```

In this example, we create two instances of **ClassA** and we give them different names. We then use the first instance whenever possible to create **ClassB**. We can also create custom qualifiers instead of the **@Named** annotation, as described in the following code:

```
import javax.inject.Qualifier

@Qualifier
@MustBeDocumented
@kotlin.annotation.Retention(AnnotationRetention.RUNTIME)
annotation class ClassA1Qualifier

@Qualifier
@MustBeDocumented
@kotlin.annotation.Retention(AnnotationRetention.RUNTIME)
annotation class ClassA2Qualifier
```

The module can be updated like this:

```
@Module
object MyModule {

    @ClassA1Qualifier
    @Provides
    fun provideClassA1(): ClassA = ClassA()

    @ClassA2Qualifier
    @Provides
    fun provideClassA2(): ClassA = ClassA()

    @Provides
    fun provideClassB(@ClassA1Qualifier classA: ClassA): ClassB =
        ClassB(classA)
}
```

SCOPES

If you want to keep track of the life cycle of your components and your dependencies, you can use scopes. Dagger offers a @**Singleton** scope. This usually indicates that your component will live as long as your application will. Scoping has no impact on the life cycle of the objects; they are built to help developers identify the life cycles of objects. It is recommended to give your components one scope and group your code to reflect that scope. Some common Dagger scopes on Android are related to the activity or fragment:

```
import javax.inject.Scope

@Scope
@MustBeDocumented
@kotlin.annotation.Retention(AnnotationRetention.RUNTIME)
annotation class ActivityScope

@Scope
@MustBeDocumented
@kotlin.annotation.Retention(AnnotationRetention.RUNTIME)
annotation class FragmentScope
```

The annotation can be used in the module where the dependency is provided:

```
@ActivityScope
@Provides
fun provideClassA(): ClassA = ClassA()
```

The code for **Component** will be as follows:

```
@ActivityScope
@Component(modules = [MyModule::class])
interface MyComponent {
}
```

The preceding example would indicate that **Component** can only use objects with the same scope. If any of the modules that are part of this **Component** contain dependencies with different scopes, Dagger will throw an error indicating that there is something wrong with the scopes.

SUBCOMPONENTS

Something that goes hand-in-hand with scopes is subcomponents. They allow you to organize your dependencies for smaller scopes. One common use case on Android is to create subcomponents for activities and fragments. Subcomponents inherit dependencies from the parent and they generate a new dependency graph for the scope of the subcomponent.

Let's assume we have a separate module:

```
class ClassC

@Module
object MySubcomponentModule {

    @Provides
    fun provideClassC(): ClassC = ClassC()
}
```

A **Subcomponent** that will generate a dependency graph for that module would look something like the following:

```
import dagger.Subcomponent

@ActivityScope
@Subcomponent(modules = [MySubcomponentModule::class])
interface MySubcomponent {

    fun inject(mainActivity: MainActivity)
}
```

The parent component would need to declare the new component, as shown in the following code snippet:

```
import dagger.Component

@Component(modules = [MyModule::class])
interface MyComponent {

    fun inject(myApplication: MyApplication)

    fun createSubcomponent(mySubcomponentModule:
      MySubcomponentModule): MySubcomponent
}
```

And you can inject **ClassC** into your activity as follows:

```
@Inject
    lateinit var classC: ClassC

    override fun onCreate(savedInstanceState: Bundle?) {
        super.onCreate(savedInstanceState)
        (application as MyApplication).component
          .createSubcomponent(MySubcomponentModule).inject(this)
}
```

With this knowledge, let's move on to an exercise.

EXERCISE 12.02: DAGGER INJECTION

In this exercise, we will write an Android application that will apply the concept of DI with Dagger. The application will have the same **Repository** and **ViewModel** defined in *Exercise 12.01, Manual Injection*. We will need to use Dagger to expose the same two dependencies:

- **Repository**: This will have the **@Singleton** scope and will be provided by **ApplicationModule**. Now, **ApplicationModule** will be exposed as part of **ApplicationComponent**.

- **ViewModelProvider.Factory**: This will have the custom-defined scope named **MainScope** and will be provided by **MainModule**. Now, **MainModule** will be exposed by **MainSubComponent**. Also, **MainSubComponent** will be generated by **ApplicationComponent**.

The app itself will display a randomly generated number each time a button is clicked:

1. Let's start by adding Dagger and the **ViewModel** libraries to the **app/build. gradle** file:

```
implementation 'com.google.dagger:dagger:2.29.1'
kapt 'com.google.dagger:dagger-compiler:2.29.1'
implementation "androidx.lifecycle:lifecycle-
    extensions:2.2.0"
```

2. We also need the **kapt** plugin in the **app/build.gradle** module. Attach the plugin as shown here:

```
apply plugin: 'kotlin-kapt'
```

3. We now need to add the **NumberRepository**, **NumberRepositoryImpl**, **MainViewModel**, and **RandomApplication** classes and build our UI with **MainActivity**. This can be done by following *Steps 2-9* from *Exercise 12.01, Manual Injection*.

4. Now, let's move on to **ApplicationModule**, which will provide the **NumberRepository** dependency:

```
@Module
    class ApplicationModule {

        @Provides
        fun provideRandom(): Random = Random()

        @Provides
```

```
        fun provideNumberRepository(random: Random):
          NumberRepository = NumberRepositoryImpl(random)
}
```

5. Now, let's create **MainModule**, which will provide the instance of
   ViewModel.Factory:

```
@Module
class MainModule {

    @Provides
    fun provideMainViewModelFactory(numberRepository:
      NumberRepository): ViewModelProvider.Factory {
        return object : ViewModelProvider.Factory {
            override fun <T : ViewModel?> create(modelClass:
              Class<T>): T {
                return MainViewModel(numberRepository) as T
            }
        }
    }
}
```

6. Now, let's create **MainScope**:

```
@Scope
@MustBeDocumented
@kotlin.annotation.Retention(AnnotationRetention.RUNTIME)
annotation class MainScope
```

7. We will need **MainSubcomponent**, which will use the preceding scope:

```
@MainScope
@Subcomponent(modules = [MainModule::class])
interface MainSubcomponent {

    fun inject(mainActivity: MainActivity)
}
```

8. Next, we will require **ApplicationComponent**:

```
@Singleton
@Component(modules = [ApplicationModule::class])
interface ApplicationComponent {

    fun createMainSubcomponent(): MainSubcomponent
}
```

9. We will need to navigate to **Build** and click on **Rebuild project** in Android Studio so that we generate the Dagger code for performing the DI.

10. Next, we modify the **RandomApplication** class in order to add the code required to initialize the Dagger dependency graph:

```
class RandomApplication : Application() {
    lateinit var applicationComponent: ApplicationComponent
    override fun onCreate() {
        super.onCreate()
        applicationComponent =
          DaggerApplicationComponent.create()
    }
}
```

11. We now modify the **MainActivity** class to inject **ViewModelProvider. Factory** and initialize **ViewModel** so that we can display the random number:

```
class MainActivity : AppCompatActivity() {

    @Inject
    lateinit var factory: ViewModelProvider.Factory

    override fun onCreate(savedInstanceState: Bundle?) {
        (application as RandomApplication).applicationComponent
          .createMainSubcomponent().inject(this)
        super.onCreate(savedInstanceState)
        setContentView(R.layout.activity_main)
        val viewModel = ViewModelProvider(this,
          factory).get(MainViewModel::class.java)
        viewModel.getLiveData().observe(this, Observer {
            findViewById<TextView>(R.id.activity_main_text_view)
              .text = it.toString()
        }
        )

        findViewById<TextView>(R.id.activity_main_button)
          .setOnClickListener {
            viewModel.generateNextNumber()
        }
    }
}
```

If you run the preceding code, it will build an application that will display a different random output when you click the button:

Figure 12.2: Emulator output of Exercise 12.02 displaying a randomly generated number

12. *Figure 12.2* shows what the application looks like. You can view the generated Dagger code in the **app/build** folder:

Figure 12.3: Generated Dagger code for Exercise 12.02

In *Figure 12.3*, we can see the code that Dagger generated in order to satisfy the relationship between dependencies. For every dependency that needs to be injected, Dagger will generate an appropriate **Factory** class (based on the **Factory** design pattern), which will be responsible for creating the dependency. Dagger also looks at the places where dependencies will need to be injected and generates an **Injector** class, which will have the responsibility of assigning the value to the dependency (in this case, it will assign the value to the members annotated with @**Inject** in the **MainActivity** class). Finally, Dagger creates implementations for the interfaces that have the @**Component** annotation. In the implementation, Dagger will handle how the modules are created and also provide a builder in which developers can specify how modules can be built.

DAGGER ANDROID

In the previous example, you have probably noticed that in the activity, you had to call the components and subcomponents to perform the injection. That tends to get repetitive in an application. It's also not recommended for activities and fragments to know who is performing the injection. All of this comes from the fundamental conflict between Dagger and the Android framework. In Dagger, you are responsible for providing and injecting your dependencies. In Android, fragments and activities are instantiated by the system. In other words, you cannot move the creation of your activity or fragment into a Dagger module and inject the dependencies, so you have to resort to building subcomponents. By using subcomponents, you then create a dependency between the subcomponent and the activity. Luckily, Dagger provides a set of libraries to address these issues for Android, which can be added to your **build.gradle** file:

```
implementation 'com.google.dagger:dagger-android:2.29.1'
implementation 'com.google.dagger:dagger-android-support:2.29.1'
kapt 'com.google.dagger:dagger-android-processor:2.29.1'
```

The Android Dagger libraries provide specialized injection methods that Dagger uses to inject dependencies into activities and fragments. This setup also simplifies the dependency setup for simpler projects by eliminating the need for subcomponents. A module that would set up the injection into an activity will look something like this:

```
@Module
abstract class ActivityProviderModule {
    @ContributesAndroidInjector(modules = [ActivityModule::class])
    @ActivityScope
    abstract fun contributeMyActivityInjector(): MyActivity
}
```

(Please note that import statements are not shown for these examples.)

One important thing here is the introduction of the @
ContributesAndroidInjector annotation, which, when applied to an abstract method, allows Dagger to create an implementation in which it will create **AndroidInjector**, which will then be used to perform the injection into the activity. The **Application** component will need a dedicated **AndroidInjectionModule** or **AndroidSupportInjection** module (if you are using the compatibility library to implement your fragments):

```
@Singleton
@Component(
    modules = [AndroidSupportInjectionModule::class,
        ApplicationModule::class,
        ActivityProviderModule::class
    ]
)
interface ApplicationComponent {

    fun inject(myApplication: MyApplication)
}
```

AndroidSupportInjectionModule comes from the Dagger Android library and provides a set of bindings that prove useful when using the Android framework classes by keeping track of the different injectors you've added to your **Application**, **Activity**, and **Fragment** classes. This is how Dagger will know how each dependency should be injected into your activity or fragment.

In your **Application** class, you will need a **HasAndroidInjector** implementation. This will be responsible for providing the injection into each of your application's activities. The same rule can be applied if you are using services or **ContentProvider**:

```
class MyApplication : Application(), HasAndroidInjector {

    @Inject
    lateinit var dispatchingAndroidInjector:
      DispatchingAndroidInjector<Any>

    lateinit var applicationComponent: ApplicationComponent

    override fun onCreate() {
        super.onCreate()
```

```
        applicationComponent = DaggerApplicationComponent.create()
        applicationComponent.inject(this)
    }


    override fun androidInjector(): AndroidInjector<Any> =
        dispatchingAndroidInjector
}
```

What Dagger will do in your **Application** class, in **onCreate()**, is to create the graph and inject an **AndroidInjector** object into the **Application** class. The **AndroidInjector** object will then be used to inject dependencies into each of the specified activities. Finally, in your activity, you can use the **AndroidInjection. inject()** method to inject the dependencies. When **inject()** gets called, Dagger will look up the injector responsible for DI. If **inject()** gets called from an activity, then it will use the application injector. This is the point where the **androidInjector()** method from the application will be called by Dagger. If the injector is valid, then DI will be performed. If **inject()** is called from a fragment, then Dagger will look for an injector in the parent activity. If **inject()** is called from a nested fragment, then Dagger will look for an injector in the parent fragment, which is why it is only limited to one nested fragment:

```
class MyActivity : AppCompatActivity() {

    @Inject
    lateinit var myClass: MyClass

    override fun onCreate(savedInstanceState: Bundle?) {
        AndroidInjection.inject(this)
        super.onCreate(savedInstanceState)
    }
}
```

In order to perform DI in your fragments, a similar principle must be followed for each of your activities that was executed previously. Let's assume that **MyActivity** has **MyFragment**. We will need to implement **HasAndroidInjector** for **MyActivity**:

```
class MyActivity : AppCompatActivity(), HasAndroidInjector {
    @Inject
    lateinit var dispatchingAndroidInjector:
        DispatchingAndroidInjector<Any>
    override fun onCreate(savedInstanceState: Bundle?) {
        AndroidInjection.inject(this)
```

```
        super.onCreate(savedInstanceState)
    }


    override fun androidInjector(): AndroidInjector<Any> =
        dispatchingAndroidInjector
}
```

Next, we will need a provider module for our fragment that is similar to the provider module for the activity:

```
@Module
abstract class FragmentProviderModule {

    @ContributesAndroidInjector(modules = [FragmentModule::class])
    @FragmentScope
    abstract fun contributeMyFragmentInjector(): MyFragment
}
```

Finally, in **ActivityProviderModule**, you need to add **FragmentProviderModule**:

```
    @ContributesAndroidInjector(modules = [ActivityModule::class,
        FragmentProviderModule::class])
    @ActivityScope
    abstract fun contributeMyActivityInjector(): MyActivity
```

This is required for every activity that has fragments that have dependencies that require injection.

Dagger Android provides a set of classes that have the **HasAndroidInjector** implementation. If you wish to avoid implementing the **HasAndroidInjector** method in your classes, use some of the following classes: **DaggerApplication**, **DaggerActivity**, **DaggerFragment**, and **DaggerSupportFragment**. Using them just requires them to be extended instead of **Application**, **Activity**, and so on.

EXERCISE 12.03: CHANGING INJECTORS

In this exercise, we will change *Exercise 12.02, Dagger Injection*, to add the Android injector features. The output will be to display a randomly generated number and the same dependencies will need to be exposed in the following way:

- **Repository**: This will have the @**Singleton** scope and will be provided by **ApplicationModule**. Now, **ApplicationModule** will be exposed as part of **ApplicationComponent** (the same as for *Exercise 12.02, Dagger Injection*).

- **ViewModelProvider.Factory**: This will have the custom-defined scope named **MainScope** and will be provided by **MainModule**. Now, **MainModule** will be exposed by **MainProviderModule**.

- The dependencies will be injected into **MainActivity** using the Android injector. The Android injector will be added to **RandomApplication** in order for the injection to work properly.

Perform the following steps to complete the exercise:

1. Let's add the Dagger Android dependencies to the **app/build.gradle** file, which will make your dependencies look something like this:

```
implementation 'com.google.dagger:dagger:2.29.1'
kapt 'com.google.dagger:dagger-compiler:2.29.1'
implementation 'com.google.dagger:dagger-android:2.29.1'
implementation 'com.google.dagger:dagger-android-
    support:2.29.1'
kapt 'com.google.dagger:dagger-android-processor:2.29.1'
```

2. Next, delete the **MainSubcomponent** class.

3. Create a **MainProviderModule** class, which will provide the **MainActivity** reference:

```
@Module
abstract class MainProviderModule {
    @MainScope
    @ContributesAndroidInjector(modules = [MainModule::class])
    abstract fun contributeMainActivityInjector(): MainActivity
}
```

4. Update **ApplicationComponent** in order to add an **inject** method to the **Application** class and to add **ActivityProviderModule** and **AndroidSupportInjectionModule**:

```
@Singleton
@Component(modules = [ApplicationModule::class,
AndroidSupportInjectionModule::class, MainProviderModule::class])
interface ApplicationComponent {

    fun inject(randomApplication: RandomApplication)

}
```

5. Change the **Application** class to implement **HasAndroidInjector** and to have Dagger inject an injector object into it:

```
class RandomApplication : Application(), HasAndroidInjector {
    @Inject
    lateinit var dispatchingAndroidInjector:
      DispatchingAndroidInjector<Any>
    lateinit var applicationComponent: ApplicationComponent

    override fun onCreate() {
        super.onCreate()
        applicationComponent =
          DaggerApplicationComponent.create()
        applicationComponent.inject(this)
    }

    override fun androidInjector(): AndroidInjector<Any> =
      dispatchingAndroidInjector
}
```

6. In **MainActivity**, replace the old injection with the **AndroidInjection.inject** method:

```
override fun onCreate(savedInstanceState: Bundle?) {
    AndroidInjection.inject(this)
    super.onCreate(savedInstanceState)
    setContentView(R.layout.activity_main)
    val viewModel = ViewModelProvider(this,
        factory).get(MainViewModel::class.java)
    viewModel.getLiveData().observe(this, Observer {
        findViewById<TextView>(R.id.activity_main_text_view)
            .text = it.toString()
    }
}
```

```
    )
    findViewById<TextView>(R.id.activity_main_button)
      .setOnClickListener {
        viewModel.generateNextNumber()
      }
    }
  }
```

The final output will be as follows:

Figure 12.4: Emulator output of Exercise 12.03 displaying a randomly generated number

Have a look at the code generated when the app is built:

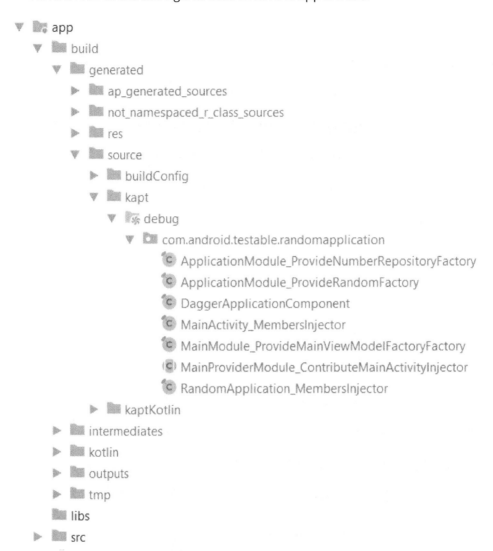

Figure 12.5: Generated Dagger code for Exercise 12.03

Running the preceding code shouldn't change the outcome of the exercise or the scope of the dependencies presented in *Figure 12.3*. You can observe how the **MainActivity** object no longer has a dependency on the **Application** class or any of the components or subcomponents. *Figure 12.5* shows the generated code with the Dagger Android injectors. Most of it is similar to the existing one, but we can see the generated code for **MainProviderModule**, which actually generates a subcomponent.

A common setup you will find for Android applications when it comes to organizing their dependencies is as follows:

- **ApplicationModule**: This is where dependencies common for the entire project are defined. Objects such as context, resources, and other Android framework objects can be provided here.

- **NetworkModule**: This is where dependencies related to API calls are stored.

- **StorageModule**: This is where dependencies related to persistence are stored. It can be split into `DatabaseModule`, `FilesModule`, `SharedPreferencesModule`, and so on.

- **ViewModelsModule**: This is where dependencies to `ViewModels` or `ViewModel` factories are stored.

- **FeatureModule**: This is where dependencies are organized for a particular activity or fragment with their own `ViewModel`. Here, either subcomponents or Android injectors are used for this purpose.

We've raised some questions about how manual DI can go wrong. Now we have seen how Dagger can address these issues. Although it does the job, and it does it quickly when it comes to performance, it is also a complex framework with a very steep learning curve.

KOIN

Koin is a lighter framework that is suitable for smaller apps. It requires no code generation and is built based on Kotlin's functional extensions. It is also a **Domain Specific language (DSL)**. You may have noticed that when using Dagger, there's a lot of code that must be written in order to set up the DI. Koin's approach to DI solves most of those issues, allowing faster integration.

Koin can be added to your project by adding the following dependency to your **build.gradle** file:

```
implementation 'org.koin:koin-android:2.2.0-rc-4'
```

In order to set up Koin in your application, you need the **startKoin** call with the DSL syntax:

```
class MyApplication : Application() {

    override fun onCreate() {
        super.onCreate()
```

```
        startKoin {
            androidLogger(Level.INFO)
            androidContext(this@MyApplication)
            androidFileProperties()
            modules(myModules)
        }
    }
}
```

Here, you can configure what your application context is (in the **androidContext** method), specify property files to define Koin configurations (in the **androidFileProperties**), state the Logger Level for Koin, which will output in **LogCat** results of Koin operations depending on the Level (in the **androidLogger** method), and list the modules your application uses. A similar syntax is used to create the modules:

```
class ClassA

class ClassB(private val classB: ClassA)

    val moduleForClassA = module {
        single { ClassA() }
    }
    val moduleForClassB = module {
        factory { ClassB(get()) }
    }


    override fun onCreate() {
        super.onCreate()
        startKoin {
            androidLogger(Level.INFO)
            androidContext(this@MyApplication)
            androidFileProperties()
            modules(listOf(moduleForClassA, moduleForClassB))
        }
    }
```

In the preceding example, the two objects will have two different life cycles. When a dependency is provided using the **single** notation, then only one instance will be used across the entire life cycle of the application. This is useful for repositories, databases, and API components, where multiple instances will be costly for the application. The **factory** notation will create a new object every time an injection is performed. This may be useful in the situation where an object needs to live as long as an activity or fragment.

The dependency can be injected using the **by inject()** method or the **get()** method, as shown in the following code:

```
class MainActivity : AppCompatActivity() {
  val classB: ClassB by inject()

}


override fun onCreate(savedInstanceState: Bundle?) {
    super.onCreate(savedInstanceState)
    val classB: ClassB = get()
}
```

Koin also offers the possibility of using qualifiers with the help of the **named()** method when the module is created. This allows you to provide multiple implementations of the same type (for example, providing two or more list objects with different content):

```
val moduleForClassA = module {
    single(named("name")) { ClassA() }
}
```

One of Koin's main features for Android applications is scopes for activities and fragments and can be defined as shown in the following code snippet:

```
val moduleForClassB = module {
    scope(named<MainActivity>()) {
        scoped { ClassB(get()) }
    }
}
```

The preceding example connects the life cycle of the **ClassB** dependency to the life cycle of **MainActivity**. In order for you to inject your instance into your activity you will need to extend the **ScopeActivity** class. This class is responsible for holding a reference as long as the activity lives. Similar classes exist for other Android components like Fragments (**ScopeFragment**) and Services (**ScopeService**)

```
class MainActivity : ScopeActivity() {
    val classB: ClassB by inject()
}
```

You can inject the instance using the **inject()** method into your activity. This is useful in situations where you wish to limit who gets to access the dependency. In the preceding example, if another activity had wanted to access the reference to **ClassB**, then it wouldn't be able to find it in the scope.

Another feature that comes in handy for Android is the **ViewModel** injections. To set this up, you will need to add the library to **build.gradle**:

```
implementation "org.koin:koin-android-viewmodel:2.2.0-rc-4"
```

If you recall, **ViewModels** require **ViewModelProvider.Factories** in order to be instantiated. Koin automatically solves this, allowing **ViewModels** to be injected directly and to handle the factory work:

```
val moduleForClassB = module {
    factory {
        ClassB(get())
    }
    viewModel { MyViewModel(get()) }
}
```

In order to inject the dependency of **ViewModel** into your activity, you can use the **viewModel()** method:

```
class MainActivity : AppCompatActivity() {
    val model: MyViewModel by viewModel()
}
```

Alternatively, you can use the method directly:

```
override fun onCreate(savedInstanceState: Bundle?) {
    super.onCreate(savedInstanceState)
    val model : MyViewModel = getViewModel()
}
```

As we can see in the preceding setup, Koin takes full advantage of Kotlin's language features and reduces the amount of boilerplate required to define your modules and their scopes.

EXERCISE 12.04: KOIN INJECTION

Here, we will write an Android application that will perform DI using Koin. The application will be based on *Exercise 12.01*, *Manual Injection*, by keeping **NumberRepository**, **NumberRepositoryImpl**, **MainViewModel**, and **MainActivity**. The following dependencies will be injected:

- **Repository**: As part of a module named **appModule**.

- **MainViewModel**: This will rely on Koin's specialized implementation for **ViewModels**. This will be provided as part of a module named **mainModule** and will have the scope of **MainActivity**.

Perform the following steps to complete the exercise:

1. The app itself will display a randomly generated number each time a button is clicked. Let's start by adding the Koin libraries:

```
implementation "androidx.lifecycle:lifecycle-extensions:2.2.0"
implementation 'org.koin:koin-android:2.2.0-rc-4'
implementation "org.koin:koin-android-viewmodel:2.2.0-rc-4"
```

2. Let's start by defining the **appModule** variable inside the **MyApplication** class. This will have a similar structure to **AppModule** with the Dagger setup:

```
class RandomApplication : Application() {

    val appModule = module {
        single {
            Random()
        }
        single<NumberRepository> {
            NumberRepositoryImpl(get())
        }
    }
}
```

3. Now, let's add the activity module variable after **appModule**:

```
val mainModule = module {
    scope(named<MainActivity>()) {
        scoped {
            MainViewModel(get())
        }
    }
}
```

4. Now, let's initialize **Koin** in the **onCreate()** method of **RandomApplication**:

```
super.onCreate()
startKoin {
    androidLogger()
    androidContext(this@RandomApplication)
    modules(listOf(appModule, mainModule))
}
```

5. Finally, let's inject the dependencies into the activity:

```
class MainActivity :  ScopeActivity() {

    private val mainViewModel: MainViewModel by inject()
    override fun onCreate(savedInstanceState: Bundle?) {
        super.onCreate(savedInstanceState)
        setContentView(R.layout.activity_main)
        mainViewModel.getLiveData().observe(this, Observer {
            findViewById<TextView>(R.id.activity_main_text_view)
                .text = it.toString()
        }
        )
        findViewById<TextView>(R.id.activity_main_button)
            .setOnClickListener {
            mainViewModel.generateNextNumber()
        }
    }
}
```

6. If you run the preceding code, the app should work as per the previous examples. However, if you check **LogCat**, you will see a similar output to this:

```
[Koin]: [init] declare Android Context
[Koin]: bind type:'android.content.Context' ~ [type:Single,primary_
type:'android.content.Context']
[Koin]: bind type:'android.app.Application' ~ [type:Single,primary_
type:'android.app.Application']
[Koin]: bind type:'java.util.Random' ~ [type:Single,primary_
type:'java.util.Random']
[Koin]: bind type:'com.android.testable.randomapplication
  .NumberRepository' ~ [type:Single,primary_type:'com.android
  .testable.randomapplication.NumberRepository']

[Koin]: total 5 registered definitions

[Koin]: load modules in 0.4638 ms
```

In *Figure 12.6*, we can see the same output as in previous exercises:

Figure 12.6: Emulator output of Exercise 12.04 displaying a randomly generated number

As we can see from this exercise, Koin is much faster and easier to integrate, especially with its **ViewModel** library. This comes in handy for small projects, but its performance will be impacted once projects grow.

ACTIVITY 12.01: INJECTED REPOSITORIES

In this activity, you are going to create an app in Android Studio that connects to a sample API, https://jsonplaceholder.typicode.com/posts, using the Retrofit library and retrieves a list of posts from the web page, which will then be displayed on the screen. You will then need to set up a UI test in which you will assert that the data is asserted correctly on the screen, but instead of connecting to the actual endpoint, you will provide dummy data for the test to display on the screen. You will take advantage of the DI concept in order to swap the dependencies when the app is executed as opposed to when the app is being tested.

In order to achieve this, you will need to build the following:

- A network component responsible for downloading and parsing the JSON file

- A repository that accesses the data from the API layer

- A **ViewModel** instance that accesses the Repository

- An activity with **RecycleView** that displays the data

- A Dagger module for providing the repository instance and one for providing the **ViewModel** factory instance, and a test module that will swap the repository dependency

- One UI test that will assert the rows and uses a dummy object to generate the API data

> **NOTE**
>
> Error handling can be avoided for this activity.

Perform the following steps in order to complete this activity:

1. In Android Studio, create an application with **Empty Activity** (**MainActivity**) and add an **api** package where your API calls are stored.

2. Define a class responsible for the API calls.

3. Create a **repository** package.

4. Define a repository interface that will have one method, returning **LiveData** with the list of posts.

5. Create the implementation for the repository class.

6. Create a **ViewModel** instance, which will call the repository to retrieve the data.

7. Create an adapter for the rows of the UI.

8. Create the activity that will render the UI.

9. Set up a Dagger module that will initialize the network-related dependencies.

10. Create a Dagger module that will be responsible for defining the dependencies required for the activity.

11. Create a subcomponent that will use the associated module and have the injection in the activity.

12. Create **AppComponent**, which will manage all of the modules.

13. Set up the UI tests and a test application and provide a separate **RepositoryModule**, class, which will return a dependency holding dummy data.

14. Implement the UI test.

> **NOTE**
>
> The solution to this activity can be found at: http://packt.live/3sKj1cp.

ACTIVITY 12.02: KOIN-INJECTED REPOSITORIES

In this activity, you will migrate the app built in *Activity 12.01, Injected Repositories*, from Dagger to Koin, keeping the requirements intact.

Assuming that the components in your code are the same as for the previous activity, the following steps need to be followed in order to complete the activity:

1. Remove the Dagger 2 dependencies from **build.gradle** and the **kapt** plugin. The compilation errors this will generate will be able to guide you in removing unnecessary code.

2. Add the standard **Koin** library and the one for **ViewModels**.

3. Delete the Dagger modules and components from your code.

4. Create the **networkModule, repositoryModule**, and **activityModule** modules.

5. Set up Koin with the preceding modules.

6. Inject **ViewModel** into **MainActivity**.

7. Override **repositoryModule** in **TestApplication** to return **DummyRepository**.

> **NOTE**
>
> The solution to this activity can be found at: http://packt.live/3sKj1cp

SUMMARY

In this chapter, we analyzed the concept of DI and how it should be applied in order to separate concerns and prevent objects from having the responsibility of creating other objects and how this is of great benefit for testing. We started the chapter by analyzing the concept of manual DI. This served as a good example of how DI works and how it can be applied to an Android application; it served as the baseline when comparing the DI frameworks.

We also analyzed two of the most popular frameworks that help developers with injecting dependencies. We started with a powerful and fast framework in the form of Dagger 2, which relies on annotation processors to generate code to perform an injection. We also looked into Koin, which is a lightweight framework written in Kotlin with slower performance but a simpler integration and a lot of focus on Android components.

The exercises in this chapter were intended to explore how the same problem can be solved using multiple solutions and compare the degrees of difficulty between the solutions. In the activities for this chapter, we leveraged Dagger's and Koin's modules in order to inject certain dependencies when running the app and other dependencies when running the tests on an application that uses **ViewModels**, repositories, and APIs to load data. This is designed to show the seamless integration of multiple frameworks that achieve different goals. The activities also represented the combination of the different skills learned in previous chapters, from the basic ones that taught you how to display data on the UI to the more complex ones, such as those to do with networking, testing, **ViewModels**, repositories, and DI.

In the following chapters, you will have the opportunity to build upon the knowledge acquired thus far by adding concepts related to threading and how to handle background operations. You will get the opportunity to explore libraries such as RxJava and its reactive approach to threading, and you will also learn about coroutines, which takes a different approach to threading. You will also observe how coroutines and RxJava can combine very effectively with libraries such as Room and Retrofit. Finally, you will be able to combine all of these concepts in a robust application that will have a high degree of scalability for the future.

13

RXJAVA AND COROUTINES

OVERVIEW

This chapter will introduce you to doing background operations and data manipulations with RxJava and coroutines. It covers how to use RxJava to retrieve data from an external API and how to do that with coroutines. You'll also learn how to manipulate and display the data using RxJava operators and LiveData transformations.

By the end of this chapter, you will be able to use RxJava to manage network calls in the background and use RxJava operators to transform data. You will also be able to perform network tasks in the background using Kotlin coroutines and manipulate data with LiveData transformations.

INTRODUCTION

You have now learned the basics of Android app development and implemented features such as RecyclerViews, notifications, fetching data from web services, and services. You've also gained skills in the best practices for testing and persisting data. In the previous chapter, you learned about dependency injection. Now, you will be learning about background operations and data manipulation.

Some Android applications work on their own. However, most apps would need a backend server to retrieve or process data. These operations may take a while, depending on the internet connection, device settings, and server specifications. If long-running operations are run in the main UI thread, the application will be blocked until the tasks are completed. The application might become unresponsive and might prompt the user to close it and stop using it.

To avoid this, tasks that can take an indefinite amount of time must be run asynchronously. An asynchronous task means it can run in parallel to another task or in the background. For example, while fetching data from a data source asynchronously, your UI can still display or interact with the users.

You can use libraries like RxJava and coroutines for asynchronous operations. We'll be discussing both of them in this chapter. Let's get started with RxJava.

RXJAVA

RxJava is a Java implementation of **Reactive Extensions (Rx)**, a library for reactive programming. In reactive programming, you have data streams that can be observed. When the value changes, your observers can be notified and react accordingly. For example, let's say clicking on a button is your observable and you have observers listening to it. If the user clicks on that button, your observers can react and do a specific action.

RxJava makes asynchronous data processing and handling errors simpler. Writing it the usual way is tricky and error-prone. If your task involves a chain of asynchronous tasks, it will be more complicated to write and debug. With RxJava, it can be done more easily and you will have less code, which is more readable and maintainable. RxJava also has a wide range of operators that you can use for transforming data into the type or format you need.

RxJava has three main components: observables, observers, and operators. To use RxJava, you will need to create observables that emit data, transform the data using RxJava operators, and subscribe to the observables with observers. The observers can wait for the observables to produce data without blocking the main thread.

OBSERVABLES, OBSERVERS, AND OPERATORS

Let's understand the three main components of RxJava in detail.

Observables

An observable is a source of data that can be listened to. It can emit data to its listeners.

The **Observable** class represents an observable. You can create observables from lists, arrays, or objects with the **Observable.just** and **Observable.from** methods. For example, you can create observables with the following:

```
val observable = Observable.just("This observable emits this string")
val observableFromList = Observable.fromIterable(listOf(1, 2, 3, 4))
```

There are more functions that you can use to create observables, such as **Observable.create**, **Observable.defer**, **Observable.empty**, **Observable.generate**, **Observable.never**, **Observable.range**, **Observable.interval**, and **Observable.timer**. You can also make a function that returns an **observable**. Learn more about creating observables at https://github.com/ReactiveX/RxJava/wiki/Creating-Observables.

Observables can be either hot or cold. Cold observables emit data only when they have subscribers listening. Examples are database queries or network requests. Hot observables, on the other hand, emits data even if there are no observers. Examples of this are UI events in Android like mouse and keyboard events.

Once you have created an observable, the observers can start listening to the data the observable will send.

Operators

Operators allow you to modify and compose the data you get from the observable before passing it to the observers. Using an operator returns another observable so you can chain operator calls. For example, let's say you have an observable that emits the numbers from 1 to 10. You can filter it to only get even numbers and transform the list into another list containing each item's square. To do that in RxJava, you can use the following code:

```
Observable.range(1, 10)
 .filter { it % 2 == 0 }
 .map { it * it }
```

The output of the preceding code will be a data stream with the values 4, 16, 36, 64, and 100.

Observers

Observers subscribe to observables and are notified when the observers emit data. They can listen to the next value or error emitted by the observable. The **Observer** class is the interface for observers. It has four methods that you can override when making an observer:

- **onComplete**: When the observable has finished sending data

- **onNext**: When the observable has sent new data

- **onSubscribe**: When an observer is subscribed to an observable

- **onError**: When the observable encountered an error

To subscribe to an observable, you can call **Observable.subscribe()** passing in a new instance of the **Observer** interface. For example, if you want to subscribe to an observable of even numbers from **2** to **10**, you can do the following:

```
Observable.fromIterable(listOf(2, 4, 6, 8, 10))
    .subscribe(object : Observer<Int> {
        override fun onComplete() {
            println("completed")
        }

        override fun onSubscribe(d: Disposable) {
            println("subscribed")
        }
        override fun onNext(t: Int) {
            println("next integer is $t")
        }
        override fun onError(e: Throwable) {
            println("error encountered")
        }
    })
```

With this code, the observer will print the next integer. It will also print text when it has subscribed, when the observable is completed, and when it encounters an error.

Observable.subscribe() has different overloaded functions wherein you can pass the **onNext, onError, onComplete**, and **onSubscribe** parameters. These functions return a **disposable** object. You can call its **dispose** function when closing an activity to prevent memory leaks. For example, you can use a variable for the **disposable** object:

```
val disposable = observable
        ...
        .subscribe(...)
```

Then, in the **onDestroy** function of the activity where you've made the observable, you can call **disposable.dispose()** to stop the observers from listening to the observable:

```
override fun onDestroy() {
    super.onDestroy()
    disposable.dispose()
}
```

Aside from the observables, observers, and operators, you also need to learn about RxJava schedulers, which will be covered in the next section.

SCHEDULERS

By default, RxJava is synchronous. This means all processes are done in the same thread. There are some tasks that take a while, such as database and network operations, which need to be made asynchronous or run in parallel in another thread. To do that, you need to use schedulers.

Schedulers allow you to control the thread where the actions will be running. There are two functions you can use: **observeOn** and **subscribeOn**. You can set which thread your observable will run on with the **subscribeOn** function. The **observeOn** function allows you to set where the next operators will be executed.

For example, if you have the **getData** function, which fetches data from the network and returns an observable, you can subscribe to **Schedulers.io** and observe the Android main UI thread with **AndroidSchedulers.mainThread()**:

```
val observable = getData()
    .subscribeOn(Schedulers.io())
    .observeOn(AndroidSchedulers.mainThread())
    ...
```

AndroidSchedulers is part of RxAndroid, which is an extension of RxJava for Android. You will need RxAndroid to use RxJava in Android app development.

In the next section, you will learn how to add RxJava and RxAndroid to your project.

ADDING RXJAVA TO YOUR PROJECT

You can add RxJava to your project by adding the following code to your **app/ build.gradle** file dependencies:

```
implementation 'io.reactivex.rxjava3:rxandroid:3.0.0'
implementation 'io.reactivex.rxjava3:rxjava:3.0.7'
```

This will add both the RxJava and RxAndroid libraries to your Android project. The RxAndroid library already includes RxJava but it is better to still add the RxJava dependency as the one bundled with RxAndroid might not be the latest version.

USING RXJAVA IN AN ANDROID PROJECT

RxJava has several benefits, one of which is handling long-running operations such as network requests in a non-UI thread. The result of a network call can be converted to an observable. You can then create an observer that will subscribe to the observable and present the data. Before displaying the data to the user, you can transform the data with RxJava operators.

If you are using Retrofit, you can convert the response to an RxJava observable by adding a call adapter factory. First, you would need to add **adapter-rxjava3** in your **app/build.gradle** file dependencies with the following:

```
implementation 'com.squareup.retrofit2:adapter-rxjava3:2.9.0'
```

With this, you can use **RxJava3CallAdapterFactory** as the call adapter in your **Retrofit** instance. You can do that with the following code:

```
val retrofit = Retrofit.Builder()
    ...
    .addCallAdapterFactory(RxJava3CallAdapterFactory.create())
    ...
```

Now, your Retrofit methods can return **Observable** objects that you can listen to in your code. For example, in your **getMovies** Retrofit method that calls your movie endpoint, you can use the following:

```
@GET("movie")
fun getMovies() : Observable<Movie>
```

Let's try what you have learned so far by adding RxJava to an Android project.

EXERCISE 13.01: USING RXJAVA IN AN ANDROID PROJECT

For this chapter, you will be working with an application that displays popular movies using The Movie Database API. Go to https://developers.themoviedb.org/ and register for an API key. In this exercise, you will be using RxJava to fetch the list of all popular movies from the movie/popular endpoint, regardless of year:

1. Create a new project in Android Studio. Name your project **Popular Movies** and use the package name **com.example.popularmovies**.

2. Set the location where you want to save the project, then click the **Finish** button.

3. Open **AndroidManifest.xml** and add the **INTERNET** permission:

```
<uses-permission android:name="android.permission.INTERNET" />
```

This will allow you to use the device's internet connection to do network calls.

4. Open your **app/build.gradle** file and add the kotlin-parcelize plugin at the end of the plugins block:

```
plugins {
    ...
    id 'kotlin-parcelize'
}
```

This will allow you to use Parcelable for the model class.

5. Add the following in the **android** block:

```
compileOptions {
    sourceCompatibility JavaVersion.VERSION_1_8
    targetCompatibility JavaVersion.VERSION_1_8
}

kotlinOptions {
    jvmTarget = '1.8'
}
```

These will allow you to use Java 8 for your project.

6. Add the following dependencies in your **app/build.gradle** file:

```
implementation 'androidx.recyclerview:recyclerview:1.1.0'
implementation 'com.squareup.retrofit2:retrofit:2.9.0'
implementation 'com.squareup.retrofit2:adapter-rxjava3:2.9.0'
```

```
implementation 'io.reactivex.rxjava3:rxandroid:3.0.0'
implementation 'io.reactivex.rxjava3:rxjava:3.0.7'
implementation 'com.squareup.retrofit2:converter-moshi:2.9.0'
implementation 'com.github.bumptech.glide:glide:4.11.0'
```

These lines will add the RecyclerView, Glide, Retrofit, RxJava, RxAndroid, and Moshi libraries to your project.

7. Create a **dimens.xml** file in the **res/values** directory and add a **layout_margin** dimension value:

```
<resources>
    <dimen name="layout_margin">16dp</dimen>
</resources>
```

This will be used for the vertical and horizontal margins of the views.

8. Create a new layout file named **view_movie_item.xml** and add the following:

view_movie_item.xml

```
9     <ImageView
10        android:id="@+id/movie_poster"
11        android:layout_width="match_parent"
12        android:layout_height="240dp"
13        android:contentDescription="Movie Poster"
14        app:layout_constraintBottom_toBottomOf="parent"
15        app:layout_constraintEnd_toEndOf="parent"
16        app:layout_constraintStart_toStartOf="parent"
17        app:layout_constraintTop_toTopOf="parent"
18        tools:src="@tools:sample/backgrounds/scenic" />
19
20    <TextView
21        android:id="@+id/movie_title"
22        android:layout_width="match_parent"
23        android:layout_height="wrap_content"
24        android:layout_marginStart="@dimen/layout_margin"
25        android:layout_marginEnd="@dimen/layout_margin"
26        android:ellipsize="end"
27        android:gravity="center"
28        android:lines="1"
29        android:textSize="20sp"
30        app:layout_constraintEnd_toEndOf="@id/movie_poster"
31        app:layout_constraintStart_toStartOf="@id/movie_poster"
32        app:layout_constraintTop_toBottomOf="@id/movie_poster"
33        tools:text="Movie" />
```

The complete code for this step can be found at http://packt.live/3sD8zmN.

This layout file, containing the movie poster and title text, will be used for each movie in the list.

9. Open **activity_main.xml**. Replace the Hello World TextView with RecyclerView:

```
<androidx.recyclerview.widget.RecyclerView
    android:id="@+id/movie_list"
    android:layout_width="match_parent"
    android:layout_height="match_parent"
app:layoutManager=
  "androidx.recyclerview.widget.GridLayoutManager"
    app:layout_constraintBottom_toBottomOf="parent"
    app:layout_constraintTop_toTopOf="parent"
    app:spanCount="2"
    tools:listitem="@layout/view_movie_item" />
```

This RecyclerView will be displaying the list of movies. It will be using **GridLayoutManager** with two columns.

10. Create a new package, **com.example.popularmovies.model**, for your model class. Make a new model class named **Movie** with the following:

```
@Parcelize
data class Movie(
    val adult: Boolean = false,
    val backdrop_path: String = "",
    val id: Int = 0,
    val original_language: String = "",
    val original_title: String = "",
    val overview: String = "",
    val popularity: Float = 0f,
    val poster_path: String = "",
    val release_date: String = "",
    val title: String = "",
    val video: Boolean = false,
    val vote_average: Float = 0f,
    val vote_count: Int = 0
) : Parcelable
```

This will be the model class representing a **Movie** object from the API.

11. Create a new activity named **DetailsActivity** with **activity_details.xml** as the layout file.

12. Open the **AndroidManifest.xml** file and add **MainActivity** as the value for the **parentActivityName** attribute of **DetailsActivity**:

```
<activity android:name=".DetailsActivity"
          android:parentActivityName=".MainActivity" />
```

This will add an up icon in the details activity to go back to the main screen.

13. Open **activity_details.xml**. Add the required views. (The code below is truncated for space. Refer to the file linked below for the full code that you need to add.)

activity_details.xml

```
9    <ImageView
10       android:id="@+id/movie_poster"
11       android:layout_width="160dp"
12       android:layout_height="160dp"
13       android:layout_margin="@dimen/layout_margin"
14       android:contentDescription="Poster"
15       app:layout_constraintStart_toStartOf="parent"
16       app:layout_constraintTop_toTopOf="parent"
17       tools:src="@tools:sample/avatars" />
18
19   <TextView
20       android:id="@+id/title_text"
21       style="@style/TextAppearance.AppCompat.Title"
22       android:layout_width="0dp"
23       android:layout_height="wrap_content"
24       android:layout_margin="@dimen/layout_margin"
25       android:ellipsize="end"
26       android:maxLines="4"
27       app:layout_constraintEnd_toEndOf="parent"
28       app:layout_constraintStart_toEndOf="@+id/movie_poster"
29       app:layout_constraintTop_toTopOf="parent"
30       tools:text="Title" />
```

The complete code for this step can be found at http://packt.live/38WyRbQ.

This will add the poster, title, release, and overview on the details screen.

14. Open **DetailsActivity** and add the following:

```
class DetailsActivity : AppCompatActivity() {

    companion object {
        const val EXTRA_MOVIE = "movie"
        const val IMAGE_URL = "https://image.tmdb.org/t/p/w185/"
    }

    override fun onCreate(savedInstanceState: Bundle?) {
        super.onCreate(savedInstanceState)
```

```
        setContentView(R.layout.activity_details)

        val titleText: TextView = findViewById(R.id.title_text)
        val releaseText: TextView = findViewById(R.id.release_text)
        val overviewText: TextView = findViewById(R.id.overview_text)
        val poster: ImageView = findViewById(R.id.movie_poster)

        val movie = intent.getParcelableExtra<Movie>(EXTRA_MOVIE)
        movie?.run {
            titleText.text = title
            releaseText.text = release_date.take(4)

            overviewText.text = "Overview: $overview"

            Glide.with(this@DetailsActivity)
                .load("$IMAGE_URL$poster_path")
                .placeholder(R.mipmap.ic_launcher)
                .fitCenter()
                .into(poster)
        }
    }
}
```

This will display the poster, title, release, and overview of the movie selected.

15. Create an adapter class for the movie list. Name the class **MovieAdapter**. Add the following:

```
class MovieAdapter(private val clickListener: MovieClickListener) :
    RecyclerView.Adapter<MovieAdapter.MovieViewHolder>() {

    private val movies = mutableListOf<Movie>()

    override fun onCreateViewHolder(parent: ViewGroup,
        viewType: Int): MovieViewHolder {
            val view = LayoutInflater.from(parent.context)
              .inflate(R.layout.view_movie_item, parent, false)
            return MovieViewHolder(view)
    }

    override fun getItemCount() = movies.size

    override fun onBindViewHolder(holder: MovieViewHolder,
      position: Int) {
```

```
        val movie = movies[position]
        holder.bind(movie)
        holder.itemView.setOnClickListener {
          clickListener.onMovieClick(movie) }
    }


    fun addMovies(movieList: List<Movie>) {
        movies.addAll(movieList)
        notifyItemRangeInserted(0, movieList.size)
    }
}
```

This class will be the adapter for your RecyclerView.

16. Add **ViewHolder** for your class after the **onBindViewHolder** function:

```
class MovieAdapter...
    ...
    class MovieViewHolder(itemView: View) :
      RecyclerView.ViewHolder(itemView) {
        private val imageUrl = "https://image.tmdb.org/t/p/w185/"
        private val titleText: TextView by lazy {
            itemView.findViewById(R.id.movie_title)
        }
        private val poster: ImageView by lazy {
            itemView.findViewById(R.id.movie_poster)
        }


        fun bind(movie: Movie) {
            titleText.text = movie.title

            Glide.with(itemView.context)
                .load("$imageUrl${movie.poster_path}")
                .placeholder(R.mipmap.ic_launcher)
                .fitCenter()
                .into(itemView.poster)
        }
    }
}
```

This will be the **ViewHolder** used by **MovieAdapter** for the RecyclerView.

17. Below the **MovieViewHolder** declaration, add **MovieClickListener**:

```
class MovieAdapter...

    ...
    interface MovieClickListener {
        fun onMovieClick(movie: Movie)
    }
}
```

This interface will be used when clicking on a movie to view the details.

18. Create another class named **PopularMoviesResponse** in the **com.example.popularmovies.model** package:

```
data class PopularMoviesResponse (
    val page: Int,
    val results: List<Movie>
)
```

This will be the model class for the response you get from the API endpoint for popular movies.

19. Create a new package, **com.example.popularmovies.api**, and add a **MovieService** interface with the following contents:

```
interface MovieService {

@GET("movie/popular")
fun getPopularMovies(@Query("api_key") apiKey: String):
  Observable<PopularMoviesResponse>
}
```

This will define the endpoint you will be using to retrieve the popular movies.

20. Create a **MovieRepository** class with a constructor for **movieService**:

```
class MovieRepository(private val movieService: MovieService) { ... }
```

21. Add the **apiKey** (with the value of the API key from The Movie Database API) and a **fetchMovies** function to retrieve the list from the endpoint:

```
private val apiKey = "your_api_key_here"


fun fetchMovies() = movieService.getPopularMovies(apiKey)
```

22. Create an application class named **MovieApplication** with a property for **movieRepository**:

```
class MovieApplication : Application() {


    lateinit var movieRepository: MovieRepository

}
```

This will be the application class for the app.

23. Override the **onCreate** function of the **MovieApplication** class and initialize **movieRepository**:

```
override fun onCreate() {
  super.onCreate()
  val retrofit = Retrofit.Builder()
    .baseUrl("https://api.themoviedb.org/3/")
    .addConverterFactory(MoshiConverterFactory.create())
    .addCallAdapterFactory(RxJava3CallAdapterFactory.create())
    .build()
  val movieService = retrofit.create(MovieService::class.java)
  movieRepository = MovieRepository(movieService)
}
```

24. Set **MovieApplication** as the value for the **android:name** attribute of the application in the **AndroidManifest.xml** file:

```
<application
    ...
    android:name=".MovieApplication"
    ... />
```

25. Create a **MovieViewModel** class with a constructor for **movieRepository**:

```
class MovieViewModel(private val movieRepository: MovieRepository) :
  ViewModel() { ... }
```

26. Add properties for **popularMovies**, **error**, and **disposable**:

```
private val popularMoviesLiveData = MutableLiveData<List<Movie>>()
private val errorLiveData = MutableLiveData<String>()

val popularMovies: LiveData<List<Movie>>
    get() = popularMoviesLiveData

val error: LiveData<String>
    get() = errorLiveData

private var disposable = CompositeDisposable()
```

27. Define the **fetchPopularMovies** function. Inside the function, get the popular movies from **movieRepository**:

```
fun fetchPopularMovies() {
    disposable.add(movieRepository.fetchMovies()
        .subscribeOn(Schedulers.io())
        .map { it.results }
        .observeOn(AndroidSchedulers.mainThread())
        .subscribe({
            popularMoviesLiveData.postValue(it)
        }, { error ->
            errorLiveData.postValue("An error occurred:
                ${error.message}")
        })
    )
}
```

This will fetch the popular movies asynchronously in the **Schedulers.io** thread when subscribed and will return an observable and with operators on the main thread.

28. Override the **onCleared** function of the **MovieViewModel** and dispose of
    the **disposable**:

```
override fun onCleared() {
    super.onCleared()
    disposable.dispose()
}
```

This will dispose of the **disposable** when the ViewModel has been cleared, like
when the activity has been closed.

29. Open **MainActivity** and add define a field for the movie adapter:

```
private val movieAdapter by lazy {
    MovieAdapter(object : MovieAdapter.MovieClickListener {
        override fun onMovieClick(movie: Movie) {
            openMovieDetails(movie)
        }
    })
}
```

This will have a listener that will open the details screen when a movie is clicked.

30. In the **onCreate** function, set the adapter for the **movie_
    list RecyclerView**:

```
val recyclerView: RecyclerView = findViewById(R.id.movie_list)
recyclerView.adapter = movieAdapter
```

31. Create a **getMovies** function on **MainActivity**. Inside, initialize
    movieRepository and **movieViewModel**:

```
private fun getMovies() {
    val movieRepository = (application as
      MovieApplication).movieRepository

    val movieViewModel = ViewModelProvider(this, object :
      ViewModelProvider.Factory {
        override fun <T : ViewModel?>
          create(modelClass: Class<T>): T {
            return MovieViewModel(movieRepository) as T
```

```
            }
        }).get(MovieViewModel::class.java)
    }
```

32. At the end of the **getMovies** function, add an observer to the
    popularMovies and **error** LiveData from **movieViewModel**:

```
private fun getMovies() {
    ...
    movieViewModel.fetchPopularMovies()
    movieViewModel.popularMovies
        .observe(this, { popularMovies ->
            movieAdapter.addMovies(popularMovies)
        })
        movieViewModel.error.observe(this, { error ->
            Toast.makeText(this, error, Toast.LENGTH_LONG).show()
        })
    }
```

33. At the end of the **onCreate** function of the **MainActivity** class, call the
    getMovies() function:

```
getMovies()
```

34. Add the **openMovieDetails** function to open the details screen when clicking
    on a movie from the list:

```
private fun openMovieDetails(movie: Movie) {
    val intent =
      Intent(this, DetailsActivity::class.java).apply {
        putExtra(DetailsActivity.EXTRA_MOVIE, movie)
    }
    startActivity(intent)
}
```

35. Run your application. You will see that the app will display a list of popular movie titles:

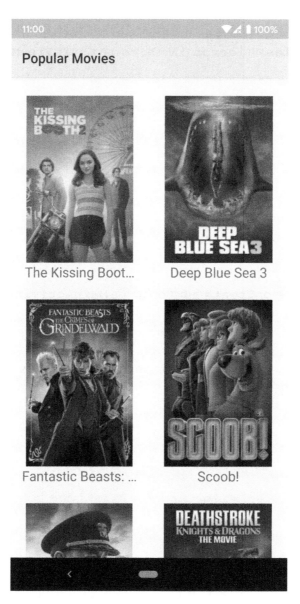

Figure 13.1: How the Popular Movies app will look

36. Click on a movie, and you will see its details, such as its release date and an overview:

Figure 13.2: The movie details screen

You have learned how to use RxJava to retrieve the response from an external API. In the next section, you will convert the data you fetched into the data that you need to display with RxJava operators.

MODIFYING DATA WITH RXJAVA OPERATORS

When you have an observable that emits data, you can use operators to modify the data before passing it to the observers. You can use a single operator or a chain of operators to get the data that you want. There are different types of operators that you can use, such as transforming operators and filtering operators.

Transforming operators can modify items from the observable into your preferred data. The **flatMap()** operator transforms the items into an observable. In *Exercise 13.01, Using RxJava in an Android Project*, you transformed the observable of **PopularMoviesResponse** into an observable of **Movies** with the following:

```
.flatMap { Observable.fromIterable(it.results) }
```

Another operator that can transform data is **map**. The **map(x)** operator applies a function **x** to each item and returns another observable with the updated values. For example, if you have an observable of a list of numbers, you can transform it into another observable list with each number multiplied by 2 with the following:

```
.map { it * 2 }
```

Filtering operators allow you to select only some of the items. With **filter()**, you can select items based on a set condition. For example, you can filter odd numbers with the following:

```
.filter { it % 2 != 0 }
```

The **first()** and **last()** operators allow you to get the first and last item, while with **take(n)** or **takeLast(n)**, you can get *n* first or last items. There are other filtering operators such as **debounce()**, **distinct()**, **elementAt()**, **ignoreElements()**, **sample()**, **skip()**, and **skipLast()**.

There are many other RxJava operators you can use. Let's try to use RxJava operators in an Android project.

EXERCISE 13.02: USING RXJAVA OPERATORS

In the previous exercise, you used RxJava to fetch the list of popular movies from The Movie Database API. Now, before displaying them in RecyclerView, you will be adding operators to sort the movies by title and only get the movies released last month:

1. Open the **Popular Movies** project you did in *Exercise 13.01, Using RxJava in an Android Project*.

2. Open **MovieViewModel** and navigate to the **fetchPopularMovies** function.

3. You will be modifying the app to only display popular movies for this year. Replace `.map { it.results }` with the following:

```
.flatMap { Observable.fromIterable(it.results) }
.toList()
```

This will convert the Observable of **MovieResponse** into an observable of Movies.

4. Before the **toList()** call, add the following:

```
.filter {
    val cal = Calendar.getInstance()
    cal.add(Calendar.MONTH, -1)
    it.release_date.startsWith(
        "${cal.get(Calendar.YEAR)}-${cal.get(Calendar.MONTH) + 1}"
    )
}
```

This will select only the movies released in the previous month.

5. Run the application. You will see that the other movies are no longer displayed. Only those released this year will be on the list:

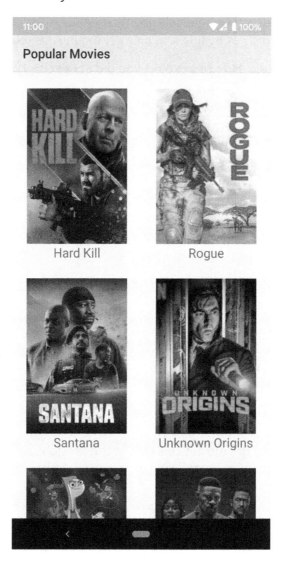

Figure 13.3: The app with the year's popular movies

6. You'll also notice that the movies displayed are not in alphabetical order. Sort the movies by using the **sorted** operator before the **toList()** call:

```
.sorted { movie, movie2 -> movie.title.compareTo(movie2.title) }
```

This will sort the movies based on their titles.

7. Run the application. You will see that the list of movies is now sorted alphabetically by title:

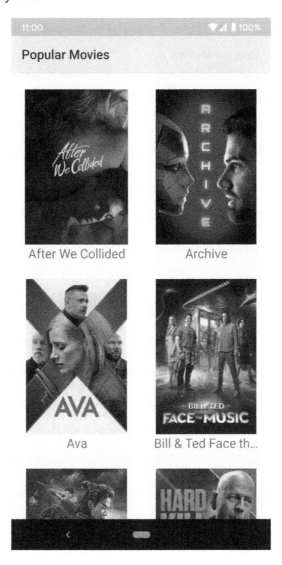

Figure 13.4: The app with the year's popular movies sorted by title

8. Before the **toList()** call, use the **map** operator to map the list of movies into another list whose title is in uppercase:

```
.map { it.copy(title = it.title.toUpperCase(Locale.getDefault())) }
```

9. Run the application. You will see that the movie titles are now in uppercase letters:

Figure 13.5: The app with the movie titles in uppercase

10. Before the **toList()** call, use the **take** operator to only get the first four movies from the list:

```
.take(4)
```

11. Run the application. You will see that the RecyclerView will only show four movies:

Figure 13.6: The app with only four movies

12. Try other RxJava operators and run the application to see the results.

You have learned how to use RxJava operators to manipulate the retrieved response from an external API before displaying them in the RecyclerView.

In the next section, you will learn how to use coroutines instead of RxJava to get data from an external API.

COROUTINES

Coroutines were added in Kotlin 1.3 for managing background tasks such as making network calls and accessing files or databases. Kotlin coroutines are Google's official recommendation for asynchronous programming on Android. Their Jetpack libraries, such as LifeCycle, WorkManager, and Room, now include support for coroutines.

With coroutines, you can write your code in a sequential way. The long-running task can be made into a suspending function, which when called can pause the thread without blocking it. When the suspending function is done, the current thread will resume execution. This will make your code easier to read and debug.

To mark a function as a suspending function, you can add the **suspend** keyword to it; for example, if you have a function that calls the **getMovies** function, which fetches **movies** from your endpoint and then displays it:

```
val movies = getMovies()
displayMovies(movies)
```

You can make the **getMovies()** function a suspending function by adding the **suspend** keyword:

```
suspend fun getMovies(): List<Movies> { ... }
```

Here, the calling function will invoke **getMovies** and pause. After **getMovies** returns a list of movies, it will resume its task and display the movies.

Suspending functions can only be called in suspending functions or from a coroutine. Coroutines have a context, which includes the coroutine dispatcher. Dispatchers specify what thread the coroutine will use. There are three dispatchers you can use:

- **Dispatchers.Main**: Used to run on Android's main thread
- **Dispatchers.IO**: Used for network, file, or database operations
- **Dispatchers.Default**: Used for CPU-intensive work

To change the context for your coroutine, you can use the **withContext** function for the code that you want to use a different thread with. For example, in your suspending function, **getMovies**, which gets movies from your endpoint, you can use **Dispatchers.IO**:

```
suspend fun getMovies(): List<Movies>  {
    withContext(Dispatchers.IO) { ... }
}
```

In the next section, we will cover how to create coroutines.

CREATING COROUTINES

You can create a coroutine with the **async** and **launch** keywords. The **launch** keyword creates a coroutine and doesn't return anything. On the other hand, the **async** keyword returns a value that you can get later with the **await** function.

async and **launch** must be created from **CoroutineScope**, which defines the lifecycle of the coroutine. For example, the coroutine scope for the main thread is **MainScope**. You can then create coroutines with the following:

```
MainScope().async { ... }
MainScope().launch { ... }
```

You can also create your own **CoroutineScope** instead of using **MainScope** by creating one with **CoroutineScope** and passing in the context for the coroutine. For example, to create **CoroutineScope** for use on a network call, you can define the following:

```
val scope = CoroutineScope(Dispatchers.IO)
```

The coroutine can be canceled when the function is no longer needed, like when you close the activity. You can do that by calling the **cancel** function from **CoroutineScope**:

```
scope.cancel()
```

A ViewModel also has a default **CoroutineScope** for creating coroutines: **viewModelScope**. Jetpack's LifeCycle also has the **lifecycleScope** that you can use. **viewModelScope** is canceled when the ViewModel has been destroyed; **lifecycleScope** is also canceled when the lifecycle is destroyed. Thus, you no longer need to cancel them.

In the next section, you will be learning how to add coroutines to your project.

ADDING COROUTINES TO YOUR PROJECT

You can add coroutines to your project by adding the following code to your **app/build.gradle** file dependencies:

```
implementation "org.jetbrains.kotlinx:kotlinx-coroutines-core:1.3.9"
implementation "org.jetbrains.kotlinx:kotlinx-coroutines-android:1.3.9"
```

kotlinx-coroutines-core is the main library for coroutines while **kotlinx-coroutines-android** adds support for the main Android thread.

You can add coroutines in Android when making a network call or fetching data from a local database.

If you're using Retrofit 2.6.0 or above, you can mark the endpoint function as a suspending function with **suspend**:

```
@GET("movie/latest")
suspend fun getMovies() : List<Movies>
```

Then, you can create a coroutine that will call the suspending function **getMovies** and display the list:

```
CoroutineScope(Dispatchers.IO).launch {
    val movies = movieService.getMovies()
    withContext(Dispatchers.Main) {
        displayMovies(movies)
    }
}
```

You can also use LiveData for the response of your coroutines. LiveData is a Jetpack class that can hold observable data. You can add LiveData to your Android project by adding the following dependency:

```
implementation 'androidx.lifecycle:lifecycle-livedata-ktx:2.2.0'
```

Let's try to use coroutines in an Android project.

EXERCISE 13.03: USING COROUTINES IN AN ANDROID APP

In this exercise, you will be using coroutines to fetch the list of popular movies from The Movie Database API. You can use the **Popular Movies** project in the previous exercise or make a copy of it:

1. Open the **Popular Movies** project in Android Studio.

2. Open the **app/build.gradle** file and remove the following dependencies:

```
implementation 'com.squareup.retrofit2:adapter-rxjava3:2.9.0'
implementation 'io.reactivex.rxjava3:rxandroid:3.0.0'
implementation 'io.reactivex.rxjava3:rxjava:3.0.7'
```

These dependencies will no longer be needed as you will be using coroutines instead of RxJava.

3. In the **app/build.gradle** file, add the dependencies for the Kotlin coroutines:

```
implementation 'org.jetbrains.kotlinx:kotlinx-coroutines-core:1.3.9'
implementation 'org.jetbrains.kotlinx:kotlinx-coroutines-android:1.3.9'
```

These will allow you to use coroutines in your project.

4. Also, add the dependencies for the ViewModel and LiveData extension libraries:

```
implementation 'androidx.lifecycle:lifecycle-livedata-ktx:2.2.0'
implementation 'androidx.lifecycle:lifecycle-viewmodel-ktx:2.2.0'
```

5. Open the **MovieService** interface and replace it with the following code:

```
interface MovieService {

    @GET("movie/popular")
    suspend fun getPopularMovies(@Query("api_key") apiKey: String):
      PopularMoviesResponse
}
```

This will mark **getPopularMovies** as a suspending function.

6. Open **MovieRepository** and add the movies and error LiveData for the list of movies:

```
private val movieLiveData = MutableLiveData<List<Movie>>()
private val errorLiveData = MutableLiveData<String>()

val movies: LiveData<List<Movie>>
    get() = movieLiveData
val error: LiveData<String>
    get() = errorLiveData
```

7. Replace the **fetchMovies** function with a suspending function to retrieve the list from the endpoint:

```
suspend fun fetchMovies() {
    try {
        val popularMovies = movieService.getPopularMovies(apiKey)
        movieLiveData.postValue(popularMovies.results)
    } catch (exception: Exception) {
```

```
                errorLiveData.postValue("An error occurred:
                    ${exception.message}")
        }
    }
```

8. Update the contents of **MovieViewModel** with the following code:

```
init {
    fetchPopularMovies()
}

val popularMovies: LiveData<List<Movie>>
get() = movieRepository.movies

fun getError(): LiveData<String> = movieRepository.error

private fun fetchPopularMovies() {
    viewModelScope.launch(Dispatchers.IO) {
        movieRepository.fetchMovies()
    }
}
```

The **fetchPopularMovies** function has a coroutine, using **viewModelScope**, that will fetch the movies from **movieRepository**.

9. Open the **MovieApplication** file. In the **onCreate** function, remove the line containing **addCallAdapterFactory**. It should look like this:

```
override fun onCreate() {
    super.onCreate()

    val retrofit = Retrofit.Builder()
        .baseUrl("https://api.themoviedb.org/3/")
        .addConverterFactory(MoshiConverterFactory.create())
        .build()

    ...
}
```

10. Open the **MainActivity** class. Delete the **getMovies** function.

11. In the **onCreate** function, remove the call to **getMovies**. Then, at the end of the **onCreate** function, create **movieViewModel**:

```
val movieRepository =
  (application as MovieApplication).movieRepository
val movieViewModel =
  ViewModelProvider(this, object: ViewModelProvider.Factory {
    override fun <T : ViewModel?>
      create(modelClass: Class<T>): T {
        return MovieViewModel(movieRepository) as T
      }

  }
}).get(MovieViewModel::class.java)
```

12. After that, add an observer to the **getPopularMovies** and **error** LiveData from **movieViewModel**:

```
        movieViewModel.popularMovies.observe(this, { popularMovies ->
            movieAdapter.addMovies(popularMovies
                .filter {
                    it.release_date.startsWith(
                        Calendar.getInstance().get(Calendar.YEAR)
                            .toString()
                    )
                }
                .sortedBy { it.title }
            )
        })
        movieViewModel.getError().observe(this, { error ->
            Toast.makeText(this, error, Toast.LENGTH_LONG).show()
})
```

This will update the activity's RecyclerView with the movies fetched. The list of movies is filtered using Kotlin's **filter** function to only include movies released this year. They are then sorted by title using Kotlin's **sortedBy** function.

13. Run the application. You will see that the app will display a list of popular movie titles from the current year, sorted by title:

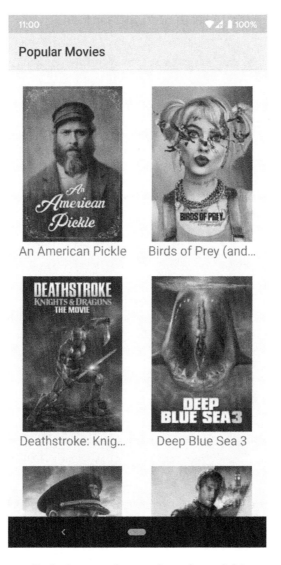

Figure 13.7: The app displaying popular movies released this year, sorted by title

You have used coroutines and LiveData to retrieve and display a list of popular movies from a remote data source without blocking the main thread.

Before passing the LiveData into the UI for display, you can also transform the data first. You will learn about that in the next section.

TRANSFORMING LIVEDATA

Sometimes, the LiveData you pass from the ViewModel to the UI layer needs to be processed first before displaying. For example, you can only select a part of the data or do some processing on it first. In the previous exercise, you filtered the data to only select popular movies from the current year.

To modify LiveData, you can use the **Transformations** class. It has two functions, **Transformations.map** and **Transformations.switchMap**, that you can use.

Transformations.map modifies the value of LiveData into another value. This can be used for tasks like filtering, sorting, or formatting the data. For example, you can transform **movieLiveData** into string LiveData from the movie's title:

```
private val movieLiveData: LiveData<Movie>
val movieTitleLiveData : LiveData<String> =
    Transformations.map(movieLiveData) { it.title }
```

When **movieLiveData** changes value, **movieTitleLiveData** will also change based on the movie's title.

With **Transformations.switchMap**, you can transform the value of a LiveData into another LiveData. This is used when you want to do a specific task involving a database or network operation with the original LiveData. For example, if you have a LiveData representing a movie **id** object, you can transform that to movie LiveData by applying the function **getMovieDetails**, which returns LiveData of movie details from the **id** object (such as from another network or database call):

```
private val idLiveData: LiveData<Int> = MutableLiveData()
val movieLiveData : LiveData<Movie> =
    Transformations.switchMap(idLiveData) { getMovieDetails(it) }

fun getMovieDetails(id: Int) : LiveData<Movie> = { ... }
```

Let's use LiveData transformations on the list of movies fetched using coroutines.

EXERCISE 13.04: LIVEDATA TRANSFORMATIONS

In this exercise, you will be transforming the LiveData list of movies before passing them to the observers in the **MainActivity** file:

1. In Android Studio, open the **Popular Movies** project you worked on in the previous exercise.

2. Open the **MainActivity** file. In the **movieViewModel.popularMovies** observer in the·**onCreate** function, remove the filter and **sortedBy** function calls. The code should look like the following:

```
movieViewModel.getPopularMovies().observe(this,
  Observer { popularMovies ->
    movieAdapter.addMovies(popularMovies)
})
```

This will now display all movies in the list without them being sorted by title.

3. Run the application. You should see all movies (even those from the past year), not sorted by title:

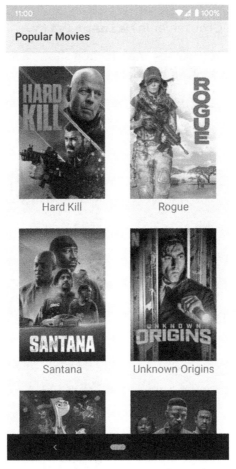

Figure 13.8: The app with unsorted popular movies

4. Open the **MovieViewModel** class and update **popularMovies** with LiveData transformations to filter and sort the movies:

```
val popularMovies: LiveData<List<Movie>>
get() = movieRepository.movies.map { list ->
list.filter {
    val cal = Calendar.getInstance()
    cal.add(Calendar.MONTH, -1)
    it.release_date.startsWith(
        "${cal.get(Calendar.YEAR)}-${cal.get(Calendar.MONTH)
        + 1}"
    )
}.sortedBy { it.title }
}
```

This will select the movies released last month and sort them by title before passing them to the UI observer in **MainActivity**.

5. Run the application. You will see that the app shows a list of popular movies from the current year, sorted by title:

Figure 13.9: The app with the movies released this year sorted by title

You have used LiveData transformations to modify the list of movies to select only the ones released this year. They were also sorted by title before passing them to the observers in the UI layer.

COROUTINES CHANNELS AND FLOWS

If your coroutine is fetching a stream of data or you have multiple data sources and you process the data one by one, you can use either Channel or Flow.

Channels allow you to pass data between different coroutines. They are a hot stream of data. It will run and emit values the moment they are called, even when there's no listeners. Flows, meanwhile, are cold asynchronous streams. They only emit values when the values are collected.

To learn more about Channels and Flows, you can go to https://kotlinlang.org.

RXJAVA VERSUS COROUTINES

Both RxJava and coroutines can be used for doing background tasks in Android, such as network calls or database operations.

Which one should you use then? While you can use both in your application, for example, RxJava for one task and coroutines for another, you can also use them together with **LiveDataReactiveStreams** or **kotlinx-coroutines-rx3**. This, however, will increase the number of dependencies you use and the size of your application.

So, RxJava or coroutines? The following table shows the differences between the two:

RxJava	Coroutines
Popular with Android developers, especially those who use reactive programming.	Google's official recommendation for asynchronous programming. Jetpack libraries already support it and their new ones are being built with it.
Has a lot of operators for modifying data from the observer.	Uses Kotlin's built-in functions for modifying data response.
Can increase the size of your application.	Lightweight.
Code is callback-based; can be complicated and harder to read.	Code is written sequentially, simpler and easier to read and debug.
The learning curve can be steep, especially if you're new to reactive programming.	Uses standard Kotlin so it's easier to learn.
Ideal to use if your project is already using RxJava or reactive programming.	Ideal to use if you are using 100% Kotlin code.

Figure 13.10: Differences between coroutines and RxJava

Let's move on to the next activity.

ACTIVITY 13.01: CREATING A TV GUIDE APP

A lot of people watch television. Most of the time, though, they are not sure what TV shows are currently on the air. Suppose you wanted to develop an app that can display a list of these shows from The Movie Database API's **tv/on_the_air** endpoint using Kotlin coroutines and LiveData.

The app will have two screens: the main screen and the details screen. On the main screen, you will display a list of the TV shows that are on the air. The TV shows will be sorted by name. Clicking on a TV show will open the details screen, which displays more information about the selected TV show.

Steps for completion:

1. Create a new project in Android Studio and name it **TV Guide**. Set its package name.

2. Add the **INTERNET** permission in the **AndroidManifest.xml** file.

3. Add the Java 8 compatibility and the dependencies for the RecyclerView, Glide, Retrofit, RxJava, RxAndroid, Moshi, ViewModel, and LiveData libraries in your **app/build.gradle** file.

4. Add a **layout_margin** dimension value.

5. Create a **view_tv_show_item.xml** layout file with **ImageView** for the poster and **TextView** for the name of the TV show.

6. In the **activity_main.xml** file, remove the Hello World TextView and add a RecyclerView for the list of TV shows.

7. Create a model class, **TVShow**.

8. Create a new activity named **DetailsActivity** with **activity_details.xml** as the layout file.

9. Open the **AndroidManifest.xml** file and add the **parentActivityName** attribute in the **DetailsActivity** declaration.

10. In **activity_details.xml**, add the views for the details of the TV show.

11. In **DetailsActivity**, add the code for displaying the details of the TV show selected.

12. Create a **TVShowAdapter** adapter class for the list of TV shows.

13. Create another class named **TVResponse** for the response you get from the API endpoint for the TV shows on air.

14. Create a **TelevisionService** class for adding the Retrofit method.

15. Create a **TVShowRepository** class with a constructor for **tvService**, and properties for **apiKey** and **tvShows**.

16. Create a suspending function to retrieve the list of TV shows from the endpoint.

17. Create a **TVShowViewModel** class with a constructor for **TVShowRepository**. Add a **getTVShows** function that returns the LiveData for the list of TV shows and **fetchTVShows** that fetches the list from the repository.

18. Create an application class named **TVApplication** with a property for **TVShowRepository**.

19. Set **TVApplication** as the value for the application in the **AndroidManifest.xml** file.

20. Open **MainActivity** and add the code to update the RecyclerView when the LiveData from **ViewModel** updates its value. Add a function that will open the details screen when clicking on a TV show from the list.

21. Run your application. The app will display a list of TV shows. Clicking on a TV show will open the details activity, which displays the show details. The main screen and details screen will be similar to the following figure:

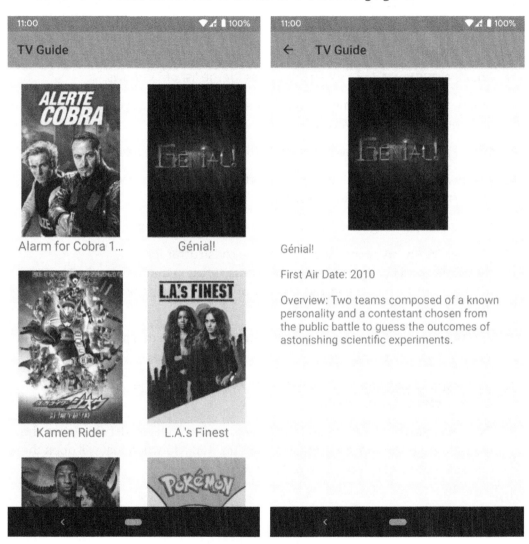

Figure 13.11: The main screen and details screen of the TV Guide app

NOTE

The solution to this activity can be found at: http://packt.live/3sKj1cp

SUMMARY

This chapter focused on doing background operations with RxJava and coroutines. Background operations are used for long-running tasks such as accessing data from the local database or a remote server.

You started with the basics of RxJava: observables, observers, and operators. Observables are the data sources that provide data. The observers listen to observables; when an observable emits data, observers can react accordingly. Operators allow you to modify data from an observable to the data you need before it can be passed to the observers.

Next, you learned how to make RxJava calls asynchronous with schedulers. Schedulers allow you to set the thread through which the required action will be done. The **subscribeOn** function is used for setting which thread your observable will run on, and the **observeOn** function allows you to set where the next operators will be executed. You then fetched data from an external API with RxJava and used RxJava operators to filter, sort, and make modifications to the data.

Next, you learned about using Kotlin coroutines, which is Google's recommended solution for asynchronous programming. You can make a background task into a suspending function with the **suspend** keyword. Coroutines can be started with the **async** or **launch** keywords.

You've learned how to create suspending functions and how to start coroutines. You also used dispatchers to change the thread where a coroutine runs. Finally, you used coroutines for doing network calls and modified the data retrieved with the LiveData transformation functions **map** and **switchMap**.

In the next chapter, you will learn about architecture patterns. You will learn about patterns such as **MVVM** (**Model-View-ViewModel**) and how you can improve the architecture of your app.

14

ARCHITECTURE PATTERNS

OVERVIEW

This chapter will introduce you to architectural patterns you can use for your Android projects. It covers using the **MVVM** (**Model-View-ViewModel**) pattern, adding ViewModels, and using data binding. You will also learn about using the Repository pattern for caching data and WorkManager for scheduling data retrieval and storage.

By the end of the chapter, you will be able to structure your Android project using MVVM and data binding. You will also be able to use the Repository pattern with Room library to cache data and WorkManager to fetch and save data at a scheduled interval.

INTRODUCTION

In the previous chapter, you learned about using RxJava and coroutines for doing background operations and data manipulation. Now, you will learn about architectural patterns so you can improve your application.

When developing an Android application, you might tend to write most of the code (including business logic) in activities or fragments. This would make your project hard to test and maintain later. As your project grows and becomes more complex, the difficulty will increase too. You can improve your projects with architectural patterns.

Architectural patterns are general solutions for designing and developing parts of applications, especially for large apps. There are architectural patterns you can use to structure your project into different layers (the presentation layer, the **user interface** (**UI**) layer, and the data layer) or functions (observer/observable). With architectural patterns, you can organize your code in a way that makes it easier for you to develop, test, and maintain.

For Android development, commonly used patterns include **MVC (Model-View-Controller)**, **MVP (Model-View-Presenter)**, and MVVM. Google's recommended architectural pattern is MVVM, which will be discussed in this chapter. You will also learn about data binding, the Repository pattern using Room library, and WorkManager.

Let's get started with the MVVM architectural pattern.

MVVM

MVVM allows you to separate the UI and business logic. When you need to redesign the UI or update the Model/business logic, you only need to touch the relevant component without affecting the other components of your app. This will make it easier for you to add new features and test your existing code. MVVM is also useful in creating huge applications that use a lot of data and views.

With the MVVM architectural pattern, your application will be grouped into three components:

- **Model**: Represents the data layer

- **View**: The UI that displays the data

- **ViewModel**: Fetches data from the `Model` and provides it to the `View`

The MVVM architectural pattern can be understood better through the following diagram:

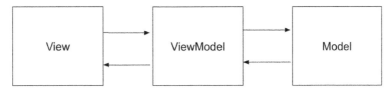

Figure 14.1: The MVVM architectural pattern

The Model contains the data and the business logic of the application. The activities, fragments, and layouts that your users see and interact are the Views in MVVM. Views only deal with how the app looks. They let the ViewModel know about user actions (such as opening an activity or clicking on a button).

The ViewModel links the View and the Model. ViewModels get the data from the Model and transform them for display in the View. Views subscribe to the ViewModel and update the UI when a value changes.

You can use Jetpack's ViewModel to create the ViewModel classes for your app. Jetpack's ViewModel manages its own life cycle so you don't need to handle it yourself.

You can add a ViewModel to your project by adding the following code in your **app/build.gradle** file dependencies:

```
implementation 'androidx.lifecycle:lifecycle-viewmodel-ktx:2.2.0'
```

For example, if you're working on an app that displays movies, you could have a **MovieViewModel**. This ViewModel will have a function that will fetch a list of movies:

```
class MovieViewModel : ViewModel() {

    private val movies: MutableLiveData<List<Movie>>
    fun getMovies(): LiveData<List<Movie>> { ... }
    ...
}
```

In your activity, you can create a ViewModel using **ViewModelProvider**:

```
class MainActivity : AppCompatActivity() {

    private val movieViewModel by lazy {
        ViewModelProvider(this).get(MovieViewModel::class.java)
    }


    ...
}
```

Then, you can subscribe to the **getMovies** function from the ViewModel and automatically update the list in the UI when the list of movies changes:

```
override fun onCreate(savedInstanceState: Bundle?) {
    ...
    movieViewModel.getMovies().observe(this, Observer { popularMovies ->
        movieAdapter.addMovies(popularMovies)
    })
    ...
}
```

Views are notified when values in the ViewModel have changed. You can also use data binding to connect the View with the data from the ViewModel. You will learn more about data binding in the next section.

DATA BINDING

Data binding links the views in your layout to data from a source such as a ViewModel. Instead of adding code to find the views in the layout file and updating them when the value from the ViewModel changes, data binding can handle that for you automatically.

To use data binding in your Android project, you should add the following in the **android** block of the **app/build.gradle** file:

```
buildFeatures {
    dataBinding true
}
```

In the layout file, you must wrap the root element with a layout tag. Inside the layout tag, you need to define the **data** element for the data to be bound to this layout file:

```
<layout xmlns:android="http://schemas.android.com/apk/res/android">
    <data>
        <variable name="movie" type="com.example.model.Movie"/>
    </data>

    <ConstraintLayout ... />
</layout>
```

The movie layout variable represents the **com.example.model.Movie** class that will be displayed in the layout. To set the attribute to fields in the data model, you need to use the **@{}** syntax. For example, to use the movie's title as the text value of the **TextView**, you can use the following:

```
<TextView
    ...
    android:text="@{movie.title}"/>
```

You also need to change your activity file. If your layout file is named **activity_ movies.xml**, the data binding library will generate a binding class named **ActivityMainBinding** in your project's build files. In the activity, you can replace the line **setContentView(R.layout.activity_movies)** with the following:

```
val binding: ActivityMoviesBinding = DataBindingUtil.setContentView(this,
  R.layout.activity_movies)
```

You can also use the **inflate** method of the binding class or the **DataBindingUtil** class:

```
val binding: ActivityMoviesBinding =
  ActivityMoviesBinding.inflate(getLayoutInflater())
```

Then, you can set the **movie** instance to bind in the layout with the layout variable named **movie**:

```
val movieToDisplay = ...
binding.movie = movieToDisplay
```

If you are using **LiveData** as the item to bind to the layout, you need to set **lifeCycleOwner** of the binding variable. **lifeCycleOwner** specifies the scope of the **LiveData** object. You can use the activity as **lifeCycleOwner** of the binding class:

```
binding.lifeCycleOwner = this
```

With this, when the values of **LiveData** in the ViewModel change their value, the View will automatically update with the new values.

You set the movie title in the TextView with **android:text="@{movie.title}"**. The data binding library has default binding adapters that handle the binding to the **android:text** attribute. Sometimes, there are no default attributes that you can use. You can create your own binding adapter. For example, if you want to bind the list of movies for **RecyclerView**, you can create a custom **BindingAdapter** call:

```
@BindingAdapter("list")
fun bindMovies(view: RecyclerView, movies: List<Movie>?) {
    val adapter = view.adapter as MovieAdapter
    adapter.addMovies(movies ?: emptyList())
}
```

This will allow you to add an **app:list** attribute to **RecyclerView** that accepts a list of movies:

```
app:list="@{movies}"
```

Let's try implementing data binding on an Android project.

EXERCISE 14.01: USING DATA BINDING IN AN ANDROID PROJECT

In the previous chapter, you worked on an application that displays popular movies using the Movie Database API. For this chapter, you will be improving the app using MVVM. You can use the Popular Movies project from the previous chapter or make a copy of it. In this exercise, you will be adding data binding to bind the list of movies from the ViewModel to the UI:

1. Open the **Popular Movies** project in Android Studio.

2. Open the **app/build.gradle** file and add the following in the **android** block:

```
buildFeatures {
    dataBinding true
}
```

This enables data binding for your application.

3. Add the **kotlin-kapt** plugin at the end of the plugins block in your **app/build.gradle** file:

```
plugins {
    ...
    id 'kotlin-kapt'
}
```

The kotlin-kapt plugin is the Kotlin annotation processing tool, which is needed for using Data Binding.

4. Create a new file called **RecyclerViewBinding** that contains the binding adapter for the **RecyclerView** list:

```
@BindingAdapter("list")
fun bindMovies(view: RecyclerView, movies: List<Movie>?) {
    val adapter = view.adapter as MovieAdapter
    adapter.addMovies(movies ?: emptyList())
}
```

This will allow you to add an **app:list** attribute for **RecyclerView** where you can pass the list of movies to be displayed. The list of movies will be set to the adapter, updating the **RecyclerView** in the UI.

5. Open the **activity_main.xml** file and wrap everything inside a **layout** tag:

```
<layout xmlns:android="http://schemas.android.com/apk/res/android"
    xmlns:app="http://schemas.android.com/apk/res-auto"
    xmlns:tools="http://schemas.android.com/tools">

    <androidx.constraintlayout.widget.ConstraintLayout
        ... >
    </androidx.constraintlayout.widget.ConstraintLayout>
</layout>
```

With this, the data binding library will be able to generate a binding class for this layout.

6. Inside the **layout** tag and before the **ConstraintLayout** tag, add a data element with a variable for the **viewModel**:

```
<data>
    <variable
        name="viewModel"
        type="com.example.popularmovies.MovieViewModel" />
</data>
```

This creates a **viewModel** layout variable that corresponds to your **MovieViewModel** class.

7. In **RecyclerView**, add the list to be displayed with **app:list**:

```
app:list="@{viewModel.popularMovies}"
```

The **LiveData** from **MovieViewModel.getPopularMovies** will be passed as the list of movies for **RecyclerView**.

8. Open **MainActivity**. In the **onCreate** function, replace the **setContentView** line with the following:

```
val binding: ActivityMainBinding =
    DataBindingUtil.setContentView(this, R.layout.activity_main)
```

This sets the layout file to be used and creates a binding object.

9. Replace the **movieViewModel** observer with the following:

```
binding.viewModel = movieViewModel
binding.lifecycleOwner = this
```

This binds **movieViewModel** to the **viewModel** layout variable in the **activity_main.xml** file.

10. Run the application. It should work as usual, displaying the list of popular movies where clicking on one will open the details of the movie selected:

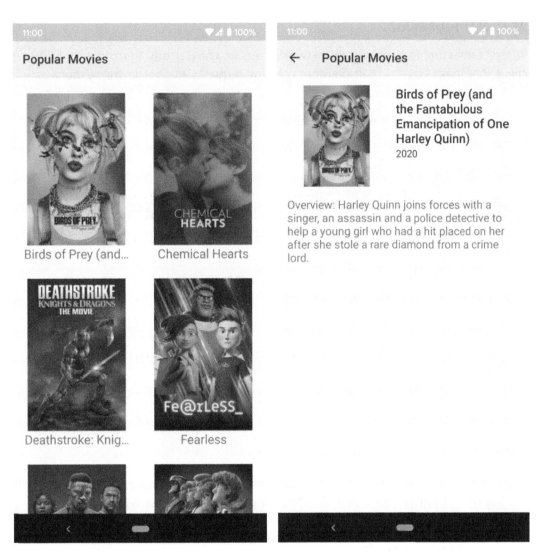

Figure 14.2: The main screen (left) with the year's popular movies sorted by title and the details screen (right) with more information about the selected movie

In this exercise, you have used data binding on an Android project.

Data binding links the Views to the ViewModel. The ViewModel retrieves the data from the Model. Some of the libraries you can use to fetch data are Retrofit and Moshi, which you will learn more about in the next section.

RETROFIT AND MOSHI

When connecting to your remote network, you can use Retrofit. Retrofit is an HTTP client that makes it easy to implement creating requests and retrieving responses from your backend server.

You can add Retrofit to your project by adding the following code in your **app/ build.gradle** file dependencies:

```
implementation 'com.squareup.retrofit2:retrofit:2.9.0'
```

You can then convert the JSON response from Retrofit by using Moshi, a library for parsing JSON into Java objects. For example, you can convert the JSON string response from getting the list of movies into a **ListofMovie** object for display and storage in your app.

You can add the Moshi Converter to your project by adding the following code to your **app/build.gradle** file dependencies:

```
implementation 'com.squareup.retrofit2:converter-moshi:2.9.0'
```

In your Retrofit builder code, you can call **addConverterFactory** and pass **MoshiConverterFactory**:

```
Retrofit.Builder()
    ...
    .addConverterFactory(MoshiConverterFactory.create())
    ...
```

You can call the data layer from the ViewModel. To reduce its complexity, you can use the Repository pattern for loading and caching data. You will learn about this in the next section.

THE REPOSITORY PATTERN

Instead of the ViewModel directly calling the services for getting and storing data, it should delegate that task to another component, such as a repository.

With the Repository pattern, you can move the code in the ViewModel that handles the data layer into a separate class. This reduces the complexity of the ViewModel, making it easier to maintain and test. The repository will manage where the data is fetched and stored, just as if the local database or the network service were used to get or store data:

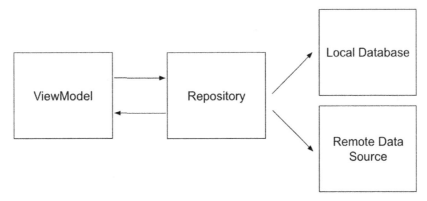

Figure 14.3: ViewModel with the Repository pattern

In your ViewModel, you can add a property for the repository:

```
class MovieViewModel(val repository: MovieRepository): ViewModel() {
    ...
}
```

The ViewModel will get the movies from the repository, or it can listen to them. It will not know where you actually got the list from.

You can create a repository interface that connects to a data source, such as in the following example:

```
interface MovieRepository {
    fun getMovies(): List<Movie>
}
```

The **MovieRepository** interface has a **getMovies** function that your repository implementation class will override to fetch movies from the data source. You can also have a single repository class that handles the fetching of data from either the local database or from your remote endpoint.

When using the local database as the data source for your repository, you can use the Room library, which makes it easier for you to work with the SQLite database by writing less code and having compile-time checks on queries.

You can add Room to your project by adding the following code to your **app/build. gradle** file dependencies:

```
implementation 'androidx.room:room-runtime:2.2.5'
implementation 'androidx.room:room-ktx:2.2.5'
kapt 'androidx.room:room-compiler:2.2.5'
```

Let's try adding the Repository pattern with Room to an Android project.

EXERCISE 14.02: USING REPOSITORY WITH ROOM IN AN ANDROID PROJECT

You have added data binding in the Popular Movies project in the previous exercise. In this exercise, you will update the app with the Repository pattern.

When opening the app, it fetches the list of movies from the network. This takes a while. You will be caching this data into the local database every time you fetch them. When the user opens the app next time, the app will immediately display the list of movies from the database on the screen. You will be using Room for data caching:

1. Open the **Popular Movies** project that you used in the previous exercise.

2. Open the **app/build.gradle** file and add the dependencies for the Room library:

```
implementation 'androidx.room:room-runtime:2.2.5'
implementation 'androidx.room:room-ktx:2.2.5'
kapt 'androidx.room:room-compiler:2.2.5'
```

3. Open the **Movie** class and add an **Entity** annotation for it:

```
@Entity(tableName = "movies", primaryKeys = [("id")])
data class Movie( ... )
```

The **Entity** annotation will create a table named **movies** for the list of movies. It also sets **id** as the primary key of the table.

4. Make a new package called **com.example.popularmovies.database**. Create a **MovieDao** data access object for accessing the **movies** table:

```
@Dao
interface MovieDao {
@Insert(onConflict = OnConflictStrategy.REPLACE)
fun addMovies(movies: List<Movie>)

@Query("SELECT * FROM movies")
fun getMovies(): List<Movie>
}
```

This class contains a function for adding a list of movies in the database and another for getting all the movies from the database.

5. Create a **MovieDatabase** class in the **com.example.popularmovies. database** package:

```
@Database(entities = [Movie::class], version = 1)
abstract class MovieDatabase : RoomDatabase() {

    abstract fun movieDao(): MovieDao

    companion object {
        @Volatile
        private var instance: MovieDatabase? = null
        fun getInstance(context: Context): MovieDatabase {
            return instance ?: synchronized(this) {
                instance ?: buildDatabase(context).also {
                    instance = it
                }
            }
        }

        private fun buildDatabase(context: Context): MovieDatabase {
            return Room.databaseBuilder(context,
                MovieDatabase::class.java, "movie-db")
                .build()
        }
    }
}
```

This database has a version of 1, a single entity for **Movie**, and the data access object for the movies. It also has a **getInstance** function to generate an instance of the database.

6. Update the **MovieRepository** class with constructors for **movieDatabase**:

```
class MovieRepository(private val movieService: MovieService,
    private val movieDatabase: MovieDatabase) { ... }
```

7. Update the **fetchMovies** function:

```
suspend fun fetchMovies() {
    val movieDao: MovieDao = movieDatabase.movieDao()
    var moviesFetched = movieDao.getMovies()
    if (moviesFetched.isEmpty()) {
        try {
            val popularMovies = movieService.getPopularMovies(apiKey)
            moviesFetched = popularMovies.results
            movieDao.addMovies(moviesFetched)
        } catch (exception: Exception) {
            errorLiveData.postValue("An error occurred:
                ${exception.message}")
        }
    }

    movieLiveData.postValue(moviesFetched)
}
```

It will fetch the movies from the database. If there's nothing saved yet, it will retrieve the list from the network endpoint and then save it.

8. Open **MovieApplication** and in the **onCreate** function, replace the **movieRepository** initialization with the following:

```
val movieDatabase = MovieDatabase.getInstance(applicationContext)

movieRepository = MovieRepository(movieService, movieDatabase)
```

9. Run the application. It will display the list of popular movies, and clicking on one will open the details of the movie selected. If you turn off mobile data or disconnect from the wireless network, it will still display the list of movies, which is now cached in the database:

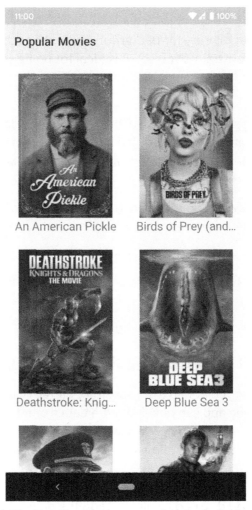

Figure 14.4: The Popular Movies app using Repository with Room

In this exercise, you have improved the app by moving the loading and storing of data into a repository. You have also used Room to cache the data.

The repository fetches the data from the data source. If there's no data stored in the database yet, the app will call the network to request the data. This can take a while. You can improve the user experience by pre-fetching data at a scheduled time so the next time the user opens the app, they will already see the updated contents. You can do this with WorkManager, which we will discuss in the next section.

WORKMANAGER

WorkManager is a Jetpack library for background operations that can be delayed and can run based on the constraints you set. It is ideal for doing something that must be run but can be done later or at regular intervals, regardless of whether the app is running or not.

You can use WorkManager to run tasks such as fetching the data from the network and storing it in your database at scheduled intervals. WorkManager will run the task even if the app has been closed or if the device restarts. This will keep your database up to date with your backend.

You can add WorkManager to your project by adding the following code to your **app/build.gradle** file dependencies:

```
implementation 'androidx.work:work-runtime:2.4.0'
```

WorkManager can call the repository to fetch and store data from either the local database or the network server.

Let's try adding WorkManager to an Android project.

EXERCISE 14.03: ADDING WORKMANAGER TO AN ANDROID PROJECT

In the previous exercise, you added the Repository pattern with Room to cache data in the local database. The app can now fetch the data from the database instead of the network. Now, you will be adding WorkManager to schedule a task for fetching data from the server and saving it to the database at scheduled intervals:

1. Open the **Popular Movies** project you used in the previous exercise.

2. Open the **app/build.gradle** file and add the dependency for the WorkManager library:

```
implementation 'androidx.work:work-runtime:2.4.0'
```

This will allow you to add WorkManager workers to your app.

3. Open **MovieRepository** and add a suspending function for fetching movies from the network using the apiKey from The Movie Database, and saving them to the database:

```
suspend fun fetchMoviesFromNetwork() {
    val movieDao: MovieDao = movieDatabase.movieDao()
    try {
        val popularMovies = movieService.getPopularMovies(apiKey)
```

```
        val moviesFetched = popularMovies.results
        movieDao.addMovies(moviesFetched)
    } catch (exception: Exception) {
        errorLiveData.postValue("An error occurred:
          ${exception.message}")
    }
}
```

This will be the function that will be called by the **Worker** class that will be running to fetch and save the movies.

4. Create the **MovieWorker** class:

```
class MovieWorker(private val context: Context,
  params: WorkerParameters) : Worker(context, params) {
    override fun doWork(): Result {
        val movieRepository =
            (context as MovieApplication).movieRepository
        CoroutineScope(Dispatchers.IO).launch {
            movieRepository.fetchMoviesFromNetwork()
        }
        return Result.success()
    }
}
```

5. Open **MovieApplication** and at the end of the **onCreate** function, schedule **MovieWorker** to retrieve and save the movies:

```
override fun onCreate() {
    ...

    val constraints =
        Constraints.Builder().setRequiredNetworkType(
          NetworkType.CONNECTED).build()
    val workRequest = PeriodicWorkRequest
        .Builder(MovieWorker::class.java, 1, TimeUnit.HOURS)
        .setConstraints(constraints)
        .addTag("movie-work")
        .build()
    WorkManager.getInstance(applicationContext).enqueue(workRequest)
}
```

This schedules **MovieWorker** to run every hour when the device is connected to the network. **MovieWorker** will fetch the list of movies from the network and save it to the local database.

6. Run the application. Close it and make sure the device is connected to the internet. After more than an hour, open the application again and check whether the list of movies displayed has been updated. If not, try again in a few hours. The list of movies displayed will be updated regularly, around every hour, even if the app has been closed.

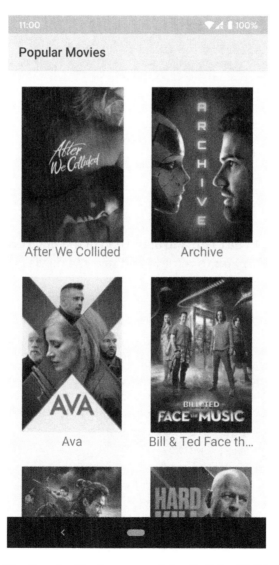

Figure 14.5: The Popular Movies app updates its list with WorkManager

In this exercise, you added WorkManager to your application to automatically update the database with the list of the movies retrieved from the network.

ACTIVITY 14.01: REVISITING THE TV GUIDE APP

In the previous chapter, you developed an app that can display a list of TV shows that are on the air. The app had two screens: the main screen and the details screen. On the main screen, there's a list of TV shows. When clicking on a TV show, the details screen will be displayed with the details of the selected show.

When running the app, it takes a while to display the list of shows. Update the app to cache the list so it will be immediately displayed when opening the app. Also, improve the app by using MVVM with data binding and adding a WorkManager.

You can use the TV Guide app you worked on in the previous chapter or download it from the GitHub repository. The following steps will help guide you through this activity:

1. Open the TV Guide app in Android Studio. Open the **app/build.gradle** file and add the **kotlin-kapt** plugin, the data binding dependency, and the dependencies for Room and WorkManager.

2. Create a binding adapter class for **RecyclerView**.

3. In **activity_main.xml**, wrap everything inside a **layout** tag.

4. Inside the **layout** tag and before the **ConstraintLayout** tag, add a data element with a variable for the ViewModel.

5. In the **RecyclerView**, add the list to be displayed with **app:list**.

6. In **MainActivity**, replace the line for **setContentView** with the **DataBindingUtil.setContentView** function.

7. Replace the observer from **TVShowViewModel** with the data binding code.

8. Add an **Entity** annotation in the **TVShow** class.

9. Create a **TVDao** data access object for accessing the TV shows table.

10. Create a **TVDatabase** class.

11. Update **TVShowRepository** with a constructor for **tvDatabase**.

12. Update the **fetchTVShows** function to get the TV shows from the local database. If there's nothing there yet, retrieve the list from the endpoint and save it in the database.

13. Create the **TVShowWorker** class.

14. Open the **TVApplication** file. In **onCreate**, schedule **TVShowWorker** to retrieve and save the shows.

15. Run your application. The app will display a list of TV shows. Clicking on a TV show will open the details activity that displays the movie details. The main screen and details screen will be similar to *Figure 14.6*:

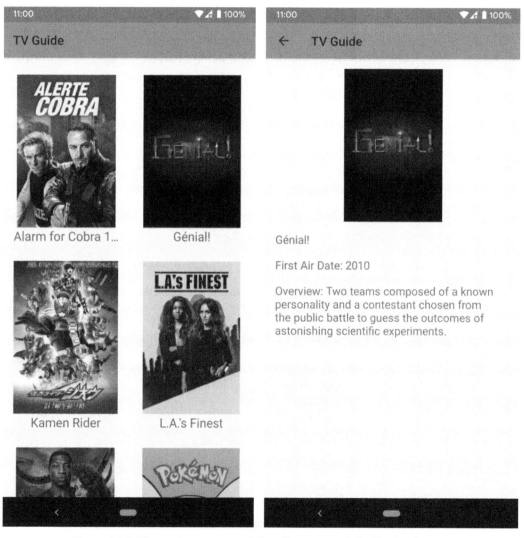

Figure 14.6: The main screen and details screen of the TV Guide app

> **NOTE**
>
> The solution to this activity can be found at: http://packt.live/3sKj1cp.

SUMMARY

This chapter focused on architectural patterns for Android. You started with the MVVM architectural pattern. You learned its three components: the Model, the View, and the ViewModel. You also used data binding to link the View with the ViewModel.

Next, you learned about how the Repository pattern can be used to cache data. Then, you learned about WorkManager and how you can schedule tasks such as retrieving data from the network and saving that data to the database to update your local data.

In the next chapter, you will be learning how to improve the look and design of your apps with animations. You will add animations and transitions to your apps with `CoordinatorLayout` and `MotionLayout`.

15

ANIMATIONS AND TRANSITIONS WITH COORDINATORLAYOUT AND MOTIONLAYOUT

OVERVIEW

This chapter will introduce you to animations and how to handle changing between layouts. It covers the description of moving objects using `MotionLayout` and the Motion Editor in Android, along with a detailed explanation of constraint sets. The chapter also covers modifying paths and adding keyframes for a frame's motion.

By the end of this chapter, you will be able to create animations using `CoordinatorLayout` and `MotionLayout` and use the Motion Editor in Android Studio to create `MotionLayout` animations.

INTRODUCTION

In the previous chapter, you learned about architecture patterns such as MVVM. You now know how to improve the architecture of an app. Next, we will learn how to use animations to enhance our app's look and feel and make it different and better than other apps.

Sometimes, the apps we develop can look a little plain. We can include some moving parts and delightful animations in our apps to make them more lively and to make the UI and user experience better. For example, we can add visual cues so that the user will not be confused about what to do next and can be guided through what steps they can take. Animations while loading can entertain the user while content is being fetched or processed. Pretty animations when the app encounters an error can help prevent users from getting angry about what has happened and can inform them of what options they have.

In this chapter, we'll start by looking at some of the traditional ways of doing animations with Android. We'll end the chapter by looking at the newer `MotionLayout` option. Let's get started with activity transitions, which are one of the easiest and most used animations.

ACTIVITY TRANSITIONS

When opening and closing an activity, Android will play a default transition. We can customize the activity transition to reflect the brand and/or differentiate our app. Activity transitions are available starting with Android 5.0 Lollipop (API level 21).

Activity transitions have two parts: the enter transition and the exit transition. The enter transition defines how the activity and its views will be animated when the activity is opened. The exit transition, meanwhile, describes how the activity and views are animated when the activity is closed or a new activity is opened. Android supports the following built-in transitions:

- **Explode**: This moves views in or out from the center.
- **Fade**: This view slowly appears or disappears.
- **Slide**: This moves views in or out from the edges.

Now, let's see how we can add activity transitions in the following section. There are two ways to add activity transitions: through XML and through code. First, we will learn how to add transitions via XML, and then via code.

ADDING ACTIVITY TRANSITIONS THROUGH XML

You can add activity transitions through XML. The first step is to enable window content transitions. This is done by adding the activity's theme in **themes.xml** the following:

```
<item name="android:windowActivityTransitions">true</item>
```

After that, you can then add the enter and exit transitions with the **android:windowEnterTransition** and **android:windowExitTransition** style attributes. For example, if you have want to use the default transitions from @ **android:transition/**, the attributes you will need to add are as follows:

```
<item name="android:windowEnterTransition">
  @android:transition/slide_left</item>
<item name="android:windowExitTransition">
  @android:@transition/explode</item>
```

Your **themes.xml** file would then look as follows:

```
    <style name="AppTheme"
      parent="Theme.AppCompat.Light.DarkActionBar">
      ...

      <item name="android:windowActivityTransitions">true</item>

      <item name="android:windowEnterTransition">
        @android:@transition/slide_left</item>
      <item name="android:windowExitTransition">
        @android:@transition/explode</item>
    </style>
```

Activity transitions are enabled with **<item name="android:windowActivityTransitions">true</item>**. The **<item name="android:windowEnterTransition">@android:transition/slide_left</item>** attribute sets the enter transition, while the @**android:@transition/explode** is the exit transition file, as set by the **<item name="android:windowExitTransition">@android:transition/explode</item>** attribute.

In the next section, you will learn how to add activity transitions through coding.

ADDING ACTIVITY TRANSITIONS THROUGH CODE

Activity transitions can also be added programmatically. The first step is to enable window content transitions. You can do that by calling the following function in your activity before the call to **setContentView()**:

```
window.requestFeature(Window.FEATURE_CONTENT_TRANSITIONS)
```

You can add the enter and exit transactions afterward with **window. enterTransition** and **window.exitTransition**, respectively. We can use the built-in **Explode()**, **Slide()**, and **Fade()** transitions from the **android. transition** package. For example, if we want to use **Explode()** as an enter transition and **Slide()** as an exit transition, we can add the following code:

```
window.enterTransition = Explode()
window.exitTransition = Slide()
```

Remember to wrap these calls with a check for **Build.VERSION.SDK_INT >= Build.VERSION_CODES.LOLLIPOP** if your app's minimum supported SDK is lower than 21.

Now that you know how to add entry and exit activity transitions through code or XML, you need to learn how to activate the transition when opening the activity. We will do that in the next section.

STARTING AN ACTIVITY WITH AN ACTIVITY TRANSITION

Once you have added activity transitions to an activity (either through XML or by coding), you can activate the transition when opening the activity. Instead of the **startActivity(intent)** call, you should pass in a bundle with the transition animation. To do that, start your activity with the following code:

```
startActivity(intent,ActivityOptions
    .makeSceneTransitionAnimation(this).toBundle())
```

The `ActivityOptions.makeSceneTransitionAnimation(this).` `toBundle()` argument will create a bundle with the enter and exit transition we specified for the activity (via XML or with code).

Let's try out what we have learned so far by adding activity transitions to an app.

EXERCISE 15.01: CREATING ACTIVITY TRANSITIONS IN AN APP

In many establishments, it is common to leave a tip (often called a gratuity). This is a sum of money given to show appreciation for a service—for example, to the waiting staff in a restaurant. The tip is provided in addition to the basic charge denoted on the final bill.

Throughout this chapter, we will be working with an application that calculates the amount that should be given as a tip. This value will be based on the amount of the bill (the basic charge) and the extra percentage that the user wants to give. The user will input both of these values, and the app will calculate the tip value.

In this exercise, we will be customizing the activity transition between the input and the output screen:

1. Create a new project in Android Studio.

2. In the **Choose Your Project** dialog, select **Empty Activity**, then click **Next**.

3. In the **Configure Your Project** dialog, as shown in *Figure 15.1*, name the project **Tip Calculator** and set the package name as **com.example. tipcalculator**:

Figure 15.1: Configure Your Project dialog

4. Set the location where you want to save the project. Choose **API 21: Android 5.0 Lollipop** for **Minimum SDK**, then click the **Finish** button. This will create a default **MainActivity** with a layout file, **activity_main.xml**.

5. Add the **MaterialComponents** dependency to your **app/build. gradle** file:

```
implementation 'com.google.android.material:material:1.2.1'
```

We will need this to be able to use **TextInputLayout** and **TextInputEditText** for the input text fields.

6. Open the **themes.xml** file and make sure that the activity's theme is using a theme from **MaterialComponents**. See the following example:

```xml
<style name="AppTheme"
    parent="Theme.MaterialComponents.Light.DarkActionBar">
```

We will need to do this as the **TextInputLayout** and **TextInputEditText** we will be using later require your activity to use a **MaterialComponents** theme.

7. Open **activity_main.xml**. Delete the **Hello World TextView** and add the input text field for the amount:

```xml
<com.google.android.material.textfield.TextInputLayout
    android:id="@+id/amount_text_layout"
    style="@style/Widget.MaterialComponents
        .TextInputLayout.OutlinedBox"
    android:layout_width="match_parent"
    android:layout_height="wrap_content"
    android:layout_marginStart="16dp"
    android:layout_marginTop="100dp"
    android:layout_marginEnd="16dp"
    android:layout_marginBottom="16dp"
    android:alpha="1"
    android:hint="Amount"
    app:layout_constraintEnd_toEndOf="parent"
    app:layout_constraintStart_toStartOf="parent"
    app:layout_constraintTop_toTopOf="parent">
    <com.google.android.material.textfield
        .TextInputEditText
        android:id="@+id/amount_text"
        android:layout_width="match_parent"
        android:layout_height="wrap_content"
        android:inputType="numberDecimal"
        android:textSize="18sp" />
</com.google.android.material.textfield.TextInputLayout>
```

8. Add another input text field for the tip percentage below the amount text field:

```xml
<com.google.android.material.textfield.TextInputLayout
    android:id="@+id/percent_text_layout"
    style="@style/Widget.MaterialComponents
        .TextInputLayout.OutlinedBox"
    android:layout_width="match_parent"
```

```
            android:layout_height="wrap_content"
            android:layout_margin="16dp"
            android:alpha="1"
            android:hint="Tip Percent"
            app:layout_constraintEnd_toEndOf="parent"
            app:layout_constraintStart_toStartOf="parent"
            app:layout_constraintTop_toBottomOf
                ="@id/amount_text_layout">

            <com.google.android.material.textfield
                .TextInputEditText
                    android:id="@+id/percent_text"
                    android:layout_width="match_parent"
                    android:layout_height="wrap_content"
                    android:inputType="numberDecimal"
                    android:textSize="18sp" />
        </com.google.android.material.textfield.TextInputLayout>
```

9. Finally, add a **Compute** button at the bottom of the tip percent text field:

```
<Button
    android:id="@+id/compute_button"
    android:layout_width="wrap_content"
    android:layout_height="wrap_content"
    android:layout_marginTop="36dp"
    android:text="Compute"
    app:layout_constraintEnd_toEndOf
        ="@+id/percent_text_layout"
    app:layout_constraintTop_toBottomOf
        ="@+id/percent_text_layout" />
```

10. Create another activity. Go to the **File** menu and click on **New | Activity | Empty Activity**. Name it **OutputActivity**. Make sure that **Generate Layout File** is checked so that **activity_output** will be created.

11. Open **MainActivity**. At the end of the **onCreate** function, add the following code:

```
val amountText: EditText =
    findViewById(R.id.amount_text)
val percentText: EditText =
    findViewById(R.id.percent_text)
val computeButton: Button =
    findViewById(R.id.compute_button)
computeButton.setOnClickListener {
    val amount =
```

```
            if (amountText.text.toString().isNotBlank())
              amountText.text.toString() else "0"
        val percent =
            if (percentText.text.toString().isNotBlank())
              percentText.text.toString() else "0"
        val intent = Intent(this,
          OutputActivity::class.java).apply {
            putExtra("amount", amount)

            putExtra("percent", percent)

        }

        startActivity(intent)

    }
```

This will add a **ClickListener** component to the **Compute** button so that when it's tapped, the system will open **OutputActivity** and pass the amount and percentage values as intent extras.

12. Open **activity_output.xml** and add a **TextView** for displaying the tip:

```
<TextView
        android:id="@+id/tip_text"
        android:layout_width="wrap_content"
        android:layout_height="wrap_content"
        app:layout_constraintBottom_toBottomOf="parent"
        app:layout_constraintEnd_toEndOf="parent"
        app:layout_constraintStart_toStartOf="parent"
        app:layout_constraintTop_toTopOf="parent"
        style="@style/TextAppearance.AppCompat.Headline"
        tools:text="The tip is " />
```

13. Open **OutputActivity**. At the end of the **onCreate** function, add the following code:

```
        val amount = intent?.getStringExtra("amount")
          ?.toBigDecimal() ?: BigDecimal.ZERO
        val percent = intent?.getStringExtra("percent")
          ?.toBigDecimal() ?: BigDecimal.ZERO
        val tip = amount * (percent.divide("100"
          .toBigDecimal()))
        val tipText: TextView = findViewById(R.id.tip_text)
        tipText.text = "The tip is $tip"
```

This will compute and display the tip based on the input amount and percentage.

14. Run the application. Tap on the **Compute** button and note what happens when opening **OutputActivity** and going back. There is a default animation while **MainActivity** is being closed and **OutputActivity** is being opened and closed.

15. Now, let's start adding transition animations. Open **themes.xml** and update the activity theme with the **windowActivityTransitions**, **windowEnterTransition**, and **windowExitTransition** style attributes:

```
<item name="android:windowActivityTransitions">
  true</item>
<item name="android:windowEnterTransition">
  @android:transition/explode</item>
<item name="android:windowExitTransition">
  @android:transition/slide_left</item>
```

This will enable the activity transition, add an explode enter transition, and add a slide left exit transition to the activity.

16. Go back to the **MainActivity** file and replace **startActivity(intent)** with the following:

```
startActivity(intent, ActivityOptions
  .makeSceneTransitionAnimation(this).toBundle())
```

This will open **OutputActivity** with the transition animation we specified in the XML file (which we set in the previous step).

17. Run the application. You will see that the animation when opening and closing **MainActivity** and **OutputActivity** has changed. When the Android UI is opening **OutputActivity**, you will notice that the text is moving toward the center. While closing, the views slide to the left:

Figure 15.2: The app screens: input screen (on the left) and output screen (on the right)

We have added an activity transition to an app. When we open a new activity, the new activity's enter transition will be played. Its exit transition will play when the activity is being closed.

Sometimes, when we open another activity from one activity, there is a common element that is present in both activities. In the next section, we will learn about adding this shared element transition.

ADDING A SHARED ELEMENT TRANSITION

There are times when an application moves from one activity to another, and there is a common element that is present in both activities. We can add an animation to this shared element to highlight to the users the link between the two activities.

In a movie application, for example, an activity with a list of movies (with a thumbnail image) can open a new activity with details of the selected movie, along with a full-sized image at the top. Adding a shared element transition for the image will link the thumbnail on the list activity to the image on the details activity.

The shared element transition has two parts: the enter transition and the exit transition. These transitions can be done through XML or code.

The first step is to enable a window content transition. You can do this by adding the activity's theme to **themes.xml** with the following:

```
<item name="android:windowContentTransitions">true</item>
```

You can also do this programmatically by calling the following function in your activity before the call to **setContentView()**:

```
window.requestFeature(Window.FEATURE_CONTENT_TRANSITIONS)
```

The **android:windowContentTransitions** attribute with a **true** value and **window.requestFeature(Window.FEATURE_CONTENT_TRANSITIONS)** will enable the window content transition.

Afterward, you can add the shared element enter transition and the shared element exit transition. If you have **enter_transition.xml** and **exit_transition.xml** in your **res/transitions** directory, you can add the shared element enter transition by adding the following style attribute:

```
<item name="android:windowSharedElementEnterTransition">
  @transition/enter_transition</item>
```

You can also do this through code with the following lines:

```
val enterTransition = TransitionInflater.from(this)
  .inflateTransition(R.transition.enter_transition)
window.sharedElementEnterTransition = enterTransition
```

The **windowSharedElementEnterTransition** attribute and **window. sharedElementEnterTransition** will set our enter transition to the **enter_ transition.xml** file.

To add the shared element exit transition, you can add the following style attributes:

```
<item name="android:windowSharedElementExitTransition">
  @transition/exit_transition</item>
```

This can be done programmatically with the following lines of code:

```
val exitTransition = TransitionInflater.from(this)
  .inflateTransition(R.transition.exit_transition)
window.sharedElementExitTransition = exitTransition
```

The **windowSharedElementExitTransition** attribute and **window. sharedElementExitTransition** will set our exit transition to the **exit_ transition.xml** file.

You have learned how to add shared element transitions. In the next section, we'll learn how to start the activity with the shared element transition.

STARTING AN ACTIVITY WITH THE SHARED ELEMENT TRANSITION

Once you have added the shared element transition to an activity (either through XML or programmatically), you can activate the transition when opening the activity. Before you do that, add a **transitionName** attribute. Set its value as the same text for the shared element in both activities.

For example, in **ImageView**, we can add a **transition_name** value for the **transitionName** attribute:

```
<ImageView
    . . .
    android:transitionName="transition_name"
    android:id="@+id/sharedImage"
... />
```

To start the activity with shared elements, we will be passing in a bundle with the transition animation. To do that, start your activity with the following code:

```
startActivity(intent, ActivityOptions
  .makeSceneTransitionAnimation(this, sharedImage,
    "transition_name").toBundle());
```

The **ActivityOptions.makeSceneTransitionAnimation(this, sharedImage, "transition_name").toBundle()** argument will create a bundle with the shared element (**sharedImage**) and the transition name (**transition_name**).

If you have more than one shared element, you can pass variable arguments of **Pair<View, String>** of **View** and the transition name **String** instead. For example, if we have the view's button and image as shared elements, we can do the following:

```
val buttonPair: Pair<View, String> = Pair(button, "button")
val imagePair: Pair<View, String> = Pair(image, "image")
val activityOptions = ActivityOptions
    .makeSceneTransitionAnimation(this, buttonPair, imagePair)
startActivity(intent, activityOptions.toBundle())
```

> **NOTE**
>
> Remember to import **android.util.Pair** instead of **kotlin.Pair** as **makeSceneTransitionAnimation** is expecting the pair from the Android SDK.

Let's try out what we have learned so far by adding shared element transitions to the *Tip Calculator* app.

EXERCISE 15.02: CREATING THE SHARED ELEMENT TRANSITION

In the first exercise, we customized the activity transitions for **MainActivity** and **OutputActivity**. In this exercise, we will be adding an image to both activities. This shared element will be animated when moving from the input screen to the output screen. We'll be using the app launcher icon (**res/mipmap/ic_launcher**) for **ImageView**. You can change yours instead of using the default one:

1. Open the **Tip Calculator** project we developed in **Exercise 15.01**, **Creating Activity Transitions in an App**.

2. Go to the **activity_main.xml** file and add an **ImageView** at the top of the amount text field:

```
<ImageView
    android:id="@+id/image"
    android:layout_width="wrap_content"
    android:layout_height="wrap_content"
    android:layout_marginTop="100dp"
    android:src="@mipmap/ic_launcher"
    android:transitionName="transition_name"
```

```
            app:layout_constraintEnd_toEndOf="parent"
            app:layout_constraintStart_toStartOf="parent"
            app:layout_constraintTop_toTopOf="parent" />
```

The **transitionName** value of **transition_name** will be used to identify this as a shared element.

3. Change the top constraint of **amount_text_layout TextInputLayout** by changing **app:layout_constraintTop_toTopOf="parent"** with the following:

```
app:layout_constraintTop_toBottomOf="@id/image"
```

This will move the amount **TextInputLayout** class below the image.

4. Now, open the **activity_output.xml** file and add an image above the tip **TextView** with a height and width of 200dp and a **scaleType** of **fitXY** to fit the image to the dimensions of the **ImageView**.

```
    <ImageView
        android:id="@+id/image"
        android:layout_width="200dp"
        android:layout_height="200dp"
        android:layout_marginBottom="40dp"
        android:src="@mipmap/ic_launcher"
        android:scaleType="fitXY"
        android:transitionName="transition_name"
        app:layout_constraintEnd_toEndOf="parent"
        app:layout_constraintStart_toStartOf="parent"
        app:layout_constraintBottom_toTopOf="@id/tip_text" />
```

The **transitionName** value of **transition_name** is the same as the value for the **ImageView** from **MainActivity**.

5. Open **MainActivity** and change the **startActivity** code to the following:

```
val image: ImageView = findViewById(R.id.image)
startActivity(intent, ActivityOptions
    .makeSceneTransitionAnimation(this, image,
        "transition_name").toBundle())
```

This will start a transition from the **ImageView** in **MainActivity** with the ID image to another image in **OutputActivity** whose **transitionName** value is also **transition_name**.

6. Run the application. Provide an amount and percentage and tap on the **Compute** button. You will see that the image in the input activity appears to enlarge and position itself in **OutputActivity**:

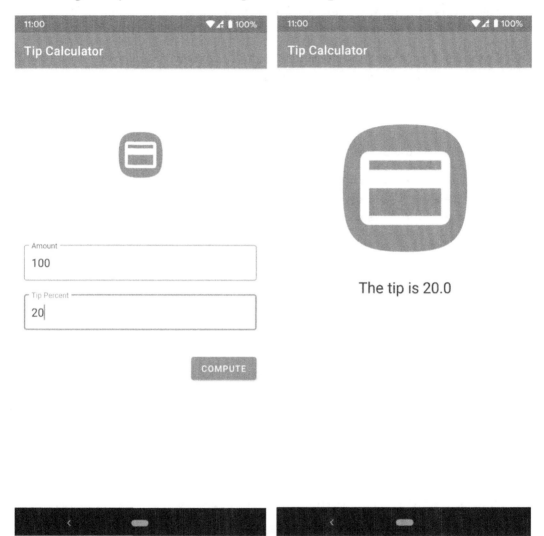

Figure 15.3: The app screens: input screen (on the left) and output screen (on the right)

We have learned about adding activity transitions and shared element transitions. Now, let's look into animating views inside a layout. If we have more than one element inside, it might be difficult to animate each element. **CoordinatorLayout** can be used to simplify this animation. We will discuss this in the next section.

ANIMATIONS WITH COORDINATORLAYOUT

CoordinatorLayout is a layout that handles the motions between its child views. When you use **CoordinatorLayout** as the parent view group, you can animate the views inside it with little effort. You can add **CoordinatorLayout** to your project by adding in your **app/build.gradle** file dependencies with the following:

```
implementation 'androidx.coordinatorlayout:coordinatorlayout:1.1.0'
```

This will allow us to use **CoordinatorLayout** in our layout files.

Let's say we have a layout file with a floating action button inside **CoordinatorLayout**. When tapping on the floating action button, the UI displays a **Snackbar** message.

> **NOTE**
>
> A **Snackbar** is an Android widget that provides a brief message to the user at the bottom of the screen.

If you use any layout other than **CoordinatorLayout**, the Snackbar with the message will be rendered on top of the floating action button. If we use **CoordinatorLayout** as the parent view group, the layout will push the floating action button upwards, display the Snackbar below it, and move it back when the Snackbar disappears. *Figure 15.4* shows how the layout adjusts to prevent the Snackbar from being on top of the floating action button:

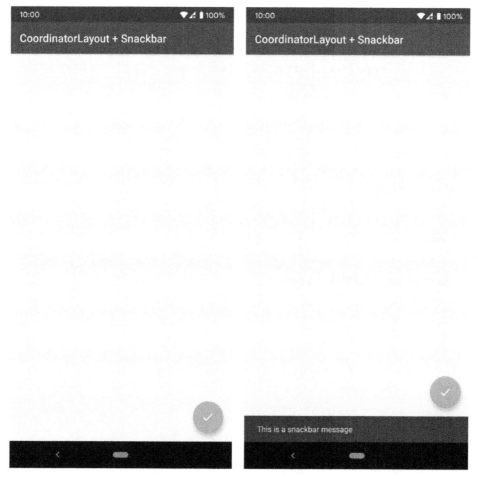

Figure 15.4: The left screenshot displays the UI before and after the Snackbar is shown. The screenshot on the right shows the UI while the Snackbar is visible

The floating action button moves and gives space to the Snackbar message because it has a default behavior called **FloatingActionButton.Behavior**, a subclass of **CoordinatorLayout.Behavior**. **FloatingActionButton.Behavior** moves the floating action button while the Snackbar is being displayed so that the Snackbar won't cover the floating action button.

Not all views have **CoordinatorLayout** behavior. To implement custom behavior, you can start by extending **CoordinatorLayout.Behavior**. You can then attach it to the view with the **layout_behavior** attribute. For example, if we have made **CustomBehavior** in the **com.example.behavior** package for a button, we can update the button in the layout with the following:

```
...
<Button
    ...
    app:layout_behavior="com.example.behavior.CustomBehavior">

    .../>
```

We have learned how to create animations and transitions with **CoordinatorLayout**. In the next section, we will look into another layout, **MotionLayout**, which allows developers more control over motion.

ANIMATIONS WITH MOTIONLAYOUT

Creating animations in Android is sometimes time-consuming. You need to work on XML and code files even to create simple animations. More complicated animations and transitions take more time to make.

To help developers easily make animations, Google created **MotionLayout**. **MotionLayout** is a new way to create motion and animations through XML. It is available starting at API level 14 (Android 4.0).

With **MotionLayout**, we can animate the position, width/height, visibility, alpha, color, rotation, elevation, and other attributes of one or more views. Normally, some of these are hard to do with code, but **MotionLayout** allows us to easily adjust them using declarative XML so that we can focus more on our application.

Let's get started by adding **MotionLayout** to our application.

ADDING MOTIONLAYOUT

To add **MotionLayout** to your project, you just need to add the dependency for ConstraintLayout 2.0. ConstraintLayout 2.0 is the new version of ConstraintLayout, which adds new features, including **MotionLayout**. Add in your app/**build. gradle** file dependencies with the following:

```
implementation 'androidx.constraintlayout:constraintlayout:2.0.4'
```

This will add the latest version of ConstraintLayout (2.0.4 as of the time of writing) to your app. For this book, we will be using the AndroidX versions. If you haven't updated your project yet, consider updating from the Support Library to AndroidX.

After adding the dependency, we can now use **MotionLayout** to create animations. We'll be doing that in the next section.

CREATING ANIMATIONS WITH MOTIONLAYOUT

MotionLayout is a subclass of our good old friend ConstraintLayout. To create animations with **MotionLayout**, open the layout file where we will add the animations. Replace the root ConstraintLayout container with **androidx. constraintlayout.motion.widget.MotionLayout**.

The animation itself won't be in the layout file but in another XML file, called **motion_scene**. **motion_scene** will specify how **MotionLayout** will animate the views inside it. **motion_scene** files should be placed in the **res/xml** directory. The layout file will link to this **motion_scene** file with the **app:layoutDescription** attribute in the root view group. Your layout file should look similar to the following:

```
<?xml version="1.0" encoding="utf-8"?>
<androidx.constraintlayout.motion.widget.MotionLayout

    ...

    app:layoutDescription="@xml/motion_scene">


    ...

</androidx.constraintlayout.motion.widget.MotionLayout>
```

To create animations with **MotionLayout**, we must have the initial state and final state of our views. **MotionLayout** will automatically animate the transition between the two. You can specify these two states in the same **motion_scene** file. If you have a lot of views inside the layout, you can also use two different layouts for the beginning and ending states of the animation.

The root container of the **motion_scene** file is **motion_scene**. This is where we add the constraints and the animation for **MotionLayout**. It contains the following:

- **ConstraintSet**: Specifies the beginning and ending position and style for the view/layout to animate.

- **Transition**: Specifies the start, end, duration, and other details of the animation to be done on the views.

Let's try adding animations with **MotionLayout** by adding it to our *Tip Calculator* app.

EXERCISE 15.03: ADDING ANIMATIONS WITH MOTIONLAYOUT

In this exercise, we will be updating our *Tip Calculator* app with a **MotionLayout** animation. In the output screen, the image above the tip text will move down when tapped and will go back to its original position when tapped again:

1. Open the *Tip Calculator* project in Android Studio 4.0 or higher.

2. Open the **app/build.gradle** file and replace the dependency for **ConstraintLayout** with the following:

```
implementation 'androidx
    .constraintlayout:constraintlayout:2.0.4'
```

With this, we will be able to use **MotionLayout** in our layout files.

3. Open the **activity_output.xml** file and change the root **ConstraintLayout** tag to **MotionLayout**. Change **androidx. constraintlayout.widget.ConstraintLayout** to the following:

```
androidx.constraintlayout.motion.widget.MotionLayout
```

4. Add **app:layoutDescription="@xml/motion_scene"** to the **MotionLayout** tag. The IDE will warn you that this file does not yet exist. Ignore that for now, as we will be adding it in the next step. Your file should look similar to this:

```
<?xml version="1.0" encoding="utf-8"?>
<androidx.constraintlayout.motion.widget.MotionLayout
    xmlns:android="http://schemas.android.com/apk/res/android"
    xmlns:app="http://schemas.android.com/apk/res-auto"
    xmlns:tools="http://schemas.android.com/tools"
    android:layout_width="match_parent"
    android:layout_height="match_parent"
    app:layoutDescription="@xml/motion_scene"
    tools:context=".OutputActivity">


    ...


</androidx.constraintlayout.motion.widget.MotionLayout>
```

5. Create a **motion_scene.xml** file in the **res/xml** directory. This will be our **motion_scene** file where the animation configuration will be defined. Use **motion_scene** as the root element for the file.

6. Add the starting **Constraint** element by adding the following inside the **motion_scene** file:

```
<ConstraintSet android:id="@+id/start_constraint">
    <Constraint
        android:id="@id/image"
        android:layout_width="200dp"
        android:layout_height="200dp"
        android:layout_marginBottom="40dp"
        app:layout_constraintBottom_toTopOf="@id/tip_text"
        app:layout_constraintEnd_toEndOf="parent"
        app:layout_constraintStart_toStartOf="parent" />
</ConstraintSet>
```

This is how the image is at the current position (constrained to the top of the screen).

7. Next, add the ending **Constraint** element by adding the following inside the **motion_scene** file:

```
<ConstraintSet android:id="@+id/end_constraint">
    <Constraint
        android:id="@id/image"
        android:layout_width="200dp"
        android:layout_height="200dp"
        android:layout_marginBottom="40dp"
        app:layout_constraintBottom_toBottomOf="parent"
        app:layout_constraintEnd_toEndOf="parent"
        app:layout_constraintStart_toStartOf="parent" />
</ConstraintSet>
```

At the ending animation, the **ImageView** will be at the bottom of the screen.

8. Let's now add in the transition for our **ImageView**:

```
<Transition
    app:constraintSetEnd="@id/end_constraint"
    app:constraintSetStart="@id/start_constraint"
    app:duration="2000">
    <OnClick
```

```
            app:clickAction="toggle"
            app:targetId="@id/image" />
    </Transition>
```

Here, we're specifying the start and end constraints, which will animate for 2,000 milliseconds (2 seconds). We also added an **OnClick** event to **ImageView**. The toggle will animate the view from the start to end, and if the view is already on the end state, it will animate back to the start state.

9. Your completed **motion_scene.xml** file should look like this:

```xml
<?xml version="1.0" encoding="utf-8"?>
<MotionScene xmlns:android
  ="http://schemas.android.com/apk/res/android"
    xmlns:app="http://schemas.android.com/apk/res-auto">

    <ConstraintSet android:id="@+id/start_constraint">
        <Constraint
            android:id="@id/image"
            android:layout_width="200dp"
            android:layout_height="200dp"
            android:layout_marginBottom="40dp"
            app:layout_constraintBottom_toTopOf="@id/tip_text"
            app:layout_constraintEnd_toEndOf="parent"
            app:layout_constraintStart_toStartOf="parent" />
    </ConstraintSet>

    <ConstraintSet android:id="@+id/end_constraint">
        <Constraint
            android:id="@id/image"
            android:layout_width="200dp"
            android:layout_height="200dp"
            android:layout_marginBottom="40dp"
            app:layout_constraintBottom_toBottomOf="parent"
            app:layout_constraintEnd_toEndOf="parent"
            app:layout_constraintStart_toStartOf="parent" />
    </ConstraintSet>

    <Transition
        app:constraintSetEnd="@id/end_constraint"
        app:constraintSetStart="@id/start_constraint"
        app:duration="2000">
```

```
        <OnClick
            app:clickAction="toggle"
            app:targetId="@id/image" />
    </Transition>
</MotionScene>
```

10. Run the application and tap on the **ImageView**. It will move straight downward in around 2 seconds. Tap it again and it will move back up in 2 seconds. *Figure 15.5* shows the start and end of this animation:

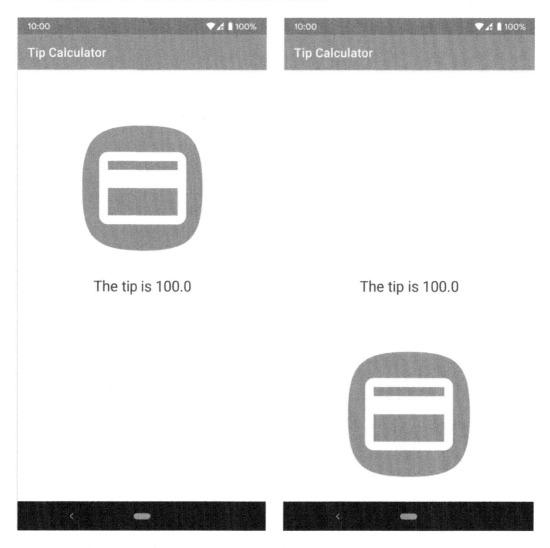

Figure 15.5: The starting animation (left) and ending animation (right)

In this exercise, we have animated an **ImageView** in **MotionLayout** by specifying the start constraint, end constraint, and the transition with a duration and **OnClick** event. **MotionLayout** automatically plays the animation from the start to the end position (which to us looks like it's moving up or down in a straight line automatically when tapped).

We have created animations with **MotionLayout**. In the next section, we will be using Android Studio's Motion Editor to create **MotionLayout** animations.

THE MOTION EDITOR

Android Studio, starting with version 4.0, includes the Motion Editor. The Motion Editor can help developers create animations with **MotionLayout**. This makes it easier for developers to create and preview transitions and other motions instead of doing it by hand and running it to see the changes. The editor will also generate the corresponding files automatically.

You can convert your ConstraintLayout to MotionLayout the Layout Editor by right-clicking the preview and clicking on the **Convert to MotionLayout** item. Android Studio will do the conversion and also create the motion scene file for you.

When viewing a layout file that has **MotionLayout** as the root in **Design** view, the Motion Editor UI will be included in the **Design** view, as in *Figure 15.6*:

Figure 15.6: The Motion Editor in Android Studio 4.0

In the upper-right window (the **Overview** panel), you can see a visualization of **MotionLayout** and the start and end constraint. The transition is displayed as an arrow from the start. The dot near the start constraint shows the click action for the transition. *Figure 15.7* shows the **Overview** panel with **start_constraint** selected:

Figure 15.7: The Motion Editor's Overview panel with start_constraint selected

The bottom-right window is the **Selection** panel, which shows the views in the constraint set or **MotionLayout** selected in the **Overview** panel. It can also show the transitions when the transition arrow is the one selected. *Figure 15.8* shows the **Selection** panel when **start_constraint** is selected:

	ConstraintSet (start_constraint)		

Constraint	ID	Source
✓	image	start_constraint
	tip_text	layout

Figure 15.8: The Motion Editor's Selection panel showing ConstraintSet for start_constraint

When you click on **MotionLayout** on the left of the **Overview** panel, the
Selection panel below will display the views and their constraints, as shown in
Figure 15.9:

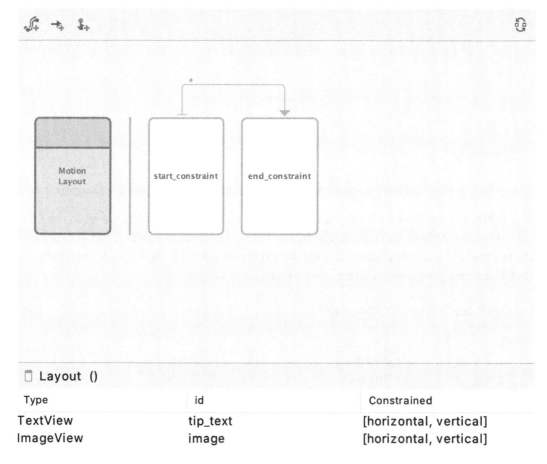

Layout ()

Type	id	Constrained
TextView	tip_text	[horizontal, vertical]
ImageView	image	[horizontal, vertical]

Figure 15.9: The Overview and Selection panel when MotionLayout is selected

When you click on **start_constraint** or **end_constraint**, the preview window on the left will display how the start or end state looks. The **Selection** panel will also show the view and its constraints. Take a look at *Figure 15.10* to see how it looks when **start_constraint** is selected:

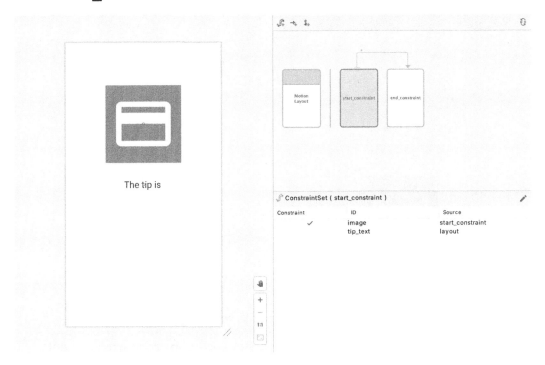

Figure 15.10: How the Motion Editor looks when start_constraint is selected

Figure 15.11 shows how the Motion Editor will look if you select **end_constraint**:

Figure 15.11: How the Motion Editor looks with end_constraint selected

The arrow connecting **start_constraint** and **end_constraint** represents the transition of **MotionLayout**. On the **Selection** panel, there are controls to play or go to the first/last state. You can also drag the arrow to a specific position. *Figure 15.12* shows how it looks in the middle (50% of the animation):

Figure 15.12: The transition in the middle of the animation

During the development of animations with **MotionLayout**, it would be better if we could debug the animations to make sure we're doing it correctly. We'll discuss how we can do this in the next section.

DEBUGGING MOTIONLAYOUT

To help you visualize the **MotionLayout** animation before running the app, you can show the motion path and the animation's progress in the Motion Editor. The motion path is the straight route that the object to animate will take from the start to the ending state.

To show the path and/or progress animation, we can add a **motionDebug** attribute to the **MotionLayout** container. We can use the following values for **motionDebug**:

- **SHOW_PATH**: This displays the path of the motion only.

- **SHOW_PROGRESS**: This displays the animation progress only.

- **SHOW_ALL**: This displays both the path and the progress of the animation.

- **NO_DEBUG**: This hides all animations.

To display the **MotionLayout** path and progress, we can use the following:

```
<androidx.constraintlayout.motion.widget.MotionLayout
    ...
    app:motionDebug="SHOW_ALL"
...>
```

The **SHOW_ALL** value will display the path and the progress of the animation. *Figure 15.13* shows how it will look when we use **SHOW_PATH** and **SHOW_PROGRESS**:

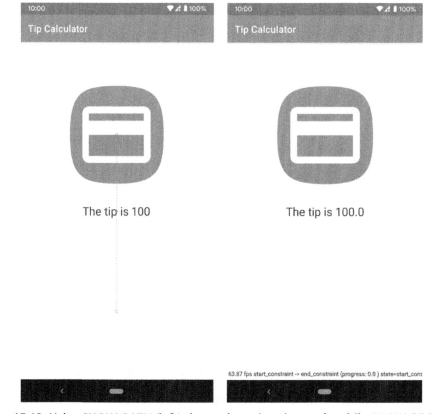

Figure 15.13: Using SHOW_PATH (left) shows the animation path, while SHOW_PROGRESS (right) shows the animation progress

While **motionDebug** sounds like something that only appears in debug mode, it will also appear in release builds, so it should be removed when you're preparing your app for publishing.

During the **MotionLayout** animation, the start constraint will transition to the end constraint, even if there's an element or elements that can block the objects in motion. We'll discuss how we can avoid this from happening in the next section.

MODIFYING THE MOTIONLAYOUT PATH

In an animation with **MotionLayout**, the UI will play the motion from the start constraint to the end constraint, even if there are elements in the middle that can block our moving views. For example, if **MotionLayout** involves text that moves from the top to the bottom of the screen and vice versa, and we add a button to the middle, the button will cover the moving text.

Figure 15.14 shows how the **OK** button is blocking the moving text in the middle of the animation:

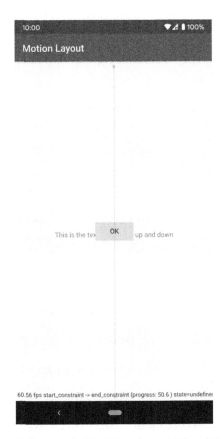

Figure 15.14: The OK button is blocking the middle of the text animation

MotionLayout plays the animation from the start to the end constraint in a straight path and adjusts the views based on the specified attributes. We can add keyframes between the start and end constraints to adjust the animation path and/or the view attributes. For example, during the animation, other than changing the position of the moving text to avoid the button, we can also change the attributes of the text or other views.

Keyframes can be added in **KeyFrameSet** as a child of the transition attribute of **motion_scene**. We can use the following keyframes:

- **KeyPosition**: This specifies the view's position at a specific point during the animation to adjust the path.

- **KeyAttribute**: This specifies the view's attributes at a specific point during the animation.

- **KeyCycle**: This adds oscillations during animations.

- **KeyTimeCycle**: This allows cycles to be driven by time instead of animation progress.

- **KeyTrigger**: This adds an element that can trigger an event based on the animation progress.

We will focus on **KeyPosition** and **KeyAttribute** as **KeyCycle**, **KeyTimeCycle**, and **KeyTrigger** are more advanced keyframes and are still subject to changes.

KeyPosition allows us to change the location of views in the middle of the **MotionLayout** animation. It has the following attributes:

- **motionTarget**: This specifies the object controlled by the keyframe.

- **framePosition**: Numbered from 1 to 99, this specifies the percentage of the motion when the position will be changed. For example, 25 means it is at one quarter of the animation, and 50 is the halfway point.

- **percentX**: This specifies how much the **x** value of the path will be modified.

- **percentY**: This specifies how much the **y** value of the path will be modified.

- **keyPositionType**: This specifies how **KeyPosition** modifies the path.

The **keyPositionType** attribute can have the following values:

- **parentRelative**: **percentX** and **percentY** are specified based on the parent of the view.

- **pathRelative**: **percentX** and **percentY** are specified based on the straight path from the start constraint to the end constraint.

- **deltaRelative**: **percentX** and **percentY** are specified based on the position of the view.

For example, if we want to modify the path of the **TextView** with the **text_view** ID at the exact middle of the animation (50%), by moving it 10% by **x** and 10% by **y** relative to the parent container of the **TextView**, we would have the following key position in **motion_scene**:

```
<KeyPosition
    app:motionTarget="@+id/text_view"
    app:framePosition="50"
    app:keyPositionType="parentRelative"
    app:percentY="0.1"
    app:percentX="0.1"
/>
```

Meanwhile, **KeyAttribute** allows us to change the attributes of views while the **MotionLayout** animation is ongoing. Some of the view attributes we can change are **visibility**, **alpha**, **elevation**, **rotation**, **scale**, and **translation**. It has the following attributes:

- **motionTarget**: This specifies the object controlled by the keyframe.

- **framePosition**: Numbered from 1 to 99, this specifies the percentage of the motion when the view attributes will be applied. For example, 20 means it is at one-fifth of the animation, and 75 is the three-quarters point of the animation.

Let's try adding keyframes to the *Tip Calculator* app. During the animation of the **ImageView**, it goes on top of the text displaying the tip. We'll fix that with keyframes.

EXERCISE 15.04: MODIFYING THE ANIMATION PATH WITH KEYFRAMES

In the previous exercise, we animated the image to move straight down when tapped (or upward when it's already at the bottom). When it is in the middle, the image is covering the tip **TextView**. We'll be solving this issue in this exercise by adding **KeyFrame** to **motion_scene** using Android Studio's Motion Editor:

1. Open the *Tip Calculator* app with Android Studio 4.0 or higher.

2. Open the **activity_output.xml** file in the **res/layout** directory.

3. Switch to the **Design** view.

4. Add **app:motionDebug="SHOW_ALL"** to the **MotionLayout** container. This will allow us to see the path and progress information in Android Studio and on our device/emulator. Your **MotionLayout** container will look like the following:

```
<androidx.constraintlayout.motion.widget.MotionLayout
    xmlns:android="http://schemas.android.com/apk/res/android"
    xmlns:app="http://schemas.android.com/apk/res-auto"
    xmlns:tools="http://schemas.android.com/tools"
    android:layout_width="match_parent"
    android:layout_height="match_parent"
    app:layoutDescription="@xml/motion_scene"
    app:motionDebug="SHOW_ALL"
        tools:context=".OutputActivity">
```

5. Run the app and make a computation. On the output screen, tap on the image. Look at the tip text while the animation is in progress. You will notice that the text is covered by the image in the middle of the animation, as shown in *Figure 15.15*:

Figure 15.15: The image hides the TextView displaying the tip

6. Go back to the **activity_output.xml** file in Android Studio. Make sure it's opened in **Design** view.

7. In the **Overview** panel at the top right, click the arrow connecting **start_constraint** and **end_constraint**. Drag the down arrow in the **Selection** panel to the middle (50%), as shown in *Figure 15.16*:

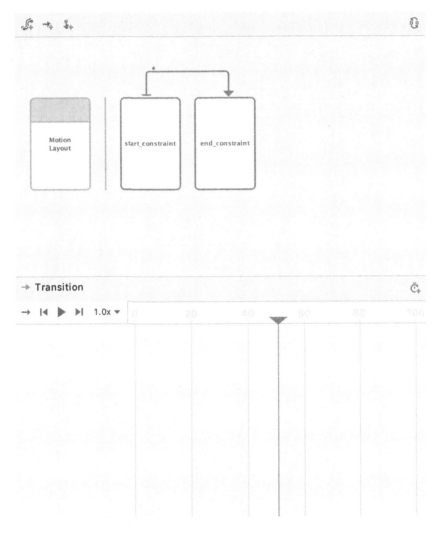

Figure 15.16: Select the arrow representing the transition between the start and end constraints

8. Click the **Create KeyFrames** icon to the right of **Transition** in the **Selection** panel (the one with a green **+** symbol). Refer to *Figure 15.17* to see the icon:

Figure 15.17: The Create KeyFrames icon

9. Select **KeyPosition**. We will be using **KeyPosition** to adjust the text position and avoid the button.

10. Select **ID**, choose **image**, and set the input position to **50**. The **Type** is **parentRelative**, and **PercentX** is **1.5**, as *Figure 15.18* shows. This will add a **KeyPosition** attribute for the image at the middle (50%) of the transition, which is at 1.5 times relative to the **x** axis of the parent:

Figure 15.18: Provide the input to the key position to be made

11. Click the **Add** button. You will see in the **Design** preview, as shown in *Figure 15.19*, that the motion path is no longer a straight line. At position 50 (the middle of the animation), the text will no longer be covered by the **ImageView**. The **ImageView** will be to the right of the **TextView**:

Figure 15.19: The path will now be curved instead of straight. The Transition panel will also have a new item for KeyPosition

12. Click the play icon to see how it will animate. Run the application to verify it on a device or emulator. You will see that the animation is now curving to the right instead of taking its previous straight path, as in *Figure 15.20*:

Figure 15.20: The animation now avoids the TextView with the tip

13. The Motion Editor will automatically generate the code for **KeyPosition**. If you go to the **motion_scene.xml** file, you will see that the Motion Editor added the following code in the transition attribute:

```
<KeyFrameSet>
    <KeyPosition
        app:framePosition="50"
        app:keyPositionType="parentRelative"
        app:motionTarget="@+id/image"
        app:percentX="1.5" />
</KeyFrameSet>
```

A **KeyPosition** attribute was added in the keyframes during the transition. At 50% of the animation, the image's **x** position will be moved by 1.5x relative to its parent view. This allows the image to avoid other elements during the animation process.

In this exercise, you have added a key position that will adjust the **MotionLayout** animation so that it will not block or be blocked by another view in its path.

Let's test everything you've learned by doing an activity.

ACTIVITY 15.01: PASSWORD GENERATOR

Using a strong password is important to secure our online accounts. It must be unique and must include uppercase and lowercase letters, numbers, and special characters. In this activity, you will develop an app that can generate a strong password.

The app will have two screens: the input screen and the output screen. In the input screen, the user can provide the length of the password and specify whether it must have uppercase or lowercase letters, numbers, or special characters. The output screen will display three possible passwords, and when the user selects one, the other passwords will move away and a button will display to copy the password to the clipboard. You should customize the transition from the input to the output screen.

The steps to complete are as follows:

1. Create a new project in Android Studio 4.0 or higher and name it **Password Generator**. Set its package name and **Minimum SDK**.

2. Add the **MaterialComponents** dependency to your **app/build. gradle** file.

3. Update the dependency for **ConstraintLayout**.

4. Make sure that the activity's theme is using a theme from **MaterialComponents** in the **themes.xml** file.

5. In the **activity_main.xml** file, remove the **Hello World TextView** and add the input text field for the length.

6. Add the code for checkboxes for uppercase, numbers, and special characters.

7. Add a **Generate** button at the bottom of the checkboxes.

8. Create another activity and name it **OutputActivity**.

9. Customize the activity transition from the input screen (**MainActivity**) to **OutputActivity**. Open **themes.xml** and update the activity theme with the **windowActivityTransitions**, **windowEnterTransition**, and **windowExitTransition** style attributes.

10. Update the end of the **onCreate** function in **MainActivity**.

11. Update the code for **androidx.constraintlayout.widget. ConstraintLayout** in the **activity_output.xml** file.

12. Add **app:layoutDescription="@xml/motion_scene"** and **app:motionDebug="SHOW_ALL"** to the **MotionLayout** tag.

13. Add three instances of **TextView** to the output activity for the three passwords generated.

14. Add a **Copy** button at the bottom of the screen.

15. Add the **generatePassword** function in **OutputActivity**.

16. Add the code to generate the three passwords based on user input and add a **ClickListener** component to the **Copy** button for the user to copy the selected password to the clipboard.

17. In **OutputActivity**, create an animation per password **TextView**.

18. Create **ConstraintSet** for the default view.

19. Add **ConstraintSet** when the first, second, and third passwords are selected.

20. Next, add **Transition** when each password is selected.

21. Run the application by going to the **Run** menu and clicking the **Run app** menu item.

22. Input a length, select uppercase, numbers, and special characters, and tap on the **Generate** button. Three passwords will be displayed.

23. Select one and the rest will move out of view. A **Copy** button will also be displayed. Click on it and check whether the password you selected is now on the clipboard. The initial and final state of the output screen will be similar to *Figure 15.21*:

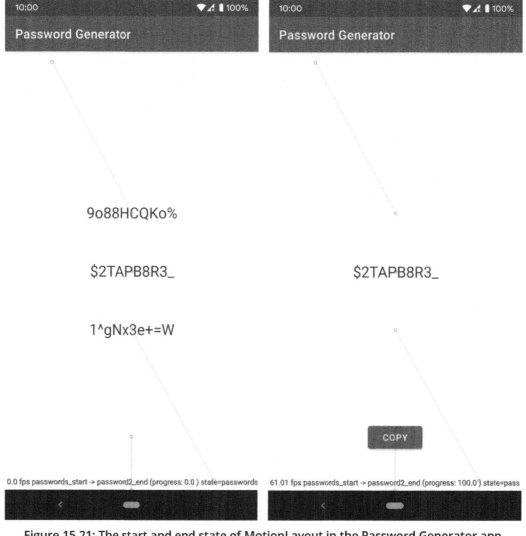

Figure 15.21: The start and end state of MotionLayout in the Password Generator app

> **NOTE**
>
> The solution to this activity can be found at: http://packt.live/3sKj1cp.

SUMMARY

This chapter covered creating animations and transitions with `CoordinatorLayout` and `MotionLayout`. Animations can improve the usability of our app and make it stand out compared to other apps.

We started by customizing the transition when opening and closing an activity with activity transitions. We also learned about adding shared element transitions when an activity and the activity that it opens both contain the same elements so that we can highlight this link between the shared elements to the users.

We learned how we can use `CoordinatorLayout` to handle the motion of its child views. Some views have built-in behaviors that handle how they work inside `CoordinatorLayout`. You can add custom behaviors to other views too. Then, we moved on to using `MotionLayout` to create animations by specifying the start constraint, end constraint, and the transition between them. We also looked into modifying the motion path by adding keyframes in the middle of the animation. We learned about keyframes such as `KeyPosition`, which can change the view's position, and `KeyAttribute`, which can change the view's style. We also looked into using the Motion Editor in Android Studio to simplify the creation and previewing of animations and modifying the path.

In the next chapter, we'll be learning about the Google Play store. We'll discuss how you can create an account and prepare your apps for release, as well as how you can publish them for users to download and use.

16

LAUNCHING YOUR APP ON GOOGLE PLAY

OVERVIEW

This chapter will introduce you to the Google Play console, release channels, and the entire release process. It covers creating a Google Play Developer account, setting up the store entry for our developed app, and creating a key store (including coverage of the importance of passwords and where to store files). We'll also learn about app bundles and APK, looking at how to generate the app's APK or AAB file. Later in the chapter, we'll set up release paths, open beta, and closed alpha, and finally we'll upload our app to the store and download it on a device.

By the end of this chapter, you will be able to create your own Google Play Developer account, prepare your signed APK or app bundle for publishing, and publish your first application on Google Play.

INTRODUCTION

You learned how to add animations and transitions with `CoordinatorLayout` and `MotionLayout` in the previous chapter. Now, you are ready to develop and launch Android applications.

After developing Android apps, they will only be available on your devices and emulators. You must make them available to everyone so they can download them. In turn, you will acquire users and you can earn from them. The official marketplace for Android apps is Google Play. With Google Play, the apps and games you release can be available to over 2 billion active Android devices globally.

In this chapter, we're going to learn about launching your apps on Google Play. We'll start with preparing the apps for release and creating a Google Play Developer account. Then, we'll move on to uploading your app and managing app releases.

Let's get started with preparing your apps for release on Google Play.

PREPARING YOUR APPS FOR RELEASE

Before publishing an app on Google Play, you must make sure that it is signed with a release key and that it has the correct version information. Otherwise, you won't be able to publish a new app or an update to an already-published app.

Let's start with adding versions to your app.

VERSIONING APPS

The version of your app is important for the following reasons:

- Users can see the version they have downloaded. They can use this when checking whether there's an update or whether there are known issues when reporting bugs/problems with the app.

- The device and Google Play use the version value to determine whether an app can or should be updated.

- Developers can also use this value to add feature support in specific versions. They can also warn or force users to upgrade to the latest version to get important fixes on bugs or security issues.

An Android app has two versions: `versionCode` and `versionName`. Now, `versionCode` is an integer that is used by developers, Google Play, and the Android system, while `versionName` is a string that the users see on the Google Play page for your app.

The initial release of an app can have a **versionCode** value of **1**, and you should increase it for each new release.

versionName can be in *x.y* format (where *x* is the major version and the *y* is the minor version). You can also use semantic versioning, as in *x.y.z*, by adding the patch version with *z*. To learn more about semantic versioning, refer to https://semver.org.

In the module's **build.gradle** files, **versionCode** and **versionName** are automatically generated when you create a new project in Android Studio. They are in the **defaultConfig** block under the **android** block. An example **build.gradle** file shows these values:

```
android {
    compileSdkVersion 29
    defaultConfig {
        applicationId "com.example.app"
        minSdkVersion 16
        targetSdkVersion 29
        versionCode 1
        versionName "1.0"
        ...
    }
    ...
}
```

When publishing updates, the new package to be released must have a higher **versionCode** value because users cannot downgrade their apps and can only download new versions.

After ensuring that the app version is correct, the next step in the release process is to get a keystore to sign the app. This will be discussed in the next section.

CREATING A KEYSTORE

Android apps, when run, are automatically signed by a debug key. However, before it can be published on Google Play Store, an app must be signed with a release key. To do so, you must have a keystore. If you don't have one yet, you can create one in Android Studio.

EXERCISE 16.01: CREATING A KEYSTORE IN ANDROID STUDIO

In this exercise, we'll use Android Studio to make a keystore that can be used to sign Android apps. Follow these steps to complete this exercise:

1. Open a project in Android Studio.

2. Go to the **Build** menu and then click on **Generate Signed Bundle or APK...**:

Figure 16.1: The Generate Signed Bundle or APK dialog

3. Make sure either **APK** or **Android App Bundle** is selected, and then click the **Next** button. Here, you can choose an existing keystore or create a new one:

Figure 16.2: The Generate Signed Bundle or APK dialog after selecting APK and pressing the Next button

4. Click the **Create new...** button. The **New Key Store** dialog will then appear:

Figure 16.3: The New Key Store dialog

5. In the **Key store path** field, choose the location where the keystore file will be saved. You can click on the folder icon at the right to select your folder and type the filename. The value will be similar to **users/packt/downloads/ keystore.keystore**

6. Provide the password in both the **Password** and **Confirm** fields.

7. In the certificate section under **Key**, input the first and last name, organizational unit, organization, city/locality, state/province, and country code. Only one of these is required but it's good to provide all the information.

8. Click the **OK** button. If there is no error, the keystore will be created in the path you provided and you will be back in the **Generate Signed Bundle or APK** dialog with the keystore values so you continue generating the APK or app bundle. You can close the dialog if you only wanted to create a keystore.

In this exercise, you have created your own keystore that you can use to sign applications that can be published to Google Play.

You can also use the command line to generate a keystore if you prefer to use that. The **keytool** command is available in the **Java Development Kit (JDK)**. The command is as follows:

```
keytool -genkey -v -keystore my-key.jks -keyalg RSA -keysize
   2048 -validity 9125 -alias key-alias
```

This command creates a 2,048-bit RSA keystore in the current working directory, with a filename of **my-key.jks** and an alias of **key-alias**; it is valid for 9,125 days (25 years). The command line will prompt you to input the keystore password, then prompt you to enter it again to confirm. It will then ask you for the first and last name, organizational unit, organization name, city or locality, state or province, and country code, one at a time. Only one of these is required; you can press the *Enter* key if you want to leave something blank. It is good practice, though, to provide all the information.

After the country code prompt, you will be asked to verify the input provided. You can type yes to confirm. You will then be asked to provide the password for the key alias. If you want it to be the same as the keystore password, you can press *Enter*. The keystore will then be generated.

Now that you have a keystore for signing your apps, you need to know how you can keep it safe. You'll learn about that in the next section.

STORING THE KEYSTORE AND PASSWORDS

You need to keep the keystore and passwords in a safe and secure place because if you lose the keystore and/or the credentials for it, you will no longer be able to release updates for your apps. If a hacker also gains access to these, they may be able to update your apps without your consent.

You can store the keystore in your CI/build server or in a secure server.

Keeping the credentials is a bit tricky, as you will need them later when signing releases for app updates. One way you can do this is by including this information in your project's **build.gradle** file.

In the **android** block, you can have **signingConfigs**, which references the keystore file, its password, and the key's alias and password:

```
android {
    ...
    signingConfigs {
        release {
            storeFile file("keystore-file")
            storePassword "keystore-password"
            keyAlias "key-alias"
            keyPassword "key-password"
        }
    }
    ...
}
```

Under the release block of the **buildTypes** in the project's **build.gradle** file, you can specify the release config in the **signingConfigs** block:

```
buildTypes {
    release {
        ...
        signingConfig signingConfigs.release
    }
    ...
}
```

Storing the signing configs in the **build.gradle** file is not that secure, as someone who has access to the project or the repository can compromise the app.

You can store these credentials in environment variables to make it more secure. With this approach, even if malicious people get access to your code, the app updates will still be safe as the signing configurations are not stored in your code but on the system. An environment variable is a key-value pair that is set outside your IDE or project, for example, on your own computer or on a build server.

To use environment variables for keystore configurations in Gradle, you can create environment variables for the store file path, store password, key alias, and key password. For example, you can use the **KEYSTORE_FILE**, **KEYSTORE_PASSWORD**, **KEY_ALIAS**, and **KEY_PASSWORD** environment variables.

On Mac and Linux, you can set an environment variable by using the following command:

```
export KEYSTORE_PASSWORD=securepassword
```

If you're using Windows, it can be done with this:

```
set KEYSTORE_PASSWORD=securepassword
```

This command will create a **KEYSTORE_PASSWORD** environment variable with **securepassword** as the value. In the app **build.gradle** file, you can then use the values from the environment variables:

```
storeFile System.getenv("KEYSTORE_FILE")
storePassword System.getenv("KEYSTORE_PASSWORD")
keyAlias System.getenv("KEY_ALIAS")
keyPassword System.getenv("KEY_PASSWORD")
```

Your keystore will be used to sign your app for release so you can publish it on Google Play. We'll be discussing that in the next section.

SIGNING YOUR APPS FOR RELEASE

When you run an application on an emulator or an actual device, Android Studio automatically signs it with the debug keystore. To publish it on Google Play, you must sign the APK or app bundle with your own key, using a keystore you made in Android Studio or from the command line.

If you have added the signing config for the release build in your **build.gradle** file, you can automatically build a signed APK or app bundle by selecting the release build in the **Build Variants** window. You then need to go to the **Build** menu, click on the **Build Bundle(s)** item and then select either **Build APK(s)** or **Build Bundle(s)**. The APK or app bundle will be generated in the **app/build/output** directory of your project.

EXERCISE 16.02: CREATING A SIGNED APK

In this exercise, we will create a signed APK for an Android project using Android Studio:

1. Open a project in Android Studio.

2. Go to the **Build** menu and then click on the **Generate Signed Bundle or APK**... menu item:

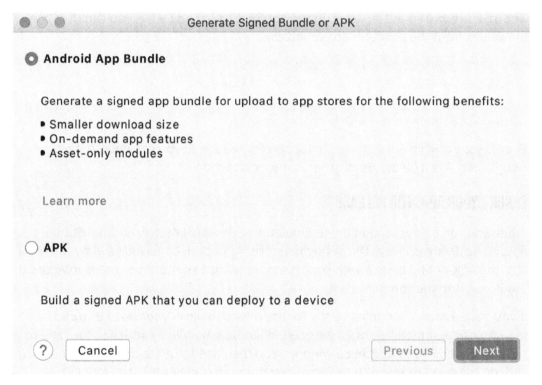

Figure 16.4: The Generate Signed Bundle or APK Dialog

3. Select **APK** and then click the **Next** button:

Figure 16.5: The Generate Signed Bundle or APK dialog after clicking the Next button

4. Choose the keystore you made in *Exercise 16.01, Creating a Keystore in Android Studio*.

5. Provide the password in the **Key store password** field.

6. In the **Key alias** field, click the icon on the right side and select the key alias.

7. Provide the alias password in the **Key password** field.

8. Click the **Next** button.

9. Choose the destination folder where the signed APK will be generated.

10. In the **Build Variants** field, make sure the **release** variant is selected:

Figure 16.6: Choose the release build in the Generate Signed Bundle or APK dialog

11. For the signature version, select both V1 and V2. **V2 (Full APK Signature)** is a whole-file scheme that increases your app security and makes it faster to install. This is only available for Android 7.0 Nougat and above. If you are targeting lower than that, you should also use **V1 (Jar Signature)**, which is the old way of signing APKs but is less secure than v2.

12. Click the **Finish** button. Android Studio will build the signed APK. An IDE notification will pop up informing you that the signed APK was generated. You can click on **locate** to go to the directory where the signed APK file is:

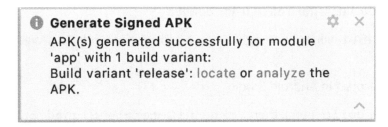

Figure 16.7: Pop-up notification for successful signed APK generation

In this exercise, you have made a signed APK that you can now publish on Google Play. In the next section, you will learn about Android App Bundle, which is a new way of packaging apps for release.

ANDROID APP BUNDLE

The traditional way of releasing Android apps is through an APK or an application package. This APK file is the one downloaded to users' devices when they install your app. This is one big file that will contain all the strings, images, and other resources for all device configurations.

As you support more device types and more countries, this APK file will grow in size. The APK that users download will contain things that would not really be needed for their device. This will be an issue for you as users with low storage might not have enough space to install your app. Users with expensive data plans or slow internet connections might also avoid downloading the app if it's too big. They might also uninstall your app to save storage space.

Some developers have been building and publishing multiple APKs to avoid these issues. However, it's a complicated and inefficient solution, especially when you target different screen densities, CPU architectures, and languages. That would be too many APK files to maintain per release.

Android App Bundle is a new way of packaging apps for publishing. You just generate a single app bundle file (using Android Studio 3.2 and up) and upload it on Google Play. Google Play will automatically generate the base APK file and the APK files for each device configuration, CPU architecture, and language. When users install your app, they will only download the necessary APKs for their device. This will be smaller in size compared to a universal APK.

This will work for devices Android 5.0 Lollipop and up; for those below it, the APK files that will be generated are only for device configuration and CPU architecture. All the languages and other resources will be included on each APK file.

EXERCISE 16.03: CREATING A SIGNED APP BUNDLE

In this exercise, we will create a signed app bundle for an Android project using Android Studio:

1. Open a project in Android Studio.

2. Go to the **Build** menu, then click on the **Generate Signed Bundle or APK**... menu item:

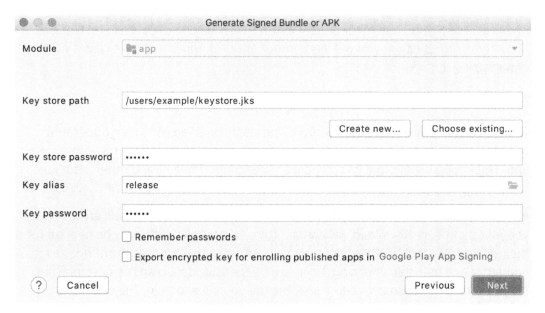

Figure 16.8: The Generate Signed Bundle or APK dialog

3. Select **Android App Bundle**, then click the **Next** button:

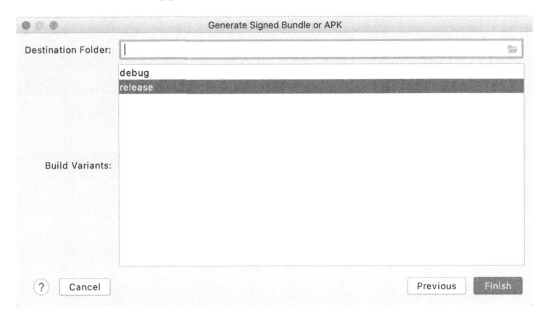

Figure 16.9: The Generate Signed Bundle or APK dialog after clicking the Next button

4. Choose the keystore you made in *Exercise 16.01, Creating a Keystore in Android Studio*.

5. Provide the password in the **Key store password** field.

6. In the **Key alias** field, click the icon at the right side and select the key alias.

7. Provide the alias password in the **Key password** field.

8. Click the **Next** button.

9. Choose the destination folder where the signed app bundle will be generated.

10. In the **Build Variants** field, make sure the **release** variant is selected:

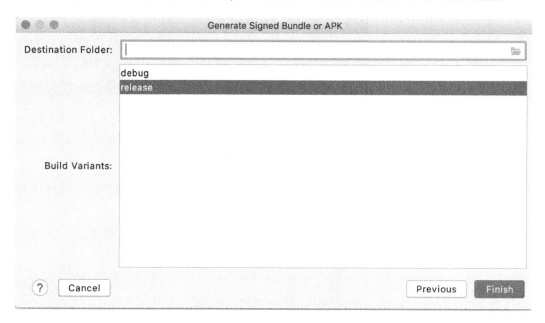

Figure 16.10: Choose the release build in the Generate Signed Bundle or APK dialog

11. Click the **Finish** button. Android Studio will build the signed app bundle. An IDE notification will pop up informing you that the signed app bundle was generated. You can click on **locate** to go to the directory where the signed app bundle file is:

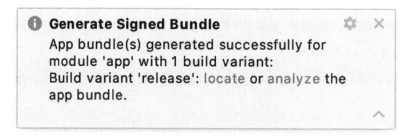

Figure 16.11: Pop up notification that the signed app bundle was generated

In this exercise, you have made a signed app bundle that you can now publish on Google Play.

To be able to publish your app with the Android app bundle format, you will need to opt in to app signing by Google Play. We will discuss Google Play app signing in the next section.

APP SIGNING BY GOOGLE PLAY

Google Play provides a service called app signing that allows Google to manage and protect your app signing keys and automatically re-sign your app for the users.

With Google Play app signing, you can either let Google generate the signing key or upload yours. You can also create a different upload key for additional security. You can sign the app with the upload key and publish the app on the Play Console. Google will check the upload key, remove it, and use the app signing key to re-sign the app for distribution to users. When app signing is enabled for the app, the upload key can be reset. If you lose the upload key or feel that it is already compromised, you can simply contact Google Play developer support, verify your identity, and get a new upload key.

It is easy to opt in to app signing when publishing a new app. In the Google Play Console (https://play.google.com/console), you can go to the `Release Management | App Releases` section and select `Continue` in the `Let Google manage and protect your app signing key` section. The key you originally used to sign the app will become the upload key and Google Play will generate a new app signing key.

You can also convert your existing apps to use app signing. This is available in the `Release | Setup | App Signing` section of the app in the Google Play Console. You would need to upload your existing app signing key and generate a new upload key.

Once you enroll in Google Play app signing, you will no longer be able to opt out. Also, if you are using third-party services, you would need to use the app signing key's certificate. This is available in `Release Management | App Signing`.

App signing also enables you to upload an app bundle, and Google Play will automatically sign and generate APK files that users will download when they install your app.

In the next section, you will be creating a Google Play developer account so you can publish an app's signed APK or app bundle to Google Play.

CREATING A DEVELOPER ACCOUNT

To publish applications on Google Play, the first step that you need to take is to create a Google Play developer account. Head over to https://play.google.com/console/signup and log in with your Google account. If you don't have one, you should create one first.

It is recommended to use a Google account that you plan to use in the long term instead of a throwaway one. Read the developer distribution agreement and agree to the terms of service.

> **NOTE**
>
> If your goal is to sell paid apps or add in-app products to your apps/games, you must also create a merchant account. This is not available in all countries, unfortunately. We won't cover this here, but you can read more about it on the registration page or at https://support.google.com/googleplay/android-developer/answer/150324.

You will need to pay a $25 USD registration fee to create your Google Play Developer account. This is a one-time payment). The fee must be paid using a valid debit/credit card, but some prepaid/virtual credit cards work too. What you can use varies by location/country.

The final step is to complete the account details, such as the developer name, email address, website, and phone number. These, which can also be updated later, will form the developer information displayed on your app's store listing.

After completing the registration, you will receive a confirmation email. It may take a few hours (up to 48 hours) for your payment to be processed and your account registered, so be patient. Ideally, you should do this in advance even if your app is not yet ready, so that once it's ready for release, you can easily publish the app.

When you have received the confirmation email from Google, you can start publishing apps and games to Google Play.

In the next section, we will be discussing uploading apps to Google Play.

UPLOADING AN APP TO GOOGLE PLAY

Once you have an app ready for release and a Google Play Developer account, you can go to the Google Play Console (https://play.google.com/console) to publish the app.

To upload an app, go to the Play Console, click `All Apps`, and then click `Create app`. Provide the name of the application and the default language. In the App or game section, set if it's an app or game. Likewise, in the Free or paid section, set if it's free or paid. Create your store listing, prepare the app release, and roll out the release. We'll have a look at the detailed steps in this section.

CREATING A STORE LISTING

The store listing is what users first see when they open your app's page on Google Play. If the app is already published, you can go to **Grow** then **Store presence** and then select **Main store listing**.

APP DETAILS

You will be navigated to the **App details** page. On the **App details** page, you need to fill in the following fields:

- **App name**: Your app's name (the maximum amount of characters is 50).

- **Short description**: Short text summarizing your app (the maximum amount of characters is 80).

- **Full description**: Long description of your app. The limit is 4,000 characters, so you can add a lot of relevant information here, such as what its features are and things users would need to know.

> ### NOTE
>
> For the product details, you can add localized versions depending on the languages/countries where you will release your app.
>
> Your app title and description must not contain copyrighted materials and spam as it might get your app rejected.

GRAPHIC ASSETS

In this section, provide the following details:

- An icon (a high-resolution icon that is 512 x 512).

- Feature graphic (1,024 x 500):

- 2-8 screenshots of the app. If your app supports other form factors (tablet, TV, or Wear OS), you should also add screenshots for each form factor:

You can also add promo graphics and promo videos, if you have any.

Your app can be rejected if you use graphics that violate Google Play policy, so ensure that the images you use are your own and don't include copyrighted or inappropriate content.

PREPARING THE RELEASE

Before preparing your release, make sure that your build is signed with a signature key. If you're publishing an app update, make sure that it is of the same package name, signed with the same key, and with a version code higher than the current one on Play.

You must also make sure you follow the developer policy (so as to avoid any violations) and make sure that your app follows the app quality guidelines. More of these are listed on the launch checklist, which you can see at https://support.google.com/googleplay/android-developer/.

APK/APP BUNDLE

You can upload an APK (an Android Package) or the newer format: Android App Bundle. Go to **Release** and then **App Releases**. This will display a summary of active and draft releases in each track.

There are different tracks where you can release the app:

- Production
- Open testing
- Closed testing
- Internal testing

We'll discuss the release tracks in detail in the **Managing App Releases** section of this chapter.

Select the track where you will create the release. For the production track, you can select **Manage** on the left. For the other tracks, click **Testing** first then select the track. To release on a Closed testing track, you must also select **Manage track** and then create a new track by clicking on **Create track**.

Once done, you can click **Create new release** at the top right of the page. In the **Android App Bundles and APKs to add** section, you can upload your APK or app bundle.

Make sure that the app bundle or APK file is signed by your release signing key. The Google Play Console will not accept it if it's not properly signed. If you're publishing an update, the version code for the app bundle or APK must be higher than the existing version.

You can also add a release name and release notes. The release name is for the developer's use to track the release and won't be visible to users. By default, the version name of the APK or app bundle uploaded is set as the release name. The release notes form the text that will be shown on the Play page and will inform users of what the updates to the app are.

The text for the release notes must be added inside the tags for the language. For example, the opening and closing tags for the default US English language are **<en-US>** and **</en-US>**. If your app supports multiple languages, each language tag will be displayed in the field for the release notes by default. You can then add the release notes for each language.

If you have already released the app, you can copy the release notes from previous releases and reuse or modify them by clicking the **Copy from a previous release** button and selecting from the list.

When you click the **Save** button, the release will be saved and you can go back to it later. The **Review release** button will take you to the screen where you can review and roll out the release.

ROLLING OUT A RELEASE

If you're ready to roll out your release, go to the Play Console and select your app. Go to **Release** and select your release track. Click the releases tab and then click on the **Edit** button next to the release:

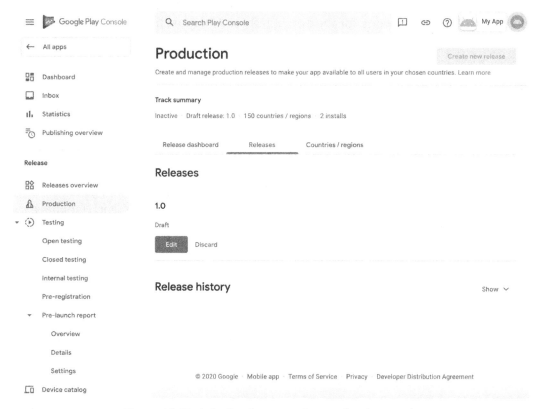

Figure 16.12: A draft release on the production track

You can review the APK or app bundle, release names, and release notes. Click the **Review release** button to start the rollout for the release. The Play Console will open the **Review and release** screen. Here, you can review the release information and check whether there are warnings and errors.

If you are updating an app, you can also select the rollout percentage when creating another release. Setting it to 100% means it will be available for all your users to download. When you set it to a lower percentage, for example, 50%, the release will be available to half of your existing users.

If you're confident with the release, you can select the **START ROLLOUT TO PRODUCTION** button at the bottom of the page. After publishing your app, it will take a while (7 days or longer for new apps) before it is reviewed. You can see the status in the top-right corner of the Google Play Console. These statuses include the following:

- Pending publication (your new app is being reviewed)

- Published (your app is now available on Google Play)

- Rejected (your app wasn't published because of a policy violation)

- Suspended (your app violated Google Play policy and was suspended)

If there are issues with your app, you can resolve them and resubmit the app. Your app can be rejected for reasons such as copyright infringement, impersonation, and spam.

Once the app has been published, users can now download it. It can take some time before the new app or the app update becomes live on Google Play. If you're trying to search for your app on Google Play, it might not be searchable. Make sure you publish it on the production or open track.

MANAGING APP RELEASES

You can slowly release your apps on different tracks so you can test it before rolling it out publicly to users. You can also do timed publishing to make the app available on a certain date, instead of automatically publishing it once approved by Google.

RELEASE TRACKS

When creating a release for an app, you can choose between four different tracks:

- Production is where everyone can see the app.

- Open testing is targeted at wider public testing. The release will be available on Google Play and anyone can join the beta program and test.

- Closed testing is intended for small groups of users testing pre-release versions.

- Internal testing is for developer/tester builds while developing/testing an app.

The internal, closed, and open tracks allow developers to create a special release and allow real users to download it while the rest of the users are on the production version. This will give you a way to quickly know whether the release has bugs and quickly fix them before rolling it out to everyone. User feedback on these tracks will also not affect the public reviews/ratings of your app.

The ideal way is to release it first on internal tracks during development and internal testing. When a pre-release version is ready, you can create a closed test for a small group of trusted people/users/testers. Then, you can create an open test to allow other users to try your app before the full launch in production.

To go to each track and manage releases, you can go to the **Release** section of the Google Play Console and select **Production** or **Testing** and then the Open, Closed, or Internal tracks.

FEEDBACK CHANNEL AND OPT-IN LINK

In the internal, closed, and open tracks, there is a section for **Feedback URL or email address** and **How testers join your test**. You can provide an email address or a website in **Feedback URL or email address** where the testers can send their feedback. This is displayed when they opt in to your testing program.

In the **How testers join your test** section, you can copy the link to share with your testers. They can then join the testing program using this link.

INTERNAL TESTING

This track is for builds while developing/testing the app. Releases here will be quickly available on Google Play for internal testers. In the **Testers** tab, there's a Testers section. You can choose an existing list or create a new one. There is a maximum of 100 testers for an internal test.

CLOSED TESTING

In the **Testers** tab, you can choose an email list or Google Groups for the testers. If you choose email lists, choose a list of testers or create a new list. There is a maximum of 2,000 testers for a closed test:

If you select Google Groups, you can provide the Google Group email address (for example, **the-alpha-group@googlegroups.com**) and all the members of that group will become testers:

OPEN TESTING

In the Testers tab, you can set **Unlimited** or **Limited number** for the testers. The minimum testers for the limited testing that you can set is 1,000:

In the open, closed, and internal tracks, you can add users to be your testers for your applications. You will learn how to add testers in the next section.

STAGED ROLLOUTS

When rolling out app updates, you can release them to a small group of users first. When the release has issues, you can stop the rollout or publish another update to fix the issues. If there are none, you can slowly increase the rollout percentage. This is called **staged rollout**.

If you have published an update to less than 100% of your users, you can go to the Play Console, select **Release**, click the track, then select the **Releases** tab. Below the release you want to update, you can see the **Manage rollout** dropdown. It will have options to update or halt the rollout.

You can select the **Manage rollout** then **Update rollout** to increase the percentage of rollout of the release. A dialog will appear where you can input the rollout percentage. You can click the **Update** button to update the percentage.

A 100% rollout will make the release available to all of your users. A percentage below that means the release will only be available to that percentage of your users.

If, during a staged rollout, a major bug or crash is found, you can go to the Play Console, select **Release**, click the track, then select the **Releases** tab. Under the release you want to update, select `Manage rollout` then `Halt rollout`. A dialog will appear with additional information. Add an optional note then click the `Halt` button to confirm:

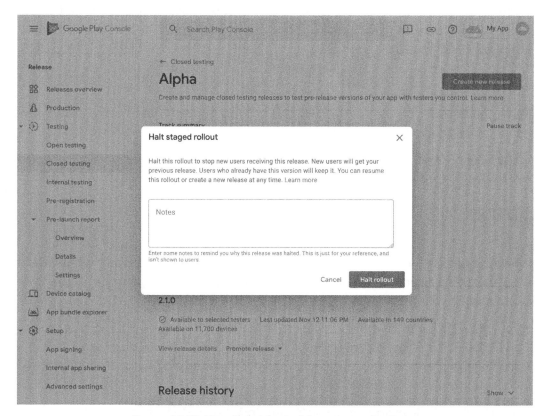

Figure 16.13: The dialog for halting a staged rollout

When a staged rollout is halted, the release page in your track page will be updated with `Rollout halted` text and a `Resume rollout` button:

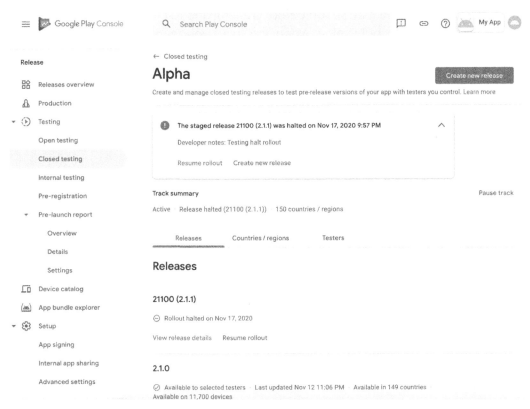

Figure 16.14: The release page for a halted staged rollout

If you have fixed the issue, for example, in the backend, and there's no need to release a new update, you can resume your staged rollout. To do that, go to the Play Console and select `Release`, click the track, then select the `Releases` tab. Choose the release and click the `Resume rollout` button. In the `Resume staged rollout` dialog, you can update the percentage and click `Resume rollout` to continue the rollout.

MANAGED PUBLISHING

When you roll out a new release on Google Play, it will be published in a few minutes. You can change it to be published at a later time. This is useful when you are targeting a specific day, for example, the same day as an iOS/web release or after a launch date.

Managed publishing must be set up before creating and releasing the update you want to control the publishing. When you select your app on the Google Play Console, you can select **Publishing Overview** on the left side. In the **Managed publishing status** section, click on the **Manage** button:

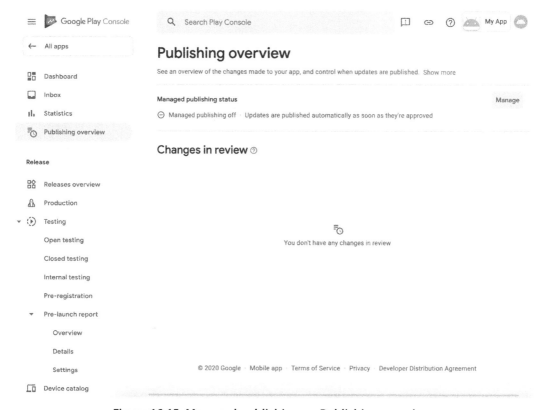

Figure 16.15: Managed publishing on Publishing overview

The Managed publishing status will be displayed. Here, you can turn managed publishing on or off then click the **Save** button.

When you turn on **Managed publishing**, you can continue adding and submitting updates to the app. You can see these changes in the **Publishing overview** under the **Changes in review** section:

Once the changes have been approved, the **Changes in review** will be empty and will be moved to the **Changes ready to publish** section. There, you can click on the **Review and publish** button. In the dialog that appears, you can click on the **Publish** button to confirm. Your update will then be published instantly.

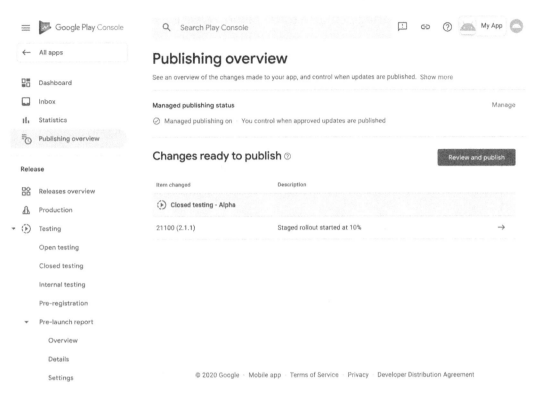

Figure 16.16: Managed publishing Changes ready to publish

ACTIVITY 16.01: PUBLISHING AN APP

As the final activity of this book, you are tasked with creating a Google Play Developer account and publishing a newly developed Android app that you have built. You could publish one of the apps you've built as part of this book, or another project that you've been developing. You can use the following steps as guidelines:

1. Go to the Google Play Developer Console (https://play.google.com/console) and create an account.

2. Create a keystore that you can use for signing the release build.

3. Generate an Android app bundle for release.

4. Publish the app on an open beta track, before releasing it to the production track.

> **NOTE**
>
> The detailed steps for publishing an app have been explained throughout this chapter, so there is no separate solution available for this activity. You can follow the exercises of this chapter to successfully complete the preceding steps. The exact steps required will be unique to your app and will depend on the settings you want to use.

SUMMARY

This chapter covered the Google Play Store: from preparing a release, to creating a Google Play Developer account, to finally publishing your app. We started with versioning your apps, generating a keystore, creating an APK file or Android app bundle and signing it with a release keystore, and storing the keystore and its credentials. We then moved on to registering an account on the Google Play Console, uploading your APK file or app bundle, and managing releases.

This is the culmination of the work done throughout this book—publishing your app and opening it up to the world is a great achievement and demonstrates the progress you've made throughout this course.

Throughout this book, you have gained many skills, starting with the basics of Android app development and building up to implementing features such as **RecyclerViews**, fetching data from web services, notifications, and testing. You have seen how to improve your apps with best practices, architecture patterns, and animations, and finally, you have learned how to publish them on Google Play.

This is still just the start of your journey as an Android developer. There are many more advanced skills for you to develop as you continue to build more complex apps of your own and expand upon what you have learned here. Remember that Android is continuously evolving, and so it is good to keep yourself up to date with the latest Android releases. You can go to https://developer.android.com/ to find the latest resources and further immerse yourself in the Android world.

INDEX

Made in the USA
Monee, IL
30 June 2022

98877293R00437